Becker Professional Education, a global leader in professional education, has been developing study materials for the ACCA for more than 20 years. Thousands of students studying for the ACCA Qualification have succeeded in their professional examinations studying with its Platinum and Gold ALP training centers in Central and Eastern Europe and Central Asia.

Nearly half a million professionals have advanced their careers through Becker Professional Education's courses. Throughout its 60-year history, Becker has earned a strong track record of student success through world-class teaching, curriculum and learning tools.

Becker Professional Education has been awarded ACCA Approved Content Provider Status for its ACCA materials, as well as materials for the Diploma in International Financial Reporting (DipIFR).

We provide a single solution for individuals and companies in need of global accounting certifications and continuing professional education.

Becker Professional Education's ACCA Study Materials

All of Becker's materials are authored by experienced ACCA lecturers and are used in the delivery of classroom courses.

Study Text: Gives complete coverage of the syllabus with a focus on learning outcomes. It is designed to be used both as a reference text and as part of integrated study. It also includes the ACCA Syllabus and Study Guide, exam advice and commentaries and a Study Question Bank containing practice questions relating to each topic covered.

Revision Question Bank: Exam style and standard questions together with comprehensive answers to support and prepare students for their exams. The Revision Question Bank also includes past examination questions (updated where relevant), model answers and alternative solutions and tutorial notes.

Revision Essentials Handbook*: A condensed, easy-to-use aid to revision containing essential technical content and exam guidance.

*Revision Essentials Handbook are substantially derived from content reviewed by ACCA's examining team.

Becker Professional Education
is an ACCA approved content provider

BECKER
PROFESSIONAL EDUCATION®

ACCA

CORPORATE REPORTING P2
(INTERNATIONAL)
STUDY TEXT

September 2017 to June 2018

BECKER
PROFESSIONAL EDUCATION®

No responsibility for loss occasioned to any person acting or refraining from action as a result of any material in this publication can be accepted by the author, editor or publisher.

This training material has been prepared and published by Becker Professional Development International Limited: www.becker.com/acca

ISBN: 978-1-78566-397-0

Copyright ©2017 DeVry/Becker Educational Development Corp. All rights reserved.
The trademarks used herein are owned by DeVry/Becker Educational Development Corp. or their respective owners and may not be used without permission from the owner.

No part of this training material may be translated, reprinted or reproduced or utilised in any form either in whole or in part or by any electronic, mechanical or other means, now known or hereafter invented, including photocopying and recording, or in any information storage and retrieval system without express written permission. Request for permission or further information should be addressed to the Permissions Department, DeVry/Becker Educational Development Corp.

LICENSE AGREEMENT

DO NOT DOWNLOAD, ACCESS, AND/OR USE ANY OF THESE MATERIALS (AS THAT TERM IS DEFINED BELOW) UNTIL YOU HAVE READ THIS LICENSE AGREEMENT CAREFULLY. IF YOU DOWNLOAD, ACCESS, AND/OR USE ANY OF THESE MATERIALS, YOU ARE AGREEING AND CONSENTING TO BE BOUND BY AND ARE BECOMING A PARTY TO THIS LICENSE AGREEMENT ("AGREEMENT").

The printed Materials provided to you and/or the Materials provided for download to your computer and/or provided via a web application to which you are granted access are NOT for sale and are not being sold to you. You may NOT transfer these Materials to any other person or permit any other person to use these Materials. You may _only_ acquire a license to use these Materials and _only_ upon the terms and conditions set forth in this Agreement. Read this Agreement carefully _before_ downloading, and/or accessing, and/or using these Materials. _Do not_ download and/or access, and/or use these Materials _unless_ you agree with _all_ terms of this Agreement.

NOTE: You may already be a party to this Agreement if you registered for a Becker Professional Education® ACCA Program (the "Program") or placed an order for these Materials online or using a printed form that included this License Agreement. Please review the termination section regarding your rights to terminate this License Agreement and receive a refund of your payment.

Grant: Upon your acceptance of the terms of this Agreement, in a manner set forth above, DeVry/Becker Educational Development Corp. ("Becker") hereby grants to you a non-exclusive, revocable, non-transferable, non-sublicensable, limited license to use (as defined below) the Materials by downloading them onto a computer and/or by accessing them via a web application using a user ID and password (as defined below), and any Materials to which you are granted access as a result of your license to use these Materials and/or in connection with the Program on the following terms:

During the Term of this Agreement, you may:

- use the Materials for preparation for the ACCA examinations (the "Exams"), and/or for your studies relating to the subject matter covered by the Materials and/or the Exams, including taking electronic and/or handwritten notes during the Program, provided that all notes taken that relate to the subject matter of the Materials are and shall remain Materials subject to the terms of this Agreement;

- download the Materials onto any single device;

- download the Materials onto a second device so long as the first device and the second device are not used simultaneously;

- download the Materials onto a third device so long as the first, second, and third device are not used simultaneously; and

- download the Materials onto a fourth device so long as the first, second, third, and fourth device are not used simultaneously.

The number of installations may vary outside of the U.S. Please review your local office policies and procedures to confirm the number of installations granted—your local office's policies and procedures regarding the number of allowable activations of downloads supersedes the limitations contained herein and is controlling.

You may not:

- use the Materials for any purpose other than as expressly permitted above;

- use the downloaded Materials on more than one device, computer terminal, or workstation at the same time;

- make copies of the Materials;

- rent, lease, license, lend, or otherwise transfer or provide (by gift, sale, or otherwise) all or any part of the Materials to anyone;

- permit the use of all or any part of the Materials by anyone other than you; or

- reverse engineer, decompile, disassemble, or create derivate works of the Materials.

Materials: As used in this Agreement, the term "Materials" means and includes any printed materials provided to you by Becker, and/or to which you are granted access by Becker (directly or indirectly) in connection with your license of the Materials and/or the Program, and shall include notes you take (by hand, electronically, digitally, or otherwise) while using the Materials relating to the subject matter of the Materials; any and all electronically-stored/accessed/delivered, and/or digitally-stored/accessed/delivered materials included under this License via download to a computer or via access to a web application, and/or otherwise provided to you and/or to which you are otherwise granted access by Becker (directly or indirectly), including, but not limited to, applications downloadable from a third party, for example Google® or Amazon®, in connection with your license of the Materials.

Title: Becker is and will remain the owner of all title, ownership rights, intellectual property, and all other rights and interests in and to the Materials that are subject to the terms of this Agreement. The Materials are protected by the copyright laws of the United States and international copyright laws and treaties.

Termination: The license granted under this Agreement commences upon your receipt of these Materials. This license shall terminate the earlier of: (i) ten (10) business days after notice to you of non-payment of or default on any payment due Becker which has not been cured within such 10-day period; or (ii) immediately if you fail to comply with any of the limitations described above; or (iii) upon expiration of the examination period for which the Materials are valid as specified on your order confirmation and in the title of the course package. For example, Materials marked, "For Examinations to August 2018," are valid for examinations from September 2017 to August 2018 and the license to these Materials terminates at the end of August 2018. All online packages and Materials will be removed after the relevant examination period and you will no longer have access to the online packages or Materials. In addition, upon termination of this license for any reason, you must delete or otherwise remove from your computer and other device any Materials you downloaded, including, but not limited to, any archival copies you may have made. The Title, Exclusion of Warranties, Exclusion of Damages, Indemnification and Remedies, Severability of Terms and Governing Law provisions, and any amounts due, shall survive termination of the license.

Your Limited Right to Terminate this License and Receive a Refund: You may terminate this license for the in-class, online, and self-study Programs in accordance with Becker's refund policy at https://becker.com/ACCA.

Exclusion of Warranties: YOU EXPRESSLY ASSUME ALL RISK FOR USE OF THE MATERIALS. YOU AGREE THAT THE MATERIALS ARE PROVIDED TO YOU "AS IS" AND "AS AVAILABLE" AND THAT BECKER MAKES NO WARRANTIES, EXPRESS OR IMPLIED, WITH RESPECT TO THE MATERIALS, THEIR MERCHANTABILITY OR FITNESS FOR A PARTICULAR PURPOSE AND NO WARRANTY OF NONINFRINGEMENT OF THIRD PARTIES' RIGHTS. NO DEALER, AGENT OR EMPLOYEE OF BECKER IS AUTHORIZED TO PROVIDE ANY SUCH WARRANTY TO YOU. BECAUSE SOME JURISDICTIONS DO NOT ALLOW THE EXCLUSION OF IMPLIED WARRANTIES, THE ABOVE EXCLUSION OF IMPLIED WARRANTIES MAY NOT APPLY TO YOU. BECKER DOES NOT WARRANT OR GUARANTEE THAT YOU WILL PASS ANY EXAMINATION.

Exclusion of Damages: UNDER NO CIRCUMSTANCES AND UNDER NO LEGAL THEORY, TORT, CONTRACT, OR OTHERWISE, SHALL BECKER OR ITS DIRECTORS, OFFICERS, EMPLOYEES, OR AGENTS BE LIABLE TO YOU OR ANY OTHER PERSON FOR ANY CONSEQUENTIAL, INCIDENTAL, INDIRECT, PUNITIVE, EXEMPLARY OR SPECIAL DAMAGES OF ANY CHARACTER, INCLUDING, WITHOUT LIMITATION, DAMAGES FOR LOSS OF GOODWILL, WORK STOPPAGE, COMPUTER FAILURE OR MALFUNCTION OR ANY AND ALL OTHER DAMAGES OR LOSSES, OR FOR ANY DAMAGES IN EXCESS OF BECKER'S LIST PRICE FOR A LICENSE TO THE MATERIALS, EVEN IF BECKER SHALL HAVE BEEN INFORMED OF THE POSSIBILITY OF SUCH DAMAGES, OR FOR ANY CLAIM BY ANY OTHER PARTY. Some jurisdictions do not allow the limitation or exclusion of liability for incidental or consequential damages, so the above limitation or exclusion may not apply to you.

Indemnification and Remedies: You agree to indemnify and hold Becker and its employees, representatives, agents, attorneys, affiliates, directors, officers, members, managers, and shareholders harmless from and against any and all claims, demands, losses, damages, penalties, costs or expenses (including reasonable attorneys' and expert witnesses' fees and costs) of any kind or nature, arising from or relating to any violation, breach, or nonfulfillment by you of any provision of this license. If you are obligated to provide indemnification pursuant to this provision, Becker may, in its sole and absolute discretion, control the disposition of any indemnified action at your sole cost and expense. Without limiting the foregoing, you may not settle, compromise, or in any other manner dispose of any indemnified action without the consent of Becker. If you breach any material term of this license, Becker shall be entitled to equitable relief by way of temporary and permanent injunction without the need for a bond and such other and further relief as any court with jurisdiction may deem just and proper.

Confidentiality: The Materials are considered confidential and proprietary to Becker. You shall keep the Materials confidential and you shall not publish or disclose the Materials to any third party without the prior written consent of Becker.

Severability of Terms: If any term or provision of this license is held invalid or unenforceable by a court of competent jurisdiction, such invalidity shall not affect the validity or operation of any other term or provision and such invalid term or provision shall be deemed to be severed from the license. This Agreement may only be modified by written agreement signed by both parties.

Governing Law: This Agreement shall be governed and construed according to the laws of the State of Illinois, United States of America, excepting that State's conflicts of laws rules. The parties agree that the jurisdiction and venue of any dispute subject to litigation is proper in any state or federal court in Chicago, Illinois, U.S.A. The parties hereby agree to waive application of the U.N. Convention on the Sale of Goods. If the State of Illinois adopts the current proposed Uniform Computer Information Transactions Act (UCITA, formerly proposed Article 2B to the Uniform Commercial Code), or a version of the proposed UCITA, that part of the laws shall not apply to any transaction under this Agreement.

ACCA and Chartered Certified Accountants are registered trademarks of the Association of Chartered Certified Accountants and may not be used without their express, written permission. Becker Professional Education is a registered trademark of DeVry/Becker Educational Development Corp. and may not be used without its express, written permission.

Paper P2

Contents

© DeVry/Becker Educational Development Corp. All rights reserved.

Contents

© DeVry/Becker Educational Development Corp. All rights reserved.

Introduction

ABOUT THIS STUDY TEXT

This Study Text has been specifically written for the Association of Chartered Certified Accountants fundamentals level examination, Paper P2 *Corporate Reporting.*

It provides comprehensive coverage of the core syllabus areas and is designed to be used both as a reference text and as an integral part of your studies to provide you with the knowledge, skill and confidence to succeed in your ACCA studies.

About the author: Phil Bradbury is Becker's lead tutor in corporate reporting and has more than 16 years' experience in delivering ACCA exam-based training.

How to Use This Study Text

You should start by reading through the syllabus, study guide and approach to examining the syllabus provided in this introduction to familiarise yourself with the content of this paper.

The sessions which follow include the following features:

Focus	These are the learning outcomes relevant to the session, as published in the ACCA Study Guide.
Session Guidance	Tutor advice and strategies for approaching each session.
Visual Overview	A diagram of the concepts and the relationships addressed in each session.
Definitions	Terms are defined as they are introduced and larger groupings of terms will be set forth in a Terminology section.
Illustrations	These are to be read as part of the text. Any solutions to numerical Illustrations are provided.
Exhibits	These extracts of external content are presented to reinforce concepts and should be read as part of the text.
Examples	These should be attempted using the pro forma solution provided (where applicable).
Key Points	Attention is drawn to fundamental rules, underlying concepts and principles.
Exam Advice	These tutor comments relate the content to relevance in the examination.
Commentaries	These provide additional information to reinforce content.
Session Summary	A summary of the main points of each session.
Session Quiz	These quick questions are designed to test your knowledge of the technical content. A reference to the answer is provided.
Study Question Bank	A reference to recommended practice questions contained in the Study Question Bank. As a minimum, you should work through the priority questions after studying each session. For additional practice, you can attempt any remaining questions.
Example Solutions	Answers to the Examples are presented at the end of each session.

SYLLABUS

Aim

To apply knowledge, skills and exercise professional judgement in the application and evaluation of financial reporting principles and practices in a range of business contexts and situations.

Main Capabilities

On successful completion of this paper, candidates should be able to:

A. Discuss the professional and ethical duties of the accountant

B. Evaluate the financial reporting framework

C. Advise on and report the financial performance of entities

D. Prepare the financial statements of groups of entities in accordance with relevant accounting standards

E. Explain reporting issues relating to specialised entities

F. Discuss the implications of changes in accounting regulation on financial reporting

G. Appraise the financial performance and position of entities

H. Evaluate current developments

Position in the ACCA Qualification

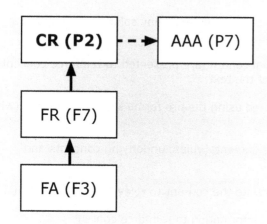

© DeVry/Becker Educational Development Corp. All rights reserved.

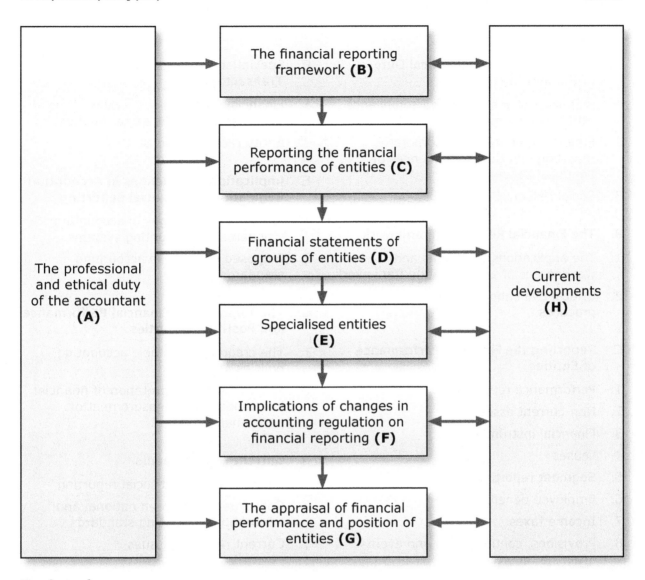

Rationale

The syllabus for Paper P2 *Corporate Reporting* assumes knowledge acquired at the Fundamentals level including the core technical capabilities to prepare and analyse financial reports for single and combined entities.

The Paper P2 syllabus takes the subject into greater depth and contextualises the role of the accountant as a professional steward and adviser/analyst by initially exploring the wider professional duties and responsibilities of the accountant to the stakeholders of an organisation.

The syllabus examines the financial reporting framework within which the accountant operates and examines detailed financial reporting requirements for entities leading to the preparation of group financial reports in accordance with generally accepted accounting practice and relevant standards.

The syllabus then deals with the nature of reporting for specialised entities including not-for-profit and small and medium-sized enterprises.

The final sections of the syllabus explore—in more depth—the role of the accountant as financial analyst and adviser through the assessment of financial performance and position of entities, and the accountant's role in assessing and advising on the implications of accounting regulation on corporate reporting.

Finally, the syllabus covers the evaluation of current developments and their implications for financial reporting.

Detailed Syllabus

A. The Professional and Ethical Duty of the Accountant

1. Professional behaviour and compliance with accounting standards
2. Ethical requirements of corporate reporting and the consequences of unethical behaviour
3. Social responsibility

B. The Financial Reporting Framework

1. The applications, strengths and weaknesses of an accounting framework
2. Critical evaluation of principles and practices

C. Reporting the Financial Performance of Entities

1. Performance reporting
2. Non-current assets
3. Financial instruments
4. Leases
5. Segment reporting
6. Employee benefits
7. Income taxes
8. Provisions, contingencies and events after the reporting date
9. Related parties
10. Share-based payment
11. Reporting requirements of small and medium-sized entities (SMEs)

D. Financial Statements of Groups of Entities

1. Group accounting including statements of cash flows
2. Continuing and discontinued interests
3. Changes in group structures
4. Foreign transactions and entities

E. Specialised Entities and Specialised Transactions

1. Financial reporting in specialised, not-for-profit and public sector entities
2. Entity reconstructions

F. Implications of Changes in Accounting Regulation on Financial Reporting

1. The effect of changes in accounting standards on accounting systems
2. Proposed changes to accounting standards

G. The Appraisal of Financial Performance and Position of Entities

1. The creation of suitable accounting policies
2. Analysis and interpretation of financial information and measurement of performance

H. Current Developments

1. Environmental and social reporting
2. Convergence between national and international reporting standards
3. Current reporting issues

© DeVry/Becker Educational Development Corp. All rights reserved.

Approach to Examining the Syllabus

The syllabus is assessed by a three-hour 15 minutes paper-based examination. It examines professional competences within the corporate reporting environment.

Students will be examined on concepts, theories and principles, and on their ability to question and comment on proposed accounting treatments.

Students should be capable of relating professional issues to relevant concepts and practical situations. The evaluation of alternative accounting practices and the identification and prioritisation of issues will be a key element of the paper. Professional and ethical judgement will need to be exercised, together with the integration of technical knowledge when addressing corporate reporting issues in a business context.

Global issues will be addressed via the current issues questions on the paper. Students will be required to adopt either a stakeholder or an external focus in answering questions and to demonstrate personal skills such as problem solving, dealing with information and decision making.

The paper also deals with specific professional knowledge appropriate to the preparation and presentation of consolidated and other financial statements from accounting data, to conform with accounting standards.

The examination will be structured in two sections:

Time allowed: 3 hours and 15 minutes

		Number of marks
Section A:	One compulsory question	50
Section B:	Choice of two out of three 25-mark questions	50
		100

Section A will consist of one scenario-based question worth 50 marks. It will deal with the preparation of consolidated financial statements including group statement of cash flows and with issues in financial reporting.

Students will be required to answer two out of three questions in Section B, which will normally comprise two questions which will be scenario or case-study based and one essay question which may have some computational element. Section B could deal with any aspects of the syllabus. New accounting standards will feature prominently in this section on initial introduction.

One of the features of the Professional level exam papers is the awarding of "professional marks". These are marks allocated not for the content of an answer, but for the degree of professionalism with which certain parts of the answer are presented. You should assume that if the question asks for a specific format of answer that some marks may be awarded for an effective presentation of that format.

Guide to Examination Assessment

For financial accounting papers ACCA will publish *examinable documents* once a year to indicate exactly what regulations and legislation could potentially be assessed within identified examination sessions.

For the P2 exam, regulation *issued* or legislation *passed* on or before 31st August annually will be examinable from 1st September of the *following* year to 31st August of the *year after* that.

Therefore any regulation issued or legislation passed by 31st August 2016 is examinable in the September 2017, December 2017, March 2018 and June 2018 examination sessions.

EXAMINABLE DOCUMENTS

International Financial Reporting Standards (IFRSs)		Study Session
IAS 1	Presentation of Financial Statements	4
IAS 2	Inventories	4
IAS 7	Statement of Cash Flows	23
IAS 8	Accounting Policies, Changes in Accounting Estimates and Errors	5
IAS 10	Events After the Reporting Period	13
IAS 12	Income Taxes	12
IAS 16	Property, Plant and Equipment	6
IAS 19	Employee Benefits	11
IAS 20	Accounting for Government Grants and Disclosure of Government Assistance	6
IAS 21	The Effects of Changes in Foreign Exchange Rates	22
IAS 23	Borrowing Costs	6
IAS 24	Related Party Disclosures	14
IAS 27	Separate Financial Statements	16
IAS 28	Investments in Associates and Joint Ventures	21
IAS 32	Financial Instruments: Presentation	8
IAS 33	Earnings per Share	24
IAS 34	Interim Financial Reporting	4
IAS 36	Impairment of Assets	7
IAS 37	Provisions, Contingent Liabilities and Contingent Assets	13
IAS 38	Intangible Assets	6
IAS 40	Investment Property	6
IAS 41	Agriculture	3
IFRS 1	First-Time Adoption of International Financial Reporting Standards	25
IFRS 2	Share-based Payment	15
IFRS 3 (revised)	Business Combinations	17, 18
IFRS 5	Non-current Assets Held for Sale and Discontinued Operations	4, 6
IFRS 7	Financial Instruments: Disclosure	8
IFRS 8	Operating Segments	10
IFRS 9	Financial Instruments	8
IFRS 10	Consolidated Financial Statements	16
IFRS 11	Joint Arrangements	21
IFRS 12	Disclosure of Interests in Other Entities	21
IFRS 13	Fair Value Measurement	3
IFRS 15	Revenue from Contracts with Customers	4
IFRS 16	Leases	9
IFRS for Small and Medium-sized Entities		1

© DeVry/Becker Educational Development Corp. All rights reserved.

Other Statements		Study Session
	The Conceptual Framework for Financial Reporting	3
	Practice Statement on Management Commentary	27
	The International <IR> Framework	27
EDs, Discussion Papers and Other Documents		
ED/2014/4	Measuring quoted investments in subsidiaries, joint ventures and associates at fair value	3
ED 2015/1	Classification of Liabilities—proposed amendments to IAS 1	4
ED 2015/3	Conceptual Framework for Financial Reporting	3
ED 2015/8	IFRS Practice Statement Application of Materiality in Financial Statements	4

ACCA Support

For examinable documents, examiner's reports, guidance, and technical articles relevant to this paper see www.accaglobal.com/gb/en/student/acca-qual-student-journey/qual-resource/acca-qualification/p2.html.

The ACCA Study Guide offers more detailed guidance on the depth and level at which the examinable documents will be examined and should therefore be read in conjunction with the examinable documents list. The ACCA's Study Guide which is reproduced as follows is referenced to the Sessions in this Study Text.

ACCA STUDY GUIDE

A. The Professional and Ethical Duties of the Accountant	Ref.
1. Professional behaviour and compliance with accounting standards	26
a) Appraise and discuss the ethical and professional issues in advising on corporate reporting.	
b) Assess the relevance and importance of ethical and professional issues in complying with accounting standards.	
2. Ethical requirements of corporate reporting and the consequences of unethical behaviour	26
a) Appraise the potential ethical implications of professional and managerial decisions in the preparation of corporate reports.	
b) Assess the consequences of not upholding ethical principles in the preparation of corporate reports.	
3. Social responsibility	27
a) Discuss the increased demand for transparency in corporate reports, and the emergence of non-financial reporting standards.	
b) Discuss the progress towards a framework for integrated reporting.	

B. The Financial Reporting Framework	Ref.
1. The applications, strengths and weaknesses of an accounting framework	3
a) Evaluate the valuation models adopted by standard setters.	
b) Discuss the use of an accounting framework in underpinning the production of accounting standards.	
c) Assess the success of such a framework in introducing rigorous and consistent accounting standards.	
2. Critical evaluation of principles and practices	
a) Identify the relationship between accounting theory and practice.	3
b) Critically evaluate accounting principles and practices used in corporate reporting.	5

C. Reporting the Financial Performance of Entities	Ref.
1. Performance reporting	
a) Prepare reports relating to corporate performance for external stakeholders.	24
b) Discuss and apply the criteria that must be met before an entity can apply the revenue recognition model to a contract.	4
c) Discuss and apply the five-step model which relates to revenue earned from a contract with a customer.	
2. Non-current assets	6
a) Apply and discuss the timing of the recognition of non-current assets and the determination of their carrying amounts including impairments and revaluations.	
b) Apply and discuss the treatment of non-current assets held for sale.	
c) Apply and discuss the accounting treatment of investment properties including classification, recognition and measurement issues.	
d) Apply and discuss the accounting treatment of intangible assets including the criteria for recognition and measurement subsequent to acquisition and classification.	
3. Financial instruments	8
a) Apply and discuss the recognition and derecognition of financial assets and financial liabilities.	
b) Apply and discuss the classification of financial assets and financial liabilities and their measurement.	
c) Apply and discuss the treatment of gains and losses arising on financial assets and financial liabilities.	
d) Apply and discuss the treatment of the expected loss impairment model.	

(continued on next page)

© DeVry/Becker Educational Development Corp. All rights reserved.

	Ref.

e) Account for derivative financial instruments, and simple embedded derivatives.

f) Outline the principles of hedge accounting and account for fair value hedges and cash flow hedges including hedge effectiveness.

4. Leases   9

a) Apply and discuss the accounting for leases by lessees including the measurement of the right of use asset and liability.

b) Apply and discuss the accounting for leases by lessors.

c) Apply and discuss the circumstances where there may be re-measurement of the lease liability.

d) Apply and discuss the reasons behind the separation of the components of a lease contract into lease and no-lease elements.

e) Discuss the recognition exemptions under the current leasing standard.

f) Account for and discuss sale and leaseback transactions.

5. Segment reporting   10

a) Determine the nature and extent of reportable segments.

b) Specify and discuss the nature of segment information to be disclosed.

6. Employee benefits   11

a) Apply and discuss the accounting treatment of short term and long term employee benefits and defined contribution and defined benefit plans.

b) Account for gains and losses on settlements and curtailments.

c) Account for the "Asset Ceiling" test and the reporting of actuarial gains and losses.

7. Income taxes   12

a) Apply and discuss the recognition and measurement of deferred tax liabilities and deferred tax assets.

b) Determine the recognition of tax expense or income and its inclusion in the financial statements.

8. Provisions, contingencies and events after the reporting date   13

a) Apply and discuss the recognition, derecognition and measurement of provisions, contingent liabilities and contingent assets including environmental provisions and restructuring provisions.

b) Apply and discuss the accounting for events after the reporting date.

c) Determine and report going concern issues arising after the reporting date.

9. Related parties   14

a) Determine the parties considered to be related to an entity.

b) Identify the implications of related party relationships and the need for disclosure.

10. Share based payment   15

a) Apply and discuss the recognition and measurement criteria for share-based payment transactions.

b) Account for modifications, cancellations and settlements of share based payment transactions.

11. Reporting requirements of small and medium-sized entities (SMEs)   1

a) Discuss the accounting treatments not allowable under the IFRS for SMEs including the revaluation model for certain assets

b) Discuss and apply the simplifications introduced by the IFRS for SMEs including accounting for goodwill and intangible assets, financial instruments, defined benefit schemes, exchange differences and associates and joint ventures.

(continued on next page)

© DeVry/Becker Educational Development Corp. All rights reserved.

D.	Financial Statements of Groups of Entities	Ref.
1.	**Group accounting including statements of cash flows**	
a)	Apply the method of accounting for business combinations including complex group structures.	18
b)	Apply the principles in determining the cost of a business combination.	18
c)	Apply the recognition and measurement criteria for identifiable acquired assets and liabilities and goodwill including step acquisitions.	18
d)	Apply and discuss the criteria used to identify a subsidiary and an associate.	16
e)	Determine and apply appropriate procedures to be used in preparing group financial statements.	18
f)	Identify and outline:	16
	• the circumstances in which a group is required to prepare consolidated financial statements.	
	• the circumstances when a group may claim an exemption from the preparation of consolidated financial statements.	
	• why directors may not wish to consolidate a subsidiary and where this is permitted.	
g)	Apply the equity method of accounting for associates.	21
h)	Outline and apply the key definitions and accounting methods which relate to interests in joint arrangements.	21
i)	Prepare and discuss group statements of cash flows.	23
2.	**Continuing and discontinued interests**	
a)	Prepare group financial statements where activities have been discontinued, or have been acquired or disposed of in the period.	20
b)	Apply and discuss the treatment of a subsidiary which has been acquired exclusively with a view to subsequent disposal.	16
3.	**Changes in group structures**	20
a)	Discuss the reasons behind a group reorganisation.	
b)	Evaluate and assess the principal terms of a proposed group reorganisation.	
4.	**Foreign transactions and entities**	22
a)	Outline and apply the translation of foreign currency amounts and transactions into the functional currency and the presentational currency.	
b)	Account for the consolidation of foreign operations and their disposal.	

E.	Specialised Entities and Specialised Transactions	Ref.
1.	**Financial reporting in specialised, not-for-profit and public sector entities**	3
a)	Apply knowledge from the syllabus to straightforward transactions and events arising in specialised, not-for-profit, and public sector entities.	
2.	**Entity reconstructions**	20
a)	Identify when an entity may no longer be viewed as a going concern or uncertainty exists surrounding the going concern status.	
b)	Identify and outline the circumstances in which a reconstruction would be an appropriate alternative to a company liquidation.	
c)	Outline the appropriate accounting treatment required relating to reconstructions.	

(continued on next page)

© DeVry/Becker Educational Development Corp. All rights reserved.

F.	Implications Of Changes In Accounting Regulation on Financial Reporting	Ref.
1.	**The effect of changes in accounting standards on accounting systems**	**25**
a)	Apply and discuss the accounting implications of the first time adoption of a body of new accounting standards.	
2.	**Proposed changes to accounting standards**	**1**
a)	Identify issues and deficiencies which have led to a proposed change to an accounting standard.	

G.	The Appraisal of Financial Performance and Position of Entities	Ref.
1.	**The creation of suitable accounting policies**	**5**
a)	Develop accounting policies for an entity which meet the entity's reporting requirements.	
b)	Identify accounting treatments adopted in financial statements and assess their suitability and acceptability.	
2.	**Analysis and interpretation of financial information and measurement of performance**	**24**
a)	Select and calculate relevant indicators of financial and non-financial performance.	
b)	Identify and evaluate significant features and issues in financial statements.	
c)	Highlight inconsistencies in financial information through analysis and application of knowledge.	
d)	Make inferences from the analysis of information taking into account the limitation of the information, the analytical methods used and the business environment in which the entity operates.	

H.	Current Developments	Ref.
1.	**Environmental and social reporting**	**27**
a)	Appraise the impact of environmental, social, and ethical factors on performance measurement.	
b)	Evaluate current reporting requirements in the area including the development of integrated reporting.	
c)	Discuss why entities might include disclosures relating to the environment and society.	
2.	**Convergence between national and international reporting standards**	**2**
a)	Evaluate the implications of worldwide convergence with International Financial Reporting Standards.	
b)	Discuss the influence of national regulators on international financial reporting.	
3.	**Current reporting issues**	**1**
a)	Discuss current issues in corporate reporting, including:	
	i) recent IFRSs	
	ii) practice and regulatory issues	
	iii) proposed changes to IFRS	
	iv) problems with extant standards	

EXAMINATION TECHNIQUE

Aim of Paper P2

"To apply knowledge, skills and exercise professional judgement in the application and evaluation of financial reporting principles and practices in a range of business contexts and situations."

There is much more to passing exams than recalling facts, terms, definitions, etc. You must practise your examination technique and be able to apply the knowledge learnt during your studies to the scenario given. Markers will be assessing you on the quality and professionalism of your answers rather than the quantity of information; you will not achieve good marks by "knowledge dumping".

The examiner expects candidates to read around and research the topic of corporate reporting and be aware of current issues related to the syllabus. You should aim to follow what is happening in the real world not just from an accounting perspective but also from economic and political perspectives. Every now and again peruse the annual accounts of a global multinational corporation, visit one of the "Big 4" audit firm's IFRS websites and the business and finance pages of The Economist (http://www.economist.com/business-finance).

Time Allocation

- As a minimum we recommend that 15 minutes is used to read and plan Section A and 7 minutes to each of the two choice questions. The more time you spend on reading and planning (within reason) the better and more structured your response to the question requirements should be. If you do not plan your answer you are more likely to answer the question you wanted to be set, not the question that the examiner set.

- Decide which of the optional questions you do not want to do.

- Decide the order in which you will answer the three questions.

- You must allow 1½ hours for Question 1 and 45 minutes for each of the Section B questions.

- Stick to this time allocation. You **MUST** attempt **all** parts of **all three** questions that you are required to answer.

- The first marks for each part of a question should be the easiest to gain, so when time is up, move to the next part.

© DeVry/Becker Educational Development Corp. All rights reserved.

Answer Planning

Things to do when reading and planning your answers:

✔ Highlight the "instruction(s)" in each requirement.

✔ Underline the "content(s)" and "context".

✔ Think about the most suitable layout—"Pro forma"? Tabulation?

✔ Register marks—time allocations for each part.

✔ Make notes that will assist you in your later answer (e.g. on the question paper).

✔ Plan discursive answers (e.g. draw a spidergram or mind map).

✔ Answer plans in your scripts should be headed up and clearly distinguished from the answer the marker should mark.

The most common **instructions** in this examination are:

▨ Prepare ... (e.g. a consolidated statement of cash flows);

▨ Discuss ... (e.g. principles, the directors' views, ethical implications);

▨ Advise ... (e.g. how transactions should be dealt with in accordance with IFRS);

▨ Explain ... (e.g. the effect of an accounting treatment on the financial statements); and

▨ Describe ... (e.g. accounting rules).

Although computational aspects (see below) are particularly relevant to the instruction "prepare", you should look out for "with suitable calculations" in instructions to explain, advise, etc.

To plan an answer during this time:

▨ Read the scenario quickly to identify:

Company name, dates, nature of business, performance.

▨ Recall the technical knowledge you have learned relating to the content from the requirements and your quick read of the scenario.

The importance of adequate planning cannot be overemphasised. Adequate planning leads to an organised logical structure to your answer, incorporating all the points you can come up with and highlighting your powers of analysis and communication. A lack of planning leads to a disorganised illogical jumble of scraps of thoughts and ideas, causing you to omit key elements of the question and repeat answer points already made.

Write any answer plans you jot down in your answer booklet so you can submit them, and perhaps earn some marks.

Clearly head up the page "answer plan" or "workings".

WARNING: Never write "half sentences"—there is **no time** for them in answer planning and **no place** for them in writing out your answer.

Computational Answers

Key Point

Clear presentation, workings and notes are essential.

- Before starting a computation, picture your route. Do this by jotting down the steps you are going to take and imagining the layout of your answer.
- Set up a pro forma structure to your answer before working the numbers.
- Use a columnar layout if appropriate. This helps to avoid mistakes and is easier for the marker to follow.
- Include all your workings and cross-reference them to the face of your answer.
- A clear approach and workings will help earn marks even if you make an arithmetic mistake.
- If you do spot a mistake in your answer, it is *not* worthwhile spending time amending the consequent effects of it. The marker of your script will *not* punish you for errors caused by an earlier mistake.
- Do not ignore marks for written recommendations or comments based on your computation. These are easy marks to gain.
- If you could not complete the calculations required for comment then *assume* an answer to the calculations. As long as your comments are consistent with your assumed answer you can still pick up all the marks for the comments.

Non-computational Answers

Key Point

Focus on exactly what is being asked for in the question.

- Are you required to discuss, advise, explain or describe? They do not mean the same thing (e.g. a discussion should take a balanced view of different perspectives).
- Who is the target audience? Advising a client will require a different tone to describing rules of IFRS. You should be thinking about this before you put pen to paper to write your answer.
- It is likely that you will need to read the scenario at least twice. During the second reading some of the following may assist you in your answer:
  - highlighting key points; or
  - noting implications in the margin; and
  - noting points on a plan of your answer.
- Draw together your technical knowledge and the points from the scenario. Do this by thinking and rearranging your plan, before you write up your answer.

© DeVry/Becker Educational Development Corp. All rights reserved.

Write Your Answer

If you have adequately read, thought and planned, this *should* be the easiest part of the whole exercise. Points to remember:

- Use underlined HEADINGS and subheadings (generated by the requirement and any breakdown of the scenario into parts) to produce a logical and structured answer.

- Use the scenario given when answering the question but do not copy the question into your answer booklet, you will not earn marks for this and you will have wasted your valuable time. As mentioned previously, apply your knowledge do not simply regurgitate facts that you may have learnt that have no bearings on the requirements of the question.

- Maintain a sentence structure and keep sentences and paragraphs short and succinct. Look to suggested solutions of past examinations for appropriate style.

Explain and define where necessary (e.g. if asked to be writing to a layman, briefly explain when an impairment arises, if relevant.

- Try to achieve a good standard of English. Although you will not lose marks for spelling mistakes and poor grammar, you may lose marks if your answer points cannot be understood by the marker.

- Allow plenty of space to present your answer and, if your writing is difficult to read,

  write on

  every

  other

  line—in CAPITALS if necessary.

WARNING: Restrict the use of underlining to headings and sub-headings (and use a ruler). Do **not** waste time underlining what you consider to be the "key" words—it is quite unnecessary and may interfere with the marking process.

- Candidates often ask, "How much should I write". The examiner is not interested in volume, he does not weigh scripts and marking is an arduous task. So do yourselves (and your markers) a favour—answer the Q set and think about the *relevance* of what you are writing. Look back to the answer plan (above).

Case Study Question 1

This question will be 50 marks broken down into a number of parts. The majority of the marks (approximately 35 marks) will be for the preparation of one or more consolidated financial statements.

One of the biggest issues with this question will be time management; you must not spend more than 90 minutes on it. It is a matter of fact that approximately 70% of the marks for this question can be achieved in the first 50% of the time available. So the second 45 minutes you spend on this will be searching for the more difficult marks.

✔ Once the time is up, move on to the next question; by all means come back to it if you have time at the end of the exam.

Keep all parts of the solution together.

✔ If, for example, you answer parts (a), (b) and (c) but want to come back to (d) later in the exam, then leave some space at the end of (c) with a heading for (d).

✗ It is a "pet hate" of the examiner to see candidates include parts of their answers elsewhere; he feels it shows a lack of professionalism.

Cross-reference all workings and keep them legible and intelligible.

✗ A simple list of numbers is not a working; you must provide sufficient narrative (albeit brief) to explain what you are doing to the marker.

Goodwill, for example, may be worth 5 marks; if your answer is wrong then the marker will go to a cross-referenced working to see if you deserve some partial credit. If the marker cannot find your working or if it does not make any sense, you cannot be given credit. Get the marker on your side. If you do not have a cross-referenced working, the marker is not required to look for one!

Once you have determined an amount that you want to include in the solution (whether from simply summing two numbers or performing a number of calculations), insert it straight away; do not wait until the very end to produce the solution.

✔ You are strongly advised to prepare the solution at the same time you are doing your workings to ensure that you earn the marks for the work you have done.

✗ Even with workings, a "blank pro forma" solution will not attract as many marks as if the required financial statement has been **prepared**.

If part way through your answer you realise you have made a mistake then simply put a neat line through the incorrect number and insert the new number at the side.

✗ Do not overwrite as it can become virtually impossible to identify the number you want to include. Remember that your script will be **scanned**.

✔ If you find an error at the end of the exam then do not try to change all your numbers; simply make a note that a certain figure is wrong and state the consequence that the change would have on the remainder of your solution.

Do not overlook the theory and discursive parts of the question, as it is often very easy to achieve a pass mark on these parts. No answer to a part is clearly zero marks. Keep your answer points clear and concise. You should not give detailed technical knowledge unless it is a requirement (i.e. to describe rules); it is the application of knowledge that the examiner is generally looking for rather than the knowledge itself.

Section B Questions

You should be able to decide quickly which optional questions you are going to attempt or, more likely, the one that you are not going to attempt. Remember that you must do two (and only two) from three; you must not attempt parts of all three.

Questions 2 and 3 are likely to be "multi-standard" questions (i.e. requiring knowledge of a number of standards).

✗ Do not look at one part of a question and dismiss it entirely without looking at other parts.

✗ Equally, do not choose a question based on just one part only to find out later that you cannot answer the remaining parts.

At this level, you are expected to be able to think about inter-relationships between standards and how they may interact for a given transaction or series of transactions; do not concentrate on individual standards in isolation. Make sure that you have planned how you are going to answer the issues and stick with your plan.

Do not write essays. Answer clearly in succinct paragraphs working on the general principle that one good and relevant point is worth 1 mark; therefore a requirement with 10 marks calls for a **minimum** of 5 relevant if you are aiming to pass.

Refer to the standard when relevant and use the standard number if you know it. If you do not know the number then do **not** guess it; refer to it instead by the topics it deals with (e.g. "the standard on leases").

Aim to demonstrate to the examiner not only that you have the knowledge but that you can apply it to a given scenario.

                 © DeVry/Becker Educational Development Corp. All rights reserved.

One question is usually structured around a specific industry (e.g. telecommunications, oil, football clubs). You are not expected to have industry-specific knowledge but you are expected to demonstrate your application skills.

Although the Conceptual Framework may not feature as a direct question the definition of assets and liabilities and the two recognition criteria will often assist with an answer, make sure that you have the definitions and the recognition criteria committed to memory.

As Question 4 should be of a "topical" nature, it is impossible to predict it with any degree of certainty. You will be expected to have read all the technical articles relating to P2 under qualification resources on ACCA's website. Also look at the CPD resources in the members' section of the website.*

Commentary

*Articles tend to be available in the members' section before they are referenced in the students' section.

Professional Marks

Each question in Section B carries 2 professional marks; ensure that you earn these marks. Be professional in your answers by:

✔ Answering every part
✔ Following the requirements
✔ Writing legibly
✔ Answering in the style and tone required (e.g. advising the directors)
✔ Cross-referencing calculations (as workings) where required.

Summary

When attempting an exam style and standard question, *always* practise exam technique so that it is second nature to you by the time of the real exam.

▨ Spend time thoroughly reviewing your answer against the "model" answer and make a note of the points you missed. (Do not be despondent if some of the answers you encounter do not follow this guidance—historically "model" answers are written solely to convey technical content rather than exam technique.)

▨ Study the examiner's comments on candidates' performance in previous exams, areas of weakness and suggestions for improvements.

▨ Practice "effective writing" throughout your studies.

Remember the key elements to examination technique:

Read: This provides the facts to trigger your knowledge.

Think: Without this planning process you will not be able to convey the skills of comprehension, application and analysis which are expected of you.

Write: Concentrate on your style of writing to address the examiners' requirements as directly as possible.

IFRS and Corporate Reporting

FOCUS

This session covers the following content from the *ACCA Study Guide.*

C. Reporting the Financial Performance of Entities

11. Reporting requirements of small and medium-sized entities (SMEs)

a) Discuss the accounting treatments not allowable under the IFRS for SMEs including the revaluation model for certain assets. ☐

b) Discuss and apply the simplifications introduced by IFRS for SMEs including accounting for goodwill and intangible assets, financial instruments, defined benefit schemes, exchange differences and associates and joint ventures. ☐

F. Implications of Changes in Accounting Regulation on Financial Reporting

2. Proposed changes to accounting standards

a) Identify issues and deficiencies which have led to a proposed change to an accounting standard. ☐

H. Current Developments

3. Current reporting issues

a) Discuss current issues in corporate reporting, including: ☐
    i)   recent IFRSs
    ii)   practice and regulatory issues
    iii) proposed changes to IFRS
    iv)   problems with extant standards

Session 1 Guidance

■ **Comprehend** that this session is generally background reading, much of which you should be familiar with from your F7 studies.

■ **Pay** attention to "Big GAAP, Little GAAP" and understand the different accounting treatment allowed/ required by IFRS for SMEs as opposed to full IFRS accounting (s.5).

■ **Be** aware that IFRICs and SICs are not examinable documents.

VISUAL OVERVIEW

Objective: To describe the concept of GAAP; the objectives of the International Accounting Standards Board (IASB) and its relationship with other bodies; and the development, scope and use of International Financial Reporting Standards (IFRSs).

GAAP

- What Is GAAP?
- Sources of GAAP
- Statute and Standards

INTERNATIONAL FEDERATION OF ACCOUNTANTS

- What Is It?
- Membership
- Technical Committees

IASB

- What Is It?
- Objectives
- Structure

SMALL AND MEDIUM-SIZED ENTITIES

- Differential Reporting
- Big GAAP/Little GAAP
- IFRS for SMEs
- Undue Cost or Effort

IFRS

- Importance
- Development
- Changes to Standards
- Work Plan
- Interpretation
- Annual Improvements
- Scope and Application

IFRS IC

- Background
- Approach
- Changes

CURRENT ISSUES

- Recent IFRSs
- Proposed Changes
- Practice and Regulation
- Extant Standards

© DeVry/Becker Educational Development Corp. All rights reserved.

1 GAAP

1.1 What Is GAAP?

- GAAP (Generally Accepted Accounting Principles) is a term used to describe how financial statements are prepared in a given environment.
- GAAP is a general term.*
- The term may or may not have legal authority in a given country.

Key Point

GAAP is a dynamic concept. It changes with time in accordance with changes in the business environment.

*UK GAAP, US GAAP are more specific statements.

1.2 Sources of GAAP

1.2.1 Regulatory Framework

- The body of rules and regulations, from whatever source, which an entity must follow when preparing accounts in a particular country for a particular purpose, will include:
  - Statute;
  - Accounting standards—Statements issued by professional accounting bodies which lay down rules on accounting for different issues. For example:
    — International Financial Reporting Standards;
    — Financial Reporting Standards (UK);
    — Financial Accounting Standards (US).

1.2.2 Other Sources

- IFRSs—In countries in which these have not been adopted they have an influence on local standards because the provisions of the IFRS will be considered by the local standard-setting body.
- Best practice—methods of accounting developed by companies (industry groups) in the absence of rules in a specific area (e.g. oil exploration costs).

1.3 Role of Statute and Standards

- Varies from country to country
  - Some countries have a very legalistic approach to drafting financial statements. The legal rules are detailed and specific and the system is often geared to the production of a profit figure for taxation purposes.
  - Some countries adopt an approach by which statute provides a framework of regulation and standards then fill in the blanks (e.g. in the UK).*
    — Statute—Companies Act 2006
    — Standards—SSAPs and FRSs.
  - Some countries have little in the way of statute and rely largely on standards (e.g. the US).

*The legislation of European Union (EU) member states is based on EU directives.

© DeVry/Becker Educational Development Corp. All rights reserved.

2 International Federation of Accountants (IFAC)

2.1 What Is It?

▦ IFAC is a non-profit, non-governmental, non-political organisation of accountancy bodies which represents the worldwide accountancy profession.

▦ Its mission is to develop and enhance the profession to provide services of consistently high quality in the public interest.

2.2 Membership

▦ Accountancy bodies recognised by law or consensus within their countries.

▦ Membership in IFAC automatically includes membership in the International Accounting Standards Board (IASB).

2.3 Technical Committees

▦ International Auditing Practices Committee (IAPC)—issues International Standards on Auditing (ISAs).

▦ Forum on Ethics—publishes a Code of Ethics for Professional Accountants.

▦ Others:
  ● Education
  ● Financial and Management Accounting
  ● Public Sector
  ● Information Technology
  ● Membership

3 The IASB

3.1 What Is It?

▦ The International Accounting Standards Board was formed in 2001. One of its major roles is the issuance of a single set of globally accepted accounting standards.*

▦ To this end:
  ● 122 jurisdictions, including UK, Afghanistan and New Zealand require public entities to use IFRSs;
  ● 13 jurisdictions, including Switzerland and Japan, permit the use of IFRS's; and
  ● Eight jurisdictions, including USA and Egypt, use National or Regional standards.*

*Commentary

*Formerly the International Accounting Standards Committee (IASC).

*Commentary

*The countries required or permitted to use IFRSs is constantly changing.

© DeVry/Becker Educational Development Corp. All rights reserved.

3.2 Objectives

Key Point

The primary objective of the IASB is to develop, in the public interest, a *single set* of high-quality, understandable and enforceable global accounting standards which require high-quality, *transparent* and *comparable* information in financial statements and other financial reporting to help participants in the world's capital markets and other *users* make *economic decisions*.

- To promote the use and rigorous application of those standards.
- To take account of the needs of a range of sizes and types of entities in diverse economic settings (e.g. emerging economies).
- To promote and facilitate adoption of IFRSs through the convergence of national accounting standards and IFRS.

3.3 Structure

3.3.1 Overview

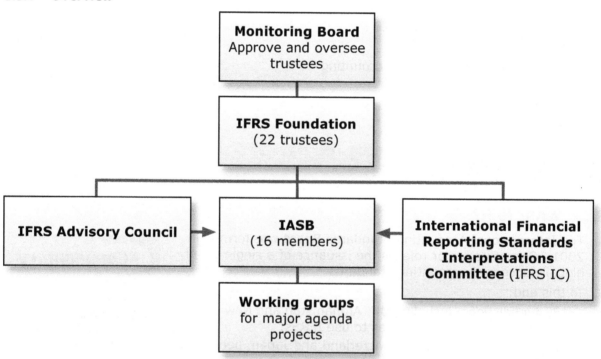

3.3.2 Monitoring Board

- This board oversees the IFRS Foundation trustees, participates in the trustee nomination process and approves appointments to the trustees.

© DeVry/Becker Educational Development Corp. All rights reserved.

3.3.3   IFRS Foundation

- Formerly known as the International Accounting Standards Committee Foundation this independent not-for-profit corporation was established under the laws of the US in 2001.
- The body oversees the IASB.
- The trustees are 22 individuals from diverse geographical and functional backgrounds.
- The trustees:
  - appoint the members of the IASB, Advisory Council and IFRS IC;
  - monitor the IASB's effectiveness;
  - secure funding;
  - approve the IASB's budgets; and
  - are responsible for constitutional change.

3.3.4   IASB

- The trustees appoint 16 members, of whom a maximum of three may be part time. Members are appointed for three- to five-year terms; the main qualification for board membership is that they must show professional competence and have the necessary practical experience.

 **Key Point**

The board has complete responsibilities for all technical matters.

- These include:
  - preparation and issue of IFRSs;
  - preparation and issue of exposure drafts;
  - setting up procedures to review comments received on documents published for comment; and
  - issuing basis for conclusions.
- Each member has one vote and the approval of 10 members is required for documents to be issued for discussion, exposure or as the final standard.

3.3.5   IFRS Council

- About 40 members all appointed by the trustees for a renewable term of three years and with diverse geographical and functional backgrounds.
- The council provides a forum for participation by organisations and individuals with an interest in international financial reporting.
- It meets at least three times a year.
- The council:
  - advises the board on agenda decisions and work priorities;
  - passes on views of the council members on the major standard-setting projects;
  - gives other advice to the trustees and the board.

4 International Financial Reporting Standards

4.1 Importance of IFRSs

Key Point

Ultimately, IFRSs will form the basis of international financial reporting.

■ The IASB concentrates on essentials. It endeavours not to make IFRSs so complex that they cannot be applied effectively on a worldwide basis.

4.2 Development of IFRSs

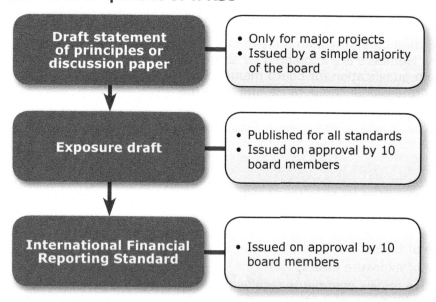

Draft statement of principles or discussion paper	• Only for major projects • Issued by a simple majority of the board
Exposure draft	• Published for all standards • Issued on approval by 10 board members
International Financial Reporting Standard	• Issued on approval by 10 board members

Key Point

Since 2001, all new standards are issued as International Financial Reporting Standards (IFRSs). Standards issued by the IASC were International Accounting Standards (IASs). Both terms are acceptable to mean accounting standards in general.

4.2.1 Financial Instruments

■ IAS 39 *Financial Instruments: Recognition and Measurement* was first issued in 1999 as part of the IASC's overall financial instruments project for the core set of standards required by IOSCO.*

■ The second part of the project, IAS 32 *Financial Instruments Presentation and Disclosure*, was delivered first. IAS 39 sought to address the recognition and measurement issues.

■ IAS 39 required derivative instruments to be recognised in the financial statements for the first time. Prior to the standard, derivatives had been kept "off balance sheet".

*Commentary

*See *Session 2* for details of the International Organisation of Securities Commission (IOSCO).

© DeVry/Becker Educational Development Corp. All rights reserved.

▨ Another effect was on the measurement of these derivatives, at fair value. This meant that any changes in fair value during the holding period of the derivative would be included in profit or loss, making profits far more volatile.

▨ IFRS 9 *Financial Instruments* was initially issued in November 2009 and only reflected the recognition and measurement of financial assets. In October 2010, the IASB amended IFRS 9 to also include the recognition and measurement of financial liabilities. The amended standard also deals with the derecognition of financial assets and liabilities.

▨ The hedging section of the standard was completed in 2013 and the impairment section followed in 2014. The standard is now complete and is applicable for periods beginning 1 January 2018; early adoption is allowed.

4.2.2 IFRS 2 *Share-based Payment*

▨ How to account for share-based payment transactions had been deliberated for many years before this standard was issued. The Financial Accounting Standards Board (FASB) had tried to introduce a compulsory standard into US GAAP previously but met with so much hostility that it reduced the requirements, eventually requiring only disclosures to be included in the financial statements.

▨ One of the major effects of IFRS 2 was that it required share options to be accounted for the first time. At that time, in the UK (for example), share options were a regular feature of remuneration packages but there were no requirements to account for them prior to IFRS 2.

▨ The IASB argued that they were the same as salary, a payment to an employee for providing a service and should therefore be accounted for in the same way as the salary.

▨ The effect of accounting for share options was that the reported profits were reduced as the cost of the share option was charged against profits. There was no change to the net asset position in the statement of financial position as the credit entry was made into equity, with that credit eventually being transferred through to the retained earnings reserve.

4.3 Changes to Standards

▨ Once issued, a standard does not always remain in its original form. For example, if issues are identified about the application of a standard which were not considered during the due process stages, then the IASB will make subsequent amendments.

▨ Amendments may be made through:
* the annual improvement project, for minor issues;
* revisions to large parts of the existing standard; or
* the issue of a new standard.

▨ IAS 39 went through many revisions and amendments after it was first issued. The topic of financial instruments is so complex that it has proved extremely difficult to incorporate all aspects of accounting for financial instruments in one standard.*

Exam Advice

IFRS 9 is the examinable document for the P2 exam.

*Commentary

*Complexities are such that full implementation of IFRS 9 (to replace IAS 39) is five years behind the original scheduled effective date.

- Accounting for leases is an area that has caused much concern for the IASB. The accounting profession has been looking at the issue since 1999, with the IASB issuing two ED's before finally issuing new standard IFRS 16 *Leases* in 2016.

- In 2011, the IASB issued a revised IAS 19 *Employee Benefits*, which drastically changed the accounting model for defined benefit schemes.

  - Until then, accounting for defined benefit schemes had been very complex and the original standard allowed different accounting treatments that led to a lack of comparability between companies.

  - Although the revised standard is still quite complex there is now only one treatment for actuarial gains and losses, which has led to greater comparability.

- The above examples show that GAAP is dynamic; it does not stand still. If an issue is identified then the IASB will look into it and, when necessary, amend or revise an existing standard, even though the process can take many years.*

4.4 Projects and Work Plan

4.4.1 Most Recent IFRSs

- In 2014 IASB issued the long-awaited IFRS 9 *Financial Instruments* and IFRS 15 *Revenue from Contracts with Customers*.

- In 2016 the IASB issued IFRS 16 *Leases*, this replaced the previous standard, IAS 17; it had taken the IASB nearly six years to get the new standard published.

4.4.2 Work Plan

- The IASB's current work plan includes:
  - Insurance contracts;
  - Disclosure initiatives; and
  - Conceptual Framework.

4.4.3 Convergence

- Convergence is a gradual process by which local GAAP approaches and is replaced with IFRS. As a step-by-step transition process it:
  - gives more time for preparation; and
  - reduces the potentially negative effects on companies trading their shares.

- The main effects on financial statements of adopting IFRSs include:
  - greater use of fair value as a measurement basis;
  - considerably greater disclosure; and
  - the need for more narrative to explain its complexities.

- Major areas of differences between local GAAP and IFRSs may be classified, for example, between those which are:*
  - fully related to day-to-day accounting (e.g. IAS 16 *Property, Plant and Equipment*);
  - partially related to day-to-day accounting (e.g. IAS 19 *Employee Benefits*); and
  - related to consolidation (e.g. IFRS 3 *Business Combinations*).

*In some circumstances, the IASB may rush through a change. For example, in 2008, when the financial crisis first hit, the IASB abandoned due process in order to expedite the "fair value opt out" amendment to IAS 39.

*Companies may, therefore, need to change their accounting systems to meet IFRS requirements.

© DeVry/Becker Educational Development Corp. All rights reserved.

4.5   Interpretation of IFRSs

* Steps taken by the IASB to achieve *consistent* interpretation include:
  * publication of draft statement of principles—to make IASB intentions clear;
  * issue of interpretations by the Standing Interpretations Committee (SIC), renamed International Financial Reporting Interpretations Committee (IFRIC), and now called International Financial Reporting Standards Interpretation Committee (IFRS IC).

4.6   Annual Improvements Project

* Since 2007, the IASB has issued, as a separate document, annual improvements to IFRSs. These improvements are initially issued as an exposure draft (ED) and then, if approved, issued as a separate standard which will eventually be embedded into the standards being amended.
* These amendments are deemed to be non-urgent but necessary to clarify any inconsistencies or ambiguities in the original standard.

4.7   Scope and Application

* IFRSs apply to the published financial statements of any commercial, industrial or business reporting entity (whether public or private sector).
* IFRSs apply to both separate and consolidated financial statements.
* Any limitation on the applicability of specific IFRSs is made clear in the IFRS.
* IFRSs are not intended to apply to immaterial items.
* An IFRS applies from a date specified in the standard and is not retroactive unless indicated to the contrary (which is often the case).

5   Small and Medium-Sized Entities

5.1   Differential Reporting

* A debate has arisen about the relevance of IFRS to all forms of business. Is financial reporting the same for:
  * Large and small companies?
  * Profit-focused and not-for-profit organisations?
  * Public sector and private sector organisations?
* Not all businesses have profit as their prime focus. The information that listed companies are required to present is likely to be of little use to the users of a charity's financial statements.
* The majority of companies in the world are not listed on a recognised stock exchange and their shares are not traded. Many of these are "insider" or owner-managed companies and therefore financial information is available immediately for the owners. In contrast, shareholders (owners) of a listed company only really get to see financial information that is published in the annual financial statements.

- There is also a cost issue involved in the debate. It is very costly to produce and present a set of financial statements in compliance with IFRS. If most businesses gain no benefit from these statements is it really cost effective for every business type to fully comply with IFRS?

- In 2009, the IASB issued *IFRS for Small and Medium-sized Entities* (IFRS for SMEs); this standard was updated and revised in 2015.

- The debate is therefore about "differential reporting"—whether "one-size-fits-all" or whether different types of business should report under different regulations. The possible options available for reporting for different businesses are:
  - All businesses to use one "IFRS GAAP".
  - Use one GAAP but limit disclosures for certain types of business.
  - Exempt some types of business from the reporting requirements.
  - Have a separate set of standards for certain businesses.

- The IASB has gone down the latter route by issuing IFRS for small and medium-sized entities. The remainder of this section focuses mainly on the SME debate.

5.2 Big GAAP/Little GAAP

- There has been a consensus for a long time that reporting requirements are biased towards larger companies and ignore the needs of small companies.

- Compliance places a burden on small companies which includes:
  - the cost of considering whether a particular standard is applicable to the entity;
  - the cost of assembling the information;
  - the cost of auditing the information; and
  - the loss of commercial advantage that may arise from increased disclosure.

- The appropriateness of applying accounting standards to small companies has been the subject of numerous studies in the UK and around the world. The debate has revolved around whether accounting standards should apply equally to all financial statements that purport to present a "true and fair view" or whether small companies should be exempted from the need to comply with certain standards.

5.2.1 Difficulties

- Difficulties include:
  - ✗ the choice of a method of determining which companies should be allowed exemption from the general GAAP; and
  - ✗ the choice of accounting rules from which such companies should be exempted.

- In considering how to distinguish between categories of companies a number of factors could be used, including:
  - the extent to which there is public interest in an entity;
  - its complexity, the separation of ownership and control; and
  - its size.*

*Although size is not the most important factor, it is the easiest to apply.

© DeVry/Becker Educational Development Corp. All rights reserved.

■ The UK Accounting Standards Board introduced a modified GAAP for certain companies based on size. This has met with much criticism as most commentators feel that the separation of ownership would be a more useful criterion.

5.2.2 Arguments For

✔ The purpose of a set of accounts is to communicate information to users of financial statements. However, for a simple concern, some of the complex rules which are in force today may serve to hinder rather than aid communication.

✔ The complex calculations, the quantity of disclosure and the technical terminology called for by accounting standards may serve to make the accounts of small companies incomprehensible to their users.

✔ The owners of public companies are not generally involved in managing the business. For this reason, a relationship of accountability exists between owners and managers. This is not the case for owner-managed entities.

✔ In short, standards fail to take adequate account of the needs of users.

- The users of public companies' financial statements include:
  - existing and potential shareholders;
  - loan creditors;
  - financial analysts and advisers;
  - the financial press; and
  - employees.
- The users of small companies' financial statements include:
  - owner-managers;
  - bankers; and
  - tax authorities.

5.2.3 Arguments Against

✗ Empirical research has not found that small companies find complying with accounting standards a matter for concern.

✗ Small entities normally have very few major accounting issues which need to be addressed, simply because of their size. In practice, this means that many of the IFRSs have a negligible effect on the small company.

✗ For those entities aiming for public ownership sometime in the future then it will prove costly to move from one method of accounting for full IFRS.

✗ For companies already in existence, accounts formats with full disclosure will already be in place.

5.3 IFRS for SMEs

■ *IFRS for Small and Medium-Sized Entities* offers possible relief from compliance with full IFRS.

■ The standard provides an alternative framework which can be applied by eligible companies in place of the full set of IFRS.

5.3.1 Definition of SME

■ IFRS for SMEs does not specifically define an SME; it leaves this up to national regulatory authorities as the bodies which will set the eligibility criteria (e.g. based on turnover, value of assets or number of employees).

5.3.2 Applicability

Key Point

IFRS for SMEs applies to general purpose financial statements of entities that have *no* public accountability.*

*Commentary

*This does not define an SME. Entities without public accountability cannot adopt the standard if they do not meet the criteria set by national regulators.

▦ This standard is therefore not relevant to entities which have securities, equities or debt, listed on a recognised market (or are in the process of obtaining a listing).

▦ An entity which holds assets in a fiduciary capacity for others (e.g. a bank) has public accountability and will not be able to apply this standard.

▦ A company which is "small" but has a listing must apply full versions of IFRS.

5.3.3 Objectives of IASB SME Standards

▦ To provide high-quality, understandable and enforceable standards suitable for SMEs globally.

▦ To focus on meeting the needs of users of SME financial statements.

▦ To be built on the same conceptual framework as IFRSs.

▦ To reduce the financial reporting burden on SMEs which want to use global standards.

▦ To allow easy transition to full IFRS for those SMEs which become publicly accountable or choose to change to full IFRS.

5.3.4 Stand-Alone Document

▦ The standard is intended to be a stand-alone document without the need to refer to the full set of IFRS.

▦ Where an item is not covered by the standard then there is no mandatory fallback to full IFRS.

▦ The standard takes the fundamental concepts from the framework document, principles and mandatory guidance from appropriate standards and modifies these to take account of users' needs and cost-benefit considerations.

5.3.5 Topics Omitted

▦ Standards that are not relevant to the "typical" SME are omitted from the standard. Therefore, if an omitted standard is relevant to the financial statements of an entity, the full IFRS must be applied.

▦ IAS 33 is not applicable as an SME's equity cannot be listed on a recognised stock market and so has no requirement to present earnings per share.

▦ Other standards omitted include those dealing with:*

- interim financial reporting;
- operating segments;
- insurance; and
- assets held for sale.

*Commentary

*The related standards would be irrelevant for most SMEs even if they prepared financial statements in compliance with full IFRS.

© DeVry/Becker Educational Development Corp. All rights reserved.

- It could be argued that there is no need for IFRS for SMEs for these areas of financial reporting as, in the majority of cases, the full IFRS would not be used. For example:
  - interim financial reports are a requirement only for listed companies (so SMEs do not prepare them);
  - it would be rare for a small company to have two or more operating segments.

5.3.6 Simpler Option Included

- Where the full standard gives a choice of policy, then only the simpler option has been included in the SME standard.
- The standard leaves it to individual jurisdictions as to whether there is an option to cross-reference to the full IFRS.
- The relevant standards include:
  - IAS 40—investment properties are valued at fair value as long as this can be measured reliably and without undue cost or effort.
  - IAS 23—requires all borrowing costs to be expensed.
  - IAS 20—requires that government grants be recognised in income when performance conditions, if any, have been met. If performance conditions have not yet been met they must be recognised as liabilities.
  - IAS 38—requires all research and development costs to be expensed.
  - IAS 38—only the cost model is available for property, plant and equipment and intangible assets.

5.3.7 Recognition and Measurement

- Certain standards have simplified recognition and measurement requirements. The relevant standards include:
  - IFRS 9—there are only two categories of financial assets—those measured at amortised cost and those at fair value through profit or loss.*
  - IAS 21—there is no need to reclassify exchange differences that are initially recognised in other comprehensive income to profit or loss on disposal of the foreign investment.
  - IFRS 3 and IAS 36—goodwill is amortised annually rather than tested for impairment.

5.4 Undue Cost or Effort

The standard allows exemption from following certain requirements if application would cause undue cost or effort. Issues covered by undue cost or effort exemption include:

- measurement of investments in equity instruments at fair value;
- recognising intangible assets separately in a business combination; and
- offsetting income tax assets and liabilities.

Guidance in the standard emphasises that undue cost or effort is not intended to be a "low hurdle" that entities can use as a "get out" clause to excuse them from following the requirements of the standard.

 **Key Point**

The 2015 version of the standard now allows an entity to use a revaluation model for property, plant and equipment; revaluation was not allowed under the 2009 version of the standard.

 **Commentary**

*There is no "fair value through other comprehensive income" category.

© DeVry/Becker Educational Development Corp. All rights reserved.

6 IFRS Interpretations Committee

Exam Advice

6.1 Background (IFRS IC)

- This committee was reconstituted in December 2001 to take over the role of the Standing Interpretations Committee. The SIC was founded in April 1997 with the objective of developing conceptually sound and practicable interpretations of IFRSs to be applied on a global basis where the standards are silent or unclear.

- It is made up of a team of accounting experts from 13 countries appointed by the IASC Foundation.

> The examiner expects candidates to know that IFRICs and SICs exist, but they are not examinable documents and so are not detailed in this Study Text.

6.2 Approach

- The IFRS IC uses the approach described in IAS 8 *Accounting Policies, Changes in Accounting Estimates and Errors* by:
  - making analogies with the requirements and guidance in IFRS dealing with similar and related issues;
  - applying the definitions, recognition and measurement criteria for assets, liabilities, income and expenses set out in the IASB Framework; and
  - taking into consideration the pronouncements of other standard-setting bodies and accepted industry practices to the extent that these are consistent with international GAAP.

- The interpretations were originally issued as SIC 1, SIC 2, etc.

- After approval by the board the interpretations become part of the IASB's authoritative literature. The pronouncements have the same status as an IFRS.

6.3 Changes

- The IASB has renamed this committee and the interpretations that it produces. The committee is now known as the International Financial Reporting Standards Interpretations Committee (IFRS IC) and it issues IFRICs. All SICs currently in existence are still known as SICs but new interpretations are IFRIC 1, IFRIC 2, etc.

© DeVry/Becker Educational Development Corp. All rights reserved.

7 Current Issues

- Accounting is dynamic; it is always on the move, trying to improve on itself and eliminate any loopholes in the accounting system.
- The IASB is continually amending or issuing new standards where problems in the accounting model have been identified.*

Commentary

*The IASB is not the only body that introduces change; financial reporting is a global issue and many bodies work together to develop it.

7.1 Recent IFRSs

- IFRS 15 *Revenue from Contracts with Customers* replaced IAS 11 *Construction Contracts* and IAS 18 *Revenue*. These old standards were not sufficiently rigorous to prevent inconsistencies in revenue reporting. The IASB project took over three years to complete, as the accountancy profession had concerns about the initial proposals.*

Commentary

*The exposure draft was revised and reissued.

- When initially issued the standard had an implementation date of 1 January 2017. However, major implementation problems were identified and both IASB and FASB decided to delay implementation to 1 January 2018.*

Commentary

*IFRS 15 is detailed in *Session 4*.

- It took the IASB five years to complete the financial instruments projects. IFRS 9 is effective from 2018. Until then entities can use either IAS 39 or IFRS 9; this will affect the comparability of financial statements.
- The final version applies a single classification approach to all financial assets on which the requirements for impairment and hedge accounting are based.*

Commentary

*The IASB's ongoing project on accounting for macro-hedge is a separate project. It is of most relevance to financial institutions.

- Accounting for financial instruments has been a highly contentious topic, with many commentators having opposing opinions on how to account for certain instruments. It is to be expected that issues will continue to emerge as the new provisions are implemented.*

Commentary

*IFRS 9 is detailed in *Session 8*.

- IFRS 16 prescribes the treatment of leases by lessees. The new standard has not changed the accounting treatment for lessors.
- The IASB first tried to introduce a new standard on leases in 2010. It took six years for the accounting profession to accept a new standard on the subject.*

Commentary

*IFRS 16 is detailed in *Session 9*.

7.2 Proposed Changes to IFRS

▦ The IASB continually reviews and updates IFRS, amending existing standards and issuing standards on new areas. The IASB publishes a regular update on its work plan.*

*See the IASB's website at http://www.ifrs.org/Current-Projects/IASB-Projects/Pages/IASB-Work-Plan.aspx for the latest update.

▦ Current issues that the IASB are working on include the following:

- Conceptual Framework—This project is aiming to bring the Framework document up to date. The update in 2010 was only relevant to two sections of the document (see *Session 3*).

- Disclosure initiative: this project is an examination of the disclosures required by an entity, aiming the focus on quality rather than quantity.

- Insurance Contracts: this topic is outside the scope of the P2 syllabus.

▦ Developing new standards and bringing them into effect can be a very slow process. For example, IFRS 9 was first issued in 2009 with the intention of being fully effective by 2013; this was put back to 2015 and is now applicable from 2018.

7.3 Practice and Regulatory Issues

7.3.1 Integrated Reporting <IR>*

▦ The International Integrated Reporting Council has issued a framework document that will result in financial statements being much more inclusive—moving the focus away from "just the numbers" to provide all stakeholders with information about all forms of capital and the influences on value creation.

*See section 3 in *Session 27*.

▦ Management will be required, for example:

- to commentate on what is happening to the company, where it has come from and where it is going; and

- to describe the nature and quality of the company's relationships with key stakeholders.

7.3.2 Harmonisation and Convergence

▦ Accounting has become a global issue over the last 10 years. Far fewer "local" GAAPs exist as many countries have moved towards the adoption, in one form or another, of an IFRS-based set of standards.*

*See *Session 2* for details.

▦ However, there is still a long way to go before the accounting profession is fully integrated into one body that covers accounting issues for all. Until then, if ever, harmonisation and convergence issues will always exist.

© DeVry/Becker Educational Development Corp. All rights reserved.

7.3.3 Other Regulation

- Companies must keep up-to-date on types of regulation that can affect their corporate reports:
    - Market regulations—the main reason why IAS 33 *Earnings per Share* and IFRS 8 *Operating Segments* exist is because market regulators require listed entities to publish earnings per share figures and segmental information.*
    - Corporate governance requirements also affect the level of reporting required by entities and changes in best practice in the area of corporate reporting have implications for financial statements.

*European Securities and Markets Authority (ESMA) is an independent EU authority which aims to regulate the EU financial markets with a single rule book.

7.4 Problems With Extant Standards

Nearly all extant standards give rise to issues for some users. However, some standards cause more problems than others. The most contentious include the following:

- IAS 8 *Accounting Policies, Changes in Accounting Estimates and Errors* can hinder rather than aid consistency and comparability.
    - There is a "grey area" between what constitutes an accounting policy and what should be regarded as an accounting estimate. For example, a change of inventory valuation from FIFO to weighted average may be regarded by some as a change in policy, but others may maintain that it is a change in estimate.
- IAS 36 *Impairment of Assets* can be difficult to implement. Preparers of financial statements may need to consider:
    - estimates of the amounts and timing of cash flows;
    - what discount rate should be applied to those cash flows;
    - whether it is acceptable to include "boilerplate" statements in disclosure notes.*
- IAS 1 *Presentation of Financial Statements* gives rise to a number of areas for debate:
    - What items should be included in profit or loss and what should be included in other comprehensive income?
    - Should those items included in other comprehensive income be reclassified through profit or loss at some point?
    - Should all gains and losses appear in profit or loss, as they all result from the performance of the entity?
    - What subtotals should be used in the statement of profit or loss and how? The inclusion of subtotals should result in greater consistency in accounting but could also lead to a manipulation of the figures to suit user needs.*

*"Boilerplate" refers to standardised text provided to comply with IFRS rather than to communicate meaningfully with users of financial statements.

*See the member magazine AB (Accounting and Business) in the members' section of ACCA's website for topical articles.

© DeVry/Becker Educational Development Corp. All rights reserved.

Summary

- GAAP is a dynamic concept.

- IFAC is a non-profit, non-governmental, non-political organisation of accountancy bodies which represents the accountancy profession.

- More than 120 countries are reported to be either permitting or requiring the use of IFRS.

- The objective of IASB is to develop a single set of high-quality, understandable and enforceable global standards which help users make economic decisions.

- The IASB is responsible for all technical matters including preparation of IFRSs and EDs.

- Convergence is a gradual process by which local GAAP approaches and is replaced with IFRS.

- Since 2007, the IASB issues annual improvements. Amendments are non-urgent but necessary to clarify inconsistencies or ambiguities.

- There has long been a consensus that reporting requirements are biased towards larger companies and ignore the needs of small companies.

- *IFRS for Small and Medium-Sized Entities* gives possible relief from compliance with full IFRS.

- *IFRS for SMEs* applies to general purpose financial statements of entities which have *no* public accountability.

- The scope of "current issues" in corporate reporting for the P2 examination is extremely broad, and wider reading is encouraged.

© DeVry/Becker Educational Development Corp. All rights reserved.

Session 1 Quiz
Estimated time: 15 minutes

1. List the sources of GAAP. (1.2)
2. Describe IFAC and state its mission. (2.1)
3. State the objectives of the IASB. (3.2)
4. List the steps the IASB takes to ensure consistent interpretation of IFRSs. (4.5)
5. Specify some of the burdens placed on small companies when complying with IFRS. (5.1)
6. List THREE major differences between full IFRS and *IFRS for SMEs*. (5.3.4–5.3.6)
7. Summarise the approach adopted by IFRIC when the committee considers issuing a new pronouncement. (6.2)
8. State who issued the International <IR> Framework. (7.3)

Study Question Bank
Estimated time: 50 minutes

Priority		Estimated Time	Completed
Q1	IFRS for SMEs	50 minutes	

© DeVry/Becker Educational Development Corp. All rights reserved.

International Issues

FOCUS

This session covers the following content from the *ACCA Study Guide.*

H. Current Developments

2. Convergence between national and international reporting standards

a) Evaluate the implications of worldwide convergence with International Financial Reporting Standards. ☐

b) Discuss the influence of national regulators on international financial reporting. ☐

Session 2 Guidance

- **Understand** how and where IFRSs fit into the global accounting framework (s.1, s.2, s.3).
- **Evaluate** the steps being taken towards international harmonisation of accounting standards (s.4, s.5). Convergence between national and international reporting standards is a subject which could be examined as part of the current issues affecting accounting.

VISUAL OVERVIEW

Objective: To discuss the advantages and disadvantages of harmonisation and to explain the reconciliation of profits obtained under different GAAPs.

INTERNATIONAL HARMONISATION
- Introduction
- Environmental Factors
- General Comment

ADVANTAGES
- Enterprises
- Accounting Firms
- Investors

BARRIERS

PROGRESS
- IASB
- IOSCO Project
- Use Around the World
- Impact on US Listing
- Problems With Adoption
- Convergence

ROLE OF OTHER ORGANISATIONS
- EU Directives
- National Standard Setters
- Others

© DeVry/Becker Educational Development Corp. All rights reserved.

1 International Harmonisation

1.1 Introduction

Key Point

The strong tendency towards globalisation has resulted in the formation of increased numbers of larger multinational companies.

▣ Operating divisions of such companies are subject to different reporting rules in each country.

1.2 Environmental Factors

The form of financial statements is influenced by the environment in the jurisdiction.

▣ Environmental factors which influence accounting (and auditing) practices include:
  - Economic development
  - Language
  - Global perspective
  - Interdependence on other economies
  - Global capital markets
  - Growth in multinational enterprises
  - Government involvement
  - Needs of users and preparers of financial statements
  - Importance of the accounting profession
  - Local orientation of accounting practice and profusion of accounting standards
  - Inflation
  - Culture
  - Legal and political system
  - Education system and academic influence
  - Historical events
  - Foreign investment in the country.

▣ In particular, the needs of users are an important influence on the accounting rules in each jurisdiction.

Jurisdiction	Comment
US and UK	Information is produced for owners and potential owners, with the stock market having an important influence.
Germany	There is often heavy institutional investment, reducing the need for information to individual shareholders as the institutions may have board representation.
France	Financial statements are used for macro-economic purposes, with the government determining the information to be included in the accounts.

© DeVry/Becker Educational Development Corp. All rights reserved.

1.3 General Comment

> **Key Point**
>
> Harmonisation of accounting would result in all companies anywhere in the world reporting in the same way on:
> - position;
> - performance; and
> - changes in financial position.

- This would lead to greater market efficiency through the quality of the information and should make raising finance cheaper and easier.

2 Advantages of Harmonisation

2.1 Multinational Enterprises

Harmonisation would benefit the multinationals in a number of ways:*

- ✔ Improved management control.
- ✔ Improved access to funds. (The provider of capital would find it easier to appraise the companies/divisions.)
- ✔ Easier appraisal of investment opportunities.
- ✔ Easier preparation of group accounts.
- ✔ Transferability of accounting expertise within the multinational between countries.
- ✔ Lower costs of complying with a single framework (compared with a large number of local regulatory frameworks).
- ✔ Reduced costs of monitoring such compliance.

*Multinational entities are a driving force in the move towards international harmonisation.

2.2 Multinational Accounting Firms

- ✔ The fact that the firm, taken as a whole, would provide services in a standardised environment should lead to improved quality control.*
- ✔ It would be easier to train staff to deal with multinational accounting issues.
- ✔ Harmonisation should lead to reduced costs of:
  - training;
  - compliance; and
  - transferring expertise.

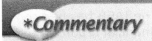

*The "Big Four" accounting firms have an important role to play in the move towards international harmonisation because of their influence in accounting matters in individual jurisdictions.

2.3 Investors

- ✔ Investor confidence should increase with the ability to compare and understand the investment opportunities presented by multinationals.
- ✔ Improved confidence should lead to a reduction in the cost of capital.

3 Barriers to Harmonisation

Key Point

Harmonisation requires the adoption of a universally accepted business language.

✗ English is the international language of business because of the importance of the US economy, but even for native speakers there is the possibility of confusion. For example, the term "stock" has a different meaning in the UK and in Australia than in the US.

✗ Countries with strong accounting traditions and professions may feel that the standards they have developed are more appropriate.

✗ Different governments place different emphasis on accounts:

  ● in some countries, the accounts are primarily used as the basis of tax computations;

  ● in others, they report performance to other parties.

✗ Different countries traditionally draft standards to serve different uses:*

  ● UK   – owners

  ● Russia   – taxation

  ● Germany – creditors

▨ True harmonisation would require the existence of a strong accounting profession in each country and a government with the will to adopt a standardised system. These factors are not always present.

*Commentary

*Companies often prepare sets of financial statements in different GAAP for different purposes.

4 Progress on Harmonisation

4.1 Adoption

The IASB has had considerable influence on the harmonisation of financial reporting:

▨ through adoption by multinationals and local regulators; and

▨ through working with the International Organisation of Securities Commissions (IOSCO).

Key Point

Large, multinational companies continue to adopt IFRSs to satisfy investor needs in the various markets from which they raise finance.

4.4.1 Adoption

▨ IFRSs are used:

  ● as national requirements or as the basis for national requirements;

  ● as an international benchmark for countries developing their own requirements;

  ● by regulatory authorities and companies; and

  ● by large multinationals for the purpose of raising finance on international capital markets.

© DeVry/Becker Educational Development Corp. All rights reserved.

4.2   The IOSCO Project

- IOSCO is the international organisation of stock exchange regulators. In 1995, the IASC agreed to produce a set of core standards covering all of the main and general issues in accounting. The two bodies continue to liaise on IASB's programme for revising standards.

- The aim was that IOSCO would then endorse them as satisfactory for use in the preparation of financial statements which could be used in worldwide, cross-border listings.

- Approval for use in individual stock exchanges is not automatic following endorsement. This will happen only when individual regulatory authorities take action at a national level. However, the endorsement was a major step towards international harmonisation.

- The US Securities and Exchange Commission (SEC), is represented in IOSCO and backed the IASB's efforts. The support of the SEC was essential as endorsement could proceed only with unanimous approval by a working party set up for the purpose. The support of the SEC is widely seen as crucial to the future success of IFRSs. Companies need and want access to US capital markets.

- Endorsement was given as IOSCO were satisfied that:
  - The core standards constitute a comprehensive, generally accepted basis of accounting.
  - The standards are of high quality, resulting in:
    — comparability;
    — transparency; and
    — full disclosure.
  - The standards can be rigorously interpreted and applied.

4.3   Use Around the World

- As previously noted (*in Session 1*) more than 120 countries are reported to either permit or require the use of IFRS.

- In Canada, IFRS was compulsory for fiscal years beginning 1 January 2011 for all public accountable entities, not just listed entities, and permitted for private sector companies.

- Australia has adopted a policy of ensuring that its accounting standards are harmonised with IFRS. Compliance with Australian standards automatically ensures compliance with IFRS.

- IFRS financial statements are not currently permitted, for example, in China, Pakistan, Saudi Arabia, Malaysia or Indonesia. However, a convergence project that is ongoing in Malaysia and China has substantially converged national standards.

- The above examples illustrate the range and extent to which the use of IFRS varies around the world. Clearly this is constantly changing.

- The harmonisation programme between IASB and FASB has been halted. During the early 2000s this programme led many to believe that US GAAP would be fully harmonised with IFRS, leading to the global community using just one GAAP— namely, IFRS.

Key Point

IOSCO endorsed core standards in 2000.

Key Point

Enforcement is a huge problem. The IASB has no power to ensure compliance. This will be up to the local regulatory authorities, and the "Big Four" have an important part to play in this respect.

Key Point

The EU has **not** given endorsement to **all** of the IASB's standards and interpretations; this has led to there being two versions of IFRS.

© DeVry/Becker Educational Development Corp. All rights reserved.

Although members of FASB and IASB still work closely together, it is very unlikely that FASB and IASB will be converging their respective accounting standards in the near future.

4.4 Impact of Endorsement on US Listings

The US SEC is a prominent member of IOSCO. It used to require a full schedule 20F reconciliation of equity and profit to a US GAAP basis. This reconciliation is no longer required if the entity prepares financial statements in accordance with IFRS.

In 2010, the SEC indicated that it would make a decision in 2011 about the use of global standards by US public companies following completion of the SEC's IFRS work plan and the convergence projects agreed to by FASB and the IASB.

In 2011, FASB and the IASB completed five projects. Inter alia, this resulted in the issue of IFRS 10 *Consolidated Financial Statements*. However, this has given rise to new proposals to define investment entities as a separate type of entity which would be exempt from the accounting requirements of IFRS 10.

4.5 Problems Associated With Further Adoption of IFRSs

Companies must apply all IFRSs before they can describe their accounts as compliant. In some countries it is felt that this will cause the loss of necessary flexibility.

Choices allowed in the IFRSs may lead to lack of comparability.

Different interpretation of the same principle may result in like items being accounted for in different ways.

Entities may feel that the disclosures will result in the loss of competitive advantage.

4.6 Convergence

Convergence is a gradual process by which local GAAP approaches and is replaced with IFRS. As a step-by-step transition process it:*

- gives more time for preparation; and
- reduces the potentially negative effect on companies trading their shares.

The main effects on financial statements of adopting IFRS include:

- greater use of fair value as a measurement basis;
- considerably greater disclosure; and
- the need for more narrative to explain its complexities.

Major areas of differences between local GAAP and IFRS may be classified, for example, between those which are:

- fully related to day-to-day accounting (e.g. IAS 16 *Property, Plant and Equipment*);
- partially related to day-to-day accounting (e.g. IAS 19 *Employee Benefits*); and
- related to consolidation (e.g. IFRS 3 *Business Combinations*).

*Commentary

*As a result of convergence, companies likely need to change their accounting systems to meet IFRS requirements.

© DeVry/Becker Educational Development Corp. All rights reserved.

5   The Role of Other Organisations

5.1   European Union Directives

▦ The EU guides legislation of member states through the issue of directives.

▦ Examples:

Directive	Area Covered
4th directive	Form and content of financial statements
7th directive	Group accounts
8th directive	Regulation of auditors

▦ The adoption of these directives by member states has resulted in the EU moving towards harmonisation.

▦ There are two further barriers to harmonisation within the EU:

Problem	Progress
✗ Lack of a single currency. ✗ Different countries still use different standards.	✔ The EU has introduced the euro. ✔ The EU requires that the consolidated accounts of listed companies must comply with IFRS.

▦ As stated, all EU listed companies were required to adopt IFRSs by 2005. This meant entities with a 31 December year end prepared an IFRS opening statement of financial position as at 1 January 2004. Problems associated with first-time adoption of IFRSs are dealt with in *Session 25.*

▦ Emergent economies in Eastern Europe are incorporating the EU directives into their accounting acts (to further their ambitions to join the EU) and often adopt IFRSs.

▦ The EU was instrumental in getting the IASB to amend IAS 39, in 2008, allowing the reclassification of certain financial assets out of the category "fair value through profit or loss".

▦ This amendment was introduced by the IASB without following due process relating to the issue of new or amended standards. Due process was "bypassed" due to the global financial crisis in 2008.

▦ EFRAG, a group within the EU, has a role of endorsing IFRSs for use by EU companies on issue. This effectively results in two sets of IFRS:

1. those issued by the IASB; and

2. those issued by the IASB and endorsed by EFRAG.

▦ Although initially issued in 2009 and finalised in 2014, IFRS 9 was not endorsed by EFRAG until November 2016. Prior to the endorsement EU companies were required to apply IAS 39.

© DeVry/Becker Educational Development Corp. All rights reserved.

5.2 IASB and National Standard Setters

■ The International Forum of Accounting Standard Setters (IFASS), formerly known as National Standard Setters (NSS), is a group of national accounting standard setters from around the world and other organisations that are closely involved in financial reporting issues.*

■ The forum meets on a regular basis to consider and comment on topical issues that affect the various users of financial statements.

■ It does not act as a direct adviser to the IASB but its views and proposals are taken into account by the IASB.

■ A recent meeting of the forum discussed the following topics:

- Rate regulation: Potential basis for recognition
- Application issues relating to IFRS 11
- Integrated reporting and the role of NSS
- Disclosure requirements for partially-owned subsidiaries on their consolidation
- Reporting on discount rate issues
- Presentation of "exceptional items" in profit or loss
- Post-implementation review of IFRS 3.

■ A major focus of the meeting was the IASB's Conceptual Framework project, especially regarding the issues of measurement and prudence.

- Regarding measurement, the key message for the IASB was that it should not use a pragmatic approach as a starting point, but that the Framework should be aspirational in nature.
- Regarding prudence, a group of the members concluded that the Framework should provide a clear definition or description of this concept.

■ In 2009, the IASB issued *IFRS for Small and Medium-sized Entities*. Shortly thereafter, ACCA carried out a survey about the implementation of the standard by NSSs. Out of 51 countries surveyed:

- 31 either planned to require or allow companies to use the standard;
- 9 were undecided; and
- 11 had no plans to require or allow use of the standard.

■ In 2013, the national standard setter in the UK, the Financial Reporting Council (FRC), issued standards that will move current Financial Reporting Standards (current FRS) towards an IFRS-based framework, thereby eliminating UK GAAP.*

5.3 Others

■ Other important international bodies have committees which advise on accounting matters, including:

- the United Nations (UN);
- the Organisation for Economic Co-operation and Development (OECD); and
- the World Trade Organisation (WTO).

*NSSs include the accounting standards boards of Australia (AASB), Germany (DRSC), UK (FRC) and US (FASB).

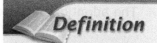

Prudence—the inclusion of a degree of caution in the exercise of the judgements needed in making estimates under conditions of uncertainty, such that assets or income are not overstated and liabilities or expenses are not understated.

*The FRC will still oversee and administer the application of IFRS by UK companies.

© DeVry/Becker Educational Development Corp. All rights reserved.

Summary

- Harmonisation of accounting would result in all companies reporting in the same way on position, performance and changes in financial position.
- Harmonisation requires adoption of a universally accepted business language.
- IOSCO endorsed IASB's core standards in May 2000.
- Enforcement is a huge problem. The IASB has no power to ensure compliance.
- The EU has not endorsed all standards and interpretations; this has led to two versions of IFRS.
- Convergence is a gradual process by which local GAAP is eventually replaced with IFRS.

Session 2 Quiz
Estimated time: 15 minutes

1. Identify TEN environmental factors which influence accounting. (1.2)
2. Identify FIVE benefits which harmonisation would have for multinational entities. (2.1)
3. Identify FIVE barriers to harmonisation. (3)
4. Outline the aim of the IOSCO project undertaken by the IASB. (4.2)
5. Specify directives the European Union has issued to help the harmonisation project. (5.1)

Study Question Bank
Estimated time: 45 minutes

Priority		Estimated Time	Completed
Q2	Autol	45 minutes	

Conceptual Framework

FOCUS

This session covers the following content from the *ACCA Study Guide.*

B. The Financial Reporting Framework

1. The applications, strengths and weaknesses of an accounting framework

a) Evaluate the valuation models adopted by standard setters. ☐

b) Discuss the use of an accounting framework in underpinning the production of accounting standards. ☐

c) Assess the success of such a framework in introducing rigorous and consistent accounting standards. ☐

2. Critical evaluation of principles and practices

a) Identify the relationship between accounting theory and practice. ☐

E. Specialised Entities and Specialised Transactions

1. Financial reporting in specialised, not-for-profit and public sector entities

a) Apply knowledge from the syllabus to straightforward transactions and events arising in specialised, not-for-profit and public sector entities. ☐

Session 3 Guidance

■ **Understand** the importance of the conceptual framework, both in real life and on the examination.

■ **Pay** particular attention to the definitions of elements given in the framework (s.1.4.1) and the recognition criteria of when these elements should be recognised in the financial statements (s.1.4.2). It is highly likely that you will need to consider these elements somewhere within the exam.

■ **Revise** the IASB's Conceptual Framework for Financial Reporting (s.2).

■ **Learn** the definitions relevant to IFRS 13 *Fair Value Measurement*, the valuation techniques and the hierarchy of inputs (s.5).

(continued on next page)

VISUAL OVERVIEW

Objective: To set out the concepts underlying the preparation and presentation of financial statements for external users.

NOT-FOR-PROFIT ORGANISATIONS
- Primary Objectives
- Value for Money
- Accounting

FRAMEWORK
- Purpose and Scope
- Objective of Financial Statements
- Underlying Assumption
- Elements
- Measurement Bases
- Success of Failure

EXPOSURE DRAFT
- Background
- Proposed Revisions

QUALITATIVE CHARACTERISTICS
- Economic Phenomena
- Fundamental Characteristics
- Relevance
- Faithful Representation
- Enhancing Characteristics
- Cost Constraint

MEASUREMENT
- Bases
- IASB Stance

IAS 41
- Objective and Scope
- Terminology
- Recognition and Measurement
- Presentation and Disclosure

SUBSTANCE OVER FORM
- Introduction
- Recognition of Assets and Liabilities
- Creative Accounting
- Accounting Theory v Practice

FAIR VALUE
- Background
- Terminology
- Price
- Non-financial Assets
- Valuation Techniques
- Hierarchy of Inputs
- Disclosure
- Benefits and Limitations

Session 3 Guidance

■ **Be aware** that this session includes topics that could be examined in the current issues question. Pay particular attention to the Exposure Draft (s.8).

■ **Understand** that biological assets can arise other than by purchase and undergo physical transformation (s.7.2).

■ **Be able** to measure biological assets at fair value and account for gains and losses (s.7.3.2).

■ **Read** the *student accountant* article "IFRS 13 *Fair Value Measurement*".

© DeVry/Becker Educational Development Corp. All rights reserved.

1 Framework

1.1 Purpose and Scope

1.1.1 Purpose*

Key Point

- Primarily, the purpose of the Framework is to assist the Board of IASB in:
  - developing future IFRSs and reviewing existing IFRSs; and
  - promoting harmonisation of regulations by providing a basis for reducing the number of alternative accounting treatments permitted by IFRSs.

- Other purposes are:*
  - to assist **national standard-setting bodies** in developing national standards;
  - to assist **preparers** of financial statements in applying IFRSs and in dealing with topics that have yet to form the subject of an IFRS;
  - to assist **auditors** in forming an opinion as to whether financial statements conform with IFRSs;
  - to assist **users** of financial statements in interpreting information contained in financial statements prepared in conformity with IFRSs; and
  - to provide those who are interested in the work of IASB with information about how IFRSs are formulated (published in a "basis of conclusion").

1.1.2 Scope

- The Framework covers the following areas, and requires them to be applied to accounting events and transactions that an entity may encounter:
  - the objective of financial statements;
  - the underlying assumption;
  - the qualitative characteristics of useful information;
  - the definition, recognition and measurement of elements; and
  - the concepts of capital and capital maintenance.

***Commentary**

*In September 2010, the IASB issued the Conceptual Framework for Financial Reporting. It supersedes the Framework for the Preparation and Presentation of Financial Statements. It reflects the completion of only the first phase of the IASB's updating of its Framework.

*In short, the Framework provides a conceptual foundation for the preparation and appraisal of accounting standards.

© DeVry/Becker Educational Development Corp. All rights reserved.

1.2   The Objective of Financial Statements

▨ To provide information about:
- ● the financial position;
- ● the financial performance; and
- ● changes in financial position of an entity;
- ● that is useful to a wide range of users in making economic decisions.

▨ This information should also show the results of management's stewardship (i.e. accountability for resources entrusted to it).

▨ This information should enable users to evaluate:
- ● the ability of an entity to generate cash and cash equivalents; and
- ● the timing and certainty of their generation.

Financial Position	Financial Performance	Changes in Financial Position
Affected by: ● economic resources control; ● financial structure; ● liquidity and solvency; and ● capacity to adapt to changes.	● In particular profitability. ● To predict capacity to generate cash flows from an existing resource base. ● To form judgements about effectiveness with which additional resources might be employed.	● To assess investing, financing and operating activities. ● To assess ability to generate cash and cash equivalents and needs to utilise those cash flows. ● Framework does not define funds.

STATEMENT OF FINANCIAL POSITION	STATEMENT OF COMPREHENSIVE INCOME	SEPARATE STATEMENT

1.3   Underlying Assumption

▨ Going concern assumes that the entity will continue in operation for the foreseeable future.*

▨ Therefore, there is neither the intention nor the need to liquidate or curtail materially the scale of operations.

 Key Point

There is only one underlying assumption of financial statements—going concern.

 *Commentary

*The going concern assumption, which concerns the basis of preparation, is presumed to apply unless users of financial statements are told otherwise (i.e. in the notes to the financial statements). If going concern is in doubt, a capital reconstruction may be necessary.

© DeVry/Becker Educational Development Corp. All rights reserved.

1.4   Elements of Financial Statements

1.4.1   Terminology

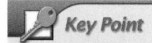

"Elements" of financial statements are broad classes of the financial effects of transactions grouped according to their economic characteristics.

*The Framework defines assets, liabilities and equity, and the definitions for income and expenses follow on from those. Therefore, the Framework is said to take a "balance sheet approach".

Asset:

- a resource *controlled* by the entity
- as a result of *past* events
- from which *future economic benefits* are expected to flow.

Liability:

- a *present obligation* of the entity
- arising from *past* events
- settlement of which is expected to result in an outflow of resources embodying economic benefits.

Equity:

- the residual interest
- in the **assets** of the entity
- after deducting all its **liabilities**.

Income:

- increases in economic benefits during the accounting period
- in the form of inflows (or enhancements) of assets or decreases of liabilities
- that result in increases in **equity**
- other than those relating to contributions from equity participants.

Expenses:

- decreases in economic benefits during the accounting period
- in the form of outflows (or depletions) of assets or incurrences of liabilities
- that result in decreases in equity
- other than those relating to distributions to equity participants.

                                    © DeVry/Becker Educational Development Corp. All rights reserved.

1.4.2 Recognition

Key Point

Recognition is the process of incorporating in the statement of financial position or statement of comprehensive **income** an item that *meets the definition* of an element and satisfies the recognition criteria.

- It involves the depiction of the item in words and by a monetary amount and the inclusion of that amount in the statement of financial position or statement of comprehensive income totals.
- Items that satisfy the recognition criteria must be recognised.
- The failure to recognise such items is not rectified by disclosure of the accounting policies used nor by notes or explanatory material.

1.4.3 Recognition Criteria

- It is *probable* that any future economic benefit associated with the item will flow to or from the entity; and
- The item has a cost or value that can be *measured* with reliability.

1.5 Measurement Bases

	Assets	Liabilities
Historical cost	• The amount paid (or the fair value of the consideration given) to acquire them at the time of their acquisition.	• The amount received in exchange for the obligation.
Current cost	• The amount that would have to be paid if the same or an equivalent asset was acquired currently.	• The undiscounted amount that would be required to settle the obligation currently.
Realisable (settlement) value	• The amount that could currently be obtained by selling the asset in an orderly disposal.	• At settlement values (i.e. the undiscounted amounts expected to be paid to satisfy the liabilities in the normal course of business).
Present cost	• Present discounted value of the future net cash inflows that the item is expected to generate in the normal course of business.	• Present discounted value of the future net cash outflows that are expected to be required to settle the liabilities in the normal course of business.

© DeVry/Becker Educational Development Corp. All rights reserved.

1.6 Success or Failure?

▣ It is very difficult to make an emphatic statement about whether a conceptual framework model is a success in introducing rigorous and consistent accounting standards.

▣ The IASB's Framework has clearly been successful in defining the elements of financial statements that underpin the standards. Financial statements are now far more rigorous in recognising, for example, assets and liabilities that might otherwise be off balance sheet (e.g. leases and provisions) and income and expenses that might otherwise be excluded from the income statement (e.g. relating to construction contracts and share option schemes).

▣ Clearly, the process of standard setting, which requires the IASB to take the Framework into account, should give a degree of consistency to the standards issued and thereby aid a user's ability to compare financial statements.*

*Consider, for example, the parallels between IAS 16 and IAS 38.

  ● IAS 2 *Inventories* was the first of many standards to be issued that offered benchmark and allowed alternative treatments (see *Session 1*). IAS 31 *Interests in Joint Ventures* (since withdrawn) was the last standard to be issued with an alternative, just shortly after the publication of the Framework. Since then the IASB has eliminated all alternatives.

  ● A standard may not appear to be sufficiently rigorous if it does not address certain issues (e.g. because they were not foreseen when the standard was issued) or unsatisfactory or conflicting interpretations develop. IFRIC IC responds to these with IFRICs. Of the 21 issued, 13 are currently extant (along with five of the 32 SICs previously issued).

  ● Rigour and consistency have been further enhanced in the last 10 years since the IASB started to publish implementation guidance with new and revised standards. This guidance, together with the basis of conclusions, assists preparers of financial statements in implementing the provisions of a standard and so minimises, if not eliminates, inconsistencies in their application.

▣ It is also a success in that it recognises the real need for the use of alternative measurement bases to historical cost in order to meet the fundamental characteristics (relevance and faithful representation).

▣ However, it could be argued that it has not been a success, as the availability of so many measurement bases to potentially choose from could lead to inconsistencies that hinder comparisons of financial statements.*

*This is of course mitigated, however, by the standards themselves, where they prescribe the bases to use.

▣ Further, the necessity of so much disclosure to support the concept of faithful representation means that the volume of notes far exceeds the "financial statements" themselves. Such information overload may impair relevance and understandability for many users.

© DeVry/Becker Educational Development Corp. All rights reserved.

- Although the part of the Framework that deals with qualitative characteristics has been relatively recently updated (see next section), as a whole it has not kept pace with the changes in accounting. There are still areas where the Framework is in conflict with accounting standards.

- Examples of areas where there is conflict include:

  ✗ Accounting for Government Grants, where deferred income may be recognised on the statement of financial position. The Framework does not consider this concept of deferred income.

  ✗ Accounting for deferred taxes under IAS 12. The standard requires full provision for all deferred tax liabilities, but in many cases the entity will not have a present obligation to pay any taxes until the tax legislation requires payments, which may be many years into the future.*

2 Qualitative Characteristics

2.1 "Economic Phenomena"

Key Point

Qualitative characteristics of financial statements are the attributes that make information provided therein useful to primary users.

- "Economic phenomena" in the Framework refers to economic resources, claims against the entity and the effects on these of transactions, conditions and other events.

2.2 Fundamental Characteristics

Key Point

The two *fundamental* characteristics are *relevance* and *faithful representation*.

- Other *enhancing* characteristics are:
  - comparability;
  - verifiability;
  - timeliness; and
  - understandability.

2.3 Relevance

- This quality concerns the decision-making needs of users. It helps users:
  - to evaluate past, present or future events (i.e. has a predictive value); and
  - to confirm or correct their past evaluations (i.e. has a confirmatory value).*

Commentary

*Absence of an actual liability conflicts with the Framework's definition of a liability. Deferred tax is not only recognised according to different criteria but also measured differently (it is not discounted).

Commentary

*Predictive and confirmatory values are interrelated (e.g. the same information may confirm a previous prediction and be used for a future prediction).

© DeVry/Becker Educational Development Corp. All rights reserved.

- Relevance of information is affected by:

Its Nature	Materiality
• Nature alone may be sufficient to determine relevance.*	• Information is material if its omission or misstatement could influence the economic decisions of users taken on the basis of the financial statements.
	• Depends on size of item or error judged in the specific circumstances of its omission or misstatement.
	• It provides a threshold or cut-off point rather than being a primary qualitative characteristic.

***Commentary**

*For example, the fact that Azure sold a property for $4 million is one piece of information. That it sold it to another company which is owned by Azure's chief executive officer is another piece of information. Such "related party" transactions are the subject of IAS 24. (See *Session 14*.)

- Both nature and materiality may be important (e.g. amounts of inventories held in each main category).
- The IASB has issued an exposure draft proposing the issue of a practice statement giving guidance on the definition and application of materiality. The full statement can be viewed on the IASB website.

2.4 Faithful Representation

- Useful information must represent faithfully that which it purports to represent (or could reasonably be expected to represent).
- To represent the economic phenomena faithfully may sometimes mean that the financial statements do more than just follow accounting standards. A transaction which falls outside the scope of all standards must still be reflected in the financial statements.*
- Faithful representation encompasses:
  - neutrality (i.e. free from bias);
  - completeness (within the bounds of materiality and cost)—an omission can cause information to be false or misleading and thus unreliable; and
  - accuracy (i.e. free from error).*

***Commentary**

*There is no specific standard on accounting for a Van Gogh painting, but an entity must faithfully represent the fact that they have acquired a painting.

***Commentary**

*The 2007 Framework included "substance over form" and "prudence" as aspects of reliability. "Faithful representation" has now replaced "reliability" as a fundamental characteristic. "Substance over form" and reliability of measurement is still crucial to the recognition of elements of financial statements. However, "prudence" is no longer mentioned in the Framework.

© DeVry/Becker Educational Development Corp. All rights reserved.

2.5   Enhancing Characteristics

2.5.1   Comparability

- Users need to be able to compare financial statements of:
    - an entity *through time*—to identify trends in financial position and performance;
    - *different* entities—to evaluate relative financial position, performance and changes in financial position.
- Comparability requires *consistent* measurement and display of the financial effect of like transactions and other events.
- An implication of this is that users must be informed of the accounting policies employed, any changes in those policies and the effects of such changes.
- Financial statements must show corresponding information for preceding periods.

2.5.2   Verifiability

- This means that knowledgeable, independent observers could reach a consensus that a particular representation has the fundamental quality of faithfulness.
- Verification may be:
    - direct (e.g. through physical inspection); or
    - indirect (e.g. using a model, formula or technique).

2.5.3   Timeliness

- Information needs to be available in time for users to make decision.*

2.5.4   Understandability

*Commentary

*Older information is generally less useful (but may still be useful in identifying and assessing trends).

- Users are assumed to have a reasonable knowledge of business and economic activities and accounting, and a willingness to study information with reasonable diligence (i.e. they are expected to have a level of financial expertise).
- Information about complex matters should not be excluded on the grounds that it may be too difficult for certain users to understand.

2.6   Cost Constraint

- The cost of providing information should not exceed the benefit obtained from it.
- This cost, though initially borne by the reporting entity, is ultimately borne by the users (e.g. through lower returns on their investment).
- Users also incur costs (e.g. in analysing and interpreting information).
- Benefits are the most difficult to quantify and assess:
    - the better the quality of information, the better decision making should be; and
    - confidence in the efficiency of capital markets lowers the cost of capital.

3 Substance Over Form

3.1 Introduction

 **Key Point**

Financial statements must reflect the economic substance of transactions if they are to show a true and fair view.

- Ultimately financial statements must follow the Framework with respect to the definition of elements and the recognition of assets and liabilities.

- Usually substance (i.e. commercial effect) = legal form. For more complex transactions, this may not be the case.

3.2 Recognition of Assets and Liabilities

- The key issue underlying the treatment of a transaction is whether an asset or liability should be shown in the statement of financial position.

- In recent years, some companies devised increasingly sophisticated "off balance sheet financing" schemes whereby it was possible to hold assets and liabilities which did not appear on the statement of financial position. This is one of the most important issues in financial reporting. Some countries have issued accounting standards to address this point specifically.

- The concept of substance over form has existed as a concept in IFRSs for many years. If companies had been following IFRSs, some of the reporting problems which have occurred may not have arisen.

- The release of IAS 39 *Financial Instruments: Recognition and Measurement* greatly improved accounting for financial instruments and complex hedging arrangements.

3.3 Creative Accounting

- Over the past 40 years companies have tried to be creative in the way they account for certain transactions. This has led to abuses of the accounting entries recording these transactions and the financial statements not reflecting the economic reality of the situation. Listed here are some of the main areas in which management have been creative in their accounting treatment.

3.3.1 Off Balance Sheet Financing

- This is where a company has a present obligation to make a payment but has been able to keep the obligation (debt) off the statement of financial position. A sale and repurchase transaction, if accounted under its legal form, is an example of off balance sheet financing.

3.3.2 Profit Manipulation or Smoothing

- Management prefer profits to be increasing at a steady rate, not going up and down each year in an uncontrolled manner. Managers may change their revenue and cost recognition in order to smooth out the profits. Examples of abuse in this area include early recognition of revenue and incorrect recognition of provisions.

© DeVry/Becker Educational Development Corp. All rights reserved.

Illustration 1 Profit Manipulation

"Hollywood accounting" is a form of profit manipulation technique used in the film industry. Many actors and screenwriters have contracts entitling them to a share of the profits of a film; many studios ensure the film makes a loss by allocating overheads against the film even though there may be no relationship between the film and the overhead. The film *Forrest Gump* is an example of this form of profit manipulation. The film made millions in the box office, but when the accountants got hold of the finances, they managed to turn it into a loss-making film, depriving the author of his share of any profits from the film.

3.3.3 Window Dressing

▨ This is where the financial statements are made "pretty" for one moment in time, normally the year end. Many ratios are calculated using figures from the statement of financial position; if these figures can be made to look good, then it will improve the related ratios and put the company in a much better light.

▨ Settling trade payables on the last day of the year, only to re-instigate them the very next day, is an example of this abuse.

Illustration 2 Window Dressing

"Repo 105" is a recent example of window dressing being used by companies. Lehman Brothers held some quite risky assets in their statement of financial position, but entered into a contract to sell these assets towards the end of the financial year only to buy them back at the beginning of the following period. Although not illegal, the ethics of a transaction of this nature must be called into question, despite the fact that the company's auditors did allow the practice.

3.4 Accounting Theory v Practice

▨ The IASB produces accounting standards that prescribe the principles to be observed when accounting for transactions, unlike US GAAP, which prescribes a set of accounting rules.

▨ Principles require application by users; one user may apply a stated principle in one particular way, while another may apply the principle in a totally different manner. Fair value, as an example, is a concept. What is fair value to one party may not be fair value to another party, leading to different valuations for the same item.

▨ Even when a principle is applied in the same manner by two reporting entities, an accounting standard may give a choice regarding valuation. IAS 16 allows subsequent measurement of non-current assets using a cost model or revaluation model. Equivalent items may be accounted for at different carrying amounts.

▨ Management will, in many cases, be looking to report the "best" profit figure possible.*

*A "best" profit figure may be the highest possible, a required profit or even a lower profit (e.g. to reduce taxation).

© DeVry/Becker Educational Development Corp. All rights reserved.

- Transactions and events may therefore be interpreted in the manner that shows the entity in this "best" light, even if this is contrary to accounting theory. For example:
  - Hotel chains have been averse to charging depreciation on hotel properties. Management has argued that to do so would be "double charging" profits and that the recoverable amount of the hotel would exceed its carrying amount.
  - WorldCom classified revenue expenditure as capital expenditure, and so capitalised costs that should have been charged to the statement of comprehensive income.
  - Enron excluded special purpose vehicles from its statement of financial position. To have included them would have shown a much higher level of debt, one that could not be sustained.
- Accounting theory cannot capture all situations that can affect an entity's results. Accounting standards do not cover every event.*
- Seasonal trends will also play a large part in how companies apply these principles. Holiday firms, historically, have been geared to selling summer holidays in the early part of the year. Should the revenue be recognised in the January/ February period, or when the client actually takes the holiday in the summer months?
- Nearly every figure relating to assets and liabilities appearing in the statement of financial position is subjective in its amount. Even the cash figure could be subjective; if a company has foreign cash deposits, then it must translate those back into its functional currency. What exchange rate does it use?
- So although the accounting theory may want a transaction to be accounted for in a particular manner, the practice may not always follow that theory.

Commentary

*How should a Van Gogh painting purchased as an investment be accounted for? As there is no standard for this type of asset, a degree of subjective judgement has to be made; different people will apply different degrees of subjectivity.

4 Measurement

4.1 Bases

- Accountants are at present spoilt for choice as to the value that should be included for an asset or liability in the statement of financial position.
- An entity buys an asset, and at that one point in time, there is really only one value that is relevant—the amount that was paid for the asset (assuming it to be an economic transaction).
- But suppose three years pass—what would be the most relevant and reliable value of that asset?
  - Historical cost: the value we originally paid for the asset.
  - Depreciated historical cost: having allocated some of its original cost over the period of the asset's use.
  - Replacement cost: how much would it cost to replace that asset, either in its original form or based on the current value of a three-year-old asset.
  - Net realisable value: what we could sell the asset for today.
  - Value in use: the present value of the future cash flows associated with using the asset.

© DeVry/Becker Educational Development Corp. All rights reserved.

⬚ Which one of those values is correct? The answer is they are all correct in one way or another. The problem for the IASB is deciding what it is that companies should report and to whom.

4.2   IASB Stance

⬚ As previously mentioned, the Framework identifies a number of valuation models—historical cost, current cost, realisable value and present value.

⬚ IFRS applies these and other models through the application of measurement bases.

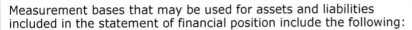

> ### Illustration 3   Measurement Bases
>
> Measurement bases that may be used for assets and liabilities included in the statement of financial position include the following:
>
> - Historical cost
>   - Land
>   - Inventory
> - Depreciated historical cost
>   - Buildings
>   - Investment property
>   - Plant and machinery
>   - Patents
> - Revalued amount
>   - Land and buildings
> - Fair value
>   - Financial assets and liabilities
>   - Investment property
> - Amortised cost
>   - Financial assets and liabilities
> - Net realisable value
>   - Inventory
> - Present value
>   - Decommissioning costs
> - Equity accounting
>   - Investment in associate or joint venture
>
> The above list is not exhaustive.

⬚ *Illustration 3* highlights that IFRS applies multi-measurement bases to its application.*

⬚ IASB recently issued IFRS 13 *Fair Value Measurement,* which is to be applied to the measurement of fair value when another standard requires the use of fair value (see next section).

⬚ There has been much debate over the past 40 years about the valuation of assets and liabilities in the statement of financial position. For example:

- In the 1970s, a voluntary accounting standard was issued in the UK for applying constant purchasing power (CPP) accounting. This was quite quickly withdrawn.
- In 1980, a new standard was issued in the UK that required listed companies to present current cost accounts (CCA) in addition to historical cost accounting.*

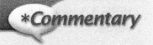

*Commentary

*There is no "one model fits all".

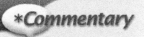

*Commentary

*Widespread non-compliance led to it being made non-mandatory in 1986, and in 1988 it was withdrawn.

© DeVry/Becker Educational Development Corp. All rights reserved.

At the extremes, measurement bases can be simple but not relevant to users (e.g. historical cost), or complex but not easily understood by users (e.g. fair value). What is important is that the financial statements reflect the *economic phenomena* relating to the events and transactions that have occurred in the period. The measurement bases used must faithfully represent the events, and the carrying amounts of assets and liabilities must be reliable and relevant to users.

- For the information relating to measurement bases used to be faithful and relevant, an entity must make numerous disclosures about how the bases have been applied and how the carrying amounts have been derived.

- Judgements and assumptions (and other major sources of estimation uncertainty) that have the most significant effect on the amount recognised must be disclosed (IAS 1).

The measurement bases selected will have a major impact on how users evaluate the financial statements:

- If fair values are used then it is highly likely that profits will be far more volatile.

- If assets are revalued, return on capital employed will be lower than if a cost model was used (assuming values are rising). Gearing also will be lower.

5 Fair Value

5.1 Background

When the Framework document was first issued, the concept of fair value was not widely used in accounting, and so was not incorporated into the Framework as a measurement of value.

Over the past 10–15 years the use of fair value in accounting has become far more widespread, with many international standards now requiring or allowing the use of fair value.

When the IASB issued new standards that required or allowed the use of fair value, there was no consistency between each standard as to how fair value should be measured.

In May 2011, the IASB issued IFRS 13 *Fair Value Measurement*, which prescribed that when a particular standard requires an item to be measured at fair value, then IFRS 13 would be the reference point in how to measure fair value.

 **Key Point**

IFRS 13 does not prescribe **when** an entity should use fair value but **how** fair value should be used. So if an entity holds investment property, it is IAS 40 that allows the use of fair value, but IFRS 13 that give the actual fair value.

© DeVry/Becker Educational Development Corp. All rights reserved.

5.2   Terminology

Fair value—the price which would be received to sell an asset or paid to transfer a liability in an orderly transaction between market participants at the measurement date.

Key Point

The definition of fair value is based on an exit price (taking the asset or liability out of the entity) rather than an entry price (bringing the asset or liability into the entity).

- When measuring fair value, all characteristics of the asset or liability that a market participant would take into account should be reflected in the valuation. This could include the condition or location of the asset and any restrictions on the use of the asset.
- The definition is market-based and is not entity-specific. It reflects the use market participants would use the asset or liability for, not what a specific entity would use the asset or liability for.

Active market—a market in which the transaction for the asset or liability takes place with sufficient frequency and volume to provide pricing information on an ongoing basis.

Highest and best use—the use of a non-financial asset by market participants which would maximise the value of the asset or the group of assets and liabilities within which the asset would be used.

Principal market—the market with the greatest volume and level of activity for the asset or liability.*

Most advantageous market—is the market that maximises the amount that would be received to sell the asset or minimise the amount paid to settle the liability, after taking account of both transaction and transport costs.

Commentary

*It is irrelevant which market the entity itself uses; if the principal market for an item is in Asia but an entity transacts in a market in Europe then the principal market as far as the definition is concerned will be that of the Asian market.

5.3   Price

- Fair value is an exit price rather than an entry price. It is the amount that would be received for an asset or paid for a liability in the principal market. Fair value can be a price that is directly observable or a price that is estimated using a valuation technique.
- Fair value includes transport costs, but does not include transaction costs.
- Fair value is not adjusted for transaction costs as these costs are not characteristics of the specific asset or liability. Any transaction costs are treated in accordance with other standards and are generally expensed as incurred.*
- Transport costs are reflected in the fair value of an asset or liability because they change the characteristics of the item (i.e. the location of the asset or liability is changed).

Commentary

*Transaction costs are ignored when measuring fair value because they are a cost of entering into the transaction rather than a cost specific to the item being measured.

© DeVry/Becker Educational Development Corp. All rights reserved.

Illustration 4 Principal Market

Jammee has business in two markets, Europe and Asia. Jammee has to place a fair value on an asset it holds for accounting purposes. The market price of the asset in the two markets is $120 and $125, respectively.

Details relating to the asset in the two markets is as follows:

	Europe	Asia
	$	$
Market price	120	125
Transaction costs	(5)	(11)
Transport costs	(5)	(2)
	110	112

If Europe was deemed to be the principal market for the asset then fair value would be $115 (price − transport cost).

If neither Europe or Asia were the principal markets for this asset then Jammee would take the most advantageous price to be fair value. This would reflect the best price available to sell the asset after deducting transaction and transport costs.

In this situation Asia is the most advantageous market giving net proceeds of $112 v $110 in Europe. However, $112 is not the fair value of the asset. The fair value is $123, the price less transport costs.

If the item was a liability then the most advantageous market would be Europe and the fair value of the liability would be $115. This reflects the amount the entity would have to pay to settle the liability, which is obviously better than having to settle at $123.

5.4 Non-financial Assets

▦ For non-financial assets (e.g. investment property) the fair value measurement requires that the highest and best use of that asset is reflected in the valuation.

▦ The highest and best use will take into account the use of the asset that is physically possible, that is legally allowed and that is financially feasible when using the asset.*

▦ Taking account of the highest and best use may require assumptions that the asset will be combined, or complementary, with other assets or liabilities available to market participants.*

5.5 Valuation Techniques

▦ The standard assumes that the transaction will occur in the principal market for the asset or liability, if one exists. If there is no principal market, then the standard requires the valuation to be based on the most advantageous market.

▦ Unless proven otherwise, the marketplace will be presumed to be the one that the entity transacts in on a regular basis.

▦ The objective of the standard is to estimate the price at which the asset or liability could exit the entity in an orderly transaction. Three common techniques that would give an accurate estimate are considered.

*Commentary

*The definition of highest and best use will not reflect illegal activities in the use of the asset; it will reflect what is economically viable, taking account of any financial constraints.

*If the entity uses the asset on its own, but the best use of the asset by market participants would be combined with other assets then the valuation would be based on using the asset in combination with others, irrespective of how the entity is currently using the asset.

© DeVry/Becker Educational Development Corp. All rights reserved.

5.5.1 Market Approach

▦ This approach uses prices and other information generated in a marketplace that involve identical or comparable assets or liabilities.

5.5.2 Cost Approach

▦ This approach reflects the amount that would be required to replace the service capacity of the asset (current replacement cost).

5.5.3 Income Approach

▦ This approach considers future cash flows and discounts those cash flows to a current value. Models that follow an income approach include:

- • present value; and
- • option pricing models (e.g. Black-Scholes-Merton).

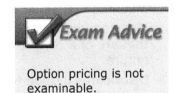

Exam Advice

Option pricing is not examinable.

5.6 Hierarchy of Inputs

Key Point

The techniques used to estimate fair values should maximise observable inputs wherever possible. The hierarchy (order) of inputs aims to increase consistency of usage and comparability in the measurement of fair values and their related disclosures.

5.6.1 Level 1 Inputs

▦ These are quoted prices in active markets for identical assets or liabilities that the entity can access at the measurement date.

5.6.2 Level 2 Inputs

▦ These are inputs other than quoted prices that are observable for the asset or liability, either directly or indirectly.

▦ These would include prices for similar, but not identical, assets or liabilities that were then adjusted to reflect the factors specific to the measured asset or liability.

5.6.3 Level 3 Inputs

▦ These are unobservable inputs for the asset or liability.*

5.6.4 ED 2014/4 Measuring Quoted Investments

▦ The exposure draft clarifies that when measuring fair value of quoted investments in subsidiaries, joint venture or associates, the unit of account that should be used is the investment as a whole.

▦ Where an active market exists for these shares, the measurement of the fair value of the investment will be based on the quoted price of the shares (Level 1 input) without any adjustments.

▦ This principal should be applied to the calculation of the recoverable amount of a cash generating unit that is a quoted entity in an active market. The fair value less costs of disposal should be based on the unadjusted quoted price of the investment.

*Commentary

*Level 1 inputs should be used wherever possible; the use of Level 3 inputs should be kept to a minimum.

© DeVry/Becker Educational Development Corp. All rights reserved.

- A second clarification is made regarding the management of financial assets and financial liabilities on a net basis. The standard allows measurement at fair value of the net position. A new example will be included in the standard to explain this situation.

5.7 Disclosure

- The disclosure requirements of IFRS 13 are very extensive and depend on whether Level 1, 2 or 3 inputs are being used in the measurement techniques. The disclosures required are of a quantitative and qualitative nature.

- The standard also distinguishes between those measurements that are of a recurring nature against those of a non-recurring nature.

- Disclosures include the following:

  - reason for using fair value;
  - the level of hierarchy used;
  - description of techniques used for Level 2 or 3 inputs;
  - for non-financial assets, disclosure is required if the highest and best use differs from what the entity is using; and
  - for Level 3 inputs a reconciliation of the opening and closing balances and any amounts included in profit or loss for the period.

The disclosures listed in this section are only a small sample of what is required; it is unlikely that the examiner will require extensive knowledge of the disclosures.

5.8 Benefits and Limitations

5.8.1 Benefits

✔ Fair values provide information about the values of assets and liabilities that is most relevant to current economic conditions. They therefore provide users with the most "accurate" information available to help them make economic decisions.

✔ Certain other aspects of accounting are generally not required. For example, there should be no need to test for impairment assets that are carried at fair value.

✔ Fair values provide a means for reliably measuring assets and liabilities that would not otherwise be recognised (e.g. derivatives and other assets that have negligible or no initial cost). This means that financial statements are more transparent.*

*Items that meet the Framework's definition of an element cannot be recognised in the absence of reliable measurement.

5.8.2 Limitations

✗ The definition of fair values is market-based but market values may not be available for many assets and liabilities. This gives rise to inconsistency in accounting treatment of similar assets which renders financial statements less comparable. For example, most entities have more than one class of tangible asset but typically only revalue property. Intangible assets can only be revalued if there is an active market on which to trade them.*

*An entity that has both traded and untraded quotas could revalue just the traded quotas.

✗ Management may need to make significant judgements about the future to measure certain fair values and some fair values are based on theoretical models. These values are less reliable because they are more subjective and subject to the limitations of the models used. The impact on the financial statements of hypothetical fair value that may never be realised may mislead users.

© DeVry/Becker Educational Development Corp. All rights reserved.

✗ Users may not comprehend the significance of how changes
   in fair value affect reported performance. In particular, the
   extent to which unrealised gains are reported in profit.*

✗ One aspect of relevance is that information should assist users
   in predicting future events and confirming past evaluations.
   That is, the users should be able to make predictions—not
   the financial statements. Increasing the use of fair values
   may lead users to place more reliance on the financial
   statements as a prediction of the future than the auditor can
   reasonably assure.

*Commentary

*When fair values
are introduced, some
users do not even
understand (as for
the revaluation model)
that not all assets are
measured on
this basis.

6 Not-for-Profit Organisations

Key Point

Not all organisations' primary objectives are to make profit.
Specialised organisations, not-for-profit and public sector
entities have other functions to perform in the economy.

▨ These types of organisations still enter into economic
   transactions and therefore still have accounting issues to deal
   with; the question is, do these organisations need to comply
   fully with IFRS?

6.1   Primary Objectives

▨ Most of these types of organisations do not have as their
   primary objective the making of profits. In many cases, these
   organisations are providing a service for the community as
   a whole. National governments have amongst their many
   objectives to provide health, education and policing to all
   members of the community; they do not seek to make a profit
   out of giving these services.

▨ Other organisations do not have profit as their primary
   objective (e.g. charities and many museums); they seek
   to provide a service to various groups within the local and
   international communities.

6.2   Value for Money

Key Point

Many not-for-profit organisations and public sector entities
follow a value for money (VFM) approach to how they perform
their services.

▨ VFM considers the "3 Es":
   ● *Economy*—seeking to minimise the cost of inputs;
   ● *Efficiency*—seeking to maximise outputs in proportion to the
      cost of the inputs; and
   ● *Effectiveness*—meeting the objectives set.

© DeVry/Becker Educational Development Corp. All rights reserved.

6.3   Accounting

▦ Most of these types of organisation enter into accounting transactions leading to the requirement for the transactions to be recorded by one means or another. Accruals accounting is used by the vast majority of these organisations, however, cash-based accounting is still used in some public sector institutions.

▦ The International Federation of Accountants (IFAC) has published International Public Sector Accounting Standards prescribing the accounting treatment to be followed by public sector bodies. These standards are derived from IFRSs, with adaptations being made to put them in a public sector context, when appropriate. The preface to these standards state that the conceptual framework of the IASB is still relevant in public sector accounting.

▦ Charitable organisations cannot do as they please with their funds; they must produce accounting records showing the stewardship of the funds that have been entrusted to them. They are required to follow a form of best practice for their accounting transactions.

7   IAS 41 *Agriculture*

7.1   Objective and Scope

▦ IAS 41 prescribes the accounting treatment and the presentation and disclosures related to agricultural activity, including:

- biological assets;
- agricultural produce at the point of harvest; and
- related government grants.

▦ It does not deal with land or intangible assets related to agricultural activity, which are addressed in IAS 16 and IAS 38, respectively.

7.2   Terminology

Biological asset: a living animal or plant.

Biological transformation: includes the processes of growth, degeneration, production and procreation that give rise to qualitative and quantitative changes in a biological asset.

Harvest: the detachment of produce from a biological asset or the cessation of a biological asset's life.

Agricultural produce: the product harvested from a biological asset.

Agricultural activity: an entity's management of biological transformation of biological assets into agricultural produce or additional biological assets.*

Fair value: the price that would be received to sell an asset (or paid to transfer a liability) in transaction between market participants at the measurement date.

Exam Advice

The inclusion of IAS 41 in the examinable documents means that this is a business sector that could be examined under learning outcome E1a).

*Commentary

*Activities include raising livestock, forestry, annual cropping and cultivation of orchards and plantations.

© DeVry/Becker Educational Development Corp. All rights reserved.

7.2.1 Agricultural Activity

Common features of agricultural activity are:

▨ Capability to change—living animals and plants are biologically transformed.

▨ Management of change—by enhancing or stabilising conditions (e.g. temperature, moisture, nutrient levels and light).

▨ Measurement of change—the change in quality (e.g. ripeness, density, fat cover, genetic merit) or quantity (e.g. number of fruits, weight, size).

7.3 Recognition and Measurement

7.3.1 Recognition

▨ A biological asset should be recognised when, and only when:

  ● the asset is controlled as a result of a past event;

  ● it is probable that future economic benefits associated with the asset will flow to the entity; and

  ● fair value can be measured reliably.*

7.3.2 Measurement

▨ A biological asset should be measured at its **fair value less costs to sell**:*

  ● on initial recognition; and

  ● at the end of each reporting period.

*Commentary

*IAS 41 presumes that fair value can be measured reliably.

*Commentary

*IFRS 13 applies.

Illustration 5 Fair Value

A farmer owns a dairy herd at 1 January 2017. The number of cows in the herd is 100. The fair value of the herd at this date is $5,000. The fair values of 2-year-old animals at 31 December 2016 and 3-year-old animals at 31 December 2017 are $60 and $75, respectively.

Separating out the value increases of the herd into those relating to price change and those relating to physical change gives the following valuation:

	$
Fair value at 1 January 2017	5,000
Increase due to price change (100 × ($60 − $50))	1,000
Increase due to physical change (100 × ($75 − $60))	1,500
Fair value at 31 December 2017	7,500

▨ Agricultural produce should be measured at its fair value less costs to sell at the **point of harvest**. This is deemed to be cost at that date when applying another IFRS (usually IAS 2).

▨ Costs to sell include commissions to dealers, levies and duties. They do **not** include transport and other costs of getting the asset to the market.

© DeVry/Becker Educational Development Corp. All rights reserved.

■ In certain cases fair value may be approximated by cost.
For example:

- when there has been little biological transformation since initial cost was incurred (e.g. tree seedlings planted shortly before the end of the reporting period);
- when the effect of the biological transformation on price is not material (e.g. initial growth in a 30-year tree plantation).

7.3.3 Reliable Measurement Presumption

■ The presumption that fair value can be measured reliably can be rebutted **only** on *initial recognition* when:

- a quoted market price is not available; and
- alternative estimates are clearly unreliable.

■ In this case, the asset should be valued at cost less accumulated depreciation (IAS 16) and any impairment losses (IAS 36).

■ When fair value can be measured reliably the asset will be carried at fair value less costs to sell.

7.3.4 Gains and Losses

■ A gain or loss arising on initial recognition of a biological asset or agricultural produce should be included in profit or loss for the period in which it arises.

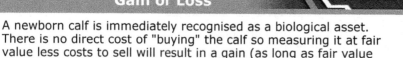

Illustration 6 Initial Recognition Gain or Loss

A newborn calf is immediately recognised as a biological asset. There is no direct cost of "buying" the calf so measuring it at fair value less costs to sell will result in a gain (as long as fair value exceeds costs to sell). This gain is recognised immediately in profit or loss.

If costs to sell exceed fair value, a loss must be recognised immediately in profit or loss.

■ Any changes in fair value less costs to sell arising at the end of each reporting period are similarly recognised in profit or loss for the period.

7.3.5 Government Grants

■ An unconditional government grant is recognised as income when, and only when, the government grant becomes receivable.

■ If a government grant is conditional, it is recognised when, and only when, the conditions are met.*

***Commentary**

*A condition may be that an entity does **not** engage in specified agricultural activity.

© DeVry/Becker Educational Development Corp. All rights reserved.

Example 1 Changes in Fair Value

As at 31 December 2016, a plantation consists of 100 Insignis Pine trees that were planted 10 years earlier. Insignis Pine takes 30 years to mature and will ultimately be processed into building material for houses or furniture.

Only mature trees have established fair values by reference to a quoted price in an active market. The fair value (inclusive of current transport costs to get 100 logs to market) for a mature tree of the same grade as in the plantation is:

As at 31 December 2016:	171
As at 31 December 2017	165

The entity's weighted average cost of capital is 6% per annum.

Required:

(a) **Estimate the fair value of the plantation as at:**

    (i) 31 December 2016; and

    (ii) 31 December 2017

(b) **Analyse the gain between the two period ends:**

    (i) a price change; and

    (ii) a physical change.

Solution

(a) **Estimate of Fair Value**

    (i) 31 December 2016

    Mature plantation =

    Immature plantation =

    (ii) 31 December 2017

    Mature plantation =

    Immature plantation =

(b) **Analysis of Gain**

    (i) Price change

    Reflects the change in price on the biological asset over the period.

                                                      $

    Prior year estimate restated at *current* price

    Less

    Prior year estimate (at prior year price)

    Gain/(Loss)

    (ii) Physical change

    Reflects the change in the state of maturity of the biological asset at current price.

                                                      $

    Current year estimate (at current price)

    Less

    Prior year estimate restated at *current* price

    Gain/(Loss)

7.4 Presentation and Disclosure

▦ The carrying amount of biological assets is presented *separately* in the statement of financial position.

▦ Disclosures include:

- The methods and assumptions used in determining fair value.
- A reconciliation of changes in the carrying amount between the beginning and the end of the current period.
- The aggregate gain or loss arising that is recognised in profit or loss.

▦ Separate disclosure of physical changes and price changes in the market is encouraged.

8 Conceptual Framework Exposure Draft

8.1 Background

▦ The conceptual framework was first issued in 1989, when accounting and reporting were very different. Two sections were updated in 2010 and since then the IASB has been looking to update the entire Framework.

▦ In May 2015, the IASB issued an exposure draft that proposes to drastically update the Framework to ensure that it keeps pace with the constant changes in the accounting profession.

▦ The proposed new framework is not an accounting standard. When the conceptual framework conflicts with an individual standard, the individual standard will always take precedence. It is hoped that the new framework will minimise any conflicts.

▦ The draft proposes to reinstate terms that were deleted from the 2010 update of the Framework. "Substance over form" and "prudence" will be incorporated in the fundamental concept of *faithful representation* and guidance given on the possible conflict between *neutrality* and *prudence*.

▦ The issue of *stewardship* has also been reintroduced; the draft states that users need information about how efficiently and effectively management has discharged its responsibilities to use the entity's resources to assess management's stewardship of those resources.

8.2 Proposed Revisions

▦ The draft proposes to include an introduction section followed by eight chapters.

Introduction

▦ The introduction provides background information, discussing the purpose of the Framework and identifying where the Framework sits in respect to the hierarchy of IFRS.

▦ It explains that the primary purpose of the Framework is to assist the IASB in its development and revision of IFRS.

▦ If, in the future, the IASB issues new documents that conflict with the Framework then the fact will be highlighted and an explanation behind the conflict will be given.

© DeVry/Becker Educational Development Corp. All rights reserved.

Chapter 1 Objective of general purpose financial reporting

▦ This chapter was one of the two chapters updated in 2010. No major changes are proposed in this update.

▦ However, the IASB felt it necessary, based on responses to the original discussion paper, to add guidance on stewardship and the primary users of financial statements.

Chapter 2 Qualitative characteristics of useful financial information

▦ This chapter was also updated in 2010 and no major changes are proposed.

▦ However, new text is proposed relating to "measurement uncertainty" and how it impacts the relevance of information. Specifically, the exposure draft clarifies that measurement uncertainty can make financial information less relevant.

▦ The draft also proposes to reintroduce the concepts of substance over form and prudence.

Chapter 3 Financial statements and the reporting entity

▦ Financial statements should be prepared from the perspective of the entity as a whole rather than any specific group of users of the financial statements.

▦ A reporting entity is defined as an entity that chooses to prepare general purpose financial statements. The boundary of the reporting entity could be based on direct control, such as a company reporting on its assets and liabilities (single entity), or indirect control, which would include a parent and its subsidiaries (group entity).

Chapter 4 Elements of financial statements

▦ This chapter defines assets, liabilities, equity, income and expenses.

▦ An asset is defined as "a present economic resource controlled by the entity as a result of past events", with economic resource defined as "a right that has the potential to produce economic benefits".

▦ The current definition requires that economic benefits be "probable" and "expected". The proposed new definition only requires that there be the potential to produce economic benefits. The new definition moves away from assets being physical in nature to assets being "a right to use something".*

▦ The new definition of a liability states that a liability is a present obligation of the entity to transfer an economic resource. Guidance is given regarding the term "present obligation", stating that two conditions must be met before a present obligation exists:

- the entity has no practical ability to avoid transfer of resources, and
- the obligation arises from past events that establish the extent of the obligation.

▦ The definition of equity will remain unchanged as will the definition of income and expenses; apart from the fact that they will change to tie in with the changes to the definition of assets and liabilities.

＊Commentary

*IFRS 16 Leases requires a lessee to recognise the "right-of-use" asset rather than the physical asset when accounting for leases.

© DeVry/Becker Educational Development Corp. All rights reserved.

Session 3 • Conceptual Framework

P2 Corporate Reporting (INT)

Chapter 5 Recognition and derecognition

▨ Recognition is the process of capturing an element for inclusion in the financial statements.

▨ The current recognition criteria focus on "probability" and "reliable measurement". The exposure draft proposes that the focus moves to the relevance of information and the faithful representation of the element in the financial statement.

▨ Derecognition is the removal from the statement of financial position of a previously recognised asset or liability.

Chapter 6 Measurement

▨ The concept of measurement remains similar to the present Framework in that it is the process of quantifying in monetary terms information about the entity's elements.

▨ The draft describes two categories of measurement bases: historical cost and current value. The current Framework also mentions realisable value and present value.

▨ An entity must select a measurement base that is both relevant and faithfully representative of the events and transactions that have occurred.*

▨ Equity as a total is not measured; it is the difference between the total of assets less liabilities. Components of equity, however, may be measured.

Chapter 7 Presentation and disclosure

▨ This chapter deals with the information to be included in the financial statements and how it is to be presented and disclosed. There is a focus on performance statements, profit or loss and other comprehensive income, and guidance is given on how other comprehensive income is presented.

▨ Without sufficient presentation and disclosure of transactions the financial statements would not faithfully represent the events of the period and could omit relevant information. Presentation and disclosure of information aids communication and enhances the qualitative, fundamental and enhancing, characteristics of financial information.

▨ The grouping of similar items, aggregation of information and elimination of "boiler-plate" disclosures is also considered.*

> ***Commentary***
>
> *Some standards require the use of current value. IFRS 9 *Financial Instruments* requires certain financial assets be measured at fair value. Other standards require items to be measured at historical cost. IAS 2 requires inventory to be measured at cost unless net realisable value (current value) is lower.

> ***Commentary***
>
> *Boiler-plate disclosures are standardised disclosures, repeating the same script year after year, without applying the requirements to the specific issues relating to the entity.
>
> For example, in relation to impairment "No reasonable possible change in a key assumption would result in an impairment loss."

Chapter 8 Concepts of capital and capital maintenance

▨ This chapter is unchanged apart from minor terminology changes. The IASB feels that capital maintenance concepts would be best dealt with in conjunction with issues relating to high inflation. At present, the IASB has not included this in its work programme.

© DeVry/Becker Educational Development Corp. All rights reserved.

Summary

- The purpose of the Framework is primarily to assist the IASB in developing and reviewing IFRSs and promoting harmonisation.
- The Framework states one underlying assumption: going concern.
- Recognition means including in the financial statements items that meet the definition of an element and satisfy the recognition criteria.
- Qualitative characteristics are attributes that make information useful to primary users.
- Fundamental characteristics are relevance and faithful representation.
- Financial statements must reflect the economic substance of transactions if they are to show a true and fair view.
- IFRS 13 does not prescribe when an entity should use fair value but how fair value should be used.
- Fair value is based on an exit price (rather than an entry price).
- Techniques used to estimate fair values should maximise observable inputs.
- Not all organisations have profit as a primary objective. Specialised organisations, not-for-profit and public sector entities have other functions to perform in the economy.
- Many not-for-profit organisations and public sector entities follow a value for money (VFM) approach, which considers economy, efficiency and effectiveness.

Session 3 Quiz
Estimated time: 40 minutes

1. State the objective of financial statements. (1.2)

2. Define asset. (1.4.1)

3. Name the TWO recognition criteria. (1.4.2)

4. Explain what is meant by the term "economic phenomena", which is used in the Framework. (2.1)

5. Explain the qualitative characteristic of faithful representation. (2.4)

6. Describe how accountants have been creative in their methods of accounting. (3.3)

7. Describe the methods available to the accountant when valuing an asset. (4.2)

8. When assessing the fair value of non-financial assets, explain what is meant by "highest and best use". (5.2)

9. When assessing fair value, state where the best place to get a Level 1 input valuation is. (5.6.1)

10. State THREE benefits and THREE limitations of fair values. (5.8)

11. List the THREE Es considered under value for money. (6.2)

12. Explain the presumption of reliable measurement in relation to IAS 41. (7.3.3)

13. List the issues addressed in the IASB's Conceptual Framework Exposure Draft. (8)

 # Study Question Bank
Estimated time: 20 minutes

Priority		Estimated Time	Completed
Q3	Timber Products	20 minutes	
Additional			
Q4	Creative Accounting		

© DeVry/Becker Educational Development Corp. All rights reserved.

EXAMPLE SOLUTION

Solution 1—Changes in Fair Value

(a) Estimate of Fair Value

(i) 31 December 2016

The mature plantation would have been valued at 17,100.

The estimate for the immature plantation is $\dfrac{17,100}{1.06^{20}} = 5,332$

(ii) 31 December 2017*

The mature plantation would have been valued at 16,500.

The estimate for the immature plantation is $\dfrac{16,500}{1.06^{19}} = 5,453$

(b) Analysis of Gain

The gain identified in (a) is analysed as follows:

(i) Price change

Reflects the change in price on the biological asset over the period.

		$
Prior year estimate restated at *current* price $\dfrac{16,500}{1.06^{20}}$	=	5,145
Less		
Prior year estimate (at prior year price) per (a)(i)		5,332
Loss		(187)

(ii) Physical change

Reflects the change in the state of maturity of the biological asset at current price.

	$
Current year estimate (at current price) per (a)(ii)	5,453
Less	
Prior year estimate restated at *current* price ((b)(i))	5,145
Gain	308

> ***Commentary**
>
> *The difference in fair value of the plantation between the two period ends is $121 ($5,453- $5,332) which will be reported as a gain in profit or loss.

Reporting Financial Performance

FOCUS

This session covers the following content from the *ACCA Study Guide.*

C. Reporting the Financial Performance of Entities

1. Performance reporting

a) Discuss and apply the criteria that must be met before an entity can apply the revenue recognition model to that contract.

c) Discuss and apply the five-step model which relates to revenue earned from a contract with a customer.

Session 4 Guidance

■ **Revise** IASs 1 and 2 (s.2, s.5).

■ **Learn** the IFRS 5 criteria (s.3) and attempt *Example 1*.

■ **Learn** the five-step model for revenue recognition (s.4.1) and understand its application to specific transactions (s.4.3). Pay particular attention to variable consideration (s.4.2).

VISUAL OVERVIEW

Objective: To describe the international financial reporting standards that predominantly affect the statement of comprehensive income.

```
                        ┌─────────────────────────────┐
                        │   FINANCIAL PERFORMANCE     │
                        └─────────────────────────────┘
```

IAS 1 PRESENTATION OF FINANCIAL STATEMENTS

- Objective
- Financial Statements
- Overall Considerations
- Financial Position
- Comprehensive Income
- Changes in Equity
- ED on materiality

IFRS 15 REVENUE FROM CONTRACTS WITH CUSTOMERS

- Principles
- Variable Consideration
- Specific Transactions

IAS 34 INTERIM FINANCIAL REPORTING

- Introduction
- Content
- Recognition and Measurement

IFRS 5 NON-CURRENT ASSETS HELD FOR SALE AND DISCONTINUED OPERATIONS

- Component of an Entity
- Discontinued Operations
- Presentation
- Continuing Operations

IAS 2 INVENTORIES

- Measurement
- Components of Cost
- Net Realisable Value
- Recognition

Session 4 Guidance

■ **Understand** the who, when and how of interim reports and learn the requirements (s.6).

■ **Read** the *student accountant* articles "Revenue revisited" and "Profit, loss and OCI".

© DeVry/Becker Educational Development Corp. All rights reserved.

1 Financial Performance

- This session considers the reporting of financial performance by an entity by looking at those standards which mostly affect the reporting of performance through the statement of total comprehensive income.
- This session deals with:*
  - IAS 1 *Presentation of Financial Statements*;
  - IAS 2 *Inventories* (as an expense against revenue recognised);
  - IFRS 15 *Revenue from Contracts with Customers*; and
  - IFRS 5 *Non-current Assets Held for Sale and Discontinued Operations*.
- The session also considers IAS 34 *Interim Financial Reporting*. Although this standard is not assumed knowledge, the level of detail required at P2 is fairly minimal.

Commentary

*The details of these standards that are assumed knowledge from F7 *Financial Reporting* are not repeated.

2 IAS 1 *Presentation of Financial Statements*

2.1 Objective

- To achieve this, the standard sets out:
  - overall considerations for the presentation;
  - guidelines for the structure; and
  - minimum requirements for content of financial statements.

Key Point

To prescribe the content of general purpose financial statements to ensure comparability with:
- the entity's own financial statements; and
- financial statements of other entities.

2.1.1 General Purpose Financial Statements

- These are financial statements intended to meet the needs of users who are not in a position to demand reports tailored to specific information needs.
- They may be presented separately or within another public document (e.g. annual report or prospectus).

2.1.2 Application

- To financial statements of individual entities and consolidated financial statements of groups.
- To all types of entities including banks, insurance and other financial institutions.
- To entities with a profit objective (including public sector business entities).

© DeVry/Becker Educational Development Corp. All rights reserved.

2.2 Financial Statements

2.2.1 Objectives of Financial Statements

▨ These are restated as in the Framework (see *Session 3*).

▨ To meet the objectives, financial statements provide information about an entity's:

- assets;
- liabilities;
- equity;
- income and expenses including gains and losses; and
- cash flows.

2.2.2 Components

▨ A complete set of financial statements includes:

- Statement of financial position
- Statement of total comprehensive income, to include:*
  — profit or loss for the period
  — other comprehensive income (e.g. revaluation surplus)
- Statement of changes in equity
- Statement of cash flows
- Accounting policies and explanatory notes.

2.2.3 Supplementary Statements

▨ Entities may present additional information on a voluntary basis, for example:

- a financial review by management;
- environmental reports; and
- value added statements.

▨ Any additional statements presented are outside the scope of IFRSs.

Commentary

*Information in the statement of total comprehensive income can be presented either as a single statement or two separate statements (see s.2.5).

2.3 Overall Considerations

2.3.1 Fair Presentation and Compliance With IFRSs

▨ Financial statements must "present fairly":

- financial position;
- financial performance; and
- cash flows.

▨ This is achieved by appropriate application of IFRSs (and any necessary additional disclosures).

▨ Where an IFRS is applied before its effective date that fact must be disclosed.

Key Point

Inappropriate accounting treatments are *not* rectified by:

- disclosure of accounting polices used; or
- notes or explanatory material.

2.3.2 Departure From IFRS

■ In *extremely* rare circumstances, if compliance would be misleading and therefore departure from a standard is necessary to achieve a fair presentation, the entity must disclose:*

*Departures from IFRS are often referred to as "true and fair override" (i.e. that a "true and fair" view takes precedence).

- that management has concluded that the financial statements fairly present the entity's financial position, performance and cash flows;
- that it has complied in all material respects with applicable IFRSs except that it has departed from a standard in order to achieve a fair presentation;
- the standard from which the entity has departed, the nature of departure, including the treatment that the standard would require together with the reason why that treatment would be misleading in the circumstances and the treatment adopted;
- the financial effect of the departure on the entity's profit or loss, assets, liabilities, equity and cash flows for each period presented.

■ The IASB does not expect departure from an IFRS in order to present information fairly.

2.3.3 Going Concern

■ If a company is not a going concern, the financial statements should be prepared on a break-up basis.

Key Point

The entity is likely to continue in business, as currently, for the foreseeable future.

2.3.4 Accrual Basis of Accounting

■ Transactions are accounted for as they occur, not when any relevant cash flows are made. Cash accounting would be the opposite model to accruals accounting.

2.3.5 Consistency of Presentation

■ An entity should maintain the same methods and policies for accounting from one period to another. The changing of any policy, from a voluntary basis, should only occur if the change would give more relevant and reliable information.

© DeVry/Becker Educational Development Corp. All rights reserved.

2.3.6   Materiality and Aggregation

 Definition

Material—omissions or misstatements of items are material if they could, individually or collectively, influence the economic decisions of users taken on the basis of the financial statements.*

Materiality—materiality depends on the size and nature of the omission or misstatement judged in the surrounding circumstances. The size or nature of the item, or a combination of both, could be the determining factor.

 *Commentary

*Understandability of financial statements must not be reduced by obscuring material information with immaterial information.

Material items	Immaterial amounts
• Present separately in financial statements.	• Aggregate with amounts of similar nature or function (in the financial statements or in notes). • Need not be presented separately.

▓ **Materiality**: provides that the specific disclosure requirements of IFRSs need not be met if a transaction is not **material**.

2.3.7   Offsetting

 Key Point

Assets and liabilities, and income and expenses, must not be offset unless another standard or interpretation requires or permits offsetting.

▓ IAS 12 *Income Taxes* is a standard which does allow, under certain circumstances, the offsetting of current tax assets against current tax liabilities and deferred tax assets against deferred tax liabilities. It does not allow the offset of current tax assets against deferred tax liabilities.

© DeVry/Becker Educational Development Corp. All rights reserved.

2.3.8 Comparative Information

Key Point

At least one year's comparative information should be included in the financial statements. If there is a change in an accounting policy, two years' comparative information should be presented.

■ If a retrospective change in accounting policy has a material effect on the statement of financial position at the beginning of the preceding period then that statement also should be presented. Other than the specified required disclosures, additional information relating to this statement is not required.

2.4 Statement of Financial Position

2.4.1 Overall Structure

■ There is no prescribed format, though IAS 1 presents a format as an illustration.
■ There are two main types of format found in practice. They differ with respect to the form of the accounting equation which they expand:
  ● Net Assets (Assets – Liabilities) = Capital
  ● Assets = Capital + Liabilities

2.4.2 Presentation of Statement of Financial Position Items

■ Certain items must be shown in the statement of financial position. The minimum requirements for these "line items" are:*
  ● Property, plant and equipment
  ● Investment property
  ● Intangible assets
  ● Financial assets
  ● Assets and assets included in disposal groups classified as held for sale
  ● Investments accounted for under the equity method
  ● Biological assets
  ● Inventories
  ● Trade and other receivables
  ● Cash and cash equivalents
  ● Trade and other payables
  ● Liabilities included in disposal groups classified as held for sale
  ● Current tax assets or liabilities
  ● Deferred tax assets or liabilities
  ● Provisions
  ● Financial liabilities
  ● Non-controlling interest, to be presented as part of equity
  ● Issued equity capital and reserves.

Commentary

*The order in which the line items in the statement of financial position appear is not prescribed.

© DeVry/Becker Educational Development Corp. All rights reserved.

▩ An entity must disclose either in the statement of financial position or in the notes further sub-classifications of the line items presented, classified in a manner appropriate to the entity's operations.*

▩ Typically, companies will present the main headings in the statement of financial position and the detail in the notes to the accounts.

*Line items can be disaggregated or aggregated as deemed necessary to faithfully represent events and transactions.

2.4.3 Classification of Liabilities, ED/2015/1

▩ In 2015 the IASB issued an exposure draft that proposes minor amendments to IAS 1 *Presentation of Financial Statements.* The proposals relate to the classification of liabilities at the reporting date.

▩ The draft clarifies that the split of liabilities into current or non-current is based on rights that are in existence at the reporting date. This clarification will resolve a slight conflict between paragraphs within the standard.

▩ It also proposes to group similar liabilities together in the financial statements.

2.5   Statement of Total Comprehensive Income

▩ All items of income and expense recognised in a period must be presented either:

- ● in a *single* statement of total comprehensive income; or
- ● in *two* statements:

1. A statement displaying components of profit or loss.

2. A second statement beginning with profit or loss and displaying components of other comprehensive income.

2.5.1   Statement of Profit or Loss

▩ The profit or loss presents the following items, in addition to any presentation required by other standards:*

- ● Revenue
- ● Finance costs
- ● Share of profits and losses of associates and joint ventures accounted for under the equity method
- ● Tax expense
- ● A single amount for the total of discontinued operations (IFRS 5)
- ● Profit or loss (i.e. the total of income less expenses, excluding the items of other comprehensive income).

*All items of income and expense in a period *must* be included in profit or loss unless an IFRS requires or permits otherwise. This statement is commonly called the income statement.

2.5.2   Other Comprehensive Income

▩ Components of other comprehensive income may be presented either:*

- ● net of related tax effects (see *Illustration 1*); or
- ● before related tax effects with one amount shown for the aggregate amount of related tax effects (see *Illustration 2*).

*The income tax relating to each component of other comprehensive income must be disclosed in the notes if not in the statement of comprehensive income.

- Items included in other comprehensive income should be grouped into those gains and losses which will be reclassified to profit or loss and those gains and losses which will not be reclassified.

- Reclassification adjustments (i.e. reclassification of amounts previously recognised in other comprehensive income to profit or loss) are included with the related component of other comprehensive income and may be presented in the statement of comprehensive income or in the notes.

- Both profit or loss and total comprehensive income must be attributed to:

  - non-controlling interest; and
  - owners of the parent.*

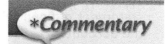

*This disclosure is required in the statement of comprehensive income.

Illustration 1 — Other Comprehensive Income Net of Tax*

Year ended 31 December 2017	Before-tax amount	Tax (expense) amount	Net-of-tax amount
Items which will not be reclassified in profit or loss:			
Gains of property revaluation	x	(x)	x
Investments in equity instruments	(x)	x	(x)
Actuarial losses on defined benefit pension plans	(x)	x	(x)
Share of other comprehensive income of associates	x	(x)	x
	x	(x)	x
Items which may be reclassified to profit or loss:			
Exchange differences on translating foreign operations	x	(x)	x
Cash flow hedges	x	(x)	x
	x	(x)	x
Other comprehensive income	x	(x)	x

*Commentary

*Disclosure of the separate attribution is required in the relevant statement(s).

© DeVry/Becker Educational Development Corp. All rights reserved.

2.5.3   Reclassification

Illustration 2 Other Comprehensive Income*		
Year ended 31 December	**2017**	**2016**
*Items which will **not** be reclassified in profit or loss:*		
Investments in equity instruments	(x)	x
Gains of property revaluation	x	x
Actuarial gains (losses) on defined benefit pension plans	x	(x)
Share of other comprehensive income of associates and joint ventures	x	x
Income tax relating to items which will not be reclassified	(x)	(x)
	x	x
*Items which **may** be reclassified to profit or loss:*		
Exchange differences on translating foreign operations	x	(x)
Cash flow hedges	x	(x)
Income tax relating to items which will be reclassified	(x)	(x)
Other comprehensive income for the year	x	(x)

*Commentary

*Using the format in *Illustration 2*, the income tax relating to each component must be disclosed in the notes.

▦ This is where a transaction reported in other comprehensive income is later reported again in profit or loss (usually when the item is realised). IFRSs may require or prohibit this:

  ● Reclassification is **required** for the cumulative foreign exchange differences arising on translation of a net investment in a foreign entity when that investment is disposed of (IAS 21 *The Effects of Changes in Foreign Exchange Rates*).

  ● Reclassification to profit or loss is **prohibited** for surpluses on the revaluation of property, plant and equipment (IAS 16, *Property, Plant and Equipment*). If the asset is sold the surplus **may** be transferred to retained earnings.

  ● The cumulative gain or loss on financial assets that must be measured at fair value through other comprehensive income **is reclassified** through profit or loss on the disposal of the financial asset.

▦ The IASB decisions on whether to report changes in values to profit or loss or other comprehensive income (and if reported initially in other comprehensive income whether they should be reclassified) have been made on an ad hoc basis.

© DeVry/Becker Educational Development Corp. All rights reserved.

2.5.4   Material Items

▨ The nature and amount of material items of income or expense should be disclosed separately. For example:
  - write-downs of assets (and reversals thereof);
  - costs of restructurings;
  - asset disposals;
  - discontinued operations; and
  - legal settlements.

2.6   Statement of Changes in Equity

▨ An entity must present, as a separate component of its financial statements, a statement showing:*
  - total comprehensive income for the period, showing separately the total amounts attributable to owners of the parent and to non-controlling interest;
  - for each component of equity, the effects of retrospective application or retrospective restatement (per IAS 8);
  - the amounts of transactions with owners in their capacity as owners, showing separately contributions and distributions; and
  - for each component of equity, a reconciliation between the carrying amount at the beginning and the end of the period, disclosing each change separately.

▨ *In addition,* an entity should present, either in this statement or in the notes, dividends recognised as distributions to owners during the period, and the related amount per share.

2.6.1   Structure

▨ The requirements are most easily satisfied in a columnar format with a separate column for each component of equity.*

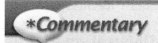

*Commentary

*Components of equity include each class of contributed equity, the accumulated balance of each class of other comprehensive income and retained earnings. Changes in equity reflect the increase or decrease in net assets. Except for changes resulting from transactions with owners (including direct transaction costs), the overall change clearly represents the total amount of income and expense, including gains and losses, generated by the entity's activities.

*Commentary

*A full year's comparative information must also be shown.

	Attributable to owners of the parent[1]					
	Share capital	Share premium	Revaluation[2] surplus	Retained earnings	Non-controlling interest	Total equity
Balance at 1 January	x	x	x	x	x	x
Change in accounting policy				(x)	(x)	(x)
Restated balance	x	x	x	x	x	x
Changes in equity for period						
Issue of share capital	x	x				x
Dividends				(x)		(x)
Total comprehensive income for the year			x	x	x	x
Transfer to retained earnings			(x)	x		
Balance at 31 December	x	x	x	x	x	x

1 A column showing the sub-total of amounts attributable to equity holders of the parent should also be included.
2 A translation reserve might similarly be presented as a separate column.

                    © DeVry/Becker Educational Development Corp. All rights reserved.

2.6.2   Transfers Within Equity

▨ Although many items cannot be reclassified from other comprehensive income into profit or loss, some standards will allow some form of transfer between components of equity.

▨ IAS 16 allows the transfer of a revaluation surplus from revaluation reserve into retained earnings.

▨ The issue of convertible debt requires the instrument to be split into debt and equity on initial issue. Although not specifically required by IAS 32 the initial amount recognised in equity, as a separate component, could subsequently be transferred into another component of equity, namely, retained earnings.

2.7   ED on Materiality

▨ ED/2015/8 *IFRS Practice Statement* - Application of Materiality to Financial Statements gives guidance to management on the application of the definition of materiality.

▨ The guidance covers three main areas:

- characteristics of materiality;
- presentation and disclosure in the financial statements; and
- omissions and misstatements.

▨ The ED proposes to ultimately issue a "practice statement" rather than a standard and will therefore not be compulsory for compliance with IFRS.

3   IFRS 5 *Non-current Assets Held for Sale and Discontinued Operations*

3.1   Component of an Entity

▨ Operations and cash flows which are clearly distinguishable from the remainder of the entity—both operationally and for financial reporting purposes.*

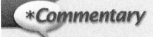

Commentary

*A component will have been a cash generating unit (or a group of cash generating units) when held for use.

3.1.1   "Distinguishable"

▨ This will be the case if:

- its operating assets and liabilities can be directly attributed to it;
- its income (gross revenue) can be directly attributed to it; and
- at least a majority of its operating expenses can be directly attributed to it.

Key Point

A discontinued operation must be distinguishable operationally and for reporting purposes.

© DeVry/Becker Educational Development Corp. All rights reserved.

3.2 Discontinued Operations

■ A discontinued operation is a component of an entity which either:

- has been disposed of; or
- is classified as held for sale, and
- represents a *separate* major line of business or geographical area of operations;
- is part of a *single coordinated* plan to dispose of that line of business or area of operations; or
- is a subsidiary acquired exclusively with a view to resale.

3.2.1 "Separate"

■ A discontinued operation must be a separate major line of business or geographical area of operations.

- An operating segment (IFRS 8 *Operating Segments*) would normally satisfy this criterion.
- A part of a segment may also satisfy the criterion.
- For an entity which does not report segment information, a major product or service line may also satisfy the criteria of the definition.

■ Business entities frequently close facilities, abandon products (or even product lines) and change the size of the workforce in response to market forces. These changes usually are not discontinued operations but they can occur in connection with a discontinued operation.

For example:

- gradual or evolutionary phasing out of a product line or class of service;
- discontinuance of several products within an on-going line of business;
- shifting of some production or marketing activities for a particular line of business from one location to another;
- closing of a facility to achieve productivity improvements or other cost savings; and
- sale of a subsidiary whose activities are similar to those of the parent or other subsidiaries or associates within a consolidated group.

3.2.2 "A Single Coordinated Plan"

■ A discontinued operation may be disposed of in its entirety or piecemeal, but always in pursuit of an overall coordinated plan to discontinue the entire component.

3.3 Presentation

3.3.1 A Single Amount

■ A single amount in the statement of profit or loss comprises:

- post-tax profit or loss of discontinued operations;
- post-tax gain or loss recognised on:
  - the measurement to fair value less costs to sell; or
  - the disposal of the assets (or disposal groups) constituting the discontinued operation.

© DeVry/Becker Educational Development Corp. All rights reserved.

3.3.2 An Analysis

▨ An analysis of the single amount in the statement of profit or loss or in the *notes* into:

- the revenue, expenses and pre-tax profit or loss of discontinued operations;
- the gain or loss recognised on:
  - the measurement to fair value less costs to sell; or
  - the disposal of the assets or disposal group(s) constituting the discontinued operation.*

▨ If presented in the statement of profit or loss it is identified as relating to discontinued operations separately from continuing operations.

3.4 Continuing Operations

▨ If an entity ceases to classify a component as held for sale, the results of operations previously presented as discontinued are presented in continuing operations for all periods presented.

▨ Gains and losses on the re-measurement of held for sale non-current assets that do not meet the definition of a discontinued operation are included in profit or loss from continuing operations.

Commentary

*Each discontinued operation is presented with the related income tax expense.

Illustration 3 Disposal

Entity X has three segments:

    A   Tobacco

    B   Alcohol

    C   Health food

The following information relates to the year ended 31 December 2017:

	A	B	C
	$000	$000	$000
Revenue	200	180	110
Expenses	120	105	115
Taxation (30%)	24	22.5	(1.5)

Segment C is felt to be inconsistent with the long-term direction of the company. Management has decided, therefore, to dispose of Segment C.

On 5 November 2017, the board of directors of X voted to approve the disposition and a public announcement was made. On that date, the carrying amount of Segment C's assets was $105,000 and it had liabilities of $15,000. The estimated recoverable amount of the assets was determined to be $85,000 and the directors of X concluded that a pre-tax impairment loss of $20,000 should be recognised. This was duly processed in November and is included in the above amounts

At 31 December 2017, the carrying amount of Segment C's assets was $85,000 and it had liabilities of $15,000. There was no further impairment between 5 November and the year end.

X decided to adopt the provisions of IFRS 5 by making the necessary disclosures in the notes to the accounts.

Required:

Show how the above information would be reflected in the financial statements of X for the year ended 31 December 2017.

© DeVry/Becker Educational Development Corp. All rights reserved.

Illustration 3 Disposal (continued)

Solution

Statement of profit or loss for the year ended 31 December 2017

	$000
Revenue	490
Expenses	(320)
Impairment loss	(20)
Profit before tax	150
Taxation (30%)	(45)
	105

Note to the financial statements

On 5 November 2017, the board of directors publicly announced a plan to dispose of Segment C, the health food division. The disposal is consistent with the company's long-term strategy to focus its activities on the manufacture and distribution of cigarettes and alcoholic drinks and to divest unrelated activities. The company is actively seeking a buyer for Segment C and hopes to complete the sale by the end of September 2018.

At 31 December 2017, the carrying amount of the assets of Segment C was $85,000 and its liabilities were $15,000.

During 2017, Segment C earned revenues of $110,000 and incurred expenses of $115,000 resulting in a pre-tax operating loss of $5,000, with a related tax benefit to the entity of $1,500.

During 2017, Segment C's cash outflow from operating activities was xx, cash outflow from investing activities was xx and cash inflow from financing activities was xx.

Example 1 Sale Contract for Business Segment

Following on from *Illustration 3*, the following information relates to the year ended 31 December 2018 before taking into account the sale of Segment C:

	A	B	C
	$000	$000	$000
Revenue	230	195	90
Expenses	130	115	100
Taxation (30%)	30	24	(3)

On 30 September 2018, X sold Segment C to Z Corporation for $60,000. The carrying amount of Segment C's net assets at that date was $70,000. The loss on disposal will attract tax relief at 30%.

The sale contract obliges X to terminate the employment of certain employees of Segment C, incurring an expected termination cost of $30,000, to be paid by 31 March 2019. This has not been accounted for as at the year end and will attract tax relief at 30%.

X has decided to make the disclosures in the statement of profit or loss.

Required:

Show how the above information would be reflected in the financial statements of X for the year ended 31 December 2018.

© DeVry/Becker Educational Development Corp. All rights reserved.

4 IFRS 15 *Revenue from Contracts with Customers*

4.1 Principles of Revenue Recognition

4.1.1 Introduction to IFRS 15

- In May 2014, the IASB and FASB jointly issued IFRS 15 *Revenue from Contracts with Customers*. The Standard replaces IAS 11 *Construction Contracts* and IAS 18 *Revenue*.

IFRS 15 outlines the five steps of the revenue recognition process:

Step 1	Identify the contract(s) with the customer
Step 2	Identify the separate performance obligations
Step 3	Determine the transaction price
Step 4	Allocate the transaction price to the performance obligations
Step 5	Recognise revenue when (or as) a performance obligation is satisfied

- The core principle of IFRS 15 is that an entity recognises revenue from the transfer of goods or services to a customer in an amount that reflects the consideration that the entity expects to be entitled to in exchange for the goods or services.

4.1.2 Identify Contracts With Customers

Definition

Contract—an agreement between two or more parties that creates enforceable rights and obligations. Contracts can be written, verbal or implied based on an entity's customary business practices.

Customer—a party that has contracted with an entity to obtain goods or services that are an output of the entity's ordinary activities in exchange for consideration.

- The revenue recognition principles of IFRS 15 apply only when a contract meets **all** of the following criteria:*
  - the parties to the contract have **approved** the contract;
  - the entity can identify each party's **rights** regarding the goods or services in the contract;
  - the **payment terms** can be identified;
  - the contract has **commercial substance**; and
  - it is **probable** that the entity will collect the **consideration** due under the contract.*

*Commentary

*These are assessed at the beginning of the contract. If met, they are **not** reassessed unless a significant change in circumstances makes the contract rights and obligations unenforceable. If not met initially, a contract can be reassessed at a later date.

Definition

Commercial substance—the event or transaction causes cash flows to change.

*Commentary

*Consideration may not be the same as the transaction price due to discounts and bonuses.

© DeVry/Becker Educational Development Corp. All rights reserved.

4.1.3 Identify Performance Obligations

Definition

Performance obligation—a promise to transfer to a customer:

- a good or service (or bundle of goods or services) that is distinct; **or**
- a series of goods or services that are substantially the same and are transferred in the same way.

- If a promise to transfer a good or service is not distinct from other goods and services in a contract, then the goods or services are combined into a single performance obligation.

Key Point

A good or service is distinct if **both** of the following criteria are met:

1. The customer can benefit from the good or service on its own or when combined with the customer's available resources; and
2. The promise to transfer the good or service is separately identifiable from other goods or services in the contract.*

*Commentary

*A transfer of a good or service is separately identifiable if it:

- is not integrated with other goods or services in the contract;
- does not modify or customise another good or service in the contract; or
- does not depend on or relate to other goods or services promised in the contract.

4.1.4 Determine the Transaction Price

- Transaction price does not include amounts collected for third parties (i.e. sales taxes or VAT).
- The effects of the following must be considered when determining the transaction price:
  - the time value of money;*
  - the fair value of any non-cash consideration;
  - estimates of variable consideration;
  - consideration payable to the customer.*

Definition

Transaction price—the amount of consideration to which an entity is entitled in exchange for transferring goods or services.

*Commentary

*The time value of money does not need to be considered if the length of the contract is less than one year.

*Commentary

*Consideration payable to the customer is treated as a reduction in the transaction price unless the payment is for goods or services received from the customer.

© DeVry/Becker Educational Development Corp. All rights reserved.

4.1.5 Allocate the Transaction Price

▥ The transaction price is allocated to all separate performance obligations in proportion to the stand-alone selling price of the goods or services.

Stand-alone selling price—the price at which an entity would sell a promised good or service separately to a customer.

- The best evidence of stand-alone selling price is the observable price of a good or service when it is sold separately.
- The stand-alone selling price should be estimated if it is not observable.

▥ The allocation is made at the beginning of the contract and is not adjusted for subsequent changes in the stand-alone selling prices of the goods or services.

4.1.6 Recognise Revenue

▥ Recognise revenue when (or as) a performance obligation is satisfied by transferring a promised good or service (an asset) to the customer.

▥ An asset is transferred when (or as) the customer gains control of the asset.

▥ The entity must determine whether the performance obligation will be satisfied over time or at a point in time.

4.2 Variable Consideration

4.2.1 Estimation

▣ If the consideration promised in a contract includes a variable amount, the variable consideration must be estimated.

▣ Examples of variable consideration include:

- volume discounts (see *Illustration 4*);
- incentives (e.g. for early completion)
- penalties (e.g. for late completion);
- customer referral bonuses;
- rebates and refunds; and
- price concessions.

▣ One of two methods should be used to estimate the amount of variable consideration (whichever method gives the best prediction):*

1. Expected value (i.e. the sum of possible amounts weighted according to their respective probabilities); or

2. Most likely amount (i.e. the single most likely amount of consideration).

▣ The chosen method should be applied consistently throughout the contract.

▣ The estimated variable consideration should be updated at the end of each reporting period; any changes in estimate are reflected in the current period financial statements (i.e. treated prospectively).

Commentary

*Expected value is more suitable for a large number of contracts with similar characteristics. The most likely amount is more suitable when there are few possible outcomes.

4.2.2 Constraints on Estimation

▣ Variable consideration should be included in the transaction price only when it is **highly probable** that there will be **no reversal** of the cumulative revenue recognised when the uncertainty associated with the variable consideration is resolved.

▣ Both the **likelihood** and **magnitude** of revenue reversal should be considered when assessing this probability. Factors that increase the likelihood or magnitude include:

- A high likelihood that the variable consideration will change due to factors that cannot be influenced by the entity (e.g. market performance);
- A long period of uncertainty about the variable consideration before it is expected to be resolved;
- Limited experience with similar types of contracts;
- A practice of offering a wide range of variable terms or a history of changing variable terms in similar circumstances;
- A contract with a large number and broad range of possible consideration amounts.

© DeVry/Becker Educational Development Corp. All rights reserved.

Illustration 4   Volume Discount

Bellway has a contract to supply components to a customer on a monthly basis. The contract price of $6 per unit is reduced to $5 per unit if the customer orders more than 10,000 units during the calendar year.

The customer ordered 1,200 units in the month of January. Bellway has significant experience with this product and the purchasing patterns of this customer. Bellway estimates that the customer's purchases will exceed the 10,000-unit threshold and concludes that it is highly probable that a significant reversal in the amount of revenue recognised will not occur when the total amount of purchases by the customer is known at year end.

Bellway will recognise revenue of $6,000 (1,200 units × $5 per unit) for the goods sold in January, as this is the most likely outcome for the year.

If at any time during the year it appears that the total number of units ordered for the year will be less than 10,000, Bellway should change the amount of revenue previously recognised to reflect the higher (non-discounted) price.

4.2.3 Allocation to Performance Obligations

▨ Variable consideration may be attributable to:

- an entire contract; or
- a specific part of a contract (e.g. part of the performance obligations or part of the distinct goods or services promised in a single performance obligation).

Illustration 5   Management Fees

Investment Management Partners (IMP) enters into a contract to provide asset management services to a client for four years. IMP receives a quarterly management fee equal to 1.5% of the client's assets at the end of each quarter. The management fee is a form of variable consideration. The contract is a single performance obligation made up of series of distinct services that are substantially the same and have the same pattern of transfer.

The management fee is highly susceptible to factors outside IMP's influence because the fee is dependent on the market. As a result, IMP cannot include the management fee in the transaction price at the inception of the contract.

At the end of each quarter, IMP updates its estimate of the transaction price. The actual management fee earned during that quarter is the transaction price, as there is no longer uncertainty related to this variable amount.

At the end of the first quarter, the assets under management are $50 million and the management fee is $750,000. The $750,000 transaction price is allocated to the services provided in the first quarter because these services are distinct from the services provide in other quarters. Therefore, IMP will record revenue of $750,000 for the first quarter.

© DeVry/Becker Educational Development Corp. All rights reserved.

4.3   Specific Transactions*

*Commentary

*The Application Guidance and Illustrative Examples of IFRS 15 include warranties, principal versus agent considerations, customer options for additional goods and services, customers' unexercised rights, non-refundable upfront fees, licensing, repurchase agreements and bill-and-hold arrangements. Principal versus agent considerations, repurchase agreements and bill-and-hold arrangements are examinable in F7 (see Appendix). The other transactions are covered in this section.

4.3.1   Warranties

Definition

Assurance-type warranty—a warranty that provides a customer with assurance that the related product will function as the parties intended because it meets agreed-upon considerations.

Service-type warranty—a warranty that provides a customer with a service in addition to the assurance that the product meets agreed-upon specifications.

▪ When a customer has the option to purchase a separate warranty it is a distinct service that is accounted for as a separate performance obligation. A portion of the transaction price is allocated to the warranty.

▪ If there is no option to purchase a warranty separately, it is accounted for in accordance with IAS 37 *Provisions, Contingent Liabilities and Contingent Assets*, unless it is a service-type warranty (wholly or in part). For a service-type warranty, the promised service is a performance obligation and a portion of the transaction price is allocated to the warranty.*

*Commentary

*A warranty including service-type and assurance-type warranties that cannot reasonably be accounted for separately is accounted for as a single performance obligation.

Illustration 6   Warranty

Delta Manufacturing offers customers an optional service warranty that covers parts and labour for any product repairs needed during the first two years of ownership. The selling price of a product is $10,000 including the warranty, or $9,500 without the warranty. If a customer purchases the product with the warranty, $9,500 of the transaction price will be allocated to the product and $500 will be allocated to the warranty.

4.3.2   Customer Options for Additional Goods and Services

▪ When a customer buys goods or services and is given an option to acquire additional goods or services at a discount (a discount voucher), the option is a separate performance obligation if it provides a material right to the customer that would not be received without entering into the contract.*

*Commentary

*For example, a discount that exceeds the discounts typically made available to all customers in that geographical area or market.

© DeVry/Becker Educational Development Corp. All rights reserved.

■ The transaction price should be allocated between the current purchase and the discount voucher based on relative stand-alone selling price. If the relative stand-alone selling price of the option is not directly observable, it should be estimated, taking into account:

  ● any discount the customer would receive *without* exercising the option; and

  ● the *likelihood* that the option will be exercised.

■ The discount voucher is an advance payment for future goods or services and revenue should be recognised when the future goods or services are provided or the option expires.

Illustration 7 Discount Voucher

Vacation Out, a hotel chain, offers customers a 30% discount on future stays with the chain when its customers spend more than $200 on a stay. The voucher is valid for three months from the date of the original stay.

The hotel plans to offer a 10% discount to all customers during that same period, so the portion of the discount that provides the customer with a material right is the additional 20% discount.

The average hotel bill has been calculated at $250 and it is estimated that the probability that a customer will use the voucher is 60%. The estimated stand-alone selling price of the discount voucher is therefore $30 ($250 × 60% × 20%).

Zena stayed with the chain and spent $400. The total stand-alone selling price is $430 and the $400 transaction price is allocated as follows:

Current stay ($400 ÷ $430 × $400) = $372
Discount voucher ($30 ÷ $430 × $400) = $28

$372 is recognised at the time of Zena's current stay at the hotel. The $28 of revenue for the discount voucher is recognised when Zena stays at the hotel again and uses the voucher, or when the voucher expires at the end of three months.

■ An option to acquire an additional good or service at the stand-alone selling price for the good or service (i.e. no discount) is a marketing offer that is not accounted for until the customer exercises the option to purchase the additional goods or services.

4.3.3 Customers' Unexercised Rights ("Breakage")

■ A non-refundable prepayment made by a customer gives the customer a right to receive a good or service in the future.*

■ If the customer does not exercise all contractual rights, the breakage amount is recognised as revenue unless there is a requirement to remit it to another party (e.g. a government under unclaimed property laws).

  ● If entitlement to the breakage amount is expected, it is recognised as revenue in proportion to the pattern of rights recognised by the customer.

  ● If entitlement is not expected, the breakage amount is recognised as revenue when the likelihood that the exercise of the customers' rights becomes remote.

***Commentary**

*For example, for hotel room and flight bookings.

© DeVry/Becker Educational Development Corp. All rights reserved.

4.3.4 Non-refundable Upfront Fees

▨ A non-refundable "upfront" fee (at contract inception) that relates to a transfer of a promised good or service should be evaluated to determine whether to account for the good or service as a separate performance obligation.

▨ If it is an advance payment for future goods or services, it should be recognised as revenue when the future goods or services are provided.

Illustration 8   **Health Club Membership Fees**

A health club enters into a one-year contract with a customer for unlimited health club access for $75 per month. The contract requires the customer to pay a non-refundable upfront fee of $120. The upfront fee does not transfer a good or service to the customer and is, in effect, an advance payment for health club access. The upfront fee will be recognised as revenue on a straight-line basis throughout the year, as the health club recognises the revenue from the contract with the customer.

The monthly revenue from the contract with this customer will be $85 (75 + ($1/12$ × 120)).

4.3.5 Licensing

▨ Licences of IP include:

- Software and technology
- Media and entertainment
- Franchises
- Patents, copyrights and trademarks.

▨ If the promise to grant a licence is distinct from the other promised goods or services, it is a separate performance obligation. Whether the separate performance obligation is satisfied at a point in time or over time depends on the right conferred:

- **Right to access**—provision of access to IP as it exists throughout the licence period; or
- **Right to use**—transfer of a right to use IP as it exists at the point in time in which the licence is granted.

▨ A licence gives a customer the **right to access** the entity's IP if it meets **all** of the following criteria:

- The contract requires or the customer (licensee) expects that the licensor will undertake activities that will significantly affect the IP.
- The customer is exposed to the positive or negative effects of these activities.
- The activities do not result in the transfer of a good or service to the customer.

▨ A licence to **access** a licensor's IP is accounted for as a performance obligation satisfied over time.

Definition

Licence—a permission that establishes a customer's rights to the intellectual property (IP) of an entity.

Key Point

If these criteria are not met, the licence gives a **right to use**.

© DeVry/Becker Educational Development Corp. All rights reserved.

Illustration 9   Access to IP

An author, C D Bowling, licenses the images and names of the characters of her series of popular children's books to a theme park for 10 years. The series is ongoing and the characters evolve over time as they age in the stories. New characters are also introduced in successive books. The theme park is required to use the latest images of the characters.

In exchange for the licence, Bowling receives $10 million per year for 10 years.

This licence gives the theme park the right to access Bowling's IP because:

■ The theme park can reasonably expect that Bowling will undertake activities that will affect the IP (i.e. the evolution of the characters over time and the introduction of new characters).

■ The theme park is exposed to any positive or negative effects of the changes in the characters because it is required to use the latest images of the characters.

■ No good or service is transferred by Bowling to the theme park.

The licence will be accounted for as a performance obligation satisfied over time. A time-based method is appropriate for measuring progress towards completion. Bowling will recognise revenue of $10 million each year for the 10-year term of the licence.

▨ A licence to **use** an entity's IP is accounted for as a performance obligation satisfied at a point in time.

Illustration 10   Use of IP

An artist licenses the right to use images of his most famous piece of artwork to a museum. The museum has the right to use the images in its advertising and merchandise for three years. The museum will pay the artist a fixed monthly fee of $15,000.

The licence gives the museum the right to use the artist's IP as it exists at the point in time that the licence is granted because the artist has no contractual or implied obligations to make changes to the artwork.

The licence will be accounted for as a performance obligation satisfied at a point in time. The artist can recognise the revenue from the licence when the museum can direct the use of and obtain the benefits of the artwork (i.e. at the beginning of the licence period). Because the payments are made by the museum to the artist over time, the contract has a significant financing component that must be considered when determining the transaction price.

▨ Regardless of whether a licence represents a right to access or a right to use IP, revenue from a sales-based or usage-based royalty promised in exchange for a licence is recognised on the **later** of the following events:
  • Sales or usage occurs;
  • The performance obligation to which the royalty has been allocated has been satisfied or partially satisfied.

Illustration 11   Sales-Based Royalty

A film studio licenses its latest movie to Big Stars Cinemas (BSC). The licence grants BSC the right to show the movie in its cinemas for two months. BSC will pay the film studio 65% of the of the cinema's ticket sales for the movie.

Regardless of whether this licence represents a right to use or a right to access the film studio's IP (the movie), the film studio will recognise revenue as the ticket sales occur because BSC is paying the film studio a sales-based royalty.

5 IAS 2 *Inventories*

5.1 Measurement

 **Key Point**

Inventories are measured at the *lower* of *cost* and *net realisable value*.

■ Cost includes all costs involved in bringing the inventories to their present location and condition.

5.2 Components of Cost

Purchase costs	Conversion costs	Other costs
• Purchase price • Import duties/non-refundable taxes • Transport/handling • *Deduct* trade discounts/rebates.	• Direct production costs • Production overheads based on normal capacity (i.e. expected on average under normal circumstances) • Joint product costs (*deduct* net realisable value of by-products).	• Only if incurred in bringing inventories to present location and condition such as non-production overheads (e.g. storage in whiskey distillers) and specific design costs. • Borrowing costs in limited circumstances (see IAS 23).

■ The following expenditures are excluded:
- abnormal amounts of wasted materials, labour and other production costs;
- storage costs unless necessary to the production process;
- administrative overheads; and
- selling costs.

■ For service providers, the cost of inventories consists primarily of labour including supervisory personnel and attributable overheads.

5.3 Net Realisable Value

■ Costs of inventories may not be recoverable due to:
- damage;
- obsolescence;
- decline in selling price; or
- an increase in estimated costs to completion/to be incurred.

■ Any necessary write-down to net realisable value is usually on an item-by-item basis.

5.3.1 Considerations

■ Estimates of net realisable value take into consideration:
- fluctuations of price or cost relating to events after the period end; and
- the purpose for which inventory is held.

© DeVry/Becker Educational Development Corp. All rights reserved.

5.3.2 Materials

▦ Materials for use in production are not written down to below cost unless cost of finished products will exceed net realisable value.

5.3.3 Timing

▦ A new assessment is made of net realisable value in each subsequent period. When circumstances causing write-down no longer exist (e.g. selling price increases), write-down is reversed. Note that reversals are rare in practice.

5.4 Recognition

5.4.1 As an Expense

▦ When inventories are sold, their carrying amount is recognised as an expense in the period in which related revenue is recognised.

▦ Any write-down to net realisable value and all losses are recognised in the period in which the write-down/loss occurs.

▦ Any reversal of any write-down is recognised as a *reduction* in expense in the period in which the reversal occurs.

▦ Inventories allocated to asset accounts (e.g. self-constructed property, plant or equipment) are recognised as an expense during the useful life of an asset.

5.4.2 As an Asset

▦ Although mentioned in IFRS 15, it is appropriate to consider here the "substance over form" issue of "consignment inventory".

▦ A consignment sale is one under which the recipient (buyer) undertakes to sell the goods on behalf of the shipper (seller).

▦ The issue is whether and when revenue should be recognised in the accounts of the shipper. An implication of this is which party should record the inventory as an asset?

▦ This will depend on whether it is the dealer or the manufacturer who bears the risks and benefits from the rewards of ownership.

▦ Treatment—is the inventory an asset of the dealer at delivery?

• **If yes**—the dealer recognises the inventory in the statement of financial position with the corresponding liability to the manufacturer.

• **If no**—do not recognise inventory in statement of financial position until transfer of title has crystallised (manufacturer recognises inventory until then).

6 IAS 34 *Interim Financial Reporting*

6.1 Introduction

6.1.1 Who?

▓ IAS 34 does not mandate which companies should be required to publish interim financial reports, how frequently, or how soon after the end of an interim period. However, the IASB strongly encourages governments, securities regulators, stock exchanges, international bodies and accountancy bodies to require companies whose debt or equity securities are publicly traded to provide interim financial reports which conform to the recognition and measurement criteria in the standard.

6.1.2 When?

▓ Entities should be encouraged to:
  ● provide interim financial reports by the end of the first half of their financial year; and
  ● make their interim financial reports available not later than 60 days after the end of the interim period.

6.1.3 Why?

▓ To prescribe the principles for preparing and reporting information about the financial position, performance and changes in financial position of an entity for less than a full financial year or for a 12-month period ending on a date other than the entity's financial year end.

6.2 Content of an Interim Financial Report

6.2.1 Minimum Components

▓ Interim financial reports should include (at a minimum):
  ● a condensed statement of financial position;
  ● a condensed statement of total comprehensive income;
  ● a condensed statement of cash flows;
  ● a condensed statement of changes in equity; and
  ● selected note disclosures.

6.2.2 Condensed Statement of Financial Position

▓ Statement of financial position should include each of the major components of assets, liabilities and equity which were presented in its most recent annual statement of financial position.

6.2.3 Condensed Statement of Total Comprehensive Income

▓ Statement of total comprehensive income should include revenue; each of the components of income and expense which were presented in the most recent annual statement of comprehensive income; and basic and diluted earnings per share.

Key Point

Interim statements provide an update on the latest set of annual financial statements and so focus on new activities, events and circumstances, and should not duplicate information previously reported.

© DeVry/Becker Educational Development Corp. All rights reserved.

6.2.4   Condensed Statement of Cash Flows

▥ Statement of cash flows should include the three major subtotals of cash flows required by IAS 7 *Statement of Cash Flows*.

6.2.5   Changes in Equity

▥ The statement of changes in equity should include each of the major components of equity which were presented in the most recent annual statement of changes in equity.

6.2.6   Selected Note Disclosures

▥ The notes should include an explanation of events and changes which are significant to an understanding of the changes in financial position and performance of the entity since the last annual reporting date.

▥ The following should be disclosed:

- a statement that the accounting policies and methods of computation followed are the same as those in the most recent annual financial statements (or a description of the nature and effect of any changes);
- explanation of the seasonality or cyclical nature of interim operations;
- the nature and amount of items affecting assets, liabilities, equity, net income or cash flows which are unusual because of their nature, size or incidence;
- information relating to the fair value of any financial instruments;
- dividends paid;
- segmental information;
- significant events subsequent to the end of the interim period;
- the effect of the acquisition or disposal of subsidiaries during the interim period;
- significant changes in a contingent liability or a contingent asset since the end of the last annual reporting period; and
- the nature and amount of any significant re-measurement of amounts reported in prior interim periods of the current financial year.

▥ Entities are encouraged to provide:

- a discussion of significant changes in business trends (e.g. in demand, market shares, prices and costs);
- a description of significant new commitments (e.g. for capital spending); and
- a discussion of prospects for the full current financial year of which the interim period is a part.

6.3 Recognition and Measurement

6.3.1 General Comment

▦ Entities should apply the same accounting recognition and measurement principles in interim financial reports as are applied in the preparation of annual financial statements, which should be measured on a year-to-date basis.

▦ The entity should apply the basic principles from the Framework in the recognition of assets, liabilities, income and expenses.

6.3.2 Tax Charge

▦ Income tax expense should be accrued using the tax rate which would be applicable to expected total annual earnings (the estimated average annual effective income tax rate applied to the pre-tax income of the interim period).

6.3.3 Use of Estimates

▦ The measurement procedures should be designed to ensure that information is reliable and relevant to an understanding of the financial position or performance of an entity. Preparation of interim financial reports generally will require a greater use of estimation methods than annual financial reports.

▦ The Framework recognises the need for trade-offs. Some degree of reliability may have to be sacrificed to enhance relevance or timeliness.

▦ Timeliness is particularly important for interim financial information, which often is published more promptly than annual financial information. To increase timeliness or reduce cost, it may be necessary to accept a lesser degree of reliability.

Examples:

- *Inventories*: Full stocktaking and valuation procedures may not be required for inventories at interim dates. Alternative methods might include:
  — estimates based on sales margins; and
  — using representative samples.
- *Provisions:* Determination of provisions (e.g. for environmental costs) may be complex, costly and time consuming. At the year end, an entity might engage outside experts to assist in the calculations. Estimates at interim dates may entail a simple updating of the prior annual provision.
- *Revaluations*: An entity may rely on professionally qualified valuers at annual reporting dates, although not at interim reporting dates.

© DeVry/Becker Educational Development Corp. All rights reserved.

Summary

- IAS 1 prescribes the content of general purpose financial statements to ensure comparability with the entity's own financial statements and those of other entities.
- Inappropriate accounting treatments are *not* rectified by:
  - disclosure of accounting polices used; or
  - notes or explanatory material.
- Assets and liabilities, and income and expenses, must not be offset unless another standard or interpretation requires or permits offsetting.
- At least one year's comparative information should be included in the financial statements. If there is a change in an accounting policy, then two years' comparative information is presented.
- A discontinued operation must be distinguishable operationally and for reporting purposes.
- The five steps of the revenue recognition process are:
  - identify the contract(s)
  - identify the separate performance obligation(s)
  - determine the transaction price
  - allocate the transaction price
  - recognise revenue.
- Variable consideration should be estimated using an expected value or most likely amount.
- Variable consideration should be included in the transaction price only when it is highly probable that there will be no reversal of the cumulative amount recognised.
- The promise of service under a warranty should be accounted for separately.
- An option to acquire an additional good or service for an undiscounted price is a marketing offer.
- Breakage is recognised as revenue unless it must be paid over to another party.
- A licence may confer a right to access at a point in time or a right to use over time.
- Inventories are measured at the *lower* of *cost* and *net realisable value*.
- Interim statements provide an update on the latest set of annual financial statements and so focus on new activities, events and circumstances.

Session 4 Quiz

Estimated time: 30 minutes

1. State the objective of IAS 1. (2.1)

2. Yes or no? Can assets be offset against liabilities on the statement of financial position? (2.3.7)

3. Name the items which must be presented in the statement of financial position. (2.4.2)

4. Name the items which must be presented in profit or loss. (2.5.1)

5. State the function of the SOCIE. (2.6)

6. Explain the concept of reclassification. (2.5.3)

7. Explain the term *discontinued operation*. (3.2)

8. State the THREE criteria that are used to determine if a performance obligation is satisfied over time. (4.2.1)

9. Give FOUR examples of variable consideration and state the methods used to estimate variable consideration. (4.2.1)

10. State the TWO types of warranty and the relevant IFRS under which each should be accounted for. (4.3.1)

11. State how breakage amounts are recognised as revenue. (4.3.3)

12. Differentiate between revenue recognition under a right to access licence and a right to use licence. (4.3.5)

13. List the minimum components of interim financial reports. (6.2.1)

Study Question Bank

Estimated time: 45 minutes

Priority		Estimated Time	Completed
Q7	Alexandra	45 minutes	
Additional			
Q5	XYZ		
Q6	Burley		
Q8	Venue		

© DeVry/Becker Educational Development Corp. All rights reserved.

EXAMPLE SOLUTIONS

Solution 1—Sale Contract for Business Segment

Statement of profit or loss for the year ended 31 December 2018

	Continuing operations (A and B)		Discontinued operations (C only)		Entity as a whole	
	2017	**2018**	*2017*	**2018**	*2017*	**2018**
	$000	**$000**	*$000*	**$000**	*$000*	**$000**
Revenue	380	**425**	110	**90**	490	**515**
Expenses	(225)	**(245)**	(95)	**(100)**	(320)	**(345)**
Impairment loss	–	**-**	(20)	–	(20)	–
Loss on disposal	–	–	–	**(10)**	–	**(10)**
Provision for termination of employment	–	–	–	**(30)**	–	**(30)**
	155	**180**	(5)	**(50)**	150	**130**
Taxation (30%)	(46.5)	**(54)**	1.5	**15**	(45)	**(39)**
	108.5	**126**	(3.5)	**(35)**	105	**91**

Note to the financial statements

On 30 September 2018, the company sold its health food operations to Z Corporation for $60,000. The company decided to dispose of Segment C because its operations are in areas apart from the core business areas (cigarette and beverage manufacture and distribution) that form the long-term direction of the company. Further, Segment C's rate of return has not been equal to that of the company's other two segments during the period.

The loss on disposal of Segment C (before income tax benefit of $3,000) was $10,000.

The company recognised a provision for termination benefits of $30,000 (before income tax benefit of $9,000) to be paid by 31 March 2019 to certain employees of Segment C whose jobs will be terminated as a result of the sale.

© DeVry/Becker Educational Development Corp. All rights reserved.

Accounting Policies, Estimates and Errors

FOCUS

This session covers the following content from the *ACCA Study Guide.*

B. The Financial Reporting Framework

2. Critical evaluation of principles and practices

b) Critically evaluate accounting principles and practices used in corporate reporting. ☐

G. The Appraisal of Financial Performance and Position of Entities

1. The creation of suitable accounting policies

a) Develop accounting policies for an entity which meet the entity's reporting requirements. ☐

b) Identify accounting treatments adopted in financial statements and assess their suitability and acceptability. ☐

Session 5 Guidance

■ **Learn** which standards are most relevant to reporting of performance (s.1).

■ **Learn** that most voluntary changes in accounting policy must be done retrospectively (s.3).

■ **Understand** the distinction between the treatment once errors have been found (retrospective adjustment) and the treatment for any changes in estimate (prospective adjustment) (s.4, s.5).

(continued on next page)

VISUAL OVERVIEW

Objective: To explain the need for guidance on reporting performance and to prescribe the classification, disclosure and accounting treatment of certain items in the statement of comprehensive income.

```
┌─────────────────────────────────┐
│           BACKGROUND            │
│  • Information Needs            │
│  • Disaggregation              │
│  • Reporting Aspects           │
│    of Performance              │
└─────────────────────────────────┘
                │
┌─────────────────────────────────┐
│             IAS 8               │
│  • Scope                        │
│  • Terminology                  │
└─────────────────────────────────┘

┌──────────────────┐  ┌─────────────────────────┐  ┌──────────────────┐
│   ACCOUNTING     │  │  CHANGES IN ACCOUNTING  │  │   PRIOR PERIOD   │
│    POLICIES      │  │        ESTIMATE         │  │      ERRORS      │
│ • Selection and  │  │  • Introduction         │  │ • Introduction   │
│   Application    │  │  • Accounting Treatment │  │ • Accounting     │
│ • Consistency    │  │                         │  │   Treatment      │
│ • Changes        │  │                         │  │                  │
└──────────────────┘  └─────────────────────────┘  └──────────────────┘

┌──────────────────┐  ┌─────────────────────────┐
│   ACCOUNTING     │  │   CRITICAL EVALUATION   │
│    SCENARIOS     │  │  • Accounting Principles│
│ • Home Delivery  │  │    and Practices        │
│   Service        │  │  • Earnings Management  │
│ • Landfill Site  │  │  • Asset Manipulation   │
│ • Chemical       │  │                         │
│   Leakage        │  │                         │
└──────────────────┘  └─────────────────────────┘
```

Session 5 Guidance

■ **Understand** the need for critical evaluation of accounting principles and practices including the need for consistency of their application (s.6).

■ **Attempt** *Examples 1–3* (s.7).

■ **Revise** F7 studies if needed. Knowledge of IAS 8 is not only assumed but examined.

© DeVry/Becker Educational Development Corp. All rights reserved.

1 Background

1.1 Information Needs

- The economic decisions taken by users of financial statements require an evaluation of an entity's ability to generate cash and cash equivalents, and of the timing and certainty of their generation.

- Users are better able to evaluate this ability to generate cash and cash equivalents if they are provided with information which focuses on the financial position, performance and changes in financial position of an entity.

- Information about the performance of an entity, in particular its profitability, is required in order to:
  - assess potential changes in the economic resources it is likely to control in the future;
  - predict the capacity of the entity to generate cash flows from its existing resource base; and
  - form judgements about how effectively the entity might employ additional resources.

- Information about variability of performance is important in this respect.

1.2 Disaggregation

- In order to make economic decisions, users of the accounts need to understand the composition of figures in as much detail as possible. There is a trend in reporting to provide more detailed information about the composition of key elements of the financial statements. In short, the information may be analysed, either in the statements or in notes to the accounts, into component parts to better aid understanding.

- For example:
  - disclosure of material and unusual items which are part of ordinary activities;
  - information on discontinued operations; and
  - segmental reporting.

- Users can use such information to make better-quality forecasts about the entity.

1.3 Reporting Aspects of Performance

In considering the reporting of financial performance, the following areas need to be covered.

- The form and content of the statement of total comprehensive income:
  - Structure (IAS 1)
  - Which items must go to the statement of total comprehensive income (IAS 1)
  - Classification of material items (IAS 1)
  - Disclosure about discontinued operations (IFRS 5).

© DeVry/Becker Educational Development Corp. All rights reserved.

- Other statements of performance:
  - Segmental reports (IFRS 8)
  - Statement of cash flows (IAS 7)
  - Statement showing changes in equity (IAS 1).*
- Other non-mandatory disclosures:
  - Operating and financial reviews.
- Corporate governance.

*Commentary

*Note that many of these areas are covered elsewhere in this text. All of these areas need to be incorporated into an understanding of how international GAAP provides information to enable users to understand performance.

2   IAS 8

2.1   Scope

Key Point

IAS 8 prescribes the *criteria* for selecting and applying *accounting policies* and the accounting *treatment* for changes in accounting policies, changes in accounting estimates and corrections of prior period errors.

2.2   Terminology

Accounting policies: the specific principles, bases, conventions, rules and practices applied by an entity in preparing and presenting financial statements.

Changes in accounting estimate: adjustments to the carrying amount of an asset or liability, or the amount of annual consumption of an asset, which result from the assessment of the present status of, and expected future benefits and obligations associated with, assets and liabilities. These changes arise due to new information or developments and are not to be classified as corrections of errors.

- Examples of **changes in accounting estimate** are:
  - a receivable balance which is subsequently not recovered; and
  - changes to the useful life of a depreciable non-current asset.

International Financial Reporting Standards: standards and interpretations adopted by the IASB (i.e. IFRSs, IASs, IFRICs and SICs).

*Commentary

*Errors may include the effects of mathematical mistakes, mistakes in application of accounting policies, oversights and fraud.

Prior period errors: omissions and misstatements relating to the financial statements of previous periods arising from a failure to use, or misuse, information which:

- was available when those financial statements were authorised for issue; and
- could reasonably be expected to have been obtained and taken into account in the preparation and presentation of the financial statements.*

3 Accounting Policies

3.1 Selection and Application

Key Point

When an IFRS applies to a transaction, the accounting policy or policies applied to that transaction are determined by applying the relevant IFRS along with any relevant implementation guidance issued by the IASB.

▢ If there is no applicable IFRS for a transaction, management must use its judgement in developing and applying an accounting policy, resulting in information that:
- is relevant to the economic decision-making needs of users;
- is reliable;
- represents faithfully;
- reflects the economic substance of the transaction;
- is neutral;
- is prudent; and
- is complete in all material aspects.

▢ Management may consider requirements of accounting standards dealing with similar transactions, the definitions and recognition criteria in the Framework, recent pronouncements of other standard-setting bodies which use a similar conceptual framework, and any other accounting literature denoting best practice in a particular industry.

Illustration 1 Appropriate Standard

Kitty has recently purchased a Van Gogh painting to display in the client reception area, with the hope that it will lead to more contracts and that the painting will appreciate in value.

There is no specific accounting standard which deals with this type of asset, but IAS 40 *Investment Property* does deal with a particular type of asset which is being held for capital appreciation.

It would, therefore, seem appropriate to use IAS 40 as justification to value the painting at fair value year on year.

© DeVry/Becker Educational Development Corp. All rights reserved.

3.2 Consistency of Accounting Policies

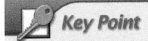

Key Point

An entity must be consistent in selecting and applying **accounting policies** to transactions of a similar nature.

▨ IAS 2 *Inventories* requires inventory to be valued at lower of cost and net realisable value. In identifying cost it allows alternative formulae (e.g. FIFO or weighted average). The same cost formula must be applied to similar items of inventory, but a different cost formula can be applied to a different classification of inventory.

3.3 Changes in Accounting Policy

3.3.1 When

Key Point

A change in accounting policy only can be made if:
- required by an IFRS or IFRIC (i.e. a *mandatory* change); or
- it would result in the financial statements providing more relevant and reliable information (i.e. a *voluntary* change).

▨ As users of financial statements will wish to see trends in an entity's financial statements, it would not be appropriate for an entity to change its accounting policy whenever it wishes.

▨ If an entity decides to adopt the revaluation model of IAS 16 *Property, Plant and Equipment,* this would be classified as a change in accounting policy.*

*Commentary

*Note, however, that accounting for this change is specifically prescribed in IAS 16.

3.3.2 How

▨ If a new IFRS is issued, the transitional provisions of that standard will be applied to any change of accounting policy. When IFRS 11 *Joint Arrangements* was issued it did not allow the use of proportionate consolidation, so the transition statement explains how to change from a policy of proportionate consolidation to a policy of equity accounting.

Key Point

If a new standard does not have transitional provisions, or it is a voluntary change, the entity must apply the change in policy *retrospectively*.

- Retrospective application means adjusting the opening balance of each affected part of equity for the earliest period presented and the comparative amounts disclosed for each prior period as if the new policy had *always* been applied.

- If it is not practicable to apply the effects of a change in policy to prior periods then the change of policy is made from the earliest period for which retrospective application is practicable.

- IAS 1 requires an entity to include an additional statement of financial position (i.e. three statements must be presented) whenever it changes an accounting policy.

Exhibit 1   **VOLUNTARY CHANGE IN ACCOUNTING POLICY**

This note, an extract from the Paladin Energy Ltd Annual Report 2011, describes a retrospective application of a voluntary change in accounting policy.

NOTE 3. Voluntary Change in Accounting Policy

The financial report has been prepared on the basis of a retrospective application of a voluntary change in accounting policy relating to exploration and evaluation expenditure.

The new exploration and evaluation expenditure accounting policy is to capitalise and carry forward exploration and evaluation expenditure as an asset.

The previous accounting policy was to charge exploration and evaluation expenditure against profit and loss as incurred; except for acquisition costs and for expenditure incurred after a decision to proceed to development was made, in which case the expenditure was capitalised as an asset.

The new accounting policy was adopted on 31 March 2011 and has been applied retrospectively. Management judges that the change in policy will result in the financial report providing more relevant and no less reliable information because it leads to a more transparent treatment of exploration and evaluation expenditure that meets the definition of an asset and is consistent with the treatment of other assets controlled by the Group when it is probable that future economic benefits will flow to the Group and the asset has a cost that can be measured reliably.

Exam Advice

The accounting treatment of exploration and evaluation expenditure is not examinable.

© DeVry/Becker Educational Development Corp. All rights reserved.

Illustration 2   Account for New Policy Retrospectively

Alpha, an incorporated entity, has previously followed a policy of capitalisation of development expenditure. It has recently decided to adopt the provisions of IAS 38 *Intangible Assets* for the year ending 31 December 2017. Alpha has been advised by the entity's auditors that the expenditure previously capitalised does not qualify for capitalisation under the recognition criteria set out in the standard.

The notes to the accounts for the year ended 31 December 2016 relating to the deferred development expenditure were as follows:

	$
Balance at 1 January	1,000
Additions	500
Amortisation	(400)
Balance at 31 December	1,100

During the year ended 31 December 2017, the company has expensed all expenditure in the period on projects, in respect of which expenditure had previously been capitalised and no amortisation has been charged to profit or loss in 2017.

The following are extracts from the draft accounts for the year ended 31 December 2017.

Statement of profit or loss	2017	2016
		(as previously published)
	$	$
Revenue	1,200	1,100
Expenses	(800)	(680)
Profit for the year	400	420
Statement of changes in equity (extract)	$	$
Balance as at 1 January	3,000	2,580
Profit for the year	400	420
Balance as at 31 December	3,400	3,000

Required:
Show how the statement of profit or loss and statement of changes in equity would appear in the financial statements for the year ended 31 December 2017, processing the necessary adjustments in respect of the change in accounting policy by applying the new policy retrospectively.

Solution*

Statement of profit or loss	2017	2016
		(as restated)
	$	$
Revenue	1,200	1,100
Expenses	(800)	(780)
Profit for the year	400	320
Statement of changes in equity (extract)	$	$
Balance as at 1 January		
As previously stated	3,000	2,580
Prior period adjustment	(1,100)	(1,000)
	1,900	1,580
Profit for the year	400	320
Balance as at 31 December	2,300	1,900

*Commentary

*1. The entity amortised $400 in 2016 but spent $500. The policy would have been to write off the amount of expenditure directly to profit or loss; therefore the entity needs to adjust last year's figures by an extra $100 expense.

The adjustment against last year's profit or loss ($100) has the effect of restating it to what it would have been if the company had been following the same policy last year. This is important because the profit or loss as presented must be prepared on a comparable basis.

2. The balance left on the deferred expenditure account at the end of the previous year ($1,100) is written off against the accumulated profit which existed at that time.

This $1,100 is made up of an amount which arose last year (the difference between the amount spent ($500) and the amount amortised ($400) and the balance which existed at the beginning of the previous year ($1,000)).

These amounts are written off against last year's profit and the opening balance on the accumulated profit last year, respectively.

4 Changes in Accounting Estimate

4.1 Introduction

▓ Many items recognised in the financial statements must be measured with an element of estimation attached to them:

- Receivables may be measured after allowing for irrecoverable debts arising.
- Inventory is measured at lower of cost and net realisable value and must allow for obsolescence etc.
- A provision under IAS 37 by its very nature may be an estimation of future economic benefits to be paid out.
- Non-current assets are depreciated; the charge takes into account the expected pattern of consumption of the asset and its expected useful life. The consumption pattern and expected life are estimates.

4.2 Accounting Treatment

 **Key Point**

When a change in circumstances occurs which affects an estimate previously made, the effect of that change is recognised *prospectively* by including in the current and future (where relevant) periods profit or loss.

▓ A change in estimate is not an error or a change in accounting policy and therefore does not affect prior period statements.

▓ If the change in estimate affects the *measurement* of assets or liabilities then the change is recognised by adjusting the carrying amount of the asset or liability.

© DeVry/Becker Educational Development Corp. All rights reserved.

5 Prior Period Errors

5.1 Introduction

Prior period errors—omissions from, and misstatements in, an entity's financial statements for one or more prior periods arising from the failure to use or, misuse of, reliable information that was available and could reasonably be expected to have been obtained when those prior period financial statements were authorised for issue.

5.2 Accounting Treatment

The amount of the correction of an **error that relates to prior periods** shall be reported by adjusting the opening balance of retained earnings and restating comparative information.

- The financial statements of the current period are presented as if the error had been corrected in the period in which the error was originally made. However, an entity does not reissue the financial statements of prior periods.
- IAS 1 requires an entity to include an additional statement of financial position (i.e. three statements) whenever it corrects a prior period error.
- If it is not practicable to determine the period-specific effects of an error on comparative information for prior periods presented, the entity shall restate the opening balances for the earliest period practicable.

6 Critical Evaluation

6.1 Accounting Principles and Practices

▦ The definition of accounting policies includes those principles and practices that an entity has applied in the preparation and presentation of its financial statements.

  • Accounting policies mostly affect assets and liabilities in the statement of financial position and so any changes in their measurement will ultimately affect reported profits.

  • For information to be useful to a wide range of users, each entity must determine the common needs of its users and, on this basis, select those policies and estimation techniques that best meet those needs but without reducing the usefulness of financial statements to other users.*

▦ If users cannot identify the principles and policies adopted:

  • they cannot hope to analyse the performance of an entity in a meaningful way; and

  • the opportunity for management to manipulate earnings increases.

▦ Although IFRS need not be applied to immaterial items, if previously immaterial items become material, an accounting policy will need to be introduced that complies with IFRS:

  • This is **not** a change in accounting policy; therefore

  • The accounting policy will be applied **prospectively**.

*Commentary

*A particular issue arises if estimation techniques are found to be invalid.

6.2 Earnings Management

▦ Management must apply consistent principles and practices in preparing the financial statements. If there is a lack of consistency, values placed on assets and liabilities become *ad hoc* and can lead to income and expense items being included in profit or loss according to management's design.

  • It becomes very easy to manipulate profits if consistency is lacking. For example, if not all depreciable assets are depreciated, profits will be inflated and return on capital employed will be higher.*

  • Earnings could be manipulated to increase profit-related bonuses of key personnel. Therefore, IFRS prescribes certain accounting policies that must be followed in order to faithfully represent the economic phenomena in the period.

▦ A change in accounting policy is applied retrospectively (unless transitional rules apply). Restating comparative information can be complex (e.g. where data was not collected in the prior period) and it can be difficult to achieve comparability. However, once a change is made it should be to provide users with "better" financial information, so there should be no reversion to old policies.

▦ A clear distinction must be made between a change in policy and a change in estimate—as only a change in policy is accounted for retrospectively. For example:

  • changing historical cost measurement to fair value is a change in policy;

  • changing a depreciation method is a change in estimate.

*Commentary

*EPS would be increased also.

Key Point

Non-compliance with IFRS and inappropriate accounting policies **cannot** be rectified either by disclosure of the accounting policies used or by notes or explanatory material.

© DeVry/Becker Educational Development Corp. All rights reserved.

6.3   Asset Manipulation

6.3.1   Non-current Assets

▓ Depreciation or non-depreciation of non-current assets affects reported earnings. Although the effect on reported profit may not be material, the cumulative effect on the carrying amount (and retained earnings) may become material if this is not corrected.

▓ Classifying non-current assets as "held for sale" can influence how users view the results of the entity.

▓ Many assets, especially intangibles, are not recognised in an entity's financial statements. Brands, copyright, and customer relationships all add value to an entity but in the absence of a purchase transaction recognition and measurement is too subjective for financial reporting.*

*Commentary

*They may be incapable of separation from goodwill even in a business acquisition.

6.3.2   Inventory

▓ Inventory valuation is a major determinant of reported profit for entities in manufacturing and retail sectors. IAS 2 *Inventories* permits a choice between the FIFO and weighted average bases for items that are ordinarily interchangeable.*

▓ The choice of method should take account of the physical movement of items in inventory (e.g. weighted average where batches are produced). Therefore, once determined, this should not change unless the production method is changed.

▓ What costs should be included in the inventory valuation? A clear distinction needs to be made between product costs and period costs. Incorrect inclusion of period costs will overstate reported profits.

▓ Where standard costs are used to approximate actual cost, are these standards up to date? What is the "normal" level of activity for the absorption of overheads?

*Commentary

*When prices are increasing, FIFO leads to higher closing inventory valuation and therefore higher profits.

6.3.3   Financial Assets

▓ The choice between measuring financial assets at fair value and amortised cost ultimately affects reported profits. In the absence of controls over this choice, entities could choose fair value when this is increasing, and then switch to amortised cost when fair value falls.

▓ When valuing at fair value a further choice is available; whether to recognise fair value changes in profit or loss or other comprehensive income. Currently, if changes are recognised in other comprehensive income, any gains or losses cannot be recycled to profit or loss.*

*Commentary

*The IASB's proposal to allow some reclassification would lead to a third treatment that might make manipulation of earnings easier.

7 Accounting Scenarios

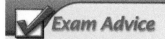

Exam Advice

In the examination you should expect to need to identify issues in order to address them.

Example 1 Home Delivery Service

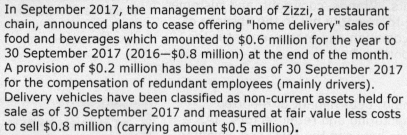

In September 2017, the management board of Zizzi, a restaurant chain, announced plans to cease offering "home delivery" sales of food and beverages which amounted to $0.6 million for the year to 30 September 2017 (2016—$0.8 million) at the end of the month. A provision of $0.2 million has been made as of 30 September 2017 for the compensation of redundant employees (mainly drivers). Delivery vehicles have been classified as non-current assets held for sale as of 30 September 2017 and measured at fair value less costs to sell $0.8 million (carrying amount $0.5 million).

Issues

- Is the home delivery service a separate component of the business?

- Is it material?

- Have the IAS 37 criteria been met to recognise a provision?

- Are the delivery vehicles correctly identified as non-current assets held for sale?

- If the vehicles are correctly identified as held for sale, have they been measured correctly?

Required:

Comment and conclude, if possible, on the issues raised.

© DeVry/Becker Educational Development Corp. All rights reserved.

Example 2 Landfill Site

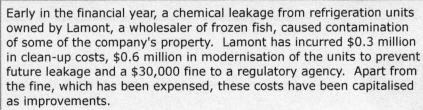

In April 2016, Keffler, a manufacturer of plastic products, bought the right to use a landfill site for a period of 15 years for $1.1 million. Keffler expects that the amount of waste that it will need to dump will increase annually and that the site will be completely filled after just 10 years. Keffler has charged the following amounts to the statement of profit or loss for the year to 31 March 2017:

- $20,000 licence amortisation calculated on a sum-of-digits basis to increase the charge over the useful life of the site; and

- $100,000 annual provision for restoring the land in 15 years' time.

Issues

- What type of asset does Keffler have?

- What is the useful life of the asset—10 years or 15 years?

- Is an increasing sum-of-digits model the most appropriate method to allocate the cost?

- What type of provision is Keffler required to set up?

- How should that provision be accounted for?

Required:

Comment and conclude, if possible, on the issues raised.

Example 3 Chemical Leakage

Early in the financial year, a chemical leakage from refrigeration units owned by Lamont, a wholesaler of frozen fish, caused contamination of some of the company's property. Lamont has incurred $0.3 million in clean-up costs, $0.6 million in modernisation of the units to prevent future leakage and a $30,000 fine to a regulatory agency. Apart from the fine, which has been expensed, these costs have been capitalised as improvements.

Issues

- Has the fine been accounted for correctly?

- What are the accounting treatments for subsequent expenditure on non-current assets?

- Have the clean-up costs been correctly accounted for?

- Have the modernisation costs been correctly accounted for?

Required:

Comment and conclude, if possible, on the issues raised.

Summary

- IAS 8 prescribes the criteria for selecting and applying accounting policies and the accounting treatment for changes in accounting policies, changes in accounting estimates and corrections of prior period errors.

- When an IFRS applies to a transaction, the accounting policy or policies applied to that transaction are determined by applying the relevant IFRS along with any relevant implementation guidance issued by the IASB.

- An entity must be consistent in selection and application of accounting policies to transactions of a similar nature.

- An entity may only change its accounting policy if required to do so by an IFRS (or IFRIC) or it would result in the financial statements providing more relevant and reliable information.

- A change in policy is applied *retrospectively* for a new standard that does not have transitional provisions and voluntary changes.

- The effects of a change in circumstances on previously made estimates are recognised *prospectively* (i.e. in current and future periods' profit or loss).

- A change in estimate which affects the measurement of an asset or liability is recognised by adjusting the carrying amount of the asset or liability.

- The amount of the correction of a prior period error is reported by adjusting the opening balance of retained earnings and restating comparative information.

- Non-compliance with IFRS and inappropriate accounting policies **cannot** be rectified through disclosure.

Session 5 Quiz
Estimated time: 25 minutes

1. Define change in accounting estimate. (2.2)

2. When there is no standard, name other sources of guidance which IAS 8 suggests that management use when developing appropriate accounting policies. (3.1)

3. State the circumstances under which a change in an accounting policy is acceptable. (3.3)

4. Identify FOUR situations when estimates are used to value assets or liabilities. (4.1)

5. The treatment for correction of prior period errors as provided by IAS 8 is that they should be adjusted retrospectively. Where this is not practicable, explain what companies may do instead. (5.2)

6. Give an example of earnings management and an example of asset manipulation and state the accounting principles and practices that may be applied to deter each. (6.2, 6.3)

Study Question Bank
Estimated time: 30 minutes

Priority		Estimated Time	Completed
Q9	Hamilton	30 minutes	

© DeVry/Becker Educational Development Corp. All rights reserved.

EXAMPLE SOLUTIONS

Solution 1—Home Delivery Service

It is unlikely that the home delivery service would be classified as a separate component of the business as the business would not be closing down any of its restaurants or kitchens.

It is not possible to conclude from the information given whether these transactions are material. (However, you should expect to be able to assess materiality (e.g. in comparison with total revenue) if it is not specified to be material in the question.)

If the employees of the business have been told of the redundancy and the directors have made the proposals public, then a provision should be recognised in accordance with IAS 37.

If the economic benefits from the delivery vehicles are to be recovered through their disposal then it is probable that they would be classified as held for sale.

However, valuation of held for sale assets is at the *lower* of carrying amount and fair value less costs to sell. A loss should be recognised immediately but any gain should not be recognised until the asset has been sold.

Solution 2—Landfill Site

The right to use the site would be classified as an intangible asset.

Although Keffler has the right to use the asset for 15 years, it expects to fill the site within 10 years so that should be the depreciation period.

The increasing sum-of-the-digits method would not be appropriate for depreciating this asset if it is likely that the site will be used in equal measure each year.

A decommissioning provision is required for the future restoration costs. The provision should initially be recognised as the present value of the future expected cash flows, so the current method is incorrect.

Solution 3—Chemical Leakage

The fine has been accounted for correctly.

Day-to-day running costs should be expensed as incurred, any major parts which are replaced should be capitalised with the old part derecognised and any major inspection or overhaul costs should be capitalised.

IAS 16 does not work on the concept of improvements. The clean-up costs should be expensed as incurred and the modernisation costs could be capitalised if an old part has been replaced by a new part; otherwise, the modernisation costs also should be expensed.

© DeVry/Becker Educational Development Corp. All rights reserved.

Non-current Assets

FOCUS

This session covers the following content from the *ACCA Study Guide.*

C. Reporting the Financial Performance of Entities

2. Non-current assets

a) Apply and discuss the timing of the recognition of non-current assets and the determination of their carrying amounts including revaluations. ☐

b) Apply and discuss the treatment of non-current assets held for sale. ☐

c) Apply and discuss the accounting treatment of investment properties including classification, recognition and measurement issues. ☐

d) Apply and discuss the accounting treatment of intangible assets including the criteria for recognition and measurement subsequent to acquisition and classification. ☐

Session 6 Guidance

■ **Recognise** that this session revises assumed F7 knowledge and does not introduce any new issues. Note that these topics are examined regularly.

■ **Revise** all definitions and the recognition and measurement principles which are summarised in the key points.

VISUAL OVERVIEW

Objective: To prescribe the accounting treatment for non-current assets.

```
                           NON-CURRENT ASSETS
```

IAS 16 PROPERTY, PLANT AND EQUIPMENT
- Recognition Criteria
- Initial Measurement
- Subsequent Measurement
- Subsequent Costs
- Non-depreciation

IAS 40 INVESTMENT PROPERTY
- Recognition
- Initial Measurement
- Subsequent Measurement

IAS 38 INTANGIBLE ASSETS
- Identifiability
- Initial Measurement
- Subsequent Measurement

IAS 23 BORROWING COSTS
- Accounting Treatment
- Capitalisation

IFRS 5 NON-CURRENT ASSETS HELD FOR SALE
- Classification
- Measurement

IAS 20 GOVERNMENT GRANTS
- Accounting Treatment
- Granted Assets

Session 6 Guidance

■ **Read** carefully *Illustrations 1* and *2* concerning the more complex aspects of IAS 16 and complete *Example 1* (s.1).

■ **Revise** IAS 40 and complete *Example 2* (s.2).

■ **Review** *Illustration 3* on IFRS 5 (s.3) and *Illustrations 4–6* on IAS 38 (s.4).

■ **Refer** back to your previous studies, if necessary, to refresh your knowledge of relevant points (i.e. if you do not sufficiently remember the details).

1 IAS 16 *Property, Plant and Equipment*

1.1 Recognition Criteria

■ An item of property, plant and equipment is recognised when:
- it is *probable* that *future economic benefits* associated with the asset will flow to the entity (satisfied when risks and rewards have passed to the entity); and
- the cost of the asset to the entity can be *measured reliably*.*

Exam Advice

Details of the standards in this session are assumed knowledge from F7 *Financial Reporting*.

*Commentary

*The criterion, measured reliably, is usually readily satisfied because exchange transaction evidencing purchase identifies cost. For a self-constructed asset, a reliable measurement of cost can be made from transactions with third parties for the acquisition of materials, labour and other inputs used.

■ In certain circumstances it is appropriate to allocate the total expenditure on an asset to its component parts and account for each component separately.

1.2 Initial Measurement

Key Point

Items of property, plant and equipment are initially measured at *cost*.

■ Cost will include the following, where relevant:
- Purchase price, including import duties and non-refundable purchase taxes (after deducting trade discounts and rebates).
- Directly attributable costs of bringing the asset to location and working condition, such as:
  - wages and salaries arising directly from construction or acquisition;
  - costs of site preparation;
  - initial delivery and handling costs;
  - installation and assembly costs;
  - costs of testing proper functioning (net of any sale proceeds of items produced);
  - professional fees (e.g. architects and engineers);
  - decommissioning costs; and
  - borrowing costs.

© DeVry/Becker Educational Development Corp. All rights reserved.

Example 1 Initial Measurement

On 1 October, Dearing acquired a machine under the following terms:

	$000
Manufacturer's base price	1,050
20% Trade discount on base price	
5% Early settlement discount taken	
(offered only on the base price)	
Freight charges	30
Electrical installation cost	28
Staff training in use of the machine	40
Pre-production testing	22
Purchase of a three-year maintenance contract	60

Required:
Determine the initial amount to be capitalised for the machine on acquisition.

1.3 Subsequent Measurement

1.3.1 Cost Model

- Carry at cost less any accumulated depreciation and any accumulated impairment losses.

1.3.2 Revaluation Model

- Carry at a revalued amount, being fair value at the date of the revaluation less any subsequent accumulated depreciation and any accumulated impairment losses.
- To use this model, fair value must be reliably measurable.

1.4 Subsequent Costs

- The issue is whether subsequent expenditure is capital expenditure (i.e. to the statement of financial position) or revenue expenditure (i.e. to the statement of profit or loss).

1.4.1 Running Costs

 Key Point

Servicing costs (e.g. labour and consumables) are recognised in profit or loss as incurred.

- Often described as "repairs and maintenance", this expenditure is made to restore or maintain future economic benefits.

© DeVry/Becker Educational Development Corp. All rights reserved.

1.4.2 Part Replacement

▦ Some items (e.g. aircraft, ships, gas turbines, etc) are a series
of linked parts which require regular replacement at different
intervals and so have different useful lives.

Key Point

The carrying amount of an item of property, plant and equipment
recognises the cost of replacing a part when that cost is incurred, if
the recognition criteria are met.

▦ The carrying amount of replaced parts is derecognised (i.e.
treated as a disposal).

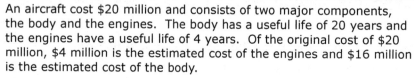

Illustration 1 Depreciating Linked Parts

An aircraft cost $20 million and consists of two major components,
the body and the engines. The body has a useful life of 20 years and
the engines have a useful life of 4 years. Of the original cost of $20
million, $4 million is the estimated cost of the engines and $16 million
is the estimated cost of the body.

The cost of the engines will be depreciated over 4 years to give an
annual charge of $1 million and the body will be depreciated over 20
years to give an annual depreciation charge of $800,000.

After 4 years, the engines will be replaced and the cost of the new
engines will be included into the cost of the asset. Those engines will
then be depreciated over the period to the next replacement.

1.4.3 Major Inspection or Overhaul Costs

▦ Performing regular major inspections for faults, regardless of
whether parts of the item are replaced, may be a condition
of continuing to operate an item of property, plant and
equipment (e.g. an aircraft).

Key Point

The cost of each major inspection performed is recognised in the carrying
amount, as a replacement, if the recognition criteria are satisfied.

▦ On initial recognition, an estimate will be made of the
inspection costs and that amount will be depreciated over the
period to the first inspection. This amount is part of the original
cost recognised and is not an additional component of cost.

▦ Any remaining carrying amount of the cost of the previous
inspection (as distinct from physical parts) is derecognised.

▦ The amount capitalised will be depreciated over the period
to the next major inspection, when the costs incurred at that
point will be capitalised.

                                      © DeVry/Becker Educational Development Corp. All rights reserved.

> **Illustration 2 Capitalising Overhaul Costs**
>
> A shipping company is required by law to bring all its ships into dry dock every 5 years for a major inspection and overhaul. Overhaul expenditure might at first sight seem to be a repair to the ships but it is actually a cost incurred in getting the ship back into seaworthy condition. As such, the costs must be capitalised.
>
> A ship which cost $20 million with a 20-year life must have a major overhaul every 5 years. The estimated cost of the overhaul at the 5-year point is $5 million.
>
> The depreciation charge for the first 5 years of the asset's life will be as follows:
>
> | | Overhaul | Capital |
> |---|---|---|
> | Cost | 5 | 15 |
> | Years | 5 | 20 |
> | Depreciation per year | 1 | 0.75 |
>
> Total accumulated depreciation for the first 5 years will be $8.75 million and the carrying amount of the ship at the end of year 5 will be $11.25 million.
>
> The actual overhaul costs incurred at the end of year 5 are $6 million. This amount will now be capitalized into the costs of the ship, to give a carrying amount of $17.25 million.
>
> The depreciation charge for years 6 to 10 will be as follows:
>
> | | Overhaul | Capital |
> |---|---|---|
> | Cost | 6 | 11.25 |
> | Years | 5 | 15 |
> | Depreciation per year | 1.2 | 0.75 |
>
> Annual depreciation for years 6 to 10 will now be $1.95 million.
>
> This process will then be continued for years 11 to 15 and years 16 to 20. By the end of year 20, the capital cost of $20 million will have been depreciated plus the actual overhaul costs incurred at years 5, 10 and 15.

1.5 Non-depreciation

1.5.1 Background

- It has long been argued that certain assets should not be subject to the general rule that all assets should be depreciated.

- Many companies in some jurisdictions have taken to the practice of not depreciating certain of their assets (e.g. hotels).

© DeVry/Becker Educational Development Corp. All rights reserved.

1.5.2 Arguments For

▓ Assets are maintained to a very high standard. This maintenance cost is charged to the statement of profit or loss in lieu of depreciation.

▓ The residual value is at least equal to the carrying amount (maybe due to maintenance).

▓ Assets have a very long, useful economic life such that depreciation is not material.

▓ Asset is not currently in use.

1.5.3 IAS 16 Accounting Treatment

▓ The standard directs that depreciation must be charged in all circumstances but a depreciation charge may be nil (where the residual value exceeds the carrying amount of the asset).

> **Key Point**
>
> Repair and maintenance policy may affect useful life but this does **not** negate the need to charge depreciation.

2 IAS 40 *Investment Property*

2.1 Recognition

▓ Investment property is recognised as an asset when:

- it is probable that the future economic benefits that are attributable to the investment property will flow to the entity; and
- the cost of the investment property can be measured reliably.

▓ Investment properties under construction are now accounted for as investment properties in accordance with IAS 40. Previously they were accounted for as property, plant and equipment under IAS 16.

2.2 Initial Measurement

▓ An investment property is measured initially at its cost, which is the fair value of the consideration given for it, which includes any transaction costs.

2.3 Subsequent Measurement

> **Key Point**
>
> An entity must choose either the fair value model or the cost model and apply that policy to all its investment properties.

2.3.1 Cost Model

▓ After initial recognition, an entity that chooses the cost model shall measure all of its investment property using the cost model in IAS 16 *Property, Plant and Equipment* (i.e. at cost less any accumulated depreciation and impairment losses).

▓ An investment property, measured under the cost model, that is subsequently classified as held for sale in accordance with IFRS 5 is measured in accordance with that standard.

© DeVry/Becker Educational Development Corp. All rights reserved.

2.3.2 Fair Value Model

▨ IAS 40 prescribes when to use fair value but IFRS 13 *Fair Value Measurement* defines fair value and identifies how to measure fair value.

▨ After initial recognition, an entity that chooses the **fair value** model must measure all of investment properties at fair value (except in exceptional circumstances).

▨ A gain or loss arising from a change in the fair value of investment property shall be included in profit or loss for the period in which it arises.

> **Definition**
>
> **Fair value**—"the price that would be received to sell an asset or paid to transfer a liability in an orderly transaction between market participants at the measurement date."
> —*IFRS 13*

Example 2 Constructed Investment Property

Conseil, an investment property company, has been constructing a new cinema. At 31 December 2017, the cinema was nearing completion, and the costs incurred to date were:

	$m
Materials, labour and subcontractors	14.8
Other directly attributable overheads	2.5
Interest on borrowings	1.3

It is Conseil's policy to capitalise interest on specific borrowings raised for the purpose of financing a construction. The amount of borrowings outstanding at 31 December 2017 in respect of this project was $18 million and the annual interest rate was 9.5%.

During the three months to 31 March 2018, in which the cinema was completed, the following additional costs were incurred:

	$m
Materials, labour and subcontractors	$1.7
Other overhead	$0.3

Conseil was not able to measure the fair value of the property reliably during the construction period and so valued it at cost pending completion (as allowed by IAS 40).

On 31 March 2018, Conseil obtained a professional appraisal of the cinema's fair value; the valuer's report put this at $24 million. The valuation fee for this appraisal was $0.1 million; this has not been included in the above amounts for costs incurred during the three months.

The cinema was taken by a national multiplex chain on an operating lease as at 1 April 2018, and was immediately welcoming capacity crowds. In a complete valuation of Conseil's investment properties at 31 December 2018, the fair value of the cinema was measured at $28 million.

Required:

Set out the accounting entries relating to the measurement of the cinema complex for the year ended 31 December 2018.

---

3 IFRS 5 *Non-current Assets Held for Sale*

3.1 Classification

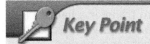

> **Key Point**
>
> A non-current asset is classified as held for sale when its carrying amount will be recovered mainly through proceeds on disposal rather than continuing use.

- The asset must be in a condition suitable for its immediate sale and the sale must meet the **highly probable** criteria:
  - Management must be committed to a plan of sale;
  - The entity must be actively seeking a buyer;
  - The asset must be marketed at a reasonable price; and
  - The sale should be completed within 12 months.*

*This period may be extended under certain circumstances.

3.2 Measurement

- Immediately before classification of an asset as held for sale, it must be measured in accordance with the relevant standard.

- On classification as held for sale, the asset is measured at the lower of its carrying amount and the asset's fair value less costs to sell. Any loss on valuing at fair value less costs to sell is charged against profit unless the asset has a revaluation surplus (in which case the loss will be taken through other comprehensive income, resulting in a decrease in the revaluation surplus).

- Once classified as held for sale, the asset will no longer be depreciated and presented separately (from continuing use assets) in the statement of financial position.

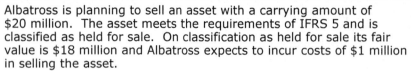

Illustration 3 Non-current Asset Held for Sale

Albatross is planning to sell an asset with a carrying amount of $20 million. The asset meets the requirements of IFRS 5 and is classified as held for sale. On classification as held for sale its fair value is $18 million and Albatross expects to incur costs of $1 million in selling the asset.

The asset should be measured at fair value less cost to sell of $17 million.

On initial recognition as a non-current asset held for sale, the expected loss is recognised:

- the asset would have been remeasured in accordance with the relevant standard (IAS 16, IAS 38 or IAS 40);
- an initial loss of $2 million is recognised in profit or loss (or a revaluation reserve, if relevant); and
- a further loss of $1 million is recognised in profit or loss, bringing the asset to its fair value less costs to sell.

If the fair value of the asset had been $21 million, it would be measured at its carrying amount of $20 million; the expected profit could not be recognised in advance.

© DeVry/Becker Educational Development Corp. All rights reserved.

4 IAS 38 *Intangible Assets*

4.1 Identifiability

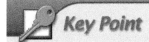

Key Point

An intangible asset, whether generated internally or acquired in a business combination, is identifiable when it:

- is separable; or
- arises from contractual or other legal rights.

▤ These criteria distinguish intangible assets from goodwill acquired in a business combination.

4.2 Initial Measurement

▤ Intangible assets should be measured initially at cost, following the same principles as for tangible assets.

▤ An intangible asset may be acquired:

- separately;
- as part of a business combination;
- by way of a government grant;
- internally generated; or
- by an exchange of assets.

Illustration 4 Initial Measurement

An entity is developing a new production process. The amount of expenditure in the year to 31 December 2017 was as follows:

	$
1 January to 30 November	2,160
1 December to 31 December	240
	2,400

On 1 December, the entity was able to demonstrate that the production process met the criteria for recognition as an intangible asset. The amount estimated to be recoverable from the process (including future cash outflows to complete the process before it is available for use) is $1,200.

Analysis

- On 31 December 2017, the production process is recognised as an intangible asset at a cost of $240 (expenditure incurred since 1 December, when the recognition criteria were met). The intangible asset is carried at this cost (being less than the amount expected to be recoverable).

- The $2,160 expenditure incurred before 1 December is recognised as an expense because the recognition criteria were not met until that date. This expenditure can **never** be recognised as an asset in the statement of financial position.

4.3 Subsequent Measurement

▓ An entity can choose either a cost or revaluation model.

4.3.1 Cost Model

▓ Cost less any accumulated amortisation and any accumulated impairment losses.

> **Illustration 5 Subsequent Measurement at Cost**
>
> Following on from *Illustration 4*:
>
> Expenditure in 2018 is $4,800. On 31 December 2018, the amount estimated to be recoverable from the process (including future cash outflows to complete the process before it is available for use) is $4,500.
>
> Analysis
>
> ■ At 31 December 2018, the cost of the production process is $5,040 (240 + 4,800). The entity recognises an impairment loss of $540 to adjust the carrying amount before impairment loss ($5,040) to its recoverable amount ($4,500).
>
> ■ This impairment loss will be reversed in a subsequent period if the requirements for the reversal of an impairment loss in IAS 36 *Impairment of Assets* are met.

4.3.2 Revaluation Model

▓ Revalued amount, being fair value at the date of the revaluation less any subsequent accumulated amortisation and any accumulated impairment losses.

▓ Fair value must be measured by reference to an active market.

▓ This is different from the treatment of revaluation under IAS 16 where depreciated replacement cost can be used when there is no evidence of market value.

▓ The revaluation model does not allow:

- the revaluation of intangible assets which have not previously been recognised as assets;
- the initial recognition of intangible assets at amounts other than their cost.

▓ The revaluation is carried out according to the same principles applied in accounting for other assets. For example:

- surplus is taken through other comprehensive income and increases the revaluation surplus;
- deficit is expensed unless covered by a previously recognised surplus;
- all intangibles in the class must be revalued, etc.

4.3.3 Active Markets

▓ The revaluation of intangibles will be uncommon in practice as it is not expected that an **active market** will exist for most intangible assets in that:

- they will not be homogeneous (most are unique);
- willing buyers and sellers may not be normally found at any time; and
- prices are not usually available to the public.

Definition

Active market—"a market in which transactions for the asset or liability take place with sufficient frequency and volume to provide pricing information on an on-going basis."—*IFRS 13*

© DeVry/Becker Educational Development Corp. All rights reserved.

- For example, active markets cannot exist for brands, newspaper mastheads, music and film publishing rights, patents or trademarks. Each item is unique, transactions are relatively infrequent and contracts are negotiated between individual buyers and sellers.

- However, examples do exist of active markets for intangible assets—freely transferable taxi licences, fishing licences and production quotas.

- The Kyoto Agreement on climate change has given rise to an active market in the buying and selling of emission rights.

Illustration 6 Active Market for an Intangible Asset

In 1990, in the United States, legislation was introduced to authorise sulphur dioxide pollution at a limited rate from power-generating systems—an emission right. Such rights are no longer granted. Organizations reducing their emissions through, for example, modernisation then had excess pollution rights (i.e. an ability to pollute which was surplus to their requirements). An active market in emission rights emerged as new plants sought to buy the excess.

5   IAS 23 *Borrowing Costs*

5.1   Accounting Treatment

Key Point

All borrowing costs related to a qualifying asset must be *capitalised* as part of the cost of that asset.

Definition

Qualifying asset—an asset that necessarily takes a substantial period of time to get ready for its intended use or sale.

- All other borrowing costs are *expensed* as and when they are incurred.

5.2   Capitalisation

- Capitalisation commences when:
  - expenditure has been incurred;
  - borrowing costs are being incurred; and
  - activity has commenced.
- Capitalisation should be suspended during extended periods in which active development is interrupted.
- Capitalisation should cease when substantially all the activities necessary to prepare the qualifying asset for its intended use or sale are complete.

6 IAS 20 *Government Grants*

IAS 20 *Accounting for Government Grants and Disclosure of Government Assistance* considers the accounting treatment for government grants that are income-based grants and asset based. This section only considers the issues relating to asset-based grants.

6.1 Accounting Treatment

The standard allows two possible methods of accounting for asset-based grants.

6.1.1 Present as Deferred Income

The grant will be presented as deferred income in the statement of financial position. Deferred income is included in the liability section of the statement of financial position, split between non-current and current elements.*

The deferred income will be credited to profits over the life of the related asset, in the same manner in which that asset is depreciated.

6.1.2 Deduct From Cost of Asset

The other option is to deduct the grant from the cost of the asset.

The effect on profits will be the same as the previous method due to the fact that the charge for depreciation will now be based on the net cost of the asset.*

6.2 Granted Asset

Some intangible assets may be acquired free of charge, or for nominal consideration, by way of a government grant (e.g. airport landing rights, licences to operate radio or television stations, import quotas, rights to emit pollution).

Under IAS 20, both the intangible asset (debit entry) and the grant (credit entry) may be recorded initially at either fair value or cost (which may be zero).

> ***Commentary***
>
> *Some accountants would argue that this method includes an item in the statement of financial position which does not meet the definition of a liability and is therefore contrary to the framework.

> ***Commentary***
>
> *Some accountants would argue that this method allows a form of offsetting in the statement of financial position and does not reflect the true cost of the asset.

Illustration 7 Measuring Intangible Granted Asset

Neelix is an entity involved in the harvest and production of foodstuffs. On 31 December, it was awarded a fishing quota of 1,000 tonnes of cod per annum for five years.

The quota requires a registration fee of $1,000. The fair value of the fishing quota is $10,000,000 (net of the registration fee).

Analysis

Measurement of the intangible asset on initial recognition is at either:

Cost	*or*	Fair value
$1,000		$10,000,000

© DeVry/Becker Educational Development Corp. All rights reserved.

Summary

- Property, plant and equipment is initially measured at cost.
- Servicing costs (e.g. labour and consumables) are recognised in profit or loss as incurred.
- The carrying amount of an item of property, plant and equipment recognises the cost of replacing a part when that cost is incurred, if the recognition criteria are met.
- The cost of each major inspection performed is recognised in the carrying amount, as a replacement, if the recognition criteria are satisfied.
- Repair and maintenance policy may affect useful life but does not negate the need to charge depreciation.
- An entity must choose either the fair value model or the cost model and apply that policy to all investment properties.
- Non-current assets are classified as held for sale when their carrying amount will be recovered mainly through proceeds of disposal rather than continuing use.
- An intangible asset is identifiable when it is separable or arises from contractual or other legal rights.
- All borrowing costs related to a qualifying asset must be capitalised as part of the cost of that asset.
- Asset-based government grants can either be presented as a deduction from the related asset or a liability.

Session 6 Quiz
Estimated time: 20 minutes

1. List the costs which may be included within the cost of PPE on initial recognition. (1.2)
2. Explain how the THREE categories of subsequent costs are accounted for under IAS 16. (1.4)
3. Explain why some accountants favour the non-depreciation of certain assets. (1.5.2)
4. Explain how the movement in the fair value of investment properties is accounted for under the fair value model. (2.3.2)
5. State how non-current assets held for disposal should be valued in the statement of financial position. (3.2)
6. List the recognition criteria for intangible assets. (4.1)
7. Specify which intangible assets may be subsequently measured using the revaluation model. (4.3.2)
8. Discuss how borrowing costs should be accounted for. (5.1)
9. Specify the TWO methods of accounting for capital-based grants, which IAS 20 allows. (6.1)

Study Question Bank
Estimated time: 45 minutes

Priority		Estimated Time	Completed
Q12	Heywood	45 minutes	
Additional			
Q10	Sponger		
Q11	Moore		

© DeVry/Becker Educational Development Corp. All rights reserved.

EXAMPLE SOLUTIONS

Solution 1—Initial Measurement

	$000
Manufacturer's base price	1,050
Less: Trade discount (20%)	(210)
Base cost	840
Freight charges	30
Electrical installation cost	28
Pre-production testing	22
Initial capitalised cost	920

- The early settlement discount is not necessary to getting the asset to a place and condition of use.
- The staff training cost cannot be capitalised, as this would be classified as revenue expenditure and expensed as incurred.
- The maintenance contract is also revenue expenditure. Two thirds of the cost will be included in the statement of financial position as a prepaid expense, but it is not a capital cost.

© DeVry/Becker Educational Development Corp. All rights reserved.

Solution 2—Constructed Investment Property

Costs incurred in the three months to 31 March

		$m	$m
Dr	Asset under construction	1.7	
	Cr Cash/Payables		1.7
Dr	Asset under construction	0.3	
	Cr Cash/Payables		0.3
Dr	Asset under construction	0.43	
	Cr Interest expense (W)		0.43

Working

Outstanding borrowings $18m

Interest for 3 months $18m × $\frac{3}{12}$ × 9.5% = $0.43m

Cost at the date of transfer into investment properties

	$m
Cost at 1 January (14.8 + 2.5 + 1.3)	18.6*
Costs to 31 March (1.7 + 0.3 + 0.43)	2.43
Investment property at cost	21.03

*The cinema was valued at cost as its fair value was not measurable during construction.

On initial recognition at fair value

		$m	$m
Dr	Investment property	3.97	
	Cr Profit or loss		3.97

*Being the increase from cost to fair value $24 million on completion of the property.**

*A professional valuation does not increase the profit-earning potential of an asset so the appraiser's fee is expensed. The property will be valued at fair value once construction is complete and the gain will be recognised in profit or loss at 31 March 2018.

On subsequent measurement at 31 December

		$m	$m
Dr	Investment property (28 – 24)	4	
	Cr Profit or loss		4

Being the increase in fair value on subsequent measurement.

© DeVry/Becker Educational Development Corp. All rights reserved.

IAS 36 *Impairment of Assets*

FOCUS

This session covers the following content from the *ACCA Study Guide.*

C. Reporting the Financial Performance of Entities

2. Non-current assets

a) Apply and discuss the timing of the recognition of non-current assets and the determination of their carrying amounts including impairments and revaluations.

Session 7 Guidance

- **Work** through all of the *Illustrations* and *Examples* in this session.
- **Define** these terms: recoverable amount of an asset, impairment loss and cash generating unit (s.1.2, s.4).
- **Know** how to calculate the recoverable amount of an asset and to compare against an asset's carrying amount and the accounting for an impairment, both in cases of a loss and any future reversal (s.2–s.6).

(continued on next page)

VISUAL OVERVIEW

Objective: To give guidance on the recognition and reversal of impairment losses.

```
              ┌─────────────────────────────────┐
              │           IMPAIRMENT            │
              │  • Objective of IAS 36          │
              │  • Terminology                  │
              └─────────────────────────────────┘
              ┌─────────────────────────────────┐
              │          BASIC RULES            │
              │  • All Assets                   │
              │  • Intangible Assets            │
              │  • Impairment Indicators        │
              └─────────────────────────────────┘
```

RECOVERABLE AMOUNT	CASH GENERATING UNITS
• Measurement Principles	• Basic Concept
• Fair Value Less Costs of Disposal	• Shared Assets
• Value in Use	

```
              ┌─────────────────────────────────┐
              │  ACCOUNTING FOR IMPAIRMENT LOSS │
              │  • Basics                       │
              │  • Allocation                   │
              └─────────────────────────────────┘
              ┌─────────────────────────────────┐
              │       SUBSEQUENT REVIEW         │
              │  • Basic Provisions             │
              │  • Reversals                    │
              └─────────────────────────────────┘
              ┌─────────────────────────────────┐
              │          DISCLOSURE             │
              └─────────────────────────────────┘
```

Session 7 Guidance

■ **Identify** circumstances indicating that an asset may be impaired (s.2.3).

■ **Return** to this session once you have studied *Session 18* on accounting for goodwill.

© DeVry/Becker Educational Development Corp. All rights reserved.

1 Impairment

1.1 Objective of IAS 36

- Prudence is a widely applied concept in the preparation of financial statements. A specific application of prudence is that assets must not be carried in the statement of financial position at a value, which is greater than the cash flows which they are expected to generate in the future.

- Several standards (including IASs 16, 28 and 38) require that if the recoverable amount of an asset is less than its carrying amount (i.e. there is "impairment") then the carrying amount is written down immediately to this recoverable amount.

- IAS 36 *Impairment of Assets* prescribes detailed procedures to be followed in terms of identifying impairments and accounting for them. It applies to all assets (including subsidiaries, associates and joint ventures) except those covered by the specific provisions of other IFRSs:

  - inventories (IAS 2);
  - assets recognised in accordance with IFRS 15 *Revenue from Contracts with Customers*;
  - deferred tax assets (IAS 12);
  - financial assets that are included in the scope of IFRS 9;
  - assets arising from employee benefits (IAS 19);
  - investment property that is measured at fair value (IAS 40);
  - biological assets measured at fair value less costs of disposal (IAS 41); and
  - non-current assets classified as held for sale (IFRS 5).

1.2 Terminology

Impairment loss: the amount by which the carrying amount of an asset exceeds its recoverable amount.

Recoverable amount: the higher of an asset's fair value less costs of disposal and its value in use.

Fair value: the price which would be received to sell an asset or paid to transfer a liability in an orderly transaction between market participants at the measurement date.

Value in use: the present value of the future cash flows expected to be derived from an asset (or cash generating unit).

Cash generating unit: the smallest identifiable group of assets which generate cash inflows that are largely independent of the cash inflows from other assets or groups of assets.

© DeVry/Becker Educational Development Corp. All rights reserved.

2 Basic Rules

2.1 All Assets

Key Point

At the end of each reporting period, an entity should assess whether there are any indicators that an asset (or cash generating unit) may be impaired. If there are such indicators, the entity should estimate the **recoverable amount** of the asset.

- If there are no indications of a potential impairment, there is no need to make a formal estimate of recoverable amount, except for intangible assets with indefinite useful lives or those which are not yet ready for use.

2.2 Intangible Assets

- Irrespective of any indication of impairment, the following intangible assets must be tested annually for impairment:
  - those with an indefinite useful life;
  - those not yet available for use; and
  - goodwill acquired in a business combination.
- The impairment tests for these assets may be performed at any time during an annual period, provided they are performed at the same time every year. All other assets (including intangibles that are amortised) are tested for impairment when there is an indication that impairment has occurred.
- If an intangible asset with an indefinite life forms part of a **cash generating unit** and cannot be separated, that cash generating unit must be tested for impairment at least annually, or whenever there is an indication that the cash generating unit may be impaired.

2.3 Indications of Potential Impairment Loss

- An entity should consider the following indications of potential **impairment loss**—both external and internal—as a minimum.

2.3.1 External Sources of Information

- Observable indications that the asset's value has declined during the period significantly more than would be expected due to the passage of time or normal use.

Illustration 1 Carrying Amount May Exceed Estimated Recoverable Value

Meade owns a subsidiary, Lee. Lee is a property development company with extensive holdings in Malaysia. The Malaysian economy has moved into a deep recession.

The recession is an indication that the carrying amount of Lee in Meade's accounts might be greater than the recoverable amount. Meade must make a formal estimate of the recoverable amount of its investment in Lee.

▨ Significant changes with an adverse effect on the entity have taken place during the period, or will take place in the near future, in the technological, market, economic or legal environment in which the entity operates.

Illustration 2 Possible Adverse Effect

Buford is an entity involved in the manufacture of steel. It owns a steel production facility, which was constructed 10 years ago. The facility has 10 blast furnaces, each of which is being written off over 30 years from the date of construction.

Recent technological innovations have resulted in a new type of furnace coming onto the market. This furnace offers efficiency improvements which the manufacturers claim will reduce the unit cost of a tonne of steel by 15% to 20%. The company which supplied the furnaces for Buford has recently introduced a series of price cutting measures to try to preserve its own market share.

The market for the grade of steel Buford produces is very price sensitive, and price is often used as a basis of competition in this market. A major competitor has announced that it is constructing a plant which will utilise the new technology.

The existence of the new technology and the announcement by the competitor are indications that Buford's blast furnaces might be impaired. Buford should make a formal estimate of the recoverable amount of its blast furnaces (or possibly the production plant as a whole if it is deemed to be a cash generating unit).

▨ Market interest rates or other market rates of return on investments have *increased* during the period, and those increases are likely to affect the discount rate used in calculating an asset's **value in use** and decrease the asset's recoverable amount materially.

Illustration 3 Effect of Higher Discount Rate

Gibbon is an entity which owns a 60% holding in Pickett, an unquoted entity. Both entities operate in a country with a stable economy. The government of the country has recently announced an increase in interest rates.

The increase in interest rates will cause a fall in value of equity holdings (all other things being equal). This is because risk-free investments offer a higher return, making them relatively more attractive. The market value of equity will adjust downwards to improve the return available on this sort of investment.

The increase in interest rates is an indication that Gibbon's holding in Pickett might be impaired. Gibbon should make a formal estimate of the recoverable amount of its interest in Pickett.

© DeVry/Becker Educational Development Corp. All rights reserved.

■ The carrying amount of the net assets of the reporting entity is more than its market capitalisation.

Illustration 4 Carrying Amount v Recoverable Amount

Sickles is a quoted entity. The carrying amount of its net assets is $100m. The market capitalisation of the entity has recently fallen to $80m.

The value of the entity as compared to the carrying amount of its net assets indicates that its assets might be impaired. Sickles should make a formal estimate of the recoverable amount of its assets.

2.3.2 Internal Sources of Information

■ Evidence is available of obsolescence or physical damage.

Illustration 5 Evidence of Obsolescence

Custer is an entity that manufactures machinery. It makes use of a large number of specialised machine tools. It capitalises the machine tools as a non-current asset and starts to depreciate the tools when they are brought into use.

A review of the non-current asset register in respect of machine tools has revealed that approximately 40% of the value held relates to machine tools purchased more than two years ago and not yet brought into use.

The age of the machine tools and the fact that they have not yet been brought into use is an indication that the asset may be impaired. Custer should make a formal estimate of the recoverable amount of its machine tools.

■ Significant adverse changes have taken place during the period, or are expected to take place in the near future, the extent to which, or manner in which, an asset is used or is expected to be used.

Illustration 6 Changes in Asset's Use

Hood is a small airline. It owns a Dash 8 aircraft, which it purchased to service a contract for passenger flights to a small island. The rest of its business is long-haul freight shipping.

It has been informed that its licence to operate the passenger service will not be renewed after the end of this current contract in six months. It is proposing to use the aircraft in a new business venture offering pleasure flights.

The change in the use of the asset which is expected to take place in the near future is an indication that the aircraft may be impaired. Hood should make a formal estimate of the recoverable amount of its Dash 8 aircraft.

© DeVry/Becker Educational Development Corp. All rights reserved.

▧ Evidence is available from internal reporting which indicates that the economic performance of an asset is, or will be, worse than expected. Evidence which indicates that an asset may be impaired includes the existence of:*

Commentary

*The list of signs of impairment is not exhaustive.

- cash flows for acquiring the asset, or subsequent cash needs for operating or maintaining it, which are significantly higher than those originally budgeted;
- actual net cash flows or operating profit or loss flowing from the asset which are significantly worse than those budgeted;
- a significant decline in budgeted net cash flows or operating profit, or a significant increase in budgeted loss, flowing from the asset; or
- operating losses or net cash outflows for the asset, when current period figures are aggregated with budgeted figures for the future.

Illustration 7 Impairment of Development Asset

Armistead is an entity in the professional training sector. It has produced a series of CD ROM-based training products which have been on sale for eight months. The entity has capitalised certain development costs associated with this product in accordance with the rules in IAS 38 *Intangible Assets*. Early sales have been significantly below forecast.

The failure of the entity to meet sales targets is an indication that the development asset may be impaired. Armistead should make a formal estimate of the recoverable amount of the capitalised development cost.

▧ Where there is an indication that an asset may be impaired, this may indicate that the remaining useful life, the depreciation (amortisation) method or the residual value for the asset needs to be reviewed and adjusted, even if no impairment loss is recognised for the asset.

© DeVry/Becker Educational Development Corp. All rights reserved.

3 Recoverable Amount

3.1 Measurement Principles

Key Point

The recoverable amount is the *higher* of the asset's fair value less costs of disposal and value in use.

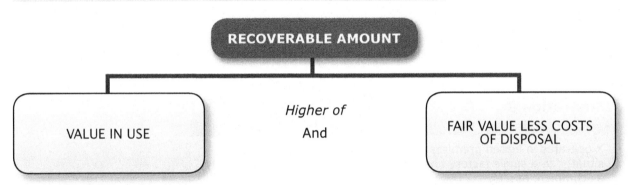

- Recoverable amount is determined for an individual asset, unless the asset does not generate cash inflows from continuing use which are largely independent of those from other assets or groups of assets. In this case, recoverable amount is determined for the cash generating unit to which the asset belongs.
- It is not always necessary to determine both an asset's fair value less costs of disposal and its value in use to determine the asset's recoverable amount if:
  - either of these amounts exceed the asset's carrying amount, the asset is not impaired so it is not necessary to estimate the other amount; or
  - there is no reason to believe that the asset's value in use materially exceeds its fair value less cost of disposal, the asset's recoverable amount is its fair value less costs of disposal.*
- Where the asset is an intangible asset with an indefinite useful life, the most recent detailed calculation of the recoverable amount made in a preceding period may be used in the impairment test in the current period.

3.2 Fair Value Less Costs of Disposal

- Fair value is assessed using the fair value hierarchy in IFRS 13 *Fair Value Measurement*. The basis of the hierarchy is as follows:
  - Level 1 inputs—quoted prices in active markets for identical assets or liabilities which the entity can access at the measurement date.
  - Level 2 inputs—inputs other than quoted prices included in Level 1 which are observable for the asset or liability, either directly or indirectly.
  - Level 3 inputs—unobservable inputs for the asset or liability.

*Commentary

*When an asset is held for imminent disposal the value in use will consist mainly of the net amount to be received for the disposal of the asset. Future cash flows from continuing use of the asset until disposal are likely to be negligible.

Definition

Active market—"a market in which transactions for the asset or liability take place with sufficient frequency and volume to provide pricing information on an on-going basis." —*IFRS 13*

Costs of disposal—incremental costs directly attributable to the disposal of an asset, excluding finance costs, income tax expense and any cost which has already been included as a liability. Examples include:*

- Legal costs
- Stamp duty
- Costs of removing the asset.

Other direct incremental costs to bring an asset into condition for its sale.

> ***Commentary***
>
> *Examples of costs which are not costs of disposal include termination benefits and costs associated with reducing or reorganising a business following the disposal of an asset.

Illustration 8 Fair Value Less Disposal Costs

X operates in leased premises. It owns a bottling plant which is situated in a single factory unit. Bottling plants are sold periodically as complete assets.

Professional valuers have estimated that the plant might be sold for $100,000. They have charged a fee of $1,000 for providing this valuation.

X would need to dismantle the asset and ship it to any buyer. Dismantling and shipping would cost $5,000. Specialist packaging would cost a further $4,000 and legal fees $1,500.

Fair value less costs of disposal:	$
Sales price	100,000
Dismantling and shipping	(5,000)
Packaging	(4,000)
Legal fees	(1,500)
Fair value less costs of disposal*	(89,500)

> ***Commentary***
>
> *The professional valuer's fee of $1,000 would not be included in the fair value less costs of disposal as this is not a directly attributable cost of selling the asset.

3.3   Value in Use

- **Value in use**—is the present value of the future cash flows expected to be derived from an asset. Estimating it involves:
  - estimating the future cash inflows and outflows to be derived from continuing use of the asset and from its ultimate disposal; and
  - applying the appropriate discount rate.

> **Key Point**
>
> Value in use is more entity specific than fair value.

© DeVry/Becker Educational Development Corp. All rights reserved.

- Fair value normally would not reflect the following factors:
  - additional value derived from the grouping of assets;
  - synergies between the asset being measured and other assets;
  - legal rights or restrictions that are specific solely to the current owner of the asset; and
  - tax benefits or burdens that is specific to the current owner of the asset.

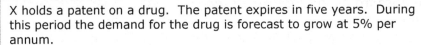

Illustration 9 Value in Use

X holds a patent on a drug. The patent expires in five years. During this period the demand for the drug is forecast to grow at 5% per annum.

Experience shows that competitors flood the market with generic versions of a profitable drug as soon as it is no longer protected by a patent. As a result, X does not expect the patent to generate significant cash flows after five years.

Net revenues from the sale of the drug were $100m last year.

The entity has decided that 15.5% is an appropriate discount rate for the appraisals of the cash flows associated with this product.

Time	Cash $m	Discount factor @15.5%	Present value ($m)
1	$100 \times 1.05 = 105$	0.86580	91
2	$100 \times 1.05^2 = 110.3$	0.74961	83
3	$100 \times 1.05^3 = 115.8$	0.64901	75
4	$100 \times 1.05^4 = 121.6$	0.56192	68
5	$100 \times 1.05^5 = 127.6$	0.48651	62
	Value in use		**379**

3.3.1 Cash Flow Projections

Key Point

Projections should be based on reasonable and supportable assumptions that represent management's best estimate of economic conditions for the remaining useful life of the asset.

- They should be based on the most recent financial budgets/ forecasts which have been approved by management.*
- Projections based on these budgets/forecasts should cover a *maximum* period of five years, unless a longer period can be justified.
- Beyond the period covered by the most recent budgets/ forecasts, the cash flows should be estimated by extrapolating the projections based on the budgets/forecasts using a steady or declining growth rate for subsequent years, unless an increasing rate can be justified.

*Commentary

*Greater weight is given to external evidence when developing forecasts and estimates.

© DeVry/Becker Educational Development Corp. All rights reserved.

▦ The growth rate should not exceed the long-term average growth rate for the products, industries, or country or countries in which the entity operates, or for the market in which the asset is used, unless a higher rate can be justified.

▦ Estimates of future cash flows should include:
- projected cash inflows including disposal proceeds; and
- projected cash outflows which are necessarily incurred to generate the cash inflows from continuing use of the asset.

▦ Estimates of future cash flows should exclude:*
- cash flows relating to the improvement or enhancement of the asset's performance;
- cash flows expected to arise from a future restructuring which is not yet committed;
- cash outflows which will be required to settle obligations which have already been recognised as liabilities;
- cash inflows or outflows from financing activities; and*
- income tax receipts or payments.

*Future cash flows are estimated based on the asset in its current condition or in maintaining its current condition.

*Cash flows from financing activities are already discounted.

Key Point

The discount rate is a *pre-tax* market rate (or rates) which reflects current market assessments of the time value of money and the *risks specific to the asset*.

▦ When an asset-specific rate is not available from the market, an entity uses surrogates to estimate the discount rate. As a starting point, the entity may take into account the following rates:
- the entity's weighted average cost of capital determined using techniques such as the Capital Asset Pricing Model;
- the entity's incremental borrowing rate; and
- other market borrowing rates.

▦ These rates are adjusted:*
- to reflect the way the market would assess the specific risks associated with the projected cash flows; and
- to exclude risks which are not relevant to the projected cash flows.

▦ Consideration is given to risks (e.g. country risk, currency risk, price risk and cash flow risk).

▦ Where value-in-use is sensitive to a difference in risks for different future periods or to the term structure of interest rates, separate discount rates for each period should be used.

*Rate adjustments do not include adjustments for risks that the estimated cash flows have already taken into account (e.g. bad debts).

© DeVry/Becker Educational Development Corp. All rights reserved.

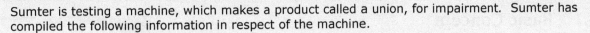

Example 1 Cash Flows

Sumter is testing a machine, which makes a product called a union, for impairment. Sumter has compiled the following information in respect of the machine.

	$
Selling price of a union	100
Variable cost of production	70
Fixed overhead allocation per unit	10
Packing cost per unit	1
All costs and revenues are expected to inflate at 3% per annum.	

Volume growth is expected to be 4% per annum. Last year, 1,000 units were sold. This is in excess of the long-term rate of growth in the industry. Sumter's management has valid reasons for projecting this level of growth.

The machine originally cost $400,000 and was supplied on credit terms from a fellow group entity. Sumter is charged $15,000 per annum for this loan.

Future expenditure

In two years' time, the machine will be subject to major servicing to maintain its operating capacity. This will cost $10,000.

In three years' time, the machine will be modified to improve its efficiency. This improvement will cost $20,000 and will reduce unit variable cost by 15%.

The asset will be sold in eight years' time. Currently the scrap value of machines of a similar type is $10,000.

All values are given in real terms (to exclude inflation).

Required:

Identify the cash flows which should be included in Sumter's estimate of the value in use of the machine. Explain the rationale of the inclusion or exclusion of each amount.

Solution

Time	Narrative		Cash flow	Comment
	Net revenue			
	Per unit	Volume		
1				
2				
3				
4				
5				
6				
7				
8				
	Other flows			
2				
8				

© DeVry/Becker Educational Development Corp. All rights reserved.

4 Cash Generating Units

4.1 Basic Concept

Definition

Cash generating unit—the smallest identifiable group of assets which generates cash inflows which are largely independent of the cash inflows from other assets or groups of assets.

- If there is any indication that an asset may be impaired, the recoverable amount (the higher of the fair value less **costs of disposal** and value in use of the asset) must be estimated for the individual asset.

- However, it may not be possible to estimate the recoverable amount of an individual asset because:
  - its value in use cannot be estimated to be close to its fair value less costs of disposal (e.g. when the future cash flows from continuing use of the asset cannot be estimated to be negligible); and
  - it does not generate cash inflows which are largely independent of those from other assets.

 **Key Point**

In this case, the recoverable amount of the cash generating unit to which the asset belongs (the asset's cash generating unit) must be determined.

- Identifying the lowest aggregation of assets which generate largely independent cash inflows may be a matter of considerable judgement.

- Management should consider various factors including how it monitors the entity's operations (e.g. by product lines, individual locations, regional areas, etc) or how it makes decisions about continuing or disposing of the entity's assets and operations.

Illustration 10 Cash Generating Unit: Dry Dock

An entity owns a dry dock with a large crane to support its activities. The crane could only be sold for scrap value, and cash inflows from its use cannot be identified separately from all of the operations directly connected with the dry dock.

It is not possible to estimate the recoverable amount of the crane because its value in use cannot be determined. Therefore, the entity estimates the recoverable amount of the cash generating unit to which the crane belongs—the dry dock as a whole.

- Sometimes it is possible to identify cash flows which stem from a specific asset but these cannot be earned independently from other assets. In such cases, the asset cannot be reviewed independently and must be reviewed as part of the cash generating unit.

© DeVry/Becker Educational Development Corp. All rights reserved.

Illustration 11 Cash Generating Unit: Airport

An entity operates an airport which provides services under contract with a government that requires a minimum level of service on domestic routes in return for licence to operate the international routes. Assets devoted to each route and the cash flows from each route can be identified separately. The domestic service operates at a significant loss.

Because the entity does not have the option to curtail the domestic service, the lowest level of identifiable cash inflows which are largely independent of the cash inflows from other assets or groups of assets are cash inflows generated by the airport as a whole. This is, therefore, the cash generating unit.

- If an **active market** exists for the output produced by an asset or a group of assets, this asset or group of assets is identified as a cash generating unit, even if some or all of the output is used internally.
- Where the cash flows are affected by internal transfer pricing, management's best estimate of future market (i.e. in an arm's length transaction) prices is used to estimate cash flows for value-in-use calculations.
- Cash generating units should be identified consistently from period to period for the same asset or types of assets, unless a change is justified.

4.2   Allocating Shared Assets

- The carrying amount of a cash generating unit should include the carrying amount of only those assets which can be directly attributed, or allocated on a reasonable and consistent basis, to it.*

4.2.1   Goodwill Acquired in a Business Combination

Key Point

Goodwill acquired in a business combination must be allocated to each of the acquirer's cash generating units which are expected to benefit from the synergies of the combination, irrespective of whether other assets or liabilities of the acquiree are assigned to those units.

Commentary

*Goodwill acquired in a business combination and corporate (head office) assets are examples of shared assets which will need to be allocated.

- If the initial allocation of goodwill cannot be completed before the end of the financial year in which the business combination is affected, the allocation must be completed by the end of the following financial year.
- Where an acquirer needs to account for a business combination using provisional values, adjustments can be made to such values within 12 months of the date of acquisition (IFRS 3). Until such provisional values have been finalised, it may not be possible to complete the initial allocation of goodwill.

© DeVry/Becker Educational Development Corp. All rights reserved.

- IFRS 3 allows 12 months from the date of acquisition in which to finalise goodwill; IAS 36 allows up to the end of the following financial period (i.e. in most cases additional time) in which to allocate goodwill.
- Each unit (or group of units) to which the goodwill is so allocated must:*
  - represent the lowest level in the entity at which the goodwill is monitored for internal management purposes; and
  - not be larger than an operating segment as defined in IFRS 8 *Operating Segments* (i.e. before the aggregation permitted by IFRS 8 when segments have similar economic characteristics).
- Once goodwill has been allocated to a cash generating unit, that unit must be tested for impairment:
  - at least annually; or
  - as soon as there is an indication of impairment of:
    - goodwill; or
    - the cash generating unit.
- Different cash generating units may be tested for impairment at different times. However, if some or all of the goodwill allocated to a cash generating unit was acquired in a business combination during the current annual period, that unit is tested for impairment before the end of the current annual period.

4.2.2 Corporate Assets

- The distinctive characteristics of **corporate assets** are that they do not generate cash inflows independently of other assets or groups of assets and their carrying amount cannot be fully attributed to the cash generating unit under review.*

*Commentary

*The standards aim to match the testing of impairment of goodwill with the monitoring level of goodwill in the entity. As a minimum, this is considered to be based on segmental reporting requirements such that listed companies will not be able to "net-off" and shield goodwill impairment at the entity level.

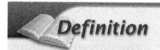

*Commentary

*Examples of corporate assets include head office or divisional buildings, a central information system or a research centre.

Definition

Corporate assets—assets, other than goodwill, that contribute to the future cash flows of both the cash generating unit under review and other cash generating units.

- Because corporate assets do not generate separate cash inflows, the recoverable amount of an individual corporate asset cannot be determined unless management has decided to dispose of the asset.
- If there is an indication that a cash generating unit may be impaired then the appropriate portion of corporate assets must be included in the carrying amount of that unit or group of units.
- Corporate assets are allocated on a reasonable and consistent basis to each cash generating unit.
- If a corporate asset cannot be allocated to a specific cash generating unit, the smallest group of cash generating units which include the unit under review must be identified.
- The carrying amount of the unit or group of units (including the portion of corporate assets) is then compared to its recoverable amount. Any impairment loss is dealt with in the same way as an impairment loss for goodwill would be dealt with.

© DeVry/Becker Educational Development Corp. All rights reserved.

5 Accounting for Impairment Loss

5.1 Basics

Key Point

If, and only if, the recoverable amount of an asset is less than its carrying amount, the carrying amount must be reduced to the recoverable amount. The reduction is an impairment loss.

▨ An impairment loss is recognised as an expense in profit or loss immediately, unless the asset is carried at revalued amount under another IFRS.

▨ Any impairment loss of a revalued asset should be treated as a revaluation decrease under that other IFRS.*

*Commentary

*An impairment loss of a revalued asset usually will mean that the fall in value must be charged to the revaluation surplus to the extent that the loss is covered by the surplus, with the fall in value reflected in other comprehensive income. Any amount not so covered is then charged to the profit or loss.

Illustration 12   Revaluation of Asset

	Carrying amount (1)	Recoverable amount	Profit or loss	Other comprehensive income
Situation 1				
Asset carried at historical cost	100	80	20 **Dr**	–
Situation 2				
Historical cost of asset = 100 but revalued to 150	150	125	–	25 **Dr**
Situation 3				
Historical cost of asset = 100 but revalued to 150	150	95	5 **Dr**	50 **Dr**

(1) Before recognition of impairment loss.

▨ After impairment, the carrying amount of the asset less any residual value is depreciated (amortised) over its remaining expected useful life.

© DeVry/Becker Educational Development Corp. All rights reserved.

5.2   Allocation Within a Cash Generating Unit

▩ If an impairment loss is recognised for a cash generating unit, the problem arises as to where to set the credit entry in the statement of financial position.

 **Key Point**

The impairment loss should be allocated between all assets of the cash generating unit in the following order:

■ goodwill allocated to the cash generating unit (if any);
■ then, to the other assets of the unit on a pro rata basis (based on their carrying amounts).

▩ In allocating an impairment loss the carrying amount of an asset should not be reduced below the highest of:

● its fair value less costs of disposal (if measurable);
● its value in use (if determinable); and
● zero.

▩ The amount of the impairment loss which would otherwise have been allocated to the asset should be allocated to the other assets of the unit on a pro rata basis.

Example 2   Impairment Loss, Part 1

At 1 January, an entity paid $2,800 for a company whose main activity consists of refuse collection. The acquired company owns four refuse collection vehicles and a local government licence, without which it could not operate.

At 1 January, the fair value less costs of disposal of each lorry and of the licence is $500. The company has no insurance cover.

At 1 February, one lorry crashed. Because of its reduced capacity, the entity estimates the value in use of the business at $2,220.

Required:

Show how the impairment loss would be allocated to the assets of the business.

Solution

	1 January	Impairment loss	1 February
Goodwill			
Intangible asset			
Lorries			

                                    © DeVry/Becker Educational Development Corp. All rights reserved.

Example 3 Impairment Loss, Part 2

At 22 May, the government increased the interest rates. The entity re-determined the value in use of the business as $1,860. The fair value less costs of disposal of the licence had decreased to $480 (as a result of a market reaction to the increased interest rates). The demand for lorries was hit hard by the increase in rates, and the selling prices were adversely affected.

Required:

Show how the above information would be reflected in the asset values of the business.

Solution

	1 February	Impairment loss	22 May
Goodwill			
Intangible asset			
Lorries			

■ If an individual asset in the cash generating unit is impaired, but the cash generating unit as a whole is not, no impairment loss is recognised even if the asset's fair value less costs of disposal is less than its carrying amount.

Illustration 13 No Impairment Loss

Two machines in a production line (the cash generating unit) have suffered physical damage, but are still able to work albeit at reduced capacities. The fair value less costs of disposal of both machines are below their carrying amount. As the machines do not generate independent cash flows and management intends to keep the machines in operation, their value in use cannot be estimated. They are considered to be part of the cash generating unit, the production line.

5.2.1 Analysis

■ Assessment of the recoverable amount of the production line as a whole shows that there has been no impairment of the cash generating unit. Therefore, no impairment losses are recognised for the machines.

■ However, because of the damage to the machines, the estimated useful life and residual values of the machines may need to be reassessed.

■ If, because of the damage, management decides to replace the machines and sell them in the near future, their value in use can be estimated as the expected sale proceeds less costs of disposal. Where this is less than their carrying amount, an impairment loss should be recognised for the individual machines.

■ No impairment will be recognised for the production line because the machines have not been replaced.

6 Subsequent Review

6.1 Basic Provisions

▣ Once an entity has recognised an impairment loss for an asset other than goodwill, it should carry out a further review in later years if there is an indication:

  • that the asset may be further impaired;
  • that the impairment loss recognised in prior years may have decreased.

▣ An entity considers, as a minimum, the following indications of both external and internal sources of information.

6.1.1 External Sources of Information

▣ Observable indications that the asset's value has increased significantly during the period.

▣ Significant favourable changes during the period, or taking place in the near future, in the technological, market, economic or legal environment in which the entity operates or in the market to which the asset is dedicated.

▣ Decrease in market interest rates or other market rates of return likely to affect the discount rate used in calculating the asset's value in use and materially increase the asset's recoverable amount.

6.1.2 Internal Sources of Information

▣ Significant favourable changes in the actual or expected extent or manner of use of the asset.*

▣ Evidence available from internal reporting indicates that the economic performance of the asset is, or will be, better than expected.

Commentary

*For example, if capital expenditure incurred enhances the asset.

6.2 Reversals of Impairment Losses

6.2.1 On Individual Assets, Other Than Goodwill

▣ The carrying amount of an asset, other than goodwill, for which an impairment loss has been recognised in prior years is increased to its recoverable amount *only* if there has been a change in the estimates used to determine the asset's recoverable amount since the last impairment loss was recognised.*

▣ The increased carrying amount of the asset should not exceed the carrying amount which would have been determined (net of amortisation or depreciation) had no impairment loss been recognised for the asset in prior years.

▣ Any increase in the carrying amount of an asset above the carrying amount which would have been determined (net of amortisation or depreciation) had no impairment loss been recognised for the asset in prior years is a revaluation and should be treated accordingly.

Commentary

*If estimates of future cash flows remain the same, the passage of time will lead to an increase in the present value of future cash flows. This increase in present value **is not** a reversal of an impairment loss.

© DeVry/Becker Educational Development Corp. All rights reserved.

Illustration 14 Reverssal of an Impairment Loss

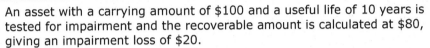

An asset with a carrying amount of $100 and a useful life of 10 years is tested for impairment and the recoverable amount is calculated at $80, giving an impairment loss of $20.

Two years later, the asset's value has recovered and the recoverable amount has been reassessed to $94. The carrying amount of the asset at this time would be $64 (80 − (80 × $\frac{2}{10}$)). The maximum value that the asset can be measured at, without revaluing the asset, would be $80 (100 − (100 × $\frac{2}{10}$)), giving a reversal of the impairment loss of $16.

- A reversal of an impairment loss for an asset is recognised in profit or loss immediately, unless the asset is carried at revalued amount under another IFRS.

- Any reversal of an impairment loss on a revalued asset is treated as a revaluation increase under the relevant IFRS, with the reversal being reflected in other comprehensive income.*

***Commentary**

*A reversal of an impairment loss on a revalued asset will usually be credited to the revaluation reserve unless it reverses an impairment which has been previously recognised as an expense in profit or loss. In this case, it is recognised in profit or loss to the extent previously recognised.

6.2.2 Reversal of an Impairment Loss for a Cash Generating Unit

Key Point

A reversal of an impairment loss for a cash generating unit should be allocated to increase the carrying amount of the assets *(but never to goodwill)* pro rata with the carrying amount of those assets.

- Increases in carrying amounts are treated as reversals of impairment losses for individual assets.

- In allocating a reversal of an impairment loss for a cash generating unit, the carrying amount of an asset is not increased above the *lower* of:*
  - its recoverable amount (if determinable); and
  - the carrying amount which would have been determined (net of amortisation or depreciation) had no impairment loss been recognised for the asset in prior years.

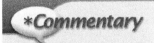

***Commentary**

*Equivalent to the "ceiling" for the reversal of an impairment loss for an individual asset.

© DeVry/Becker Educational Development Corp. All rights reserved.

6.2.3 Reversal of an Impairment Loss on Goodwill

▇ An impairment loss recognised for goodwill *cannot* be reversed in a subsequent period.

▇ IAS 38 prohibits the recognition of internally generated goodwill. Any increase in the recoverable amount of goodwill in the periods following the recognition of an impairment loss is likely to be an increase in internally generated goodwill, rather than a reversal of the impairment loss recognised for the acquired goodwill.

7 Disclosure

▇ Extensive disclosure is required by IAS 36, especially for the key assumptions and estimates used to measure the recoverable amount of cash generating units containing goodwill or intangible assets with indefinite useful lives.

▇ Impairment losses or any reversals recognised during the period and the line item(s) of the statement of total comprehensive income in which those impairment losses or reversals are included. The information is broken down by segment if the entity applies IFRS 8 *Operating Segments*.

▇ If any portion of the goodwill acquired in a business combination during the period has not been allocated to a cash generating unit at the reporting date, the amount of the unallocated goodwill disclosed and the reasons why that amount remains unallocated.

© DeVry/Becker Educational Development Corp. All rights reserved.

Summary

- Indications of impairment of an asset should be assessed at the end of each reporting period. If indications exist the recoverable amount of the asset should be estimated.

- The recoverable amount is the *higher* of fair value less costs of disposal and value in use.

- Value in use differs from fair value; value in use is more entity specific whereas fair value only reflects the assumptions of market participants.

- Projections should be based on reasonable and supportable assumptions representing management's best estimate of the economic conditions for the remaining useful life of the asset.

- The discount rate used in the value-in-use calculation is a pre-tax market rate that reflects the current time value of money and the *risks specific to the asset*.

- If the recoverable amount of a single asset cannot be calculated the recoverable amount of the cash generating unit to which the asset belongs must be determined.

- Goodwill acquired in a business combination must be allocated to cash generating units that are expected to benefit from the synergies of the combination.

- If the recoverable amount is less than the carrying amount, the carrying amount is reduced to its recoverable amount. The reduction is an impairment loss.

- The impairment loss of a CGU is allocated between all assets of the CGU; firstly to goodwill and then to other assets on a pro rata basis.

- Impairment of goodwill can *never* be reversed.

- A reversal of an impairment loss for a CGU is allocated to increase the carrying amount of the assets *(but never goodwill)* pro rata with the carrying amount of those assets.

Session 7 Quiz
Estimated time: 20 minutes

1. Define recoverable amount of an asset. (1.2)
2. List the types of intangible assets which should be tested annually for impairment. (2.2)
3. Specify the categories of "costs" which are included in costs of disposal for the purposes of calculating "fair value less costs of disposal." (3.2)
4. Specify which cash flows to include with the value-in-use calculations. (3.3.1)
5. Define cash generating unit. (4)
6. Explain how an impairment loss is allocated to assets in a cash generating unit. (5.2)
7. State when the impairment loss relating to goodwill may be reversed. (6.2.3)

Study Question Bank
Estimated time: 25 minutes

Priority		Estimated Time	Completed
Q13	Wilderness	25 minutes	

EXAMPLE SOLUTIONS

Solution 1—Cash Flows

Time	Narrative		Cash flow*	Comment
	Net revenue			
	Per unit	Volume		
1 (W1)	29.87	1,040	31,065	*Net revenue per unit inflates at 3%*
2	30.77	1,082	33,293	*per annum for 8 years.*
3	31.69	1,125	35,651	*Volume inflates at 4% per annum for*
4	32.64	1,170	38,189	*5 years. After this, IAS 36 prohibits the use of a growth rate which*
5	33.62	1,217	40,916	*exceeds the industry average. In the*
6	34.63	1,217	42,145	*absence of further information, zero*
7	35.67	1,217	43,410	*growth has been assumed.*
8	36.74	1,217	44,713	*Efficiency improvements from the future capital improvement are not included.*
	Other flows			
2	*Service* $(10{,}000 \times 1.03^2)$		10,609	*The capital improvement is not included in the estimate of future cash flows.*
8	*Disposal* $(10{,}000 \times 1.03^8)$		12,668	

Working

(1) In the first year

Net revenue per unit = $(100 - (70+1)) \times (1.03) = 29.87$
Volume = $1{,}000 \times 1.04 = 1{,}040$

*Commentary

*The finance cost of $15,000 is ignored. All cash flows have been inflated to money terms.

© DeVry/Becker Educational Development Corp. All rights reserved.

Solution 2—Impairment Loss, Part 1

	1 January	Impairment loss	1 February
Goodwill	300	(80)	220
Intangible asset	500	–	500
Lorries	2,000	(500)	1,500
	2,800	(580)	2,220

An impairment loss of 500 is recognised first for the lorry which crashed, because its recoverable amount can be assessed individually. (It no longer forms part of the cash generating unit which was formed by the four lorries and the licence.)

The remaining impairment loss (80) is attributed to goodwill.

Solution 3—Impairment Loss, Part 2

	1 February	Impairment loss	22 May	
Goodwill	220	(220)	–	
Intangible asset	500	(20)	480	Note 1
Lorries	1,500	(120)	1,380	Note 2
	2,220	(360)	1,860	

Note 1

220 is charged to the goodwill to reduce it to zero. The balance of 140 must be pro rated between the remaining assets in proportion to their carrying amount.

The ratio that the remaining assets bear to each other is 500:1,500. This implies that 25% × 140 = 35 should be allocated to the intangible asset. However, this would reduce its carrying amount to below its fair value less costs of disposal and this is not allowed. The maximum which may be allocated is 20 and the remaining 15 must be allocated to the lorries.

Note 2

The amount which is allocated to the lorries is 75% × 140 = 105 + 15 =120.

© DeVry/Becker Educational Development Corp. All rights reserved.

Financial Instruments

FOCUS

This session covers the following content from the *ACCA Study Guide.*

C. Reporting the Financial Performance of Entities

3. Financial instruments

a) Apply and discuss the recognition and derecognition of financial assets and financial liabilities. ☐

b) Apply and discuss the classification of financial assets and financial liabilities and their measurement. ☐

c) Apply and discuss the treatment of gains and losses arising on financial assets and financial liabilities. ☐

d) Apply and discuss the treatment of the expected loss impairment model. ☐

e) Account for derivative financial instruments and simple embedded derivatives. ☐

f) Outline the principles of hedge accounting and account for fair value hedges and cash flow hedges including hedge effectiveness. ☐

Session 8 Guidance

■ **Recognise** that this topic is very important both in terms of the exam and real life. You should be familiar with the subject from your F7 studies *but*, at this level, the questions are likely to be significantly more involved.

■ **Understand** the need for standards in this area (s.1) and **revise** the scope of each IFRS (s.2).

■ **Revise** the effective interest rate method (s.3.2), the accounting for convertible bonds (s.4.4) and the categories of financial assets (s.5.2). **Attempt** *Examples 2 and 3.*

■ **Understand** the impairment implications (s.6).

■ **Revise** the subsequent measurement rule for financial liabilities (s.7.2)

■ **Read** through hedging carefully (s.8). **Work** through *Illustrations 14 and 15.* **Attempt** *Example 4.*

■ **Read** the *student accountant* article "Impairment of financial assets".

VISUAL OVERVIEW

Objective: To explain the rules for measurement, recognition, presentation and disclosure of financial instruments.

BACKGROUND

- Traditional Accounting
- Financial Instruments
- History

APPLICATION AND SCOPE

- IAS 32 Presentation
- IFRS 7 Disclosure
- IFRS 9 Financial Instruments

TERMINOLOGY

- IAS 32 Definitions
- Executory Contracts
- IFRS 9 Definitions

PRESENTATION (IAS 32)

- Liabilities and Equity
- Own Equity Instruments
- Offset
- Compound Instruments
- Treasury Shares

FINANCIAL ASSETS (IFRS 9)

- Initial Measurement
- Subsequent Measurement
- Amortised Cost
- Gains and Losses
- Embedded Derivatives
- Reclassification
- Derecognition

FINANCIAL LIABILITIES (IFRS 9)

- Recognition
- Measurement
- Derecognition

HEDGING (IFRS 9)

- Hedging Instruments
- Hedged Items
- Hedge Accounting
- Fair Value Hedges
- Cash Flow Hedges
- Net Investment

DISCLOSURE (IFRS 7)

- Rules
- Assets and Liabilities
- Gains and Losses
- Other Disclosures
- Nature and Extent of Risks

IMPAIRMENT

- Terminology
- General Approach
- Credit Risk
- Trade Receivables

© DeVry/Becker Educational Development Corp. All rights reserved.

1 Background

1.1 Traditional Accounting

▨ Traditional accounting practices are based on serving the needs of manufacturing companies. Accounting for such entities is concerned with accruing costs to be matched with revenues. A key concept in such a process is revenue and cost recognition.

▨ The global market for financial instruments has expanded rapidly over the last 20 years, not only in the sheer volume of such instruments but also in their complexity. Entities have moved from using "traditional" instruments (e.g. cash, trade receivables, long-term debt and investments) to highly sophisticated risk management strategies based on derivatives and complex combinations of instruments.

▨ The traditional cost-based concepts are not adequate to deal with the recognition and measurement of financial assets and liabilities. Specifically:

  ● Traditional accounting bases recognition on the transfer of risks and rewards. It is not designed to deal with transactions that divide up the risks and rewards associated with a particular asset (or liability) and allocate them to different parties.

  ● Some financial instruments have no or little initial cost (e.g. options) and are not adequately accounted for (if at all) under traditional historical cost-based systems.

 **Key Point**

If a transaction has no cost it cannot be accounted for (there is no Dr and Cr). Further, the historical cost of financial assets and liabilities has little relevance to risk management activities.

1.2 Financial Instruments

 **Definition**

Financial instrument—any contract which gives rise to both a financial asset of one entity and a financial liability or equity instrument of another entity.

▨ **Financial instruments** include:

  ● *primary* instruments (e.g. receivables, payables and equity securities); and

  ● *derivative* instruments (e.g. financial options, futures and forwards, interest rate swaps and currency swaps).

© DeVry/Becker Educational Development Corp. All rights reserved.

1.3   History

- IAS 32 *Financial Instruments: Disclosure and Presentation* was first issued in 1995.

- IAS 39 *Financial Instruments: Recognition and Measurement* was first issued in 1998.

- Both standards have been revised and updated since they were first issued.

- IFRS 7 *Financial Instruments: Disclosure* was issued in 2005 to replace IAS 30 *Disclosures for Banks* and the disclosure requirements of IAS 32. IAS 32 now only deals with *presentation* issues.

- The subsequent revisions reflect the "learning process" of dealing with the complexities of financial instruments and new issues which have been raised since the standards were first issued.

- IFRS 9 *Financial Instruments* was issued in 2009. This standard deals with the recognition and measurement of financial *assets* and replaces those corresponding sections of IAS 39.

- IFRS 9 was revised in 2010 to include the recognition and measurement issues relating to financial *liabilities*.

- The IASB finalised the hedge accounting section in 2013 and issued the impairment section in 2014.

- IFRS 9 is now complete and effective from 1 January 2018.*

Exam Advice

IFRS 9 is the examinable document although IAS 39 is still being used in practice.

*Commentary

*Early adoption is permitted.

2   Application and Scope

2.1   IAS 32: Presentation

2.1.1   Application

- Classification of financial instruments between:
  - financial assets;
  - financial liabilities; and
  - equity instruments.
- Presentation and offset of financial instruments and the related interest, dividends, losses and gains.

2.1.2   Scope

IAS 32 should be applied in presenting information about all types of financial instruments, both recognised and unrecognised, *except for financial instruments that are dealt with by other standards.* For example:

- interests in subsidiaries, associates and joint ventures accounted for under IFRS 10 and IAS 28;

- contracts for contingent consideration in a business combination under IFRS 3 (only applies to the acquirer);

- employers' rights and obligations under employee benefit plans (IAS 19 applies);

- financial instruments, contracts and obligations under share-based payment transactions to which IFRS 2 applies.

© DeVry/Becker Educational Development Corp. All rights reserved.

2.2 IFRS 7 *Financial Instruments: Disclosure*

2.2.1 Application

▤ IFRS 7 applies to the disclosure of:

- factors affecting the amount, timing and certainty of cash flows;
- the use of financial instruments and the business purpose they serve; and
- the associated risks and management's policies for controlling those risks.

2.2.2 Scope

IFRS 7 should be applied in presenting and disclosing information about all types of financial instruments, both recognised and unrecognised, except for financial instruments that are dealt with by other standards.*

2.3 IFRS 9 *Financial Instruments*

▤ This standard applies to all financial instruments except those that are specifically scoped out by the standard.

▤ Specific exclusions include:

- Rights and obligations under leases to which IFRS 16 applies;
- Employer's rights and obligations under employee benefit plans to which IAS 19 applies;
- Interests in subsidiaries, associates and joint ventures which are accounted for under IFRS 3 and IAS 28 respectively;*
- Rights and obligations within the scope of IFRS 15 that are financial instruments.

*Commentary

*Essentially as for IAS 32.

*Commentary

*IFRSs 10, 11 and 12 are also relevant.

3 Terminology

3.1 From IAS 32

Financial asset: any asset that is:

▤ cash;

▤ a contractual right to receive cash or another financial asset from another entity;

▤ a contractual right to exchange financial instruments with another entity under conditions that are potentially favourable;

▤ an equity instrument of another entity; or

▤ certain contracts that will (or may) be settled in the entity's own equity instruments.

© DeVry/Becker Educational Development Corp. All rights reserved.

Financial liability: any liability that is a contractual obligation:

- to deliver cash or another **financial asset** to another entity;
- to exchange financial instruments with another entity under conditions that are potentially unfavourable; or
  - certain contracts that will (or may) be settled in the entity's own equity instruments.*

*Commentary

*Physical assets (e.g. prepayments), liabilities that are not contractual in nature (e.g. taxes), operating leases and contractual rights and obligations relating to non-financial assets that are not settled in the same manner as a financial instrument) are not financial instruments.

Preferred shares that provide for mandatory redemption by the issuer, or that give the holder the right to redeem the share, meet the definition of liabilities and are classified as such even though, legally, they may be equity.

Equity instrument: any contract that evidences a residual interest in the assets of an entity after deducting all of its liabilities.

Fair value: the price that would be received to sell an asset or paid to transfer a liability in an orderly transaction between market participants at the measurement date.

3.2 Executory Contracts

- Contracts to buy and sell a non-financial item that can be settled net in cash are not financial instruments if the contract satisfies normal sale and purchase requirements of the two parties. They are executory contracts.
- Some executory contracts may be settled net in cash. That is, the value of the item given up is matched against the value of the item to be received and the holder of the net asset position receives the net cash figure.*

Illustration 1   Executory Contract

BA agrees to exchange 1 million litres of fuel oil for 750,000 litres of diesel with DT in three months' time. The value of the initial contract is nil as 1 million litres of fuel oil has the same value as 750,000 litres of diesel. BA intends to settle the contract net in three months. This is an executory contract. As the price of fuel oil fluctuates against the price of diesel, BA will recognise either a net asset or net liability position.

BA has also entered into a forward contract to buy 500,000 litres of diesel at a specified price on a specified date. BA will not take delivery of the diesel. This contract **will** give rise to a financial instrument and BA must recognise, as a financial liability, the obligation to deliver cash on the commitment date.

Definition

Executory contract— a contract in which the terms are set to be fulfilled at a later date. Both sides must fulfil their obligation before a contract is fully executed.

*Commentary

*Accounting for a net position is being considered as part of the IASB's *Conceptual Framework* project.

© DeVry/Becker Educational Development Corp. All rights reserved.

3.3   From IFRS 9

Derivative: a financial instrument:

▪ whose value changes in response to the change in a specified interest rate, financial instrument price, commodity price, foreign exchange rate, index of prices or rates, credit rating or credit index, or other variable (sometimes called the "underlying");

▪ which requires little or no initial net investment relative to other types of contracts that would be expected to have a similar response to changes in market conditions; and

▪ that is settled at a future date.

Amortised cost of a financial asset or financial liability:

▪ the amount at which it was measured at initial recognition;
  minus

▪ principal repayments;
  plus or minus

▪ the cumulative amortisation of any difference between that initial amount and the maturity amount; and

▪ for financial assets, adjusted for any loss allowance.

Effective interest method: a method of calculating the amortised cost of a financial asset or a financial liability, using the *effective interest rate* and of allocating the interest.

Effective interest rate: the rate that exactly discounts estimated future cash payments or receipts through the expected life of the financial instrument to the gross carrying amount of a financial asset (or amortised cost of a financial liability). The computation includes all cash flows (e.g. fees, transaction costs, premiums or discounts) between the parties to the contract.

The effective interest rate is sometimes termed the "level yield-to-maturity" (or to the next re-pricing date) and is the internal rate of return of the financial asset (or liability) for that period.

Illustration 2   Effective Interest Rate

A company issues a $100,000 zero coupon bond redeemable in five years at $150,000.

The internal rate of return (the yield) on these flows is 8.45%. This should be used to allocate the expense.

Period	Opening balance	Interest @ 8.45%	Closing balance
1	100,000	8,450	108,450
2	108,450	9,164	117,614
3	117,614	9,938	127,552
4	127,552	10,778	138,330
5	138,330	11,689	150,019

This should be 150,000. The difference of 19 is due to rounding

---

Transaction costs: incremental costs that are directly attributable to the acquisition, issue or disposal of a financial asset (or financial liability).*

***Commentary**

*An incremental cost is one that would not have been incurred if the entity had not acquired, issued or disposed of the financial instrument. Examples include fees and commissions paid to agents.

© DeVry/Becker Educational Development Corp. All rights reserved.

4　Presentation (IAS 32)

4.1　Liabilities and Equity

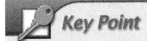

Key Point

On issue, financial instruments should be classified as liabilities or equity in accordance with the substance of the contractual arrangement on initial recognition.

▨ Some financial instruments may take the legal form of equity, but are in substance liabilities.

An equity instrument is any contract which evidences a residual interest in the assets of an entity after deducting all of its liabilities.

Illustration 3　Preference Shares

Redeemable preference shares are not classified as equity under IAS 32, as there is a contractual obligation to transfer financial assets (e.g. cash) to the holder of the shares. They are therefore a financial liability.

If such shares are redeemable at the option of the issuer, they would not meet the definition of a financial liability as there is no present obligation to transfer a financial asset to the holder of the shares. When the issuer becomes obliged to redeem the shares, the shares become a financial liability and will then be transferred out of equity.

For *non-redeemable* preference shares, the substance of the contract would need to be studied. For example, if distributions to the holders of the instrument are at the discretion of the issuer, the shares are equity instruments.

4.2　Settlement in Own Equity Instruments

▨ A contract is not an equity instrument solely because it may result in the receipt or delivery of the entity's own equity instruments.

▨ A *financial liability* will arise when:

● there is a contractual obligation to deliver cash or another financial asset, to exchange financial assets or financial liabilities, under conditions that are potentially unfavourable to the issuer;

● there is a non-derivative contract to deliver, or the requirement to deliver, a variable number of the entity's own equity instruments;

● there is a **derivative** that will or may be settled *other* than by issuing a fixed number of the entity's own equity instruments.

▨ An *equity instrument* will arise when:

● there is a non-derivative contract to deliver, or the requirement to deliver, a *fixed* number of the entity's own equity instruments;

● there is a derivative that will or may be settled by issuing a *fixed* number of the entity's own equity instruments.

© DeVry/Becker Educational Development Corp. All rights reserved.

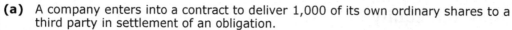

Illustration 4 Settlement in Own Equity Instruments

(a) A company enters into a contract to deliver 1,000 of its own ordinary shares to a third party in settlement of an obligation.

As the number of shares is *fixed* in the contract to meet the obligation, it is an equity instrument. There is no obligation to transfer cash, another financial asset or an equivalent value.

(b) The same company enters into another contract that requires it to settle a contractual obligation using its own shares in an amount that equals the contractual obligation.

In this case, the number of shares to be issued will *vary* depending on, for example, the market price of the shares at the date of the contract or settlement. If the contract was agreed at a different date, a different number of shares may be issued. Although cash will not be paid, the equivalent value in shares will be transferred. The contract is a financial liability.

(c) Company G has an option contract to buy gold. If exercised, it will be settled, on a net basis, in the company's shares based on the share price at the date of settlement.

As the company will deliver as many shares (i.e. variable) as are equal to the value of the option contract, the contract is a financial asset or a financial liability.

This will be so even if the amount to be paid was fixed or based on the value of the gold at the date of exercising the option.

In both cases, the number of shares issued would be variable.

4.3 Offset

Key Point

Financial assets and liabilities must be offset where the entity:

- has a legal right of offset; and*
- intends to settle on a net basis or to realise the asset and settle the liability simultaneously.

*Commentary

*An offset might be of trade receivables and payables, or of accounts in debit and credit at a bank.

4.4 Compound Instruments

4.4.1 Presentation

Illustration 5 Convertible Bonds, a Compound Instrument

Convertible bonds are primary financial liabilities of the issuer which grant an option to the holder to convert them into equity instruments in the future. Such bonds consist of:

- the obligation to repay the bonds, which is presented as a liability; and
- the option to convert, which is presented in equity.

The economic effect of issuing such an instrument is substantially the same as issuing simultaneously a debt instrument with an early settlement provision and warrants to purchase ordinary shares.

4.4.2 Carrying Amounts

▨ The equity component is the residual amount after deduction of the more easily measurable debt component from the value of the instrument as a whole.

▨ The liability is measured by discounting the stream of future payments at the prevailing market rate for a similar liability without the associated equity component.

© DeVry/Becker Educational Development Corp. All rights reserved.

Key Point

Financial instruments which contain both a liability and an equity element are classified into separate component parts.

Example 1 Convertible Bond

An entity issues 2,000 convertible, $1,000 bonds at par on 1 January 2016.

Interest is payable annually in arrears at a nominal interest rate of 6%.

The prevailing market rate of interest at the date of issue of the bond was 9%.

The bond is redeemable 31 December 2018.

Required:

Calculate the values at which the bond will be included in the financial statements of the entity at initial recognition.

4.5 Treasury Shares

Key Point

The entity's own equity instruments acquired by the entity itself ("treasury shares") are deducted from equity.

- No gain or loss is recognised in profit or loss on the purchase, sale, issue or cancellation of treasury shares.*
- Treasury shares may be acquired and held by the entity or by other members of the consolidated group.*

*Any difference between what was paid for treasury shares and the value placed on them if they are reissued is taken directly to equity.

*Commentary

*Treasury shares are often acquired by an entity so they can be reissued to holders of share options, when the holders exercise their options.

- Consideration paid or received is recognised directly in equity.
- The amount of treasury shares held is disclosed separately either in the statement of financial position or in the notes, in accordance with IAS 1.
- If treasury shares are acquired from related parties, IAS 24 disclosure requirements apply.

5 Financial Assets

5.1 Initial Measurement

▩ On initial recognition, financial assets (except trade receivables) are measured at **fair value**. If the financial asset is not classified as fair value through profit or loss, any directly attributable transaction costs are adjusted against the fair value.

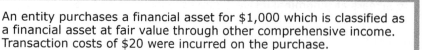

Illustration 6 Transaction Costs

An entity purchases a financial asset for $1,000 which is classified as a financial asset at fair value through other comprehensive income. Transaction costs of $20 were incurred on the purchase.

The asset is initially measured at $1,020.

If the asset had been classified as fair value through profit or loss it would be measured at $1,000 and the $20 would be expensed to profit or loss immediately.

▩ Trade receivables, which do not have a major financing element, are measured at their transaction price in accordance with IFRS 15.*

*Commentary

*That is, "the amount of consideration expected in exchange for the transfer of promised goods or services to a customer".

5.2 Subsequent Measurement

▩ Once recognised, a financial asset is subsequently measured at either:

- amortised cost;
- fair value through other comprehensive income; or
- fair value through profit or loss.

▩ Classification requires consideration of:

- the entity's **business model**. This refers to how the entity manages its financial assets to generate cash flows. (Does it intend to collect contractual cash flows (i.e. interest and principal repayments), sell financial assets or both?); and
- the contractual cash flow characteristics of the financial asset.

5.2.1 Amortised Cost

▩ A financial asset is subsequently measured at **amortised cost** if it meets two conditions:*

1. It is held within a business model whose objective is achieved through holding financial assets to collect contractual cash flows; and

2. Its contractual terms give rise to cash flows on specified dates which are solely payments of principal and interest (on the outstanding principal).

*Commentary

*These conditions capture simple debt instruments that are intended to be held for the long term, maybe until maturity.

© DeVry/Becker Educational Development Corp. All rights reserved.

Illustration 7   Amortised Cost

An entity purchased a debt instrument for $1,000. The instrument pays interest of $60 annually and had 10 years to maturity when purchased. The business model test was met and the instrument was classified as a financial asset at amortised cost.

Nine years have passed and the entity is suffering a liquidity crisis and needs to sell the asset to raise funds.

The sale was not expected on initial classification and does not affect the classification (i.e. there is no retrospective reclassification).

5.2.2   Fair Value Through Other Comprehensive Income

- A financial asset is subsequently measured at fair value through other comprehensive income if it meets two conditions:*

  1. It is held within a business model whose objective is achieved through collect contractual cash flows **and sell** financial assets; and

  2. Its contractual terms give rise to cash flows on specified dates, which are solely payments of principal and interest.

> *Commentary*
>
> *There is no commitment to keep the asset until maturity. Cash may be realised by selling the asset at any time. This category also captures debt instruments, but without intention to hold until maturity.

Illustration 8   Business Model

An entity anticipates the purchase of a large property in eight years' time. The entity invests cash surpluses in short- and long-term financial assets. Many of the financial assets purchased have a maturity in excess of eight years.

The entity holds the financial assets for their contractual cash flows but will sell them and reinvest the cash for a higher return as and when an opportunity arises.

The objective of the business model is achieved by collecting contractual cash flows and selling the financial assets. The entity's decisions to hold or sell aim to maximise returns from the portfolio of financial assets.

- The asset is measured at fair value in the statement of financial position, and interest income, based on the amortised cost of the asset, is recognised in the statement of profit or loss. Any difference, after allowing for impairment (see s.5), is recognised in other comprehensive income.

Illustration 9   Expected Credit Losses

An entity purchases a debt instrument for $2,000. The entity's business model is to hold financial assets for contractual cash flows and sell them when conditions are favourable. The asset has a coupon rate of 5%, which is also the effective interest rate.

At the end of the first year the fair value of the asset has fallen to $1,920; part of the fall in value is due to 12-month expected credit losses on the asset of $60.

Of the fall in value $60 will be expensed to profit or loss as an impairment loss and $20 will be debited to other comprehensive income.

© DeVry/Becker Educational Development Corp. All rights reserved.

5.2.3 Fair Value Through Profit or Loss

◾ All other financial assets are measured at fair value through profit or loss, with one possible exception:

On **initial recognition** an entity may **elect** to designate an **equity instrument** in **another entity** at fair value through other comprehensive income.

◾ Also, an entity can opt to designate **any** financial asset at fair value through profit or loss in order to eliminate an accounting mismatch (i.e. where a linked financial liability is measured at fair value through profit or loss).*

5.2.4 Classification and Measurement Summary

The diagram below summarises the application of the classification and measurement model for financial assets as described above:

Key Point

This election is irrevocable.

***Commentary**

*This so-called fair value option is also irrevocable.

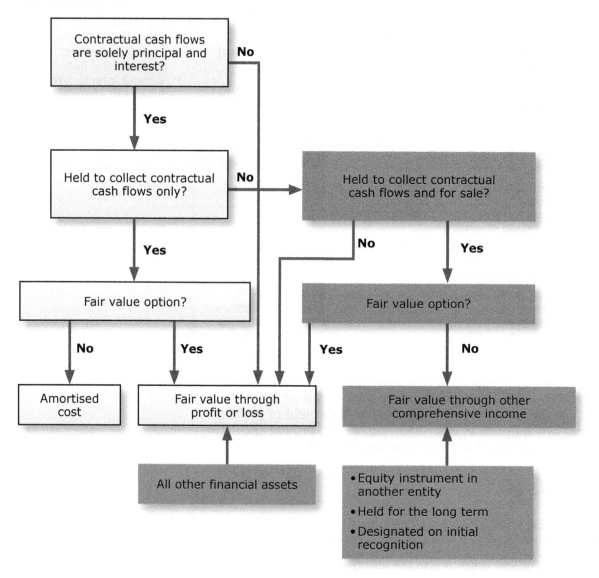

© DeVry/Becker Educational Development Corp. All rights reserved.

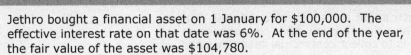

Example 2 Financial Asset Investments

Jethro bought a financial asset on 1 January for $100,000. The effective interest rate on that date was 6%. At the end of the year, the fair value of the asset was $104,780.

Required:

Explain how the financial asset should be classified under each of the following business models:

(a) Held to collect contractual cash flows, which are solely payments of principal and interest on the principal amount;

(b) Held to collect contractual cash flows and those from the sale of assets when circumstances are advantageous.

5.3 Amortised Cost

▓ Measuring a financial asset at amortised cost means that interest revenue will be calculated using the effective interest method:

- The credit to profit or loss is based on the effective interest rate.
- The cash flow is based on the instrument's coupon (nominal) rate of interest.*

▓ Any difference between the interest credited to profit or loss and the cash received is added to the value of the financial asset.

*For many instruments the two rates may be the same.

5.4 Gains and Losses

▓ Interest income is recognised in **profit or loss** using the instrument's effective interest rate.

▓ Dividend income is recognised in **profit or loss** when the entity's right to the dividend has been established.

▓ Gains and losses on financial assets measured at **amortised cost** are recognised in **profit or loss**.

▓ Generally, gains and losses on financial assets that are measured at **fair value** are recognised in **profit or loss** with the following **exceptions:**

- If it is part of a **hedging relationship**.
- If it is an **equity** investment measured at fair value through other comprehensive income.*
- If it is a **debt** instrument measured at fair value through other comprehensive income some fair value changes will be recognised in other comprehensive income:
  - impairment gains and losses and foreign exchange gains and losses are recognised in profit or loss; **but**
  - changes due to the movement in fair value of the instrument are recognised in other comprehensive income.*

*Cumulative gains and losses in other comprehensive income are **not reclassified** on derecognition (but can be transferred to retained earnings).

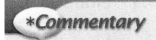

*These fair value changes are reclassified through profit or loss on derecognition.

Illustration 10 Accounting for Gains and Losses

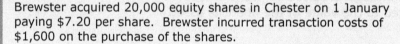

An entity purchased a debt instrument at its fair value, $1,000. The entity classified the asset at fair value through other comprehensive income as its business model is to collect contractual cash flows and sell financial assets.

The instrument had five years to maturity and a contractual par value of $1,250. It pays fixed interest of 4.7% and its effective interest rate is 10%.

At the end of the first year the fair value of the instrument is $1,020. The entity has calculated the impairment loss on the asset to be $8.

Dr Cash – interest received ($1,250 x 4.7%)	$ 59
Dr Financial asset (increase in fair value)	$ 20
Dr Profit or loss – impairment (as given)	$ 8
Dr Other comprehensive income (fair value change)	$ 13
Cr Profit or loss – interest income ($1,000 x 10%)	$ 100

The change in fair value recognised in other comprehensive income (in this case a balancing loss of $13) will be reclassified through profit or loss on derecognition.

Example 3 Equity Investments

Brewster acquired 20,000 equity shares in Chester on 1 January paying $7.20 per share. Brewster incurred transaction costs of $1,600 on the purchase of the shares.

In November, Chester paid a dividend of $0.04 per share.

On 31 December, the share price of Chester had risen to $7.47.

Required:

Explain how the investment in Chester should be accounted if:

(a) Brewster intends to hold the shares for a maximum of two years.

(b) Brewster has stated that it wants to recognise the investment at fair value through other comprehensive income.

5.5 Embedded Derivatives

Key Point

An embedded derivative is a component of a combined instrument which includes a non-derivative host contract.

- The effect will be that some of the cash flows of the combined instrument will vary in a manner that is similar to that of a stand-alone derivative.

- A derivative that is attached to a financial instrument but can be transferred separately from that instrument (e.g. a warrant) *is not* an embedded derivative, but a separate financial instrument.

© DeVry/Becker Educational Development Corp. All rights reserved.

- If the instrument contains a host contract that falls within the scope of IFRS 9 then the entire contract will be accounted for in accordance with IFRS 9; it is not separated.*

- If the host contract is not a financial instrument under IFRS 9 then the embedded derivative will have to be separated, and accounted for as a separate derivative, if:

  - the economic characteristics and risks of the derivative are not closely related to the host;

  - a separate instrument with the same terms as the embedded derivative would meet the definition of a derivative; and

  - the hybrid contract is not measured at fair value with changes recognised in profit or loss.

> ***Commentary**
>
> *A purchased convertible instrument would be an embedded derivative that is not separated because the host instrument (the debt asset) falls within the scope of IFRS 9.

Illustration 11   Embedded Derivative

A company with $ as its functional currency buys raw materials for use in production from a UK company that has £ as its functional currency. The transaction is denominated in €, not the functional currency of either party to the transaction, and so an embedded derivative has been included in the purchase contract.

There are now two elements to the contract:

(1) Contract to buy/sell goods; and
(2) Movement on the $/€ and £/€ exchange rates.

5.6   Reclassification

- If an entity changes its business model for managing financial assets it must reclassify all affected financial assets **prospectively,** from the date of the change.

- Amounts previously recognised based on the financial assets original classification are **not restated**.

5.7   Derecognition

5.7.1   Basic Derecognition Criteria

- An entity derecognises a financial asset (or a part of it) when, and only when:

  - the contractual rights to the cash flows from the financial asset expire; or

  - it transfers the financial asset and the transfer qualifies for derecognition.

- In many cases, derecognition of a financial asset is straightforward—if there are no longer any contractual rights, the asset is derecognised. If contractual rights remain, the standard requires three further steps to be considered (i.e. transfer, risks and rewards, control).

© DeVry/Becker Educational Development Corp. All rights reserved.

5.7.2   Transfer of a Financial Asset

■ An entity transfers a financial asset if, and only if, it *either*:
- gives the contractual rights to receive the cash flows to a third party; *or*
- retains the contractual rights to receive the cash flows, but assumes a contractual obligation to pay the cash to a third party.

5.7.3   Transfer of Risks and Rewards of Ownership

■ When the entity establishes that a transfer has taken place, it must then consider risks and rewards of ownership.

■ If substantially all the risks and rewards of ownership of the financial asset have been transferred, the financial asset is derecognised.

■ However, if the entity neither transfers nor retains substantially all the risks and rewards of ownership, the entity determines whether it has retained control.

5.7.4   Control

■ If control has not been retained, the financial asset is derecognised.

■ If the third party is able to use the asset as if it owned it (e.g. sell the asset without attaching conditions such as a repurchase option), the entity has not retained control.

■ In all other cases, the entity has retained control.

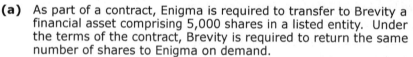

Illustration 12 Control

(a) As part of a contract, Enigma is required to transfer to Brevity a financial asset comprising 5,000 shares in a listed entity. Under the terms of the contract, Brevity is required to return the same number of shares to Enigma on demand.

As the shares are listed and are therefore freely traded in an active market, Brevity can sell the shares when received and repurchase 5,000 shares when required to return them to Enigma.

Enigma should derecognise the shares when transferred to Brevity as it has lost control.

(b) The same situation, except that the "shares" transferred are rare collector's items of shares issued by a Russian railroad entity in the late 1800s.

In this situation, the shares are not freely available on an active market and, if sold, could not be repurchased (without attaching a repurchase option). Control has not been passed and the financial asset would not be derecognised.

■ Where a financial asset is transferred to another entity but control has not been lost, the transferor accounts for the transaction as a collateralised borrowing.

If control passes, the asset may be treated as sold.

    Dr   Cash

        Cr   Disposals

If control does not pass, then the asset has not been sold but rather it has been used as collateral (security) for borrowing.

    Dr   Cash

        Cr   Loan

© DeVry/Becker Educational Development Corp. All rights reserved.

5.7.5   Profit or Loss on Derecognition

▦ On derecognition, the gain or loss included in profit or loss for the period is the difference between:

  ● the carrying amount of an asset (or portion of an asset) transferred to another party; and

  ● the consideration received, adjusted for any new asset received or new liability assumed.

6   Impairment

6.1   Terminology

▦ **Past due:** a financial asset is past due when the debtor has failed to make a payment that was contractually due.

▦ **Impairment gain or loss:** gains or losses recognised in profit or loss that arise from the impairment requirements of IFRS 9.

▦ **Credit loss:** the present value of the difference between all contractual cash flows due to be received and those expected to be received (i.e. all cash shortfalls).*

▦ **Lifetime expected credit losses:** losses that result from all possible default events over the expected life of a financial instrument.

▦ **Loss allowance:** the allowance for expected credit losses on:

  ● financial assets measured at amortised cost or fair value through other comprehensive income;

  ● lease receivables;

  ● contract assets (under IFRS 15), loan commitments and financial guarantee contracts.

Commentary

*Discounted at the original effective interest rate.

6.2   General Approach

▦ Financial assets measured at amortised cost and financial assets measured at fair value through other comprehensive income according to the entity's business model are subject to impairment testing.

▦ A loss allowance for any expected credit losses must be recognised in **profit or loss**.

▦ The loss allowance is measured at each reporting date. The amount depends on whether or not the instrument's credit risk has *increased significantly* since initial recognition:

  ● If significant, the loss allowance is the amount of the lifetime expected credit losses.

  ● If not significant, the loss allowance is 12-month expected credit losses.*

Commentary

*A credit loss can arise even if all cash flows due are expected to be received in full; if receipts are expected to be late the expected present value will fall.

▦ Practical methods may be used to measure expected credit losses as long as they are consistent with the principles prescribed by the standard (e.g. see trade receivables in s.6.4).

© DeVry/Becker Educational Development Corp. All rights reserved.

6.3   Credit Risk

■ The credit risk associated with a financial asset must be assessed at each reporting date:*

- If it has increased significantly the loss is measured based on the lifetime of the asset.
- If it has not increased significantly the loss is measured based on the 12-month expected credit losses.

■ The probability of a significant increase in credit risk will be higher for assets with a low credit risk on initial recognition than for those with a high credit risk on initial recognition.

■ Factors that could significantly increase credit risk include:

- An actual or forecast deterioration in the economic environment which is expected to have a negative effect on the debtor's ability to generate cash flows.
- The debtor is close to breaching covenants which may require restructuring of the loan.
- A decrease in the trading price of the debtor's bonds and/ or significant increases in credit risk on other bonds of the same debtor.
- The fair value of an asset has been below its amortised cost for some time.
- A reassessment of the entity's own internal risk grading of loans given.
- An actual or expected decline in the debtor's operating results.

■ There is a rebuttable presumption that any asset that is more than 30 days past due is an indicator that lifetime expected credit losses should be recognised.*

*Comparison is with the risk of default assessed on initial recognition.

*This presumption can only rebutted if reasonable and supportable information demonstrates that the credit risk is not significantly increased.

6.4   Trade Receivables

■ The standard allows a simplified impairment approach to an entity's trade receivables. The simplification allows the entity to measure the loss allowance as an amount equal to lifetime expected credit losses for trade receivables or contract assets resulting from transactions under IFRS 15 *Revenue from Contracts with Customers.**

Commentary

*There is a proviso that the contract does not contain a significant financing element, or if it does the entity has elected an accounting policy that measures the loss allowance at an amount equal to lifetime expected credit losses.

■ A **provision matrix** is a practical method of calculating expected credit losses on trade receivables. This is based on percentages (using appropriately adjusted historical experience) of the number of days past due. (For example, 1% if not past due, 2% if less than 30 days past due, 5% if more than 30 but less than 90, etc.)

© DeVry/Becker Educational Development Corp. All rights reserved.

Illustration 13 Provision Matrix

An entity has receivables of $1 million analysed as follows:

	Balance outstanding	Default risk	Expected credit loss
	$	%	$
Current	326,000	0.25	815
1–30 days past due	427,000	1.3	5,551
31–60 days past due	198,000	2.4	4,752
More than 60 days past due	49,000	10.5	5,145
Loss allowance			16,263

7 Financial Liabilities (IFRS 9)

7.1 Initial Recognition

■ A financial liability is recognised only when an entity becomes a party to the contractual provisions of the instrument.

7.2 Measurement

7.2.1 Initial Measurement

■ If the liability is classified at fair value through profit or loss, any relevant transaction costs will be charged immediately to profit or loss.

7.2.2 Subsequent Measurement

Key Point

The liability will initially be recognised at fair value less any directly attributable transaction costs.

Key Point

Most financial liabilities will subsequently be measured at amortised cost using the **effective interest method**, with the interest expense being charged to profit or loss.

■ The groups of financial liabilities which are not measured at amortised cost will include:

• Those at fair value through profit or loss (to include derivatives) which are measured at fair value.

• Commitment to provide a loan at below-market interest rate—these liabilities will be measured at the higher of the amount determined under IAS 37 or the initial amount recognised less any cumulative amortisation.

© DeVry/Becker Educational Development Corp. All rights reserved.

7.3 Derecognition

- An entity removes a financial liability from the statement of financial position when, and only when, it is extinguished—that is, when the obligation specified in the contract is discharged, cancelled or expires.

- This condition is met when either:
  - the debtor discharges the liability by paying the creditor, normally with cash, other financial assets, goods or services; or
  - the debtor is legally released from primary responsibility for the liability (or part thereof) either by process of law or by the creditor.*

- If the liability is renegotiated with the original lender at substantially different contractual terms, then the original liability will be derecognised and a new liability will be recognised.

- The difference between:
  - the carrying amount of a liability (or portion) extinguished or transferred to another party (including related unamortised costs); and
  - the amount paid for it, including any non-cash assets transferred or liabilities assumed, is included in profit or loss for the period.

Commentary

*The fact that the debtor may have given a guarantee does not necessarily mean that the condition of legal release is not met.

8 Hedging

Definition

Hedging—for accounting purposes, means designating one or more hedging instruments so that their change in fair value is an offset, in whole or in part, to the change in fair value or cash flows of a hedged item.

A hedged item—an asset, liability, firm commitment or highly probable forecast transaction which:
- exposes the entity to the risk of changes in fair value or changes in future cash flows; and
- is designated as being hedged.

A hedging instrument—a designated derivative (or, in limited circumstances, another financial asset or liability) whose fair value or cash flows are expected to offset changes in the fair value or cash flows of a designated hedged item.

Hedge effectiveness—the degree to which changes in the fair value or cash flows of the hedged item which are attributable to a hedged risk are offset by changes in the fair value or cash flows of the hedging instrument.

Hedge ratio—the quantity of the hedging instrument and the quantity of the hedged item in terms of their relative weighting.

© DeVry/Becker Educational Development Corp. All rights reserved.

8.1   Objective of Hedge Accounting

- Most entities are exposed to risks that could affect profit or loss or other comprehensive income. Hedging is just one of the strategies that management may adopt to reduce exposure to risk.
- IFRS 9 allows an entity to account for an economic hedge using hedge accounting; this will eliminate some of the volatility in the movement in value of the hedged item or hedging instrument that would otherwise be reflected in profit or loss.

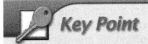
Key Point

Hedge accounting is **voluntary**. If hedge accounting is **not** used hedged items and hedging instruments are accounted for in the same manner as other financial asset and liabilities.

8.2   Hedging Instruments

- All derivatives (except written options, because the writer has accepted risk rather than reducing risk) may be designated as a hedging instrument.*

*Commentary

*To "write" is to sell an option. The investor who sells the option is called the writer.

- Non-derivative financial instruments (e.g. foreign currency loans) may be designated as a hedging instrument.

8.3   Hedged Items

- A hedged item can be:
  - a recognised asset or liability;
  - an unrecognised firm commitment; or
  - a highly probable forecast transaction.
- The hedged item can be:*
  - a single asset, liability, firm commitment or forecast transaction; or
  - a group of assets, liabilities, firm commitments or forecast transactions with similar risk characteristics.

*Commentary

*For hedge accounting purposes, only instruments involving a party *external* to the reporting entity can be designated as hedging instruments. Hedge accounting is not applied to transactions between entities or segments in the same group, neither in the consolidated nor separate financial statements.

© DeVry/Becker Educational Development Corp. All rights reserved.

8.4 Hedge Accounting

8.4.1 Hedging Relationships

There are three types of hedging relationships:

1. **Fair value hedge**: a hedge of the exposure to changes in the fair value of a recognised asset (or liability or an identified portion of such an asset or liability) which:
    - is attributable to a particular risk; and
    - will affect reported profit or loss.

2. **Cash flow hedge:** a hedge of the exposure to variability in cash flows which:
    - is attributable to a particular risk associated with a recognised asset or liability (e.g. all or some future interest payments on variable rate debt) or a highly probable forecast transaction (e.g. an anticipated purchase or sale); and
    - will affect reported profit or loss.

3. **Hedge of a net investment in a foreign operation** as defined in IAS 21.*

8.4.2 Hedge Accounting Criteria

A hedge relationship qualifies for hedge accounting if **all** the following criteria are met:

- The relationship consists **only** of eligible hedging instrument and hedged items.

- At inception, there is a **formal designation** of the relationship and of the entity's risk management objective.

- The relationship meets all the hedge effectiveness requirements:
    - there is an economic relationship between the hedged item and hedging instrument;
    - the effect of credit risk does not dominate the value changes that result from the economic relationship; and
    - the hedge ratio of the relationship is the same as the hedge ratio of the *actual* quantity of the hedging instrument used to the *actual* quantity of the hedged item.

Key Point

Hedge accounting recognises the *offsetting effects* on profit or loss of changes in the fair values of the hedging instrument and the related item being hedged. The hedge accounting rules do **not** relate to the offset of any asset and liability.

*Commentary

*The hedge of a net investment in a foreign operation is accounted for in a similar manner to that of a cash flow hedge.

© DeVry/Becker Educational Development Corp. All rights reserved.

8.5   Fair Value Hedges

▧ The gain or loss on the hedged item attributable to the hedged risk adjusts the carrying amount of the hedged item and is recognised immediately in profit or loss.

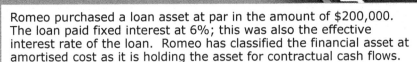

Illustration 14   Fair Value Hedge

Romeo purchased a loan asset at par in the amount of $200,000. The loan paid fixed interest at 6%; this was also the effective interest rate of the loan. Romeo has classified the financial asset at amortised cost as it is holding the asset for contractual cash flows.

Romeo was concerned that interest rates were about to rise and cause the fair value of the loan to fall (as new loan issues would be more attractive as they would pay a higher rate of interest).

Romeo decided to hedge its exposure to the risk of an increase in interest rates by entering into a fixed for variable interest rate swap with a counterparty, a financial institution, designating the loan asset as the hedged item and the swap contract as the hedging instrument. When interest rates rose to 6.5%, Romeo received interest from the issuer of the loan of $12,000 ($200,000 × 6%) and $1,000 ($200,000 × 0.5%) from the counterparty.

Romeo calculated that the hedge was perfectly effective, leading to the recognition of a derivative asset in respect of the swap contract of $2,500 and the fair value of the loan asset falling to $197,500.

Analysis

If **hedge accounting is not** used then the swap contract will be recognised as a derivative asset at a value of $2,500 and the loan asset will still be measured at amortised cost of $200,000.

The accounting entries, if hedge accounting **is not** used, would be:

Dr	Derivative asset	2,500	
	Cr Profit or loss		2,500

The gain on the swap contract is recognised immediately in profit or loss but no loss would be recognised on the value of the loan asset, causing a mismatch.

If **hedge accounting is** used then the swap contract will still be recognised as a derivative asset of $2,500 but the loan asset will now be measured at fair value of $197,500, matching the gain and loss in profit or loss in the same period.

The accounting entries, if hedge accounting *is* used, would be:

Dr	Derivative asset	2,500	
	Cr Profit or loss		2,500
Dr	Profit or loss	2,500	
	Cr Loan asset		2,500

This time both the gain and the loss affect profit or loss in the same period; hedge accounting has facilitated matching the upside with the downside.

▧ If the hedged item is **required** to be measured at fair value through other comprehensive income, any gain or loss on the hedged item will be recognised in profit or loss.

▧ If the hedged item is an equity instrument that is **voluntarily** classified at fair value through other comprehensive income, the gain or loss on the item will be recognised in **other comprehensive income**.

8.6 Cash Flow Hedges

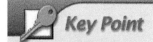 **Key Point**

The portion of the gain or loss on the hedging instrument which is determined to be an effective hedge is recognised in other comprehensive income.

- Any ineffective portion should be reported immediately in profit or loss if the hedging instrument is a derivative.

- If the hedge transaction results in the recognition of a financial asset or liability, the amount previously recognised in other comprehensive income will be reclassified to profit or loss to match the interest income or expense from the financial asset or liability.

- If the hedge transaction results in the recognition of a non-financial asset or liability the hedge reserve will be included in the initial cost of that asset or liability.*

*Commentary

*This treatment used to be called "the basis adjustment".

Illustration 15 Cash Flow Hedge

Romeo has items of inventory whose selling price is based on the fair value of its commodity content. Management is concerned that the fair value of the commodity will fall and so reduce the cash flow on the sale of the inventory. It enters into a forward contract to sell the inventory at a fixed price in the future. The forecast sale of inventory is the designated hedge item and the forward contract is designated as the hedging instrument. The hedge is effective and qualifies as a cash flow hedge.

If the fair value of the commodity falls by $600, then the fair value of the forward contract will increase by $600 and create a derivative asset.

The accounting entries, if hedge accounting *is not* used, would be:

Dr	Derivative asset	600	
	Cr Profit or loss		600

The sale proceeds will be $600 lower (or more) when the inventory is sold, presumed to be in the following period in this example. Therefore, there is a mismatch in profit.

The accounting entries, if hedge accounting *is* used would be:

Dr	Derivative asset	600	
	Cr Other comprehensive income		600

The $600 gain, which was included as other comprehensive income, will be reclassified through profit or loss when the cash flow effect of the inventory affects profit or loss (i.e. when the inventory is sold). Using hedge accounting has allowed the gain to be matched with the loss.

© DeVry/Becker Educational Development Corp. All rights reserved.

Example 4 Foreign Exchange Hedge

30 September

- X contracted to buy a plane for Swiss Francs (SwFr)1,000,000 (a future transaction). The spot rate at this date was 2.5 SwFr = $1.
- X is worried about changes in the rate, so on the same day it enters into a forward exchange contract to buy SwFr/sell $ at a rate of 2.5 SwFr = $1.

Year end 31 December

- The spot rate is 2.4 SwFr = $1.

The fair value of the forward is given as:

	$
1,000,000 @ 2.4 =	416,667
1,000,000 @ 2.5 =	400,000
	16,667

31 March

- The plane is purchased. The rate is 2.3 SwFr = $1.

The fair value of the forward is given as:

	$
1,000,000 @ 2.3 =	434,783
1,000,000 @ 2.5 =	400,000
	34,783

Required:

Write up the necessary ledger accounts to record the hedge transaction.

8.7 Hedges of Net Investment in a Foreign Operation

- If an entity has an investment in a foreign operation, as defined by IAS 21, then it will be exposed to movements in foreign exchange rates.
- The entity can minimise its exposure to foreign exchange rate movements by having an opposite exposure. In other words it may have a foreign-denominated asset (investment) but also have a foreign-denominated liability. Its exposure is therefore matched.
- Hedge accounting can be used for this type of exposure; the accounting treatment is similar to that of a cash flow hedge.

© DeVry/Becker Educational Development Corp. All rights reserved.

9 Disclosure (IFRS 7)

9.1 Rules

- The purpose of disclosure is to:
  - enhance understanding of the significance of financial instruments to an entity's financial position, performance and cash flows;
  - assist in assessing the factors affecting the amount, timing and certainty of future cash flows associated with those instruments; and
  - provide information to assist users of financial statements in assessing the extent of related risks.
- Information sufficient to allow reconciliation to the line items in the statement of financial position must be provided.
- The information disclosed should facilitate users evaluating the significance of financial instruments on an entity's financial position and performance.

9.2 Assets and Liabilities

9.2.1 Categories of Financial Assets and Liabilities

- An entity must disclose the carrying amounts analysed into the following categories:
  - financial assets at fair value through profit or loss, showing separately:
    - —those designated on initial recognition, and
    - —those which must be measured at fair value;
  - financial liabilities at fair value through profit or loss, showing separately:
    - —those designated on initial recognition, and
    - —those which meet the definition of held for trading;
  - financial assets measured at amortised cost;
  - financial liabilities measured at amortised cost; and
  - financial assets measured at fair value through other comprehensive income.
- Disclosure may be on the face of the statement of financial position or in the notes.

9.2.2 Financial Assets or Liabilities at Fair Value Through Profit or Loss

- If an entity has measured a financial asset at fair value which otherwise would be measured at amortised cost, it should disclose:
  - the maximum exposure to credit risk at the end of the period;
  - the amount by which any credit derivatives or similar instruments cancel out the exposure to credit risk;
  - the amount of change in the period (and cumulatively) in the fair value of the asset which is attributable to changes in credit risk; and
  - the amount of change in fair value of any related credit derivatives, or similar instruments, both during the period and cumulatively.

Exam Advice

IFRS 7 goes into great detail about how to measure this exposure and change in fair value. This is outside the scope of the syllabus.

© DeVry/Becker Educational Development Corp. All rights reserved.

- If a financial liability is designated at fair value through profit or loss, an entity should disclose:
  - the amount of change, both in the period and cumulatively, in the fair value of the instrument that is attributable to any change in credit risk;
  - the difference between the carrying amount of the instrument and the amount contractually required to settle the instrument at maturity.

9.2.3 Financial Assets Measured at Fair Value Through Other Comprehensive Income

- If an entity has designated investments in equity instruments at fair value through other comprehensive income, it must disclose:
  - which investments it has so designated;
  - the reason for presenting in this way;
  - the fair value of each investment at the end of the period;
  - dividends recognised in the period, and
  - any transfers of cumulative gain or loss between equity components during the period and the reason for the transfer.
- If an entity disposed of investments which had been designated at fair value through other comprehensive income, it must disclose:
  - the reason for the disposal;
  - the fair value of the instrument at the disposal date; and
  - any cumulative gain or loss on disposal.

9.2.4 Reclassification

- If an entity reclassifies a financial asset during the current or previous period, it must disclose:
  - the date of reclassification;
  - a detailed explanation of the change in business model leading to the reclassification and a qualitative description of the effect on the entity's financial statements; and
  - the amount reclassified into and out of each category.

9.2.5 Derecognition

- If an entity transfers financial assets which do not meet the derecognition criteria, partially or wholly, it must disclose:
  - the nature of the assets;
  - any risks and rewards to which the entity is still exposed;
  - the carrying amount of the asset and any associated liability which remains wholly or partially recognised; and
  - for those assets which are partially derecognised, the carrying amount of the original asset.

9.2.6 Collateral

- An entity must disclose:
  - the carrying amount of financial assets pledged as collateral for liabilities; and
  - the terms and conditions of the pledge.

9.2.7 Allowances for Credit Losses

▨ Impairment of financial assets which are accounted for by recording the loss in a separate account (rather than against the asset) will require an entity to disclose a reconciliation of the movement in the account for the period.*

9.3 Gains and Losses

▨ The following will be disclosed, on the face of the statement of comprehensive income or in the notes:*

- net gains or losses on:
  - —financial assets or liabilities at fair value through profit or loss;
  - —financial assets and liabilities measured at amortised cost; and
  - —financial assets measured at fair value through other comprehensive income.
- total interest income and expense on financial assets measured at amortised cost and liabilities not at fair value through profit or loss;
- interest income on impaired financial assets; and
- amount of impairment loss for each class of financial asset.

9.4 Other Disclosures

9.4.1 Hedge Accounting

▨ An entity discloses the following for each category of hedge:
- a description of each type of hedge;
- a description of the designated hedging instruments along with their fair values; and
- the nature of the risks being hedged.

▨ The following require separate disclosure:
- gains and losses in respect of fair value hedges:
  - —on the hedging instrument, and
  - —the hedged item;
- the ineffectiveness included in profit or loss for cash flow hedges and hedges of net investments in foreign operations.

9.4.2 Fair Value

▨ Subject to certain exceptions, an entity discloses the fair value of each class of financial asset and liability to allow comparison with the instruments' carrying amounts.

▨ An entity must disclose:
- methods used and assumptions made in arriving at fair value; and
- whether fair values have been arrived at using published price quotations in active markets or are estimations.

*Commentary

*Allowance accounts for credit losses were previously called "provision for bad and doubtful debt" accounts.

*Commentary

*The disclosed amounts should be split between those initially designated and those items held for trading.

Exam Advice

Additional disclosures required in respect of cash flow hedges under IFRS 7 are not examinable.

© DeVry/Becker Educational Development Corp. All rights reserved.

9.5   Nature and Extent of Risks

■ An entity discloses information about the nature and extent of risks arising from financial instruments.

■ Credit risk, liquidity risk and market risk should be disclosed as a *minimum*.

9.5.1   Qualitative Disclosures

■ For each type of risk:

- the exposure to risk and how it arises;
- management's objectives, policies and processes for managing the risk and methods used to measure the risk; and
- any changes in the above occurring since the previous period.

9.5.2   Quantitative Disclosures

■ For each type of risk:*

- summary quantitative data about exposure to risk at the reporting date; and
- any concentrations of risk.

*Commentary

*Quantitative disclosures regarding risk should be based on information provided internally to key management personnel of the entity. If the data at the reporting date is unrepresentative of an entity's normal exposure, further disclosure of a representative nature is required.

© DeVry/Becker Educational Development Corp. All rights reserved.

Summary

- Traditional accounting cannot account for a transaction which does not have a monetary amount.

- On issue, financial instruments should be classified as liabilities or equity in accordance with the substance of the contractual arrangement.

- Contracts allowing net settlement in cash for non-financial items that are normal sale and purchase requirements are executory contracts, not financial instruments.

- Financial assets and liabilities must be offset where the entity has a legal right of offset; *and* intends to settle on a net basis.

- Distributions to holders of equity instruments are debited directly to equity. Dividends are presented in the statement of changes in equity.

- Financial instruments that contain both a liability and an equity element are classified into separate components.

- Own equity instruments acquired ("treasury shares") are deducted from equity.

- On initial recognition, a financial asset is measured at fair value.

- Financial assets are subsequently measured at either fair value or amortised cost, depending on the entity's business model.

- An embedded derivative is a component of a combined instrument which includes a non-derivative host contract.

- At the end of each reporting period, an entity assesses whether there is any objective evidence that a financial asset measured at amortised cost has become impaired.

- Financial liabilities will initially be recognised at fair value less any directly attributable transaction costs.

- Most financial liabilities will subsequently be measured at amortised cost using the effective interest method, with the interest expense being charged to profit or loss.

- Hedge accounting recognises symmetrically the *offsetting effects* on profit or loss of changes in the fair values of the hedging instrument and the related item being hedged.

- The gain or loss from remeasuring the hedging instrument at fair value is recognised immediately in profit or loss.

- In a cash flow hedge the portion of the gain or loss on the hedging instrument is recognised in other comprehensive income.

© DeVry/Becker Educational Development Corp. All rights reserved.

Session 8 Quiz
Estimated time: 20 minutes

1. Specify the THREE accounting standards which deal with financial instruments. (1.3)

2. Define a financial asset under IAS 32. (3.1)

3. Explain why preference shares generally are treated as a financial liability. (3.1)

4. Define *compound instrument* and give an example. (4.4)

5. Suppose an entity purchases its own equity shares in the market. Give the account name for those shares and explain how they are presented in the entity's statement of financial position. (4.5)

6. Identify the THREE categories of financial asset. (5.2)

7. Define embedded derivative and explain how it is accounted for. (5.6)

8. Specify which financial assets are tested for impairment and when. (6.2)

9. Define hedging. (8)

10. List the THREE types of hedging relationships. (8.4.1)

11. Explain how the gain or loss on the hedging instrument in a cash flow hedge should be dealt with. (8.4)

Study Question Bank
Estimated time: 40 minutes

Priority		Estimated Time	Completed
Q15	Ambush	40 minutes	
Additional			
Q14	Artright		

© DeVry/Becker Educational Development Corp. All rights reserved.

EXAMPLE SOLUTIONS

Solution 1—Convertible Bond

	$
Present value of the principal repayable in 3 years' time	
$2,000,000 × 0.772 (year 3 discount factor @ 9%)	1,544,000
Present value of the interest stream	
$120,000 × 2.531 (3-year cumulative discount factor @9%)	303,720
Total liability component	1,847,720
Equity component (taken as a balancing figure)	152,280
Proceeds of the issue	2,000,000

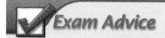

Exam Advice

A simple discount factor is $\frac{1}{r}$ where r is the discount rate.

A cumulative discount factor is the sum of simple discount factors. You will not have to calculate discount factors in the examination.

Solution 2—Financial Asset Classification

(a) As the financial asset has an amortised cost, it must be a loan asset. If Jethro is holding for contractual cash flows it is classified at amortised cost.

(b) As Jethro has sold this type of asset in the past it must be classified at fair value through other comprehensive income.

Solution 3—Equity Investments

(a) Held for Short Term

The equity investment is measured at fair value in the statement of financial position with the increase in fair value being credited to profit or loss. The transaction costs are expensed immediately to profit or loss and the dividend received in the period is credited to profit or loss.

Statement of financial position

Equity investments (20,000 × $7.47) = $149,400

Profit or loss

Increase in fair value (20,000 ×($7.47 − $7.20)) = $5,400
Dividend income (20,000 × $0.04) = $800
Transaction costs ($1,600)

(b) Fair Value Through Other Comprehensive Income

The equity investment is initially measured in the statement of financial position at fair value plus the transaction costs on initial measurement, $145,600 ((20,000 x $7.20) + $1,600). At the end of the year, it is remeasured at fair value of $149,400 and the increase of $3,800 is credited to other comprehensive income. Dividend income of $800 is credited to profit or loss.

© DeVry/Becker Educational Development Corp. All rights reserved.

Statement of financial position

Equity investments $149,400

Profit or loss

Dividend income $800

Other comprehensive income

Increase in fair value ($149,400 − ($144,000 + $1,600)) = $3,800

Solution 4—Foreign Exchange Hedge

	Note	Forward			Reserve	
30 September	(1)					
31 December	(2)	16,667				16,667
31 March	(3)	18,116				18,116
	(5)		34,783			
	(6)				34,783	
		Cash			**Plane—Asset**	
30 September						
31 December						
31 March	(4)		434,783		434,783	
	(5)	34,783				
	(6)					34,783
Bal c/f						400,000
					434,783	434,783
Bal b/f					400,000	

Notes
1. Spot rate is 2.5, which is the same as the forward, therefore the fair value of the forward is zero.
2. Fair value of forward (based on the difference between the spot rate and contracted rate) at the year end.
3. Increase in fair value of the forward to the date of purchase of the asset.
4. Purchase of asset at spot rate.
5. Recognising the amount by which the forward reduces the cash flow.
6. "Basis adjustment". Recognises that the asset's real cost was just $400,000.

© DeVry/Becker Educational Development Corp. All rights reserved.

IFRS 16 *Leases*

FOCUS

This session covers the following content from the *ACCA Study Guide.*

C. Reporting the Financial Performance of Entities

4. Leases

a) Apply and discuss the accounting for leases by lessees including the measurement of the right of use asset and liability. ☐

b) Apply and discuss the accounting for leases by lessors. ☐

c) Apply and discuss the circumstances where there may be re-measurement of the lease liability. ☐

d) Apply and discuss the reasons behind the separation of the components of a lease contract into lease and no-lease elements. ☐

e) Discuss the recognition exemptions under the current leasing standard. ☐

f) Account for and discuss sale and leaseback transactions. ☐

Session 9 Guidance

■ **Understand** IFRS 16 *Leases* is a specific standard that covers the concept of substance v form (s.1).

■ **Note** that the P2 syllabus covers lease accounting by both lessee and lessor.

■ **Understand** the accounting requirements of leases in both the books of the lessee and lessor (s.2 and s.5)

(continued on next page)

VISUAL OVERVIEW

Objective: To describe the accounting for leases from the viewpoint of the lessee and the lessor.

INTRODUCTION

- Lease v Buy
- Need for a Standard
- Terminology

LEASE IDENTIFICATION

- Inception
- Separation
- Recognition and Measurement
- Remeasurement
- Lease Modification

LESSOR ACCOUNTING

- Terminology
- Finance Lease
- Operating Lease
- Disclosures

SALE AND LEASEBACK

- Recognising a Sale
- Sale Not Recognised

PRESENTATION AND DISCLOSURE

- Presentation
- Disclosure

Session 9 Guidance

■ **Practise** the accounting rules for sale and leaseback transactions (s.3).

■ **Read** the article "All change for accounting for leases".

1 Introduction

1.1 Lease v Buy

- An entity may choose to buy or lease an asset.

- The main advantage of leasing is not having to find the upfront cash for large capital expenditure. Leasing may be cheaper than borrowing funds to buy the asset. Although a leased asset may never be owned outright a lease arrangement may allow for upgrading or replacement of assets without the expense of buying newer models.

- Although any kind of equipment can be leased common examples are vehicles, computers and printers, power tools, etc.

1.2 Need for a Standard

- IFRS 16 *Leases* was issued by the IASB in 2016 and is effective from 1 January 2019. Before IFRS 16 the relevant standard was IAS 17 *Leases*.

- IAS 17 defined two types of lease:
  - Operating leases; and
  - Finance leases.

- If a lease met the definition of a finance lease, the asset and liability were recognised in the statement of financial position. If the lease was an operating lease, no asset or liability were recognised and any lease rental was expensed to profit or loss as incurred.

- This accounting model resulted in many leases being excluded from the statement of financial position, even though the lessee had a present obligation, and therefore a liability, to make regular payments to the lessor.*

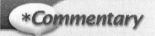

Commentary

*The IASB has now eliminated such "off balance sheet financing" by requiring entities to account for the substance of the transaction rather than the legal form.

Key Point

As a result of IFRS 16, more leased assets and lease obligations will appear in the statement of financial position. The annual expense arising from a lease now reduces over time; operating leases were previously accounted for on a straight-line basis.

IFRS 16 will therefore affect two key accounting ratios:

- Return on capital employed (higher); and
- Gearing (lower).

1.3 Terminology

Lease: a contract for the right to use an asset for a period of time.

Right-of-use asset: an asset that the lessee has the right to use under the terms of the lease.

© DeVry/Becker Educational Development Corp. All rights reserved.

Interest rate implicit in the lease: the rate of interest at which the present value of the lease payments and any unguaranteed residual value equals the fair value of the leased asset (including any initial direct costs of the lessor).*

Fair value: the amount for which an asset could be exchanged, or liability settled, between knowledgeable, willing parties in an arm's length transaction.*

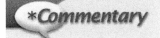

*That is, the internal rate of return of the lessor's cash flows.

*This is not the same as the IFRS 13 definition.

Short-term lease: of 12 months or less. A lease with a purchase option is **not** a short-term lease.

Underlying asset: the subject of a lease.

2 Lease Identification

2.1 Inception

- When entering into a contract the entity assesses if the contract is a lease or contains a lease.
- A contract is a lease, or contains a lease, if the lessee has the right to **control** a specified asset for a period of time in return for payment of consideration.
- There is control if the lessee has the rights:
  - to obtain most of the economic benefits from use of the contracted asset; and
  - to direct the use of the contracted asset.

Example 1 Identifying a Lease

Jerbyn has entered a contract to lease 10 trucks for a period of six years. The trucks will be used to transport goods across Europe. When not in use these trucks will be kept at Jerbyn's premises. If the trucks are damaged or require maintenance they will be sent back to the supplier to repair or replace them.

The contract also provides for the renting of additional trailers on an ad-hoc basis; these trailers will be kept by the supplier.

Required:

Discuss whether Jerbyn has entered into a leasing contract for the trucks and trailers.

2.2 Separation

- Each component of a contract must be considered separately (e.g. two distinct buildings rented under the same contract).
- Any non-lease components must also be treated separately (e.g. a cleaning and maintenance contract of leased buildings). The lessee can, however, elect not to separate the non-lease components if this is impractical.

© DeVry/Becker Educational Development Corp. All rights reserved.

Illustration 1 Separation of Lease

Thermay has entered into a lease agreement to rent three shop units in a retail village. The contract includes a non-lease clause relating to the cleaning of the units. The total consideration in the contract is $1,200,000 and the stand-alone prices for the leasing of the three units and cleaning service are as follows:

	$000
Unit 1	$375
Unit 2	$420
Unit 3	$145
Cleaning services	$260

Thermay chooses not to account for each lease and non-lease component as a single lease (as would be allowed under IFRS 16 as a practical expedient). Therefore, Thermay accounts for the three units as three separate leases and the non-lease component will be expensed to profit or loss over the course of the lease agreement.

2.3   Recognition and Measurement

2.3.1   Recognition

■ On commencement of the lease the lessee recognises:
  • a right-of-use **asset**; and
  • a lease **liability**.
■ Exceptions to this are:
  • short-term leases; and
  • leases of assets with a low value (e.g. laptops).*

Commentary

*Although the standard does not specify a monetary amount, up to $5,000 is indicated in the Basis for Conclusions.

Key Point

The previous standard on leases recognised the *physical* asset leased. IFRS 16 recognises the *right to use* the asset, which will result in more leases being capitalised under IFRS 16.

■ Rental payments for short-term leases and low-value assets are expensed to profit or loss (normally on a straight-line basis); no asset or liability is recognised other than rent prepayments or accruals.

2.3.2   Liability Measurement

■ The liability is initially measured at the commencement of the lease at the present value of the future lease payments.
■ Lease payments are discounted using the interest rate implicit in the lease, if known, or the lessee's incremental cost of borrowing.
■ Cash flows used in the present value calculation include:
  • Fixed payments less any lease incentives;
  • Variable payments that are based on a specified index (e.g. a consumer price index) or rate (e.g. LIBOR);
  • The value of any purchase option the lessee is likely to exercise; and
  • Penalties the lessee expects to pay to cancel the lease.

© DeVry/Becker Educational Development Corp. All rights reserved.

▓ As time passes, the liability is increased by any interest on the outstanding liability (the so-called "unwinding of the discount") and decreased by the lease payments made.

▓ The liability may require remeasurement if the terms of the lease are modified or the payment schedule is changed.

Illustration 2 Trade-In
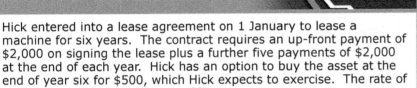

Hick entered into a lease agreement on 1 January to lease a machine for six years. The contract requires an up-front payment of $2,000 on signing the lease plus a further five payments of $2,000 at the end of each year. Hick has an option to buy the asset at the end of year six for $500, which Hick expects to exercise. The rate of interest implicit in the lease is 10%.

The initial amount of liability recognised will be calculated as:

End of year	Cash flow $	10% discount factor	Present value $
1	2,000	0.91	1,820
2	2,000	0.83	1,660
3	2,000	0.75	1,500
4	2,000	0.68	1,360
5	2,000	0.62	1,240
6	500	0.56	280
			7,860

The initial payment of $2,000 is not included in the schedule as it has been paid and therefore is not a liability.

Illustration 3 Interest Allocation

Following on from *Illustration 2* interest is allocated as follows:

Period	Liability $	Interest @ 10% $	Rental $	Closing balance $
1	7,860	786	(2,000)	6,646
2	6,646	665	(2,000)	5,311
3	5,311	531	(2,000)	3,842
4	3,842	384	(2,000)	2,226
5	2,226	223	(2,000)	449
6	449	51*	(500)	-
		2,640		

*Includes rounding difference.

At the end of year 1, the lease liability is $6,646 of which $5,311 is non-current (the amount outstanding at the end of year 2) and $1,335 is current.

© DeVry/Becker Educational Development Corp. All rights reserved.

2.3.3 Asset Measurement

▨ The right-of-use asset is initially measured at cost which includes:

- The initial amount of the liability recognised;
- Payments made before the lease commenced (e.g. a deposit) less any incentives received;
- Direct costs incurred by the lessee (e.g. installation costs); and
- Decommissioning costs expected to be incurred in dismantling or removing the asset at the end of its economic life.*

▨ The asset is subsequently measured using the cost model. However, it may be revalued if it belongs to a class of assets that are revalued.

▨ Depreciation is charged on the same basis as assets which are owned.

▨ If there is no reasonable certainty that the lessee will obtain ownership at the end of the lease term, the asset is depreciated over the shorter of:

- the lease term; and
- its useful life.

▨ If the lessee will retain ownership at the end of the lease term, the asset is depreciated over its useful life.

▨ If the lessee uses the fair value model of IAS 40 Investment Property, a right-of-use investment property will also be subsequently measured at fair value.

> ***Commentary**
>
> *The present value of these costs is recognised as a provision in accordance with IAS 37.

Illustration 4 Initial Asset

Following on from *Illustration 2*.

Hick incurs installation costs of $600. Based on the expectation that Hick will exercise the option to buy the asset, Hick will depreciate the asset over eight years on a straight line basis.

The initial amount capitalised will be:

	$
Initial liability	7,860
Deposit paid	2,000
Installation costs	600
	10,460

Annual depreciation for the asset will be $10,460 ÷ 8 years = $1,308 per annum.

© DeVry/Becker Educational Development Corp. All rights reserved.

Example 2 Right-of-use Asset

Delta entered into a contract to lease an asset on 1 January 20X8. The terms of the lease are six annual payments of $2,000 with the first payment on 31 December 20X8. Delta will incur a further $1,000 installation costs. Delta will return the asset to the lessor at the end of year six.

The initial measurement of the liability has been calculated at $8,710 using the interest rate implicit in the lease of 10%.

Required:

(a) Show the interest allocation over the six-year term of the lease.

(b) Show how the lease should be accounted for in the financial statements of Delta as at 31 December 20X8.

Exam Advice

The interest rate implicit in the lease will always be given in the exam; there will be no requirement to calculate it.

2.4 Remeasurement

- A lessee is required to remeasure the lease liability under the following circumstances:

  i) A change in expected amount payable under a residual value agreement.

  ii) A change in future lease payments that reflects changes to specified indices that are used to dictate those payments.

  iii) A change in lease term that results from a change in the non-cancellable period of the lease.*

Definition

Residual value agreement—a guarantee given to the lessor that the value of the underlying asset will be at least a specified amount.

*Commentary

*For example not exercising an option to extend or terminate the contract that was included in the initial assessment.

  iv) A change in the assessment of an option to purchase the underlying asset at the end of the lease term.

- Any remeasurement of the lease liability will be adjusted against the carrying amount of the right-of-use asset.

- The right-of-use asset cannot be reduced below zero. Any further adjustment of the lease liability is taken to profit or loss.

© DeVry/Becker Educational Development Corp. All rights reserved.

2.4.1 Original Discount Rate

▩ Changes resulting from either i) or ii) above will require an entity to apply the original discount rate to any changes in the payment schedule.

Illustration 5 **Rental Based on Price Index**

On 1 January 20X3 PQR enters into an eight year lease of office space, being one floor of a 10 storey building. The contract states that the lease rental for the first two years of the contract will be $30,000. After two years the rental will be re-assessed using a retail price index (RPI), which at 1 January 20X3 was 126.

The asset will be depreciated on a straight line basis over the eight year term of the lease.

PQR's incremental cost of borrowing is 5%.

On 1 January 20X3 the initial accounting entries were:

Dr Right-of-use asset	$203,580
Cr Lease liability (30,000 x 5.786)	$173,580
Cr Cash	$30,000

Interest expense for 20X3 is calculated at $8,679 and for 20X4 it is $7,613.

On 1 January 20X5, the lease liability is $159,872 and the value of the right-of-use asset is $152,685.

On 1 January 20X5, prior to making the third payment, the lease liability is adjusted to $32,000 to reflect the current RPI of 134.4.

1 x $32,000	$32,000
4.329 (5 year AF @ 5%) x $32,000	$138,528
	$170,528

The lease liability is increased by $10,656, the double entry will be a debit to the right-of-use asset. The adjusted value of the asset, $163,341, will now be depreciated on a straight line basis over the remaining six years of the lease to give an annual depreciation charge of $27,223.

2.4.2 Revised discount rate

▩ Changes resulting from either iii) or iv) above require an entity to apply to any changes in the payment schedule the interest rate implicit in the lease for the remainder of the lease term or, if the implicit rate is not known, the lessee's incremental borrowing rate at the date of reassessment.

© DeVry/Becker Educational Development Corp. All rights reserved.

Illustration 6 Extension Option

On 1 January 20X3 LMN enters into a five year lease of shop premises. The contract gives LMN an option to extend the lease for a further five years.

The lease rental for the first five years is $40,000 each year, payable in advance, and if LMN takes up the option the lease rentals will increase to $50,000 each year.

Due to uncertainty about the level of revenue to be generated from the shop LMN initially determines that the extension option will not be taken up. LMN uses an incremental cost of borrowing of 5% as the interest rate implicit in the lease is not available.

Based on the above information the value of the liability and asset on 1 January 20X6, immediately after the fourth instalment, would be $38,098 and $72,736 respectively.

On 1 January 20X6 the directors of LMN decided that they would take up the offer of the five year extension because sales had exceeded expectations. At this date LMN's incremental cost of borrowing was 6%.

On 1 January 20X6 the present value of future cash flows was calculated:

1 payment of $40,000	0.943	$37,720
5 payments of $50,000	3.974	$198,700
		$236,420

The amount of lease liability has increased by $198,322, the double entry being debit to right-of-use asset.

The value of the asset is now $271,058 and this would be depreciated on a straight line basis over the next seven years.

2.5 Lease Modification

Definition

A lease modification—arises when there is a change in the scope of a lease, or the consideration for a lease, that was not part of the original terms and conditions of the lease.*

- The lessee must account for any lease modification as a separate lease if:
  - The modification increases the scope of the lease by adding the right to use one or more underlying assets; and
  - The consideration increases by an amount that corresponds to the stand-alone price of the increase in scope of the lease, after adjusting for any specifics of the new contract.
- For any modification that is not accounted for as a separate lease, the lessee should:
  - Remeasure the lease liability by discounting the revised lease payments using the interest rate implicit in the lease for the remainder of the lease term. If the rate implicit in the lease cannot be determined, the lessee's incremental borrowing rate on the date of modification should be used.
  - Make a corresponding adjustment to the right-of-use asset.*

*Commentary

*This could be adding or terminating the right to use one or more underlying assets, or extending or shortening the lease term.

*Commentary

*For lease modifications that decrease the scope of the lease, the carrying amount of the right-of-use asset should be decreased to reflect the partial or full termination of the lease and any gain or loss on the partial or full termination of the lease should be recognised in profit or loss.

Illustration 7 Modification

On 1 January 20X3 FGH entered into a lease contract to lease 2 floors of a 10 storey office building. The lease is for a period of 10 years at an annual rent of $100,000, payable in arrears.

FGH's incremental cost of borrowing is 6% and the asset will be depreciated over the 10 year life of the lease.

On initial recognition the right-of-use asset and lease liability will be measured at $736,000 ($100,000 x 7.36).

On 1 January 20X7 the lease liability is $491,722 and the carrying amount of the right-of-use asset is $441,600. On this date FGH arranged, with the lessor, to continue the lease for just one of the floors, reducing the office space leased by 50%. The lease rental for the remaining six years of the lease will be $55,000 each year. FGH's incremental cost of borrowing has increased to 7%.

The lease liability and right-of-use asset are reduced by 50% to reflect the new lease terms, the difference taken to profit or loss.

DR Lease liability	$245,861	
CR Right-of-use Asset		$220,800
CR Profit or loss		$25,061

The lease liability is remeasured to reflect the new terms of the lease:

$55,000 x 4.767 (6 year AF @ 7%) $262,185

The difference in the new liability of $16,324 (262,185 – 245,861) is added to the value of the asset, to give an adjusted carrying amount of $237,124.

3   Sale and Leaseback

3.1   Recognising a Sale

■ If the revenue recognition criteria of IFRS 15 are met the seller (lessee) will:

- Recognise the cash received;
- Derecognise the asset sold;
- Recognise a right-of-use asset for the asset leased back;
- Recognise the lease liability; and
- Recognise any gain or loss, but only on the portion of the asset transferred to the buyer (lessor).

■ If the asset is sold at a price that differs from its fair value the seller must adjust the sale proceeds to fair value by:

- adding a prepayment, if sold at a below-market price; or
- deducting additional financing if sold at an above-market price.

3.2   Sale Not Recognised

■ If the criteria of IFRS 15 are not met then no sale can be recognised and the asset **cannot** be derecognised.

■ Instead the seller must apply IFRS 9 *Financial Instruments* and recognise a financial liability in respect of the proceeds received (i.e. account for it as a loan).

 Key Point

The treatment of a sale and leaseback of an asset depends on whether the revenue recognition criteria of IFRS 15 have been met.

© DeVry/Becker Educational Development Corp. All rights reserved.

Illustration 8 Sale and Leaseback

On 1 January 20X8 Juno enters into a sale and leaseback contract to sell for $1,000,000 an asset that has a carrying amount of $600,000 and a fair value of $900,000.

A contract exists, benefits are to be transferred, a price is given and a performance obligation has been satisfied; therefore the criteria of IFRS 15 have been met and Juno can treat the transaction as a sale and leaseback in accordance with IFRS 16.

Juno will make 10 annual lease payments of $115,000; the interest rate implicit in the lease is 5%. The cumulative discount factor (annuity factor) for years 1 to 10 is 7.72.

The present value of the 10 payments is $887,800. $100,000 of this relates to the additional finance provided by the buyer (the excess of $1,000,000 over the asset's fair value, $900,000). The remaining $787,800 relates to the lease liability.

The right-of-use asset is measured as a proportion of its carrying amount as follows:

$$\text{Present value of lease liability} \times \frac{\text{Carrying amount}}{\text{Fair value of asset}}$$

$$= 787,800 \times \frac{600,000}{900,000} = \$525,200$$

Although the gain on the sale is $300,000 (900 – 600), only the portion that relates to the rights transferred to the buyer is recognised as follows:

$$\text{Gain} \times \frac{\text{Fair value of asset - lease liability}}{\text{Fair value of asset}}$$

$$300,000 \times \frac{(900,000 - 787,800)}{900,000} = \$37,400$$

In summary, on 1 January 20X8 Juno will account for the sale and leaseback transaction as follows:

	$	$
Cash	1,000,000	
Right-of-use asset	525,200	
Asset sold		600,000
Liability recognised		887,800
Gain on rights transferred		37,400

The right-of-use asset will be depreciated over its 10 year life, usually on a straight-line basis, giving an annual charge of $52,520.

Interest on the liability will be calculated using the interest rate implicit in the lease of 5%. In 20X8 this will lead to a finance charge of $44,390 (5% × 887,800) to profit or loss.

4 Presentation and Disclosure

4.1 Presentation

4.1.1 Statement of Financial Position

▪ Right-of-use assets are presented separately from other assets in the statement of financial position or in the disclosure notes.

▪ A right-of-use asset classified as investment property is included with any other owned investment property.

▪ The lease liability should be presented separately from all other liabilities in the statement of financial position or the disclosure notes, separated into a non-current and a current liability (in accordance with IAS 1).

© DeVry/Becker Educational Development Corp. All rights reserved.

4.1.2 Statement of Profit or Loss

- Depreciation of right-of-use assets and rent payments for short-term and low-cost assets are expensed as operating costs.
- Interest relating to a right-of-use asset is presented as a finance cost.

4.1.3 Statement of Cash Flows

- Repayment of the capital element of a lease is classified under financing activities.
- Interest paid may be classified as an operating or financing cash flow (in accordance with IAS 7).
- Payments relating to short-term leases and low-cost assets are classified as an operating cash flow.

4.2 Disclosure

- Extensive disclosure requirements allow users of financial statements to assess how leases affect financial performance, financial position and cash flows.
- Disclosures include:
  - Depreciation of right-of-use assets;
  - Interest expense on lease liabilities;
  - Expense relating to short-term leases and lease of low-cost assets; and
  - Any gains or losses on sale and leaseback contracts.
- Disclosures should also include qualitative information such as the nature of leasing activities and any restrictions or covenants included in leasing contracts.

5 Lessor Accounting

5.1 Terminology

Definition

Finance Lease—a lease that transfers substantially all risks and rewards incidental to ownership of the underlying asset.

Operating Lease—A lease that does not transfer substantially all the risks and rewards incidental to ownership of the underlying asset.

- The accounting of leases by the lessor is fundamentally the same as it was under the previous standard (IAS 17), in that the lease contract is accounted for either as a finance lease or as an operating lease.
- The substance of the transaction dictates whether the lease is a finance lease or an operating lease.

© DeVry/Becker Educational Development Corp. All rights reserved.

5.2   Finance Lease

5.2.1   Indicators

■ The following are indicators that a lease would be classified as a finance lease:

- Underlying asset is transferred to lessee at the end of the contract;
- Lessee has an option to purchase underlying asset as a price below that fair value;
- Lease term is for the majority of the underlying asset's useful life;
- Present value of future lease payments is substantially equal to the fair value of the underlying asset; and
- The underlying asset is of a specialised nature and can only be used by the lessee.

5.2.2   Accounting

■ The lessor will derecognise the underlying asset and record an "asset held under finance lease" equal to the present value of lease payments to be received.

■ If the lessor is a manufacturer/dealer, gross profit (loss) on the sale of the asset is recognised at the inception of the lease.

■ The lessor will apply the interest rate implicit in the lease to all lease payments receivable plus any unguaranteed residual value that would accrue to the lessor.

■ Rentals received by the lessor will be split into a repayment of capital element and an interest element. Interest will be calculated to give a constant periodic rate of return on the lessor's investment in the lease.*

> ***Commentary**
>
> *The interest income credited to profit or loss will also decrease each year as the "asset held under finance lease" receivable is reduced.

Illustration 9   Finance Lease

Ivy leased an asset to Holly under a finance lease arrangement on 1 July 20X6. The terms of the lease were six payments of $200 payable annually in arrears. The cash price of the asset was $870.

The interest rate implicit in the lease is 10%.

Sale of asset

As the transaction is a finance lease, the physical asset should be derecognised through a sale transaction, with any profit or loss on sale included in profit or loss for the period.

A receivable asset should be recognised instead of the physical asset sold. The receivable recognised at lease inception is equal to the cash price of the asset, $870.

Annual rent

The $200 rent needs to be split into the interest element and the repayment of capital. In this example the interest income for year ended 30 June 20X7 would be $87 ($870 x 10%) and the receivable would be reduced to $757 ($870 + $87 - $200).

5.3　Operating Lease

▓ The lessor will maintain the recognition of the underlying asset and will depreciate that asset based on normal depreciation policy for similar assets.

▓ Operating lease rentals will be credited to profit or loss on a straight line basis, unless a more systematic basis is deemed appropriate.

Illustration 10　Operating Lease

Under a lease agreement Cartright receives a non-returnable deposit of $100,000 and then three years rental income of $100,000 paid on the first day of each year. The asset has a life of 10 years and the lease agreement is classified as an operating lease.

Statement of profit or loss

$$\frac{(\$100,000) + (\$300,000)}{3 \text{ years}} = \$133,333$$

Statement of financial position

At end of 1st year	$	
	200,000	received
	(133,333)	credited
	66,667	unearned income

5.4　Disclosures

▓ Information should be disclosed that gives users of the financial statements knowledge of an entity's leasing activities and the effect those leases have on an entity's statement of financial position, statement of profit or loss and statement of cash flows.

▓ Information disclosed will include:

- Profit or loss on the sale of an asset under a finance lease contract;
- Finance income earned on a finance lease;
- A maturity analysis for lease payments receivable under both finance and operating leases;
- Operating lease income; and
- Quantitative and qualitative disclosures necessary to give users an understanding of the entity's leasing activities.

　　　　　　　　　　© DeVry/Becker Educational Development Corp. All rights reserved.

Summary

Lessee Accounting

■ All leases are capitalised except for leases of less than 12 months duration and leases of assets with low value.

■ What the lessee is capitalising is the right-of-use asset rather than the physical asset.

■ The initial lease liability will be the present value of future lease payments using the interest rate implicit in the lease. Any upfront deposits are not included in the calculation.

■ The initial right-of-use asset is measured at the initial lease liability plus any initial deposit plus any direct costs incurred plus any future decommissioning costs.

■ Lease payments will be split into the repayment of capital and interest using the interest rate implicit in the lease.

■ The right-of-use asset is depreciated over the useful life of the lease, unless it is expected that ownership of the asset will be transferred at the end of the lease term, in which case the asset will be depreciated over the useful life of the asset.

■ Short-term leases and leases where the underlying asset is of a low value will expense any rental payments, normally on a straight-line basis.

■ The requirements of IFRS 15 *Revenue from Contracts with Customers* will be applied to sale and leaseback transactions.

■ If the revenue recognition criteria of IFRS 15 are met in a sale and leaseback, a sale of the asset will be recognised and replaced with a right-of-use asset and a lease liability.

■ If the revenue recognition criteria of IFRS 15 are not met in a sales and leaseback, a financial liability is recognised in accordance with IFRS 9 *Financial Instruments.*

Lessor Accounting

■ The lessor classifies leases as either finance leases or operating leases, dependant on the substance of the contract.

■ For finance leases, the underlying asset is derecognised and replaced with a receivable asset.

■ Rentals are split, using the interest rate implicit in the lease, into interest income and the repayment of the capital element of the lease.

■ Operating leases recognise rental income on a straight line basis and continue to depreciate the underlying asset.

© DeVry/Becker Educational Development Corp. All rights reserved.

Session 9 Quiz
Estimated time: 30 minutes

1. State the effect on Return on Capital Employed and Gearing if a leased asset and liability were excluded from the statement of financial position. (1.2)

2. Identify the two circumstances when a lessee would not recognise a right-of-use asset and lease liability when entering a lease contract. (2.3.1)

3. Describe how the right-of-use asset is initially measured. (2.3.2)

4. State the circumstances when an entity must remeasure any lease liabilities. (2.4)

5. State the accounting entries necessary when an entity modifies a lease contract that does not give rise to a new lease. (2.5)

6. Describe what happens to sale proceeds in a sale and leaseback transaction, if the asset is sold at a price that differs from its fair value. (3.1)

7. State the accounting treatment of a sale and leaseback transaction when the asset sold is not derecognised. (3.2)

8. State the presentation in the statement of cash flows of payments relating to low-cost assets. (4.1.3)

9. From the lessor's perspective distinguish between a finance lease and an operating lease. (5.1)

10. Describe the accounting entries to be made by a lessor on initial recognition of a finance lease contract. (5.2.2)

Study Question Bank
Estimated time: 45 minutes

Priority		Estimated Time	Completed
Q17	Router	45 minutes	
Additional			
Q16	Arrochar		

© DeVry/Becker Educational Development Corp. All rights reserved.

EXAMPLE SOLUTIONS

Solution 1—Identifying a Lease

The contract for the rent of 10 trucks is a lease as the trucks have been explicitly identified in the contract. They remain on Jerbyn's premises and are under the control of Jerbyn. If damaged or in need of maintenance, the supplier will deliver a replacement.

The trailers are not an identified asset as the supplier can deliver any trailer it has available and the trailers are kept at the supplier's premises; Jerbyn has no control over the trailers. Any payments for rent of the trailers will be expensed over the period of use; the right-of-use of the trailer will not be capitalised.

Solution 2—Right-of-use Asset

(a) Interest allocation

	$
Rentals	12,000
Initial liability recognised	(8,710)
Interest expense	3,290

Year	Amount owed at the start of the year	Interest @ 10%	Rental	Amount owed at the end of the year
1	8,710	871	(2,000)	7,581
2	7,581	758	(2,000)	6,339
3	6,339	634	(2,000)	4,973
4	4,973	497	(2,000)	3,470
5	3,470	347	(2,000)	1,817
6	1,817	183	(2,000)	0
		3,290		

(b) Financial statements
Analysis of payable

Current (2,000 − 758 (W))	1,242	
		= 7,581
Non-current	6,339	

Right-of-use asset	$
Cost (8,710 lease liability + 1,000 installation)	9,710
Depreciation (9,710 ÷ 6)	(1,618)
Carrying amount	8,092

WORKING

Finance lease payable

		1/1/X8 Right-of-use asset	8,710
31/12/X8 Cash	2,000	31/12/X8 Interest	871
31/12/X8 Bal c/d	7,581		
	9,581		9,581
		01/01/X9 Bal b/d	7,581
31/12/X9 Cash	*2,000*	*31/12/X9 Interest*	*758*

© DeVry/Becker Educational Development Corp. All rights reserved.

IFRS 8 *Operating Segments*

FOCUS

This session covers the following content from the *ACCA Study Guide.*

C. Reporting the Financial Performance of Entities

5. Segment reporting
a) Determine the nature and extent of reportable segments.
b) Specify and discuss the nature of segment information to be disclosed.

Session 10 Guidance

■ **Understand** the scope of IFRS 8 and learn the relevant definitions (s.1.1, s.1.2).
■ **Learn** the rules for aggregation and the quantitative thresholds (s.1.3). **Attempt** *Example 1.*

(continued on next page)

VISUAL OVERVIEW

Objective: To provide information to users of financial statements about the nature and financial effects of the business activities in which an entity engages and the economic environment in which it operates.

```
                          ┌─────────────────────────────┐
                          │     OPERATING SEGMENTS      │
                          │  ─────────────────────────  │
                          │   • Scope                   │
                          │   • Definitions             │
                          │   • Reportable Segments     │
                          └─────────────────────────────┘
                           /                           \
```

DISCLOSURE	REVIEW OF THE STANDARD
• Core Principle	• Reason for Issue
• General Information	• Advantages and Disadvantages
• Profit or Loss, Assets and Liabilities	• IASB Review
• Basis of Measurement	
• Reconciliations	
• Restatement of Previously Reported Information	
• Entity-wide Disclosures	

Session 10 Guidance

■ **Understand** the core principle and disclosure requirements (s.2).

■ **Work** through the *Illustrations* which identify a number of the disclosures required by an entity with operating segments and **attempt** *Example 2* (s.2).

© DeVry/Becker Educational Development Corp. All rights reserved.

1   Operating Segments

1.1   Scope

> **Key Point**
>
> IFRS 8 applies to the separate financial statements of entities whose debt or equity instruments are publicly traded (or are in the process of being issued in a public market).

- IFRS 8 also applies to the consolidated financial statements of a group whose parent is required to apply IFRS 8 to its separate financial statements.

- Where an entity is not required to apply IFRS 8, but chooses to do so, it must not describe information about segments as "segment information" unless it complies with IFRS 8.

- Where a parent's separate financial statements are presented with consolidated financial statements, segment information is required only in the consolidated financial statements.

1.2   Definitions

1.2.1   Operating Segment

- This is a component that meets the following three criteria:

  1. It engages in business activities from which it may earn revenues and incur expenses (including intersegment revenues and expenses arising from transactions with other components of the same entity);*

  2. its operating results are regularly reviewed by the entity's "chief operating decision-maker" to make decisions (about resources to be allocated) and to assess its performance.

  3. Discrete financial information is available.*

- An entity's post-employment benefit plans are *not* **operating segments.**

- Corporate headquarters or other departments that do not earn revenues (or only incidental revenues) are *not* operating segments.

1.2.2   "Chief Operating Decision-Maker"

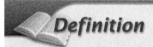

> **Definition**
>
> **Chief operating decision-maker (CODM)**—describes the function which allocates resources to and assesses the performance of operating segments (e.g. a CEO or board of directors).*

*A start-up operation not yet earning revenues may be an operating segment.

*A component, by definition, should meet the criterion of available discrete information (see IFRS 5).

> ***Commentary**
>
> *An operating segment will generally have a segment manager who is directly accountable to and maintains regular contact with the CODM to discuss operating activities, financial results, forecasts, etc.

© DeVry/Becker Educational Development Corp. All rights reserved.

1.3   Reportable Segments

1.3.1   Separate Information

Key Point

■ Separate information must be reported for each operating
   segment that:
   • meets the definition criteria or *aggregation criteria* for two or
      more segments; and
   • exceeds the *quantitative thresholds*.

1.3.2   Aggregation Criteria

▦ Two or more operating segments may be aggregated into a
   single operating segment if:*
   ◦ aggregation is consistent with the core principle of this IFRS;
   ◦ the segments have similar economic characteristics; and
   ◦ the segments are similar in respect of:
      — products and services (e.g. domestic or industrial);
      — the production process (e.g. maturing or production
         line);
      — types or class of customer (e.g. corporate or individual);
      — distribution method (e.g. door-to-door or Web
         sales); and
      — the regulatory environment (e.g. in shipping,
         banking, etc).

1.3.3   Quantitative Thresholds

▦ Separate information must be reported for an operating
   segment that meets *any one* of the following quantitative
   thresholds:*
   ◦ reported revenue is 10% or more of the combined revenue
      (internal and external) of all operating segments;
   ◦ profit or loss is 10% or more, in absolute amount, of the
      greater of:
      (i) the combined profit of all operating segments that did
         not report a loss; and
      (ii) the combined loss of all operating segments that
         reported a loss;
   ◦ assets are 10% or more of the combined assets of all
      operating segments.
▦ At least 75% of revenue must be included in reportable
   segments. Thus operating segments that fall below the
   quantitative thresholds may need to be identified as
   reportable.*
▦ Information about other business activities and operating
   segments that are not reportable are combined and disclosed
   in an "all other segments" category.
▦ When an operating segment is first identified as a reportable
   segment according to the quantitative thresholds, comparative
   data is presented, unless the necessary information is not
   available and the cost to develop it would be excessive.*

---

*Commentary

*An operating segment
that does not meet a
qualitative threshold
may be aggregated
with another segment
that does only if they
have similar economic
characteristics and
share a majority of the
aggregation criteria.

*Commentary

*IFRS 8 is the only
International Financial
Reporting Standard
with a "materiality
rule".

*Commentary

*Segments that fall
below the threshold
may also be considered
reportable, and
separately disclosed, if
management believes
that the information
would be useful to
users of the financial
statements.

*Commentary

*The standard
suggests 10 as a
practical limit to the
number of reportable
segments separately
disclosed, as segment
information may
otherwise become
too detailed.

Example 1 Reportable Segments

Fireball group has:

- three significant business lines which make up about 70% of combined revenue; and
- five small business lines, each of them contributing about 6% to the combined revenue.

Required:

Explain how many segments Fireball group should report.

2 Disclosure

2.1 Core Principle

Key Point

■ An entity must disclose information to enable users of financial statements to evaluate:
- the nature and financial effects of its business activities; and
- the economic environments in which it operates.

▨ This includes:*
- general information;
- information about reported segment profit or loss, segment assets, segment liabilities and the basis of measurement; and
- reconciliations.

2.2 General Information

▨ The factors used to identify reportable segments, including:
- the basis of organisation (e.g. around products and services, geographical areas, regulatory environments, or a combination of factors and whether segments have been aggregated); and

*Commentary

*Information for segments must be disclosed for every period for which a statement of comprehensive income is presented. Reconciliations of statement of financial position amounts are required for each end of reporting period presented.

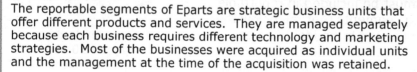

Illustration 1 Basis of Organisation

The reportable segments of Eparts are strategic business units that offer different products and services. They are managed separately because each business requires different technology and marketing strategies. Most of the businesses were acquired as individual units and the management at the time of the acquisition was retained.

- types of products and services from which each reportable segment derives its revenues.

© DeVry/Becker Educational Development Corp. All rights reserved.

Illustration 2 Types of Products and Services

Eparts has five reportable segments: machine parts, laser, prototyping, water jet and finance. The machine parts segment produces parts for sale to aviation equipment manufacturers. The laser segment produces laser cutters to serve the petrochemical industry. The prototyping segment produces plastics for sale to the pharmaceutical industry. The water jet segment produces cutting equipment for sale to car manufacturers and jewellers. The finance segment is responsible for certain aspects of financial operations, including financing customer purchases of products from other segments and car leasing operations.

2.3   Profit or Loss, Assets and Liabilities

▦ The following must be reported for each reportable segment:*

- ● A measure of profit or loss and total assets and liabilities.
- ● Disclosure is **only required** if such information is regularly reported to the CODM.

2.3.1   Profit or Loss

▦ The following must also be disclosed if regularly provided to the CODM (even if not included in the measure of segment profit or loss):

- ● revenues from external customers;
- ● intersegment revenues;
- ● interest revenue;*

> *Commentary*
>
> *Segment cash flow information is voluntary (IAS 7) and therefore unlikely to be produced, as it would provide information to an acquirer to value and target for a takeover bid.

> *Commentary*
>
> *May be reported net of its interest expense if the majority of the segment's revenues are from interest and the CODM relies primarily on reporting of net interest revenue.

- ● interest expense;
- ● depreciation and amortisation;
- ● other material items of income and expense required by IAS 1 (i.e. write-downs, restructurings, disposals, discontinued operations, litigation settlements and reversals of provisions);*

> *Commentary*
>
> *Impairment losses also have to be disclosed (but as an IAS 36 requirement).

- ● entity's interest in the profit or loss of associates and joint ventures accounted for by the equity method;
- ● income tax expense or income; and
- ● material non-cash items other than depreciation and amortisation.

2.3.2 Assets

▦ The following must also be disclosed if the specified amounts are regularly provided to the chief operating decision-maker (even if not included in the measure of segment assets):

  ● the investment in associates and joint ventures accounted for by the equity method; and

  ● additions to non-current assets (other than financial instruments, deferred tax assets and post-employment benefit assets).

Illustration 3 Profit or Loss, Assets and Liabilities*

	Machine parts $	Laser $	Proto-typing $	Water jet $	Finance $	All other $	Totals $
Revenues from external customers	7,200	12,000	22,800	28,800	12,000	2,400[a]	85,200
Intersegment revenues	–	–	7,200	3,600	–	–	10,800
Interest revenue	1,080	1,920	2,400	3,600	–	–	9,000
Interest expense	840	1,440	1,680	2,640	–	–	6,600
Net interest revenue[b]	–	–	–	–	2,400	–	2,400
Depreciation and amortisation	480	240	120	3,600	2,640	–	7,080
Reportable segment profit	480	168	2,160	5,520	1,200	240	9,768
Other material non-cash items: Impairment of assets	–	480	–	–	–	–	480
Reportable segment assets	4,800	12,000	7,200	28,800	136,800	4,800	194,400
Expenditures for reportable segment non-current assets	720	1,680	1,200	1,920	1,440	–	6,960
Reportable segment liabilities	2,520	7,200	4,320	19,200	72,000	–	105,240

(a) Revenues from segments below the quantitative thresholds are attributable to three operating segments of Eparts. Those segments include a small warehouse leasing business, a car rental business and a design consulting practice. None of those segments has ever met any of the quantitative thresholds for determining reportable segments.

(b) The finance segment derives a majority of its revenue from interest. Management primarily relies on net interest revenue, not the gross revenue and expense amounts, in managing that segment. Therefore only the net amount is disclosed.

---

*Commentary

*The company in *Illustration 3* does not allocate tax expense or non-recurring gains or losses to reportable segments. Also, not all reportable segments have material non-cash items other than depreciation and amortisation.

© DeVry/Becker Educational Development Corp. All rights reserved.

2.4   Basis of Measurement

Key Point

- The amount of each segment item reported is the measure reported to the chief operating decision-maker.
- Segment information is no longer required to conform to the accounting policies adopted for preparing and presenting the consolidated financial statements.

■ If the chief operating decision-maker uses more than one measure of an operating segment's profit or loss, the segment's assets or the segment's liabilities, the reported measures should be those that are most consistent with those used in the entity's financial statements.

Illustration 4   Measurement

The accounting policies of the operating segments are the same as those described in the summary of significant accounting policies except that pension expense for each operating segment is recognised and measured on the basis of cash payments to the pension plan. Eparts evaluates performance on the basis of profit or loss from operations before tax expense not including non-recurring gains and losses and foreign exchange gains and losses.

Eparts accounts for intersegment sales and transfers at current market prices (i.e. as if the sales or transfers were to third parties).

■ An explanation of the measurements of segment profit or loss, segment assets and segment liabilities must disclose, as a minimum:
  - the basis of accounting for intersegment transactions;
  - the nature of any differences between the measurements of the reportable segments and the entity's financial statements (if not apparent from the reconciliations required);*
  - the nature of any changes from prior periods in the measurement methods used and the effect, if any, of those changes on the measure of segment profit or loss and
  - the nature and effect of any asymmetrical allocations to reportable segments.*

*Commentary

*Explanation of differences could include accounting policies and policies for allocation of centrally incurred costs, jointly used assets or jointly utilised liabilities.

*Commentary

*An example of an asymmetrical allocation to reportable segments is the allocation of depreciation expense with the related depreciable assets.

2.5   Reconciliations

■ Reconciliations of the total of the reportable segments with the entity are required for all of the following:

- revenue;
- profit or loss (before tax and discontinued operations);
- assets;
- liabilities (if applicable); and
- every other material item.

■ All material reconciling items must be separately identified and described (e.g. arising from different accounting policies).

Illustration 5   Revenue Reconciliation

	$
Total revenues for reportable segments	93,600
Other revenues	2,400
Elimination of intersegment revenues	(10,800)
Entity's revenues	85,200

Illustration 6   Profit or Loss

	$
Total profit or loss for reportable segments	9,528
Other profit or loss	240
Elimination of intersegment profits	(1,200)
Unallocated amounts:	
Litigation settlement received	1,200
Other corporate expenses	(1,800)
Adjustment to pension expense in consolidation	(600)
Income before income tax expense	7,368

Illustration 7   Other Material Items

Other material items	Reportable segment totals	Adjustments	Entity totals
	$	$	$
Interest revenue	9,000	180	9,180
Interest expense	6,600	(120)	6,480
Net interest revenue (finance segment only)	2,400	–	2,400
Expenditures for assets	6,960	2,400	9,360
Depreciation and amortisation	7,080	–	7,080
Impairment of assets	480	–	480

The reconciling item is the amount incurred for the company head office building which is not included in segment information.

© DeVry/Becker Educational Development Corp. All rights reserved.

2.6 Restatement of Previously Reported Information

▨ Where changes in the internal organisation structure result in a change in the composition of reportable segments, corresponding information must be restated unless the information is not available and the cost to develop it would be excessive.

▨ If not restated, the current period segment information must be disclosed on both the old and new bases, unless the necessary information is not available and the cost to develop it would be excessive.

2.7 Entity-wide Disclosures

▨ All entities subject to this IFRS are required to disclose information about the following, if it is not provided as part of the required reportable segment information:*

- ● products and services:
- ● geographical areas; and
- ● major customers.

▨ The only exemption for not providing information about products and services and geographical areas is if the necessary information is not available and the cost to develop it would be excessive, in which case that fact must be disclosed.

Commentary

*The required reportable segment information includes those entities that have only a single reportable segment.

2.7.1 By Product and Service

▨ Revenues from external customers for each product and service (or each group of similar products and service) based on the financial information used to produce the entity's financial statements.

Exhibit 1   REPORTING BY PRODUCT GROUP

Rio Tinto reported the following segment information in its *2015 Annual Report and Financial Statements:*

2   Operating segments (extract)

Gross sales revenue[a]	2015 US$m	2014 US$m	2013 US$m
Iron Ore	15,305	23,281	25,994
Aluminium	10,117	12,123	12,463
Copper & Coal	7,705	9,957	10,434
Diamonds & Minerals	3,674	4,783	5,129
Other Operations	13	241	1,761
Reportable segments total	36,814	50,385	55,781
Inter-segment transactions	(29)	(344)	(1,182)
Product group total	36,785	50,041	54,599
Items excluded from underlying earnings	(1)	—	(24)
Gross sales revenue	36,784	50,041	54,575
Share of equity accounted units and adjustments for inter-subsidiary/equity accounted units sales	(1,955)	(2,377)	(3,404)
Consolidated sales revenue per income statement	34,829	47,664	51,171

2.7.2   By Geographical Area

- Revenues from external customers attributed to:
  - the entity's country of domicile;
  - all foreign countries in total; and
  - individual foreign countries, if material.
- Similarly, non-current assets (other than financial instruments, deferred tax assets and post-employment benefit assets).*

*Commentary

*Again based on the financial information used to produce the financial statements.

Illustration 8   Geographical Area

Geographical information	Revenues[a]	Non-current assets
	$	$
United States	45,600	26,400
Canada	10,080	–
China	8,160	15,600
Japan	6,960	8,400
Other countries	14,400	7,200
Total	85,200	57,600

(a) Revenues are attributed to countries on the basis of the customer's location.

2.7.3   Major Customers

- An entity discloses the extent of its reliance on major customers by stating:*
  - if revenues from a single external customer amount to 10% or more of the entity's total;
  - the total revenues from each such customer; and
  - the segment(s) reporting the revenues.
- An entity need not disclose the identity of a major customer or the amount of revenues that each segment reports from that customer.

*Commentary

*For this purpose, a group of entities known to be under common control (including control of a government) is a single customer.

Illustration 9   Concentration of Revenue Sources

Revenues from one customer of the prototyping and water jet segments of Eparts represent approximately $12,000 of the company's total revenues.

Example 2   Comparative Information

Silver is applying IFRS 8 for the first time in financial statements for the year ending 31 December. This will cause changes in the identification of Silver's reportable segments and require additional disclosures.

Required:

Comment on whether Silver should restate the comparative information.

          © DeVry/Becker Educational Development Corp. All rights reserved.

3 Review of the Standard

3.1 Reason for Issue of IFRS 8

▣ The IASB saw the subject of segmental reporting as one that would fit into its short-term convergence project with FASB. It considered that the project was stand-alone and could be completed in a relatively short time frame.

3.2 Advantages and Disadvantages

✗ Many accountants have criticised the move to a management-based approach from the more objective segments-based approach on products and geographical regions.

✗ The management approach means that the identification of a segment is a subjective internal decision that leads to a lack of comparability between entities. The approach may also give rise to inconsistency from one reporting period to the next; if internal reporting is changed the information for segment reporting will also change.

✔ The IASB counters this argument by pointing out that information requested by the CODM should also be useful to the external users of the financial statements.

✗ The standard does not define segment profit. This will again lead to a lack of comparability between entities if there are variations in how they determine profit.

✔ The disclosure requirements of the standard should be cost effective. As the information is already being provided to the CODM there should be very little extra cost in incorporating this in the financial statements.

✗ Many argue that the disclosures required are commercially sensitive and therefore could give competitors an unfair advantage. This may be true.

3.3 IASB Review

▣ The IASB post-implementation review of IFRS was completed in 2013. The review found that the benefits of applying the standard were mainly as expected and concluded that the standard has improved the quality of segment reporting in financial statements.

▣ Areas in which improvements could be made relate to:*

  ● The concept of the CODM—this is seen as confusing and outdated and difficult to identify in some entities.

  ● The presentation of reconciliations—there is some uncertainty about presentation and some investors find the reconciliations confusing.

Commentary

*IASB staff will follow up these issues and consider whether any changes or clarification to the standard are necessary.

Summary

- IFRS 8 applies to the separate financial statements of entities whose debt or equity instruments are publicly traded.

- An operating segment is a component of a business that engages in business activities, earning revenues and incurring expenses, whose results are regularly reviewed and provides discrete financial information.

- The chief operating decision-maker describes the function of allocating resources to and assessing the performance of operating segments.

- Separate information must be reported for each operating segment that meets the definition or aggregation criteria for at least two segments and exceeds the quantitative thresholds.

- Quantitative thresholds relate to revenue, profit or loss and assets. A reportable segment accounts for at least 10% of one of these.

- An entity must disclose information for the evaluation of the nature and financial effects of business activities and the economic environment.

- The amount of each segment item reported is the measure reported to the chief operating decision-maker; it does not need to conform to IFRS measurement principles.

- Reconciliations are required to the entity's reported figures, including any measurement reconciliations.

 Session 10 Quiz
Estimated time: 30 minutes

1. Describe which companies are required to apply IFRS 8. (1.1)
2. State why the chief operating decision-maker is important in respect of IFRS 8. (1.2.2)
3. Specify the quantitative thresholds when considering whether or not a segment is reportable. (1.3.3)
4. State the core principle when considering the disclosure requirements of IFRS 8. (2.1)
5. List the required disclosures regarding the assets of an operating segment. (2.3.2)
6. When reporting segmental information, state the types of items for which reconciliations are required. (2.5)
7. Yes or no? Is an entity required to disclose information relating to its customers? If yes, specify what the required information is. (2.7.3)
8. The IASB recently reviewed IFRS 8; suggest which areas require improvement. (3.3)

 Study Question Bank
Estimated time: 40 minutes

Priority		Estimated Time	Completed
Q18	AZ	40 minutes	

© DeVry/Becker Educational Development Corp. All rights reserved.

EXAMPLE SOLUTIONS

Solution 1—Reportable Segments

The issue is whether or not it is acceptable to report the three major business lines separately and to include the rest for reconciliation purposes as "all other segments".

- Since the reported revenues attributable to the three business lines that meet the separate reporting criteria constitute less than 75% of the combined revenue, additional segments must be identified as reportable, even though they are below the 10% threshold, until at least 75% of the combined revenue is included in reportable segments.

- If at least one of the small segments meets the aggregation criteria to be aggregated with one of the three reportable segments, there will be four reportable segments (including "all other segments").

- Alternatively, two or more of the smaller segments may be aggregated, if they meet the aggregation criteria. In this case, there will be five reportable segments.

- If none of the small segments meets the criteria to be aggregated with any of the other business lines, one of them must be identified as reportable, though it does not meet the 10% threshold. In this case, there will be five reportable segments also.

Solution 2—Comparative Information

- Comparative information for all periods presented should be restated (IAS 1) in conformity with IFRS 8.

- If the necessary information is not available and the cost to develop it would be excessive, this fact should be disclosed.

  In this case, there is no requirement to disclose current period segment information on both the old and new bases of segmentation (as there is when there is a change in composition of reportable segments). This is because the adoption of IFRS 8 is a mandatory change for those complying with IFRS, whereas an internal reorganisation is voluntary.

© DeVry/Becker Educational Development Corp. All rights reserved.

IAS 19 *Employee Benefits*

FOCUS

This session covers the following content from the *ACCA Study Guide.*

C. Reporting the Financial Performance of Entities

6. Employee benefits

a) Apply and discuss the accounting treatment of short-term and long-term employee benefits and defined contribution and defined benefit plans. ☐

b) Account for gains and losses on settlements and curtailments. ☐

c) Account for the "Asset Ceiling" test and the reporting of actuarial gains and losses. ☐

Session 11 Guidance

■ **Recognise** that *IAS 19 Employee Benefits* is a complex standard and is not included in the F7 syllabus.

■ **Understand** the terminology (s.1.4) and **learn** the distinction between the different types of benefits (s.2).

■ **Understand** how the two types of pension schemes are accounted for (s.4, s.5).

(continued on next page)

VISUAL OVERVIEW

Objective: To explain the accounting treatment and the disclosures for employee benefits.

```
                        ┌──────────────────────────┐
                        │        INTRODUCTION        │
                        │  • Key Problem             │
                        │  • Objective               │
                        │  • Scope                   │
                        │  • Terminology             │
                        └──────────────────────────┘
                          /                        \
      ┌──────────────────────────┐      ┌──────────────────────────────┐
      │     EMPLOYEE BENEFITS      │      │   POST-EMPLOYMENT BENEFITS     │
      │  • Short Term              │      │  • Benefit Plans               │
      │  • Long Term               │      │  • Classification              │
      │  • Termination Benefits    │      │                                │
      └──────────────────────────┘      └──────────────────────────────┘
                                          /                          \
              ┌──────────────────────────────┐      ┌──────────────────────────────┐
              │  DEFINED CONTRIBUTION PLANS     │      │     DEFINED BENEFIT PLANS      │
              │  • Introduction                │      │  • Introduction                │
              │  • Recognition and             │      │  • Accounting Principles       │
              │    Measurement                 │      │  • Detailed Accounting         │
              │                                │      │  • Disclosure                  │
              └──────────────────────────────┘      └──────────────────────────────┘
```

Session 11 Guidance

■ **Work** carefully through all the illustrations, especially *Illustration 5*.

■ **Attempt** *Example 1* to understand how the figures are used to calculate the expense and the asset or liability to be recognised.

© DeVry/Becker Educational Development Corp. All rights reserved.

1 Introduction

1.1 Key Problem

- Companies remunerate their staff by means of a wide range of benefits. These include wages and salaries, and retirement benefits.

- The cost to the employer needs to be matched with benefits derived from employees' services.

1.2 Objective

- The objective of IAS 19 is to prescribe the accounting and disclosure for employee benefits.

- An entity must recognise:
  - a liability when an employee has provided service in exchange for employee benefits to be paid in the future; and
  - an expense when the entity consumes the economic benefit arising from service provided by an employee in exchange for employee benefits.

1.3 Scope

 **Key Point**

IAS 19 applies to all employee benefits except those which relate to share-based payments (to which IFRS 2 applies).

- Employee benefits include:
  - short-term employee benefits which are expected to be settled within 12 months of the reporting date (e.g. wages, salaries and social security contributions, paid annual leave and paid sick leave, etc);
  - post-employment benefits (e.g. pensions, other retirement benefits, post-employment life insurance and post-employment medical care);
  - other long-term employee benefits (e.g. long-service leave or sabbatical leave); and
  - termination benefits.

1.4 Terminology

Employee benefits: all forms of consideration given by an entity in exchange for service rendered by employees, or for the termination of employment.

Short-term employee benefits: employee benefits (other than termination benefits) that are expected to be settled within 12 months after the end of the period in which the employees render the related service.

Other long-term employee benefits: all employee benefits other than short-term employee benefits, post-employment benefits and termination benefits.

© DeVry/Becker Educational Development Corp. All rights reserved.

Post-employment benefits: employee benefits (other than termination benefits) which are payable after the completion of employment.

Post-employment benefit plans: formal or informal arrangements under which an entity provides post-employment benefits for one or more employees.

Defined contribution plans: post-employment benefit plans under which an entity pays fixed contributions into a separate entity (a fund) and will have no legal or constructive obligation to pay further contributions if the fund does not hold sufficient assets to pay all employee benefits relating to employee service in the current and prior periods.

Defined benefit plans: post-employment benefit plans other than defined contribution plans.

Present value of a defined benefit obligation: the present value, without deducting any plan assets, of expected future payments required to settle the obligation resulting from employee service in the current and prior periods.

Current service cost: the increase in the present value of the defined benefit obligation resulting from employee service in the current period.

Past service cost: the change in present value of the defined benefit obligation for employee service in prior periods, resulting from a plan amendment or a curtailment.*

Net interest in the net defined liability (asset): the change during the period in the net defined benefit liability (asset) that arises from the passage of time.

> *Commentary*
>
> *Total service cost is made up of both current and past service cost plus any gain or loss on settlement.

- Actuarial gains and losses are changes in the present value of the defined benefit obligation resulting from:
  - experience adjustments (the effects of differences between the previous actuarial assumptions and what has actually occurred); and
  - the effects of changes in actuarial assumptions.

2 Employee Benefits

2.1 Short-Term Employee Benefits

2.1.1 Types

- Wages, salaries and social security contributions.
- Short-term compensated absences (e.g. paid annual leave and paid sick leave) where the absences are expected to occur within 12 months after the end of the period in which the employees render the related employee service.
- Profit sharing and bonuses payable within 12 months after the end of the period in which the employees render the related service.
- Non-monetary benefits (e.g. medical care, housing, cars and free or subsidised goods or services) for current employees.

2.1.2 Accounting for Short-Term Benefits

When an employee has rendered service to an entity during an accounting period, the entity recognises the amount of short-term employee benefits expected to be paid in exchange for that service:

- as a liability (accrued expense), after deducting any amount already paid; and
- as an expense (unless another IFRS requires or permits the inclusion of the benefits in the cost of an asset).

2.2 Long-Term Employee Benefits

Key Point

The entity must account for the expense on an accruals basis.

2.2.1 Types

Other types of long-term employee benefits are those which are not expected to be settled in full before 12 months after the end of the reporting period in which the service was given by the employee. The types of benefit will include:

- long-term paid absences (e.g. long-service and sabbatical leave);
- jubilee awards;
- long-term disability benefits;
- profit sharing and bonuses; and
- deferred remuneration.

2.2.2 Accounting for Long-Term Benefits

There is not as much uncertainty about the measurement of other long-term employee benefits as there is with post-employment benefits and so the standard requires a much simpler accounting model for these other long-term benefits. As an example, there is no need to recognise any remeasurement in other comprehensive income (unlike post-retirement benefits).

The principle to be applied in accounting for long-term benefits is similar to the accounting model for post-retirement benefits in that there may still be deficits or surpluses arising.

Key Point

Although the benefit is earned in the future (more than 12 months), the cost of the benefit is accrued when the employee provides the service.

The following items will be recognised in profit or loss for the period:

- service cost;
- net interest on the defined benefit asset or liability; and
- any remeasurements of the defined benefit asset or liability.

If the benefit is a long-term disability benefit and the amount paid depends on the length of service, the obligation arises when the service has been rendered and the amount recognised should reflect the probability of payment. If the benefit is fixed irrespective of the period of service, the amount is recognised when an obligating event arises.

© DeVry/Becker Educational Development Corp. All rights reserved.

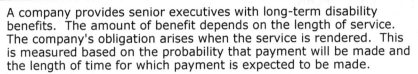

Illustration 1   Long-Term Benefits

A company provides senior executives with long-term disability benefits. The amount of benefit depends on the length of service. The company's obligation arises when the service is rendered. This is measured based on the probability that payment will be made and the length of time for which payment is expected to be made.

The same company provides all other employees with disability benefits regardless of length of service. The expected cost of those benefits is recognised only when an event occurs that causes a long-term disability.

2.3   Termination Benefits*

*Commentary

*This term does not cover any benefits if the employee terminates the employment other than in response to an offer of termination.

2.3.1   Types

- Typically lump sum payments;
- Enhanced post-employment benefits (e.g. pensions);
- Salary to the end of a notice period during which the employee renders no service (e.g. "gardening leave").

2.3.2   Recognition and Measurement

- A liability and expense is recognised:
    - when the entity cannot withdraw the offer of benefits (e.g. because it is accepted by the employee); or
    - on recognising a restructuring (under IAS 37) involving termination payments, if earlier.
- A termination benefit to be settled wholly within 12 months after the end of the reporting period is treated as a short-term benefit.
- Otherwise it is treated as a long-term benefit (i.e. with remeasurement at the end of each reporting period).

3   Post-Employment Benefits

3.1   Benefit Plans

- Arrangements whereby an entity provides post-employment benefits are post-employment benefit plans.
- An entity may, or may not, establish a separate entity to receive contributions and to pay benefits, although it is convenient to think of the plan as a separate entity.

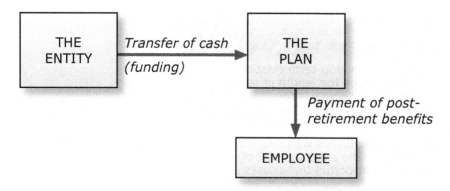

3.2   Classification

> **Key Point**
>
> Post-employment benefit plans are classified as either **defined contribution plans** or defined benefit plans, according to the economic substance of the plan.

4   Defined Contribution Plans

4.1   Introduction

▦ The entity must make a contribution into a separate fund for it to meet the definition of a defined contribution plan. If no contribution is made, then it is automatically classified as a defined benefit plan.

▦ The entity's obligation is limited to the amount it agrees to contribute to the fund.

▦ Thus, the amount of the post-employment benefits received by the employee is determined by the amount of contributions paid to the plan, together with investment returns arising from the contributions.

▦ In consequence, any risks with regard to the size of the pension paid fall on the employee.

> **Key Point**
>
> Accounting for defined contribution plans is straightforward because the reporting entity's obligation for each period is determined by the amounts to be contributed for that period.

4.2   Recognition and Measurement

▦ The accruals concept is applied:

  ● Charge contributions payable in respect of period to the statement of profit or loss.

  ● The statement of financial position will reflect any outstanding or prepaid contributions.

  ● An expense will be recognised for the contribution, unless another standard allows the cost to be included as part of an asset.*

*Commentary

*Employee costs are included in the cost of goods manufactured and so the contribution will be included as part of the inventory cost.

© DeVry/Becker Educational Development Corp. All rights reserved.

5 Defined Benefit Plans

5.1 Introduction

 **Key Point**

The entity's obligation is to provide the agreed benefits to current employees.

▓ There is a risk that the fund will be insufficient to pay the agreed pension. If this happens then the entity will have to provide for any shortfall (e.g. plans in which an employee is guaranteed a specified return).

▓ The entity will set cash aside which is invested to earn a return; this will grow and hopefully enable the entity to meet its future obligations.

▓ Clearly, the estimation of the amount to set aside is very difficult. Usually companies will use the services of an actuary (an expert in post-retirement benefits). The actuary will perform a calculation which includes estimates of all the variables that could affect the growth of assets and liabilities. These include:
  * required post-retirement benefits;
  * rate of return on the stock market;
  * interest rate;
  * inflation;
  * rate of leavers; and
  * death in service probability.

▓ The actuary will then tell the company how much it needs to set aside to meet the obligation. This is usually stated as a percentage of salary and is usually paid to the plan on a monthly basis.

▓ The actuary will never be absolutely accurate in the estimates. This means that the value of the plan assets and liabilities at each year end will be different from that forecast at the last actuarial valuation. The standard gives rules on how (or whether) to account for such differences.

5.2 Accounting Principles

▓ An entity makes payments to a fund (a separate legal entity). This cash is invested and used to pay retirement benefits when they fall due for payment. The fund is an entity with assets and liabilities (to the pensioners).

© DeVry/Becker Educational Development Corp. All rights reserved.

Key Point

At the end of each reporting period the assets and liabilities of the fund are valued and the entity recognises the net liability (or, more rarely, the net asset) in the statement of financial position.*

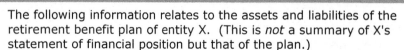

Illustration 2 Retirement Benefit Plan

The following information relates to the assets and liabilities of the retirement benefit plan of entity X. (This is *not* a summary of X's statement of financial position but that of the plan.)

	2016 $m	2017 $m
Market value of plan assets	100	110
Present value of plan obligations	(120)	(135)
Net liability of the plan	(20)	(25)

The basic rule (simplified for this illustration) is that:

In 2016 X must recognise a liability of	$20m
In 2017 X must recognise a liability of	$25m

If X had made a payment of $1m to the fund in 2017 the full journal would be:

Dr Profit or loss	6	
Cr Liability (25 – 20)		5
Cr Cash		1

Commentary

*The entity is recognising a net liability of a separate legal entity. This seems a little strange at first. But remember that the ultimate obligation to the employees is owed by the entity. The fund is merely a vehicle which allows the entity to meet this obligation. In substance, the assets and liabilities of the fund are a special area of the entity's own statement of financial position even though they are held by a separate entity.

5.3 Detailed Accounting

▣ A net defined liability (asset) is recognised in the statement of financial position and actuarial gains or losses in the statement of profit or loss and other comprehensive income.

5.3.1 Statement of Financial Position

▣ The statement of financial position must recognise the net defined benefit liability or asset.*

▣ If the net position results in an asset, then the amount of asset that can be recognised is limited to the lower of:

• the surplus in the plan; and

• the asset ceiling.

Commentary

*In *Illustration 2* this is the net liability of $25 million at the end of 2017.

© DeVry/Becker Educational Development Corp. All rights reserved.

5.3.2 Asset Ceiling

Definition

Asset ceiling—the present value of any economic benefits available to the entity in the form of refunds from the plan or future reductions in contributions to the plan.

- If a fund is "in surplus", assets exceed liabilities. A degree of prudence is attached to the recognition of this net asset position.*
- A net asset position can arise due to:
  - actuarial assumptions being over pessimistic; or
  - asset returns being higher than expected.
- The asset meets the Framework definition of an asset, as the entity controls a resource that is expected to generate future economic benefits.
- The maximum amount that can be recognised for this asset is the **lower** of:
  - the fund surplus; and
  - the asset ceiling.

*Commentary

*There is no liability ceiling equivalent, so a net liability position must be recognised in full.

Illustration 3 Asset Ceiling

A defined benefit fund has obligations of $720,000 and plan assets of $868,000 leading to a surplus of $148,000. The terms of the fund state that any surplus must be split 50:50 between the fund and the entity. The present value of $148,000 using an appropriate discount rate is $84,000.

The asset ceiling restricts the amount of the surplus of $148,000 that can be recognised. As only 50% of the surplus can be refunded, the entity recognises only 50% of the present value (i.e. $42,000).

5.3.3 Statement of Comprehensive Income

- The statement of comprehensive income will recognise components of defined benefit cost, unless another standard requires the cost be included as part of the cost of an asset.
- The defined benefit cost is made up of three components:
  - **service cost,** which itself will comprise current service cost, past service cost and any gains or losses on settlement. Service cost will be expensed to profit or loss.
  - **net interest** on the net defined benefit liability, or asset. This cost is calculated by taking the net liability, or asset, at the start of the period and applying the respective discount rate. The interest is expensed, credited, to profit or loss.
  - **remeasurements** of the net defined liability or asset. This includes actuarial gains and losses on the defined benefit liability, the return on plan assets excluding the amount included in the net interest calculation, and any change in the asset ceiling. This element of cost is included in other comprehensive income.

5.3.4 Actuarial Assumptions

▧ It is likely that an entity will use the services of an actuary in calculating the defined benefit obligation and current service cost.

▧ An actuary is a statistician who computes insurance risks and premiums, and will have expertise in the area of pension issues.

▧ When calculating the defined benefit liability and current service cost the actuary uses the projected unit credit method.

▧ This model assumes each period of service gives rise to an additional benefit and measures each additional benefit separately working towards the final obligation.

▧ The actuary is trying to predict the future and will need to make assumptions about what he expects to happen in the future. Any assumptions made must be unbiased and mutually compatible.

▧ The assumptions fall into two broad categories:

- demographic assumptions about employees, to include:
  — mortality;
  — employee turnover;
  — dependants of employees who will be eligible for benefits.
- financial assumptions, to include:
  — discount rate;
  — benefit levels and future salary;
  — future medical costs for any medical benefits.

5.3.5 Past Service Cost

▧ A past service cost arises when there is a change in the present value of the defined benefit liability caused by an amendment to the plan or a curtailment.

▧ An amendment arises when an entity changes the benefits payable under a defined benefit plan. For example, increasing the plan's payout from 1% to 1.2% of final salary for each year of service including past service (i.e. back-dated) would increase the liability. The increase in the liability is charged to profit or loss in the year of change.

▧ A curtailment occurs when the number of employees covered by a plan is significantly reduced (e.g. if part of the business was terminated and the employees made redundant). This will usually lead to some settlement of the obligation to the employees.

▧ Any gain or loss on settlement is included in profit or loss in the year of settlement.

Definition

Settlement—a transaction that eliminates all further legal or constructive obligations for all or part of the benefits provided under a defined benefit plan.

Key Point

- Past service cost should be recognised as an expense on the earlier of:
  - the date when the plan amendment or curtailment occurs; and
  - the date when the entity recognises any related restructuring costs or termination benefits.

                    © DeVry/Becker Educational Development Corp. All rights reserved.

Illustration 4 Curtailment

An entity is making redundant 100 employees who have pension entitlements under the entity's defined benefit scheme. As a result of the redundancy, an obligation of $1.2 million is to be settled with immediate payouts amounting to $0.9 million. The gain on the settlement of $0.3 million is recognised in profit or loss immediately.

5.3.6 Fair Value of Plan Assets

▓ In a funded scheme the trustees of the fund will invest any contributions into various forms of assets. These assets will include property, shares, debt assets and cash.

▓ IFRS 13 applies to the measurement of the fair value of the plan assets. If no market price exists for a particular asset then the fair value should be estimated by discounting expected future cash flows.

▓ The fair value of the plan assets will then be deducted from the defined benefit liability to identify the net liability, or asset, that will be recognised by the entity.

▓ The plan assets exclude any unpaid contributions due from the entity as well as any non-transferable financial instruments issued by the entity and held by the fund.*

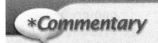

*Commentary

*One of the issues of the Enron accounting disaster was that the Enron pension fund was holding equity shares of Enron as part of their assets. This had the effect of propping up Enron's share price.

Illustration 5 Defined Benefit Scheme

The following information relates to the assets and liabilities of the defined benefit plan of Draycott for three years:

	2015 $000	2016 $000	2017 $000
Current service cost	125	140	155
Benefits paid	130	150	170
Contributions paid	80	90	100
Present value of the obligation at 31 December	1,215	1,386	1,400
Fair value of the plan assets at 31 December	1,147	1,137	1,200
Discount rate at the start of the year	9%	8%	8%

The present value of the obligation and the fair value of the plan assets were both $1 million at 1 January 2015.

In December 2016, a segment of the entity was sold and this resulted in a number of employees being made redundant and the pension scheme for these employees was curtailed. Most of the employees found new jobs and took the option to transfer their benefits to their new employers. As a result of this, Draycott transferred assets with a value of $27,000 to the new employers' pension schemes in full settlement of the employees' pension entitlements; this settlement reduced the pension obligation of Draycott by $31,000. The settlement has not yet been reflected in the 2016 balances given above.

© DeVry/Becker Educational Development Corp. All rights reserved.

Illustration 5 Defined Benefit Scheme (continued)

Required:

(a) Reconcile the present values of the obligation to determine the actuarial loss or gain for each year.

(b) Reconcile the fair values of the plan assets to determine the remeasurement gain or loss for each year.

(c) Calculate the net liability (or asset) that should be recognised in the statement of financial position at the end of each year.

(d) Calculate the amounts to be included in the statement of comprehensive income for each year.

(e) Present a journal summarising the accounting entries for each year.

Solution

(a) Present Value of Obligation

	2015 $000	2016 $000	2017 $000
Present value	1,000	1,215	1,355
Interest (9%/8%/8%)	90	97	108
Current service cost	125	140	155
Benefits paid	(130)	(150)	(170)
Settlement	—	(31)	—
Expected value	1,085	1,271	1,448
Actuarial loss/gain (to balance)	130	84	(48)
Present value at 31 December	1,215	1,355	1,400

(b) Fair Value of Asset

	2015 $000	2016 $000	2017 $000
Fair value	1,000	1,147	1,110
Interest (9%/8%/8%)	90	92	89
Contributions	80	90	100
Benefits paid	(130)	(150)	(170)
Settlement	—	(27)	—
Expected value	1,040	1,152	1,129
Gain/(loss) on remeasurement to other comprehensive income (to balance)	107	(42)	71
Fair value at 31 December	1,147	1,110	1,200

(c) Net Liability

	2015 $	2016 $	2017 $
Present value of the obligation	1,215	1,355	1,400
Fair value of the plan assets	1,147	1,110	1,200
Net liability	68	245	200

© DeVry/Becker Educational Development Corp. All rights reserved.

Illustration 5 Defined Benefit Scheme (continued)

(d) Statement of Comprehensive Income

Profit or loss	2015	2016	2017
	$000	$000	$000
Current service costs	125	140	155
Net interest on opening net liability	—	5	19
Gain on settlement (31 − 27)	—	(4)	—
Profit or loss expense	125	141	174

Other comprehensive income

Remeasurement

	2015	2016	2017
Actuarial loss/(gain) on obligation	130	84	(48)
Actual (gain)/loss on asset	(107)	42	(71)
Net other comprehensive income	23	126	(119)
Total other comprehensive income	148	267	55

(e) Accounting Entries

	Dr	Cr	Dr	Cr	Dr	Cr
Dr Comprehensive income	148		267		55	
Dr/Cr Liability (W)		68		177	45	
Cr Cash (contributions paid)		80		90		100

WORKING

Movements on net liability:	$	$	$
Opening net liability	—	68	245
Net movement	68	177	(45)
Closing net liability	68	245	200

Example 1 Defined Benefit Pension Scheme

Daktari provides a defined benefit pension scheme for its employees. The following information relates to the balances on the fund's assets and liabilities at the beginning and end of the year ending 31 December:

	1 Jan	31 Dec
Present value of benefit obligation	1,270	1,450
Fair value of plan assets	1,025	1,130
Service cost for year		70
Contributions to the plan		100
Benefits paid		–
Discount rate		3%
Expected return on fund assets		5%

Required:

(a) Identify the balance to be included in Daktari's statement of financial position at 31 December.

(b) Calculate the amounts to be included in the statement of comprehensive income for the year ended 31 December.

(c) Present a journal summarising the accounting entries.

5.4 Disclosure

▥ The following information about defined benefit plans:

- the characteristics of the defined benefit plan and any risks associated with them;
- explanations relating to the figures included in the financial statements; and
- a description as to how the entity's defined benefit plan may affect the timing and uncertainty of the entity's future cash flows.

▥ When meeting the disclosure requirements, an entity should consider the following:

- the level of detail necessary to meet the disclosure requirements;
- what emphasis to place on each of the disclosure requirements;
- how much aggregation or disaggregation to undertake; and
- whether users need additional information to evaluate the qualitative information disclosed.

© DeVry/Becker Educational Development Corp. All rights reserved.

Summary

- IAS 19 applies to all employee benefits except those relating to share-based payments (IFRS 2).
- Short-term employee benefits are accounted for on an accrual basis.
- The cost of long-term benefits is accrued when the employee provides the service.
- Post-employment benefit plans are classified, according to their economic substance, as either defined contribution plans or defined benefit plans.
- Accounting for defined contribution plans is straightforward; the reporting entity's obligation for each period is determined by the amounts of contributions for that period.
- At the end of each reporting period the assets and liabilities of defined benefit plans are valued and the net liability (or asset) recognised in the statement of financial position).
- The maximum amount that can be recognised for an asset is the **lower** of:
  - the fund surplus; and
  - the asset ceiling.
- Profit or loss includes past and current service cost and net interest on the opening net defined liability or asset.
- Other comprehensive income includes remeasurements for the period, including actuarial gains and losses.
- Past service is recognised as an expense when the plan amendment or curtailment occurs or when the entity recognises any related restructuring costs or termination benefits, if earlier.

© DeVry/Becker Educational Development Corp. All rights reserved.

Session 11 Quiz
Estimated time: 30 minutes

1. List the types of employee benefits IAS 19 addresses. (1.3)

2. Define the phrase "defined benefit plans" as it is used in IAS 19. (1.4)

3. Describe the accounting for short-term employee benefits. (2.1)

4. Describe the accounting for defined contribution schemes. (4.2)

5. Name the party which bears the risk in a defined benefit scheme. (5.1)

6. Suppose the fund of a defined benefit scheme has a net asset position to be recognised. Specify the limit placed on the amount of the asset to be recognised. (5.3.1)

7. Explain the restrictions on recognising actuarial losses of a scheme through other comprehensive income. (5.3)

8. List the THREE components which make up the defined benefit cost that appears in the statement of comprehensive income. (5.3.3)

9. Briefly explain "past service cost." (5.3.5)

Study Question Bank
Estimated time: 40 minutes

Priority		Estimated Time	Completed
Q19	Kelly	40 minutes	

© DeVry/Becker Educational Development Corp. All rights reserved.

EXAMPLE SOLUTION

Solution 1—Defined Benefit Pension Scheme

(a) Statement of financial position

Closing net defined liability (1,450 − 1,130)   320

(b) Statement of comprehensive income

Service cost	70
Net interest (W1)	7
Profit or loss	77
Other comprehensive income:	
Remeasurements (W2)	98
Total comprehensive income	175

Workings

(1) Net Interest
 3% × 245 opening net defined benefit liability (i.e. 1,270 − 1,025).

(2) Remeasurements:

Actuarial gain or loss on defined benefit liability:

Opening liability	1,270	
Current service cost	70	
Interest on opening liability (1,270 × 3%)	38	
Actuarial loss	72	to balance
Closing liability	1,450	

Actual return on plan assets:

Opening asset	1,025	
Cash contribution	100	
Actual return	5	to balance
Closing asset	1,130	

Net interest on opening plan asset is 31, (1,025 × 3%), and so decrease in plan assets due to remeasurement is 26 (5 − 31).

Net remeasurement is 98, (72 losses on liability + 26 losses on return).

(c) Journal entries

Dr Profit or loss	77	
Dr Other comprehensive income	98	
Cr Cash (contribution)		100
Cr Net defined benefit liability (W)		75

Working

Opening net liability (1,270 − 1,025)	245
Closing net liability as (a)	320
Increase in liability	75

IAS 12 *Income Taxes*

FOCUS

This session covers the following content from the *ACCA Study Guide.*

C. Reporting the Financial Performance of Entities

7. Income taxes

a) Apply and discuss the recognition and measurement of deferred tax liabilities and deferred tax assets. ☐

b) Determine the recognition of tax expense or income and its inclusion in the financial statements. ☐

Session 12 Guidance

■ **Recognise** that this is a very important topic for the examination. You should be familiar with the subject from your F7 studies, but at this level you should expect to be examined on the more complex issues of deferred tax, particularly those relating to group issues (s.4).

■ **Revise** the terminology (s.1.2) and the basics (s.2) using the *Illustrations*. **Attempt** *Example 1*.

VISUAL OVERVIEW

Objective: To describe the rules for recognition and measurement of taxes.

```
                        ┌─────────────────────────┐
                        │        TAXATION         │
                        │  • Overview             │
                        │  • Terminology          │
                        │  • Current Tax          │
                        │  • Deferred Taxation    │
                        └─────────────────────────┘
```

TAXATION
- Overview
- Terminology
- Current Tax
- Deferred Taxation

DEFERRED TAXATION
- Perspective
- Asset/Liability Amounts
- Terminology

BUSINESS COMBINATIONS
- Introduction
- Goodwill
- Carrying Amount of Investment
- Intra-group Transactions

PRESENTATION AND DISCLOSURE
- Presentation
- Disclosure

DETAILED RULES
- Liabilities
- Assets
- Accounting for Movements
- Tax Rates
- Change in Rates

APPROACH SUMMARY
- Calculations

Session 12 Guidance

■ **Learn** the rules for deferred tax liabilities (s.3.1), deferred tax assets (s.3.2), movements therein (s.3.3) and changes in tax rates (s.3.4), and understand the accounting issues which relate to these. **Attempt** *Examples 2–5*.

■ **Return** to the groups section (s.4) when you have completed *Session 18*.

© DeVry/Becker Educational Development Corp. All rights reserved.

1 Taxation

1.1 Overview

- In financial reporting, the financial statements need to reflect the effects of taxation on a company. Guidance is provided by the fundamental accounting concepts of accruals and prudence. Tax rules determine the cash flows; these must be matched to the revenues which gave rise to the tax and tax liabilities must be recognised as they are incurred, not merely when they are paid.

- The consistency must be applied in the presentation of income and expenditure.

1.2 Terminology

Accounting profit: profit or loss for a period before deducting tax expense.

Taxable profit (tax loss): the profit (loss) for a period, determined in accordance with the rules established by the taxation authorities, on which income taxes are payable (recoverable).

Tax expense (tax income): the aggregate amount included in the determination of profit or loss for the period in respect of current tax and deferred tax.

Current tax: the amount of income taxes payable (recoverable) in respect of the taxable profit (tax loss) for a period.

Deferred tax liabilities: the amounts of income taxes payable in future period in respect of taxable temporary differences.

Deferred tax assets: the amounts of income taxes recoverable in future periods in respect of:

- deductible temporary differences;
- the carry forward of unused tax losses; and
- the carry forward of unused tax credits.

Temporary differences: differences between the carrying amount of an asset or liability and its tax base. Temporary differences may be either:

- **taxable temporary differences:** temporary differences that will result in taxable amounts in determining taxable profit (tax loss) of future periods when the carrying amount of the asset or liability is recovered or settled; or

- **deductible temporary differences:** temporary differences that will result in amounts that are deductible in determining taxable profit (tax loss) of future periods when the carrying amount of the asset or liability is recovered or settled.

Tax base of an asset or liability: the amount attributed to that asset or liability for tax purposes.

© DeVry/Becker Educational Development Corp. All rights reserved.

1.3   Recognition of Current Tax Liabilities and Current Tax Assets

▨ **Current tax** for current and prior periods should, to the extent unpaid, be recognised as a liability. If the amount already paid in respect of current and prior periods exceeds the amounts due for those periods, the excess should be recognised as an asset.

▨ The benefit relating to a tax loss that can be carried back to recover current tax of a previous period should be recognised as an asset.

▨ A company is a separate legal entity and is therefore liable to income tax.

Key Point

The income tax charged in the statement of comprehensive income is an estimate. Any over/under provisions are cleared in the following period's statement of comprehensive income and do *not* give rise to a prior period adjustment.

1.4   Deferred Taxation

▨ In most jurisdictions, **accounting profit** and taxable profit differ, meaning that the tax charge may bear little relation to profits in a period.

Key Point

Differences arise due to the fact that tax authorities follow rules which differ from IFRS rules in arriving at taxable profit.

▨ Transactions which are recognised in the accounts in a particular period may have their tax effect deferred until a later period.

Illustration 1 Contribution Tax Effects v Accounting Effects
Many non-current assets are depreciated.
Most tax authorities will allow companies to deduct the cost of purchasing non-current assets from their profit for tax purposes, but only according to a set formula. If this differs from the accounting depreciation, then the asset will be written down by the tax authority and by the company, but at different rates.
Thus, the tax effect of the transaction (which is based on the tax laws) will be felt in a different period to the accounting effect.

- It is convenient to envisage two separate sets of accounts:
  - one set constructed following IFRS rules; and
  - a second set following the tax rules of the jurisdiction in which the company operates.*

*Commentary

*The second set of accounts is referred to as the "tax computations".

- The differences between the two sets of rules will result in different numbers in the financial statements and in the tax computations. These differences may be viewed from the perspective of:
  - the statement of financial position (balance sheet); or
  - the statement of profit or loss.
- The current tax charge for the period will be based on the tax authority's view of the profit, not the accounting view. This will mean that the relationship between the accounting profit before tax and the tax charge will be distorted. It will not be the tax rate applied to the accounting profit figure, but the tax rate applied to a tax computation figure.

2 Deferred Taxation—Basics

2.1 A "Balance Sheet" Perspective

- IAS 12 takes a "balance sheet" perspective. Accounting for deferred taxation involves the recognition of a liability (or an asset) in the statement of financial position. The difference between the liabilities at each year end is taken to the statement of comprehensive income.*

*Commentary

*Exceptions to this perspective are rare. Unless indicated otherwise all changes in deferred tax balances are taken through the statement of comprehensive income.

Illustration 2 Deferred Taxes*	
	$
Deferred taxation balance at the start of the year	1,000
Transfer to the statement of comprehensive income *(as a balancing figure)*	500
Deferred taxation balance at the end of the year	1,500

---

*Commentary

*Most of the effort in accounting for deferred taxation goes into the calculation of the deferred tax balance at the end of the year.

2.2 Asset or Liability Amounts

- The calculation of the balance to be included in the statement of financial position is, in essence, very simple. It involves the comparison of the carrying amounts of items in the accounts to the tax authority's view of the amount (known as the **tax base of the item**). The difference generated in each case is called a **temporary difference.***

*Commentary

*The basic temporary difference calculation, which compares the carrying amounts of items, is a simplification; complications are covered in s.4.

© DeVry/Becker Educational Development Corp. All rights reserved.

Key Point

Deferred taxation is provided on all **taxable temporary differences.**

Illustration 3 Temporary Differences

	Carrying amount in financial statements	Tax base	Temporary differences	Deferred tax balance required at 30%
	$	$	$	$
Non-current assets	20,000	14,000	6,000	1,800
Other transactions				
A (accrued income)	1,000	–	1,000	300
B (an accrued expense)	(2,000)	–	(2,000)	(600)
			5,000	1,500

Transactions A and B are taxed on a cash basis; therefore, the tax authority's statement of financial position would not recognise accrued amounts in respect of these items.

2.3 Terminology

Definition

Tax base of an asset or liability—the amount attributed to that asset or liability for tax purposes.

- The **tax base of an asset** is the amount that will be deductible for tax purposes against any taxable economic benefit that will flow to an entity when it recovers the carrying amount of the asset.

Definition

Temporary difference—a difference between the carrying amount of an asset or liability in the statement of financial position and its tax base.

- **Temporary differences** may be either:
  - debit balances in the financial statements compared to the tax computations. These will lead to deferred tax credit balances, known as taxable temporary differences; or
  - credit balances in the financial statements compared to the tax computations. These will lead to deferred tax debit balances, known as **deductible temporary differences.**

© DeVry/Becker Educational Development Corp. All rights reserved.

Key Point

As an examination rule, if the carrying amount of an asset is greater than the tax base of an asset, then a taxable temporary difference arises leading to a **deferred tax liability.**

Illustration 4	Tax Base of an Asset	
		$
Carrying amount of asset		6,000
Tax base of the asset		(5,000)
Temporary difference*		1,000
Deferred tax balance required (@30%)		300

Commentary

*Does the liability of $1,000, the temporary tax difference, meet the definition of a liability from the Framework?

IFRS says yes, but there are many accountants who believe that the definition of a liability has not been met, and therefore deferred tax should not be provided for.

▨ The difference between the carrying amount of the asset and the tax authority's value is described as a temporary difference because it is temporary in nature—it will disappear in time.

▨ The IAS 12 justification is that ownership of this asset will lead to income of $6,000 in the future. The company will only have $5,000 as an expense to charge against this for tax purposes. The $1,000 that is not covered will be taxed and should be provided for now.

▨ Temporary differences may lead to deferred tax assets or liabilities; IAS 12 imposes tougher recognition criteria for asset balances.

▨ Deferred tax accounting is about accounting for items where the tax effect is deferred to a later period. Circumstances under which temporary differences arise include:

● When income or expense is included in accounting profit in one period but included in the taxable profit in a *different* period. For example:

— items which are taxed on a cash basis but which will be accounted for on an accruals basis;

Illustration 5	Taxed on a Cash Basis

The accounts of Bill show interest receivable of $10,000. No cash has yet been received and interest is taxed on a cash basis. The interest receivable has a tax base of nil. *Deferred tax will be provided on the temporary difference of $10,000.*

— situations where the accounting depreciation does not equal tax allowable depreciation;

                                         © DeVry/Becker Educational Development Corp. All rights reserved.

Illustration 6 Accounting v Tax Purposes Depreciation

Bill has non-current assets at 31 December with a cost of $4,000,000. Aggregate depreciation for accounting purposes is $750,000. For tax purposes, depreciation of $1,000,000 has been deducted to date. The non-current assets have a tax base of $3,000,000. The provision for deferred tax will be provided on the taxable temporary difference of $250,000.

- *Revaluation* of assets where the tax authorities do not amend the tax base when the asset is revalued.
- Unfortunately, the definition of temporary difference captures other items which should **not** result in deferred taxation accounting (e.g. accruals for items which are not taxed or do not attract tax relief).
- IAS 12 therefore includes rules to exclude such items. For example, *"If those economic benefits will not be taxable, the tax base of the asset is equal to its carrying amount"*.
- The wording seems a little strange, but the effect is to exclude such items from the deferred taxation calculations.

Illustration 7 Exclude From Tax Calculations

Bill provided a loan of $250,000 to John. At 31 December, Bill's accounts show a loan payable of $200,000. The repayment of the loan has no tax consequences. Therefore, the loan payable has a tax base of $200,000. No temporary taxable difference arises.

© DeVry/Becker Educational Development Corp. All rights reserved.

Example 1   Deferred Tax Provision

The following information relates to Boniek as at 31 December 2017:

	Note	Carrying amount	Tax base
Non-current assets		$	$
Plant and machinery		200,000	175,000
Receivables			
Trade receivables	1	50,000	
Interest receivable		1,000	
Payables			
Fine		10,000	
Interest payable		2,000	

Note 1
The trade receivables balance in the accounts is made up of the following amounts:

	$
Balances	55,000
Credit loss allowance	(5,000)
	50,000

Further information:

(1) The deferred tax liability as at 1 January 2017 was $1,200.

(2) Interest is taxed on a cash basis.

(3) Allowances for trade receivables are not deductible for tax purposes. Amounts are only deductible on application of a court order to a specific amount.

(4) Fines are not tax deductible.

(5) Deferred tax is charged at 30%.

Required:

Calculate the deferred tax provision which is required at 31 December 2017 and the charge to the profit or loss for the period.

                    © DeVry/Becker Educational Development Corp. All rights reserved.

3   Deferred Tax—Detailed Rules

3.1   Deferred Tax Liabilities

3.1.1   The Rule

▨ A deferred tax liability is recognised for all **taxable temporary differences** unless it arises from:
  ● the initial recognition of goodwill; or
  ● the initial recognition of an asset or liability in a transaction which:
    — is not a business combination; and
    — at the time of the transaction, affects neither accounting profit nor taxable profit.

▨ If the economic benefits are not taxable the tax base of the asset is equal to its carrying amount.

3.1.2   Issues

▨ "all taxable temporary differences"
  ● Temporary differences include all differences between accounting rules and tax rules, not just those which are temporary. IAS 12 contains other provisions to correct this anomaly and excludes items where the tax effect is not deferred, but rather, is "permanent" in nature.

▨ "initial recognition—not a business combination"
  ● If the initial recognition is a business combination, deferred tax may arise.

▨ "affects neither accounting profit nor taxable profit (tax loss)"
  ● This rule is an application of the idea that if an item is not taxable, it should be excluded from the calculations.

▨ Taxable temporary differences also arise in the following situations:
  ● Certain IFRSs permit assets to be carried at a fair value or to be revalued.
    — if the revaluation of the asset is also reflected in the tax base, then no temporary difference arises.
    — if the revaluation does not affect the tax base, then a temporary difference does arise and deferred tax must be provided.
  ● When the cost of acquiring a business is allocated by reference to fair value of the assets and liabilities acquired, but no equivalent adjustment has been made for tax purposes.*

*Basically the same rule applies to a group accounting situation.

© DeVry/Becker Educational Development Corp. All rights reserved.

Example 2 Lato

The following information relates to Lato:

	Carrying amount $	Tax base $
At 1 January 2017	1,000	800
Depreciation	(100)	(150)
At 31 December 2017	900	650

At the year end, the company decided to revalue the asset to $1,250. The tax base is not affected by this revaluation.

Required:

Calculate the deferred tax provision required in respect of this asset as at 31 December 2017.

3.2 Deferred Tax Assets

3.2.1 The Rule

▨ A **deferred tax asset** is recognised for all *deductible temporary differences* to the extent that it is probable that taxable profit will be available against which the deductible temporary difference can be utilised, unless the deferred tax asset arises from:

- the *initial* recognition of an asset or liability in a transaction which:
  - — is not a business combination; and
  - — at the time of transaction, affects neither accounting profit nor taxable profit (tax loss).

▨ The carrying amount of a deferred tax asset is reviewed at the end of each reporting period. The carrying amount of a deferred tax asset is reduced to the extent that it is no longer probable that sufficient taxable profit will be available to utilise the asset.

3.2.2 Issues

▨ Most of the comments made about deferred tax liabilities also apply to deferred tax assets.

▨ Major difference between the recognition of deferred tax assets and liabilities is in the use of the phrase "to the extent that it is probable that taxable profit will be available against which the deductible temporary difference can be utilised".*

▨ An asset should only be recognised when the company expects to receive a benefit from its existence. The existence of deferred tax liability (to the same jurisdiction) is strong evidence that the asset will be recoverable.

Commentary

*IAS 12 brings a different standard to the recognition of deferred tax assets than it does to deferred tax liabilities. In short, liabilities will always be provided in full (subject to the specified exemptions), but assets may not be provided in full or in some cases at all. This is an application of the concept of prudence.

© DeVry/Becker Educational Development Corp. All rights reserved.

Illustration 8 Recognition*

The following budgeted information is presented concerning the costs and revenues in respect of product B, based on producing and selling 10,000 units per week:

	Situation 1	Situation 2
	$	$
Deferred tax liability	10,000	5,000
Deferred tax asset	(8,000)	(8,000)
Net position	2,000	(3,000)

- In situation 1, the existence of the liability ensures the recoverability of the asset and the asset should be provided.
- In situation 2, the company would provide for $5,000 of the asset, but would need to consider carefully the recoverability of the $3,000 net debit balance.
- In short, debit balances which are covered by credit balances will be provided (as long as the tax is payable/recoverable to/from the same jurisdiction), but net debit balances will be subject to close scrutiny.

> *Commentary*
>
> *Any deferred tax asset balance that is not recognised will be disclosed in the notes to the financial statements. If circumstances change in future periods, then the recognition of the asset will be reconsidered.

3.2.3 Debt Instruments Measured at Fair Value

- IAS 12 was amended in 2016 to reflect concern over debt instruments measured at fair value and the recognition of a deferred tax asset.
- The amendment clarifies that unrealised losses arising when the fair value falls below cost will give rise to a deductible temporary difference.
- The recogniiton of the difference is regardless of whether the holder expects to recover the carrying amount of the instrument by holding till maturity or by sale.

3.3 Accounting for the Movement on the Deferred Tax Balance

- Deferred tax is recognised as **tax expense or income** and included in the *profit or loss* for the period, except to the extent that the tax arises from:
  - a transaction or event which is recognised, in the same or a different period, outside of profit or loss, either in other comprehensive income or directly in equity; or
  - a business combination that is an acquisition.*

> *Commentary*
>
> *The deferred tax income or expense will follow the transaction to which it relates. If an entity has revalued land and the surplus has been credited to other comprehensive income, then the deferred tax effect of the revaluation will be charged through other comprehensive income.

© DeVry/Becker Educational Development Corp. All rights reserved.

Key Point

Deferred tax is charged or credited to other comprehensive income or directly to equity if the tax relates to items that are credited or charged, in the same or different period, to other comprehensive income or directly to equity.

■ Deferred tax should be debited to goodwill in respect of the difference in the fair value and the carrying amount of the subsidiaries net assets acquired. This will only relate to the year of acquisition of the subsidiary.

Example 3   Deferred Taxation Charge

Following on from *Example 2*:

	Carrying amount $	Tax base $
At 1 January 2017	1,000	800
Depreciation	(100)	(150)
At 31 December 2017	900	650

At the year end, the company decided to revalue the asset to $1,250. The tax base is not affected by this revaluation.

	Carrying amount $	Tax base $	Temporary difference
	1,250	650	600
Deferred tax at 30%			180

Required:

Assuming that the only temporary difference that the company has relates to this asset, construct a note showing the movement on the deferred taxation and identify the charge to profit or loss in respect of deferred taxation for the year ended 31 December 2017.

3.4   Tax Rates

Key Point

The tax rate used is the rate that is expected to apply to the period when the asset is realised or the liability is settled, based on tax rates that have been enacted by the end of the reporting period.

© DeVry/Becker Educational Development Corp. All rights reserved.

▨ The tax rate used should reflect the tax consequences of the manner in which the entity expects to recover or settle the carrying amount of its assets and liabilities.

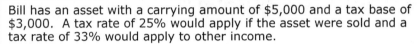

Illustration 9 Tax Rate

Bill has an asset with a carrying amount of $5,000 and a tax base of $3,000. A tax rate of 25% would apply if the asset were sold and a tax rate of 33% would apply to other income.

Bill recognises a deferred tax liability of $500 ($2,000 @ 25%) if he expects to sell the asset without further use and a deferred tax liability of $660 ($2,000 @33%) if he expects to retain the asset and recover its carrying amount through use.

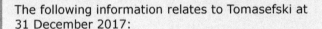

Example 4 Deferred Tax Provision

The following information relates to Tomasefski at 31 December 2017:

	Carrying amount $	Tax base $
Non-current assets	460,000	320,000
Tax losses	90,000	

Further information:

1. Tax rates (enacted by the 2017 year end)

2017	2018	2019	2020
36%	34%	32%	31%

2. The loss above is the tax loss incurred in 2017. The company is very confident about the trading prospects in 2018.

3. The temporary difference in respect of non-current assets is expected to grow each year until beyond 2020.

4. Losses may be carried forward for offset, one-third into each of the next three years

Required:

Calculate the deferred tax provision that is required at 31 December 2017.

© DeVry/Becker Educational Development Corp. All rights reserved.

3.5   Change in Tax Rates

▨ Companies are required to disclose the amount of deferred taxation in the tax expense that relates to change in the tax rates.

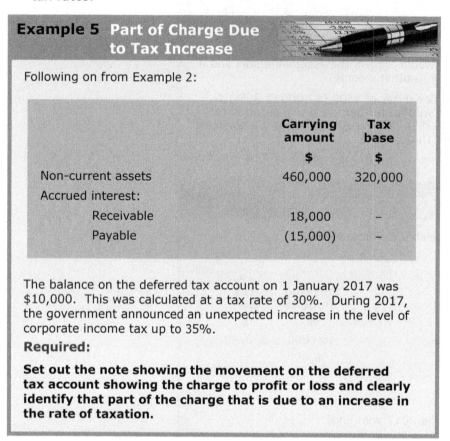

> ### Example 5   Part of Charge Due to Tax Increase
>
> Following on from Example 2:
>
> | | Carrying amount $ | Tax base $ |
> |---|---|---|
> | Non-current assets | 460,000 | 320,000 |
> | Accrued interest: | | |
> | Receivable | 18,000 | – |
> | Payable | (15,000) | – |
>
> The balance on the deferred tax account on 1 January 2017 was $10,000. This was calculated at a tax rate of 30%. During 2017, the government announced an unexpected increase in the level of corporate income tax up to 35%.
>
> **Required:**
>
> **Set out the note showing the movement on the deferred tax account showing the charge to profit or loss and clearly identify that part of the charge that is due to an increase in the rate of taxation.**

4   Business Combinations

4.1   Introduction

4.1.1   Background

▨ Acquisition accounting and equity accounting share certain features which are relevant to an understanding of the deferred taxation consequences of employing these techniques.

▨ Each involves the replacement of cost with a share of net assets and goodwill arising on acquisition. The subsequent impairment of the goodwill and the crediting of post-acquisition growth in equity balances to the equivalent equity balances of the group.

© DeVry/Becker Educational Development Corp. All rights reserved.

Illustration 10   Acquisition

	P's own financial statements		P group financial statements		
	Cost		*Share of net assets*		*Goodwill*
At the date of acquisition	600	=	450	+	150
	Cost		*Share of net assets*		Goodwill
At a subsequent statement of financial position	600	=	520	+	150
			Also		(30)
					120
			Through profit or loss to equity		
			= 70		(30)
			= a net debit of 600		

- This is effectively what takes place under each of the techniques. They differ in the way that the share of net assets is reflected in the "group" financial statements.

- Note that the carrying amount of the investment in Illustration 10 is $640 (520+120).

4.1.2 Sources of Temporary Differences

- Temporary differences may arise due to the following reasons:
  - The calculation of goodwill requires a fair valuation exercise. This exercise may change the carrying amounts of assets and liabilities, but not their tax bases. The resulting deferred tax amounts will affect the value of goodwill.
  - Retained earnings of subsidiaries, branches, associates and joint ventures are included in consolidated retained earnings, but income taxes will be payable if the profits are distributed to the reporting parent.
- Furthermore, IFRS 10 *Consolidated Financial Statements* requires the elimination of unrealised profits/losses resulting from intra-group transactions. This treatment will generate temporary differences.

4.2 Temporary Differences and Goodwill

▨ The cost of the acquisition is allocated to the identifiable assets and liabilities acquired by reference to their fair values at the date of the exchange transaction.

▨ Temporary differences arise when the tax bases of the identifiable assets and liabilities acquired are not affected by the business combination or are affected differently.

▨ Deferred tax must be recognised for the temporary differences. This will affect the share of net assets and thus the goodwill (one of the identifiable liabilities of S in Illustration 11 is the deferred tax balance).

▨ The goodwill itself is also a temporary difference, but IAS 12 prohibits the recognition of deferred tax on this item.

Illustration 11	**Goodwill and Temporary Differences—Part I**

Entity P paid $600 for 100% of S on 1 January.

S had not accounted for deferred taxation up to the date of its acquisition.

The following information is relevant to S:

	Fair value at the date of acquisition	**Tax base**	**Temporary differences**
Property plant and equipment	270	155	115
Accounts receivable	210	210	–
Inventory	174	124	50
Retirement benefit obligations	(30)	–	(30)
Accounts payable	(120)	(120)	–
	504		135

Goodwill		**$**
Cost of investment		600
Fair value of net assets acquired		
Per illustration	504	
Deferred tax liability arising in the fair valuation exercise (40%× 135)	(54)	(450)
Goodwill		150

© DeVry/Becker Educational Development Corp. All rights reserved.

4.3 Temporary Differences and the Carrying Amount of the Investment

4.3.1 Background

▨ Temporary differences arise when the carrying amount of investments in subsidiaries (branches and associates or joint arrangements) becomes different from the tax base (which is often cost) of the investment or interest.

▨ The carrying amount is the parent or investor's share of the net assets plus the carrying amount of goodwill. Such differences may arise in a number of different circumstances.

Illustration 12 Goodwill and Temporary Differences—Part II

Entity P paid $600 for 100% of S on 1 January 2017. At this date, the carrying amount in P's consolidated financial statements, of its investment in S was made up as follows:

Fair value of the identifiable net assets of S (including deferred taxation)	450
Goodwill	150
Carrying amount	600

> The carrying amount at the date of acquisition equals cost. This must be the case as the cost figure has been allocated to the net assets to leave goodwill as a residue.

The tax base in P's jurisdiction is the cost of the investment. Therefore, there is no temporary difference at the date of acquisition.

During the year ended 31 December 2017, S traded profitably and accumulated earnings of $70. This was reflected in the net assets of the entity and in its equity.

Since acquisition, goodwill has been impaired by 30.

At 31 December 2017, the carrying amount in P's consolidated financial statements, of its investment in S was made up as follows:

Fair value of the identifiable net assets of S (450 + 70)	520
Goodwill (150 - 30)	120
Carrying amount	640

This means that there is a temporary difference of $40 (640 - 600).

▨ An entity should recognise a deferred tax liability for all taxable temporary differences associated with investments in subsidiaries, branches and associates, and interests in joint arrangements, except to the extent that both of the following conditions are satisfied:

- the parent, investor, joint venture (or operator) is able to control the timing of the reversal of the temporary difference; and
- it is probable that the temporary difference will not reverse in the foreseeable future.

© DeVry/Becker Educational Development Corp. All rights reserved.

4.3.2 Subsidiaries and Branches

▪ A parent controls the dividend policy of its subsidiary (and branches). It is able to control the timing of the reversal of temporary differences associated with that investment. When the parent has determined that those profits will not be distributed in the foreseeable future, the parent does not recognise a deferred tax liability.

Illustration 12   Goodwill and Temporary Differences—Part III

If P has determined that it will not sell the investment in the foreseeable future and that S will not distribute its retained profits in the foreseeable future, no deferred tax liability is recognised in relation to P's investment in S (P discloses the amount (40) of the temporary difference for which no deferred tax is recognised).

If P expects to sell the investment in S, or that S will distribute its retained profits in the foreseeable future, P recognises a deferred tax liability to the extent that the temporary difference is expected to reverse.

The tax rate reflects the manner in which P expects to recover the carrying amount of its investment.

4.3.3 Associates

▪ An investor in an associate does not control that entity and is usually not in a position to determine its dividend policy.

▪ Therefore, in the absence of an agreement requiring that the profits of the associate will not be distributed in the foreseeable future, an investor recognises a deferred tax liability arising from taxable temporary differences associated with its investment in the associate.

Illustration 12   Goodwill and Temporary Differences—Part IV

If S were an associate of P, it would need to provide for deferred tax in respect of the $40, unless there was an agreement that the profits of S would not be distributed in the future.

The tax rate must reflect the manner in which P expects to recover the carrying amount of its investment.

4.3.4 Joint Arrangements

▪ The arrangement between the parties to a joint arrangement usually deals with the distribution of the profits and identifies whether decisions on such matters require the consent of all the parties or a group of the parties. When the joint venturer (or operator) can control the timing of the distribution of its share of the profits of the joint arrangement and it is probable that its share of profits will not be distributed in the foreseeable future, a deferred tax liability is not recognised.

                                      © DeVry/Becker Educational Development Corp. All rights reserved.

4.4   Intra-group Transactions

▇ IFRS 10 requires that unrealised profits and losses arising on Intra-group trading must be eliminated in full on consolidation. Such adjustments may give rise to temporary differences. In many tax jurisdictions, it is the individual members of the group that are the taxable entities. As far as the tax authorities are concerned, the tax base of an asset purchased from another member of the group will be the cost that the buying company has paid for it. Furthermore, the selling company will be taxed on the sale of the asset even though it is still held within the group.

▇ Note that the deferred tax is provided for at the buyer's tax rate.

Illustration 13 Intra-group Transaction

S has sold inventory to P for $700. The inventory cost S $600 originally. S has therefore made a profit of $100 on the transaction. S will be liable to tax on this amount at say 30%. Thus S will reflect a profit of $100 and a tax expense of $30 in its own financial statements.

If P has not sold the inventory at the year end, it will include it in its closing inventory figure at a cost (to itself) of $700.

On consolidation the unrealised profit must be removed by:

   Dr Profit or loss $100
     Cr Inventory $100

In the consolidated financial statements, the inventory will be measured at $600 (700 - 100), but its tax base is still $700. There is a deductible temporary difference of $100.

This requires the recognition of a deferred tax asset of $30 (30% × 100).

The other side of the entry to set this up will be a credit to profit or loss. This will remove the effect of the tax on the transaction. However, if P operated in a different tax environment and was taxed at, say, 40%, the deferred tax asset would be $40 (40% × 100).

---

5   Presentation and Disclosure

5.1   Presentation

Key Point

Tax assets and tax liabilities are presented separately from other assets and liabilities in the statement of financial position. Deferred tax assets and liabilities are distinguished from current tax assets and liabilities.

▇ When an entity makes a distinction between current and non-current assets and liabilities in its financial statements, it should not classify deferred tax assets (liabilities) as current assets (liabilities).

© DeVry/Becker Educational Development Corp. All rights reserved.

- An entity offsets current tax assets and current tax liabilities if, and only if, the entity:
  - has a legally enforceable right to set off the recognised amounts; and
  - intends either to settle on a net basis, or to realise the asset and settle the liability simultaneously.
- An entity offsets deferred tax assets and deferred tax liabilities if, and only if:
  - the entity has a legally enforceable right to set off current tax assets against current tax liabilities; and
  - the deferred tax assets and the deferred tax liabilities relate to income taxes levied by the same taxation authority on either:
    - the same taxable entity; or
    - different taxable entities which intend either to settle current tax liabilities and assets on a net basis, or to realise the assets and settle the liabilities simultaneously, in each future period in which significant amounts of deferred tax liabilities or assets are expected to be settled or recovered.
- The tax expense (income) related to profit or loss is presented in the statement of comprehensive income.

5.2   Disclosure

The following are disclosed separately.

- The major components of tax expense (income). These include:
  - current tax expense (income);
  - adjustments in respect of a prior period;
  - deferred tax expense/income;
  - deferred tax expense/income arising due to a change in tax rates; and
  - deferred tax consequence of a change in accounting policy or a correction of an error.
- The aggregate current and deferred tax relating to items that are charged or credited directly to equity and the amount charged or credited to other comprehensive income.
- An explanation of the relationship between tax expense (income) and accounting profit in either or both of the following forms:
  - A numerical reconciliation between tax expense (income) and the product of accounting profit multiplied by the applicable tax rate(s) disclosing also the basis on which the applicable tax rate(s) is (are) computed; or
  - A numerical reconciliation between the average effective tax rate and the applicable tax rate, disclosing also the basis on which the applicable tax rate is computed.

                    © DeVry/Becker Educational Development Corp. All rights reserved.

Exhibit 1   INCOME TAX RECONCILIATION

The following is from the notes to the consolidated financial statements of Bayer Group's Annual Report 2015.

14. Taxes (extract)

The reconciliation of expected to reported income tax expense and of the expected to the effective tax rate for the Group was as follows:

Reconciliation of Expected to Actual Income Tax Expense

	2014		2015	
	€ million	%	€ million	%
Expected income tax expense and expected tax rate	**1,129**	**25.6**	**1,346**	**25.7**
Reduction in taxes due to tax-free income				
Income related to the operating business	(92)	(2.1)	(155)	(3.0)
Income from affiliated companies and divestiture proceeds	(2)	–	(10)	(0.2)
First-time recognition of previously unrecognized deferred tax assets on tax loss carryforwards	(15)	(0.3)	(30)	(0.6)
Use of tax loss carryforwards on which deferred tax assets were not previously recognized	(1)	–	(6)	(0.1)
Increase in taxes due to non-tax-deductible expenses				
Expenses related to the operating business	149	3.4	148	2.8
Impairment losses on investments in affiliated companies	2	–	7	0.1
New tax loss carryforwards unlikely to be usable	57	1.3	81	1.5
Existing tax loss carryforwards on which deferred tax assets were previously recognized but which are unlikely to be usable	7	0.2	16	0.3
Tax income (−) and expenses (+) relating to other periods	(119)	(2.7)	(95)	(1.8)
Tax effects of changes in tax rates	(10)	(0.2)	(25)	(0.5)
Other tax effects	(34)	(0.9)	(50)	(0.8)
Actual income tax expense and effective tax rate	**1,071**	**24.3**	**1,227**	**23.4**

2014 figures restated

—Notes to the Consolidated Financial Statements of the Bayer Group 2015

▪ An entity discloses the amount of a deferred tax asset and the nature of the evidence supporting its recognition, when:

   ● The utilisation of the deferred tax asset is dependent on future taxable profits in excess of the profits arising from the reversal of existing taxable temporary differences; and

   ● The entity has suffered a loss in either the current or preceding period in the tax jurisdiction to which the deferred tax asset relates.

© DeVry/Becker Educational Development Corp. All rights reserved.

6 Approach Summary

6.1 Deferred Taxation Calculations

(a) *Debits* in the financial statements compared to the taxman's view give rise to deferred tax *credits*.

Credits in the financial statements compared to the taxman's view give rise to deferred tax *debits*.

(b) Full provision accounting is easy.

DT = TAX RATE x TEMPORARY DIFFERENCE = DEFERRED TAX ASSET/ LIABILITY

(c) Steps

Step 1: Summarise the accounting carrying amounts and the tax base for every asset and liability.

Step 2: Calculate the temporary difference by deducting the tax base from the carrying amount using the following pro forma:

Asset/Liability	Carrying Amount $	Tax Base $	Temporary Difference $

Step 3: Calculate the deferred tax liability and asset. To calculate the deferred tax liabilities, sum all positive temporary differences and apply the tax rate. To calculate the deferred tax asset, sum all negative temporary differences and apply the tax rate.

Step 4: Calculate the net deferred tax liability or asset by summing the two amounts in Step 3. This will be the *asset or liability* carried in the statement of financial position.

Step 5: Deduct the opening deferred tax liability or asset. The difference will be this year's charge/credit to *profit or loss* (or other comprehensive income) or directly to equity.

(d) Where there has been a change in the tax rate, it is necessary to calculate the effect of this change on the opening deferred tax provision. Follow steps one through five, calculating the required closing deferred tax liability or asset and the charge/ credit to the relevant statement. The charge/credit is then analysed in the amount that relates to the change in the tax rate and the amount that relates to the temporary differences.

The amount that relates to the change in tax rate will equal the amount of the temporary difference in the previous period x the change in the tax rate.

© DeVry/Becker Educational Development Corp. All rights reserved.

Summary

- The current tax charge in the statement of comprehensive income is an estimate. Any over/under provisions are cleared in the following period's statement of comprehensive income.
- Differences arise because tax rules differ from IFRS rules in arriving at taxable profit.
- *Temporary differences* are differences between the carrying amount of an asset or liability in the statement of financial position and its tax base.
- Deferred tax is provided on *all* taxable temporary differences.
- If the financial value of an asset exceeds its tax base, then a taxable temporary difference arises, leading to a deferred tax liability.
- Most deferred tax liabilities are recognised in the statement of financial position.
- A degree of prudence is applied in recognising deferred tax assets.
- Deferred tax is charged or credited to wherever the related gain or loss has been recognised.
- The tax rate used is the rate that is expected to apply to the period when the asset is realised or the liability is settled, based on tax rates that have been enacted by the end of the reporting period.
- Tax assets and tax liabilities are presented separately from other assets and liabilities. Deferred tax assets and liabilities are distinguished from current tax assets and liabilities.

Session 12 Quiz
Estimated time: 30 minutes

1. Identify and define the TWO types of temporary differences. (1.2)
2. Explain the IAS 12 perspective on accounting for deferred tax. (3.1)
3. State when a deferred tax asset should be recognised in the financial statements. (3.2)
4. State the possible double entries for the movement on the deferred tax balance. (3.3)
5. State the tax rate which should be applied to temporary differences. (4.1.2)
6. Yes or no? Should a parent recognise a deferred tax liability in respect of the investment in a subsidiary? (4.3.2)
7. In cases of unrealised profit in a group situation, specify which tax rate should be used when calculating deferred tax. (4.4)
8. State when deferred tax asset and liability balances may be offset. (5.1)

Study Question Bank
Estimated time: 40 minutes

Priority		Estimated Time	Completed
Q21	Kerensky	40 minutes	

EXAMPLE SOLUTIONS

Solution 1—Deferred Tax Provision

	Carrying amount $	Tax base $	Temporary difference
Non-current assets			
Plant and machinery	200,000	175,000	25,000
Receivables:			
Trade receivables	50,000	55,000	(5,000)
Interest receivable	1,000	0	1,000
Payables			
Fine	10,000	10,000	0
Interest payable	2,000	0	(2,000)

	Temporary difference	Deferred tax @ 30%
Deferred tax liabilities	26,000	7,800
Deferred tax assets	(7,000)	(2,100)
		5,700

	Deferred tax @ 30% $
Deferred tax as at 1 January 2017	1,200
Profit or loss (balancing figure)	4,500
Deferred tax as at 31 December 2017	5,700

Solution 2—Lato

	Carrying amount $	Tax base $	Temporary difference
	1,250	650	600
Deferred tax at 30%			180

Solution 3—Deferred Taxation Charge

		Deferred tax @ 30% $
Deferred tax as at 1 January 2017	(1,000 - 800) × 30%	60
To other comprehensive income	30% × (1,250 - 900)	105
Profit or loss	Balancing figure (or as (150 - 100) × 30%)	15
Deferred tax as at 31 December 2017		180

© DeVry/Becker Educational Development Corp. All rights reserved.

Solution 4—Deferred Tax Provision

		Temporary difference $
Non-current assets	(460,000 - 320,000)	140,000
Losses		(90,000)
Deferred tax liability	(31% × 140,000)	43,400
Deferred tax asset		
Reversal in 2018	(30,000 × 34%)	(10,200)
Reversal in 2019	(30,000 × 32%)	(9,600)
Reversal in 2020	(30,000 × 31%)	(9,300)
Deferred tax		14,300

Solution 5—Part of Charge Due to Tax Increase

		Deferred tax $
Deferred tax as at 1 January 2017		10,000
Profit or loss—rate change		1,667
Opening balance restated	$(10,000 \times {}^{35}\!/_{30})$	11,667
Profit or loss—origination of temporary differences	(Balancing figure)	38,383
Deferred tax as at 31 December 2017	(W)	50,050

WORKING	Carrying amount $	Tax base $	Temporary difference
Non-current assets	460,000	320,000	140,000
Accrued interest:			
Receivable	18,000	0	18,000
Payable	(15,000)	0	(15,000)
Deferred tax liability			143,000
Deferred tax at 35%			50,050

© DeVry/Becker Educational Development Corp. All rights reserved.

Provisions and Contingencies

FOCUS

This session covers the following content from the *ACCA Study Guide.*

C. Reporting the Financial Performance of Entities

8. Provisions, contingencies and events after the reporting date

a) Apply and discuss the recognition, derecognition and measurement of provisions, contingent liabilities and contingent assets including environmental provisions and restructuring provisions. ☐

b) Apply and discuss the accounting for events after the reporting date. ☐

c) Determine and report going concern issues arising after the reporting date. ☐

Session 13 Guidance

- **Recognise** that IAS 37 is an extremely important standard both in practice and for the examination.
- **Revise** the relevant terminology (s.1.3) and that a provision is recognised in the financial statements, whereas a contingent liability is only disclosed. Learn the one exception to the non-recognition of contingent liabilities (s.2.3).
- **Understand** the recognition issues (s.2.2).
- **Revise** the general measurement rules (s.3.1) and understand how they are applied to specific circumstances (s.4).
- **Revise** the definitions of IAS 10 (s.6). Refer to your F7 text if you have any doubts about the distinction between adjusting and non-adjusting events and their accounting treatments.

VISUAL OVERVIEW

Objective: To define and explain the recognition of provisions, contingent liabilities and contingent assets as well as to consider the effect of events after the reporting period on the financial statements.

IAS 37

- Objective
- Scope
- Terminology
- Relationship

IAS 10 EVENTS AFTER THE REPORTING PERIOD

- Adjusting Events
- Non-adjusting Events
- Dividends
- Going Concern

RECOGNITION

- Provisions
- Issues
- Contingent Assets and Liabilities
- Self-Insurance

DISCLOSURES

- Provisions
- Contingent Liabilities
- Contingent Assets

MEASUREMENT

- General Rules
- Specific Points
- Changes in Provisions

SPECIFIC CIRCUMSTANCES

- Future Operating Losses
- Onerous Contracts
- Restructuring
- Repairs and Maintenance
- Decommissioning Costs

1 IAS 37

1.1 Objective

■ To ensure that appropriate recognition criteria and measurement bases are applied to:

- provisions;
- contingent liabilities; and
- contingent assets.

■ To ensure that sufficient information is disclosed in the notes to the financial statements in respect of each of these items.

1.2 Scope

■ The rules will apply to all provisions and contingencies except for those covered by more specific requirements in other IFRSs. For example:

- IFRS 15 *Revenue from Contracts with Customers;* *
- IAS 19 *Employee Benefits;*
- IAS 12 *Income Taxes*
- IFRS 16 *Leases; and*
- IFRS 3 *Business Combinations.*

■ IAS 37 addresses only provisions that are liabilities (i.e. not allowances for depreciation, irrecoverable debts, etc).

*IFRS 15 has no specific requirements for contracts that are onerous; IAS 37 will be applied.

1.3 Terminology

Provisions: liabilities of uncertain timing or amount.

Liability: a present obligation of the entity arising from past events, the settlement of which is expected to result in an outflow from the entity of resources embodying economic benefits.

Obligating event: an event which creates a legal or constructive obligation which results in an entity having no realistic alternative to settling that obligation.*

Legal obligation: an obligation which derives from:

- a contract;
- legislation; or
- other operation of law.

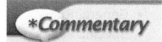

*Obligating event is a key concept in the IAS 37 approach to the recognition of provisions.

Constructive obligation: an obligation which derives from an entity's actions where:

- by an established pattern of past practice, published policies or a sufficiently specific current statement, the entity has indicated to other parties that it will accept certain responsibilities; and
- as a result, the entity has created a valid expectation on the part of those other parties that it will discharge those responsibilities.

© DeVry/Becker Educational Development Corp. All rights reserved.

Contingent liability:

- a *possible* obligation which arises from past events and whose existence will be confirmed only on the occurrence or non-occurrence of one or more uncertain future events, which are *not wholly within the control* of the entity; or
- a *present* obligation which arises from past events but is not recognised because:
  - it is not probable that an outflow of benefits embodying economic benefits will be required to settle the obligation; or
  - the amount of the obligation cannot be measured with sufficient reliability.*

Contingent asset: a possible asset which arises from past events and whose existence will be confirmed only on the occurrence or non-occurrence of one or more uncertain future events not wholly within the control of the entity.

Onerous contract: a contract in which the unavoidable costs of meeting the obligations under the contract exceed the economic benefits expected to be received from it.

Restructuring: a programme which is planned and controlled by management, and materially changes either:

- the scope of a business undertaken by an entity; or
- the manner in which that business is conducted.

*IAS 37 stresses that an entity will be unable to measure an obligation with sufficient reliability only on very rare occasions.

1.4 Relationship Between Provisions and Contingent Liabilities

▨ In a general sense, all provisions are contingent because they are uncertain in timing or amount.

Key Point

IAS 37 distinguishes between provisions and contingent liabilities by using the term *contingent* for assets and liabilities, which are not recognised because their *existence* will be confirmed only on the occurrence or non-occurrence of one or more uncertain future events not wholly within the control of the entity.

▨ The standard distinguishes between:

- *provisions,* which are present obligations; and
- *contingent liabilities,* which are not recognised because they are either:
  - only *possible* obligations; or
  - present obligations, which *cannot be measured* with sufficient reliability.

© DeVry/Becker Educational Development Corp. All rights reserved.

2 Recognition

2.1 Recognition of Provisions

▨ A provision should be recognised when:

- an entity has a present legal or constructive obligation to transfer economic benefits as a result of past events; *and*
- it is probable that an outflow of resources embodying economic benefits will be required to settle the obligation; *and*
- a reliable estimate of the obligation can be made.

▨ If these conditions are not met a provision should not be recognised.

2.2 Recognition Issues

2.2.1 Present Obligation

Key Point

A present obligation exists when the entity has no realistic alternative but to make the transfer of economic benefits because of a past event (the "obligating event").

Illustration 1 Warranty Provision

Scenario

A manufacturer gives warranties at the time of sale to purchasers of its product. Under the terms of the contract for sale, the manufacturer undertakes to make good, by repair or replacement, manufacturing defects which become apparent within three years from the date of sale. Based on past experience, it is probable (i.e. more likely than not) that there will be some claims under the warranties.

Present obligation as a result of a past obligating event?	Sale of the product with a warranty gives rise to a **legal obligation.**
An outflow of resources?	Probable.
Conclusion	Provide for the best estimate of the cost of making good under the warranty of the goods sold by the end of the reporting period.

▨ A provision is made only if the **liability** exists independent of the entity's future actions. The mere intention, or necessity to undertake expenditure related to the future, is not sufficient to give rise to an obligation.

© DeVry/Becker Educational Development Corp. All rights reserved.

- If the entity retains discretion to avoid making any expenditure, a liability does not exist and no provision is recognised:
  - the mere existence of environmental contamination (even if caused by the entity's activities) does not in itself give rise to an obligation because the entity could choose not to clean it up;
  - a board decision alone is not sufficient for the recognition of a provision because the board could reverse the decision;
  - if a decision was made that commits an entity to future expenditure no provision need be recognised as long as the board have a realistic alternative.*
- In rare cases it is not clear whether there is a present obligation. In these cases a past event should be deemed to give rise to a present obligation when it is more likely than not that a present obligation exists at the end of the reporting period.*

Commentary

*Until the board makes public a decision or commits itself in some other way to making repairs, there is no obligation beyond that to satisfy the existing statutory and contractual rights of customers.

*Clearly, recognising a present obligation after a past event requires judgement after taking into account all available evidence.

Illustration 2 Obligating Event

Scenario

After a wedding in 2017, 10 guests died, possibly as the result of food poisoning from products sold by Tin-Tin. Legal proceedings are seeking damages from Tin-Tin, which disputes liability. Up to the date of approval of the financial statements for the year to 31 December 2017, Tin-Tin's lawyers advise that it is probable that Tin-Tin will not be found liable. However, when preparing financial statements for the year to 31 December 2018, the lawyers advise that, because of developments in the case, it is probable that Tin-Tin will be found liable.

At 31 December 2017:

Present obligation as a result of a past obligating event?	On the basis of the evidence available when the financial statements were approved, there is no obligation as a result of past events.
An outflow of resources?	Irrelevant, as no present obligation.
Conclusion	No provision.

At 31 December 2018:

Present obligation as a result of a past obligating event?	On the basis of the evidence available, there is a present obligation.
An outflow of resources?	Probable.
Conclusion	Provision should be recognised.

2.2.2 Past Event

- A past event that leads to a present obligation is called an obligating event.
- An obligating event exists when the entity has no realistic alternative but to make the transfer of economic benefits. This may be due to:
  - legal obligations; or
  - constructive obligations.

▦ Examples of constructive obligations include:

- a retail store that habitually refunds purchases by dissatisfied customers even though it is under no legal obligation to do so, but could not change its policy without incurring unacceptable damage to its reputation; and

- an entity that has identified contamination in land surrounding one of its production sites. The entity is not legally obliged to clean up, but because of concern for its long-term reputation and relationship with the local community, and because of its published policies or past actions, is obliged to do so.

Illustration 3 Refund Policy

Scenario

A retail store has a policy of refunding purchases by dissatisfied customers, even though it is under no legal obligation to do so. Its policy of making refunds is generally known.

Present obligation as a result of a past obligating event?	The obligating event is the sale of the product, which gives rise to a constructive obligation because the conduct of the store has created a valid expectation on the part of its customers that the store will refund purchases.
An outflow of resources?	Probable, a proportion of goods are returned for refund.
Conclusion	A provision is recognised for the best estimate of the costs of refunds.

Illustration 4 Clean-up Costs

Scenario

An entity in the oil industry causes contamination and operates in a country in which there is no environmental legislation. However, the entity has a widely published environmental policy in which it undertakes to clean up any contamination it causes. The entity has a record of honouring this published policy.

Present obligation as a result of a past obligating event?	The obligating event is the contamination of the land, which gives rise to a constructive obligation because the conduct of the entity has created a valid expectation on the part of those affected by it that the entity will clean up contamination.
An outflow of resources?	Probable.
Conclusion	A provision is recognised for the best estimate of the costs of clean-up.

▦ Provisions are not made for general business risks since they do not give rise to obligations that exist at the end of the reporting period.

▦ It is not necessary to know the identity of the party to whom the obligation is owed in order for an obligation to exist.

© DeVry/Becker Educational Development Corp. All rights reserved.

2.2.3   Reliable Estimate of the Obligation

A reasonable estimate can always be made where an entity can determine a reasonable range of possible outcomes.

- Only in extremely rare cases will it be *genuinely* impossible to make any quantification of the obligation and therefore impossible to provide for it. (In these circumstances disclosure of the matter would be necessary).

2.3   Contingent Assets and Liabilities

Contingent assets and contingent liabilities cannot be recognised in the statement of financial position.

- They are dependent on the occurrence or non-occurrence of an uncertain future event not wholly within the control of the entity. It follows, therefore, that they are not obligations which exists at the end of the reporting period.

- There is one exception to the non-recognition of contingent liabilities. IFRS 3 *Business Combinations* requires that contingent liabilities of a subsidiary, that are present obligations, be recognised and measured at fair value as part of the acquisition process.*

*See s.3 in *Session 18*.

- The exception gives rise to inconsistency; a contingent liability that does not meet the recognition criteria of IAS 37 for a single entity is recognised as a "provision" when that entity is acquired (in the consolidated accounts).

- Many of the large tobacco companies do not recognise provisions for class actions taken against them by smokers, but classify them as contingent liabilities. The 2015 financial statements of Philip Morris, for example, included nearly 10 pages on contingent liabilities, many relating to actions taken against the company by smokers.*

*In comparison, many companies have a maximum of two pages detailing their contingent liabilities.

- Does it really matter whether a transaction is classified as a provision or a contingent liability? Clearly it matters that failure to recognise an expense until an obligation is settled is contrary to the accruals basis, and reported profits and net assets will be overstated until the expense is recognised. However, extensive disclosure on such complex issues as class actions may provide more relevant information to users on the potential effects than if they are reduced to a single amount recognised as a provision.

2.4   Self-Insurance

▨ Costs of insurance have become prohibitive for many businesses. Instead, they may choose to "self-insure" rather than take out insurance policies against the various risks that they face.

▨ Rather than pay insurance premiums, they may set aside cash funds to meet future expenses associated with uninsured risks. (There is nothing to prevent an entity "ring-fencing" cash to meet any future uninsured costs.)

▨ IAS 37 does **not** permit the recognition of a provision for such future expenses. Therefore, the cost of being self-insured will only be recognised in the period in which actual expense is incurred.*

▨ If accounting for self-insurance by setting up a provision were permitted, profits could be manipulated.

Commentary

*The cost of self-insurance is a future operating cost.

3   Measurement

3.1   General Rules

Key Point

The amount provided should be the *best estimate* at the end of the reporting period of the expenditure required to settle the obligation.

▨ The amount is often expressed as
  - the amount which could be spent to settle the obligation immediately; or
  - to pay to a third party to assume it.

▨ The best estimate may derive from the judgement of the management supplemented by
  - experience of similar transactions; and
  - evidence provided from experts (in some cases).

▨ Taking account of the uncertainty surrounding the transaction may involve:
  - an expected value calculation. This is suitable in situations where there is a large population (e.g. determining the size of warranty provisions);
  - the use of the most likely outcome in situations where a single obligation is being measured (as long as there is no evidence to indicate that the liability will be materially higher or lower than this amount).

3.1.1   Size of the Obligation—Factors to Be Considered

▨ The time value of money (the amount provided should be the present value of the expected cash flows).

▨ Evidence of expected future events such as:
  - change in legislation;
  - improvements in technology.

▨ Prudence.

© DeVry/Becker Educational Development Corp. All rights reserved.

3.2   Specific Points

- *Reimbursement*: If some (or all) of the expected outflow is expected to be reimbursed from a third party, the reimbursement will be recognised only when it is virtually certain that the reimbursement will be received if the entity settles the obligation.

  - The expense in respect of the provision may be presented net of the amount recognised for a reimbursement.
  - The reimbursement is treated as a separate asset and must not exceed the provision in terms of its value.

- Gains from the expected disposal are *not* taken into account when measuring a provision.

- The provision is measured as a *pre-tax amount.*

- This amount is to be the *lowest* of the following amounts:

  - *the present value* of the resources required to *fulfil* the obligation; or
  - the amount an entity would have to *pay* to *cancel* the obligation; or
  - the amount the entity would have to *pay* to *transfer* the obligation to another party.

- Any change in the carrying amount of the liability caused by the passage of time is to be treated as a finance cost.

3.3   Changes in Provisions

Key Point

A provision can be used *only* for expenditures that relate to the matter for which the provision was originally recognised.

- Historically, many companies abused provisions both in their initial recognition and then by not using them for their original purpose.

- Changes in provision affect reported profits. If a provision is recognised in one year, profit will be reduced. If the provision is released the following year, profit will be increased.*

- Provisions must be reviewed regularly and if the estimate of the obligation has changed, the amount recognised as a provision must be revised accordingly.

*Commentary

*IAS 37 prohibits such "profit smoothing" abuses.

4 Specific Circumstances

4.1 Future Operating Losses

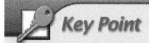

> **Key Point**
>
> Provisions are not recognised for future operating losses because:
> - they do not arise out of a past event; and
> - they are not unavoidable.

■ An expectation of future losses is an indication that the assets of the entity may be impaired. The assets should therefore be tested for impairment according to IAS 36 (see *Session 7*).

4.2 Onerous Contracts

> **Key Point**
>
> The present obligation of an **onerous contract** is recognised as a provision.

Illustration 5 Take or Pay Contract

ZY energy has entered into a contract with GasB to purchase units of gas at $50 per unit. The contract requires ZY to pay a penalty of $15 per unit of gas that it does not purchase.

The market price of gas has fallen to $30 per unit and ZY has decided to purchase gas from another supplier and incur the penalty.

ZY should recognise an onerous contract at $15 per unit of gas that it has decided not to purchase.

4.3 Restructuring

4.3.1 Examples

■ Examples of **restructurings** include:
- sale or termination of a line of business;
- closure of business locations in a region;
- relocation from one region to another;
- changes in management structure;
- fundamental reorganisations that have a material effect on the nature and focus of the entity's operations.

© DeVry/Becker Educational Development Corp. All rights reserved.

4.3.2 Recognition

 **Key Point**

A provision for a liability for restructuring is only recognised when the general recognition criteria are met.

- A constructive obligation to restructure arises only when an entity:
  - has a sufficiently detailed formal plan for the restructuring; and
  - has raised a "valid expectation" that it will carry out the restructuring by starting to implement the plan or announcing its main features to those affected by it.
- The detailed formal plan must identify as a minimum:
  - the business or part of a business concerned;
  - the principal locations affected;
  - the location, function and approximate number of employees who will be compensated for terminating their services;
  - the expenditures that will be undertaken; and
  - when the plan will be implemented.*
- A management decision to restructure does *not* give rise to constructive obligation unless the entity has (before the end of the reporting period):
  - started to implement the restructuring plan (e.g. by the sale of assets); or
  - announced the main features of the plan to those affected in a sufficiently specific manner to raise a valid expectation in them that the restructuring will occur.
- No obligation arises for the sale of an operation until there is a binding sales agreement.
- IFRS 3 *Business Combinations* does *not* allow a provision to be set up for the restructuring of a subsidiary on initial acquisition. The only restructuring provision that can be recognised on acquisition will be those of the subsidiary that had met the IAS 37 requirements and had been provided for before acquisition.

 ***Commentary**

*If there is a long delay before the plan will be implemented then it is unlikely that the plan will raise a valid expectation that the entity is committed to the restructuring.

Illustration 6 No Announcement of Board Decision

Scenario

On 12 December, the board of an entity decided to close down a division. Before the end of the reporting period (31 December), the decision was not communicated to any of those affected and no other steps were taken to implement the decision.

Present obligation as a result of a past obligating event? No.

An outflow of resources? Irrelevant, as no present obligation.

Conclusion No provision is recognised.

© DeVry/Becker Educational Development Corp. All rights reserved.

Illustration 7 Announcement of Board Decision

Scenario

On 12 December, the board of an entity decided to close down a division making a particular product. On 20 December, a detailed plan for closing down the division was agreed by the board; letters were sent to customers warning them to seek an alternative source of supply. Redundancy notices were sent to the staff of the division.

Present obligation as a result of a past obligating event?	The obligating event is the communication of the decision to the customers and employees. This gives rise to a constructive obligation from that date because it creates a valid expectation that the division will be closed.
An outflow of resources?	Probable.
Conclusion	A provision is recognised at 31 December for the best estimate of the costs of closing the division.

- Provisions for restructuring should include only those expenditures that are both:
  - necessarily entailed by a restructuring; and
  - not associated with the on-going activities of the entity.

4.4 Provisions for Repairs and Maintenance

- Some assets require, in addition to routine maintenance, substantial expenditure every few years for major refits or refurbishment and the replacement of major components. IAS 16 *Property, Plant and Equipment* gives guidance on allocating expenditure on an asset to its component parts where these components have different useful lives or provide benefits in a different pattern (see *Session 6*).

4.5 Decommissioning Costs

- An entity may be committed to incur a substantial cost when it decommissions certain assets (i.e. takes them out of operating use).*

- IAS 37 requires that a provision be made when there is a present obligation to incur these costs. This could be on initial recognition of the asset or during its useful life.

Commentary

*Substantial decommissioning costs are very common in the oil industry when an oil rig at the end of its useful life must be dismantled and the environment restored to its natural condition.

Key Point

- Initial recognition is at the present value of the future expected cash outflow for the obligation.
- The double entry is completed with a debit to the asset account (see *Session 6*).

- As time passes the present value of the provision will increase (in a similar manner to interest). This "unwinding of the discount" is charged as a finance expense to the statement of profit or loss of the period.

© DeVry/Becker Educational Development Corp. All rights reserved.

▧ Many argue that the recognition of the debit entry as an asset is contrary to the Framework.*

  ○ Is something controlled?

  ○ Was there a past event?

  ○ Are future economic benefits due?

▧ Before IAS 37, such provisions were built up annually (Debit Profit or loss and Credit Provision). This "accretion" approach is not allowed under IAS 37.

*The answer to past event question should be easily determined, but the other two questions can be problematic.

Illustration 8 Provision Accounting

An entity purchased an asset on 1 January.

The entity is committed to expenditure of $10 million in 10 years' time in respect of this asset. The obligation satisfies the recognition criteria in IAS 37.

An appropriate discount factor is 8%.

1 January
Initial measurement of the provision

$$\$10m \times \frac{1}{(1+0.08)^{10}} = 4,631,935$$

Dr Asset	4,631,935	
Cr Provision		4,631,935

31 December
Remeasurement of the provision

$$\$10m \times \frac{1}{(1+0.08)^{9}} = 5,002,490$$

	$
Presented as follows:	
Balance brought forward	4,631,935
Borrowing cost (8% × 4,631,935)	370,555
Carried forward	5,002,490

			Profit or loss
Provision			
Dr Profit or loss	370,555		370,555
Cr Provision		370,555	
Asset			
Dr Profit or loss	463,193		463,193
Cr Accumulated depreciation		463,193	
4,631,935 × 1/10			
			833,748

5   Disclosures

5.1   For Each Class of Provision

▥ The carrying amount at the beginning and end of the period along with any movements.

▥ A brief description of the nature of the obligation and expected timing of the expenditure.

▥ An indication of the nature of the uncertainties about the amount or timing of the outflows.

▥ The amount of any expected reimbursement with details of asset recognition.

5.2   For Each Class of Contingent Liability

▥ An entity discloses the following for each class of **contingent liability** unless the contingency is remote:

- a brief description of the nature of the contingency; and where practicable;
- the uncertainties expected to affect the ultimate outcome of the contingency;
- an estimate of the potential financial effect; and
- the possibility of any reimbursement.

5.3   For Each Class of Contingent Asset

▥ An entity should disclose the following for each class of contingent asset when the inflow of economic benefits is probable:

- a brief description of the nature of the contingency; and
- an estimate of the potential financial effect (where practicable).

▥ In extremely rare cases, disclosure of some or all of the information required might seriously prejudice the position of the entity in its negotiations with other parties in respect of the subject matter for which the provision, contingent liability or asset is made. In such cases the information need not be disclosed, but entities should:

- explain the general nature of the dispute; and
- explain the fact, and reason why, that information has not been disclosed.

© DeVry/Becker Educational Development Corp. All rights reserved.

6   IAS 10 *Events after the Reporting Period*

6.1   Adjusting Events

 **Key Point**

The effects of adjusting events after the end of the reporting period are recognised in the financial statements at the reporting date.

▨ Recognition affects the amounts of assets and/or liabilities in the statement of financial position.

▨ Examples of adjusting events are:

- the resolution after the end of the reporting period of a court case which, because it confirms that an entity already had a present obligation at the end of the reporting period, requires the entity to recognise a provision instead of merely disclosing a contingent liability or adjusting the provision already recognised;

- the bankruptcy of a customer which occurs after the end of the reporting period and which confirms that a loss already existed at the end of the reporting period on a trade receivable account;

- the discovery of fraud or error that shows that the financial statements were incorrect; and

- the sale of inventories after the year end at an amount below their cost.

6.2   Non-adjusting Events

 **Key Point**

The effects of *non*-adjusting events after the end of the reporting period are *not* recognised at the reporting date.

▨ The following are examples of non-adjusting events that may be of such importance that non-disclosure would affect the ability of the users of the financial statements to make proper evaluations and decisions:

- a major business combination after the end of the reporting period;

- the destruction of a major production plant by a fire after the end of the reporting period;

- abnormally large changes after the end of the reporting period in asset prices or foreign exchange rates; and

- a decline in market value of investments between the end of the reporting period and the date on which the financial statements are authorised for issue.*

 ***Commentary**

*A fall in market value does not normally relate to the condition of the investments at the end of the reporting period, but reflects circumstances, which have arisen in the following period. Therefore, an entity does not adjust the amounts recognised in its financial statements for that investment.

© DeVry/Becker Educational Development Corp. All rights reserved.

6.3 Dividends

▩ If dividends are proposed or declared after the end of the reporting period, an entity cannot recognise them as a liability.

▩ IAS 1 requires an entity to disclose the amount of dividends that were proposed or declared after the end of the reporting period, but before the financial statements were authorised for issue. This disclosure is made in the notes to the accounts and not within the statement of financial position.

6.4 Going Concern

 Key Point

> If the going concern assumption is no longer appropriate IAS 1 requires that the going concern basis of accounting be changed (e.g. to a break-up basis).

▩ An entity should not prepare its financial statements on a going concern basis if management determines after the end of the reporting period:

- it intends to liquidate the entity or to cease trading; or
- it has no realistic alternative but to do so.

▩ Deterioration in operating results and financial position after the end of the reporting period may indicate a need to consider whether the going concern assumption is still appropriate.

© DeVry/Becker Educational Development Corp. All rights reserved.

Summary

- IAS 37 distinguishes between provisions and contingent liabilities. Contingent liabilities (and contingent assets) are not recognised because their *existence* is not confirmed at the reporting date.

- A provision is recognised when there is an obligation, the outflow of economic benefits is probable and a reliable estimate can be made.

- A reliable estimate can always be made if a reasonable range of possible outcomes is determinable.

- The amount provided should be a best estimate.

- Provisions can only be used for the purpose for which they were made.

- Provision cannot be made for future operating losses (they do not arise out of a past event and can be avoided).

- Provision should be made for a present obligation under an onerous contract.

- A provision for a liability for restructuring can only be recognised when the general recognition criteria are met.

- A decommissioning provision is initially recognised at the present value of the future expected cash outflows. This amount is an increase in the cost of the related asset.

- Only adjusting events after the end of the reporting period are recognised in the financial statements. Any material non-adjusting events are disclosed in the notes.

- If the going concern assumption is no longer appropriate the basis of accounting is changed.

Session 13 Quiz
Estimated time: 20 minutes

1. Define obligating event and constructive obligation. (1.3)
2. List the THREE conditions which must be satisfied for a provision to be recognised. (2.1)
3. Describe the initial amount at which a provision should be measured. (3.1)
4. Specify how often the value of the provision should be remeasured. (3.3)
5. State the maximum amount of a provision for a future operating loss. (4.1)
6. Describe the circumstances under which an obligation for future restructuring might exist at the end of the reporting period (and so qualify for a provision). (4.3)
7. Give THREE examples of an adjusting event. (6.1)
8. Explain the accounting for a proposed dividend. (6.3)

Study Question Bank
Estimated time: 50 minutes

Priority		Estimated Time	Completed
Q22	Genpower	50 minutes	

© DeVry/Becker Educational Development Corp. All rights reserved.

Related Parties

FOCUS

This session covers the following content from the *ACCA Study Guide.*

C. Reporting the Financial Performance of Entities

9. Related Parties

a) Determine the parties considered to be related to an entity.

b) Identify the implications of related party relationships and the need for disclosure.

Session 14 Guidance

■ **Recognise** that the disclosure of related parties and the transactions that take place between them is important to users of financial statements.

■ **Be aware** that although the standard, and the session, are quite short, the standard does play a major role in accounting.

(continued on next page)

VISUAL OVERVIEW

Objective: To evaluate related party involvement and explain the disclosure of related parties and transactions between them.

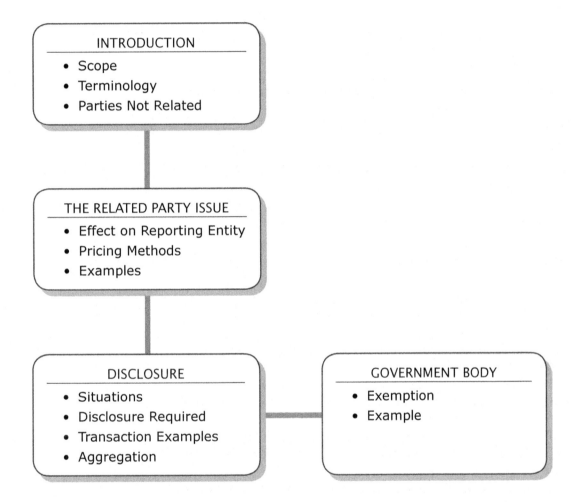

INTRODUCTION
- Scope
- Terminology
- Parties Not Related

THE RELATED PARTY ISSUE
- Effect on Reporting Entity
- Pricing Methods
- Examples

DISCLOSURE
- Situations
- Disclosure Required
- Transaction Examples
- Aggregation

GOVERNMENT BODY
- Exemption
- Example

Session 14 Guidance

■ **Learn** who is and who is not a related party (s.1) and understand the types of related party relationships (s.2.3).

■ **Understand** the need for the disclosures required by the standard (s.3) and the government body exemption (s.4).

© DeVry/Becker Educational Development Corp. All rights reserved.

1 Introduction

1.1 Scope

▨ IAS 24 is applied in:

- Identifying related party relationships and related party transactions.
- Identifying any outstanding balances between an entity and its related party.
- Determining the disclosures to be made relating to these transactions and outstanding balances.

1.2 Terminology

Related party: a person or entity that is related to the entity that is preparing its financial statements.

a. **Person** (or a close family member): related party to a reporting entity if that person:

- has control or joint control over the reporting entity;
- has significant influence over the reporting entity; or
- is a member of the key management personnel of the reporting entity or of a parent of the reporting entity.

b. **Entity:** related party to a reporting entity if any of the following conditions applies:

- The entity and the reporting entity are members of the same group; this means a parent, subsidiary and fellow subsidiaries are related to each other.
- One entity is an associate or joint venture of the other entity (or an associate or joint venture of a member of a group of which the other entity is a member).
- Both parties are joint ventures of the same third party.
- One entity is a joint venture of a third party and the other entity is an associate of the third entity.
- The entity is a post-employment benefit plan for the employees of the reporting entity (or an entity related to the reporting entity).
- The entity is controlled or jointly controlled by a **person** described in (a).
- A person having control or joint control of the reporting entity has significant influence over the entity or is a member of the key management personnel of the entity.*

*Commentary

*Substance of relationship, not merely legal form, should be considered. One party has the ability to control the other party or exercise **significant** influence over the other party in making financial and operating decisions.

© DeVry/Becker Educational Development Corp. All rights reserved.

Related party transactions: a transfer of resources, services or obligations between a reporting entity and a related party, regardless of whether a price is charged.

Government: government, government agencies and similar bodies whether local, national or international.

Government related entity: an entity that is controlled, jointly controlled or significantly influenced by a government.*

1.3 Parties Deemed Not to Be Related

▨ The following parties are deemed *not* to be related:

- Two companies, simply because they have a director or other member of key management personnel in common, or because a member of key management personnel of one **entity** has significant influence over the other entity.
- Two venturers, simply because they share joint control over a joint venture.
- Providers of finance, trade unions, public utilities, **government** departments and agencies, in the course of their normal dealings with an entity (even though they may restrict business activities).
- A customer, supplier, franchisor, distributor, etc with whom a significant volume of business is transacted as a result of economic dependence.

2 The Related Party Issue

2.1 Effect on Reporting Entity

▨ **Related party** relationships are a normal feature of commerce and business.

▨ A related party relationship could have an effect on financial position and operating results:

- Entering into transactions which unrelated parties would not.
- Transactions not at the same amounts as for unrelated parties.
- Even if **related party transactions** do not occur, mere existence of the relationship may affect transactions with other parties.

2.2 Methods for Pricing Related Party Transactions

▨ **Comparable uncontrolled price**—price of comparable goods sold in an economically comparable market to a buyer unrelated to the seller.

▨ Resale price reduced by a margin to arrive at a transfer price.

▨ **Cost-plus method**—supplier's cost plus an appropriate mark-up.

▨ No price (e.g. free provision of management services and interest-free credit).

Commentary

*The terms *control*, *significant influence* and *joint control* are defined in IFRS 10, 11 and IAS 28 and are used in IAS 24 with the meanings as specified in those standards (see *Session 21*).

2.3 Examples of Related Party Relationships

2.3.1 Person as an Investor

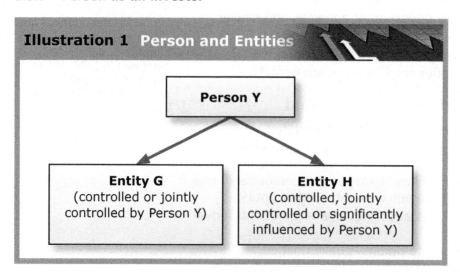

Illustration 1 Person and Entities

Person Y

Entity G
(controlled or jointly
controlled by Person Y)

Entity H
(controlled, jointly
controlled or significantly
influenced by Person Y)

- Y controls or has joint control over entity G and has control, joint control or significant influence over entity H.

- In terms of the financial statements of entity G, entity H is a related party and the same would be true of entity G in entity H's financial statements.

- If Y only had significant influence over both entities G and entity H, then the two entities would not be related parties in each other's financial statements.

2.3.2 Investments of Members of Key Management Personnel

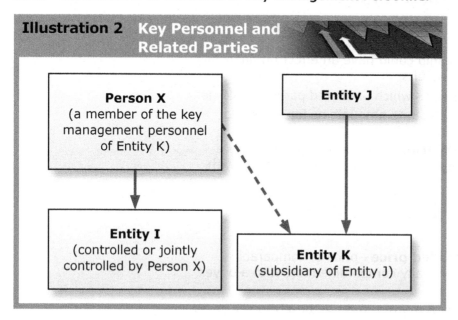

Illustration 2 Key Personnel and Related Parties

Person X
(a member of the key
management personnel
of Entity K)

Entity J

Entity I
(controlled or jointly
controlled by Person X)

Entity K
(subsidiary of Entity J)

© DeVry/Becker Educational Development Corp. All rights reserved.

■ Entity K would be a related party of entity I within I's financial statements because X has control (or joint control) of entity I and is a key management personnel in entity K.

■ The same would be true in entity K's financial statements; entity I would be a related party.

■ If X were a member of the key management personnel of entity J, the outcome in both I and K's financial statements would be the same.

2.3.3 Close Family Members

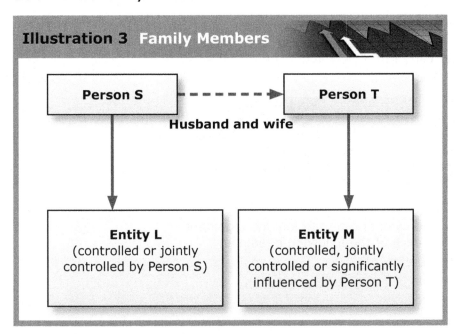

Illustration 3 Family Members

Person S - - - - - → Person T

Husband and wife

Entity L
(controlled or jointly controlled by Person S)

Entity M
(controlled, jointly controlled or significantly influenced by Person T)

■ Both entity L and entity M would be related parties under IAS 24.

■ If S and T only have significant influence over entity L and M respectively, then entity L and M would not be related parties.

3 Disclosure

3.1 Situations in Which Related Party Transactions May Lead to Disclosures

■ Purchases or sales of goods, property and other assets

■ Rendering or receiving of services

■ Agency arrangements

■ Leasing arrangements

■ Transfer of research and development

■ Licence agreements

■ Finance (including loans and equity contributions)

■ Guarantees and collaterals

■ Management contracts.

3.2 Disclosure Required

Key Point

Relationships between a parent and its subsidiaries are disclosed even if there have been *no transactions* between them.

- The name of the entity's parent must be disclosed and the ultimate parent, if different.
- Related party relationships where control exists (irrespective of whether there have been transactions between them) must be disclosed so a reader can form a view about the effects of related party relationships.

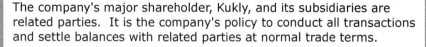

Illustration 4 Disclosing Related Parties

The company's major shareholder, Kukly, and its subsidiaries are related parties. It is the company's policy to conduct all transactions and settle balances with related parties at normal trade terms.

- An entity also must disclose compensation to key management personnel, in total and for each of the following headings:
  - Short-term employee benefits
  - Post-employment benefits
  - Other long-term benefits
  - Termination benefits
  - Equity compensation benefits.

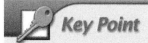

Key Point

Disclosure of *transactions* between related parties is required, along with any outstanding *balances* and *commitments*.

- As a minimum, these disclosures will include:
  - the amount of the transaction;
  - the amount of any outstanding balances, including terms and conditions; whether they are secured; the nature and means of settlement; and whether any guarantees have been given or received;
  - any allowances for irrecoverable debts relating to the outstanding balances; and
  - any expense recognised in the period in respect of irrecoverable debts due from related parties.

© DeVry/Becker Educational Development Corp. All rights reserved.

◻ Disclosures are made separately for each of the following classifications of related parties:

- Parent
- Subsidiaries
- Associates
- Joint ventures
- Key management personnel
- Parties with joint control or significant influence over the entity
- Other.

Illustration 4	Disclosing Related Parties (continued)

The following transactions were carried out with related parties:

	2018	2017
	$m	$m
Sale of goods		
Kukly	70	50
Kuklochka	40	35
Mishka	20	22
	130	107

Sales were carried out on commercial terms and conditions and at market prices.

	$m	$m
Purchases of goods		
Tass	60	50
	60	50

Purchases were carried out on commercial terms and conditions. Tass is a fellow subsidiary of Kukly.

	$m	$m
Year-end balances relating to related parties		
Receivables from related parties		
Kukly	10	15
Mishka	5	2
	15	17
Payables to related parties		
Tass	20	5

Exhibit 1 — RELATED PARTY TRANSACTIONS

The following disclosures are made in Nokia's 2015 annual report:

34. Related party transactions (extracts)

The Group had borrowings amounting to EUR 69 million (EUR 69 million in 2014 from Nokia Unterstützungskasse GmbH, the Group's German pension fund, a separate legal entity. The loan bears interest at 6% per annum and its duration is pending until further notice by the loan counterparties even though they have the right to terminate the loan with a 90-day notice period. The loan is included in long-term interest bearing liabilities in the consolidated statement of financial position.

The Group has guaranteed a loan of EUR 15 million (EUR 13 million in 2014) for an associated company.

No loans have been granted to the members of the Group Leadership Team and the Board of Directors in 2015, 2014 or 2013.

NOKIA

3.3 Examples of Transactions

- The following are examples of transactions which would be disclosed if they were made with a related party:
  - Purchases or sales of property or other assets
  - Purchases or sale of goods, or rendering or receiving of services
  - Leases
  - Transfer of research and development knowledge
  - Provision of guarantees or collateral.

3.4 Aggregation

- Items of a similar nature may be disclosed in aggregate except when separate disclosure is necessary for an understanding of the effects of the related party transactions.

4 Government Body

- The requirements of IAS 24 are quite onerous for many **government-related** entities.
- In a country such as China, many thousands of government entities would be related to each other, so IAS 24 has relaxed the disclosures for some related parties.

© DeVry/Becker Educational Development Corp. All rights reserved.

4.1   Exemption

▓ A reporting entity is exempt from disclosure requirements in relation to related party transactions and outstanding balances with:

- ● a government which has control, joint control or significant influence over the reporting entity; and
- ● another entity which is a related party because the same government has control, joint control or significant influence over both the reporting entity and the other entity.

▓ If an entity applies the exemption, it discloses the following about the transactions and outstanding balances:

- ● the name of the government and the nature of the relationship with the reporting entity; and
- ● the following information in sufficient detail to enable users to understand the effect of the related party transactions on its financial statements:

  —the nature and amount of each individually significant transaction; and

  —for other transactions which are collectively significant, a qualitative or quantitative indication of their extent.

▓ An entity must use its judgement to determine the level of detail to be disclosed, taking account of the closeness of the related party and other factors relevant to the level of significance (e.g. non-market terms or outside normal day-to-day business operations).

4.2   Example of Exemption

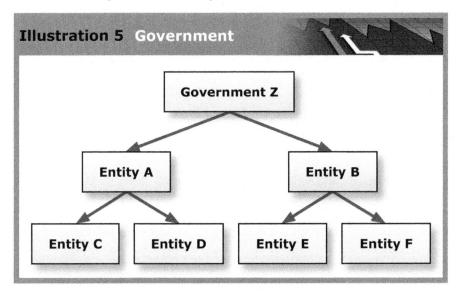

Illustration 5   Government

▓ Government body Z has control, either directly or indirectly, over entities A through F.

▓ Entity C would be able to claim the disclosure exemptions available under IAS 24 in respect of transactions with Government Z and entities A, B and D through F.

▓ If entity C entered into a transaction with a person who was a key management personnel within entity A, then the exemption would not apply.

Summary

- A related party is a *person* or *entity* related to the reporting entity.

- A person (or close family member) is related on grounds of control, joint control or significant influence or key management role.

- An entity is related on grounds of control, joint control or significant influence or if it is a pension plan for employees.

- Some parties are deemed not to be related (e.g. common directorships).

- A transfer of resources, services or obligations between related parties is a related party transaction, regardless of whether a price is charged.

- Disclosure requirements are extensive.

- Similar items may be aggregated.

- There is an exemption for reporting entities for transactions with government-related entities only. However, individually and collectively *significant* transactions still must be disclosed.

Session 14 Quiz
Estimated time: 10 minutes

1. Define related party in accordance with IAS 24. (1.2)
2. Explain what parties are deemed not related. (1.3)
3. Describe pricing methods available regarding related party transactions. (2.2)
4. Identify FIVE possible situations in which related party transactions may lead to disclosures. (3.1)
5. True or False? IAS 24 allows the aggregation of transactions concerning related parties. (3.4)

Study Question Bank
Estimated time: 50 minutes

Priority		Estimated Time	Completed
Q23	Connect	50 minutes	

© DeVry/Becker Educational Development Corp. All rights reserved.

NOTES

© DeVry/Becker Educational Development Corp. All rights reserved.

IFRS 2 *Share-based Payment*

FOCUS

This session covers the following content from the *ACCA Study Guide.*

C. Reporting the Financial Performance of Entities

10. Share-based payment

a) Apply and discuss the recognition and measurement criteria for share-based payment transactions. ☐

b) Account for modifications, cancellations and settlements of share-based payment transactions. ☐

Session 15 Guidance

■ **Recognise** the need for a standard and that share-based transactions include the issue of share options.

■ **Learn** the types of transaction which fall within the scope of IFRS 2 (s.2.2).

■ **Learn** the initial recognition rule (s.3.1) and **understand** that only the credit entry depends on the type of transaction.

■ **Understand** how fair value is measured (s.3.2, s.3.3) and the implications of vesting conditions (s.3.4). **Attempt** *Example 1.*

■ **Understand** why the liability for cash-settled transactions is remeasured at each reporting date (s.3.7).

■ **Work** carefully through *Illustration 6* to understand the deferred tax issue (s.4).

VISUAL OVERVIEW

Objective: To explain how to account for the granting of shares and share options to executives, employees and other parties.

SHARE-BASED PAYMENTS
- Need for a Standard
- Key Issues
- Objective of IFRS 2
- Scope

TERMINOLOGY
- Share-based Payment Arrangement
- Types of Transactions

RECOGNITION AND MEASUREMENT
- Initial Recognition
- Fair Value Measurement
- Equity-Settled
- Granting Equity Instruments
- Indirect Measurement
- Valuation Technique
- Cash-Settled
- Modifications to Terms

DISCLOSURES
- Schemes
- Fair Value
- Expenses Arising

DEFERRED TAX
- Issue
- Accounting

1 Share-based Payments

1.1 Need for a Standard

▪ Share plans and share option plans have become a common feature of remuneration packages for directors, senior executives and other employees in many countries.

▪ Shares and share options also may be used to pay suppliers (e.g. for professional services).

▪ IFRS 2 *Share-based Payment* fills a gap in accounting for the recognition and measurement of such transactions under IFRS.

▪ IAS 19 *Employee Benefits* prescribed certain disclosures to enable users of financial statements to assess the effect of equity compensation benefits (i.e. shares, share options and cash payments linked to future share prices) on an entity's financial performance and cash flows. However, IAS 19 did not seek to address the recognition and measurement issues.

1.2 Key Issues

▪ Recognition: When to recognise the charge for share-based payments?*

*Commentary

*Recognition must reflect accrual accounting in keeping with the Framework.

▪ Measurement: How much expense to recognise?*

*Commentary

*IFRS 2 limits the measurement possibilities. In principle, share-based payment transactions are accounted for to reflect the "value" of goods or services received. However, the measurement method depends on the type of transaction and with whom it is made.

1.3 Objective of IFRS 2

▪ To specify the financial reporting of share-based payment transactions.*

▪ In particular, to show the effects of such transactions (including associated expenses) on profit or loss and financial position.

*Commentary

*In summary, IFRS 2 requires the recognition of all share-based payment transactions measured at fair value.

                 © DeVry/Becker Educational Development Corp. All rights reserved.

1.4   Scope

- *All* share-based payment transactions. Transactions may be:
  - settled in cash, other assets or equity instruments of the entity; and
  - with employees or other parties.
- There are no exceptions for employee share purchase plans.
- IFRS 2 applies regardless of whether the entity can identify specifically some or all of the goods or services received.

2   Terminology

2.1   Share-based Payment Arrangement

Share-based payment arrangement: an agreement between the entity and an employee (or other party) to enter into a *share-based payment transaction* which entitles the other party to receive:

- *equity instruments* (including shares or share options) of the entity (or another group entity); or
- cash (or other assets) for amounts based on the price (or value) of the equity instruments of the entity (or another group entity),
- provided that any specified *vesting* conditions are met.

Vest: to become an entitlement. A party's right to shares of an entity may be free or at a prearranged exercise price.

Share-based payment transaction: a transaction in a share-based payment arrangement in which the entity:*

- receives goods or services from a supplier (including an employee); or
- incurs an obligation (to the supplier) when another group entity receives those goods or services.

Equity instrument: a contract that gives a residual interest in the assets of an entity after deducting all of its liabilities.

Share option: a contract that gives the holder the right, but *not* the obligation, to subscribe to the entity's shares at a fixed (or determinable) price for a specified period of time.

Vesting conditions: the conditions that must be satisfied for a person to become entitled to receive cash, other assets or equity instruments under a **share-based payment arrangement**.*

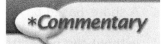

*As many entities mostly receive services (e.g. from their executives and employees), references to "goods or services" are simplified to "services" in this session.

*Examples of vesting conditions include completion of a specified service period and meeting **performance targets** (e.g. a specified increase in revenue over a specified period of time).

© DeVry/Becker Educational Development Corp. All rights reserved.

Service condition: a vesting condition requiring the director or employee to complete a specified period of service. If the director (or employee) ceases to provide service during the vesting period he fails to satisfy the condition.

Performance condition: a vesting condition that requires:

- a service condition; and
- specified performance targets to be met in rendering that service.

Performance target: refers to the entity's operations or the price of its shares. It may relate to the performance of the entity as a whole or a component (e.g. a division).

2.2 Types of Transactions

 **Key Point**

There are three types of **share-based payment transactions**:

    (1) equity-settled share-based payment transactions;

    (2) cash-settled share-based payment transactions; and

    (3) share-based payment transactions with cash alternatives.

2.2.1 Equity-Settled

▓ The entity receives services as consideration for its own **equity instruments**, or has no obligation to settle the transactions with the supplier.

▓ A share-based payment transaction settled on a net basis is classified as equity-settled if it would have been so classified without the net settlement feature.

2.2.2 Cash-Settled

▓ The entity acquires goods or services by incurring liabilities for amounts which are based on the price (or value) of the equity instrument(s) of the entity or another group entity.

2.2.3 Equity-Settled With Cash Alternative

▓ Where the counterparty to the transaction has a choice in the method of settlement a compound instrument will be recognised.

▓ This means that the value of the instrument will be split between the liability component and the equity component.

▓ Where the entity has a choice of settlement it considers whether it has a present obligation to settle the transaction in cash; if it does, a liability should be recognised.

▓ A present obligation occurs if the choice of settlement in equity instruments has no commercial substance or the entity has a past practice or stated policy of settling in cash.

© DeVry/Becker Educational Development Corp. All rights reserved.

3 Recognition and Measurement

3.1 Initial Recognition

▨ Normal recognition rules apply to the goods or services received:*

Dr   Expense (e.g. purchases, labour)

▨ If settlement by **equity-settled** share-based payment, then increase **equity:**

Cr   Equity

▨ If settlement by **cash-settled** share-based payment, then recognise a **liability**:

Cr   Trade (or other) payables

Commentary

*Or debit an asset account.

3.2 Fair Value Measurement

Key Point

Goods or services are measured at fair value (i.e. the amount for which an asset could be exchanged, a liability settled or an equity instrument granted, between knowledgeable, willing parties in an arm's length transaction).

▨ IFRS 13 *Fair Value Measurement* deals with the measurement and disclosure of fair value transactions.

▨ It also recognises that the use of fair value for share-based transactions differs from fair value for other transactions and therefore "scopes out" any fair value share-based transactions; IFRS 2 should be followed instead.

3.3 Equity-Settled Transactions

Key Point

The fair value of the services received (and the corresponding increase in equity) is measured either:

• *directly* at the fair value of the services received; or

• *indirectly* by reference to the fair value of the equity instruments granted.

▨ Direct measurement is at the date the entity receives the services (or obtains the goods).

▨ Indirect measurement, as a surrogate, is at the grant date.

▨ The grant date is the date when the parties to the arrangement have a shared understanding of its terms and conditions. The right to cash, other assets or equity instruments are conferred at grant date (provided any **vesting conditions**).*

Commentary

*If an agreement is subject to approval (e.g. by shareholders) the grant date is when that approval is obtained.

© DeVry/Becker Educational Development Corp. All rights reserved.

3.3.1 Employees' Remuneration

▣ Direct measurement of services received for particular components of a remuneration package (e.g. cash, shares and other employee benefits) may not be possible.

▣ Also, it may not be possible to measure the fair value of a total remuneration package without measuring directly the fair value of the equity instruments granted.

▣ Measurement will be further complicated where equity instruments are granted as part of a bonus arrangement (e.g. a loyalty bonus to stay with the entity) rather than as a part of basic remuneration.

▣ Granting equity instruments is paying additional remuneration to obtain additional benefits. Estimating the fair value of the additional benefits is likely to be more difficult than measuring the fair value of the equity instruments granted.*

Commentary

*The transaction, therefore, will be measured at the fair value of the equity instrument granted.

3.3.2 Transactions With Others

▣ For transactions with parties other than employees, there is a rebuttable presumption that the fair value of the goods or services received can be estimated reliably.*

▣ That fair value is measured at the date the goods are obtained or the supplier renders the service.

Commentary

*In rare cases, if the presumption of reliable estimate is rebutted, measurement will be indirect, at the date the entity obtains the goods or service (rather than at the grant date).

3.3.3 Unidentifiable Services

▣ If the identifiable consideration received appears to be less than the fair value of the equity instruments granted or liability incurred, this suggests that other consideration (i.e. unidentifiable services) has been received.

▣ Unidentifiable services are measured on the grant date as the difference between the fair values of the share-based payment and the identifiable services.

3.4 Granting of Equity Instruments

3.4.1 Without Vesting Conditions

▣ When equity instruments granted vest immediately, employees (executives or other suppliers) are not required to complete a specified period of service before becoming unconditionally entitled to those equity instruments.

▣ Unless there is evidence to the contrary, the entity presumes that services rendered by the employee have been received. So, on grant date the entity recognises:

  • the services received in full; and

  • a corresponding increase in equity.

▣ Recognition is immediate when equity instruments are granted for past performance.

Key Point

Services must then be accounted for as rendered by the employee during the vesting period, with a corresponding increase in equity.

3.4.2 With Vesting Conditions

▣ If the equity instruments granted do not vest until a specified period of service has been completed, it is presumed that the services to be rendered as consideration will be received over the future vesting period.

                                      © DeVry/Becker Educational Development Corp. All rights reserved.

> ### Illustration 1   Share Options for Period of Service
>
> An employee is granted share options conditional upon completing three years of service.
>
> The entity presumes that the services to be rendered by the employee as consideration for the share options will be received in the future, over that three-year vesting period.

> ### Illustration 2   Share Options for Performance
>
> An employee is granted share options conditional upon:
>
> - the achievement of a performance condition; and
> - remaining in the entity's employ until that performance condition is satisfied.
>
> Thus, the length of the vesting period varies depending on when that performance condition is satisfied. The entity therefore presumes that the services to be rendered for the share options will be received over an *expected* vesting period.

3.4.3   Expected Vesting Period

- The expected vesting period at grant date is estimated based on the most likely outcome of the performance condition.

- A performance condition may be a market condition (i.e. a condition upon which the exercise price, vesting or exercisability of an equity instrument is related to the market price of the entity's equity instruments).*

*Commentary

*An example of a market condition is achieving a specified share price.

- If the performance condition is a **market** condition, the estimate of length of vesting period must be consistent with the assumptions used in estimating the fair value of the options granted. This period is **not** subsequently revised.

- If the performance condition is **not** a market condition, the estimate of the length of the vesting period is revised, if necessary.*

*Commentary

*That is, if subsequent information indicates that the length of the vesting period differs from previous estimates.

Illustration 3 Accounting for Share Option Expense

Omega grants 120 share options to each of its 460 employees. Each grant is conditional on the employee working for Omega over the next three years. Omega has estimated that the fair value of each share option is $12.

Omega estimates that 25% of employees will leave during the three-year period and forfeit their rights to the share options.*

Everything turns out exactly as expected.

Required:

Calculate the amounts to be recognised for services received as consideration for the share options during the vesting period.

Solution

Year	Calculation	Remuneration expense for period $	Cumulative remuneration expense $
1	55,200 options × 75% × $12 × ⅓ years	165,600	165,600
2	(55,200 options × 75% × $12 × ⅔ years) − $165,600	165,600	331,200
3	(55,200 options × 75% × $12 × ⅓ years) − $331,200	165,600	496,800

✳Commentary

*Estimates of leavers could be made on the basis of a weighted average probability applied to a historical pattern of leavers adjusted for expected changes in that pattern.

Example 1 Changes in Expectations

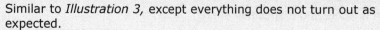

Similar to *Illustration 3,* except everything does not turn out as expected.

Year 1: 25 employees leave. Omega revises its estimate of total leavers over the three-year period from 25% (115 employees) to 20% (92 employees).

Year 2: Another 22 employees leave. Omega revises its estimate of total leavers over the three-year period from 20% to 15% (69 employees).

Year 3: A further 13 employees leave.

Required:

Calculate the amounts to be recognised for services received as consideration for the share options during the vesting period.

© DeVry/Becker Educational Development Corp. All rights reserved.

Illustration 4 Executive Stock Options

On 1 January 2016, Kappa granted 1,000 options to an executive, conditional on his remaining in Kappa's employment for three years. The exercise price is $35, but falls to $25 if earnings increase by 12% on average over the three-year period.*

On grant date, the estimated fair value of an option is:

- $12 for an exercise price of $25;
- $9 if the exercise price is $35.

2016 earnings increase by 14%. This increase is expected over the next two years, giving an expected exercise price of $25.

2017 earnings increase by 13%. The earnings target is still expected to be achieved.

2018 earnings increase by only 7%. The earnings target is not achieved.*

On 31 December 2018, the executive completes three years' service. Rights to the 1,000 options are now vested at an exercise price of $35.

Required:

Calculate the remuneration expense arising from the share options over the three-year period.

The performance condition is not a market condition.

Solution

Year	Calculation	Remuneration expense	
		Period	Cumulative
		$	$
1	1,000 options × $12 × $\frac{1}{3}$ years	4,000	4,000
2	(1,000 options × $12 × $\frac{2}{3}$ years) − $4,000	4,000	8,000
3	(1,000 options × $9) − $8,000	1,000	9,000

Commentary

*The exercise price is the price at which the executive can buy the shares under the option contract.

Commentary

*As the performance condition was not actually met in year 3, the exercise price will become $35, resulting in a $9 fair value of the option at grant date.

3.5 Indirect Measurement

▨ Fair value of equity instruments granted is based on:

- market prices, if available; otherwise
- a valuation technique.

▨ The measurement date is the grant date for employees and others providing similar services. For transactions with parties other than employees it is the date the goods are received (or the services rendered).

Key Point

Vesting conditions *other than market conditions* are *not* taken into account when estimating fair value.*

Commentary

*Instead, vesting conditions other than market conditions are reflected in the estimate of the likely outcome of these conditions and hence the number of equity instruments expected to vest.

© DeVry/Becker Educational Development Corp. All rights reserved.

▓ Services received measured at the grant date fair value of equity instruments granted is the minimum amount recognised (unless the equity instruments do not vest due to forfeiture).*

3.6   Valuation Technique

▓ It is highly unlikely that market prices will be available for employee share options because the terms and conditions under which they are granted do not apply to options which are actively traded.

Where similar traded options do not exist, the fair value of options granted is estimated by applying an option-pricing model.

▓ As a minimum, an option-pricing model should reflect:
- ● exercise price of option;
- ● life of option;
- ● current price of underlying;
- ● expected volatility of share price;
- ● expected dividends; and
- ● risk-free interest rate over life of the option.

3.7   Cash-Settled Transactions

For cash-settled transactions, the goods or services acquired and the liability incurred are measured at the fair value of the liability.

▓ The liability is remeasured to fair value at each reporting date, with any changes in value recognised in profit or loss, until it is settled.*

▓ A common example of a cash-settled share-based payment transaction is that of **share appreciation rights** (SARs).

▓ These are granted to employees and give the employee an entitlement to a future cash payment based on the increase in the entity's share price from a determined level and for a specific period of time.

▓ The SAR means that the entity will be required to make a cash payment to the employee and will therefore be required to recognise a liability based on the estimated value of the SAR.

▓ As the transaction is cash-settled, the liability will be remeasured each reporting date with any change in value being taken to profit or loss.

▓ When the SAR is exercised by the employee this will also be expensed to profit or loss.

*The rule for the minimum amount recognised applies, irrespective of any modifications to the terms and conditions on which the equity instruments were granted, including cancellations and settlement.

*Contrast the liability remeasurement with equity-settled, where there is no remeasurement.

                    © DeVry/Becker Educational Development Corp. All rights reserved.

Illustration 5 SARs

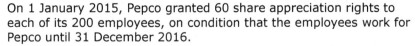

On 1 January 2015, Pepco granted 60 share appreciation rights to each of its 200 employees, on condition that the employees work for Pepco until 31 December 2016.

During 2015, 12 employees leave and Pepco estimates that a further 15 will leave during 2016.

During 2016, a further 14 employees leave.

On 31 December 2016, 61 employees exercise their SARs, another 77 employees exercise their SARs on 31 December 2017, and the remaining 36 employees exercise their SARs on 31 December 2018.

The fair value of the SARs for the years in which Pepco has a liability and the intrinsic value of the SARs are shown below:*

	Fair value $	Intrinsic value $
2015	16.20	–
2016	18.10	15.70
2017	20.50	19.80
2018	–	22.00

Required:

Calculate the liability to be included in the statement of financial position for each of the four years and calculate the expense to be recognised in profit or loss for each of the four years.

Solution

Year	Calculation	Liability $	Expense $
2015	(200 – 27) × 60 × $16.20 × ½ years	84,078	84,078[1]
2016	Not yet exercised ((200 – 26 – 61) × 60 × $18.10)	122,718	38,640[2]
	Exercised (61 × 60 × $15.70)		57,462
			96,102
2017	Not yet exercised ((200 – 26 – 61 – 77) × 60 × $20.50)	44,280	(78,438)
	Exercised (77 × 60 × $19.80)		91,476
			13,038
2018		Nil*	(44,280)
	Exercised (36 × 60 × $22.00)		47,520
			3,240

Notes to accounting entries:

1	Dr	Profit or loss	84,078	
	Cr	Liability		84,078
2	Dr	Profit or loss	96,102	
	Cr	Liability (122,718 – 84,078)		38,640
	Cr	Cash		57,462

*The fair value of the SARs would be identified from using an option-pricing model. The fair value would be given to you in an exam.

The intrinsic value of the SAR would be the cash value of the SAR at the exercise date; again this value would be given to you in the exam.

*Commentary

*The liability is derecognised at 31 December 2018, as the exercise period of the SARs has now lapsed; all SARs in this example were exercised.

© DeVry/Becker Educational Development Corp. All rights reserved.

3.8   Modifications to Terms

▣ An entity may modify the terms of a share-based payment or decide to cancel or settle the payment early.

 **Key Point**

The full amount of the expense originally calculated must still be recognised, but over a shorter period.

▣ Reducing the exercise price, for example, will lead to an increase in the fair value of the share option. This increase in fair value will have to be accounted for from the repricing date to the vesting date.

▣ Modifications will have a significant effect on profits. Not only will the original cost have to be expensed but also the effect of the modification.

▣ If a cash-settled transaction is changed to an equity-settled transaction:

  • the original liability is derecognised and the equity-settled payment recognised at fair value for services rendered to the modification date; and

  • any difference between the liability derecognised and the amount of equity recognised is recognised in profit or loss.

4   Deferred Tax

4.1   Issue

▣ In many jurisdictions the legislation allows for the recovery of tax for the share option expense.

▣ In many cases the amount of benefit will be based on the intrinsic value of the share option and will only be available once the options have been exercised.

▣ The intrinsic value of a share option is the difference between the exercise price of the option and the market price of the share; therefore, the intrinsic value of the option will move as the market price of the share moves.

 **Key Point**

The timing difference and difference in value give rise to a deductible temporary difference, which will result in the recognition of a deferred tax asset in the statement of financial position (if the IAS 12 recognition requirements are met).

                          © DeVry/Becker Educational Development Corp. All rights reserved.

4.2   Accounting

- The tax expense within the profit or loss will be credited with the double entry to the recognition of the deferred tax asset.

- The amount that can be credited within profit or loss is set as a maximum, being the cumulative share option expense × tax rate. Any additional benefit will be credited direct to equity.

Illustration 6   Deferred Tax Implications of Share-based Payment

On 1 January 2017, Robinson granted 10,000 share options to an employee vesting two years later on 31 December 2018. The fair value of each option measured at the grant date was $4.

Tax legislation in the country in which the entity operates allows a tax deduction of the intrinsic value of the options when they are exercised. The intrinsic value of the share options was $2.20 at December 2017 and $4.40 at 31 December 2018, at which point the options were exercised.

Assume a tax rate of 30%.

Show the deferred tax accounting treatment of the share options in the financial statements for the years ending 31 December 2017 and 31 December 2018.

Solution

	31 December	
	2017	**2018**
Carrying amount of share-based payment expense	0	0
Less: Tax base of share-based payment expense		
(10,000 × $2.20 × ½)	(11,000)	
(10,000 × $4.40)		(44,000)
Temporary difference	(11,000)	(44,000)
Deferred tax asset @ 30% (Asset balance)	3,300	13,200

Credit entry:

Deferred tax 31 Dec 2017

Profit or loss	3,300	
Equity	0	

Deferred tax 31 Dec 2018

Profit or loss (13,200 − 3,300 − (W) 1,200)		8,700
Equity (W)		1,200

Illustration 6 Deferred Tax Implications of Share-based Payment (continued)

The maximum benefit which can be credited to profit or loss is the cumulative expense charged against profits of $40,000 (10,000 options × $4) by the tax rate of 30%, which is $12,000. Any benefit above the $12,000 must be credited directly to equity.

On exercise, the deferred tax asset is replaced by a current tax one. The double entry is:

Dr Profit or loss (deferred tax expense)	12,000	
Dr Equity	1,200	
Cr Deferred tax asset		13,200
Dr Current tax asset	13,200	
Cr Profit or loss		12,000
Cr Equity		1,200

Working

Accounting expense recognised (10,000 × $4 × ½) ÷ (10,000 × $4)	20,000	40,000
Tax deduction (10,000 × $2.20 × ½) (10,000 × $4.40)	(11,000)	(44,000)
Excess temporary difference	0	(4,000)
Excess deferred tax asset to equity @ 30%	0	1,200

5 Disclosures

5.1 Nature and Extent of Schemes in Place

- A description of each type of scheme which existed at any time during the period, including:
  - general terms and conditions (e.g. vesting requirements);
  - the maximum term of options granted; and
  - the settlement method (i.e. cash or equity).
- The number and weighted average exercise prices of share options:
  - outstanding at the beginning of the period;
  - granted during the period;
  - forfeited during the period;
  - exercised during the period;
  - expired during the period;
  - outstanding at the end of the period; and
  - exercisable at the end of the period.
- For share options exercised during the period, the weighted average share price at the date of exercise.
- For share options outstanding at the end of the period, the range of exercise prices and weighted average remaining contractual life.

© DeVry/Becker Educational Development Corp. All rights reserved.

5.2　How Fair Value Was Determined

◾ Where fair value has been determined indirectly, by reference to the fair value of the equity instruments granted, the following extensive disclosure is required, as a minimum.

5.2.1　Share Options

◾ The weighted average fair value of share options granted during the period at the measurement date and information on how that fair value was measured.

5.2.2　Other Equity Instruments

◾ The number and weighted average fair value of other equity instruments at the measurement date and information on how that fair value was measured.

5.2.3　Direct Measurement

◾ Where the fair value of goods or services received during the period has been measured directly, disclose how that fair value was determined (e.g. whether at a market price).*

5.3　Effect of Expenses Arising

◾ The total expense recognised for the period where the goods or services received did not qualify for recognition as assets.

◾ Separate disclosure of that portion of the total expense which arises from equity-settled transactions.

◾ For liabilities arising from cash-based transactions:
  - the total carrying amount at the end of the period; and
  - any vested share appreciation rights.

*In rare cases, where the presumption that direct measurement can be made is rebutted, that fact is disclosed with an explanation why the presumption was rebutted.

Summary

- IFRS 2 identifies three types of share-based payment transactions: equity-settled, cash-settled and share-based with cash alternatives.
- On initial recognition the accounting entries are:
  Dr Expense (e.g. purchases, labour) or Asset
  Cr Equity (if equity-settled); or
  Cr Liability (if case-settled)
- Goods or services are measured at fair value.
- The fair value of services received is measured either *directly* or *indirectly* (i.e. at the fair value of the equity instruments granted).
- Any service required is accounted for when rendered during the vesting period, with a corresponding increase in equity.
- Vesting conditions other than market conditions are ignored when estimating fair value.
- Where similar traded options do not exist, the fair value of options granted is estimated using an option-pricing model.
- For cash-settled transactions, the goods or services acquired and the liability incurred are measured at the fair value of the liability.
- Any changes in the terms of the original share-based payment contract will still require the recognition of the full amount of the expense originally calculated; this must be recognised over a shorter period.
- Differences between the accounting and tax treatments give rise to a deductible temporary difference, which may lead to the recognition of a deferred tax asset.

Session 15 Quiz
Estimated time: 20 minutes

1. Define share-based payment transaction. (2.1)
2. List the THREE types of share-based payment transactions identified by IFRS 2. (2.2)
3. Explain how to measure the fair value of services received in an equity-settled transaction. (3.2)
4. If share options are issued to employees without vesting conditions, state when the services rendered should be recognised in the statement of comprehensive income. (3.4.1)
5. Fair value of equity instruments may be based on a valuation model if no market price exists. List the minimum variables which this valuation model must take into account. (3.6)
6. State what the acronym SAR stands for and define its meaning in IFRS 2. (3.7)
7. Discuss the effect on the financial statements when the terms of a share option agreement is modified. (3.8)
8. Give the maximum credit which can be made to profit or loss in respect of deferred tax relating to share options. (4.2)

Study Question Bank
Estimated time: 45 minutes

Priority		Estimated Time	Completed
Q24	Lima	45 minutes	

© DeVry/Becker Educational Development Corp. All rights reserved.

EXAMPLE SOLUTION

Solution 1—Description

Year	Calculation	Remuneration expense for period $	Cumulative remuneration expense $
1	55,200 options × 80% × $12 × 1/3 years	176,640	176,640
2	(55,200 options × 85% × $12 × 2/3 years) − $176,640	198,720	375,360
3	(48,000 options × $12) − 375,360	200,640	576,000

A total of 60 employees (25 + 22 + 13) forfeited their rights to the share options during the three-year period. Therefore, a total of 48,000 share options (400 employees × 120 options per employee) vested at the end of year 3.

© DeVry/Becker Educational Development Corp. All rights reserved.

Conceptual Principles
of Group Accounting

FOCUS

This session covers the following content from the *ACCA Study Guide.*

D. Financial Statements of Groups of Entities

1. Group accounting including statements of cash flows

d) Apply and discuss the criteria used to identify a subsidiary and an associate. ☐

f) Identify and outline: ☐

   i) the circumstances in which a group is required to prepare consolidated financial statements.

   ii) the circumstances when a group may claim an exemption from the preparation of consolidated financial statements.

   iii) why directors may not wish to consolidate a subsidiary and where this is permitted.

2. Continuing and discontinued interests

b) Apply and discuss the treatment of a subsidiary which has been acquired exclusively with a view to subsequent disposal. ☐

Session 16 Guidance

▪ **Revise** the definitions that are assumed knowledge (s.1.1).

▪ **Learn** the requirement to consolidate subsidiaries and the exclusions and exemptions (2.3); these are especially important. **Attempt** *Example 1*.

▪ **Pay** particular attention to special purpose entities; it is an area which looks at the concept of control rather than ownership (s.2.1).

(continued on next page)

VISUAL OVERVIEW

Objective: To describe the provisions of IFRS 10 *Consolidated Financial Statements*, to list the disclosure requirements of IFRS 12 *Disclosure of Interests in Other Entities* and to explain the provisions of IAS 27 *Separate Financial Statements*.

INTRODUCTION

- Terminology
- IAS 27 *Separate Financial Statements*
- Truth and Fairness

PARENT AND CONTROL

- Inclusions
- Potential Voting Rights
- Exclusions and Exemptions
- Transition to IFRS 10
- Acquisition Method

SUNDRY PROVISIONS OF IFRS 10

- Intra-group Trading
- Accounting Year Ends
- Accounting Policies
- Date of Acquisition or Disposal

EXEMPTION

- Rule
- Rationale
- Investment Entities

DISCLOSURES

- Judgement and Assumptions
- Interest in Subsidiaries
- Non-controlling Interest

Session 16 Guidance

■ **Revise** the sundry provisions of IFRS 10 (s.3).

■ **Be aware** that the examiner is quite keen to include theoretical issues relating to group accounts in the exam so it is not an area that should be treated lightly.

1 Introduction

1.1 Terminology

Business combination: a transaction or other event in which the acquirer obtains control of one or more businesses. Transactions sometimes referred to as "true mergers" or "mergers of equals" are also business combinations, as that term is used in this standard.

Acquisition date: the date the acquirer obtains control of the acquiree.

Control of an investee: arises when the investor is exposed, or has rights, to variable returns from its involvement with the investee and has the ability to affect those returns through its power over the investee.

Subsidiary: an entity controlled by another entity (the parent).

Parent: an entity which controls one or more entities.

Group: a parent and its subsidiaries.

Consolidated financial statements: the financial statements of a group in which the assets, liabilities, equity, income, expenses and cash flows of the parent and its subsidiaries are presented as those of a single economic entity.

Non-controlling interest: the equity in a subsidiary which is not attributable, directly or indirectly, to a parent.

Goodwill: an asset representing the future economic benefits arising from other assets acquired in a business combination, which are not individually identified and separately recognised.

1.2 IAS 27 *Separate Financial Statements*

Separate financial statements: "those presented by a parent ... or an investor with joint control of, or significant influence over, an investee, in which the investments are accounted for at cost or in accordance with IFRS 9 Financial Instruments".

When an investment is classified as held for sale:

- If it was carried at cost—IFRS 5 becomes the relevant standard;
- If it was carried at fair value—IFRS 9 is still the relevant standard;
- Any dividends received from the investment will be included in profit or loss once the investor's right to receive the dividend is established.

© DeVry/Becker Educational Development Corp. All rights reserved.

1.3   Truth and Fairness

▓ Group accounts aim to give a true and fair view to the owners of the parent company of what their investment represents (i.e. control and ownership of the net assets of subsidiary companies).

▓ Rules are needed to ensure that the consolidation *includes* all entities controlled by the parent company—the definition of subsidiaries attempts to do this.

▓ On occasion no useful purpose is served by a parent company producing group accounts. Thus in certain circumstances parent companies are exempt from the general requirement.

Key Point

IAS 27 requires that investments in subsidiaries, associates or joint ventures be carried either at cost or fair value (IFRS 9) in the **separate financial statements.**

2   Parent and Control

2.1   Inclusions

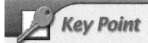

Key Point

A parent which issues consolidated financial statements must consolidate all subsidiaries, foreign and domestic, other than those excluded for the reasons specified in IFRS 10.

▓ IFRS 10 changed the previous definition of control that was included in IAS 27 (pre-2011) and also the guidance given in SIC 12 *Consolidation—Special Purpose Entities.**

∗Commentary

∗SIC 12 was withdrawn when IFRS 10 became effective.

Definition

Control—exists when the investor is exposed, or has rights, to variable returns from its involvement with the investee and has the ability to affect those returns through its power over the investee.

▓ The standard considers the substance of the transaction, being the ability to control, rather than the legal ownership of shares as the driving force when considering if control exists.

2.1.1   Power

Key Point

The investor has power over the investee if the investor has rights giving it the ability to direct activities that significantly affect returns from the investee.

▓ In many straightforward situations power is gained by holding more than 50% of the voting rights in the investee (subsidiary).

▓ But power is not always straightforward and can result from one or more contractual arrangements, without holding a majority of voting rights.

© DeVry/Becker Educational Development Corp. All rights reserved.

- An investor can have power over an investee even if other entities have rights allowing them to participate in the activities of the investee (e.g. if another investor has *significant influence*).

- The rights could be in the form of voting rights or the rights to appoint, or remove, members of the key management personnel of the investee (e.g. the board of directors).

- The assessment of rights should take into account any potential voting rights that the investor holds in the investee (e.g. share options or convertible instruments).*

*Commentary

*Potential voting rights are considered in more detail in section 2.2.

Illustration 1 Control

Entity A holds 40% of the voting right in entity B. It also holds share options which, if it were to exercise them, would take its share-holding in entity B to 80%.

Ignoring any other issues, it would be probable that entity A had control over entity B through both its current share-holding and its potential future shares. Entity B would be recognised as a subsidiary of entity A.

In this situation, recognising entity B as a subsidiary would mean that the non-controlling interest would be based on a 60% holding (i.e. the actual percentage).

2.1.2   Returns

- An investor is exposed to variable returns from the investee when there is potential for variable performance from the investee.

 Key Point

In other words the returns, dividends and profits, from the investee will depend on the performance of the subsidiary. There will be no fixed right to a specific return.

2.1.3   Link Between Power and Returns

 Key Point

To have control over the investee, the investor will have power and exposure to variable returns but must also have the ability to use that power to affect the returns from the investee.

- So an investor with decision-making rights shall determine if it is acting as either a principal or an agent. The investor will only control its investee if it is acting as a principal. An agent would need powers delegated to it by its controlling body.

© DeVry/Becker Educational Development Corp. All rights reserved.

2.2 Potential Voting Rights

Key Point

When assessing whether one entity has control over another take into account any potential voting rights (i.e. options or convertibles), that are presently exercisable or convertible, that the parent may have.

- An entity may own share options or convertible instruments that if exercised or converted will give the entity voting power over the financial and operating policies of the other entity.
- Potential voting rights that are not presently exercisable or convertible are ignored in assessing control.

Example 1 Entities in the Group

Identify the entities to be included in the group, as defined by IFRS 10, in each of the following situations:

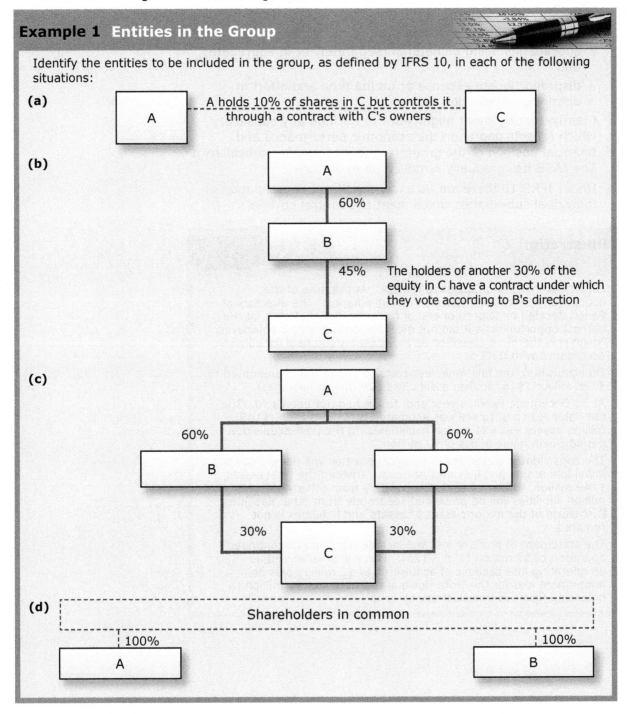

2.3 Exclusions and Exemptions

 **Key Point**

A subsidiary which has been acquired *exclusively* with the intention to resell it is not *consolidated* provided that it meets the IFRS 5 criteria of a disposal group *on acquisition*. In this case, it is carried at fair value less costs to sell and disclosed separately.

■ Previously, and still in some countries, grounds for excluding individual subsidiaries from consolidation have included:
  ● long-term restrictions over the parent's rights to control a subsidiary;
  ● a subsidiary having sufficiently different activities from the parent;
  ● temporary control of a subsidiary;
  ● subsidiaries being immaterial (separately or in aggregate); and
  ● disproportionate expense or undue time and effort in obtaining information required.

■ Clearly, management might want to exclude any subsidiary which reflects poorly on the economic performance and financial position of the group (e.g. a loss-making subsidiary). The IASB has gradually removed all exclusions.

■ Under IFRS 10 there are *no exclusions* from consolidation of individual subsidiaries which meet the control criteria.

Illustration 2 Subsidiary Acquired for Resale

On 28 October, Panon acquired Centax. At the time of the acquisition, Centax controlled three subsidiaries. The directors of Panon decided to dispose of one of the subsidiaries, Nokin, at the earliest opportunity as it did not meet Panon's strategic objectives. Nokin was therefore classified as a disposal group held for sale in accordance with IFRS 5.

On acquisition, the fair value less costs to sell of Nokin amounted to $128 million ($157 million assets less $29 million liabilities).

At 31 December, Panon's year end, Nokin had not been sold. The fair value less cost to sell was estimated at $125 million ($149 million assets less $24 million liabilities). In the post-acquisition period Nokin made a loss of $2 million.

The consolidated statement of financial position will not include the individual assets and liabilities of Nokin. Instead the total assets, $149 million, will be presented separately from other assets and $24 million liabilities will be presented separately from other liabilities. Disclosure of the major classes of assets and liabilities is not required.

The statement of profit or loss will include a loss on discontinued operation of $3 million (128 – 125). This will be analysed as an operating loss because of acquisition of $2 million plus an impairment loss for the write-down of net assets of $1 million (a balancing figure in this illustration).

© DeVry/Becker Educational Development Corp. All rights reserved.

2.4   Transition From IAS 27 to IFRS 10

▓ As a result of the issue of IFRS 10 some companies might be consolidated that were not consolidated under IAS 27.

▓ IFRS 10 clarifies that assets, liabilities and non-controlling interest should be measured as if IFRS 3 had been applied at the date when the investor gained control in accordance with the requirements of IFRS 10.

▓ The prior period would be adjusted to reflect this change in classification.

▓ If the date of control, under IFRS 10, was prior to the preceding period then any difference between carrying amounts of assets, liabilities and non-controlling interest would be recognised directly in equity.

2.5   Acquisition Method

▓ IFRS 3 requires that all **business combinations** be accounted for using the acquisition method of accounting.

▓ This involves:

• identifying an acquirer;

• determining the acquisition date;

• recognising and measuring the identifiable assets acquired, the liabilities assumed and any non-controlling interest in the acquiree; and

• recognising and measuring goodwill or a gain from a bargain purchase.

3   Sundry Provisions of IFRS 10

3.1   Results of Intragroup Trading

▓ Intragroup balances and intragroup transactions and resulting unrealised profits should be eliminated in full.

3.2   Accounting Year Ends

3.2.1   Coterminous Year Ends

▓ The financial statements of the parent and its subsidiaries used in the preparation of the consolidated financial statements are usually drawn up to the same date.

3.2.2   Different Reporting Dates

▓ Either the *subsidiary* must prepare special statements as at the same date as the group.

▓ Or, if it is impracticable to do this, financial statements drawn up to different reporting dates may be used if:

• the difference is no greater than three months; and

• adjustments are made for the effects of significant transactions or other events that occur between those dates and the date of the parent's financial statements.

3.3 Accounting Policies

■ Consolidated financial statements are prepared using uniform accounting policies for similar transactions and events.

Key Point

If a group member uses different accounting policies (e.g. a foreign subsidiary following local GAAP) then appropriate adjustments must be made at the consolidation stage.

3.4 Date of Acquisition or Disposal

■ The results of operations of a subsidiary are included in the consolidated financial statements as from the date the parent gains control of the subsidiary.

■ The date of acquisition and the date of disposal are based on when control passes not necessarily the legal date of acquisition or date of disposal.

■ The results of operations of a subsidiary disposed of are included in the consolidated statement of comprehensive income until the date of disposal, which is the date on which the parent ceases to have control of the subsidiary.

■ If a subsidiary is acquired in stages then the date of acquisition will be the date when the parent acquires control, which will normally be when the 50% threshold has been met. Any previous shareholdings will be remeasured to fair value on that acquisition date.

4 Exemption From Preparing Group Accounts

4.1 Rule

■ A parent need not present consolidated financial statements if:*

  • it is a wholly-owned or partially-owned subsidiary;*

*Commentary

*Non-controlling shareholders must give their consent. "Partially owned" is usually taken to mean 90% in many countries.

  • the parent's debt or equity instruments are not traded on a public market;
  • the parent has not filed its financial statements with a recognised stock market;
  • the ultimate (or intermediate) parent presents consolidated financial statements in accordance with IFRSs.

*Commentary

*National rules may specify exemptions subject to conditions being met. For example, in the UK an intermediate parent company is exempt if, inter alia, its parent entity prepares consolidated financial statements in accordance with the Seventh EU Directive or in an equivalent manner.

© DeVry/Becker Educational Development Corp. All rights reserved.

4.2 Rationale

▦ Users of the financial statements of a parent are usually concerned with, and need to be informed about, the financial position, results of operations and changes in financial position of the group as a whole.

▦ This need is served by consolidated financial statements, which present financial information about the group as that of a single entity without regard for the legal boundaries of the separate legal entities.

▦ A parent that is wholly owned by another entity may not always present consolidated financial statements since such statements may not be required by its parent and the needs of other users may be best served by the consolidated financial statements of its parent.

4.3 Investment Entities

▦ IFRS 10 makes an exception to the consolidation of certain subsidiaries for investment entities.

Investment entity—an entity which:

■ obtains funds from one or more investors in connection with its business of providing investment management services;

■ commits to those investors that those funds will be invested solely for returns from capital appreciation or investment income (or both); and

■ measures and evaluates the performance of substantially all of its investments on a fair value basis.*

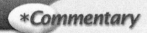

*An investment entity does not invest in the subsidiary's net assets but in its dividend income and capital appreciation. The investment is assessed in terms of its growth in market price and any dividends paid rather than its physical operations and outputs.

▦ An investment entity would typically have some, or all, of the following characteristics:

 ● More than one investment;

 ● More than one investor;

 ● Investors who are not related parties (*see Session 14*);

 ● Ownership interests in the form of equity or similar interests.

 **Key Point**

An investment entity (as defined above) must not consolidate its subsidiaries or apply IFRS 3 when it obtains control of another entity.

 ***Commentary**

▩ It must, instead, apply IFRS 9 *Financial Instruments* and measure those instruments at fair value through other comprehensive income.

▩ This exception does **not** apply to a parent of an investment entity. Such a parent is still required to consolidate all its subsidiaries (including investment entity subsidiaries).*****

*Unless the parent is an investment entity.

5 Disclosures

▩ The disclosure requirements are stated in IFRS 12 *Disclosure of Interests in Other Entities.*

▩ The standard requires disclosure in respect of all subsidiaries, joint arrangements and associates.

 **Key Point**

An entity is required to disclose any significant judgement and assumptions that it made in identifying its interest in other entities.

5.1 Judgements and Assumptions

▩ An entity must disclose how it determined it has control over another entity. This should include statements relating to the fact it holds more than 50% of voting rights but does not control, or it holds less than 50% of the entity and does control.

▩ It should disclose whether it is acting as an agent or principal.

5.2 Interest in Subsidiaries

▩ An entity must disclose information that enables users to understand the structure of the group and the share that **non-controlling** interest has in the activities and cash flows of the subsidiary.

▩ If reporting dates of the parent and subsidiary are different then this must be stated, along with the reason why and the date of the subsidiary's year end.

▩ The name of each subsidiary and place of business must be disclosed.

5.3 Non-controlling Interest

▩ Information must be disclosed in respect of the non-controlling interest in the activities of the group and its share of any cash flows. Disclosures include:

- proportion of ownership and voting rights held by the non-controlling interest;

- any profit or loss allocated to non-controlling interest during the period; and

- accumulated non-controlling interest at the beginning and end of the period.

© DeVry/Becker Educational Development Corp. All rights reserved.

Summary

- In the financial statements of a separate entity, investments are accounted for at cost or in accordance with IFRS 9.
- Group accounts should truthfully reflect the assets and liabilities under the control of the parent.
- Control exists if an investor has the ability to exercise power to control variable returns from the investee.
- Control can be achieved through voting rights or other power (e.g. of the board of directors).
- A parent which is part of a larger group may be excluded from presenting group accounts.
- Group accounts are prepared using the acquisition method.
- Intragroup balances, transactions and unrealised profits are eliminated on consolidation.
- Accounting policies within the group must be uniform.

Session 16 Quiz
Estimated time: 15 minutes

1. Define control. (1.1)

2. Explain how to determine the value of an investment in a subsidiary carried in the parent's books. (1.2)

3. State the conditions when IAS 27 allows a subsidiary to be excluded from consolidation. (2.3)

4. Explain how potential voting rights should be considered when assessing the ability to control. (2.2)

5. Yes or no? Must the parent and subsidiaries reporting dates be the same? (3.2.2)

6. Give the conditions required for a parent to be exempt from producing consolidated accounts. (4.1)

Study Question Bank
Estimated time: 10 minutes

Priority		Estimated Time	Completed
Q25	Danny	10 minutes	
Additional			
Q26	Picant		

© DeVry/Becker Educational Development Corp. All rights reserved.

EXAMPLE SOLUTION

Solution 1—Entities in the Group

(a) Even though A only holds 10% of the equity in C it is highly likely that C will be a subsidiary due to the fact that A has contractual arrangements with the owners of C to control the entity.

(b) A is the parent of B. A is also the parent of C as it has control of 75% of the voting rights of C.

(c) A is the parent of B and D. It may therefore appear to control C through a 60% indirect shareholding. In which case A would be the parent. However, A effectively owns only a 36% interest in C. The substance of this relationship would therefore require scrutiny.

(d) There is no group in this situation as A and B fall within the ownership of shareholders in common, which are scoped out of consolidated accounts. A and B however may be related parties and would have make necessary disclosures in accordance with IAS 24 (see *Session 14*).

© DeVry/Becker Educational Development Corp. All rights reserved.

NOTES

© DeVry/Becker Educational Development Corp. All rights reserved.

Basic Group Accounts

FOCUS

This session is a revision of F7 and covers the following content from the F7 *ACCA Study Guide*.

D. Business Combinations

3. Preparation of consolidated financial statements

a) Prepare a consolidated statement of financial position for a simple group (parent and one subsidiary) dealing with pre- and post-acquisition profits, non-controlling interests and consolidated goodwill. ☐

b) Prepare a consolidated statement of profit or loss and consolidated statement of profit or loss and other comprehensive income for a simple group dealing with an acquisition in the period and non-controlling interest. ☐

d) Account for the effects in the financial statements of intra-group trading. ☐

f) Account for goodwill impairment. ☐

Session 17 Guidance

■ **Revise** thoroughly group accounting principles and **understand** all the key points.

■ **Work** through *Example 1* to confirm that you have the knowledge assumed from F7 (s.3.2).

VISUAL OVERVIEW

Objective: To revise the basic techniques of consolidation before moving on to more complex issues in later sessions.

```
                    ┌─────────────────────────┐
                    │       BACKGROUND        │
                    │  • The Issue            │
                    │  • Terminology          │
                    │  • Rule                 │
                    │  • Types of             │
                    │    Consolidation        │
                    │  • Conceptual           │
                    │    Background           │
                    └─────────────────────────┘


┌─────────────────────────┐         ┌─────────────────────────┐
│      CONSOLIDATED       │         │      CONSOLIDATED       │
│      STATEMENT OF       │         │      STATEMENT OF       │
│   FINANCIAL POSITION    │         │     COMPREHENSIVE       │
│                         │         │        INCOME           │
│  • Specific Steps       │         │  • Control and          │
│  • Question Approach     │         │    Ownership            │
│                         │         │  • Unrealised Profit    │
│                         │         │    on Trading           │
│                         │         │  • Non-current Asset    │
│                         │         │    Transfer             │
│                         │         │  • Mid-year             │
│                         │         │    Acquisitions         │
└─────────────────────────┘         └─────────────────────────┘


                    ┌─────────────────────────┐
                    │    UNREALISED PROFIT    │
                    │  • Elimination          │
                    │  • Exception            │
                    │  • Deferred Tax         │
                    └─────────────────────────┘
```

1 Background

1.1 The Issue

▦ Many companies carry on part of their business through the ownership of other companies which they control. Such companies are known as subsidiaries.

▦ Controlling interests in such companies would appear at cost in the statement of financial position of the investing company. Such interests may result in the control of assets of a very different value to the cost of investment. In other words, the accounts will not provide the shareholders of the parent (or holding) company with a true and fair view of what their investment actually represents.

▦ The substance of the relationship is not reflected.

1.2 Terminology

Consolidated financial statements: the financial statements of a group in which the assets, liabilities, equity, income, expenses and cash flows of the parent and its subsidiaries are presented as those of a single economic entity.

Group: a parent and all its subsidiaries.*

Subsidiary: an entity controlled by another entity (the "parent").

Parent: an entity which controls one or more entities.

Non-controlling interest: equity in a subsidiary not attributable, directly or indirectly, to a parent.

*The definition of a group does not include associates or joint arrangements.

1.3 Rule

A company which has a subsidiary on the last day of its accounting period must prepare consolidated financial statements in addition to its own individual accounts.

▦ In practice, a parent company will usually prepare (and publish) the following:

- Its own statement of financial position with relevant notes.
- Consolidated versions of its statement of financial position, statement of comprehensive income and statement of cash flows, all with relevant notes.

1.4 Types of Consolidation

▦ IFRS 3 *Business Combinations* only allows the acquisition method of consolidation.

▦ Prior to IFRS 3 being issued, the IASB also allowed the use of the Uniting of Interest method of consolidation if certain criteria were met.*

*This session is only concerned with acquisition accounting.

© DeVry/Becker Educational Development Corp. All rights reserved.

1.5   Conceptual Background

 **Key Point**

Consolidation replaces the cost of investment with what it represents.

▦ That is:
- share of net assets at the end of the reporting period and goodwill at the date of acquisition; and
- credit reserves with parent company P's share of the post-acquisition growth in subsidiary S's reserves.

2   Consolidated Statement of Financial Position

2.1   Specific Steps

▦ There are two main steps:

1. Process individual company adjustments.

2. Consolidate.

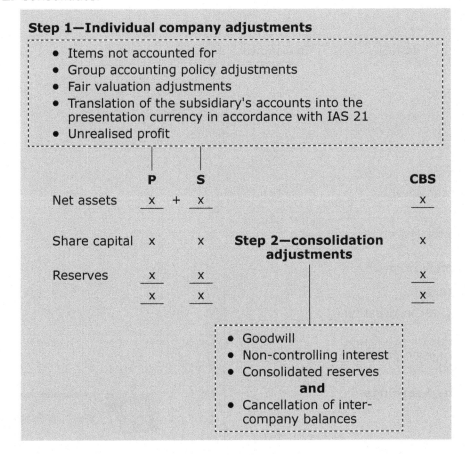

2.2 Question Approach

1. Establish group structure.

2. Pro forma the answer—fill in easy figures (e.g. share capital).

3. Process individual company adjustments:

- **do double entry** on face of question as far as possible;
- tick off points on paper as they are dealt with.

4. Prepare a net assets summary for each subsidiary:

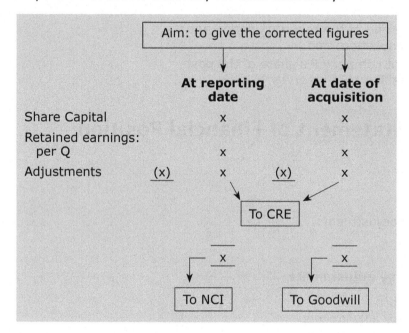

	At reporting date		At date of acquisition
Share Capital	x		x
Retained earnings: per Q	x		x
Adjustments	(x) x	(x)	x

To CRE

To NCI   To Goodwill

5. Consolidation schedules:

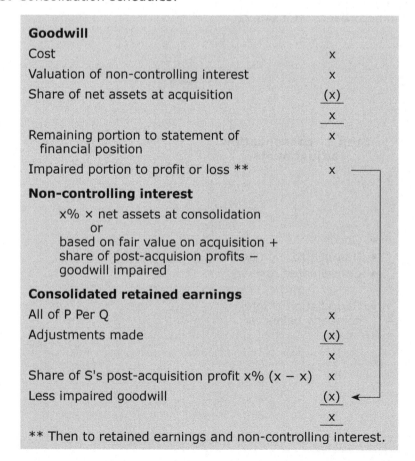

Goodwill

Cost	x
Valuation of non-controlling interest	x
Share of net assets at acquisition	(x)
	x
Remaining portion to statement of financial position	x
Impaired portion to profit or loss **	x

Non-controlling interest

x% × net assets at consolidation
    or
based on fair value on acquisition +
share of post-acquision profits −
goodwill impaired

Consolidated retained earnings

All of P Per Q	x
Adjustments made	(x)
	x
Share of S's post-acquisition profit x% (x − x)	x
Less impaired goodwill	(x)
	x

** Then to retained earnings and non-controlling interest.

Exam Advice

Be prepared to calculate S's net assets from either the equity or net asset position; both have been examined.

© DeVry/Becker Educational Development Corp. All rights reserved.

Key Point

IFRS 3 allows the non-controlling interest, at the acquisition date, to be based on either:

- fair value; or
- the proportionate share of the subsidiary's identifiable net assets.

Exam Advice

P2 consolidation questions require non-controlling interests to be valued at fair value on acquisition. Proportionate share may also be required for the purpose of making a comparison between the two bases.

▦ This choice can be made independently for **each acquisition**.

▦ The implication of this choice is that if non-controlling interest is valued at fair value then the goodwill included in the consolidated statement of financial position will reflect 100% of the subsidiary's goodwill.

▦ If non-controlling interest is valued at fair value then both goodwill and non-controlling interest will be higher to the extent of the non-controlling interest's share of goodwill.

2.2.1 Goodwill Calculation

▦ If non-controlling interest is valued at **fair value** on acquisition, goodwill is calculated as:

- consideration given; plus
- fair value of non-controlling interest; less
- fair value of identifiable net assets (100%).

▦ If non-controlling interest is to be valued at its **proportionate share** of the identifiable net assets then goodwill is calculated as:*

- consideration given; plus
- non-controlling interest share of identifiable net assets; less
- fair value of identifiable net assets (100%).

Key Point

Any impairment loss is shared between the parent and non-controlling interest in the same proportion as to which profits are shared.

*Commentary

*A short-cut for calculating goodwill of a non-controlling interest valued at proportionate share is:

- consideration given; less
- P's share of the fair value of identifiable net assets.

Key Point

Any impairment loss is charged solely to the parent through consolidated retained earnings.

© DeVry/Becker Educational Development Corp. All rights reserved.   17-**5**

2.2.2 Non-controlling Interest in the Statement of Financial Position

- If valued at *fair value* on acquisition, it is calculated as:
  - fair value on acquisition; plus
  - share of post-acquisition profits; less
  - any goodwill impaired in respect of the non-controlling interest's share.
- If valued at its *proportionate share* of the identifiable net assets, then it is calculated as:
  - the non-controlling interest's percentage of net assets at reporting date.

3 Unrealised Profit

3.1 Elimination

Key Point

IFRS 10 requires that unrealised profit on intra-group trading and sale of assets must be removed in full. This will result in the restatement of the asset to the cost to the group.

- There are two common ways of reflecting the write downs:
  1. Charge the whole amount to consolidated reserves; or
  2. Charge the non-controlling interest with its share of any adjustment where appropriate.
- IFRS 10 gives no guidance on which treatment to adopt.

3.1.1 Group Suffers the Whole Charge

- Process the following entry in the consolidated accounts:

  Dr Closing inventory in the consolidated statement of profit or loss

      Cr Closing inventory in the consolidated statement of financial position

© DeVry/Becker Educational Development Corp. All rights reserved.

3.1.2   Shared With Non-controlling Interest

▨ It is appropriate where S has made the sale to P.

▨ The double entry required is:

Dr Closing inventory in the consolidated statement of profit or loss

    Cr Closing inventory in the consolidated statement of financial position

AND

Dr Statement of financial position (non-controlling interest)

    Cr Statement of comprehensive income (non-controlling interest)

With the non-controlling share.

▨ The effect in the statement of financial position is:

Cr Closing inventory in the consolidated statement of financial position

    Dr Retained earnings

    Dr Statement of financial position (non-controlling interest)

▨ In most statement of financial position questions, this is easily carried out by treating the write down as an individual company adjustment in the books of the selling company. The non-controlling interest will then automatically share in the adjustment when necessary.

3.2   Exception

▨ This will usually work, but there is a rare circumstance in which this would not give the correct answer.

▨ The exception is when there is a piecemeal acquisition and P's percentage holding in S has changed after the date of the intra-group transfer of the inventory in question.

Illustration 1   Piecemeal Acquisition

As at 31 December 2017, P owned 80% of S. This holding consisted of 75%, which was acquired many years ago, and 5%, which was acquired on 31 December 2017. S has made sales to P and P holds inventory at the year end which S had sold to it at a mark-up of $1,000.

If the adjustment is processed in the accounts of S and the year-end non-controlling interest percentage (20%) is applied to the resultant net assets figure, this would mean that the group had been charged with 80% of the adjustment.

There is no need to charge the group with unrealised profit on transfers before S became a subsidiary. By extension, there is no need to charge the group with that part of the unrealised profit which relates to the latest acquisition.

The solution to this problem is to carry out the consolidation without the adjustment and then to process the following double entry in the consolidated accounts.

Dr Retained earnings	750	
Dr Non-controlling interest	250	
Cr Inventory		1,000

Example 1 Consolidated Statement of Financial Position

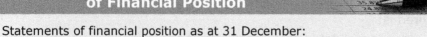

Statements of financial position as at 31 December:

	P $	S $
Non-current assets		
Cost of investment in S	10,000	
Tangible assets	8,000	2,000
Current assets	5,000	7,000
	23,000	9,000
Share capital	1,000	500
Retained earnings	21,000	5,500
Payables	1,000	3,000
	23,000	9,000

Further information

1 P acquired 80% of S two years ago when the balance on S's retained earnings was $4,000.

2 At acquisition, S's assets included one with a carrying amount of $1,200 and a fair value of $1,500. This asset was being written off over 10 years.

3 During the year, S had sold goods to P. At the year end, P retained goods at a value of $450 above the cost to S. It is group policy to charge the non-controlling interest with its share of any adjustments for unrealised profit.

4 Non-controlling interest is valued at its proportionate share of the subsidiary's identifiable net assets.

5 Goodwill had been impaired by $2,464 since the acquisition occurred.

Required:

(a) **Prepare the consolidated statement of financial position as at 31 December.**

(b) **Calculate the non-controlling interest and goodwill if valued at fair value. This fair value can be based on the market price of the subsidiary's share on acquisition, which was $23.**

© DeVry/Becker Educational Development Corp. All rights reserved.

Example 1 Consolidated Statement of Financial Position (continued)

Solution

(a) Consolidated statement of financial position

	$
Intangibles (Goodwill)	
Non-current assets	
Current assets	
	_____
	_____
Share capital	
Retained earnings	
	_____
Non-controlling interest	
	_____
Other payables	
	_____
	_____

(b) Non-controlling interest

(W1) Goodwill

	$
Cost	
Non-controlling interest	
S's net assets	
	_____
	_____
Asset	
Impaired	

(W2) Non-controlling interest

	$
On acquisition	
Share of post-acquisition profits:	
Goodwill impaired	_____
	_____

3.3 Deferred Tax

■ Unrealised profit in the group accounts will give rise to a deductible temporary difference. The tax base of the inventory will reflect the cost to the buying company whereas the carrying amount in the consolidated accounts will be based on cost.

■ IAS 12 requires the buyer's tax rate to be applied to the deductible temporary difference. This requirement is different from other tax regimes (e.g. UK) which tax the difference at the seller's tax rate.

4 Consolidated Statement of Comprehensive Income

4.1 Control and Ownership Principles

Group accounts reflect control and ownership.

Key Point

The consolidated statement of comprehensive income is prepared on a basis that is consistent with the consolidated statement of financial position.

The consolidated statement of comprehensive income:

- Shows income generated from net assets under P's control.
- Reflects ownership by deducting the non-controlling interest's share of S's profit after tax in the consolidated statement of comprehensive income.
- Discloses the non-controlling share of both consolidated profit or loss for the year and total comprehensive income. Eliminates the effect of intragroup transactions.

4.2 Unrealised Profit on Trading Adjustment

- Closing inventory needs reducing to lower of cost and NRV to group.

  Dr Statement of comprehensive income $x

      Cr Statement of financial position $x

- This normally should be done in the accounts of the *selling* company.

4.3 Non-current Asset Transfer

Adjustments

- Again, this needs to be consistent with treatment in the consolidated statement of financial position.
- Eliminate profit or loss on transfer and adjust depreciation in full.
- The profit or loss normally will be adjusted in the records of the selling company and the depreciation adjustment normally will be reflected in the records of the buying company.

4.4 Mid-year Acquisitions

- Inclusion of S's results:
  - Consolidate S from date of acquisition.
  - Assume revenue and expenses accrue evenly over time unless contradicted.

© DeVry/Becker Educational Development Corp. All rights reserved.

Summary

■ A company which has a subsidiary on the last day of its accounting period must prepare consolidated financial statements.

■ Cost of investment is replaced with net assets of the subsidiary plus goodwill.

■ IFRS 3 allows the non-controlling interest to be based on either *fair value* or the *proportionate share* of the subsidiary's identifiable net assets.

■ If non-controlling interest is valued at fair value on acquisition any impairment loss in respect of goodwill is shared between the parent and the non-controlling interest (in their shareholding proportion).

■ IFRS 10 requires that unrealised profit on intercompany trading and sale of assets be removed in full.

■ The consolidated statement of comprehensive income is prepared on a basis which is consistent with the consolidated statement of financial position.

Session 17 Quiz
Estimated time: 10 minutes

1. Specify the only method of consolidation allowed under IFRS 3. (1.4)

2. Before performing a consolidation, state the adjustments which should be made to the financial statements of the subsidiaries. (2)

3. Explain how the non-controlling interest in the assets of subsidiaries may be valued under IFRS 3. (2.2.2)

4. Give the double entry made when dealing with unrealised profit of goods sold between group companies. (3)

Study Question Bank
Estimated time: 1 hour, 30 minutes

Priority		Estimated Time	Completed
Q27	Bacup	45 minutes	
Q28	Holding	45 minutes	

© DeVry/Becker Educational Development Corp. All rights reserved.

EXAMPLE SOLUTION

Solution 1—Consolidated Statement of Financial Position

(a) Consolidated statement of financial position as at 31 December

	$
Intangibles (Goodwill)	3,696
Non-current assets (8,000 + 2,000 + 300 − 60)	10,240
Current assets (5,000 + 7,000 − 450)	11,550
	25,486
Share capital	1,000
Retained earnings (W4)	19,328
	20,328
Non-controlling interest (W2)	1,158
	21,486
Other payables	4,000
	25,486

Workings

(W1) Net assets summary

	$ At reporting date	$ At date of acquisition
Share capital	500	500
Retained earnings per Q	5,500	4,000
Extra depreciation	(60)	
Unrealised profit	(450)	
Fair value difference	300	300
	5,790	4,800

(W2) Non-controlling interest 20% × 5,790 (W1) = $1,158

(W3) Goodwill

	$
Cost	10,000
S's net assets 80% × 4,800 (W1)	(3,840)
	6,160
Asset	3,696
Impaired	2,464

(W4) Consolidated retained earnings

	$
All of P per Q	21,000
Share of S 80% (4,990 - 4,000) (W1)	792
Goodwill (W3)	(2,464)
	19,328

© DeVry/Becker Educational Development Corp. All rights reserved.

(b)   Non-controlling interest at fair value*

Goodwill

	$
Cost	10,000
Non-controlling interest (500 × 20%) × $23	2,300
S's net assets	(4,800)
	7,500
Asset	5,036
Impaired	2,464

Of the impairment loss 20% (493) is charged to non-controlling interest.

Non-controlling interest

	$
On acquisition	2,300
Share of post-acquisition profits: (990 × 20%)	198
Goodwill impaired	(493)
	2,005

*Commentary

*As compared with (a) goodwill is increased $1,340, non-controlling interest is increased by $847 and hence retained earnings is increased by $493. (Consolidated retained earnings includes only 80% of the goodwill impairment and would therefore be $19,821.)

© DeVry/Becker Educational Development Corp. All rights reserved.

Goodwill

FOCUS

This session covers the following content from the *ACCA Study Guide.*

D. Financial Statements of Groups of Entities

1. Group accounting

b) Apply the principles in determining the cost of a business combination. ☐

c) Apply the recognition and measurement criteria for identifiable acquired assets and liabilities and goodwill. ☐

e) Determine and apply appropriate procedures to be used in preparing group financial statements. ☐

Session 18 Guidance

- **Revise** the IFRS 3 definition and calculation of goodwill (s.1).
- **Understand** the difference between deferred consideration and contingent consideration and how transaction costs should be accounted for (s.2).
- **Understand** the exception to the IAS 37 recognition rule (s.3.1) and the need for provisional accounting (s.3.4). **Attempt** *Example 1.*
- **Consider** carefully the effect of *Illustrations 4* and *5.* The examiner seems keen on examining the calculation of the impairment loss related to goodwill (s.3, s.5).

(continued on next page)

VISUAL OVERVIEW

Objective: To describe GAAP applied to the measurement and recognition of goodwill and to examine the rationale behind GAAP and its recent revisions.

```
                           ┌─────────────────────────┐
                           │         GOODWILL         │
                           ├─────────────────────────┤
                           │  • Acquisition Method    │
                           │  • What Is Goodwill      │
                           │  • Features              │
                           └─────────────────────────┘
        ┌────────────────────────┐  ┌──────────────────────┐  ┌─────────────────────────┐
        │  FAIR VALUE OF PURCHASE │  │  IDENTIFIABLE ASSETS │  │      ACCOUNTING         │
        │     CONSIDERATION       │  │    AND LIABILITIES   │  ├─────────────────────────┤
        ├────────────────────────┤  ├──────────────────────┤  │  • Positive Goodwill    │
        │  • Deferred            │  │  • Recognition       │  │  • Partially-Owned      │
        │    Consideration       │  │  • Measurement       │  │    Subsidiary           │
        │  • Contingent          │  │  • Provisional       │  │  • Bargain Purchase     │
        │    Consideration       │  │    Accounting        │  └─────────────────────────┘
        │  • Share Exchange      │  └──────────────────────┘
        │  • Transaction Costs   │
        └────────────────────────┘
                           ┌─────────────────────────┐
                           │       FAIR VALUE         │
                           │   IN ACCOUNTS OF         │
                           │      SUBSIDIARY          │
                           ├─────────────────────────┤
                           │  • Exam Complication     │
                           │  • Accounting for Fair   │
                           │    Value                 │
                           └─────────────────────────┘
```

Session 18 Guidance

■ **Understand** and be able to discuss the various accounting treatments for goodwill which have been used over the past 30 years (s.6).

■ **Refer** back to *Session 7* on impairment of assets.

■ **Return** to the deferred tax implications in *Session 12*.

© DeVry/Becker Educational Development Corp. All rights reserved.

1 Goodwill

Definition

Goodwill—"an asset representing the future economic benefits arising from other assets acquired in a business combination that are not individually identified and separately recognised."

—*IFRS 3*

1.1 Acquisition Method

▦ A combination that is an acquisition should be accounted for in the consolidated accounts using the acquisition method.

▦ As at the date of the acquisition the acquirer should:

  • incorporate the results of the acquiree into the statement of comprehensive income;

  • recognise the identifiable assets and liabilities of the acquiree and any goodwill arising (positive or negative) into the statement of financial position.

1.2 What Is Goodwill

▦ In essence it is the difference between the cost of the acquisition and the acquirer's interest in the fair value of its identifiable assets and liabilities at the date of the exchange transaction. This can be reflected in consolidation workings as:

	$
Cost (the value of the part of the business owned)	X
Acquirer's share of the fair value of the identifiable assets and liabilities of the subsidiary as at the date of acquisition	(X)
Goodwill	X

▦ As a result of the revisions to IFRS 3 the non-controlling interest's share of **goodwill** may be recognised as part of the acquisition process. The choice for measuring non-controlling interests is allowed on a transaction-by-transaction basis.

▦ IFRS 3 specifies the goodwill calculation as:

	$
Acquisition date fair value of consideration transferred	X
Amount of any non-controlling interest in the entity acquired	X
Fair value (at acquisition date) of any previous shareholding (see *Session 20*)	X
Less: Acquisition date amounts of identifiable assets acquired and liabilities assumed measured in accordance with IFRS	(X)
Goodwill	X

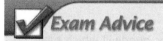

Exam Advice

Non-controlling interest should be valued at fair value on acquisition in the consolidation question. You may also be required to calculate it as a proportion of identifiable net assets to make a comparison (see *Session 17*).

© DeVry/Becker Educational Development Corp. All rights reserved.

Illustration 1 Goodwill Measurement

Parent acquires 80% of Subsidiary for $120,000. The fair value of the non-controlling interest's share in Subsidiary is $28,000, while the value of non-controlling interest based on the proportionate share of identifiable net assets acquired would give a value of $25,000. The fair value of the subsidiary's net assets on acquisition has been determined as $125,000.

Goodwill can be calculated as either:	(a)	(b)
	$	$
Cost of investment	120,000	120,000
Non-controlling interests	28,000	25,000
	148,000	145,000
Fair value of net assets acquired	(125,000)	(125,000)
Goodwill	23,000	20,000

If non-controlling interest is valued at fair value (a), then the value of goodwill and non-controlling interest will be higher to the extent of the non-controlling interest's share of the fair value of the subsidiary.

The non-controlling interest's share of goodwill is $3,000 of the total of $23,000; this represents 13% of total goodwill. It is highly likely that the percentage of goodwill owned by the non-controlling interest will be in a different proportion to the actual shareholding (20% in this illustration). This would be due to the parent paying a premium to acquire control.

▦ Therefore there are several issues to address:
- What is included in the cost of acquisition?
- The meaning of the term "identifiability".
- Calculation of the fair value.
- Accounting for the revaluation in the accounts of the subsidiary.
- Accounting for the goodwill arising on consolidation.

1.3   Features of Goodwill

▦ It cannot be realised separately.

▦ Its value has no reliable relationship to cost.

▦ Its value may fluctuate widely over time.

▦ Valuation can be highly subjective.

▦ It exists because of factors which are difficult to identify with precision.

▦ Goodwill may be internally-generated or it may arise on acquisition.

2 Fair Value of Purchase Consideration

- An acquisition should be accounted for at its cost. Cost is:
  - amount of cash or cash equivalents paid; and
  - the fair value of the other purchase consideration given.

2.1 Deferred Consideration

Key Point

Any deferred consideration is measured at its present value, taking into account any premium or discount likely to be incurred in settlement (and not the nominal value of the payable).

- If cash is to be paid sometime in the future, then the amount will need to be discounted to present value and that amount included as the fair value in the cost calculation.
- The increase in present value, through the passage of time, will be a finance cost charged to profit or loss.

Illustration 2 Goodwill and Deferred Consideration

Parent acquired 60% of Subsidiary on 1 January 2017 for $100,000 cash payable immediately and $121,000 after two years. The fair value of Subsidiary's net assets at acquisition amounted to $300,000. Parent's cost of capital is 10%. The deferred consideration was completely ignored when preparing group accounts as at 31 December 2017.

Required:

Calculate the goodwill arising on acquisition and show how the deferred consideration should be accounted for in Parent's consolidated financial statements.

Solution:

Cost of investment in Subsidiary at acquisition:
$100,000 + $121,000/1.21 = $200,000

Goodwill	$000
Cost	200
Share of net assets acquired (60% × 300,000)	(180)
	20

Deferred consideration Double entry at 1 January:

Dr	Cost of Investment in Subsidiary	$100,000	
	Cr	Deferred consideration	$100,000

On 31 December, due to unwinding of discount, the deferred consideration will equal $121,000/1.1 = 110,000

Dr	Parent retained earnings	$10,000	
	Cr	Deferred consideration	$10,000

- In the consolidated statement of financial position, the cost of investment in Subsidiary will be replaced by the goodwill of $20,000, and the deferred consideration will be $110,000.

                          © DeVry/Becker Educational Development Corp. All rights reserved.

2.2 Contingent Consideration

Key Point

When a business combination agreement provides for an adjustment to the cost, contingent on future events, the acquirer includes the acquisition date fair value of the contingent consideration in the calculation of the consideration paid.

- If the contingent settlement is to be in cash, then a liability will be recognised.
- If settlement is to be through the issue of additional equity instruments, then the credit entry will be to equity.
- Any changes to the contingent consideration recognised, after the measurement period, will be accounted for in accordance with the relevant IFRS and will not affect the original calculation of goodwill.
- If settlement will be in cash, then the consideration will be remeasured at each reporting date and any changes in value will be recognised in profit or loss. If settlement will be through an equity issue, then the consideration is not remeasured and any change in value on eventual issue will be included within equity.

2.3 Share Exchange

- It is quite common for a parent to acquire shares in the subsidiary by issuing its own shares to the previous shareholders in a share exchange.
- The cost of acquisition is determined multiplying the number of shares issued by the parent by the market price of the parent's shares at the date of acquisition.

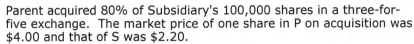

Illustration 3   Share Exchange

Parent acquired 80% of Subsidiary's 100,000 shares in a three-for-five exchange. The market price of one share in P on acquisition was $4.00 and that of S was $2.20.

Cost of investment = $100,000 \times 80\% \times \frac{3}{5} \times \$4.00 = \$192,000$
The value of S's share is irrelevant.

2.4 Transaction Costs

Key Point

Transaction costs (e.g. legal fees, advisory costs or valuation fees) incurred in the acquisition of a subsidiary are expensed in the period they are incurred.*

- Costs related to the issue of shares or debt in respect of the acquisition are treated in accordance with IAS 32 or IFRS 9. This will generally mean that they are recognised within equity.

*Commentary

*The treatment of transaction costs is a change from the previous version of IFRS 3 which required directly attributable costs to be included in the cost of investment. As a result of this change, the amount of goodwill recognised will be smaller.

© DeVry/Becker Educational Development Corp. All rights reserved.

3 Identifiable Assets and Liabilities

3.1 Recognition

3.1.1 Introduction

▦ The identifiable assets and liabilities acquired are recognised separately at the date of acquisition (and therefore featured in the calculation of goodwill).

▦ This may mean that some assets, especially intangible assets, will be recognised in the consolidated statement of financial position that were not recognised in the subsidiary's single entity statement of financial position.

▦ Any future costs that the acquirer expects to incur in respect of plans to restructure the subsidiary must not be recognised as a provision at the acquisition date. They will be treated as a post-acquisition costs.

Key Point

Expected restructuring costs of an acquisition are not liabilities of the acquiree at the date of acquisition. Therefore, they are not relevant in allocating the cost of acquisition.

Historically, companies recognised large provisions on acquisition, and this had the effect of reducing net assets and thereby increasing goodwill. Goodwill was then charged against profits (through amortisation) over a much longer period than through immediate recognition as an expense. IFRS 3 and IAS 37 have virtually eliminated these so-called big bath provisions.

3.1.2 Contingent Liabilities of the Acquiree

▦ IAS 37 *Provisions, Contingent Liabilities and Contingent Assets* does not allow contingent liabilities to be recognised in the financial statements of a single entity.

▦ However, if a contingent liability of the subsidiary has arisen due to a present obligation that has not been recognised (because an outflow of economic benefits is not probable), IFRS 3 requires this present obligation to be recognised in the consolidated financial statements as long as fair value can be measured reliably.

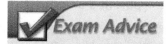

Exam Advice

If a question states that a subsidiary has a contingent liability, on acquisition, then recognise as a provision in the consolidated accounts.

© DeVry/Becker Educational Development Corp. All rights reserved.

3.2   Measurement

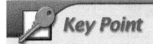

All assets and liabilities of the subsidiary which are recognised in the consolidated statement of financial position are measured at their acquisition date fair values.*

*Commentary

*IFRS 3 requires that certain assets and liabilities, for example Deferred Taxes, Employee Benefits, Share-based Payment Transactions and Held-for-Sale Non-Current Assets, are measured in accordance with their respective standards.

- Each asset (and liability) is measured as if it was separately acquired on the date of acquisition. This reduces the amount of goodwill that would otherwise be recognised (e.g. if book values were used instead).
- The non-controlling interest in the subsidiary is measured at either:*
  - fair value; or
  - the non-controlling interest's proportionate share of the subsidiary's identifiable net assets.

*The choice of measuring the non-controlling interest of the subsidiary can be made for each acquisition, so a parent does not have to be consistent in its measurement of non-controlling interests relating to separate acquisitions.

Example 1   Computation of Goodwill on Acquisition

On 1 October 2017, Hawaii purchased 8 million of Texas's 12 million equity shares. The acquisition was financed as follows:

A cash payment of $2.00 per share; $1.20 per share being payable on 1 October 2017 and $0.80 being payable on 30 September 2018. Any discounting calculations should be performed using a cost of capital of 8% per annum.

A share exchange of 1 equity share in Hawaii for every 2 shares acquired in Texas. The market value of a Texas share was $3.90 on 1 October 2017. The market values of a Hawaii share were $4 on 1 October 2017 and $4.20 on 31 March 2018.

A further share issue by Hawaii on 30 September 2018 of 1 share for every 8 shares acquired in Texas provided the profits after tax of Texas exceeded a given figure. Estimates indicate that this share issue is likely to be made. The fair value of this contingent consideration on 1 October 2017 was $4 million; this has increased to $4.2 million at 31 March 2018.

Hawaii incurred acquisition costs of $600,000. $350,000 of these costs were external due diligence costs, $100,000 were Hawaii's best estimate of management time spent in negotiating the acquisition, and $150,000 were costs incurred in connection with the issue of Hawaii's shares.

The directors of Hawaii carried out a fair value exercise on 1 October 2017 and the following matters emerged:

The net assets of Texas that were recognised in Texas's own financial statements were $30 million based on their carrying amounts in the individual financial statements of Texas.

On 1 October 2017 the carrying amount of Texas's freehold property was $15 million. The property had been purchased on 1 October 2007 for $17.5 million and the buildings element of the property (allocated cost $10 million) was being depreciated over its estimated useful economic life of 40 years. On 1 October 2017 the market value of the property was $22 million, of which $12 million related to the buildings element. The original estimate of the useful economic life of the buildings is still considered valid.

On 1 October 2017, Texas was engaged in contracts with three different customers under which it supplied each customer for a five-year-period from 1 October 2017. The directors of Hawaii believe that this creates an intangible asset with a fair value of $7.5 million. In addition the directors of Hawaii believe that the fair value of the assembled workforce of Texas creates an intangible asset with a fair value of $15 million. The average remaining working life of the employees of Texas at 1 October 2017 is 15 years. Neither of these intangible assets has been recognised in the individual financial statements of Texas.

At 1 October 2017, Texas was engaged in a legal dispute with a customer. The directors of Texas consider that the case can be successfully defended and have made no provision for legal costs in its financial statements. The directors of Hawaii estimated that the fair value of the claim at 1 October 2017 was $600,000. Events since 1 October 2017 have reduced this estimate to $500,000 by 31 March 2018 (these events do not affect the fair value of the claim at 1 October 2017).

Due to the acquisition of Texas the directors of Hawaii intend to reorganise the group, starting in June 2019. The estimated cost of this reorganisation is $20 million.

In the year ended 31 March 2018, Texas reported a post-tax profit of $6 million (accruing evenly over the period) and paid a dividend of $1.5 million on 31 December 2017 out of post-acquisition profits. The retained earnings of Hawaii at 31 March 2018 were $18 million. This figure includes the dividend received from Texas but does not include any other adjustments to its own earnings that are required as a result of the acquisition of Texas. The acquisition costs of $600,000 referred to above have been charged to retained earnings by Hawaii. Hawaii has no subsidiaries other than Texas and no associates or joint venture entities.

The non-controlling interest in Texas was valued at $17.5 million on acquisition by Hawaii.

Required:

Compute the goodwill on acquisition of Texas as initially measured at 1 October 2017.

© DeVry/Becker Educational Development Corp. All rights reserved.

3.3   Provisional Accounting

3.3.1   Estimates

- If accurate figures cannot be assigned to elements of the business combination then estimated and provisional amounts are assigned to those elements at the date of acquisition.

- Any new information that becomes available, relating to acquisition date assets and liabilities, is retrospectively adjusted against the initial provisional amounts recognised as long as the information is known within the "measurement period".

3.3.2   Measurement Period

- The measurement period cannot exceed one year after the acquisition date.

3.3.3   Subsequent Adjustments

- Any other adjustments are treated in accordance with IAS 8 *Accounting Policies, Changes in Accounting Estimates and Errors:*
  - an error in acquisition values is treated retrospectively;*
  - a change in estimate is treated prospectively.

Key Point

The measurement period is the period after the acquisition date during which the parent may adjust the provisional amounts recognised for the acquisition of a subsidiary.

*Commentary

*These retrospective adjustments are an exception to the normal requirement of IAS 8 which requires prospective application.

Illustration 4 Provisional Accounting

Parent acquires 80% of Subsidiary for $60,000. The subsidiary's net assets at date of acquisition were $62,500. At the end of the first year, goodwill has been impaired by $1,000.

In the year following acquisition, but within 12 months of the acquisition date, it was identified that the value of land was $2,500 greater than that recognised on acquisition. The value of goodwill at the end of Year 2 was valued at $7,400.

Year 1:

Cost of investment	60,000
Net assets on acquisition (62,500 × 80%)	50,000
Goodwill	10,000
Goodwill charge to profit or loss	1,000

Year 2:

Cost of investment	60,000
Net assets on acquisition (65,500 × 80%)	52,000
Goodwill on acquisition	8,000
Goodwill at year end	7,400
Goodwill charge to profit or loss	600

Journal

Dr	Land	2,500	
Dr	Profit or loss (goodwill)	600	
Cr	Goodwill (9,000 – 7,400)		1,600
Cr	Non-controlling interest (2,500 × 20%)		500
Cr	Opening retained earnings		1,000
	(prior year charge for goodwill reversed)		

© DeVry/Becker Educational Development Corp. All rights reserved.

4 Fair Value in Accounts of Subsidiary

4.1 Exam Complication

▦ The fair value adjustments may or may not have been reflected in the financial statements of S at the date of acquisition. In the exam they will not have been.

▦ If S has not reflected fair values in its accounts, this must be done before consolidating.*

▦ For an adjustment upwards create a fair value reserve in net assets working (fair value less carrying amount of net assets at acquisition) at acquisition and the end of the reporting period.

  ● For an adjustment downwards create a provision against retained earnings in net assets working (carrying amount less fair value of net assets at acquisition) at acquisition and end of the reporting period.

▦ Goodwill in S's statement of financial position is not part of identifiable assets and liabilities acquired. If S's own statement of financial position at acquisition includes goodwill, this must be written off:

  ● reduce retained earnings at acquisition and the end of the reporting period by goodwill in S's statement of financial position at acquisition. Do this in the net assets working.

4.2 Accounting for Fair Value

▦ IFRS 3 requires the fair value to be reflected in the consolidated group accounts. The non-controlling interest balance will reflect their share of the adjusted value.*

▦ Results:

  ● Goodwill calculation is based on fair value;

  ● Non-controlling interest at the date of acquisition is based on fair value;

  ● Non-controlling interest subsequent to acquisition is based on fair value at the date of acquisition plus the non-controlling interest's share in the post-acquisition growth in the assets (reserves).

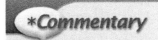

*If an adjustment is made, post-acquisition depreciation may also need to be adjusted to reflect a fair value adjustment.

*The non-controlling interest shares in both the fair value adjustment and any consequential depreciation adjustment.

© DeVry/Becker Educational Development Corp. All rights reserved.

Example 2 Fair Valuations

As at 31 December 2017

	Parent	Subsidiary
Non-current assets:	$	$
Tangibles	1,800	1,000
Cost of investment in Subsidiary	1,000	
Current assets	400	300
	3,200	1,300
Share capital ($1 nominal value)	100	100
Retained earnings	2,900	1,000
Current liabilities	200	200
	3,200	1,300

Further information:

Parent bought 80% of Subsidiary on the 31 December 2015.

At the date of acquisition Subsidiary's retained earnings stood at $600 and the fair value of its net assets was $1,000. The fair value difference was due to an asset that had a remaining useful economic life of 10 years as at the date of acquisition.

Non-controlling interest is valued at fair value on acquisition. The market price of Subsidiary's shares on acquisition was $12.40 a share. Goodwill has been impaired by $40 since acquisition.

Required:

Prepare the consolidated statement of financial position of Parent as at 31 December 2017.

5 Accounting for Goodwill

 **Key Point**

5.1 Positive Goodwill

- Goodwill reflects the future economic benefits arising from assets that are not capable of being identified individually or recognised separately.

- It is initially measured at cost (i.e. the excess of the cost of the acquisition over the acquirer's interest in the fair value of the identifiable assets and liabilities acquired) and recognised as an asset.

- Goodwill on acquisition must be allocated to a cash generating unit (CGU) that benefits from the acquisition. A CGU need not necessarily be a unit of the subsidiary acquired; it could be a unit of the parent or another subsidiary in the group.

- The unit must be at least that of an operating segment as defined by IFRS 8 *Operating Segments.*

- Subsequent to initial recognition goodwill is carried at cost less any accumulated impairment losses.

> **Key Point**
>
> Each CGU must be tested annually for impairment. The test must be carried out at the same time each year, but does not have to be carried out at the year end; any impairment loss is expensed to profit or loss.

© DeVry/Becker Educational Development Corp. All rights reserved.

5.2 Partially-Owned Subsidiary

5.2.1 Non-controlling Interest Valued at Proportionate Share of Identifiable Net Assets

- Any impairment will firstly be allocated against this grossed up goodwill figure.

- Any impairment in excess of this grossed up goodwill will then be allocated against the remaining assets of the CGU on a pro rata basis.

Key Point

Any goodwill in a partially owned subsidiary must be grossed up to include the non-controlling share of goodwill for the purposes of the impairment test.

Exam Advice

Impairment of goodwill has been examined on a number of occasions at P2; each time goodwill has been grossed up on a shareholding proportionate basis.

Illustration 5 Impairment of Goodwill

Parent acquired 75% of Subsidiary. The carrying amount of the subsidiary's net assets on the reporting date was $1,800, this included $300 of goodwill. The recoverable amount of the subsidiary on that date was $1,640.

Impairment:

Goodwill grossed up (300 × 100 ÷ 75)	400
Other net assets	1,500
	1,900
Recoverable amount	1,640
Impairment	260

Of the impairment amount 75% ($195) will be allocated against the goodwill recognised in the group financial statements, leaving goodwill included in the consolidated statement of financial position of $105. The carrying amount of the subsidiary's net assets, including goodwill, will now be $1,605.

Any impairment loss above $400, then the amount above $400 would have been recognised in full.

5.2.2 Non-controlling Interest Valued at Fair Value

- There will be no need to gross up goodwill for the impairment test as the non-controlling interest's share of goodwill has already been recognised and included in the total goodwill figure.

- Any impairment of goodwill is shared amongst the owners of the subsidiary in the same proportion in which the profits of the subsidiary are shared.

- An 80% owned subsidiary will reflect 80% of the impairment loss against consolidated retained earnings and 20% against non-controlling interest.

© DeVry/Becker Educational Development Corp. All rights reserved.

5.3 Bargain Purchase

▦ If on initial measurement the fair value of the acquiree's net assets exceeds the cost of acquisition (excess), then the acquirer reassesses:

- the value of net assets acquired;
- that all relevant assets and liabilities have been identified; and
- that the cost of the combination has been correctly measured.

▦ If there still remains an excess after the reassessment then that excess is recognised immediately in profit or loss. This excess (gain) could have arisen due to:

- future costs not being reflected in the acquisition process;
- measurement of items not at fair value, if required by another standard (e.g. deferred tax being undiscounted);
- bargain purchase.

© DeVry/Becker Educational Development Corp. All rights reserved.

Summary

- Goodwill is an asset that represents the future economic benefits arising from other assets acquired in a business combination that are not individually identified and separately recognised.

- Deferred consideration is measured at its present value.

- The acquirer includes the fair value of any contingent consideration as at the acquisition date in the calculation of the consideration paid.

- Transaction costs incurred in the acquisition of a subsidiary are expensed in the period they are incurred.

- All assets and liabilities of the subsidiary are measured at their acquisition date fair values.

- A parent may adjust the provisional amounts recognised for an acquisition of a subsidiary during the measurement period; this cannot exceed 12 months.

- Goodwill is allocated to a CGU and that CGU must be tested annually for impairment.

- Any goodwill in a partially-owned subsidiary must be grossed up to include the non-controlling share of goodwill for the impairment test.

- A gain on a bargain purchase, once confirmed, is immediately credited to profit or loss.

Session 18 Quiz
Estimated time: 20 minutes

1. Define goodwill. (1.2)

2. State the measurement used to determine deferred consideration. (2.1)

3. If the acquisition of a subsidiary is paid for by issuing shares to the shareholders of the subsidiary company, explain how the costs of issuing the shares should be treated. (2.3)

4. Describe the accounting for contingent liabilities of a subsidiary account. (3.1.2)

5. Specify the period of time allowed by IFRS 3 for assessing fair value of net assets acquired. (3.3.2)

6. When calculating the fair value of the assets of a new subsidiary at the date of acquisition, explain how goodwill is treated in the statement of financial position of the subsidiary. (4.1)

7. State how often goodwill must be tested for impairment. (5.1)

8. Briefly explain the method of calculating any impairment loss for a partially owned subsidiary. (5.2)

9. Suppose on initial calculation of goodwill, it appears that the fair value of the acquired assets less liabilities of the subsidiary exceeds the cost of acquisition. Explain what the acquirer should do. (5.3)

Study Question Bank
Estimated time: 25 minutes

Priority		Estimated Time	Completed
Q29	Guido Electronics	25 minutes	

© DeVry/Becker Educational Development Corp. All rights reserved.

EXAMPLE SOLUTIONS

Solution 1—Computation of Goodwill on Acquisition

	$000
Fair value of consideration given (**W1**)	35,526
Non-controlling interest	17,500
Fair value of net assets acquired (**W2**)	(44,500)
Goodwill	8,526

Workings

(1) Fair value of consideration given

	$000	Explanation
Immediate cash payment	9,600	Actual amount paid.
Deferred cash payment	5,926	Present value of actual amount payable (8m × $0.80/1.08).
Share exchange	16,000	4m shares issued at market value of $4 each. Include at fair value on acquisition date.
Contingent consideration	4,000	Any change in fair value does not affect the original cost of investment.
Acquisition costs	Nil	IFRS 3 requires any transaction costs related to the acquisition to be expensed immediately.
	35,526	

(2) Fair value of net assets acquired

	$000	Explanation
As per financial statements of Texas	30,000	
Adjustment for property	7,000	Market value exceeds carrying amount by 7,000.
Adjustment for customer relationships	7,500	An identifiable intangible asset with a measurable fair value.
Adjustment for workforce	Nil	Per IAS 38 *Intangible Assets* assembled workforce fails the "control test".
Adjustment for re-organisation	Nil	Per IFRS 3 *Business Combinations* must treat as post-acquisition items.
Adjustment for contingency	Nil	IFRS 3 only requires contingent liabilities that are a present obligation to be recognised.
	44,500	

© DeVry/Becker Educational Development Corp. All rights reserved.

Solution 2—Fair Valuations

Non-current assets:	$
Goodwill (W2)	208
Tangibles	
(1,800 + (1,000 + 300 – [2/10 × 300]))	3,040
Current assets (400 + 300)	700
	3,948
Share capital	100
Retained earnings (W4)	3,140
Non-controlling interest (W3)	308
Current liabilities (200 + 200)	400
	3,948

Workings

(1) Net assets summary

	At consolidation	At acquisition
	$	$
Share capital	100	100
Retained earnings	1,000	600
Fair value adjustments (300 × $^8/_{10}$)	240	300
Net assets	1,340	1,000

(2) Goodwill

Cost	1,000
Fair value of non-controlling interest (100 x 20% x $12.40)	248
Net assets acquired	(1,000)
	248
Asset	208
Impaired	40

(3) Non-controlling interest

Fair value on acquisition	248
Share of post-acquisition profits (340 × 20%)	68
Share of goodwill impairment (40 × 20%)	(8)
	308

(4) Consolidated retained earnings

P	2,900
Share of S run on calculation (80% ...)	
80% (1,340 – 1,000)	272
Goodwill impairment (80% × 40)	(32)
	3,140

Complex Groups

FOCUS

This session covers the following content from the *ACCA Study Guide.*

D. Financial Statements of Groups of Entities
1. Group accounting
a) Apply the method of accounting for business combinations, including complex group structures. ☐

■ **Recognise** that this session introduces the problem of sub-subsidiaries and sub-associates. There is nothing new to learn in this session apart from how to apply the workings and techniques to these relationships.

■ **Calculate** the correct percentage to be used under the various possible relationship scenarios (s.2, s.3) and learn when to apply those percentages.

(continued on next page)

VISUAL OVERVIEW

Objective: To consolidate more complicated group structures.

```
┌─────────────────────────────────┐
│        TYPES OF STRUCTURE        │
│                                  │
│   • Chains of Control            │
└─────────────────────────────────┘
                 │
┌─────────────────────────────────┐
│      STATUS OF THE INVESTMENT    │
│                                  │
│   • Importance of Control        │
│   • Effective Ownership          │
└─────────────────────────────────┘
                 │
┌─────────────────────────────────┐
│            TECHNIQUE             │
│                                  │
│   • Approaches                   │
│   • Direct Technique             │
│   • Timing of Acquisitions       │
│   • D-Shaped Groups              │
│   • Statement of                 │
│     Comprehensive Income         │
└─────────────────────────────────┘
```

Session 19 Guidance

■ **Work** carefully through the *Illustrations* and **attempt** the *Examples* (s.3).

© DeVry/Becker Educational Development Corp. All rights reserved.

1 Types of Structure

1.1 Chains of Control

- A subsidiary is a company controlled by another.
  - In practice this control might be achieved through complicated chains of control.

- Example

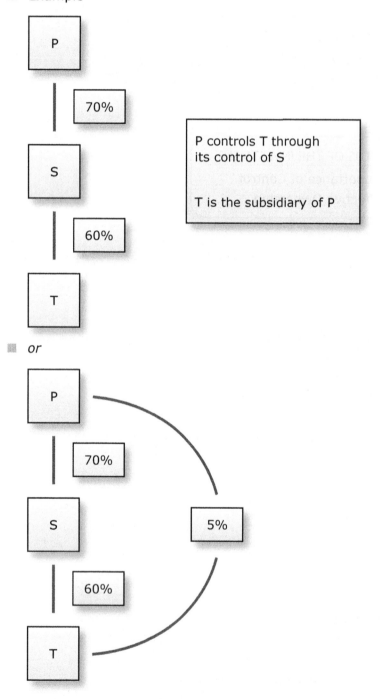

P controls T through
its control of S

T is the subsidiary of P

- *or*

                          © DeVry/Becker Educational Development Corp. All rights reserved.

Similarly, significant influence may be exercised over an associate indirectly.

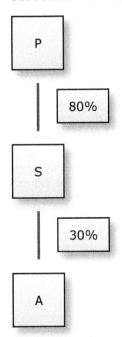

2 Status of the Investment

2.1 Importance of Control

🔑 **Key Point**

Status is *always* based on control.

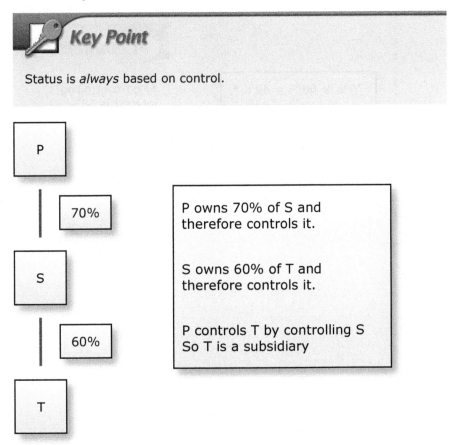

P owns 70% of S and therefore controls it.

S owns 60% of T and therefore controls it.

P controls T by controlling S
So T is a subsidiary

© DeVry/Becker Educational Development Corp. All rights reserved.

2.2 Effective Ownership

▥ As illustrated in section 2.1, P effectively owns:

70% × 60% = 42% of T.

▥ This is a useful tool to bring to the consolidation, *but* it is irrelevant in deciding the status of the investment.

3 Technique

3.1 Approaches to Consolidations Involving Sub-subsidiaries

3.1.1 Indirect Approach (Two Stages)

1. Consolidate T into S to give the S group accounts; and

2. Consolidate the S group into P.

▥ However, the indirect method *must* be used to consolidate sub-associates.

3.1.2 Direct Approach

▥ Carry out the consolidation using the effective rate.

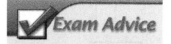

Always use the direct method. The indirect approach is too slow for exam purposes.

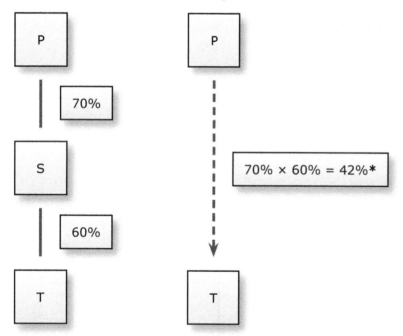

*Non-controlling interest is 58%.

© DeVry/Becker Educational Development Corp. All rights reserved.

■ In effect, this is changed to:

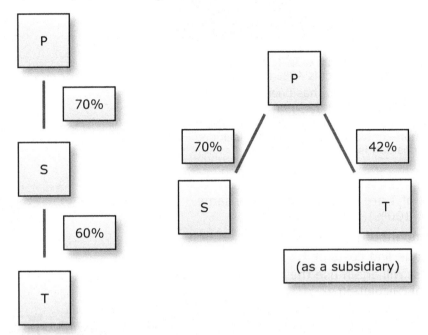

3.2   Direct Technique

■ Calculate the effective holding in the sub-subsidiary (T) by multiplying the parent's (P's) share in subsidiary with the subsidiary's (S's) share in sub-subsidiary:

  ● add in any direct holding that P has in T (see s.3.4);

  ● non-controlling interest in T is 100% less P's effective control percentage.

■ Goodwill in T is calculated as:

  ● only P's percentage of the cost of investment; **plus**

  ● fair value of non-controlling interest (based on percentage as calculated above); **less**

  ● T's net assets on acquisition.

■ Non-controlling interest of both S and T at the reporting date are calculated as normal (i.e. fair value on acquisition plus share of post-acquisition profits less a share of goodwill impaired). However, this initial calculation must be **adjusted** for the cost of investment in T held in S's books to the extent of the non-controlling interest in S. The adjustment is necessary to eliminate the double-counting that arises from the following:

  ● Cost of investment = Net assets plus goodwill (at acquisition);

  ● S's net assets include the cost of investment in T;

  ● T's net assets are *also* included in the calculation of the non-controlling interest of T—leading to this double-counting.

Illustration 1 — Non-controlling Interest in Sub-subsidiary

P has an 80% stake in S and S has a 60% stake in T. S paid $200 for the investment in T. The effective control is 48% (80 × 60).

Non-controlling interest at the reporting date has been calculated for S to be $900 and for T to be $600 (before adjustment).

Non-controlling interest of $1,500 (900 + 600) must be decreased by $40 ($200 × 20%). The non-controlling interest to be included in the statement of financial position is therefore $1,460.

- The assets and liabilities of T are consolidated in the same manner as that of S (i.e. 100%).
- In the consolidated statement of profit or loss:
  - Include 100% of revenue and costs of T;
  - Non-controlling interest will again use the percentage based on the effective control calculation.

Example 1 Sub-subsidiary

Statements of financial position as at 31 December

	P $	S $	T $
Cost of investment			
in S	700		
in T		450	
Other assets	1,100	900	600
	1,800	1,350	600
Share capital	200	100	100
Retained earnings	1,600	1,250	500
	1,800	1,350	600

Further information

P bought 70% of S two years ago when S's retained earnings stood at $500. One year ago, S bought 60% of T when T's retained earnings were $200.

Non-controlling interests are valued at fair value on acquisition. This was valued at $300 in respect of S and the 58% non-controlling interest in T was measured at $324.

Goodwill of $112 has been impaired in respect of the holding in S and $40 for the holding in T.

Required:

Prepare the consolidated statement of financial position of the P group as at 31 December.

© DeVry/Becker Educational Development Corp. All rights reserved.

Example 2 Sub-associate

Statements of financial position as at 31 December

	P $	S $	A $
Cost of investment			
in S	700		
in A		450	
Other assets	1,100	900	600
	1,800	1,350	600
Share capital	200	100	100
Retained earnings	1,600	1,250	500
	1,800	1,350	600

Further information:

P bought 70% of S two years ago when S's retained earnings stood at $500. One year ago, S bought 25% of A when A's retained earnings were $200.

The non-controlling interest was valued at fair value on acquisition at $300.

Goodwill to the extent of $112 has been impaired in respect of the holding in S. There is no impairment in the investment in the associate.

Required:

Prepare the consolidated statement of financial position of the P group as at 31 December.

3.3   Timing of Acquisitions

▨ The parent has control over the sub-subsidiary on the later of the following dates:

  ● The date the parent acquired the subsidiary; and
  ● The date the subsidiary acquired the sub-subsidiary.

Illustration 2 Use Date S Acquired T

P bought 80% of S at 31 March 2014. S bought 60% of T on 14 July 2017.
Date of acquisition of T is 14 July 2017.

Illustration 3 Use Date P Acquired S

P bought 80% of S at 31 March 2017. S already owned 60% of T.
Date of acquisition of T is 31 March 2017.

3.4   D-Shaped Groups

■ A "D-shaped group" describes the structure where a parent has a direct interest in a sub-subsidiary. For example:

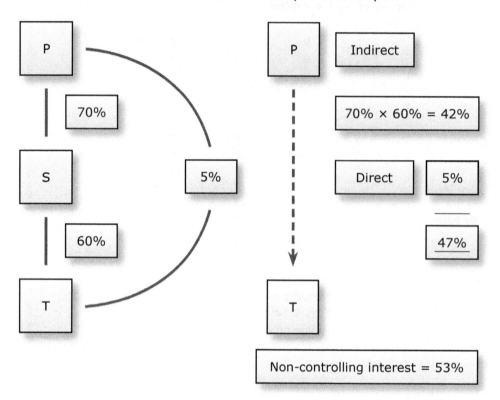

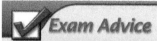

Having ascertained the structure and the non-controlling interests, the procedure is the same as the sub-subsidiary situation (see *Example 1*).

3.5   Statement of Comprehensive Income

■ These present no real problem. Calculate the effective rate and consolidate as normal.

■ There is one complication:

- ● If the sub-subsidiary has declared a dividend and the main subsidiary has accounted for its share through profit or loss this will be part of the subsidiary's profit before tax.

- ● It must be eliminated (as a consolidation adjustment) during the non-controlling interest calculation.

© DeVry/Becker Educational Development Corp. All rights reserved.

Illustration 4 Comprehensive Income Consolidation

	P	S	T	CIS
Operating profit	1,200	600	500	2,300
Dividend receivable from T	–	120	–	–
	1,200	720	500	2,300
Taxation	(400)	(250)	(100)	(750)
PAT	800	470	400	1,550
Non-controlling interest (W)				(278)
	800	470	400	1,272
Statement of changes in equity (extract)				
Dividends	(300)	(200)	(200)	(300)

Working

P

P

80%

S

48%

60%

Non-controlling interest = 52%

T

T

Non-controlling interest

In S	20% × (470 − 120)*	70
In T	52% × 400	208
		278

*Commentary

*The dividend is not consolidated.

© DeVry/Becker Educational Development Corp. All rights reserved.

Summary

- Many groups include vertical relationships of three or more layers.
- A subsidiary of a subsidiary (sub-subsidiary) is still controlled by the ultimate parent.
- Normal consolidation procedures are followed to incorporate the results of the sub-subsidiary.
- A sub-associate is equity accounted for by the subsidiary and then consolidated upwards into the group accounts as an asset of the subsidiary.
- A parent controls a subsidiary from the *later* of the date the parent acquires the subsidiary and the date the subsidiary acquires the sub-subsidiary.

 ## Session 19 Quiz
Estimated time: 10 minutes

1. If the parent owns 70% of a subsidiary, which itself owns 60% of a sub-subsidiary, state what the non-controlling interest percentage of the sub-subsidiary would be. (3.1)

2. State the TWO possible techniques to be used for consolidating a sub-subsidiary. (3.1)

3. Specify the date a parent gains control of its sub-subsidiary. (3.3)

4. Briefly describe what is meant by a "D-shaped" group. (3.4)

 ## Study Question Bank
Estimated time: 25 minutes

Priority		Estimated Time	Completed
Q30	H, S and T	25 minutes	
Additional			
Q31	Jane		

© DeVry/Becker Educational Development Corp. All rights reserved.

EXAMPLE SOLUTIONS

Solution 1—Sub-subsidiary

Consolidated statement of financial position as at 31 December

	$
Assets	
Goodwill (288 + 299) (W3)	587
Other assets (1,100 + 900 + 600)	2,600
	3,187
Share capital	200
Retained earnings (W5)	2,156
Non-controlling interest (W4)	831
	3,187

(W1) Group structure

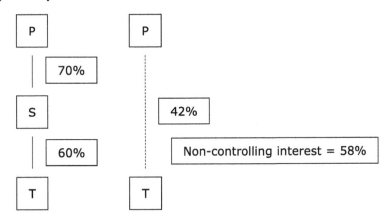

(W2) Net assets summary

S

	At consolidation	At acquisition
Share capital	100	100
Retained earnings	1,250	500
	1,350	600

T

	At consolidation	At acquisition
Share capital	100	100
Retained earnings	500	200
	600	300

© DeVry/Becker Educational Development Corp. All rights reserved.

Solution 1—Sub-subsidiary (continued)

(W3) Goodwill

	In S	In T
Cost	$	$
Investment in S	700	
Investment in T (70% × 450)		315
Non-controlling interest at fair value	300	324
Net assets on acquisition (W2)	(600)	(300)
	400	339
Asset (balance)	288	299
Impaired (given)	112	40

(W4) Non-controlling interests

	30% in S	58% in T	Total
Fair value on acquisition	300	324	
Share of post-acquisition profit (750 x 30%) and (300 x 58%)	225	174	
Goodwill impaired (112 x 30%) and (40 x 58%)	(34)	(23)	
	491	475	
Non-controlling share of investment in T (450 x 30%)	(135)		
			831

(W5) Consolidated retained earnings

All of P	1,600
Share of S	
70% (1,250 − 500) **(W2)**	525
Share of T	
42% (500 − 200) **(W2)**	126
Goodwill ((70% x 112) + (42% x 40)) **(W3)**	(95)
	2,156

© DeVry/Becker Educational Development Corp. All rights reserved.

Solution 2—Sub-associate

Consolidated statement of financial position as at 31 December

Goodwill	288
Investment in associate	525
Other assets	2,000
	2,813
Share capital	200
Retained earnings	2,100
Non-controlling interest	513
	2,813

(W1) Group structure

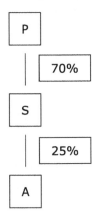

P

70%

S

25%

A

(W2) Net assets summary

S	At consolidation	At acquisition
Share capital	100	100
Retained earnings	1,250	500
	1,350	600
Share of A's post-acquisition reserves (600 − 300) × 25%	75	
	1,425	600
A		
Share capital	100	100
Retained earnings	500	200
	600	300

Solution 2—Sub-associate (continued)

(W3) Goodwill

	In S	In A
	$	$
Cost		
Investment in S	700	
Investment in A		450
Non-controlling interest at fair value	300	
Net assets acquired	(600)	
Share of net assets (25% x 300) **(W2)**		(75)
	400	375
Asset (balance)	288	
Impaired (given)	112	

(W4) Non-controlling interest

	$
Fair value on acquisition	300
Share of post-acquisition profit (825 x 30%)	247
Goodwill impaired (112 x 30%)	(34)
	513

(W5) Consolidated retained earnings

All of P	1,600
Share of S	
70% (1,425 − 600) **(W2)**	578
Goodwill impairment (70% x 112)	(78)
	2,100

© DeVry/Becker Educational Development Corp. All rights reserved.

NOTES

© DeVry/Becker Educational Development Corp. All rights reserved.

Changes in Shareholdings

FOCUS

This session covers the following content from the *ACCA Study Guide.*

D. Financial Statements of Groups of Entities

1. Group accounting

c) Apply the recognition and measurement criteria for identifiable acquired assets and liabilities and goodwill including step acquisitions. ☐

2. Continuing and discontinued interests

a) Prepare group financial statements where activities have been discontinued, or have been acquired or disposed of in the period. ☐

3. Changes in group structures

a) Discuss the reasons behind a group reorganisation. ☐

b) Evaluate and assess the principal terms of a proposed group reorganisation. ☐

E. Specialised Entities and Specialised Transactions

2. Entity reconstructions

a) Identify when an entity may no longer be viewed as a going concern or uncertainty exists surrounding the going concern status. ☐

b) Identify and outline the circumstances in which a reconstruction would be an appropriate alternative to a company liquidation. ☐

c) Outline the appropriate accounting treatment required relating to reconstructions. ☐

Session 20 Guidance

■ **Recognise** that this session focuses on disposing of shareholdings and acquiring shares on a piecemeal basis, buying shares "bit by bit".

■ **Learn** the treatment in the parent's own accounts (s.1.2).

■ **Understand** how the pattern of ownership changes the accounting treatment in the consolidation financial statements (s.2.2).

(continued on next page)

VISUAL OVERVIEW

Objective: To describe the accounting for disposal of subsidiaries, for shares purchased in a step acquisition and for a capital reconstruction scheme.

SHARE CAPITAL CHANGES

DISPOSALS

- Possibilities
- In Parent's Accounts

PIECEMEAL ACQUISITIONS

- Introduction
- Investment to Subsidiary
- Associate to Subsidiary
- Subsidiary to Subsidiary
- Investment to Associate or Joint Venture

REORGANISATION

- Forms
- Reasons
- Types

TREATMENT IN GROUP ACCOUNTS

- Summary
- Pattern of Ownership
- Profit/Loss on Disposal
- Discontinued Operation

CORPORATE RECONSTRUCTIONS

- Background
- Forms of Reconstruction
- Exam Approach
- Appraisal of Scheme
- Order of Ranking

Session 20 Guidance

■ **Work** very carefully through the *Illustrations* and **attempt** *Examples 1* and *2* (s.2, s.3).

■ **Understand** the accounting issues relating to a demerger (s.4.2).

■ **Understand** the need for corporate reconstruction and attempt *Examples 1* and *2* (s.5).

© DeVry/Becker Educational Development Corp. All rights reserved.

1 Disposal

1.1 Possibilities

■ When a group disposes of all or part of its interest in a subsidiary, this needs to be reflected in the parent's books and, more importantly, in the group accounts.*

■ Group accounts reflect:

● inclusion of results and cash flows of entity disposed of;

● calculation and presentation of profit or loss on disposal; and

● inclusion in group accounts of any remaining interest in the company after a part-disposal.

■ Disposal may be:

● full disposal (i.e. sell entire holding); or

● part disposal, retaining some interest in the undertaking.

■ Part disposal possibilities are:

● retention of control (i.e. undertaking remains a subsidiary); and

● retention of significant influence (i.e. undertaking becomes an associate).

*Commentary

*As always, the single entity concept is applied to the group as a whole.

1.2 Treatment in Parent's Own Accounts

■ Parent will carry its investment in a subsidiary in its own statement of financial position as a non-current asset investment, usually at cost.

Key Point

The sale of all or part of an investment is recorded as a disposal in the parent's own accounts and will usually give rise to a profit or loss on disposal (i.e. proceeds less cost of investment sold). An accrual may be required for tax on any gain on disposal.

■ To record disposal:

	$	$
Dr Cash/receivables (proceeds)	X	
Cr Investment in S (cost of investment sold)		X
Dr P or L loss on disposal (*or* Cr profit on disposal)	X	X

If required

	$	$
Dr P or L tax charge (tax on gain on disposal)	X	
Cr Tax payable		X

© DeVry/Becker Educational Development Corp. All rights reserved.

2 Treatment in Group Accounts

2.1 Summary

2.1.1 Consolidated Statement of Financial Position

Key Point

The consolidated statement of financial position should simply reflect the closing position.

▦ There is one potential problem area. This is when the parent has not yet accounted for the disposal in its own accounts. In this case, profit or loss on disposal must be calculated from the parent's viewpoint and processed into the parent's accounts as an individual company adjustment.

	$
Proceeds	X
Cost of investment disposed of	X
Profit or loss	X

▦ Also note that in most jurisdictions, it is this view of profit that will be taxed, and you may need to provide for the tax liability.

2.1.2 Consolidated Statement of Comprehensive Income

Key Point

The consolidated statement of comprehensive income must reflect the pattern of ownership in the period.

▦ Profit or loss on disposal must be calculated from the group's perspective. This will be different to that recognised by the parent because:

- The group recognises 100% of profit (or loss) whereas the parent recognises only dividends received; and
- The group will recognise impairment of goodwill (the parent does not).

© DeVry/Becker Educational Development Corp. All rights reserved.

2.2 Pattern of Ownership

Status of Investment Before disposal	After disposal	Treatment in Statement of Comprehensive Income	Treatment in Statement of Financial Position
Subsidiary → e.g. 90%	zero 0%	• Consolidate up until the date of disposal	No action needed
Subsidiary → e.g. 90%	Subsidiary e.g. 60%	• Consolidate for the whole year • Calculate non-controlling interest in two parts: e.g. $\dfrac{x}{12}$ profit × 10% + $\dfrac{12-x}{12}$ profit × 40%	Consolidate as normal with closing non-controlling interest based on year-end holding
Subsidiary → e.g. 90%	Associate e.g. 40%	• Prorate S's results and consolidate up to the date of disposal • After disposal equity account	Equity account as at the year end, based on year-end holding

2.3 Profit or Loss on Disposal

▧ The amount of profit or loss to be recognised, and where, is dependent on whether or not control is lost.

2.3.1 Disposal With No Loss of Control

Key Point

Any disposal without loss of control (e.g. 80% holding to 60% holding) is accounted for as a transaction within equity between the shareholders of the group, the shareholders of the parent and the non-controlling shareholders of the subsidiary.

▧ *No* profit or loss is recognised in profit or loss in this situation.

▧ The carrying amounts of the controlling and non-controlling interests are adjusted to reflect their relative interests in the subsidiary.

▧ Any difference between the adjustment to non-controlling interest and the fair value of consideration paid is recognised directly in equity, probably retained earnings, and attributed to the owners of the parent.

▧ The carrying amount of goodwill is not adjusted to reflect the change in shareholding.

© DeVry/Becker Educational Development Corp. All rights reserved.

Illustration 1   Movement in Equity

Disposal—S to S

- A acquired 100% of B a number of years ago for $125,000.
- Fair value of B's net assets on acquisition was $100,000, giving goodwill of $25,000.
- Since acquisition, B's net assets have increased in value by $20,000.
- A then disposed of 30% of its shareholding for $40,000.

Solution—Movement in Equity

	$
Fair value of consideration received	40,000
Movement in non-controlling interest (120,000 × 30%)	(36,000)
Cr to equity	4,000

- Ignoring the issue of impairment, the value of goodwill remains unchanged at $25,000.

2.3.2   Disposal With Loss of Control

Key Point

Any disposal of a shareholding that results in the loss of control will give rise to profit or loss on disposal being recognised in profit or loss.

- On the date that control is lost the following adjustments must be made:*

  - Derecognise the carrying amount of assets, including goodwill, liabilities and non-controlling interest from the consolidated statement of financial position.
  - Recognise the fair value of the consideration received on the disposal of the shareholding.
  - Recognise any distribution of shares to owners.
  - Recognise the fair value of any residual interest held after disposal; this will become the valuation going forward in respect of the remaining holding.
  - If the remaining investment results in the parent having significant influence over the entity then an associate relationship will now exist. The fair value of the remaining holding at the date of disposal will become the cost of investment in associate going forward.
  - Reclassify to profit or loss any amounts that relate to the subsidiary's net assets previously recognised in other comprehensive income, where required.
  - Recognise any resulting difference as a gain or loss in profit or loss attributable to the parent.

*Commentary

*Loss of control may result in associate status, a joint venture, an IFRS 9 investment or an entire disposal.

Illustration 2 Disposal

Disposal—S to A

- A acquired 100% of B a number of years ago for $125,000.
- Fair value of B's net assets on acquisition was $100,000, giving goodwill of $25,000.
- Since the acquisition, B's net assets have increased in value by $20,000, of which $3,000 represents an increase in a financial asset classified at fair value through other comprehensive income.
- A then disposed of 75% of its shareholding for $115,000.
- The fair value of the remaining 25% was identified as $38,000.

Solution—Profit or Loss

	$
Fair value of consideration received	115,000
Fair value of remaining 25%	38,000
Fair value of net assets and goodwill derecognised	(145,000)
Profit on disposal	8,000

- As a result of the issue of IFRS 9, the gain on the financial asset classified at fair value through other comprehensive income is not reclassified through profit or loss.

- If the disposal results in a remaining holding that would be covered by IFRS 9 (e.g. a 15% holding), then the remaining investment will be valued at fair value at the disposal date and accounted for under IFRS 9 from that point onwards.

2.4 Discontinued Operation

- It is highly likely that the disposal of a subsidiary will be classified as a discontinued operation.

Key Point

In this case, the results for the subsidiary to the date of disposal will be presented separately from the results of the continuing operations.

- IFRS 5 requires that the revenue and costs to the date of disposal and any profit or loss on the actual disposal of the operation are presented as a single item in the profit or loss, and then analysed further either in the profit or loss or in the disclosure notes.

© DeVry/Becker Educational Development Corp. All rights reserved.

Example 1 Disposal Scenarios

The draft accounts of two companies at 31 March 2018 were as follows.

Statements of financial position

	Hamble Group	Jemima
	$	$
Investment in Jemima at cost	3,440	–
Sundry assets	36,450	6,500
	39,890	6,500
Share capital ($1 ordinary shares)	20,000	3,000
Retained earnings	11,000	3,500
	31,000	6,500
Sale proceeds of disposal (suspense a/c)	8,890	–
	39,890	6,500

Statements of comprehensive income

	Hamble Group	Jemima
	$	$
Profit before tax	12,950	3,800
Tax	(5,400)	(2,150)
Profit after tax	7,550	1,650
Retained earnings b/d	3,450	1,850
Retained earnings c/f	11,000	3,500

Hamble and Jemima are both incorporated enterprises.

Hamble had acquired 90% of Jemima when the reserves of Jemima were $700. Goodwill of $110 arose on the acquisition. This had been fully impaired by 31 March 2017.

Non-controlling interest is valued at its percentage of the identifiable net assets of Jemima. The carrying amount of Jemima's net assets on disposal and at the year end closely equates to its fair value.

On 31 December 2017, Hamble sold shares in Jemima.

Required:

Prepare extracts from the Hamble Group statement of financial position and Hamble Group statement of comprehensive income on the basis that Hamble sold the following shares in Jemima:

(a) Its entire holding;

(b) A 15% holding (75% remaining);

(c) A 50% holding (40% remaining with significant influence).

Note: Ignore tax on the disposal.

Example 1 Disposal Scenarios (continued)

Solution
Workings
(1) Net assets

	Reporting date $	Disposal $	Acquisition $
Share capital			
Retained earnings			

(2) Retained earnings at date of disposal

$

B/fwd	
Profit for year to disposal	

(3) Retained earnings b/d

$

Hamble Group	
Jemima	
Less: Goodwill written off	

(4) Profit on disposal of Jemima (individual company view)

	(a) $	(b) $	(c) $
Sale proceeds			
Less: Cost of investment			
Profit on disposal			

(5) Consolidated retained earnings

	(a) $	(b) $	(c) $
Retained earnings of **Hamble**			
Per the question			
Profit on disposal (W4)			
Share of **Jemima**			
Goodwill			

© DeVry/Becker Educational Development Corp. All rights reserved.

Example 1 Disposal Scenarios (continued)

Solution

(6) Profit on disposal of Jemima (group view)

	(a) $	(b) $	(c) $
Sale proceeds	8,890	8,890	8,890
Less: Net assets at disposal **(W1)**			
Profit on disposal			

(7) Operating profit

	(a)	(b)	(c)
Hamble Group			
Jemima			

(8) Taxation—group

	(a) $	(b) $	(c) $
Hamble Group			
Jemima			

(9) Non-controlling interest in Jemima

Operating profit **(W7)**			
Tax **(W8)**			
× 10 %			
× 25 %			

(a) Hamble Group

Consolidated statement of financial position as at 31 March 2018

	H Group $	Adjustments $	Consolidated $
Sundry assets			
Share capital			
Retained earnings			

Example 1 Disiposal Scenarios (continued)

Consolidated statement of comprehensive income for the year ended 31 March 2018*

	H Group $	Jemima $	Consolidated $
Operating profit (W7)			
Profit on disposal of operations (W6)			
Profit before taxation			
Taxation—group (W8)			
Profit after taxation			
Non-controlling interest (W9)			
Profit for the year			
Retained earnings b/f (W3)			
Retained earnings c/f			

*Commentary

*In the case of a full disposal, the results of the disposed subsidiary should be kept separate from the results of the continuing operations.

(b) Hamble Group
Consolidated statement of financial position as at 31 March 2018

	H Group $	Jemima $	Consolidated $
Sundry assets			
Share capital			
Retained earnings			
Non-controlling interest			

© DeVry/Becker Educational Development Corp. All rights reserved.

Example 1 Disposal Scenarios (continued)

Consolidated statement of comprehensive income for the year ended 31 March 2018

	H Group $	Jemima $	Consolidated $
Operating profit (W7)			
Profit on disposal of operations (W6)			
Profit before taxation			
Taxation—group (W8)			
Profit after taxation			
Non-controlling interest (W9)			
Profit for the year			
Retained earnings b/f (W3)			
Movement in equity (W6)			
Retained earnings c/f			

(c) Hamble Group
Consolidated statement of financial position as at 31 March 2018

	H Group $	Jemima $	Consolidated $
Investment in associate			
Sundry assets			
Share capital			
Retained earnings			

Consolidated statement of comprehensive income for the year ended 31 March 2018

	H Group $	Jemima $	Consolidated $
Operating profit (W7)			
Income from interests in associate			
Profit on disposal of operations (W6)			
Profit before taxation			
Taxation—group (W8)			
Profit after taxation			
Non-controlling interest (W9)			
Profit for the year			
Retained earnings b/f (W3)			
Retained earnings c/f			

3 Piecemeal Acquisitions

3.1 Introduction

- A step or piecemeal acquisition occurs where the investment in a subsidiary (or an associate) is acquired in several stages, rather than in one go.

- Investments may be carried at cost or this may be replaced by a share of net assets and goodwill when appropriate. This is when the investing company has a holding which gives it:

  - control—when consolidation is used; or
  - significant influence—when equity accounting is used.

- In order to calculate goodwill and reserves at acquisition, net assets acquired need to be established. Hence, the *date* on which to identify the net assets of the subsidiary at acquisition is needed.

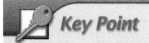

Key Point

IFRS 3 requires that any previous shareholding is remeasured to fair value at the date the parent acquires either:

- significant influence in an associate; or
- control of a subsidiary.

- As a result of this, goodwill is only calculated once a significant event occurs (e.g. on obtaining control).

- Any increase in a company that is already a subsidiary will only affect the equity of the group. No profit or loss is recognised and there will be no change to the amount of goodwill calculated on the original controlling event.

- Thus, there are several piecemeal acquisition possibilities, depending on the size of the stake purchased at each stage. Those relevant to this session are summarised in the following sections, with example percentages of control shown in the illustrations.

3.2 Investment to Subsidiary

- Any previous shareholding which qualified as a financial asset under IFRS 9 is treated as if it were disposed and then reacquired, at the acquisition date, at fair value.

- Any resulting gain or loss on the remeasurement will be included in profit or loss.

- Any changes in value of the instrument that had been reported previously in other comprehensive income will *not* be reported in profit or loss under IFRS 9.

Exam Advice

The P2 examiner has only ever examined step acquisitions in two stages.

© DeVry/Becker Educational Development Corp. All rights reserved.

Illustration 3 Step Acquisition: Investment to Subsidiary

- A acquires 75% control of B in two stages.
- 15% of B was acquired a number of years ago, for $10,000.
- The investment was classified as at fair value through other comprehensive income. A fair value gain has been reported in other comprehensive income of $2,000.
- During the current year, a further 60% was acquired for $60,000.
- Net assets of B on acquisition date were $80,000.
- Non-controlling interest is to be measured at A's share of B's net assets. On the acquisition date, the fair value of the 15% holding was $12,500.

Solution—Other Comprehensive Income

- On acquisition, A will recognise a further gain of $500 in other comprehensive income.
- This is the increase in fair amount from previous value to date of acquisition.
- The $2,000 previously recognised in other comprehensive income is not reclassified to profit or loss.

Solution—Goodwill

	$
Fair value of consideration given	60,000
Non-controlling interest ($80,000 × 25%)	20,000
Fair value of previous 15%	12,500
Fair value of net assets of B	(80,000)
Goodwill	12,500

3.3 Associate to Subsidiary

- A previous investment that was accounted for as an associate under IAS 28, or a joint venture under IFRS 11, is treated in a similar manner to that of a simple investment.
- It is presumed that the previous investment was disposed of and then reacquired at acquisition date fair value.
- Any difference between the previous carrying amount and the reacquired fair value will be recognised in profit or loss at the acquisition date.
- Goodwill will be calculated as:
  - consideration given to obtain control; *plus*
  - value of non-controlling interest (using either valuation model); *plus*
  - fair value, at acquisition date, of previous shareholding; *less*
  - fair value of the identifiable net assets of the subsidiary at the acquisition date (100%).

Illustration 4 Step Acquisition: Associate to Subsidiary

- A acquires 75% control of B in two stages.
- 40% was acquired a number of years ago for $40,000, and the fair value of B's net assets was $80,000.
- Since acquisition, A has recognised $5,000 of post-acquisition profits in respect of B and $3,000 of revaluation gain relating to IAS 16 property.
- The carrying amount of the investment was therefore $48,000.
- During the current year, a further 35% was acquired for $55,000.
- Net assets of B on the acquisition date were $110,000.
- Non-controlling interest is to be measured at its fair value of $30,000.
- On the acquisition date, the fair value of the 40% holding was $50,000.

Solution—Profit or Loss

- On acquisition, A will recognise a gain of $2,000 in profit or loss, being the difference between:
  - the fair value of the previously held 40% stake of $50,000; and
  - the previous carrying amount of the investment in associate of $48,000.
- The revaluation gain of $3,000 is not reclassified, as this gain would never be reclassified on disposal.

Solution—Goodwill

	$000
Fair value of consideration given	55
Non-controlling interest @ fair value	30
Fair value of previous 40%	50
Fair value of net assets of B	(110)
Goodwill	25

3.4 Subsidiary to Subsidiary

- Once control has been obtained, any further acquisition of shares are accounted for within equity and no profit or loss will be recognised.
- The carrying amount of non-controlling interest is adjusted to reflect its new percentage holding, if any, in the subsidiary.
- Any difference between the amount paid and the amount of adjustment to non-controlling interest will be recognised directly within equity, probably retained earnings.
- There will be no recalculation of goodwill; this will still be valued based on the original calculation of when control was achieved.
- The adjustment within equity following an increase in the percentage held will be affected by the choice of measurement basis for the non-controlling interest at the measurement date.
- If the fair value model has been chosen, then the amount of adjustment within equity will be lower than if the percentage of identifiable net assets valuation model has been chosen.

© DeVry/Becker Educational Development Corp. All rights reserved.

Illustration 5 Step Acquisition: Subsidiary to Subsidiary

- A acquires 75% control of B, a number of years ago, for $90,000.
- On acquisition, the fair value of B's net assets was $100,000.
- Fair value of non-controlling interest on acquisition was $28,000.
- Since the initial acquisition, the fair value of B's net assets has increased by $20,000.
- A further 15% of shares were then acquired for $21,000.

Solution—Goodwill

	$
Fair value of consideration given	90,000
Non-controlling interest @ fair value	28,000
Fair value of B's net assets	(100,000)
Goodwill	18,000

Solution—Non-controlling Interest

	$
Non-controlling interest (28,000 + (20,000 × 25%))	33,000
Transfer to A ($^{15}/_{25}$)	(19,800)
Remaining non-controlling interest	13,200

3.5 Investment Becoming an Associate or Joint Venture

- The standard does not detail how to deal with an equity investment, accounted for under IFRS 9 that is increased and leads to an associate or joint control status.

- IAS 28 states that many of the procedures relevant to equity accounting are similar to the consolidation procedures described in IFRS 10. Furthermore, the underlying concepts used in equity accounting are the same as those used in acquisition accounting.

- However, IAS 28 also states that an investment in an associate is initially recognised at cost, which may be taken to mean that any remeasurement under IFRS 9 should be reversed when equity accounting is used for the first time.

- This issue was considered by the IASB during the drafting process of the revised standard, but no definitive answers were given.

Exam Advice

When this was examined the published answer showed that the original holding was remeasured to fair value when control was acquired.

© DeVry/Becker Educational Development Corp. All rights reserved.

Example 2 Consolidated Statement of Financial Position

The statements of financial position of Portion and its subsidiary, Slice, at 31 December 2018 are as follows:

	Portion	Slice
	$000	$000
Investment in Slice	410	–
Sundry assets	590	550
	1,000	550
Share capital: $1 ordinary shares	200	100
Retained earnings	800	450
	1,000	550

Portion acquired its holding in Slice as follows:

Date	Proportion acquired	Cost of investment	Slice retained earnings
	%	$000	$000
30 September 2017	30	150	300
1 July 2018	50	260	400

The fair value of non-controlling interest on acquisition was $100,000.

The fair value of the previous 30% shareholding on the acquisition date was $180,000. The value of the investment in associate immediately prior to the increase in shareholding was $176,000. Goodwill has not been impaired since acquisition.

Required:

Prepare the consolidated statement of financial position of Portion at 31 December 2018.

4 Reorganisation

4.1 Forms

■ Group reorganisations can take many forms:

- The transfer of shares in a subsidiary between companies within the group;
- Creation of a new ultimate parent company;
- Combining two or more companies that share the same shareholders; or
- A reverse acquisition through which the legal subsidiary becomes the parent and the legal parent becomes the subsidiary.*

*Effected through a share exchange between the parent and subsidiary.

© DeVry/Becker Educational Development Corp. All rights reserved.

4.2   Reasons

■ There are many reasons for reorganisations:
- A private company may acquire a listed company as a short cut to obtaining a listing.
- Tax benefits or incentives may be available to the new organisation.
- As a result of a decision to sell a subsidiary.
- To simplify or rationalise the group structure by transferring assets or trade between companies.
- A demerger of a company (i.e. splitting it into parts) may increase shareholder value (i.e. the sum of the parts exceeds the value of the whole company before the demerger).

4.3   Types

4.3.1   Demerger

■ Before the demerger, the Parent (P) controls Subsidiary (S).

■ The Parent pays a dividend to shareholders in the form of **shares** in S instead of cash (i.e. such a dividend *in specie* is also called a *scrip dividend*). The Parent accounts for this dividend in the normal way except that the credit is to "Investment in S" (rather than cash).

■ The shareholders of P are now also the shareholders of S.*

■ This creates two companies. If the sum of the value of the two companies is greater than that of the group, shareholder value is increased.

> *Commentary*
>
> *P has distributed the investment in S to its shareholders.

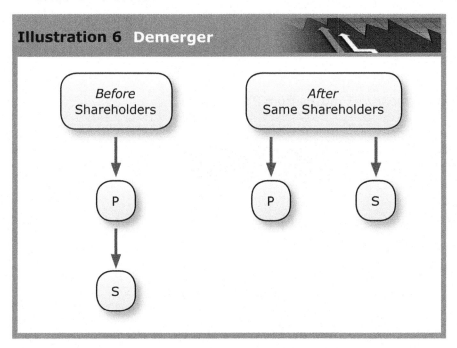

Illustration 6   Demerger

Before Shareholders → P → S

After Same Shareholders → P   S

4.3.2   Subsidiary Moved Along

■ This may be a desirable outcome when a Parent (P) is trying to sell a Subsidiary (S), but wishes to retain control of one or more sub-subsidiaries (Z).

■ This is effected by another subsidiary (T) exchanging assets with S (normally cash) for the investment in Z. This leaves S to be sold off separately.

© DeVry/Becker Educational Development Corp. All rights reserved.

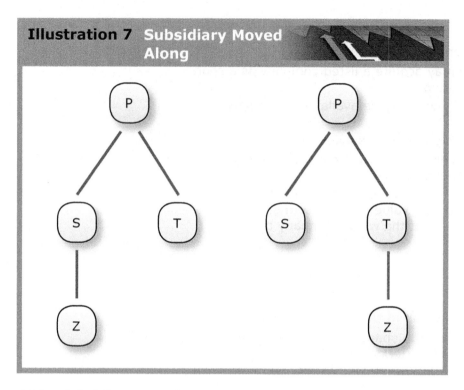

Illustration 7 Subsidiary Moved Along

4.3.3 Subsidiary Moved Down

▨ A subsidiary (T) may be moved down the chain for tax purposes or to create a smaller group based on geographical location (e.g. where two subsidiaries, S and T, operate in the same country, which is different to that of the ultimate parent).

▨ The form of the transaction could be:

- a share exchange (i.e. S issues shares to P in return for the shares in T); or
- for cash.

The end result is that *Investment in T* moves from P's books to S's books.

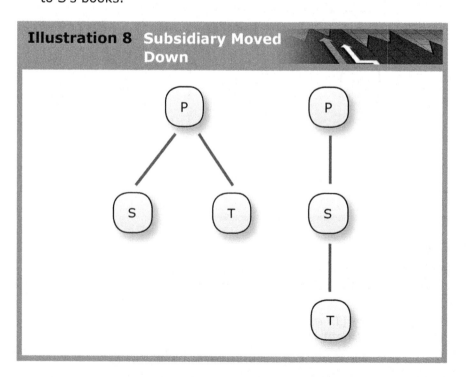

Illustration 8 Subsidiary Moved Down

© DeVry/Becker Educational Development Corp. All rights reserved.

▨ The reverse situation could also be engineered so that T moves up the chain to become a direct subsidiary of P. This may again be effected through S paying a dividend *in specie*.*

4.3.4 Divisionalisation

▨ When the assets and/or trade of a subsidiary are transferred to another group company, the defunct subsidiary becomes a dormant company.*

▨ The amount for which one company acquires the assets or trade of the other company is typically unpaid (to avoid leaving a cash balance in the dormant company). This gives rise to a liability in the buying company and an amount receivable in the selling company. Such balances must be cancelled on consolidation.

▨ The sale of the assets will lead to the write down of the value of the investment in P's books (i.e. recognise as an impairment loss) if the value of the dormant company falls below the cost of the investment.

4.3.5 Reverse Acquisition

▨ In this situation the legal parent acquires shares in the legal subsidiary through a share exchange. The share exchange results in the legal subsidiary becoming the parent in substance.

▨ This form of acquisition is used to obtain a stock market listing for the subsidiary.*

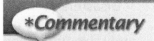

*Commentary

*A share exchange between S and P may be prohibited by legislation.

*Commentary

*It still exists in law but does not trade or carry out any form of operations.

*Commentary

*As this is quicker and much cheaper than through an initial public offering (IPO).

Illustration 9   Reverse Acquisition

P has 100 $1 shares in issue. P issues a further 300 $1 shares to acquire 100% of the 50 $1 shares of S.

P now has 400 shares in issue, 300 of which are owned by the shareholders of S, who have given up the 50 shares they held in return for the shares in P.

The shareholders of S now own 75% of P and therefore control P. Although P is the legal parent, for accounting purposes it is deemed to be the subsidiary.

---

5   Corporate Reconstruction

5.1   Background

▨ Under the Framework, financial statements are normally prepared on the going concern basis. However, when an entity appears no longer viable in its present state, that basis will not present reliable and relevant information.

▨ Not every company is successful; many make losses or find themselves in a net liability position. Many such companies will ultimately end up being liquidated if there is no way to return them to profitability.

- Indications that a company is struggling may include the following:
  - Operating losses
  - Negative cash flows
  - Poor or even adverse financial ratios such as ROCE
  - Loss of major market or customer
  - High staff turnover
  - Pending legal claim against the company
  - Disasters such as fire or flood.

- Not all struggling companies will be forced into liquidation; if a profitable future appears possible, some form of reconstruction will be used to get the company back on a level footing.*

- The various stakeholders must therefore compare what their position will be if the company is liquidated against their position if a reconstruction scheme goes ahead.

Commentary

*Factors that may contribute to a successful future include new management and new products.

Illustration 10 **Creditors as Stakeholders in a Reconstruction**

The trade creditors of GHI are owed a total of $1 million. GHI has no other debts but is struggling financially. The estimated liquidation value of its assets is just $400,000 and the share price has fallen to $0.25.

Therefore GHI would only be able to pay out $0.40 for every $1 owed if forced into liquidation.

However, a capital reconstruction has been proposed by the firm's directors and approved by the existing shareholders. Upon reconstruction the entire $1-million liability would be cancelled and replaced with:

- A $300,000 long-term loan carrying 5% interest and secured over property; and

- 500,000 equity shares.

The creditors therefore have a choice:

- Force GHI into liquidation and quickly receive $400,000 with reasonable certainty; or

- Accept the $300,000 secured loan and equity shares.

5.2 Forms of Reconstruction

- For all forms of reconstruction, it is important that all stakeholders are consulted and treated in a fair and equitable manner. However, the ordinary shareholders bear the major risk and so will suffer the greater proportion of any losses, compared with secured creditors (for example).

- In all reconstructions, the protection of the creditors is crucial. Although this stakeholder group will be required to share in any losses this will be proportionately less than that of the equity shareholders.

5.2.1 Internal Reconstruction

- In this situation, management identifies the need to reconstruct the company (e.g. to effect economies or make the company financially viable). In order to get stakeholders on board there must be some indications that the company has a future.

                     © DeVry/Becker Educational Development Corp. All rights reserved.

- Creditors will probably have to accept a loss on the amount due to them. This may be compensated with shares in the company.
- Current shareholders will have to accept a dilution in their shareholdings.
  - This could be to such an extent that they no longer have any say in the running of the company.
  - Unwillingness to accept the dilution may force the company into liquidation.*
- Shareholders may be required to inject additional cash into the business.
- All assets will be written down to their recoverable amount and any debit balances on retained earnings will be eliminated.
- It is likely that the share capital will be revised and old shares will be replaced with new shares (possibly with a lower, nominal value). The ownership structure will change, with the former creditors having a much greater say in the ownership and the running of the company.

*Commentary

*Which could result in the loss of their entire investment.

5.2.2 External Reconstruction

- External reconstruction involves *liquidation* of the existing company and the transfer of its business to a new company formed for this purpose.
  - Only one company is involved in a reconstruction—the existing company that is replaced with a new one.*
  - The aim of external reconstruction is to rectify a poor financial structure and eliminate accumulated losses and worthless assets to give a "clean" start to the new company.
  - Existing shares are cancelled and new shares are issued that potentially give a majority holding to the ex-creditors and just a minority stake to the previous shareholders.
  - The financial accounting is through a reconstruction account against which the likely debit balance on retained earnings may also be written off (to allow dividends to be paid again in future).
  - Replacing debt in the old company with equity in the new company does not raise new finance, so fresh capital injections would also be needed.

*Commentary

*Whereas two or more companies would be involved in an amalgamation.

5.3 Exam Approach

- There are two types of scheme that may be examined:
  - Internal reorganisation—a restructuring of the statement of financial position; and
  - External reorganisation:
    - winding up of a company;
    - setting up of a new company to take over trade/assets.
- You may be required to:
  - Prepare the financial statements after the reorganisation has taken place:
    - this may involve a bookkeeping exercise;
    - i.e. process the scheme of reorganisation.
  - Appraise the scheme, either in general or for a specified stakeholder:
    - For this there will be no single correct answer;
    - It is more important to apply principles.

© DeVry/Becker Educational Development Corp. All rights reserved.

Example 3 Reconstruction Scheme

The following scheme has been proposed:

1. Assets are to be revalued:

   Tangibles   980
   Goodwill   –
   Receivables   290
   Inventory   350

2. Ordinary share capital to be surrendered and reissued as $0.25 ordinary shares on a 1-for-1 basis.

3. Existing ordinary shareholders are to subscribe for 1,000 $0.25 ordinary shares at $0.75.

4. Preference share capital is to be reduced by 25% through surrender and reissue.

5. Debenture holders are to exchange debs with a value of $250 for 500 $0.25 ordinary shares.

Required:

Execute the scheme of reconstruction.

Solution

	$000	$000
Non-current assets		
Tangibles	1,000	
Goodwill	500	
	1,500	
Current assets		
Cash	–	
Receivables	300	
Inventory	400	
	2,200	
Share capital		
Ordinary shares	1,500	
Reserves		
Share premium		
Capital reserve		
Retained earnings	(300)	
Liabilities		
10% debenture (secured on the tangible non-current assets)	500	
4% Preference shares	200	
Bank overdraft	300	
	2,200	

© DeVry/Becker Educational Development Corp. All rights reserved.

5.4   Appraisal of the Scheme

A scheme must be approved by each group of stakeholders. It must therefore be appraised from each of their perspectives comparing, for example, their capital and income positions:

		Position on wind up*	Position with scheme
E		x	x
A			
C	C		
H	L	x	x
	A		
	S		
	S	x	x

*The alternative to the scheme is usually taken as being to liquidate the business.

As a general point in the appraisal of the scheme, the parties with the most to lose on winding up (and therefore to gain on the scheme) should contribute most to its success.

5.5   Order of Ranking

The capital position without the scheme is established by calculating the amount of cash that would be available and then distributing it on the basis specified in the regulatory environment in which the entity operates. Typically, stakeholders would share in the following order:

- Holders of a fixed charge (e.g. a mortgage on property);
- Preferential creditors:
  - Tax authorities (for unpaid taxes);
  - Employees (for unpaid salaries);
- Holders of a floating charge (e.g. over inventory);
- Unsecured creditors;
- Preference shareholders;
- Ordinary shareholders.

Example 4 Distribution of Cash on a Wind Up

Following on from the previous example:

Asset values on a forced sale basis are as follows:	$000
Tangibles	460
Receivables	200
Inventory	200
	860

Required:

Appraise the scheme from the point of view of the ordinary shareholders, the preference shareholders and the debenture holders.

Solution

	$000
Cash available	
Paid out to debenture holders	
Bank	
Preference shareholders—owed 200 but limited to	
Left for ordinary shareholders	

Appraisals

Ordinary	With scheme	Without scheme
Capital		
Income		

Preference	With scheme	Without scheme
Capital		
Income		

Debentures	With scheme	Without scheme
Capital		
Income		

© DeVry/Becker Educational Development Corp. All rights reserved.

Summary

- The sale of all or part of an investment is recorded as a disposal in the parent's own accounts and will usually give rise to a profit or loss on disposal.

- If a disposal occurs part way through the year, then the statement of financial position simply reflects the closing position.

- The consolidated statement of comprehensive income must reflect the pattern of ownership for the period.

- Any disposal without loss of control is accounted for as a transaction within equity between the shareholders of the group, the shareholders of the parent and the non-controlling shareholders of the subsidiary.

- Any disposal of a shareholding that results in the loss of control will give rise to profit or loss on disposal, which is recognised in profit or loss.

- Disposal of a subsidiary will usually amount to a discontinued operation, and therefore is presented separately.

- In a step acquisition, any previous shareholding is remeasured to fair value at the date the parent acquires control of a subsidiary.

- If the parent gains control through a step acquisition, then the accounting model pretends to sell the previous holding and buy the new holding.

- If control had been gained previously, then any gain or loss on the step acquisition would be recognised directly in equity.

- A demerger occurs where an existing group divides into two or more separate groups.

- Schemes of reconstruction will affect the rights of the various stakeholders in the entity. In most jurisdictions the regulatory environment will have processes to protect the rights of each class of interested party.

Session 20 Quiz

Estimated time: 20 minutes

1. Describe how the profit or loss on the disposal of shares is calculated in the parent's single entity accounts. (1.2)

2. Suppose a disposal takes the shareholding from 80% to 60%. State how much of the subsidiary's revenue should be included in consolidated profit or loss. (2.2)

3. Suppose control of a subsidiary is lost. Describe the required adjustments in the consolidated accounts. (2.3.2)

4. Give the classification for a disposal of a subsidiary in the consolidated financial statements. (2.4)

5. Describe how, in a step acquisition, any previous shareholding is valued once control is achieved. (3.1)

6. Explain how goodwill is calculated when the status of the investment moves from associate to subsidiary. (3.3)

7. In a case of moving from a 60% to 80% shareholding and non-controlling interest measured at fair value, describe the effect on the amount recognised within equity. (3.4)

8. Give THREE reasons for a corporate reorganisation. (4)

9. Give the typical order of ranking for stakeholders in the winding up of an entity. (5.5)

Study Question Bank

Estimated time: 30 minutes

Priority		Estimated Time	Completed
Q32	Harley	30 minutes	
Additional			
Q33	Renewal		

© DeVry/Becker Educational Development Corp. All rights reserved.

EXAMPLE SOLUTIONS

Solution 1—Disposal Scenarios

Consolidated statement of financial position as at 31 March 2018

	(a) $	(b) $	(c) $
Investment in associate (6,500 × 40%)	—	—	2,600
Sundry assets	36,450	42,950	36,450
	36,450	42,950	39,050
Share capital	20,000	20,000	20,000
Retained earnings	16,450	21,325	19,050
	36,450	41,325	39,050
Non-controlling interest (6,500 × 25%)	—	1,625	—
	36,450	42,950	39,050

Consolidated statement of comprehensive income for the year ended 31 March 2018

	(a) $	(b) $	(c) $
Operating profit **(W7)**	15,800	16,750	15,800
Income from interests in associate (40% × $\frac{3}{12}$ × 1,650)	—	—	165
Profit on disposal of operations **(W6)**	3,411		5,846
Profit before taxation	19,211	16,750	21,811
Taxation—group **(W8)**	(7,012)	(7,550)	(7,012)
Profit after taxation	12,199	9,200	14,799
Non-controlling interest **(W9)**	(124)	(227)	(124)
Profit for the year	12,075	8,973	14,675
Retained earnings b/f **(W3)**	4,375	4,375	4,375
Movement in equity **(W6)**		7,977	
Retained earnings c/f	16,450	21,325	19,050

Workings
(1) Net assets

	Reporting date $	Disposal $	Acquisition $
Share capital	3,000	3,000	3,000
Retained earnings	3,500	3,088	700
	6,500	6,088	3,700

(2) Retained earnings at date of disposal

	$
B/fwd	1,850
Profit for year to disposal (1,650 × $\frac{9}{12}$)	1,238
	3,088

© DeVry/Becker Educational Development Corp. All rights reserved.

(3) Retained earnings b/f

	$
Hamble Group	3,450
Jemima 90% (1,850 − 700)	1,035
Less: Goodwill written off	(110)
	4,375

(4) Profit on disposal of Jemima (individual company view)

	(a) $	(b) $	(c) $
Sale proceeds	8,890	8,890	8,890
Less: Cost of investment			
3,440	(3,440)		
3,440 × $^{15}/_{90}$		(573)	
3,440 × $^{50}/_{90}$			(1,911)
Profit on disposal	5,450	8,317	6,979

(5) Consolidated retained earnings

	(a) $	(b) $	(c) $
Retained earnings of Hamble			
Per the question	11,000	11,000	11,000
Profit on disposal **(W4)**	5,450	8,317	6,979
	16,450	19,317	17,979
Share of Jemima			
75% × (3,500 − 700)		2,100	
40% × (3,500 − 700)			1,120
Goodwill 110 × $^{75}/_{90}$		(92)	
110 × $^{40}/_{90}$			(49)
	16,450	21,325	19,050

(6) Profit on disposal of Jemima (group view)

	(a) $	(b) $	(c) $
Sale proceeds	8,890	8,890	8,890
Less: Net assets at disposal **(W1)**			
6,088 × 90%	(5,479)		
6,088 × 15%		(913)	
6,088 × 50%			(3,044)
Profit on disposal*	3,411	7,977	5,846

> ***Commentary**
>
> *In situation (b) no profit or loss on disposal will be recognised in the consolidated statement of comprehensive income, instead the amount will be recognised as a movement within equity.

© DeVry/Becker Educational Development Corp. All rights reserved.

(7) Operating profit

	(a) $	(b) $	(c) $
Hamble Group	12,950	12,950	12,950
Jemima	2,850	3,800	2,850
	15,800	16,750	15,800

(8) Taxation—group

	(a) $	(b) $	(c) $
Hamble Group	5,400	5,400	5,400
Jemima	1,612	2,150	1,612
	7,012	7,550	7,012

(9) Non-controlling interest in Jemima

	(a) $	(b) $	(c) $
Operating profit (W7)	2,850	3,800	2,850
Tax (W8)	(1,612)	(2,150)	(1,612)
	1,238	1,650	1,238
× 10%	124		124
× 10% × $\frac{9}{12}$		124	
× 25% × $\frac{3}{12}$		103	
	124	227	124

Solution 2—Consolidated Statement of Financial Position

Portion: Consolidated statement of financial position as at 31 December 2018

	$000
Goodwill	40
Sundry assets (590 + 550)	1,140
	1,180
Share capital: $1 ordinary shares	200
Retained earnings (W4)	870
	1,070
Non-controlling interest (W3)	110
	1,180

Workings
(1) Net assets working

	Reporting date $000	1 July 2018 Acquisition $000	1 July 2018 Post-acquisition $000	30 September 2017 Acquisition $000	30 September 2017 Post-acquisition $000
Share capital	100	100		100	
Retained earnings	450	400	50	300	150
	500	500		400	

© DeVry/Becker Educational Development Corp. All rights reserved.

(2) Goodwill

	$000
Cost of investment	260
Fair value of previous holding	180
Fair value of non-controlling interest	100
Less: Fair value of net assets on acquisition	(500)
	40

(3) Non-controlling interest

	$000
Fair value on acquisition	100
Share of post-acquisition profits (20% × 50)	10
	110

(4) Retained earnings

			$000
Portion			800
Share of Slice	30% × 100 (400 − 300)	30	
	80% × 50 (450 − 400)	40	
			70
			870

Solution 3—Reconstruction Scheme

	$000	$000
Non-current assets		
Tangibles	1,000	980
Goodwill	500	–
	1,500	980
Current assets		
Cash	–	450
Receivables	300	290
Inventory	400	350
	2,200	2,070
Share capital		
Ordinary shares	1,500	750
Reserves		
Share premium	–	500
Capital reserve	–	420
Retained earnings	(300)	–
Liabilities		
10% debenture (secured on the tangible non-current assets)	500	250
4% Preference shares	200	150
Bank overdraft	300	–
	2,200	2,070

© DeVry/Becker Educational Development Corp. All rights reserved.

The reconstruction account is used to record the double entry of any write-downs of assets and surrender of capital. Ideally it should balance to zero but may generate a credit balance which will be presented as a capital reserve. It should never generate a debit balance.

Reconstruction account

	$		$
Write offs of:			
Tangibles	20		
Goodwill	500		
Receivables	10		
Inventory	50		
Retained earnings	300		
Issue of:		Surrender of:	
New ordinary shares	375	Old ordinary shares	1,500
New preference shares	150	Old preference shares	200
Ordinary shares to debenture holders	125	Debentures	250
Bal c/d as capital reserve	420		
	1,950		1,950

Solution 4—Distribution of Cash on a Wind Up

	$000
Cash available	860
Paid out to debenture holders	(500)
	360
Bank	(300)
	60
Preference shareholders—owed 200 but limited to	(60)
Left for ordinary shareholders	–

Appraisals

Ordinary	With scheme	Without scheme
Capital	625/750 = 83% of the company	zero
Income	83% of profit stream (after other distributions)	zero

Preference	With scheme	Without scheme
Capital	150	60
Income	4% x 150	return on 60

Debentures	With scheme	Without scheme
Capital	375	500
Income	17% of dividend stream; 10% × 250 interest	return on 500

© DeVry/Becker Educational Development Corp. All rights reserved.

Associates and Joint Arrangements

FOCUS

This session covers the following content from the *ACCA Study Guide.*

D. Financial Statements of Groups of Entities

1. Group accounting including statements of cash flows

d) Apply and discuss the criteria used to identify an associate.

g) Apply the equity method of accounting for associates.

h) Outline and apply the key definitions and accounting methods which relate to interests in joint arrangements.

Session 21 Guidance

■ **Recognise** that joint ventures are now accounted for in the same manner as investments in associates (i.e equity accounting).

■ **Be aware** that the use of proportionate consolidation is no longer permitted since IAS 31 has been withdrawn (s.1.1).

■ **Learn** the definitions of joint arrangement, joint control and joint venture (s.1.2) and the factors that provide evidence of significant influence (s.1.3).

■ **Learn** the key points of the relevant standards (s.2).

■ **Revise** equity accounting, which has not changed as a result of the new and revised standards, so the techniques are the same as for F7 (s.3). **Attempt** *Examples 1* and *2.*

VISUAL OVERVIEW

Objective: To explain what associates and joint arrangements are and how to account for them.

BACKGROUND

- Relationship
- Terminology
- Significant Influence
- Separate Financial Statements

RELEVANT STANDARDS

- IAS 28 *Investments in Associates and Joint Ventures*
- IFRS 11 *Joint Arrangements*
- IFRS 12 *Disclosure of Interests in Other Entities*

EQUITY ACCOUNTING

- Basic Rule
- Accounting Treatment
- Consolidated Financial Position
- Consolidated Comprehensive Income
- Recognising Losses
- Accounting Policies
- Impairment
- Exemptions
- Recent Change

JOINT OPERATIONS

- Relationship
- Accounting

INTRA-GROUP ITEMS

- Trading
- Dividends
- Unrealised Profit

IFRS 12

- Application
- Disclosure

1 Background

1.1 Relationship

- Where one company has a controlling investment in another company, a parent-subsidiary relationship is formed and accounted for as a group. Companies also may have substantial investments in other entities without actually having control. Thus, a parent-subsidiary relationship does not exist between the two.

 **Key Point**

An investing company which can exert significant influence over the financial and operating policies of the investee company will have an active interest in its net assets and results.

- Including the investment at cost in the company's accounts would not fairly present the investing interest.

- So that the investing entity (which may be a single company or a group) fairly reflects the nature of the interest in its accounts, the entity's interest in the net assets and results of the company, the *associate*, should be reflected in the entity's accounts. This is achieved through the use of equity *accounting*.

- A third relationship exists where an entity shares control with one or more other entities. This shared or joint control does not give any dominant or significant influence and all parties that share control must agree on how the shared entity is to be run.

- Prior to 2011, associates were accounted for under the equity accounting model and for joint ventures an entity could choose to use either equity accounting or proportionate consolidation.

- The use of proportional consolidation never had the support of the accounting profession, and in 2011 the IASB withdrew IAS 31, which allowed its use, and replaced it with IFRS 11 *Joint Arrangements.* This standard only allows joint ventures to be accounted for using equity accounting.

1.2 Terminology

Associate: an entity over which the investor has significant influence.

Joint arrangement: an arrangement in which two or more parties have joint control.

Joint control: the contractually agreed sharing of control of an arrangement, which exists only when the decisions about the relevant activities require the unanimous consent of the parties sharing control.

© DeVry/Becker Educational Development Corp. All rights reserved.

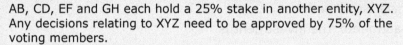

Example 1 Joint Control

AB, CD, EF and GH each hold a 25% stake in another entity, XYZ. Any decisions relating to XYZ need to be approved by 75% of the voting members.

Required:

Explain whether XYZ is jointly controlled by the four parties to the arrangement.

Joint venture: a joint arrangement whereby the parties which have joint control of the arrangement have rights to the net assets of the arrangement.

Significant influence: the power to participate in the financial and operating policy decisions of the investee but is not control or joint control of those policies.

Equity accounting: a method of accounting whereby the investment is initially recognised at cost and adjusted thereafter for the post-acquisition change in the investor's share of the investee's net assets. The investor's profit or loss includes its share of the investee's profit or loss and, similarly, other comprehensive income.

1.3 Significant Influence

▦ The term *significant influence* means that an investor is involved, or has the right to be involved, in the financial and operating policy decisions of the investee.

▦ The existence of significant influence by an investor is usually evidenced in one or more of the following ways:

- Representation on the board of directors or equivalent governing body
- Participation in policymaking;
- Material transactions between the investor and the investee;
- Interchange of managerial personnel;
- Provision of essential technical information.

▦ Conversely, a holding of less than 20% presumes that the holder does not have significant influence, unless such influence can be clearly demonstrated (e.g. representation on the board).

▦ The existence and effect of potential voting rights that are currently exercisable or convertible by the investor should be considered.*

▦ When significant influence is lost, any remaining investment will be measured at fair value. Any difference between the carrying amount of the investment in **associate** and the remeasured amount will be included within profit or loss. From that point on, the investment will be accounted for in accordance with IFRS 9.

Key Point

A holding of 20% or more of the voting rights of the investee indicates significant influence, unless it can be demonstrated otherwise.

*Commentary

*Potential voting rights may occur through holding share warrants, share call options, debt or equity instruments (or other similar instruments) which are convertible into ordinary shares.

1.4   Separate Financial Statements

▦ In the separate financial statements, an investment in an associate or a **joint venture** is accounted for in accordance with IAS 27 *Separate Financial Statements*.

▦ In the separate financial statements, the investment is accounted for:

   • under IFRS 5 if classified as held for sale;

   • at cost or in accordance with IFRS 9.

▦ The emphasis in the separate financial statements will be on the performance of the assets as investments.

2   Relevant Standards

2.1   IAS 28 *Investments in Associates and Joint Ventures*

▦ The objective of IAS 28 is to prescribe the accounting for associates and to describe the use of the equity method for both associates and joint ventures.

▦ The standard identifies when significant influence exists and the practical issues around the use of **equity accounting.**

2.2   IFRS 11 *Joint Arrangements*

Key Point

The objective of IFRS 11 is to establish principles for financial reporting by entities which have an interest in arrangements that are controlled jointly (i.e. **joint arrangements**).

▦ A joint arrangement must be classified as either:

   • a joint operation; or

   • a joint venture.

▦ The classification between a joint operation and a joint venture is dependent on the rights and obligations of parties within the arrangement.

▦ A joint operation exists if the parties have rights to assets and obligations for liabilities, relating to the arrangement.

Key Point

IFRS 11 is the relevant standard for joint operations. IAS 28 is the relevant standard for joint ventures.

                    © DeVry/Becker Educational Development Corp. All rights reserved.

Illustration 1 Joint Operation

Texon shares the use, in equal measure, of an oil pipeline with four other oil companies. The joint operation states that the maintenance of the pipeline will also be shared on an equal basis by all five parties.

The pipeline will be treated as a joint operation in accordance with IFRS 11, and therefore Texon will recognise 20% of the pipeline asset in its statement of financial position. It will also include 20% of the maintenance costs as an expense in its statement of profit or loss for the period.

■ A joint venture exists where the parties have rights to the net assets of the arrangement.

Illustration 2 Joint Venture

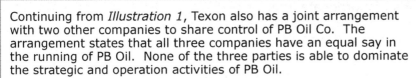

Continuing from *Illustration 1*, Texon also has a joint arrangement with two other companies to share control of PB Oil Co. The arrangement states that all three companies have an equal say in the running of PB Oil. None of the three parties is able to dominate the strategic and operation activities of PB Oil.

This arrangement would be treated as a joint venture in accordance with IFRS 11. Texon would then apply the equity method of IAS 28 when accounting for PB Oil:

■ a single asset representing the cost of the investment in PB Oil adjusted for the post-acquisition changes in PB Oil's net assets;
■ a single amount of income from joint ventures would be included in Texon's profit or loss for the period.

2.3 IFRS 12 *Disclosure of Interests in Other Entities*

■ The objective of IFRS 12 is to require an entity to disclose information enabling users to evaluate:

• the nature of, and risks associated with, interests in other entities; and
• the effects of those interests on the financial statements.

Key Point

IFRS 12 requires disclosures of investments in subsidiaries, associates and joint arrangements.

3 Equity Accounting

3.1 Basic Rule

Key Point

An investment in an associate should be accounted for using the equity method.

■ Associates must be accounted for using the equity method regardless of the fact that the investor may not have investments in subsidiaries and does not therefore prepare consolidated financial statements.*

*Commentary

*Any reference to associates and equity accounting also applies to joint ventures and equity accounting.

3.2   Accounting Treatment

Key Point

■ The investment in an associate is initially recognised at cost.

■ The carrying amount is increased or decreased to recognise the investor's share of the profit or loss of the investee after the date of acquisition.

▦ This is equivalent to taking the investor's share of the net assets of the associate at the date of the financial statements plus goodwill.

▦ Distributions received from the associate reduce the carrying amount of the investment.

▦ Adjustments to the carrying amount also may be necessary for changes in the investor's proportionate interest in the associate arising from changes in the associate's equity which have not been recognised in the profit or loss.

▦ Such changes include those arising from the revaluation of property, plant and equipment and from foreign exchange translation differences.

▦ The investor's share of the current year's profit or loss of the associate is recognised in the investor's profit or loss.

▦ The associate is not consolidated line-by-line. Instead, the group's share of the associate's net assets is included in the consolidated statement of financial position in one line and share of profits (after tax) in the consolidated statement of comprehensive income in one line.

3.3   Treatment in a Consolidated Statement of Financial Position

Exam Advice

If the examiner states that there is no impairment of the investment in the associate then there is no need to calculate goodwill.

▦ The methods described next apply equally to the financial statements of a non-group company which has an investment in an associate and to group accounts.

▦ In group investments, replace the investment as shown in the individual company statement of financial position with:

● the group's share of the associate's net assets at the end of the reporting period; plus

● the goodwill arising on acquisition, less any impairment losses.

▦ As for business combinations under IFRS 3, IAS 28 does not permit the amortisation of goodwill.

▦ Do not consolidate line-by-line the associate's net assets. The associate is not a subsidiary; therefore, the net assets are not controlled as they are for a subsidiary.

▦ In group reserves, include the parent's share of the associate's post-acquisition reserves (the same as for subsidiary).

▦ Cancel the investment in associate in the individual company's books against the share of the associate's net assets acquired at fair value. The difference is goodwill.

© DeVry/Becker Educational Development Corp. All rights reserved.

▨ The fair values of the associate's assets and liabilities must be used in calculating goodwill. Any change in reserves, depreciation charges, etc due to fair value adjustments must be taken into account (as they are when dealing with subsidiaries).

▨ Where the share of the associate's net assets acquired at fair value is in excess of the cost of investment, the difference is included as income in determining the investor's share of the associate's profits or losses.

▨ To calculate amounts for net assets and post-acquisition reserves, use a net assets working for the associate (the same as for the subsidiary).

▨ The amount to be placed in the statement of financial position at the end of the reporting period will be:

	$
Cost of investment	x
Share of post-acquisition profits of A	x
Less any impairment loss	(x)
	x

Example 2 Consolidated Statement of Financial Position

P owns 80% of S and 40% of A. Statements of financial position of the three companies at 31 December 2017 are as follows:

	P	S	A
	$	$	$
Investment: shares in S	800	–	–
Investment: shares in A	600	–	–
Other non-current assets	1,600	800	1,400
Current assets	2,200	3,300	3,250
	5,200	4,100	4,650
Issued capital—$1 ordinary shares	1,000	400	800
Retained earnings	4,000	3,400	3,600
Liabilities	200	300	250
	5,200	4,100	4,650

P acquired its shares in S seven years ago when S's retained earnings were $520 and P acquired its shares in A on the 1 January 2017 when A's retained earnings were $400.

Non-controlling interest is not credited with goodwill, which was fully written off after five years.

There were no indications during the year that the investment in A was impaired.

Required:

Prepare the consolidated statement of financial position at 31 December 2017.

3.4 Treatment in a Consolidated Statement of Comprehensive Income

▨ Treatment is consistent with consolidated statement of financial position and applies equally to a non-group company with an associate:

- Include group share of the associate's profits after tax in the consolidated statement of comprehensive income. This replaces dividend income shown in the investing company's own statement of comprehensive income.
- Do not add in the associate's revenue and expenses line-by-line as this is not a consolidation and the associate is not a subsidiary.
- Time-apportion the associate's results if acquired mid-year.

▨ Note that the associate statement of financial position is *not* time apportioned as the statement of financial position reflects the net assets at the period end to be equity accounted.

Example 3 Consolidated Comprehensive Income

P has owned 80% of S and 40% of A for several years. Statements of comprehensive income for the year ended 31 December 2017 are as follows:

	P	S	A
	$	$	$
Revenue	14,000	12,000	10,000
Cost of sales	(9,000)	(4,000)	(3,000)
Gross profit	5,000	8,000	7,000
Administrative expenses	(2,000)	(6,000)	(3,000)
	3,000	2,000	4,000
Dividend from associate	400	–	–
Profit before taxation	3,400	2,000	4,000
Income taxes	(1,000)	(1,200)	(2,000)
Profit after taxation	2,400	800	2,000
Statement of changes in equity (extract)			
Dividends (paid)	(1,000)	–	(1,000)

Goodwill was fully written off three years ago.

Required:

Prepare the consolidated statement of comprehensive income for the year ended 31 December 2017.

© DeVry/Becker Educational Development Corp. All rights reserved.

3.5 Recognition of Losses

- If an investor's share of losses of an associate equals or exceeds its interest in the associate, the investor discontinues recognising its share of further losses.

- The interest in the associate is its value under the equity method plus any long-term interest which forms part of the investor's net investment.

- Such interests may include preference shares and long-term receivables or loans but do not include trade receivables, trade payables or any long-term receivables for which adequate collateral exists (e.g. secured loans).

- After the investor's interest is reduced to zero, additional losses are provided for, and a liability is recognised, only to the extent that the investor has incurred legal or constructive obligations or made payments on behalf of the associate.

- If the associate subsequently reports profits, the investor resumes recognising its share of those profits only after its share of the profits equals the share of losses not recognised.

- The investment in the associate can be reduced to nil but no further (i.e. the investment in associate cannot be negative, even if there are post-acquisition losses of the associate).

> **Illustration 3 An Unprofitable Associate**
>
> A parent company has a 40% associate, which was acquired a number of years ago for $1m. A long-term loan also was made to the associate of $250,000.
>
> Since the acquisition, the associate's losses have totalled $5m.
>
> The parent's share of those losses would be $2m.
>
> The parent would only be required to recognise the losses to the extent of the investment of $1m plus $250,000; the remaining share of losses ($750,000) would not be recognised unless the parent had a present obligation to make good those losses.
>
> If the associate then became profitable, the parent would not be able to recognise those profits until its share of unrecognised losses had been eliminated.

- However, the investor continues to recognise losses to the extent of any guarantees made to satisfy the obligation of the associate. This may require recognition of a provision in accordance with IAS 37.

- Continuing losses of an associate is objective evidence that financial interests in the associate other than those included in the carrying amount may be impaired.

3.6 Accounting Policies and Year Ends

3.6.1 Accounting Policies

■ If an associate uses accounting policies other than those of the investor, adjustments must be made to conform the associate's accounting policies to those of the investor in applying the equity method.

3.6.2 Year Ends

■ The most recent available financial statements of the associate are used by the investor.

■ When the reporting dates of the investor and the associate are different, the associate prepares, for the use of the investor, financial statements as of the same date as the financial statements of the investor.

■ When it is not practicable to produce statements as at the same date, adjustments must be made for the effects of significant transactions or events which occur between that date and the date of the investor's financial statements.

■ In any case, the difference between the reporting date of the associate and that of the investor must not be more than three months.

■ The length of the reporting periods and any difference in the reporting dates must be the same from period to period.

3.7 Impairment

Key Point

The entire carrying amount of the investment is tested for impairment by comparing it with its recoverable amount.

■ After application of the equity method, including recognising the associate's losses, the investor applies the requirements of IFRS 9 to determine whether it is necessary to recognise any additional impairment loss.

■ Because goodwill that is included in the carrying amount of an investment in an associate is not separately recognised, it is not tested for impairment separately.

■ In determining the value in use of the investment, an entity estimates:*

● its share of the present value of the estimated future cash flows expected to be generated by the associate, including the cash flows from the operations of the associate and the proceeds on the ultimate disposal of the investment; or

● the present value of the estimated future cash flows expected from dividends to be received from the investment and from its ultimate disposal.

■ If the associate is profitable, it is unlikely there will be any impairment in its value.

*Commentary

*Under basic assumptions, either method of investment valuation will give the same result.

© DeVry/Becker Educational Development Corp. All rights reserved.

3.8 Exemptions to Equity Accounting

▓ An associate which is classified as held for sale is accounted for under IFRS 5 *Non-current Assets Held for Sale and Discontinued Operations*.

▓ Under IFRS 5, if an associate is acquired and held with a view to disposal within 12 months, it will be measured at the lower of its carrying amount (e.g. cost) or fair value less costs of disposal.

▓ If the investor is also a parent company which has elected not to present consolidated financial statements, the investment in the associate will be measured at cost or in accordance with IFRS 9.

▓ The investment in the associate will be measured at cost or in accordance with IFRS 9 if *all* of the following apply:

  • the investor is a wholly-owned subsidiary (or partially-owned and other owners do not object);

  • the investor's debt or equity instruments are not traded in a public market;

  • the investor does not file its financial statements with a securities regulator; and

  • the ultimate (or any intermediate) parent of the investor produces consolidated financial statements available for public use under IFRS.

▓ This allows investors who do not have investments in a subsidiary, but only have an investment in an associate, to be exempt from the requirement to account for equity on the same basis as parents under IFRS 10.

3.9 Recent Change

▓ The 2011 changes in standards relating to business combinations, associates and joint ventures resulted in a conflict of accounting treatments when dealing with a sale or contribution of assets by an investor to an associate or joint venture.

▓ In 2015, the IASB issued an amendment to IFRS 10 and IAS 28. The amendment deals with the sale or contribution of assets between an investor and its joint venture or associate.

  • If the sale or contribution is of a business (as defined by IFRS 3), any gain or loss from the transaction is recognised in full in the investor's financial statements. For example, if an associate has a subsidiary and that subsidiary is sold to the parent of the associate, then the associate will recognise the profit or loss in full.

  • If the transaction is not of a business, then the investor will only recognise its share of any gain or loss. For example, if the parent sells inventory to the associate then the amount of profit recognised will exclude the percentage of the parent's investment in the associate.

4 Intra-group Items*

*Commentary

*Any reference to associates and equity accounting also applies to joint ventures and equity accounting.

4.1 Intra-group Trading

▦ Members of the group can sell to or make purchases from the associate. This trading will result in the recognition of receivables and payables in the individual company accounts.

▦ *Do not* cancel intra-group balances on the statement of financial position and *do not* adjust sales and cost of sales for trading with the associate.

▦ In consolidated statement of financial position, show balances with the associate separately from other receivables and payables.

▦ The associate is not part of the group. It is, therefore, appropriate to show amounts owed to the group by the associate as assets and amounts owed to the associate by the group as liabilities.

4.2 Dividends

▦ Consolidated statement of financial position:

• Ensure that dividends payable/receivable are fully accounted for in an individual company's books.

• Include receivable in the consolidated statement of financial position for dividends owed to the *group* from the associates.

• Do not cancel intra-group balance for dividends.

▦ Consolidated statement of comprehensive income:

• Do not include dividends from the associate in the consolidated statement of comprehensive income. The parent's share of the associate's profit after tax (hence before dividends) is included under equity accounting in the income from the associate.

4.3 Unrealised Profit

Key Point

Unrealised profits are eliminated to the extent of the investor's interest in the associate.

▦ If the parent sells goods to the associate and the associate still has these goods in stock at the year end, their carrying amount will include the profit made by the parent and recorded in its books. Hence, profit is included in inventory value in the associate's net assets (profit is unrealised) and the parent's revenue.

▦ If the associate sells to the parent, a similar situation arises, with the profit being included in the associate's revenue and the parent's inventory.

▦ To avoid double counting when equity accounting for the associate, this unrealised profit is eliminated.

▦ Unrealised losses are not eliminated if the transaction provides evidence of an impairment in the value of the asset which has been transferred.

▦ To eliminate unrealised profit, deduct the profit from the associate's profit before tax and retained earnings in the net assets working before equity accounting for the associate, irrespective of whether the sale is from the associate to the parent or vice versa.

© DeVry/Becker Educational Development Corp. All rights reserved.

Illustration 4   Eliminate Unrealised Profit

The parent has a 40% associate.

The parent sells the goods to the associate for $150; the goods originally cost the parent $100. The goods are still in the associate's inventory at year end.

Required:

State how the unrealised profit will be dealt with in the consolidated accounts.

Solution

To eliminate unrealised profit:

Deduct $50 from associate's profit before tax in the statement of comprehensive income, thus dealing with the profit or loss effect.

Deduct $50 from retained earnings at the end of the reporting period in the net assets working for the associate, thus dealing with the effect of the statement of financial position.*

*Commentary

*Share of net assets and post-acquisition profits included under equity accounting will then be $20 (50 × 40%) lower.

5   Joint Operations

5.1   Relationship

- A joint operation exists when the entity only has a share in the individual assets or liabilities of the joint arrangement (e.g. an oil company sharing the control of a pipeline).

Key Point

It is the rights to individual assets (or obligations for liabilities) that drive a joint operations relationship rather than rights to the net asset position of the joint arrangement.

5.2   Accounting

- For joint operation, the joint operator recognises:
  - its assets, to include a share of any jointly held assets;
  - its liabilities, to include a share of any liabilities jointly incurred;
  - its revenue from the sale of its share of any output from the joint operation;
  - its expenses, to include a share of any jointly incurred expenses.
- The accounting for any assets, liabilities, revenue and expenses will be in accordance with the relevant standard. When accounting for property, IAS 16 will be the relevant standard.
- IFRS 11 is also applicable to an entity which participates in a joint operation but does not have **joint control,** as long as that entity has rights to the assets or obligations for the liabilities of the joint operation.

5.2.1 Sales or Contributions of Assets to Joint Operation

▧ If a joint operator sells goods to the joint operation at a profit or loss then the joint operator will only recognise the profit or loss to the extent of the other parties' interests in the joint operation.

Illustration 5 Sale to Joint Operation

Entities A, B, C and D each hold a 25% stake in the joint operation of Z. Entity A sells goods to Z, making a profit of $1,000. Entity A will only recognise $750 (75%) of profit in its financial statements.

5.2.2 Purchases of Assets From a Joint Operation

▧ If a joint operator purchases goods from a joint operation to which it is a party, it must **not** recognise its share of any gains or losses until it resells the assets to an external party.

6 IFRS 12

6.1 Application

▧ IFRS 12 should be applied by an entity if it has an interest in a subsidiary, an associate or a joint operation.

▧ It is not applicable to the following:
  - post-employment benefit plans (IAS 19);
  - separate financial statements (IAS 27);
  - participation in a joint arrangement which does not have joint control;
  - an interest which is accounted for under IFRS 9.

6.2 Disclosure

▧ An entity will disclose information which allows users to evaluate:
  - the nature, extent and financial effects of any interest in an associate or joint arrangement;
  - the nature and effects of any contractual relationship with other investors who have joint control or significant influence over the associate or joint arrangement; and
  - the nature of, and changes in, the risks associated with its joint ventures and associates.

▧ The disclosures will include:
  - the name of the joint arrangement or associate;
  - the nature of the relationship;
  - the proportion of ownership;
  - any significant restrictions on the ability of the associate or joint venture to transfer funds to the entity;
  - commitments it has relating to its joint ventures; and
  - unrecognised share of losses of a joint venture or an associate.

© DeVry/Becker Educational Development Corp. All rights reserved.

Summary

- An investing company which can exert significant influence over the financial and operating policies of an investee company has an active interest in its net assets and results.
- Joint control is the contractually agreed sharing of control of an arrangement where unanimous consent is required by all parties.
- A holding of 20% or more of the voting rights of the investee indicates significant influence, unless it can be demonstrated otherwise.
- IFRS 11 establishes principles for financial reporting by entities which have an interest in arrangements that are controlled jointly.
- IFRS 12 requires disclosures of investments in subsidiaries, associates and joint arrangements.
- An investment in an associate is accounted for using the equity method under which:
  - initial recognition is at cost; and
  - the carrying amount is increased by a share of the associate's post-acquisition profits.
- Consolidated profit or loss only includes a share of the associate's profit for the period; no income or expense items are included.
- The entire carrying amount of the investment is tested for impairment by comparing it with its recoverable amount.
- Unrealised profits are eliminated to the extent of the investor's interest in the associate.
- It is the rights to individual assets or obligations for liabilities which drive the joint arrangement relationship.
- Disclosure requirements are extensive and include the nature of the relationship and the percentage of ownership.

© DeVry/Becker Educational Development Corp. All rights reserved.

Session 21 Quiz
Estimated time: 15 minutes

1. Define the equity method of accounting. (1.2)

2. State evidence which may indicate that significant influence exists. (1.3)

3. Under equity accounting, explain how to measure investment in an associate in the consolidated financial statements. (3.3, 3.4)

4. Specify how much revenue of the associate is included within the consolidated profit or loss. (3.4)

5. Explain the difference between the impairment tests of goodwill in an associate v goodwill in a subsidiary. (3.7)

6. Yes or no? Is there a need to recognise unrealised profits on transactions between parent and associate? (4.3)

Study Question Bank
Estimated time: 20 minutes

Priority		Estimated Time	Completed
Q35	Assocks	20 minutes	
Additional			
Q34	Holly		

© DeVry/Becker Educational Development Corp. All rights reserved.

EXAMPLE SOLUTIONS

Solution 1—Joint Control

XYZ is not jointly controlled by the four parties; any combination of three of the four parties is required to vote through any decisions relating to XYZ. The relationship is that of "collective control" as defined in IFRS 11.

Each of the four parties will recognise their share of XYZ as an associated undertaking as each has significant influence over XYZ. Therefore, each party will apply equity accounting measurement principles to its investment in XYZ.

Solution 2—Consolidated Statement of Financial Position

Consolidated statement of financial position as at 31 December 2017

	$
Investment in associate	1,880
Non-current assets (1,600 + 800)	2,400
Current assets (2,200 + 3,300)	5,500
	9,780
Issued capital	1,000
Retained earnings (W5)	7,520
	8,520
Non-controlling interest (W4)	760
Liabilities	500
	9,780

Workings

(1) Group structure

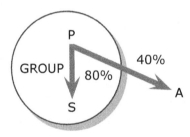

(2) Net assets working

	Reporting date	Acquisition
S	$	$
Issued capital	400	400
Retained earnings	3,400	520
	3,800	920
A	$	$
Issued capital	800	800
Retained earnings	3,600	400
	4,400	1,200

© DeVry/Becker Educational Development Corp. All rights reserved.

Solution 2—Consolidated Statement of Financial Position (continued)

(3) Goodwill

S	$
Cost of investment	800
Net assets acquired (80% × 920 (W2))	(736)
	64

A	$
Cost of investment	600
Net assets acquired (40% × 1,200 (W2))	(480)
	120

(4) Non-controlling interest

	$
S only − (20% × 3,800)	760

(5) Retained earnings

	$
P − from question	4,000
Share of S [80% × (3,400 − 520) (W2)]	2,304
Share of A [40% × (3,600 − 400) (W2)]	1,280
Less: Goodwill impaired (W3 per Activity)	(64)
	7,520

(6) Investment in associate

	$
Share of net assets (40% × 4,400)	1,760
Goodwill	120
	1,880
Proof	
Cost	600
Share of post-acquisition profits	1,280
	1,880

© DeVry/Becker Educational Development Corp. All rights reserved.

Solution 3—Consolidated Comprehensive Income

Consolidated statement of comprehensive income for the year ending 31 December 2017

	$	$
Revenue		26,000
Cost of sales		(13,000)
Gross profit		13,000
Administrative expenses		(8,000)
Operating profit		5,000
Income from associate		800
Profit before taxation		5,800
Income taxes		(2,200)
Profit after taxation		3,600
Non-controlling interest (W3)		160
Profit for shareholders of P		3,440
Statement of changes in equity (extract)		
Dividends (paid)		(1,000)

Workings

(1) Group structure

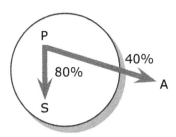

(2) Consolidation schedule

	P	S	Adjustment*	Consolidation
	$	$	$	$
Revenue	14,000	12,000		26,000
Cost of sales	(9,000)	(4,000)		(13,000)
Administration expenses	(2,000)	(6,000)		(8,000)
Income from associate	800			800
40% × 2,000				
Tax – group	(1,000)	(1,200)		(2,200)
Profit after tax		800		

(3) Non-controlling interest

	$
S only 20% × 800	$160

*Commentary

*The adjustment column that has been shown for completeness would, in an exam question, require some adjustments.

© DeVry/Becker Educational Development Corp. All rights reserved.

Foreign Currency Transactions

FOCUS

This session covers the following content from the *ACCA Study Guide.*

D. Financial Statements of Groups of Entities

4. Foreign transactions and entities

a) Outline and apply the translation of foreign currency amounts and transactions into the functional currency and the presentational currency. ☐

b) Account for the consolidation of foreign operations and their disposal. ☐

Session 22 Guidance

■ **Learn** the terminology relevant to IAS 21 (s.1.4) and the recognition rules for individual companies (s.2.1).

■ **Work** through *Examples 1* and *2* on foreign-denominated transactions (s.2.1) before moving onto foreign subsidiaries.

■ **Learn** the factors which drive an entity's functional currency (s.3.2).

(continued on next page)

VISUAL OVERVIEW

Objective: To prescribe translation rules for transactions in a currency different from the presentation currency and to prescribe the accounting treatment for exchange differences.

ACCOUNTING ISSUES

- Introduction
- Key Issues
- Scope
- Terminology

INDIVIDUAL COMPANY STAGE

- Basic Transactions
- Net Investment in a Foreign Operation

CONSOLIDATED FINANCIAL STATEMENTS

- Nature of Exchange Difference
- Functional Currency

DISCLOSURE

FOREIGN OPERATIONS

- Presentation Currency
- Supplementary Information
- Translation technique
- Exchange Difference
- Goodwill
- Foreign Associates

DISPOSAL

- Cumulative Exchange Differences
- Partial Disposal

Session 22 Guidance

■ **Work carefully** through *Example 3*, which covers the basic principles of consolidating a foreign subsidiary (s.4.5).

■ **Learn** the basic principles involved in dealing with the disposal of a foreign subsidiary (s.5).

1 Accounting Issues

1.1 Introduction

- A company may engage in foreign currency operations in two ways:
  1. Entering directly into transactions which are denominated in foreign currencies.
  2. Conducting foreign operations through a foreign entity (subsidiary or associate).
- Resultant transactions and balances must be translated into the presentation currency of the entity for inclusion in financial statements.

1.2 Key Issues

- Exchange rate to be used for translation.
- Treatment of exchange differences (which arise because exchange rates vary over time).

1.3 Scope

- IAS 21 *The Effects of Changes in Foreign Exchange Rates* is applied:
  - to account for transactions in foreign currencies; and
  - to translate the financial statements of foreign operations that are included in the financial statements of the entity by consolidation or by the equity method.
- This standard does not deal with hedge accounting for foreign currency.

1.4 Terminology

Functional currency: the currency of the primary economic environment in which the entity operates.

Presentation currency: the currency in which the financial statements are presented.

Foreign currency: a currency other than the functional currency of the entity.

Closing rate: the spot exchange rate at the end of the reporting period.

Net investment in a foreign entity: the amount of the reporting entity's interest in the net assets of that operation.

Monetary items: money held and assets and liabilities to be received or paid in fixed or determinable number of units of currency.

Spot exchange rate: the exchange rate for immediate delivery.

Foreign operation: a subsidiary, associate, joint venture or branch of the reporting entity, the activities of which are based or conducted in a country or currency other than the country of the reporting entity.

© DeVry/Becker Educational Development Corp. All rights reserved.

2   Individual Company Stage

2.1   Basic Transactions

2.1.1   Initial Recognition

▥ A **foreign currency** transaction is initially recorded in an entity's **functional currency** using the **spot exchange rate** on the date of the transaction.

 **Key Point**

Exchange differences arising on settlement of a foreign currency transaction in the same reporting period must be recognised in profit or loss for the period.

2.1.2   Subsequent Recognition

 **Key Point**

At the end of each reporting period, any foreign currency monetary item must be retranslated using the **closing exchange rate.**

▥ Exchange differences arising on retranslation of a foreign currency balance are recognised in profit or loss for the period.

▥ Non-monetary items measured at historical cost are translated at the exchange rate at the *date of the transaction*.

▥ Non-monetary items measured at fair value are translated using the exchange rate when the *fair value was measured*.

© DeVry/Becker Educational Development Corp. All rights reserved.

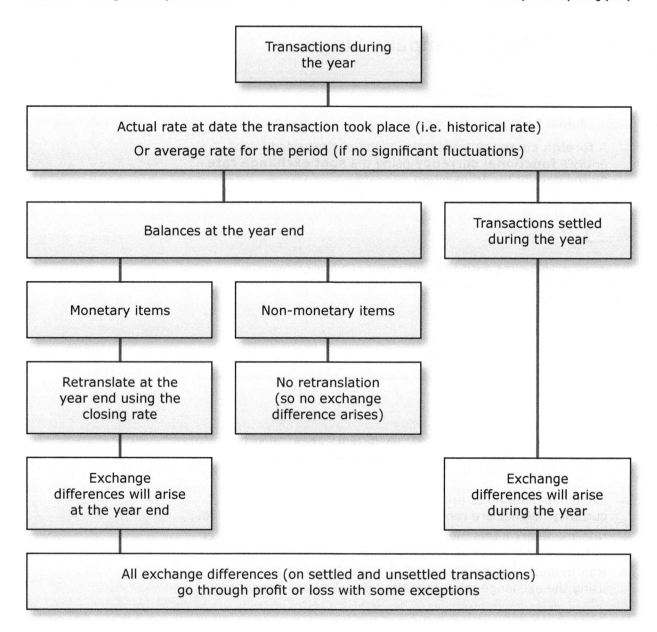

© DeVry/Becker Educational Development Corp. All rights reserved.

Example 1 Purchase of Goods on Credit

Aston has a year end of 31 December. On 25 October, Aston bought goods from a Mexican supplier for 286,000 pesos.

The goods were still in inventory at the year end.

Exchange rates	Pesos to $
25 October	11.16
16 November	10.87
31 December	11.02

Required:

Show the accounting entries for the transactions in each of the following situations:

(a) on 16 November Aston pays the Mexican supplier in full;

(b) the supplier remains unpaid at the year end.

Example 2 Loan

Warrior has a year end of 31 December. On 29 November Warrior received a loan from an Australian bank of AUD 1,520,000.

The proceeds are used to finance in part the purchase of a new office block. The loan remains unsettled at the year end.

Exchange rates	AUD to $
29 November	1.52
31 December	1.66

Required:

Show the accounting entries for these transactions.

2.2   Net Investment in a Foreign Operation

▨ An entity may have a monetary item that is receivable from (or payable to) a foreign operation.

▨ Such monetary items, where settlement is neither planned nor likely to occur in the foreseeable future, is in substance part of a "net investment in the operation".*

▨ Exchange differences on such items are included in profit or loss in the separate financial statements of the reporting entity or foreign operation.

▨ In the consolidated financial statements, these exchange differences are included in other comprehensive income and reclassified through profit or loss on disposal of the investment.

Commentary

*Monetary items unlikely to be settled do not include trade receivables and trade payables.

© DeVry/Becker Educational Development Corp. All rights reserved.

3 Consolidated Financial Statements

3.1 Nature of Exchange Difference

> **Illustration 1 Exchange Difference**
>
> | | € | Rate | $ |
> |---|---|---|---|
> | Net assets at start of the year | 1,000 | 2 | 500 |
> | Retained profit | 500 | 1.9 | 263 |
> | Net assets at year-end | 1,500 | 1.85 | 811* |
> | | | | *This column does not add up |
>
> - The closing net assets figure comes from two sources:
>   - last year's net assets;
>   - profit for the period.
> - The closing figure has been translated at a different rate to its component figures.
> - Exchange difference on consolidation comes from two sources:
>   - Restatement of opening net assets;
>   - Translating retained profit at one rate and the net assets (the other side of the double entry) at another rate

3.2 Identifying the Functional Currency

Key Point

The functional currency of an entity is dictated by the primary economic environment in which the entity operates.

- An entity should consider the following in determining its functional currency:
  - The currency that mainly influences the selling price of goods or services and the currency of the country whose regulations mainly determine the selling price of goods and services.
  - The currency that affects labour, material and other costs of providing goods and services.
- Secondary factors to consider in determining the functional currency are:
  - the currency in which funds from financing activities are generated; and
  - the currency in which monies from operating activities are kept.

© DeVry/Becker Educational Development Corp. All rights reserved.

- The following factors are also to be considered in determining the functional currency of a foreign operation and whether that currency is the same as the reporting entity:
  - Are transactions carried out as an extension of the reporting entity or does the foreign operation carry out its activities with a significant degree of autonomy?
  - Are transactions between the reporting entity and foreign operation a high percentage of total transactions?
  - Do cash flows of the foreign operation directly affect the cash flows of the reporting entity and is cash available for remittance to the reporting entity?
  - Is the foreign operation dependent upon the reporting entity to help service debt obligations, both existing and those of the future?
- If the functional currency is not obvious, management must use its judgement in identifying the currency that most faithfully represents the economic effects of the underlying transactions.

 **Key Point**

Once a functional currency has been identified, it should only be changed if there is a change to the economic climate in which it was initially identified.

4 Foreign Operation

4.1 Presentation Currency

 **Key Point**

Assets and liabilities are translated, at the end of each reporting period, at the closing exchange rate.

- The financial statements of a foreign operation are translated into the **presentation currency** of the parent entity.
- Income and expenses are translated using exchange rates when the transaction occurred. An average exchange rate that approximates actual exchange rates may be used.
- The parent's share of any exchange difference is included in other comprehensive income and reclassified through profit or loss when the foreign operation is disposed of. The non-controlling share is included within non-controlling interest in the consolidated statement of financial position.

4.2 Supplementary Information

- The standard does not prohibit an entity providing additional supplementary information translated using a different currency, prepared in a manner other than that required by the standard.
- If an entity does present additional information, it should be clearly identified as supplementary and the fact that translation is not in accordance with the standard.

4.3 Translation Technique

▣ Translation rules are summarised as follows:

4.3.1 Statement of Financial Position

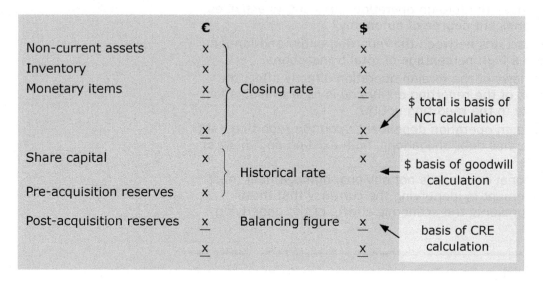

4.3.2 Statement of Comprehensive Income

> **Key Point**
>
> All items in the statement of comprehensive income are translated at the actual rate ruling at the date of the transaction. For practical reasons, a rate that approximates the rate ruling (e.g. an average rate) may be used.

▣ If, however, the foreign entity operates in a hyper-inflationary economy, the closing rate should be used.

4.3.3 Exchange Difference

> **Key Point**
>
> ■ Recognise in other comprehensive income and allocate between shareholders of parent and non-controlling interest.
> ■ Reclassify through profit or loss on disposal of the related asset.

© DeVry/Becker Educational Development Corp. All rights reserved.

4.4   Calculation of Exchange Difference

Either		$
Net assets of S:		
Closing (at closing rate)		x
Opening (at opening rate)		(x)
		x
Retained profit (average rate)		(x)
Exchange difference		x → Take P's share
Or		
Opening net assets (opening rate)		x
Opening net assets (closing rate)		x
		x
Retained profit		
as per profit or loss (average rate)		x
as per net assets (closing rate)	(x)	x
		x → Take P's share

4.5   Goodwill

▨ Goodwill arising on the acquisition of a foreign entity and any fair value adjustments to the carrying amounts of assets and liabilities arising on that acquisition are treated as assets and liabilities of the foreign operation and translated at the closing rate. This requires the recognition of goodwill in the investee's own accounts. This may mean that the level to which goodwill is allocated for foreign currency purposes is different from that which is annually tested for impairment purposes.

Key Point

Recognising goodwill in the investee's own accounts gives rise to a further exchange difference, which will be reported in other comprehensive income.

Illustration 2 **Decrease in Currency Value of Goodwill**

P acquired 100% of S on 30 September at a cost of €4m. The fair value of the net assets of S at that date was €3m. The exchange rate at the date of acquisition was €2 = $1. At 31 December (P's accounting year end) the exchange rate was € 2.1=$1.

Goodwill is an asset denominated in a foreign currency that is subject to retranslation as follows:*

	€	Rate	$
On acquisition	1,000,000	2	500,000
31 December	1,000,000	2.1	476,190

Goodwill has fallen in value by $23,810. This amount is credited to goodwill and debited directly to a separate component of equity.

---

*Commentary

*The argument for this treatment is that the amount of consideration would have been based on the expected future earnings stream expressed in foreign currency (€). Goodwill relates to a business which operates in the economic environment of another country. Any impairment will be matched as a € cost against € revenues.

© DeVry/Becker Educational Development Corp. All rights reserved.

Example 3 Closing Rate Method

Gobbo bought 80% of Sly three years ago for €6,000 when the exchange rate was €4 to $1. The reserves of Sly at that date were €2,000. Non-controlling interest is valued at the proportionate share of the identifiable net assets. Since acquisition there has been no impairment of goodwill.

On 31 December 2018 the statements of financial position were as follows:

Closing rate method

	G $	S €	Rate	S $	Consolidated financial position $
Non-current assets					
Goodwill					
Tangible	9,000	12,000			
Investment in Sly	1,500	—			
Current assets					
Inventory	1,000	1,914			
Other	500	4,986			
	12,000	18,900			
Long term loans	—	(6,000)			
	12,000	12,900			
Share capital	2,000	4,000			
Retained earnings	10,000	8,900			
Pre-acquisition					
Post-acquisition					
Exchange loss reserve					
Non-controlling interest					
	12,000	12,900			

The statements of comprehensive income for the year ended 31 December 2018 were as follows:

Closing rate method

	G $	S €	Rate	S $	Consolidated comprehensive income $
Revenue	35,250	28,215			
Cost of sales and other expenses	(28,200)	(19,515)			
Depreciation	(1,350)	(1,500)			
Profit before tax	5,700	7,200			
Tax	(2,700)	(3,600)			
Profit after tax	3,000	3,600			
Non-controlling interest					
Retained profit					

Exchange rates	€ to $
31 December 2018	3.00
31 December 2017	2.50
Average for 2018	2.85

Required:

Prepare the consolidated statement of financial position and consolidated statement of comprehensive income.

                                                            © DeVry/Becker Educational Development Corp. All rights reserved.

4.6   Foreign Associates

◾ Foreign associates are translated using the closing rate method and the standard workings.

5   Disposal of Foreign Operation

5.1   Cumulative Exchange Differences

◾ On the disposal of a foreign operation, the cumulative amount of the exchange differences which have been deferred and which relate to that foreign entity are recognised as income or as expenses in the same period in which the gain or loss on disposal is recognised.

5.2   Partial Disposal

◾ In the case of a partial disposal, only the proportionate share of the related accumulated exchange differences is included in the gain or loss.

Example 4   Disposal of Foreign Operation

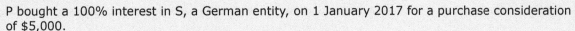

P bought a 100% interest in S, a German entity, on 1 January 2017 for a purchase consideration of $5,000.

P disposed of the holding for $10,000 on 31 December 2018.

Goodwill has been impaired by €600 since acquisition.

	Rate	
	€	**€ to $**
Net assets at the date of acquisition	7,000	1.8
Net assets at the date of disposal	10,000	2.1
Retained profit for the years ending:		
31 December 2017	1,400	1.85
31 December 2018	1,600	2

Required:
Calculate the effects of the disposal of the interest in S on the statement of comprehensive income.

---

6   Disclosure

◾ The amount of exchange differences included in profit or loss for the period.

◾ Net exchange differences shown within other comprehensive income and a reconciliation of the amount of such exchange differences at the beginning and end of the period.

◾ When presentation currency is different to the functional currency, that fact must be stated along with what the functional currency is and the reason for using a different reporting currency.

◾ Any changes in functional currency and the reasons for the change.

© DeVry/Becker Educational Development Corp. All rights reserved.

Summary

- Foreign currency transactions are initially recorded using the spot exchange rate.

- Exchange differences arising on settlement in the same reporting period are recognised in profit or loss for the period.

- At each reporting date, any foreign currency monetary item is retranslated using the closing exchange rate.

- An entity's functional currency is dictated by the primary economic environment in which it operates.

- A functional currency can only be changed if there is a change to the economic climate in which it was initially identified.

- Assets and liabilities of a foreign subsidiary are translated at each reporting period at the closing exchange rate.

- Income and expense items are translated at the rate ruling at the date of the transaction. An average rate can be used in practice.

- Exchange differences are taken through other comprehensive income and reclassified through profit or loss on disposal of the related asset.

- Goodwill is treated as a foreign denominated asset, which will give rise to a further exchange difference reported in other comprehensive income.

© DeVry/Becker Educational Development Corp. All rights reserved.

Session 22 Quiz
Estimated time: 20 minutes

1. Define presentation currency in accordance with IAS 21. (1.4)

2. State how to determine the initial recognition value of a foreign currency transaction. (2.1.1)

3. Explain what happens at the end of the reporting period to any monetary balances denominated in a foreign currency. (2.1.2)

4. Discuss the factors an entity should consider when determining its functional currency. (3.2)

5. For consolidated financial statements, give the exchange rate used for translating the assets and liabilities of a foreign subsidiary. (4.1)

6. Explain how to calculate a foreign exchange difference. (4.4)

7. Explain how to treat goodwill arising on the acquisition of a foreign subsidiary. (4.5)

8. Explain how to treat any cumulative exchange difference on the disposal of a foreign subsidiary. (5)

Study Question Bank
Estimated time: 20 minutes

Priority		Estimated Time	Completed
Q36	Bertie	20 minutes	
Additional			
Q37	Memo		

EXAMPLE SOLUTIONS

Solution 1—Purchase of Goods on Credit

(a) Supplier Paid

		$	$
25 October	Dr Purchases (W1)	25,627	
	Cr Trade payables		25,627
16 November	Dr Trade payables	25,627	
	Dr Profit or loss – other operating expense	684	
	Cr Cash (W2)		26,311

The goods will remain in inventory at the year end at $25,627.

Workings
(1) peso 286,000 ÷ 11.16 = $25,627
(2) peso 286,000 ÷ 10.87 = $26,311

(b) Supplier Unpaid

		$	$
25 October	Dr Purchases (W1)	25,627	
	Cr Trade payables		25,627
31 December	Dr Profit or loss – other operating expense	326	
	Cr Trade payables (W2)		326

The goods will remain in inventory at the year end at $25,627.

Workings

	$
(1) peso 286,000 ÷ 11.16	25,627
(2) peso 286,000 ÷ 11.02	25,953
	326

Solution 2—Loan

		$000	$000
29 November	Dr Cash	1,000	
	Cr Loan		1,000
31 December	Dr Loan	84	
	Cr Profit or loss – other operating income		84

Workings

	$000
(1) AUD 1,520,000 ÷ 1.52	1,000
(2) AUD 1,520,000 ÷ 1.66	916
	84

© DeVry/Becker Educational Development Corp. All rights reserved.

Solution 3—Closing Rate Method

Statement of financial position at 31 December 2018

	G	S	Rate	S	Consolidated financial position
	$	€		$	$
Non-current assets					
Goodwill		1,200	3.0		400
Tangible	9,000	12,000	3.0	4,000	13,000
Investment in Sly	1,500	—		—	
Current assets					
Inventories	1,000	1,914	3.0	638	1,638
Other	500	4,986	3.0	1,662	2,162
	12,000	18,900		6,300	17,200
Long term loans	—	(6,000)	3.0	(2,000)	(2,000)
	12,000	12,900		4,300	15,200
Share capital	2,000	4,000			2,000
Retained earnings			4.0	1,500	12,887
Pre-acquisition	2,000	2,000			
Post-acquisition	10,000	6,900		2,800	
Exchange loss reserve					(547)
Non-controlling interest					860
	12,000	12,900		4,300	15,200

Statement of comprehensive income for the year ended 31 December 2018

	G	S	Rate	S	Consolidated comprehensive income
	$	€		$	$
Revenue	35,250	28,215	2.85	9,900	45,150
Cost of sales and other expenses	(28,200)	(19,515)	2.85	(6,847)	(35,047)
Depreciation	(1,350)	(1,500)	2.85	(526)	(1,876)
Profit before tax	5,700	7,200		2,527	8,227
Tax	(2,700)	(3,600)	2.85	(1,263)	(3,963)
Profit after tax	3,000	3,600		1,264	4,264
Non-controlling interest					(253)
Retained profit					4,011

Solution 3—Closing Rate Method (continued)

Workings

Either

(1) Exchange difference

	$
Closing net assets	4,300
Opening net assets	
(12,900 – 3,600) @ 2.5	(3,720)
	580
Retained profit	(1,264)
Exchange difference	(684)

or

	$	$
Retranslation of opening net assets		
9,300 @ Closing rate (3.00)		3,100
@ Opening rate (2.50)		(3,720)
		(620)
Retranslation of retained profit		
3,600 @ Closing rate (3.00)	1,200	
@ Average rate (2.85)	(1,264)	
		(64)
		(684)

(2) Consolidated retained earnings

	$
G	10,000
S post-acquisition (2,800 x 80%)	2,240
Restatement of goodwill (300 x 4/3) – 300	100
Exchange loss to separate equity component (684 x 80%)	547
	12,887

© DeVry/Becker Educational Development Corp. All rights reserved.

Solution 4—Disposal of Foreign Operation

Working—Goodwill

			$
Cost of investment			5,000
Net assets on acquisition (€7,000 @ 1.8) x 100%			(3,889)
			1,111
		@1.8	€2,000
Impaired			(€600)
Unimpaired on disposal			€1,400
		@2.1	$667

		$
Proceeds		10,000
Share of net assets disposed of (10,000 @ 2.1)		(4,762)
Unimpaired goodwill (W)		(667)
Profit on disposal		**4,571**

	€	Rate	$
Net assets at date of disposal	10,000	2.1	4,762
Net assets at date of acquisition	7,000	1.8	(3,889)
			873
Retained profit			
31 December 2017	1,400	1.85	(757)
31 December 2018	1,600	2	(800)
Exchange loss			**(684)**

© DeVry/Becker Educational Development Corp. All rights reserved.

IAS 7 *Statement of Cash Flows*

FOCUS

This session covers the following content from the *ACCA Study Guide.*

D. Financial Statements of Groups of Entities

1. Group accounting including statements of cash flows
i) Prepare and discuss group statements of cash flows. ☐

Session 23 Guidance

- **Revise** the terminology (s.1), classification of activities (s.2) and format of the cash flow statement, focusing mainly on the indirect cash flow format (s.3) for a single entity.
- **Understand** the additional cash flows which are specific to a consolidated statement of cash flows (s.4). **Attempt** *Examples 1–4*.
- **Use** *Illustration 1* to think about the interpretation of cash flows identified in the statement.

VISUAL OVERVIEW

Objective: To provide information about historical changes in cash and cash equivalents by means of a statement of cash flows which classifies cash flows during the period into operating, investing and financing activities.

STATEMENT OF CASH FLOWS

- Application
- Importance of Cash Flow
- Benefits of Information
- Terminology

PRESENTATION

- Classification
- Examples
- Operating Activities
- Investing and Financing

PRO FORMA

- Direct Method
- Indirect Method
- Notes to the Statement

GROUP STATEMENT OF CASH FLOWS

- Preparation
- Non-controlling Interests
- Associated Undertakings
- Acquisitions and Disposals

DISCLOSURES

- Cash and Cash Equivalents
- Major Non-cash Transactions
- Liability disclosures

INTERPRETATION

- Information
- Comments

© DeVry/Becker Educational Development Corp. All rights reserved.

1 Statement of Cash Flows

1.1 Application

▨ Users of financial statements are interested in cash generation regardless of the nature of the entity's activities. IAS 7 *Statement of Cash Flows* therefore applies to *all* entities.

▨ Entities need cash for essentially the same reasons:

- to conduct operations;
- to pay obligations;
- to provide returns to investors.

1.2 Importance of Cash Flow

▨ To show that profits are being realised (e.g. that trade receivables are being recovered).*

▨ To pay dividends.

▨ To finance further investment (which will generate more cash).

*Profit ≠ cash therefore profitability ≠ liquidity. Even profitable companies "crash".

1.3 Benefits of Cash Flow Information

▨ Provides information that enables users to evaluate changes in:*

- net assets;
- financial structure (including its liquidity and solvency);
- ability to affect amounts and timing of cash flows (to adapt to changing circumstances and opportunities).

▨ Useful in assessing ability to generate cash and cash equivalents.

▨ Users can develop models to assess and compare the present value of future cash flows of different entities.

▨ Enhances comparability of reporting operating performance by different entities (by eliminating effects of alternative accounting treatments).

*Focus on cash management can also improve results, for example, reducing interest charges and having cash resources available on a timely basis (e.g. for investment).

Key Point

Historical cash flow information may provide an indicator of the amount, timing and certainty of future cash flows.

© DeVry/Becker Educational Development Corp. All rights reserved.

1.4   Terminology

Cash: comprises cash on hand and demand deposits.

Cash equivalents: short-term, highly liquid investments that are readily convertible to known amounts of cash subject to an insignificant risk of changes in value (e.g. overnight deposits and government bonds).*

*Equity investments are excluded from cash equivalents unless they are, in substance, cash equivalents (e.g. preferred shares acquired within a short period of their maturity and a specified redemption date).

Included in cash and cash equivalents are bank overdrafts which are repayable on demand and form an integral part of cash management. Cash balances characteristically fluctuate between debit and credit.

Cash flows: inflows and outflows of cash and cash equivalents.*

*Cash flows excludes movements between cash or cash equivalents (an aspect of cash management rather than part of operating, investing and financing activities).

Operating activities: the principal revenue-producing activities of the entity and other activities that are not investing or financing activities.

Investing activities: the acquisition and disposal of long-term assets and other investments not included in cash equivalents.

Financing activities: activities that result in changes in the size and composition of equity capital and borrowings.

© DeVry/Becker Educational Development Corp. All rights reserved.

2 Presentation of a Statement of Cash Flows

2.1 Classification of Activities

The statement of cash flows classifies cash flows into three categories of activities:

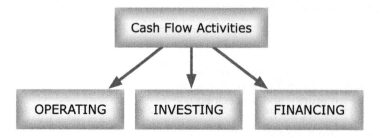

1. Operating Activities or Cash Flow From Operating (CFO)

CFO, without recourse to external sources of finance, is a key indicator of the sufficiency of cash flows to:

- repay loans;
- maintain operating capability;
- pay dividends; and
- make new investments.

It is useful in forecasting future operating cash flows.

Since it is primarily derived from principal revenue-producing activities, it generally results from transactions and events that generate profit or loss.

2. Investing Activities or Cash Flow From Investing (CFI)*

Separate disclosure is important—as investing cash flows represent the amount spent on resources that are intended to generate future income and cash flows.

3. Financing Activities or Cash Flow From Financing (CFF)

Separate disclosure is useful in predicting the claims which providers of capital and long-term finance may make on future cash flows.

*Commentary

*Some transactions (e.g. sale of an item or plant) may result in a gain or loss being included in profit or loss. However, such gains or losses are not cash flows. Actual cash flows relating to these transactions (e.g. disposal proceeds) are classified under investing activities.

© DeVry/Becker Educational Development Corp. All rights reserved.

2.2 Examples

Examples of cash inflows and outflows across the three activities are depicted in the table below.

TRANSACTIONS	CFO	CFI	CFF
Cash Flows From Operations			
1. Cash receipts from sale of goods/ rendering services	x		
2. Cash receipts from royalties, fees and commissions	x		
3. Cash payments to suppliers for goods/ services	x		
4. Cash payments to and on behalf of employees (e.g. pension contributions)	x		
Investing Cash Flows			
5. Payments to acquire/receipts from sales of property, plant and equipment, intangibles		x	
6. Payments to acquire/receipts from sales of shares, loan notes, etc of other entities		x	
7. Cash advances and loans made to other parties and repayments thereof		x	
Financing Cash Flows			
8. Cash proceeds from issuing shares			x
9. Cash proceeds from debentures, loans, notes, bonds, and other borrowings			x
10. Cash payments to owners to acquire or redeem own (i.e. the entity's) shares			x
11. Cash repayments of borrowings			x
Dividends and Interest*			
12. Interest paid			
• when recognised as an expense or capitalised (e.g. in the cost of constructing an asset)	x		
• when it is a cost of obtaining financial resources			x
13. Interest and dividends received			
• when taken into account of in the determination of profit or loss	x		
• when they are returns on investments		x	
14. Dividends paid			
• when they are a cost of obtaining financial resources			x
• when they assist users in determining the company's ability to pay dividends out of operating cash flow	x		

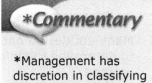

*Management has discretion in classifying cash flows as either CFO, CFI or CFF as appropriate.

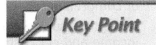

Cash flows from interest and dividends received and paid should be disclosed **separately** and classified **consistently** from one period to another.

© DeVry/Becker Educational Development Corp. All rights reserved.

2.3   Operating Activities

2.3.1   Direct Method

▨ Discloses major classes of gross cash receipts and gross cash payments.*

▨ Information is obtained either from accounting records or by adjusting sales, cost of sales for:

  • changes in inventories, operating receivables and payables during the period;

  • other non-cash items; and

  • other items for which cash effects are investing or financing cash flows.

Technique	Calculation
1. Cash receipts from customers.	Cash receipts from customers
2. Deduct cash paid to suppliers and employees.	– cash paid to suppliers – cash paid to employees
⊃ Cash generated from operations	⊃ Cash generated from operations
3. Payments for interest and income taxes.	– payments for interest – income taxes paid
⊃ Net cash from operating activities	⊃ Net cash from operating activities

*Commentary

*The direct method provides additional information that is useful in estimating future cash flows (which is not available under indirect method).

2.3.2   Advantages of the Direct Method

✔ Reporting the major classes of operating cash receipts and payments better reveals an entity's ability to generate sufficient cash from operations to pay debts, reinvest in operations and make distributions to owners. Thus it better fulfils information needs for decision-making purposes.*

✔ The format is simpler to understand.

2.3.3   Disadvantages of the Direct Method

✗ Many entities do not collect information that would allow them to determine the information necessary to prepare the direct method.

✗ It effectively presents statement of comprehensive income information on a cash basis rather than an accrual basis. This may suggest, incorrectly, that net cash flow from operations is a better measure of performance than profit per the statement of comprehensive income.

✗ It requires supplemental disclosure of a reconciliation of net income and net cash. (However, the incremental cost of providing the additional information disclosed in the direct method is not significant.)

2.3.4   Indirect Method

Adjusts profit or loss for effects of:

▨ non-cash transactions (e.g. depreciation);

▨ any deferrals or accruals of past or future operating cash receipts or payments; and

▨ items of income or expense associated with investing or financing cash flows.

*Commentary

*Being able to see cash paid is particularly important information to many users.

🔑 Key Point

Both methods give the same result.

The calculations for cash generated from operations are different, but both methods show line item deductions for interest payments and income taxes paid to determine net cash from operating activities.

© DeVry/Becker Educational Development Corp. All rights reserved.

Technique	Calculation
1. Start with profit before tax.	Profit before tax
2. Adjust for non-cash items, investing items, and financing items accounted for on the accruals basis (e.g. interest).	+ non-cash expenses/losses − non-cash income/gains
⮑ Operating profit before working capital changes	⮑ Operating profit before working capital changes
3. Make working capital changes.	+ increases (decreases) in operating liabilities (assets) − increases (decreases) in operating assets (liabilities)
⮑ Cash generated from operations	⮑ Cash generated from operations

2.3.5 Advantages of the Indirect Method

✔ It focuses on the difference between profit per the statement of comprehensive income and net cash flow from operations.

✔ It provides a useful link between cash flows, the statement of comprehensive income and the statement of financial position.*

2.4 Investing and Financing Activities

2.4.1 Separate Reporting

▨ Major classes of gross cash receipts and gross cash payments arising from investing and **financing activities** are reported separately.

2.4.2 Investing Activities

▨ Purchase of property plant and equipment—this must represent actual amounts *paid*. (Any trade-in/part-exchange will reduce amount paid.)

▨ Proceeds from sales of tangible assets (excludes trade-in allowance).

▨ Only expenditure that results in the recognition of an asset, capital expenditure, can be classified under **investing activities**.

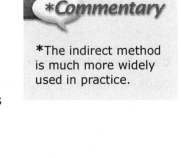

*Commentary

*The indirect method is much more widely used in practice.

Illustration 1 Trade-in

A new car is acquired at full list price of $50,000. $10,000 is allowed by way of part-exchange against the cost of the car when an old car is traded in.

Solution

Payment to acquire tangible asset	$40,000
Receipts from sale of tangible asset	Nil

© DeVry/Becker Educational Development Corp. All rights reserved.

2.4.3 Financing Activities

▓ Proceeds from issuance of share capital

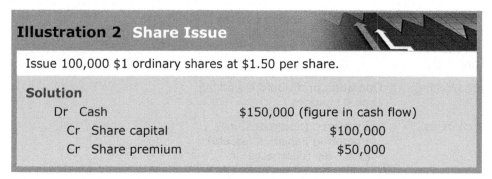

Illustration 2 Share Issue

Issue 100,000 $1 ordinary shares at $1.50 per share.

Solution

Dr Cash	$150,000 (figure in cash flow)
Cr Share capital	$100,000
Cr Share premium	$50,000

▓ Proceeds from long-term borrowings
▓ Dividends paid

3   Pro Forma

3.1   Direct Method

	$	$
Cash flows from operating activities		
Cash receipts from customers	x	
Cash paid to suppliers and employees	(x)	
Cash generated from operations (see next for alternative)	x	
Interest paid	(x)	
Income taxes paid	(x)	
Net cash from operating activities		x
Cash flows from investing activities		
Purchase of property, plant and equipment	(x)	
Proceeds from sale of equipment	x	
Interest received	x	
Dividends received	x	
Net cash used in investing activities		x
Cash flows from financing activities		
Proceeds from issuance of share capital	x	
Proceeds from long-term borrowings	x	
Dividends paid*	(x)	
Net cash used in financing activities		x
Net increase in cash and cash equivalents		x
Cash and cash equivalents at beginning of period		x
Cash and cash equivalents at end of period		x

> ****Commentary***
>
> *Dividends paid could be shown as an operating cash flow.

© DeVry/Becker Educational Development Corp. All rights reserved.

3.2   Indirect Method

	$
Cash flows from operating activities	
Profit before taxation	x
Adjustments for	
Depreciation	x
Investment income	(x)
Interest expense	x
Operating profit before working capital changes	x
Increase in trade and other receivables	(x)
Decrease in inventories	x
Decrease in trade payables	(x)
Cash generated from operations	x
...remainder as for the direct method	

3.3   Notes to the Statement of Cash Flows

Cash and cash equivalents

Cash and **cash equivalent**s consist of cash on hand and balances with banks and investments in money market instruments. Cash and cash equivalents included in the statement of cash flows comprise the following statement of financial position amounts.

	2018	2017
	$	$
Cash on hand and balances with banks	x	x
Short-term investments	x	x
	x	x

4   Group Statements of Cash Flows

4.1   Preparation

 **Key Point**

The group statement of cash flows is prepared from the consolidated financial statements and therefore reflects the cash flows of the group (i.e. the parent and its subsidiaries).

- The method of preparation is the same as for the individual company statement but additional cash flows may arise:
  - dividends paid to the *non-controlling interest*;
  - dividends received from *associates* (and other equity accounted entities);
  - cash consequences of acquisition or disposal of *subsidiaries*.

4.2   Non-controlling Interest

▨ Use a T account to calculate dividends paid to non-controlling interest.

Non-controlling Interest				
	$			**$**
		B/d —Non-controlling interest		x
% of foreign exchange losses	x	—Dividends payable		
Dividends paid to				
non-controlling interest (ß)	x	% of profit after tax		x
C/d —Non-controlling interest	x			
—Dividends payable	x	% of revaluation surplus		x
	x			x

4.3   Associates and Joint Ventures

▨ Use a T account to calculate dividends from associate/joint venture.

Investment in Associate/Joint Venture			
	$		**$**
B/d —Investment	x		
—Dividends debtor from A	x		
% of profit after tax	x		
Cost of new shares	x	Dividends received from A (ß)	x
	x	C/d —FA Investment	
	x	—Dividends debtor from A	x
	x		x

© DeVry/Becker Educational Development Corp. All rights reserved.

Example 1 Group Statement of Cash Flows

Extracts from group accounts

Statements of financial position

	2018	2017
	$000	**$000**
Investments		
Interests in associated undertakings	280	271
(share of net assets only)		
Current liabilities		
Dividends payable to members of parent	66	68
Dividends payable to non-controlling interest	5	7
Non-controlling interest	55	35

Statement of comprehensive income	**2018**
	$000
Income from interests in associate	29
Non-controlling interest	(43)
Statement of changes in equity	
Ordinary dividends	(98)

Required:

Show how the above would be reflected in the statement of cash flows of the company.

4.4 Acquisition and Disposal of a Subsidiary

- Show separately the cash flow arising on the acquisition or disposal as an investing activity.

- Disclose, as a summary, the effect of the acquisition or disposal, indicating how much of the consideration was cash.

© DeVry/Becker Educational Development Corp. All rights reserved.

Example 2 Marr Group Statement of Cash Flows (I)
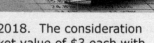

Marr acquired Corben for $22,224,000 during 2018. The consideration comprised 3,173,000 $0.25 shares with a market value of $3 each with the balance in cash.

The net assets of Corben on acquisition were as follows:

Statements of financial position

	$000
Tangible non-current assets	12,194
Inventories	9,385
Receivables	15,165
Cash at bank and in hand	1,439
Payables	(25,697)
Bank overdrafts	(6,955)
Non-controlling interest	(9)
	5,522

Required:

Show how the acquisition should be reflected in the group statement of cash flows and notes.

Each of the individual net assets of a subsidiary acquired/disposed of during the period must be excluded when comparing group statements of financial position for cash flow calculations. Their net cash effect is already dealt with (as purchase of subsidiary and net cash/overdraft acquired) in the statement.

- Subsidiary acquired in the period
  subtract inventory, receivables, payables, etc at date of acquisition from movement on these items when calculating the operating cash flow

- Subsidiary *sold* in the period
  add inventory, receivables, payables, etc at date of acquisition from movement on these items when calculating the operating cash flow

© DeVry/Becker Educational Development Corp. All rights reserved.

Example 3 Marr Group Statement of Cash Flows (II)

Continuing from *Example 2*, Marr, the following additional information is supplied.

The profit before tax of the Marr group for the year (including the post-acquisition profit of Corben) was $20,199,000. Depreciation for the year was $3,158,000. Plant and machinery with a carrying amount of $1,002,000 was disposed of for $1,052,000.

Extracts from consolidated statements of financial position		
	2018	2017
	$000	$000
Tangible non-current assets	160,064	148,518
Inventory	99,481	77,834
Receivables	42,874	25,264
Trade payables	80,326	48,939

Required:

Show how the above information would affect the statement of cash flows of the company.

Solution

Group statement of cash flows (extracts)

	$000	$000
Profit before tax		
Gain or loss on disposal		
Depreciation charges		
Increase in inventories		
Increase in receivables		
Increase in payables		
Net cash inflow from operating activities		
Capital expenditure		
Purchase of tangible fixed assets		
Sale of plant and machinery		
Acquisitions and disposals		
Purchase of subsidiary undertaking		
Net overdrafts acquired with subsidiary		

© DeVry/Becker Educational Development Corp. All rights reserved.

Illustration 3 Sale of a Subsidiary

Gita had held a 75% investment in Meena for many years. On 31 August 2018 it disposed of the investment in full for $1,000,000 cash.

Meena's statement of financial position at 31 August 2018 included:

	$000
Inventory	473
Receivables	520
Cash	100

Gita's year end is 31 December and the consolidated statement of financial position included:

	2018	2017
	$000	$000
Inventory	1,668	2,082
Receivables	4,041	4,876
Cash	392	183

Required:

Indicate how the disposal will affect the consolidated statement of cash flows of Gita for the year ended 31 December 2018.

Solution

Group statement of cash flows (extracts)

	$000
Profit before tax	x
Increase in inventories (1,668 + 473 − 2,082)	(59)
Decrease in receivables (4,041 + 520 − 4,876)	315
Net cash inflow from operating activities	x
Acquisitions and disposals	
Disposal of subsidiary undertaking	1,000
Net cash disposed of with subsidiary	(100)

Notes to the group statement of cash flows (extracts)

(x) Disposal of subsidiary undertaking

Net assets disposed of

	$000
Inventories	473
Receivables	520
Cash	100
Non-controlling interest	(x)
	x
Profit/(loss) on disposal	x/(x)
	1,000
Satisfied by	
Cash	1,000

© DeVry/Becker Educational Development Corp. All rights reserved.

5 Disclosures

- There are a number of disclosures which should be made in most cases to support the statement of cash flows. These are:
  - Analysis of cash and cash equivalents;
  - Major non-cash transactions;
  - Cash and cash equivalents held by the group;
  - Reporting futures, options and swaps;
  - Voluntary disclosures.

The first two of these are discussed briefly in this section.

5.1 Analysis of Cash and Cash Equivalents

- A note should be presented that reconciles amounts held as cash and cash equivalents at the start and end of the period.

Illustration 4	Reconciliation of Cash/Cash Equivalents		
Cash and cash equivalents			
	2018	**2017**	**Change**
	$	**$**	**$**
Cash on hand	—	1,300	(1,300)
Bank overdraft	(11,000)	—	(11,000)
	(11,000)	(1,300)	(12,300)

5.2 Major Non-cash Transactions

- Examples of such transactions include:
  - the issue of shares in order to acquire assets;
  - the conversion of debt to equity;
  - the inception of significant lease arrangements.
- In each case a brief description of the nature and purpose of the transaction should be given.

Key Point

Non-cash transactions should be excluded from the statement of cash flows. However some of these do have a major effect on investing and financing activities and should be disclosed in a note.

5.3 Liability disclosures

A recent amendment to IAS 7 requires entities to provide disclosures that enable users to evaluate changes in liabilities arising from financing activities. The disclosures should include changes arising from cash flow and non-cash flow changes.

The IASB did not prescribe the format of the disclosure but does indicate that the disclosure may be achieved by providing a reconciliation between opening and closing liability balances.

© DeVry/Becker Educational Development Corp. All rights reserved.

6   Interpretation of Statements of Cash Flows

6.1   Information Provided

■ Statements of cash flows are a vital source of information about an entity's financial health.

■ The statement of cash flows can be used to obtain information about an entity's:

- Liquidity (ability to service short term obligations);
- Solvency (ability to continue in business over the longer term);
- Financial adaptability (ability to meet cash demands and take advantage of new future opportunities).

■ The user of cash flow information should be able to break the statement down and consider the effect of the following:

- Unusual or discretionary cash flows;
- Non-cash changes.

> **Key Point**
>
> The statement of cash flows should be read in conjunction with the other primary statements. None of these statements in isolation is sufficient.

Illustration 5   Statement of Cash Flows

Cash flows from operating activities	$	
Net profit before taxation	14,400	
Adjustments for:		
Depreciation	4,000	
Profit on sale of equipment	(100)	
Interest expense	1,000	
Operating profit before working capital charges	19,300	
Increase in trade and other receivables	(7,250)	
Increase in inventories	(5,000)	
Decrease in trade payables	(3,000)	
Cash generated from operations	4,050	
Interest paid	(500)	
Income taxes paid	(1,200)	
Net cash from operating activities		2,350
Cash flows from investing activities		
Purchase of property, plant and equipment	(11,000)	
Proceeds from sale of equipment	350	
Net cash used in investing activities		(10,650)
Cash flows from financing activities		
Repayment of long term borrowings	(4,000)	
Net cash used in financing activities		(4,000)
Net decrease in cash and cash equivalents		(12,300)
Cash and cash equivalents at beginning of period		1,300
Cash and cash equivalents at end of period		(11,000)

                    © DeVry/Becker Educational Development Corp. All rights reserved.

6.2   Comments on *Illustration 5*

▨ Overall decrease in cash and cash equivalents of ($12,300) looks poor, but this figure needs further analysis using the rest of the statement as follows:

- Cash from operations $4,050 is reasonably strong; however, this is only 28% of profit before taxation ($14,400).

- Low "quality" of profits can be ascribed to significant increases in working capital (e.g. inventories and receivables). The reasons for this need investigating.

- Unusual or one-off cash flows include $11,000 to purchase new property and plant. This could represent the replacement of old assets or the acquisition of new ones as part of an expansion. A similar large cash outflow may not be anticipated next year.

- The repayment of long term borrowings ($4,000) has improved the solvency of the business and will reduce interest payments in future years.

- In conclusion, with tight working capital management and fewer one-off outflows next year, the cash flow position should improve. However the large cash outflow this year presents management with an immediate liquidity problem (overdraft $11,000) which will need to be monitored carefully.

© DeVry/Becker Educational Development Corp. All rights reserved.

Summary

- A statement of cash flows shows that profits are being realised, that there is enough cash to pay dividends and identifies the need for finance for future investments.
- Historical cash flow information may provide an indicator of the amount, timing and certainty of future cash flows.
- IASB encourages, but does not require, the direct method.
- Investing cash flows focus mainly on cash flows relating to non-current assets.
- Financing cash flows focus mainly on the issue and redemption of capital, both equity and debt.
- The group statement of cash flows is prepared from the consolidated financial statements and therefore reflects the cash flows of the group.
- Cash flow on acquisition or disposal of a subsidiary should take into account the cash and cash equivalent balances of the subsidiary on acquisition or disposal.
- Non-cash transactions are excluded from the statement of cash flows but those that have a major effect on investing and financing activities should be disclosed in a note.
- The statement should be read in conjunction with the other primary statements. None of these statements in isolation is sufficient.

 ## Session 23 Quiz
Estimated time: 15 minutes

1. Define cash equivalents. (1.4)
2. When calculating cash flows from operations using the indirect method, state which profit line is normally taken as the starting point. (2.3.4)
3. Give the advantages of using the indirect method of presenting cash flows. (2.3.5)
4. Identify the subtotal line used in both methods of cash flow calculations. (2.2)
5. List additional cash flows which may appear in a consolidated statement of cash flows that would not appear in a single entity statement. (4.1)
6. Name the types of cash flows included in calculating cash paid to acquire a subsidiary. (4.4)

 ## Study Question Bank
Estimated time: 50 minutes

Priority		Estimated Time	Completed
Q38	Ladway	50 minutes	
Additional			
Q39	Lovey		

© DeVry/Becker Educational Development Corp. All rights reserved.

EXAMPLE SOLUTIONS

Solution 1—Group Statement of Cash Flows

Group statement of cash flows (extracts)

	$000
Dividends from associate	20
Dividends paid to non-controlling shareholders in subsidiary undertaking (W2)	(25)
Equity dividends paid (W3)	(100)

Workings

(1)

Investment in Associate

	$000		$000
B/d	271	Dividends received from A (β)	20
Share of profit	29	C/d	280
	300		300

(2)

Non-controlling Interest

	$000		$000
Dividends paid (β)	25	B/d (7 + 35)	42
C/d (5 + 55)	60	Profit or loss	43
	85		85

(3)

Dividends

	$000		$000
Dividends paid to group (β)	100	B/d	68
C/d	60	Final dividend (declared)	98
	166		166

© DeVry/Becker Educational Development Corp. All rights reserved.

Solution 2—Marr Group Statement of Cash Flows (I)

Group statement of cash flows (extracts)

	$000
Acquisitions and disposals	
Purchase of subsidiary	(12,705)
Net overdrafts acquired with subsidiary	
(6,955 − 1,439)	(5,516)

Notes to the group statement of cash flows (extracts)

(1) Purchase of subsidiary undertakings

	$000
Net assets acquired	
Tangible fixed assets	12,194
Inventories	9,385
Receivables	15,165
Cash at bank and in hand	1,439
Creditors	(25,697)
Bank overdrafts	(6,955)
Non-controlling interest	(9)
	5,522
Goodwill (β)	16,702
	22,224
Satisfied by	
Shares allotted (3,173 × 3)	9,519
Cash (β)	12,705
	22,224

The subsidiary acquired during the year contributed $x to the group's net operating cash flows, paid $x in respect of net returns on investments and servicing of finance, paid $x in respect of taxation and utilised $x for capital expenditure.

© DeVry/Becker Educational Development Corp. All rights reserved.

Solution 3—Marr Group Statement of Cash Flows (II)

Group statement of cash flows (extracts)

	$000	$000
Profit before tax		20,199
Gain or loss on disposal (1,052 − 1,002)		(50)
Depreciation charges		3,158
Increase in inventories (99,481 − (77,834 + 9,385))		(12,262)
Increase in receivables (42,874 − (25,264 + 15,165))		(2,445)
Increase in payables (80,326 − (48,939 + 25,697))		5,690
Net cash inflow from operating activities		14,290
Capital expenditure		
Purchase of tangible fixed assets	(3,512)	
Sale of plant and machinery	1,052	
		(2,460)
Acquisitions and disposals		
Purchase of subsidiary undertaking	(12,705)	
Net overdrafts acquired with subsidiary	(5,516)	
		(18,221)

Working

<table>
<tr><th colspan="4">Non-current Assets</th></tr>
<tr><th></th><th>$</th><th></th><th>$</th></tr>
<tr><td>B/d</td><td>148,518</td><td>Depreciation</td><td>3,158</td></tr>
<tr><td>Subsidiary acquired</td><td>12,194</td><td>Disposals</td><td>1,002</td></tr>
<tr><td>Additions (β)</td><td>3,512</td><td>C/d</td><td>160,064</td></tr>
<tr><td></td><td>164,224</td><td></td><td>164,224</td></tr>
</table>

© DeVry/Becker Educational Development Corp. All rights reserved.

Analysis and Interpretation

FOCUS

This session covers the following content from the *ACCA Study Guide.*

C. Reporting the Financial Performance of Entities

1. Performance reporting

a) Prepare reports relating to corporate performance for external stakeholders. ☐

G. The Appraisal of Financial Performance and Position of Entities

2. Analysis and interpretation of financial information and measurement of performance

a) Select and calculate relevant indicators of financial and non-financial performance. ☐

b) Identify and evaluate significant features and issues in financial statements. ☐

c) Highlight inconsistencies in financial information through analysis and application of knowledge. ☐

d) Make inferences from the analysis of information taking into account the limitation of the information, the analytical methods used and the business environment in which the entity operates. ☐

Session 24 Guidance

■ **Revise** users of financial statements and understand their information needs (s.2).

■ **Understand** the limitations on the use ratios in interpreting financial statements (s.2).

■ **Calculate** the primary ratios and be able to discuss the implications of these ratios and how they may influence the results of an entity going forward.

VISUAL OVERVIEW

Objective: To describe the need for analysis of financial statements and the approach to interpreting financial information as well as to explain the purpose and calculation of earnings per share.

USERS AND USER FOCUS

- Introduction
- Investors
- Employees
- Lenders
- Suppliers
- Customers
- Government
- Public

INTERPRETATION OF FINANCIAL STATEMENTS

- Financial Statements
- Ratios
- Limitations
- Influences
- Accounting Policies
- Business Factors
- Performance Indicators
- Other Indicators
- Trend Analysis
- Interpretation Technique

EARNINGS PER SHARE

- Evaluating Equity Instruments
- Earnings
- Basic EPS
- Diluted EPS

CREATIVE ACCOUNTING

- Meaning
- Examples
- Accounting Policies

Session 24 Guidance

■ **Understand** the effects of creative accounting (s.3) and the impact it can have on the financial statements

■ **Understand** the dilutive and anti-dilutive (also called non-dilutive) effect of potential shares and options (s.4).

© DeVry/Becker Educational Development Corp. All rights reserved.

1 Users and User Focus

Key Point

The objective of financial reporting is to provide information about an entity to external users of its financial statements. The needs of users are central to financial reporting principles.

1.1 Introduction

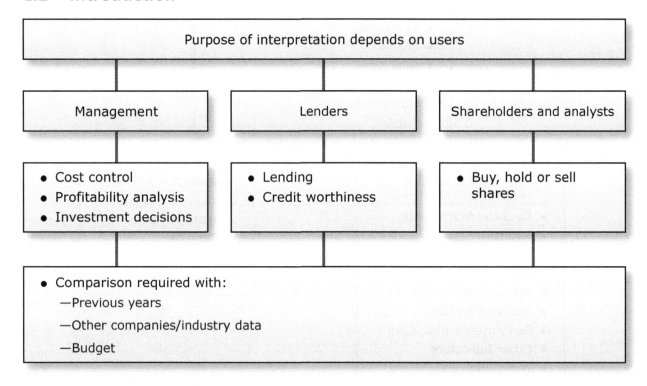

1.2 Investors

▨ The providers of risk capital and their advisers are concerned with risk inherent in, and return provided by, their investment. They need information:

- to help them determine whether they should buy, hold or sell; and
- that enables them to assess the performance of management.

▨ The aspect of the performance that will be of interest to the investor, and the type of analysis performed to provide the basis for decision-making depends on the nature of the investor and/or the size of the holding (potential holding).

                 © DeVry/Becker Educational Development Corp. All rights reserved.

1.2.1 Potential Takeover Bidder

Aspects of business performance of concern

- Value of business on basis of earnings and assets.
- Disposal value of assets in contrast with carrying amount.
- Financial and dividend policy and availability of cash.

Analysis

- Several years' accounts with particular reference to:
  - profits including any one-off or other unusual items;
  - return on capital with reference to separate divisions where possible;
  - indications of true asset values; and
  - liquid assets.

1.2.2 Potential Small Investor

Aspects of business performance of concern

- Possible enrichment by capital gain and/or dividends.
- May wish for "safe" investment or be prepared to accept "risk" for higher returns.

Analysis

- Several years' accounts with particular reference to:
  - trend of sales, costs and earnings;
  - dividend record; and
  - dividend cover.

1.2.3 Potential Institutional Investor

Aspect of business performance of concern

- Good growth prospects coupled with financial stability.

Analysis

- Several years' accounts, paying particular attention to trends in:
  - sales, costs and profits;
  - dividend record; and
  - dividend cover.
- Attention will also be paid to:
  - maintenance of adequate liquid funds;
  - general control over net current assets; and
  - gearing.
- This analysis will be carried out by experienced investment analysts.

1.3 Employees

- Employees and their representative groups are interested in information:
  - about the stability and profitability of their employers; and
  - that enables them to assess the ability of the entity to provide remuneration, retirement benefits and employment opportunities.

Aspect of business performance of concern

- Relative movements in wage levels, profits and dividends.

Analysis

- Where there is a profit sharing scheme, the level of profits. Interest is generally limited to profit or loss, although this may not give enough information.
- Controversy exists as to the extent to which employees and/ or their representatives should receive financial information above and beyond the financial statements.

1.4 Lenders

- Lenders are interested in information that enables them to determine whether their loans, and the interest attached to them, will be paid when due.

Aspect of business performance of concern

- Sufficiency of cash flow to repay and adequacy of security.

Analysis

- Will be more concerned with management accounts and budgeted cash flows.
- Published accounts will indicate:
  - adequacy of profit levels; and
  - creation of other charges.
- Despite the fact that published accounts may be a year or more out of date, debenture holders will look at:
  - the extent to which interest is covered by profits; and
  - the priority of repayment and likely adequacy of security in the event of liquidation.

1.5 Suppliers and Other Creditors

- Suppliers and other creditors are interested in information that enables them to determine whether amounts owed to them will be paid when due.*
- Trade creditors are likely to be interested in an entity over a shorter period than lenders unless they are dependent upon the continuation of the entity as a major customer.

Aspect of business performance of concern

- Ability to pay for credit purchases on due date.

Analysis

- Net current assets.
- Make-up of net current assets.
- Priority of payment on possible liquidation.
- Earnings and growth record.

*Commentary

*The financial statements may be used by specialist credit agencies on behalf of suppliers at large.

© DeVry/Becker Educational Development Corp. All rights reserved.

1.6   Customers

▨ Customers have an interest in information about the continuation of an entity, especially when they have a long-term involvement with, or are dependent on, the entity.

1.7   Government and Their Agencies

▨ Governments and their agencies are interested in the allocation of resources, and therefore the activities of the entity.

▨ They also require information in order to regulate the activities of entities, determine taxation policies and provide a basis for national income and similar statistics.

1.8   Public

▨ Entities affect members of the public in a variety of ways. For example, an entity may make a substantial contribution to the local economy in many ways, including the number of people they employ and their patronage of the suppliers. Financial statements may assist the public by providing information about the trends and recent developments in the prosperity of the entity and the range of its activities.

2   Interpretation of Financial Statements

2.1   Financial Statements

▨ Clearly, financial statements can be analysed, quite separately from the analysis and interpretation of ratios, as they provide information about profitability, liquidity and cash flows.

▨ It is important to look at the statements as a whole, as they are inter-related, rather than individual statements in isolation. For example, the tax expense in profit or loss needs to be considered alongside the tax paid in the cash flow statement.

2.1.1   Statement of Financial Position

▨ What is the net asset position? An excess of liabilities over assets would strongly suggest liquidity problems.

▨ How do non-current liabilities compare to equity? This will give a rough idea of the level of gearing before making a more precise calculation.

▨ Are assets owned or are they leased? Excessive reliance on leased assets may mean that the entity does not have much collateral if looking to raise further debt finance.

▨ Is there a positive cash balance or a bank overdraft? Are there any cash equivalents?

2.1.2 Statement of Profit or Loss and Other Comprehensive Income

▣ The most obvious amount to note is the profit for the period; an entity cannot continue in business long if it is making losses.

▣ Compare gross profit to profit for the period, to get an idea of the overheads and other expenses that the entity has to meet.

▣ Look at finance costs; they can give an idea of the level of gearing from the profit perspective.

▣ Does the entity revalue certain classes of assets? This should be apparent if gains and losses are reported in other comprehensive income.

▣ The tax expense can give an idea of whether or not the entity is taking advantage of tax reliefs.

2.1.3 Statement of Changes in Equity

▣ Has a dividend been paid in the period? Is it more than adequately covered by profit for the period? Ideally a company should not be distributing all profits to shareholders, as some funds should be kept for reinvestment.

▣ Has cash been injected through a share issued? This could be for a planned expansion programme.

2.1.4 Statement of Cash Flows*

▣ An entity cannot stay in operational existence with negative operating cash flows for too long. This statement will show how operating profits have materialised as operating cash flows. These cash flows need to be sufficient to pay tax, interest and dividends.

▣ Investing cash flows will show whether the entity is replacing assets or buying additional assets as part of an expansion programme.

▣ Financing cash flows should show the amount for payments of lease liabilities. An increase in these should be reflected in an increase in non-current assets in the statement of financial position.

***Commentary**

*It is more difficult to manipulate cash flows than profit, so this statement provides very important information.

2.1.5 Notes to the Financial Statements

▣ The notes to the financial statements also provide a huge volume of information that assists in analysis and interpretation. For example:

  ● The first disclosure note is usually the entity's accounting policies;

  ● Reconciliations of movements (e.g. tangible non-current assets and provisions);

  ● Timing of expected cash flows (e.g. for lease liabilities);

  ● Information will be analysed into reportable segments (where relevant);

  ● Extensive disclosure about how the entity is managing its exposure to risks.

                    © DeVry/Becker Educational Development Corp. All rights reserved.

2.2   Use of Ratios

▨ Ratios are of no use in isolation. To be useful, a basis is needed for comparison, for example:

- previous years;
- other companies;
- industry averages; or
- budgeted v actual (for management use).

2.3   Limitations of Ratios

✗ Comparisons of ratios between entities can be very difficult:

- Ratios may be distorted by differences in accounting policies and also by the use of creative accounting techniques.
- Comparisons between different types of business are difficult because of differing structures and market characteristics.

✗ Ratios use historical data which may not be predictive, as this ignores future actions by management and changes in the business environment.

✗ The environment within which the business is operating may change. If the business environment or the rate of inflation changes, then performance over time using ratio analysis may be distorted.

✗ The ratios are based on an information set (i.e. financial statements) which may be flawed or incomplete:

- Creative accounting can hide the true situation.
- Currently, entities must still leave certain assets and liabilities off the statement of financial position.*

2.4   Influences on Ratios

▨ The "story" of the performance and position told by a set of financial statements is a function of:

- business factors (including the results of management actions); and
- accounting policies.

▨ Users will be interested in the business factors (i.e. the underlying performance of the entity).

▨ Users need to understand the effects that accounting policy can have on reported figures. This understanding will then allow the user of the accounts to adjust or rebase figures, as necessary, onto a basis which is consistent for the comparison being undertaken.

▨ In analysing sets of financial statements, the following are important:

- changes of accounting policy; and
- creative accounting techniques.

▨ The project which produced the core set of standards adopted by IOSCO removed many areas of choice in financial reporting. This enhances comparability and makes the use of creative accounting more difficult.

▨ The improvements project, whereby the IASB revised a large number of standards in December 2003, also removed areas of choice in financial reporting.*

Key Point

Ratios are a tool to assist analysis. They focus attention on trends and weaknesses and facilitate comparison over time and between companies.

***Commentary**

*For example, internally-generated brands and contingent liabilities.

***Commentary**

*Choice does still exist; a company can choose to measure property, plant and equipment using the cost model or the revaluation model.

© DeVry/Becker Educational Development Corp. All rights reserved.

2.5   Accounting Policies

▨ Choice of accounting policies can significantly affect the view presented by the accounts, and the ratios computed, without affecting the business's core ability to generate profits and cash. For example:

● Revaluations v historical cost.

▨ If a business revalues its assets rather than carrying them at historical cost, this will usually increase capital employed and reduce profit before tax (due to higher depreciation). Thus, return on capital employed (ROCE), profit margins and gearing are all likely to be lower if a business revalues its assets.

2.6   Business Factors

▨ Ratios may change over time or differ between companies because of the nature of the business, or management actions in running the business. Such factors include:

● **The type of business (e.g. retailer v manufacturer):** This affects the nature of the assets employed and the returns earned (e.g. a retailer may have higher asset turnover but lower margins than a manufacturer).

● **The quality of management:** Better-managed businesses are likely to be more profitable and have better working capital management than businesses where management is weak.

● **The state of economy and market conditions:** If a market or the economy in general is depressed, this is likely to adversely affect companies and make most or all of their ratios appear worse.

● **Management actions:** These will be reflected in changes in ratios. For example, price discounting to increase market share is likely to reduce margins but increase asset turnover; withdrawing from unprofitable market sectors is likely to reduce turnover but increase profit margins.

● **Changes in the business:** If the business diversifies into wholly new areas, this is likely to change the resource structure and thus affect key ratios. A new acquisition near the year end will mean that capital employed will include all the assets acquired, but profits of the new acquisition will only be included in the statement of comprehensive income for a small part of the year, thus tending to depress ROCE.

                    © DeVry/Becker Educational Development Corp. All rights reserved.

2.7   Performance Indicators

■ Performance can be measured based on financial information or non-financial information. Since the 1980s the use of non-financial performance indicators (NFPIs) has become far more prevalent.

■ Traditional financial measures have been shown to be weak and unreliable as they tend to focus on "the bottom line" of profit without taking into account other possible indicators that may well drive the success of a business.

■ Financial performance indicators by their nature are derived from the financial statements. The amounts included in those statements are based on an entity's accounting policies that can be very subjective and open to abuse.*

■ NFPIs are now used in conjunction with financial measures to give a more rounded picture of how a business is performing.

*Commentary

*See discussion in
Session 5 (s.6).

2.7.1   Non-financial Performance Indicators

■ Although financial performance indicators may be a measure of success, they do not ensure success. In contrast, NFPIs can be used to drive a business forward in the long run. NFPIs can be used to measure, for example:

- Quality
- Delivery
- Customer satisfaction
- After sales service
- Employee satisfaction.

■ Examples of NFPIs include:

- *Staff turnover* (i.e. the rate at which employees leave each year)—higher turnover might indicate poor employee morale, which can lead to low-quality products.

- *Repeat custom* (e.g. the percentages of returning customers)—a high percentage indicates satisfaction with the product and customer service provided.

- *Product returns*—a lower percentage of returns may indicate a high-quality product and, again, satisfaction with the customer service.

- *Number of complaints*—although this should be as low as possible, any measure (absolute or relative) will not take into account those customers who do not complain.

■ Advantages of NFPIs include the following:

✔ They are usually easier to calculate than financial reports, so they can be provided much more quickly.

✔ Flexibility—organisations can come up with any measures that are appropriate to their objectives.

✔ They are less easily manipulated than financial measures.

© DeVry/Becker Educational Development Corp. All rights reserved.

▦ However, placing too much emphasis on NFPIs also has disadvantages:

✗ Ignoring financial performance entirely is clearly not appropriate when the objective of an organisation is to maximise the wealth of its shareholders.

✗ Developing too many NFPIs, some of which are likely to conflict, can be confusing for managers who are trying to achieve the measures.*

✗ It is difficult to make good decisions based on qualitative data alone.

*And result in a lack of goal congruence.

Illustration 1 Performance Measures About Employment

A wide range of measures can be used to measure aspects of employment, such as knowledge and skills, attitude and morale.

Knowledge and skills
- Number of staff with relevant qualifications (e.g. number of qualified ACCA staff in the finance function).
- Number of days training per year provided to employees.
- Total number of years' experience of all staff.

Attitude
- Rankings from customer feedback forms.
- Absentee records (number of days off work due to sickness per year).
- Punctuality records.
- Rankings from colleagues and managers.

Morale
- Staff turnover.
- Confidential staff surveys conducted by independent third parties.

2.7.2 Financial Performance Indicators

▦ These ratios can be broken down into four broad categories: profitability, liquidity (short- and long-term), efficiency (or turnover) and investment-based ratios.

✗ These ratios can be calculated using the financial information but their interpretation can be quite subjective when there is no universally accepted basis of the calculation.

✗ As they are calculated on historical information, great care must be taken in trying to make predictions of future performance.

✗ As they are based on financial information, they are capable of being manipulated depending on an entity's accounting policies.

The calculation of traditional accounting ratios is assumed knowledge from F7.

© DeVry/Becker Educational Development Corp. All rights reserved.

▓ Examples of financial performance measures include:

- *Return on capital employed (ROCE)*—the ratio of profit to capital, both equity and debt, employed in the business. It is the primary measure of profitability. It can be analysed into two ratios—profit margin and asset turnover.

- *Gearing*—a measure of the level of debt to equity capital. The more debt capital a business has then the higher its gearing. High gearing alone is not a "bad" thing: More highly geared companies face more business risk, especially in a fluctuating economy.

- *Receivable days*—a measure of the time it takes for customers to settle their debts. The shorter this time period the more quickly a business collects cash. Selling goods on credit effectively gives customers an interest-free loan; the seller clearly would be better off with the cash in its bank account.

- *Price earnings ratio (P/E)*—the ratio of market price per share to earnings (profit) per share. This multiple can be quite difficult to interpret. If market price is rising the ratio will increase; but falling profit will also lead to a higher ratio (if the market has not yet factored low profits into the market price).

2.8   Other Indicators

▓ Ratios are a key tool of analysis, but other sources of information are also available.

- Absolute comparisons can provide information without computing ratios. For example, comparing the current statement of financial position with the prior year may show that new shares have been issued to repay borrowings or finance new investment, which may in turn affect gearing and ROCE.

- Background information supplied about the nature of the business may help to explain changes or trends (e.g. if the business has made an acquisition).

- The statement of cash flows provides information as to how a business has generated and used cash so that users can obtain a fuller picture of liquidity and financial adaptability.

- What is the staff turnover like within a business? A high turnover would indicate that employees are not happy there and that can have a major effect on the performance of the entity. It will also be costly having to continually recruit new staff.

© DeVry/Becker Educational Development Corp. All rights reserved.

2.9 Trend Analysis

2.9.1 Introduction

▨ Financial statements provide information, which can be used to assess the performance of an entity over time. The picture given may be affected by inflation.

▨ There are two possible methods of dealing with this problem:

(1) Use specific cost and price indices; or

(2) Use a general price index.

2.9.2 Specific Cost and Price Indices

▨ This is difficult to apply in practice as it involves the generation of a completely new set of accounts for past periods at each year end.

▨ This may lead to fluctuations in profits that could be difficult to interpret.

2.9.3 General Price Indices

▨ This method focuses on financial changes.

▨ It is easier to apply because the information is readily available and involves a single inflation index rather than a combination of specific rates.

2.10 Interpretation Technique

▨ If asked to interpret accounts:

- make comments pertinent to the *user*; identify the audience from the requirement;
- only compute ratios that can be used (and always define ratios calculated);
- make comparisons and suggest reasons;
- also compare absolute numbers to identify differences (e.g. changes year-on-year);
- look for influence of business factors and accounting policies;
- be able to link different pieces of information and see what they point towards;
- indicate any need for further information; and
- be aware of limitations of ratios.

▨ Most marks in the exam are likely to be for specific, relevant comments rather than solely for computations.

▨ If asked to write a report, put a table of ratios in an appendix and refer to them in the text as appropriate.

▨ Use the requirement to structure your report/answer. If the requirement asks for a report on the profitability and liquidity of two entities, your headings should include:

Profitability		Liquidity
Entity A	AND	Entity A
Entity B		Entity B

▨ Use short, punchy sentences.

© DeVry/Becker Educational Development Corp. All rights reserved.

3 Creative Accounting

3.1 Meaning

 **Key Point**

Creative accounting means choosing an accounting treatment to allow the accounts to show a desired picture. The treatment chosen will probably not reflect the true substance of the transaction.

▧ Accounting policies can significantly affect the view presented by accounts, and ratios computed, without affecting the core ability of a business to generate profits and cash.

3.2 Examples

Effect	EPS	ROCE	Gearing
Revaluation of non-current assets v inclusion at historical cost	Reduced	Reduced	Reduced
Apply foreign currency hedging provisions (where presentation currency depreciates against foreign currency)	Increased	Reduced	Reduced

3.3 Accounting Policies

▧ Potential impact is especially important where:
- ● accounting standards permit a choice;
- ● judgement is needed in making accounting estimates; or
- ● there is no accounting standard.

▧ Examples include:

Accounting standard	Choice	Judgement
IAS 2	Method of inventory valuation	
IAS 16	Method of depreciation	
IAS 38		Development criteria met?

© DeVry/Becker Educational Development Corp. All rights reserved.

4 Earnings Per Share (EPS)

4.1 Evaluating Equity Investments

- Investors, potential investors and analysts examine earnings generated for shareholders to determine, for example, whether an investment is worthwhile and whether a share price accurately reflects the value of the company.

- Generally, earnings represent the profit made for particular period and should be examined in context. For example, negative earnings in a small or rapidly growing company does not mean that the company has no value.

- When large companies recognised on a stock market experience a fall in reported earnings, their share price will also fall.

- Expectations regarding future earnings have a significant effect on share prices. For example, companies with negative earnings may maintain high stock prices if investors and the market believe in its future profitability. If, however, investors and the market do not have a positive attitude towards a company, its share price may decrease regardless of positive earnings.

- Earnings are often viewed as a basis for analysing a company's "health". They also:
  - indicate whether the company will be able to pay dividends; and
  - signify the potential for company growth by capital appreciation.

- IAS 33 *Earnings per Share* sets out the principles for determining and presenting earnings per share to improve comparability between:
  - different entities in the same reporting period; and
  - the same entity in different reporting periods.

- Every company that falls within the scope of IAS 33 is required to calculate and present "Basic EPS". Those companies that have potential ordinary shares (see later) must also calculate and present "Diluted EPS".

 **Key Point**

Basic EPS is calculated by dividing the profit or loss for the period attributable to ordinary shareholders by the weighted average number of ordinary shares outstanding during the period.

© DeVry/Becker Educational Development Corp. All rights reserved.

4.2   Earnings

▨ Basic EPS should be based on the consolidated profit or loss for the period attributable to ordinary shareholders. This is the consolidated profit after tax after allowing for any non-controlling interest.

▨ The aim is to use that part of the total profit that is left for the equity shareholders after all other claims on profit have been accounted for.

4.3   Basic EPS

▨ The number of ordinary shares should be the weighted average number of ordinary shares outstanding during the period.*

4.3.1   Issues for Consideration

▨ The number in existence at the beginning of the period is adjusted for shares that have been issued for consideration during the period. These issues are described as issues at full market price.

▨ Consideration may be received in a number of ways:

- ◦ issue for cash;
- ◦ issue to acquire a controlling interest in another entity; or
- ◦ redemption of debt.

▨ In each case, the earnings will be boosted from the date of issue. To ensure consistency (i.e. matching of like with like) in the numerator and denominator of the basic EPS calculation, the shares are also included from the date of issue.

▨ The number of shares is therefore weighted.

4.3.2   Issues of Shares Where No Consideration Is Received

▨ The weighted average number of ordinary shares outstanding during the period and for all periods presented is adjusted for events that have changed the number of ordinary shares outstanding, without a corresponding change in resources. For example:

- ◦ bonus issues;
- ◦ bonus elements in another issue (e.g. a rights issue);
- ◦ share splits; or
- ◦ reverse share splits.

▨ Bonus issues:

- ◦ Treat as if the new shares have been in issue for the whole of the period.
- ◦ Multiply the number of shares in issue by the bonus fraction.
- ◦ The EPS will fall (all other things being equal), because the earnings are being spread over a larger number of shares. This would mislead users when they compare this year's figure to those from previous periods.
- ◦ The comparative figure and any other figures from earlier periods which are being used in an analysis must be adjusted. This is done by multiplying the comparative EPS by the *reciprocal* of the bonus fraction.

Commentary

*IAS 33 focuses on determining the weighted average number of ordinary shares outstanding during the period. This denominator in the calculation of EPS is assumed knowledge from F7.

© DeVry/Becker Educational Development Corp. All rights reserved.

4.3.3 Rights Issues

▓ A rights issue has features in common with a bonus issue *and* with an issue at full market price. A rights issue gives a shareholder the right to buy shares from the company at a price set below the market value. Thus:

   - the company will receive a consideration which is available to boost earnings (i.e. like an issue at full price); and
   - the shareholder receives part of the shares for no consideration (i.e. like a bonus issue).

▓ The method of calculating the number of shares in periods when there has been a rights issue reflects this.

▓ A bonus fraction is applied to the number of shares in issue before the date of the rights issue and the new shares issued are prorated as for issues for consideration.

▓ For presentation purposes, the comparative figure for EPS is restated to account for the bonus element of the issue (to ensure consistency). This is achieved by multiplying last year's EPS by the reciprocal of the rights issue bonus fraction.

4.4 Diluted EPS

4.4.1 Purpose

 **Key Point**

Diluted EPS is calculated as a warning to existing shareholders that the EPS in the future may fall.

▓ Potential ordinary shares, whose owners may become shareholders in the future, may currently exist (i.e. holders of share options).

▓ If these parties become equity shareholders the earnings will be spread over a larger number of shares (i.e. they will become *diluted*).

▓ Potential ordinary shares should be treated as dilutive **only** if their conversion to ordinary shares would decrease profit per share *from continuing ordinary operations*.

© DeVry/Becker Educational Development Corp. All rights reserved.

4.4.2 New Number of Ordinary Shares

▨ This is the weighted average number of ordinary shares used in the basic EPS calculation, plus the weighted average number of ordinary shares, which would be issued on the conversion of all the dilutive potential ordinary shares into ordinary shares.

▨ Dilutive potential ordinary shares should be deemed to have been converted into ordinary shares at the beginning of the period, or if later, the date of the issue of the potential ordinary shares (i.e. potential shares should be treated as shares when issued).

▨ New number of shares

Basic number   x

No of shares which could rank in the future:
    from the later of
    – 1st day of accounting period
    – date of issue   <u>x</u>

                                                                       <u>x</u>

4.4.3 New Earnings Figure

▨ The amount of profit or loss for the period attributable to ordinary shareholders, used in the basic EPS calculation, should be adjusted by the after-tax effect of the potential ordinary shares becoming ordinary shares. This means adding back:

  ● any dividends on dilutive potential ordinary shares which have been deducted in arriving at the profit or loss for the period attributed to ordinary shareholders;

  ● interest after tax recognised in the period for the dilutive potential ordinary shares; and

  ● any other changes in income or expense that would result from the conversion of the dilutive potential ordinary shares.

4.4.4 Further Adjustment

▨ When there has been an actual conversion of the dilutive potential ordinary shares into ordinary shares in the period, a further adjustment has to be made.

▨ The new shares will have been included in the basic EPS from the date of conversion. These shares must then be included in the diluted EPS calculation up to the date of conversion.

4.4.5 Options

- An entity should assume the exercise of dilutive options and other dilutive potential ordinary shares of the entity.
  - The assumed proceeds from these issues should be considered to be received from the issue of shares at fair value.
  - The difference between the number of shares issued and the number of shares that would have been issued at fair value should be treated as an issue of ordinary shares for no consideration.*
- Options will be dilutive **only** when they result in the entity issuing shares at below fair value.
- Each issue of shares under an option is deemed to consist of two elements:
  (1) A contract to issue a number of shares at a fair value (this is taken to be the average fair value during the period).
     - These are *non-dilutive*.
  (2) A contract to issue the remaining ordinary shares granted under the option for no consideration (a bonus issue).
     - These are *dilutive*.

*The number of shares calculated to have been issued for no consideration is the bonus element of the share options.

Illustration 2 Dilutive Options

An entity has 200,000 options in issue with an exercise price of $4. The average fair value of the shares during the period was $5.

Proceeds on exercise = $800,000

Number of shares if proceeds received by issuing at average fair value = $800,000 ÷ $5 = 160,000 shares

Bonus element = 200,000 − 160,000 = 40,000. This is added to the basic EPS share figure.

Options − (options x $\frac{Exprice}{AvgFV}$) = 200,000 − (200,000 x $\frac{4}{5}$) = 40,000

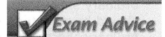

Calculations are examined at F7, not at P2. This illustration is provided to explain the dilutive effect of options with numbers.

                     © DeVry/Becker Educational Development Corp. All rights reserved.

5   Reports on Corporate Performance

5.1   Corporate Performance

- Corporate performance is generally assessed by the profit or loss that has been made in a period, including items recognised in other comprehensive income.*

- That profit or loss must be presented in the statement of profit or loss and other comprehensive income (IAS 1). However, various other parties are interested in how an entity has performed and so corporate performance reports can be structured differently for different parties.

- Corporate performance in a broader sense has many definitions and meanings. For example:

  - All the processes, methodologies, metrics and systems needed to measure and manage the performance of an organisation;

  - Fundamental measures of organisational aptitude used to assess the "health" of the organisation and to provide focused direction to operations while supporting managers; and

  - A firm's level of achievement in creating value for market constituents.

*Commentary

*IFRS only requires this performance information to be reported on an annual and six-month (interim) basis.

5.2   Purpose

- Many performance reports over and above those that are needed to meet GAAP requirements are prepared on an ad hoc basis.*

- As well as occasionally reporting to external parties, there is usually a need to report performance internally to board members on a regular basis (e.g. quarterly, monthly or even weekly).

- These internal reports must be timely and accurate, and provide information about past performance and how the company is moving forwards. It should report more than what has happened and provide information that helps management make choices about the direction of the company.

- Although such reports are usually not required to follow GAAP, measurement bases, for example, should be made clear in the report.

- Historically, some GAAPs required a form of "value added statement" to be presented to stakeholders. This report looked at the value added to different providers of "capital"— the term capital being used in a general sense to mean more than financial capital.

- The Integrated Reporting <IR> model incorporates performance reporting as part of its remit. It looks at all the "capitals" and examines how value is created.*

*Commentary

*For example, to support a loan application or to present to a meeting of employee representatives.

*Commentary

*See Session 27.

© DeVry/Becker Educational Development Corp. All rights reserved.

5.3 Content

- Corporate performance reports take many forms and their contents are extremely varied. For example:
  - A condensed statement of profit or loss that focuses on the points most relevant to the stakeholders that receive it.
  - An employment report might detail employee remuneration, in terms of wages and salaries, pension benefits, share-based schemes and other forms of benefits. This may be compared to the performance for the period and the added wealth that the employees have created.
- Reports may compare performance over a number of periods and reflect the percentage change of the periods viewed.
- The information included in reports could be based on the accounting data for the period(s) under review, or the information could be more market based. Accounting data is somewhat restricted by GAAP requirements, whereas market-based data can reflect how the organisation is perceived in the market place.*

5.4 Characteristics of Good Information

5.4.1 The Need for Good Information

- A report will be most useful to the recipient(s) if it provides good and **clear** information that is directed to the **relevant** issue(s).
- Performance reporting should be a "means to an end", rather than "an end in itself". The purpose of the information provided should be to promote action. The report, therefore, is the document that **integrates** all the relevant information with balance and objectivity.
- A good report should contain all the information necessary to facilitate decision-making. It should lead the recipient to ask the right questions and initiate a chain of actions that will help the entity achieve its short- and long-term aims and create sustainable value.
- Finance departments are particularly important in this context, because the information they provide reflects the overall health of a company. Finance directors have a crucial role to play in ensuring that **reliable**, **comparable** and unbiased information issued is provided on a **timely** basis.

5.4.2 Relevant

- Information should be sharply focused and reflect the defined objectives and the overall strategy of an organisation. It must not obscure the overall picture with irrelevant detail.
- The information should be sufficient to allow the consideration of as many alternatives as are necessary for impartial decisions to be taken.
- It may be hard for those who prepare the information to know what level of detail they should go into when compiling board reports. The right balance must be struck between too much and too little detail.

*Commentary

*One of the problems of using non-GAAP-based data is that the information could be used to serve the best purpose of the preparer of the report and therefore may not give a fair perspective of how the organisation has performed in the period.

© DeVry/Becker Educational Development Corp. All rights reserved.

5.4.3 Integrated

- Organisations are obliged to produce information for a range of internal and external purposes. Systems and processes used to provide this information should, as far as possible, be integrated. In other words, the data collected internally should be managed in a way that satisfies both internal and external reporting needs.*

- The information needs of directors are broadly similar to those of investors, except in the level of detail required.

- Some of the information that boards require (e.g. for benchmarking against competitors) cannot be generated internally but will have to be collected from external sources.

5.4.4 Timely

- It is better for recipients to have information that is imperfect (but within acceptable tolerances of precision) in good time rather than completely accurate information too late.

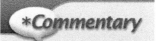

Illustration 3 • Timely Information

The collapse of Marconi in 2001 in the UK was principally due to a misguided strategy. One of the company's main failings was that the board did not receive timely information. It was not simply a case of incompetence or flawed risk assessment, as is often stated. The simple truth is that the company's directors may not have had the chance to act, because they did not find out what was going on until it was too late.

- Information should, as far as possible, be available in parallel with the activities to which it relates. The report should be available promptly enough to plan from it and/or take action to consolidate gains and recover shortfalls.

- Important information, such as key performance indicators (KPIs), should be presented monthly to enable a succinct and useful report to be produced.*

5.4.5 Reliable

- Information must be of sufficient quality for the recipient to have confidence in it. This will depend on its source, integrity and comprehensiveness.

- Information that has been generated from internal sources should be clearly distinguished from that from other sources (e.g. business publications, formal and informal contacts with staff below board level, etc).

*Commentary

*The underlying principle of IFRS 8 is a good example of this (see *Session 10*).

*Commentary

*Recent research sponsored by KPMG has highlighted the danger of reporting KPIs by exception only. Many non-executive directors in the survey blamed this approach for their limited understanding of business processes, value creation and customer satisfaction, which are crucial strategic areas for a company.

© DeVry/Becker Educational Development Corp. All rights reserved.

5.4.6　Comparable

▧ For financial performance, comparing what happens (actual) with what should have happened (e.g. budget, plan or rolling forecast) and in some cases what happened previously (e.g. last month or year) is valuable.

- Presenting a forecast year-end position will focus minds on the effectiveness of an organisation, rather than just its economy and efficiency.
- Comparison with budget is a widely used management tool. However, the emphasis should be on the future, which can be influenced, rather than on the past, which cannot.
- Comparison against budget will identify variances that should then be investigated, with the results incorporated into any future reports or budgets.

5.4.7　Clear

▧ Reports should always be written clearly and simply. Everyday language should be used wherever possible and jargon or acronyms should be avoided.

▧ Used judiciously, graphs and charts can be an effective communication medium for key indicators. They also enable trends to be identified more easily.

　　　　　　　　© DeVry/Becker Educational Development Corp. All rights reserved.

5.4.8 Best Practice

Principle	Good Practice	Poor Practice
Relevant	Focused financial report of three to six pages in length. A good report summarises the issues and highlights the overall position. It makes use of graphs and charts to replace lengthy tabular information where appropriate.	Detailed analysis of profit and expenses and variances for all departments in a 32-page report. Limited narrative. No corrective actions identified.
Integrated	Activity data linked to financial performance. Variances calculated and explained. The report integrates non-financial and financial reporting.	No activity data presented. No balance between qualitative and quantitative factors.
Timely	Report available within five working days of period end.	Information presented 28 days after period end.
Reliable	Every key issue identified with sufficient explanation.	No key issues identified or no explanation offered.
Comparable	Consistent style across reports. Performance indicators used to illustrate trends in liquidity, asset utilisation, etc. Comparison with budget or prior year.	Inconsistent format and style of report. Performance indicators not given.
Clear	Appropriate use of graphs, colour-coding and clear headings.	Copious financial tables at the beginning of the report. No title or contents pages. Information presented in complex spreadsheets.

Summary

- The objective of financial reporting is to provide information about an entity to external users of its financial statements.

- There are many different groups of users, each with different needs.

- Ratios are a tool to assist analysis. They focus attention on trends and weaknesses and facilitate comparison over time and between companies.

- Ratios are only one of the tools available to analysts when considering the results of a company.

- Analysts need to be aware that there are limitations to how ratios can be used and analysed.

- Creative accounting means choosing an accounting treatment so that the accounts show a desired picture. The treatment chosen will probably not reflect the true substance of the transaction.

- Basic EPS is calculated as:

$$\frac{\text{Profit or loss for the period attributable to ordinary shareholders}}{\text{Weighted average number of ordinary share outstanding during the period}}$$

- Diluted EPS is calculated as a warning to existing shareholders that the EPS in the future may fall.

- Potential ordinary shares should be treated as dilutive only if their conversion to ordinary shares would decrease profit per share from *continuing ordinary operations*.

© DeVry/Becker Educational Development Corp. All rights reserved.

Session 24 Quiz
Estimated time: 15 minutes

1. Explain why employees should be interested in analysing financial statements. (1.3)

2. Give the limitations of ratio analysis. (2.2)

3. Give sources of information, other than ratios, which are available for analysts. (2.7)

4. Describe the effect revaluing NCA could have on key ratios compared to valuing at historical cost. (2.4)

5. If a rights issue was made during the year, explain how the share figure is calculated in the basic EPS. (4.3.3)

6. Describe the changes for calculating diluted EPS if convertible debt is issued. (4.4)

Study Question Bank
Estimated time: 30 minutes

Priority		Estimated Time	Completed
Q40	Heywood Bottlers	30 minutes	
Additional			
Q41	NFP Organisations		
Q42	Radan		

© DeVry/Becker Educational Development Corp. All rights reserved.

IFRS 1 *First-time Adoption*

FOCUS

This session covers the following content from the *ACCA Study Guide.*

<table>
<tr><td colspan="2">F. Implications of Changes in Accounting Regulation on Financial Reporting</td></tr>
<tr><td colspan="2">1. The effect of changes in accounting standards on accounting systems</td></tr>
<tr><td>a) Apply and discuss the accounting implications of the first-time adoption of a body of new accounting standards.</td><td>☐</td></tr>
</table>

Session 25 Guidance

- **Comprehend** that IFRS 1 *First-time Adoption* is very important for entities adopting IFRSs. It explains the procedures required for setting up an opening IFRS statement of financial position.
- **Understand** who is a first-time adopter (s.1) and learn the stages in transition to IFRS (s.1.6).
- **Learn** the recognition and measurement principles (s.2.1) and **appreciate** the need for optional exemptions (s.2.2).
- **Pay attention** to the optional exemptions for tangible assets (s.2.3) and business combinations (s.2.4).

(continued on next page)

VISUAL OVERVIEW

Objective: To explain how an entity's first-time IFRS financial statements should be prepared and presented in accordance with IFRS 1 *First-time Adoption of International Financial Reporting Standards*.

```
┌────────────────────────────────┐      ┌────────────────────────────────┐
│         INTRODUCTION           │      │      PRACTICAL MATTERS         │
│  ────────────────────────      │      │  ────────────────────────      │
│   • Background                 │      │   • Overview                   │
│   • Objective                  │      │   • Making the Transition      │
│   • Scope                      │      │                                │
│   • Terminology                │      │                                │
│   • Stages in Transition       │      │                                │
│   • Transition Overview        │      │                                │
└────────────────────────────────┘      └────────────────────────────────┘

┌────────────────────────────────┐
│   OPENING IFRS STATEMENT       │
│   OF FINANCIAL POSITION        │
│  ────────────────────────      │
│   • Recognition and Measurement│
│   • Exemptions From Other IFRSs│
│   • Property, Plant and Equipment│
│   • Business Combinations      │
│   • Translation Differences    │
│   • Government Loans           │
│   • Exceptions to Retrospective│
│     Application                │
└────────────────────────────────┘

┌────────────────────────────────┐
│        PRESENTATION            │
│       AND DISCLOSURE           │
│  ────────────────────────      │
│   • Explanation of Transition  │
│   • Reconciliations            │
│   • Other Disclosures          │
└────────────────────────────────┘
```

Session 25 Guidance

■ **Learn** the list of items for which there are mandatory exceptions (s.2.7).

■ **Understand** the need for reconciliations to explain transition (s.3.1) and **appreciate** the wider implications of first-time adoption in practice (s.4).

© DeVry/Becker Educational Development Corp. All rights reserved.

1 Introduction

1.1 Background

- The European Union's requirement that all listed companies in the European Economic Area publish their consolidated financial statements in accordance with IFRS by 2005 meant that entities with a financial year end of 31 December needed to have an IFRS statement of financial position as at 1 January 2004 (for comparative purposes).

- IFRS 1 *First-time Adoption of International Financial Reporting Standards* permits certain exemptions from recognition and measurement requirements where compliance would otherwise cause undue cost or effort in application.

- However, there are *no* exemptions from IFRS 1's enhanced disclosure requirements detailing how the change to IFRSs has affected financial position, performance and cash flows.

1.2 Objective

Key Point

To ensure that an entity's first IFRS contain high-quality information which is:

- transparent for users;
- comparable over all periods presented;
- a starting point for accounting under IFRS; and
- generated at a cost which does not exceed the benefit (to users).

- A first-time adopter uses the provisions of IFRS 1 and not the transitional provisions of other standards unless IFRS 1 specifies otherwise.

1.3 Scope

- This standard applies to:
  - first IFRS financial statements; and
  - any interim financial statements presented under IAS 34 for any part of the period covered by the first IFRS financial statements.*
- It may be reapplied where an entity has previously applied IFRS 1 but then stopped applying IFRS.

*Commentary

*For example, if an entity's first IFRS financial statements are to be prepared to 31 December 2018, interim financial statements for the 6 months to 30 June 2018 will also fall within the scope of IFRS 1.

          © DeVry/Becker Educational Development Corp. All rights reserved.

1.4   Terminology

First IFRS financial statements: the first annual financial statements in which IFRSs are adopted by an explicit and unreserved statement of compliance.*

First-time adopter: an entity which presents its first IFRS financial statements. If an explicit and unreserved statement of compliance has already been made an entity is *not* a first-time adopter.*

Opening IFRS statement of financial position: an entity's statement of financial position at the date of transition to IFRSs. This may be published or unpublished.

Previous GAAP: the basis of accounting used immediately before the adoption of IFRS.

Reporting date: the end of the latest period covered by financial statements (or by an interim financial report).

Date of transition: the beginning of the earliest period for which an entity presents full comparative information under IFRSs in its first IFRS financial statements.

Deemed cost: an amount used as a surrogate for cost or depreciated cost at a given date.

> ***✲Commentary***
>
> *"Explicit and unreserved statement of compliance" means in compliance with all IFRSs, IASs and applicable interpretations.
>
> *The explicit and unreserved statement of compliance is made only once, even if there was non-compliance and the auditor's report carried a qualified opinion.

Illustration 1   Transition Date

An entity with a 31 December year end presenting its financial statements for 2018 will have a date of transition as 1 January 2017.

1.5   Stages in Transition to IFRSs

1.5.1   Accounting Policies

▨ Select accounting policies which will comply with IFRSs.

▨ The same accounting policies are used for all periods presented including the opening IFRS statement of financial position.

▨ The version of an IFRS which is extant at the *reporting date* (i.e. 31 December 2018 in *Illustration 1*) is used subject to the exemptions permitted under IFRS 1. Different versions effective at earlier dates must **not** be applied.

▨ If a new IFRS permits early application then a first-time adopter may adopt that standard early, but it is not required to do so.

▨ The transitional arrangements in other IFRSs apply to entities which already use IFRSs. They do not apply to first-time adopters except in relation to the derecognition of financial assets and financial liabilities and hedge accounting in accordance with IFRS 9.

1.5.2   Opening IFRS Statement of Financial Position

▨ Prepare an opening IFRS statement of financial position (i.e. at the date of transition). This is the starting point to accounting under IFRS.

1.5.3 Estimates

- Make estimates in accordance with IFRSs for the opening statement of financial position and all other periods covered by the financial statements.

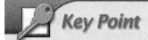 **Key Point**

Estimates must be made consistent with estimates made as at the same date under previous GAAP, after adjustments to reflect different accounting policies, unless there is objective evidence that those estimates were in error.

- Information received after the date of transition relevant to estimates made under previous GAAP is treated as for non-adjusting events (IAS 10).

Illustration 2 New Information

An entity's date of transition to IFRSs is 1 January 2018.

New information on 15 July 2018 requires an increase in the estimate of the allowance for slow-moving inventory made under previous GAAP at 31 December 2017.

The entity does not reflect that new information in its opening IFRS statement of financial position. The increase in estimate will be reflected as an additional expense in profit or loss for the year ended 31 December 2018.

 ***Commentary**

*Conditions an entity might estimate are market prices, interest rates, foreign exchange rates, etc.

- An entity may need to make estimates under IFRSs at the date of transition which were not required at that date under previous GAAP (e.g. if there was no requirement to state inventory at the lower of cost and net realisable value). Such estimates must reflect conditions which existed *at the date of transition* to IFRSs.*

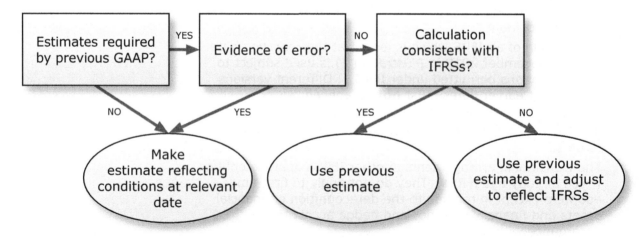

- These same principles apply to estimates made for any comparative period presented in **first IFRS** financial statements.

                        © DeVry/Becker Educational Development Corp. All rights reserved.

1.5.4 Presentation and Disclosure

■ Make presentation and disclosure requirements in accordance with IFRS 1.

■ At least three statements of financial position and two of each other statement must be included for comparison purposes (IAS 1).

■ Historical summaries of selected data need not comply with recognition and measurement requirements of IFRS 1. However, such summaries and comparative information under previous GAAP must be clearly labelled as not being prepared under IFRS and the *nature* of the main adjustments to comply with IFRS disclosed. The adjustments are not required to be quantified.

> **Key Point**
>
> IFRS 1 does not provide exemptions from the presentation and disclosure requirements of other accounting standards.

1.6 Transition Overview

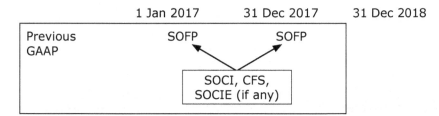

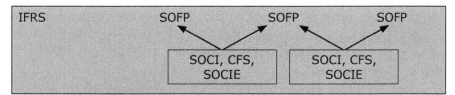

■ The financial statements to 31 December 2017 are published under previous GAAP. The financial statements to 31 December 2018 will be prepared under IFRS with the comparatives information restated.

2 Opening IFRS Statement of Financial Position

2.1 Recognition and Measurement Principles

■ Recognise all assets and liabilities required by IFRSs (e.g. assets held under leases and lease obligations).

■ Do not recognise assets and liabilities that are not allowed to be recognised under IFRSs (e.g. "provisions" which do not meet the definition of a liability).

■ Reclassify items as current/non-current, liability/equity in accordance with IFRSs as necessary (e.g. preferred shares with fixed maturity as debt rather than equity).

■ Measure all recognised assets and liabilities in accordance with IFRSs (e.g. at cost, "fair value" or a discounted amount).

■ Because the adjustments which result from changes in accounting policy on transition arise from events and transactions before the date of transition they are recognised directly in retained earnings (or, if appropriate, elsewhere in equity) at the date of transition.

2.2 Exemptions From Other IFRSs

▨ IFRS 1 essentially requires full retrospective application of all extant IFRSs on first-time adoption with limited exemptions that include:

- property, plant and equipment;*
- business combinations;
- cumulative translation differences;
- compound financial instruments;
- assets and liabilities of subsidiaries, associates and joint ventures;
- designation of previously recognised financial instruments;
- share-based payment transactions;
- insurance contracts;
- decommissioning liabilities;
- leases;
- fair value measurement of financial assets or liabilities at initial recognition; and
- borrowing costs.

2.3 Property, Plant and Equipment

▨ Cost-based measurement of some items of property, plant and equipment may involve undue cost or effort, especially if the entity has not kept up-to-date fixed-asset registers.

▨ Items of property, plant and equipment can therefore be measured at their fair value at the date of transition, and that value deemed to be cost (i.e. "deemed cost").

▨ If an entity has revalued assets under its previous GAAP and the revaluation is broadly in line with IFRSs, then that revalued amount can be taken to be the deemed cost.*

▨ If an entity has carried out a fair value exercise of all (or some) of its assets and liabilities for a particular event (e.g. an IPO or privatisation), then that fair value may be as the deemed cost at the event date.

▨ Comparing revaluation under IFRS 1 with that under IAS 16:

- for IFRS 1 it is a "one-off" exercise—under IAS 16, revaluations must be kept up to date;
- any revaluation to deemed cost under IFRS 1 is taken to retained earnings whereas revaluation under IAS 16 is credited to a revaluation surplus; and
- the IFRS 1 exemption can be applied to any item(s)—under IAS 16, all items in the same class must be revalued.

▨ Any borrowing costs capitalised in accordance with previous GAAP before the date of transition may be carried forward in the opening statement of financial position.*

*Also investment properties and intangible assets.

A first-time adopter may elect to use **any** one or more of the available exemptions.

As the individual exemptions are unlikely to be examined only the more common issues are detailed further.

*The same exemptions apply to assets accounted for under IAS 38 and IAS 40.

*Any borrowing costs incurred after the date of transition must be accounted for in accordance with IAS 23.

© DeVry/Becker Educational Development Corp. All rights reserved.

2.4   Business Combinations

2.4.1   Electing Not to Apply IFRS 3

▓ A first-time adopter does not have to apply IFRS 3 *Business Combinations* retrospectively to past business combinations (i.e. business combinations which occurred before the date of transition to IFRSs).

▓ If, however, a first-time adopter restates *any* business combination to comply with IFRS 3, all later business combinations *must* be restated and IAS 36 (Revised) and IAS 38 (Revised) applied.

> **Illustration 3   Business Combinations**
>
> A first-time adopter reporting at 31 December 2018 elects to restate a business combination which occurred 30 June 2014. It must restate all business combinations which occurred between 30 June 2014 and 1 January 2017.

▓ This exemption also applies to past acquisitions of investments in associates and of interests in joint ventures.

2.4.2   Goodwill Adjustments

▓ The carrying amount of goodwill in the opening IFRS statement of financial position is the same as under previous GAAP at the date of transition after the following adjustments (if applicable):

Commentary

*If applicable, deferred tax and non-controlling interest will be adjusted also.

  ● Increasing the carrying amount of goodwill for an item previously recognised as an intangible asset which does not meet IFRS criteria.

  ● Decreasing the carrying amount of goodwill if an intangible asset previously subsumed in recognised goodwill meets IFRS criteria for recognition.*

  ● Adjustment for the amount of a contingency affecting the purchase consideration for a past business combination which is resolved before the date of transition to IFRS. A reliable estimate of the contingent amount is needed and its payment must be probable.

  ● The carrying amount should similarly be adjusted if a previously recognised contingent adjustment can no longer be measured reliably or its payment is no longer probable.

Key Point

This is regardless of whether there are any indications the goodwill may be impaired.

  ● An impairment test at the date of transition. Any impairment loss is adjusted in retained earnings (or revaluation surplus if required by IAS 36).

▓ No other adjustments are made to the carrying amount of goodwill at the date of transition.

> **Example 1   Exclusion From Consolidation**
>
> Suggest THREE reasons why a subsidiary may not have been consolidated under previous GAAP.

2.4.3   Deferred Tax and Non-controlling Interest

▧ The measurement of deferred tax and non-controlling interest follows from the measurement of other assets and liabilities.

▧ All these adjustments to recognised assets and liabilities therefore affect non-controlling interest and deferred tax.

2.5   Cumulative Translation Differences

▧ All translation adjustments arising on the translation of the financial statements of foreign entities can be recognised in accumulated profits at the date of transition.

▧ The gain or loss on subsequent disposal of the foreign entity will then be adjusted only by those accumulated translation adjustments arising after the date of transition.

▧ If this exemption is not used, an entity must restate the translation reserve for all foreign entities since they were acquired or created.

Key Point

That is, any translation reserve included in equity under previous GAAP is reset to zero.

2.6   Government Loans Below Market Rates of Interest

▧ An entity may use a previous GAAP valuation for a government loan on first-time adoption. Subsequent measurement is based on the requirements of IFRS 9.

2.7   Mandatory Exceptions to Retrospective Application

▧ As well as the optional exemptions, there are seven mandatory exceptions, concerning:

1. derecognition of financial assets and financial liabilities;

2. hedge accounting;

3. non-controlling interest;

4. classification and measurement of financial assets;

5. impairment of financial assets;

6. embedded derivatives; and

7. government loans

2.7.1   Derecognition of Financial Assets and Financial Liabilities

▧ A first-time adopter must apply the derecognition requirements in IFRS 9 *Financial Instruments* for any transactions occurring on or after the date of transition to IFRS.

▧ Financial assets or financial liabilities derecognised under previous GAAP cannot be recognised on the adoption date of IFRS.

2.7.2   Hedge Accounting

▧ The hedging requirements of IFRS 9 must be applied prospectively from the date of transition. This means that any hedge accounting practices previously used cannot be retrospectively changed.

▧ A transaction cannot be designated as a hedge if it was not so designated under previous GAAP. Only designated hedges under previous GAAP will be recognised and measured under IFRS 9 (irrespective of whether there is hedge documentation or hedge effectiveness).

                    © DeVry/Becker Educational Development Corp. All rights reserved.

2.7.3   Non-controlling Interest

▦ Total comprehensive income must be split between owners of the parent and non-controlling interest, even if this results in a *deficit* balance for non-controlling interest.

▦ Any change in control status between the owners of the parent and non-controlling interest is accounted for from the date of transition unless the adopter has elected to apply IFRS 3 retrospectively to past business combinations.*

2.7.4   Classification and Measurement of Financial Assets

▦ An entity must assess whether a financial asset meets the conditions of IFRS 9 on the basis of facts and circumstances existing at the date of transition.

2.7.5   Impairment of Financial Assets

▦ The impairment requirements of IFRS 9 are applied retrospectively on adoption of IFRSs.

▦ On transition, an entity uses reasonable and supportable information to determine the credit risk of financial instruments when they were first recognised.

2.7.6   Embedded Derivatives

▦ An embedded derivative will be separated from its host based on the conditions which existed at the later of the date it first became a party to the contract and the date a reassessment is required by IFRS 9.

2.7.7   Government Loans

▦ A first-time adopter must classify all government loans as either financial liability or equity instrument, in accordance with IAS 32.

▦ IFRS 1 allows IAS 20 and IFRS 9 to be applied retrospectively to the loan as long as the relevant information had been obtained when the loan was received.

Commentary

*If the adopter has elected to apply IFRS 3 retrospectively, then IFRS 10 requirements must also be applied retrospectively to the past business combinations.

3   Presentation and Disclosure

3.1   Explanation of Transition

Key Point

An entity must explain how the transition to IFRSs has affected its reported financial position, performance and cash flows. This is achieved through reconciliations and disclosure and there are no exemptions to the requirements for these.

3.2   Reconciliations

▦ The following are required to enable users to understand the material adjustments to the statement of financial position and statement of comprehensive income:

- A reconciliation of equity under IFRSs and previous GAAP as at:
  — the transition date; and
  — the end of the latest period presented under previous GAAP.
- A reconciliation of profit or loss reported under previous GAAP to that under IFRS for the latest period's statement of comprehensive income presented under previous GAAP.

▦ These reconciliations must distinguish between changes in accounting policies and errors. IAS 8 disclosure requirements do not apply.

▦ Similar reconciliations are required for interim financial reports for part of the period covered by the first IFRS financial statements.

3.3   Other Disclosures

▦ If a statement of cash flows was presented under previous GAAP, material adjustments must be explained.

▦ If an entity uses fair value as deemed cost for any items of property, plant and equipment (or investment property or intangible asset) as an alternative to cost-based measurement, the following must be disclosed for each line item:

- the aggregate of those fair values; and
- the aggregate adjustment to carrying amounts reported under previous GAAP.

4   Practical Matters

4.1   Overview

▦ The finance director is most likely to be responsible for the conversion process. In large entities, a steering committee may be formed to manage the process across the business.

▦ Matters to be considered when making a preliminary assessment of the effect of conversion will include:

- the level of readily available IFRS competence of staff, internal audit and non-executive directors;
- whether specialist help may be needed and, if so, who can provide it;
- identifying agreements, contracts and reports affected by the change in the financial reporting framework;
- making an initial estimate of the financial effect of changes in key accounting policies;
- assessing the significance of fair values (e.g. for IAS 40 and IFRS 9);
- reviewing any existing weaknesses in internal financial reporting systems; and
- deciding the extent to which the previous year's financial information (prior to the date of transition) is to be restated.

                    © DeVry/Becker Educational Development Corp. All rights reserved.

Example 2 Arrangements Affected

Suggest FOUR contractual arrangements which could be affected by the change.

4.2 Making the Transition

4.2.1 Accounting

Key Point

Accounting policies should be selected after a detailed review of the choices available (especially on transition).*

Commentary

*A test run with prior period information may be advisable before the audit committee (if any) confirms management's choice of accounting policies.

- Changes may need to be made to the accounting system to collect the information necessary to meet disclosure requirements (e.g. of segment reporting).
- The group accounting manual should be updated to reflect changes in terminology as well as changes in accounting policies, measurement bases, etc.
- Accounting policies used for internal reporting (e.g. in budgeting systems) may need to be standardised or made compatible with those used for external financial reporting.

4.2.2 Treasury

- Treasury managers will need to review treasury policy and how they hedge risk.
- Some entities may not be able to hedge account in accordance with IFRS 9 even if they change their hedging strategy.
- Loan agreements may need to be renegotiated to avoid breaching covenant limits.

4.2.3 IT and Systems

- Accounting system changes may be required as a direct result of the change to IFRS.
- Changes in IT and systems also may be required in response to the identification of business improvement opportunities.

4.2.4 Human Resources

- Resource planning should take account of:
  - the effect of the change on long-term recruitment plans;
  - how day-to-day responsibilities of seconded staff will be covered; and
  - temporary specialist assistance needed.
- Remuneration schemes will need to be reviewed and renegotiated.
- Staff will need to be trained.

4.2.5   Training

▨ Internal experts with specialist IFRS knowledge will need to be
involved in the training of others in the organisation. This may
require that they be trained as trainers.

▨ Subsidiary finance managers will need a broad understanding
of the effect of IFRS on the entity and changes in policy
and procedure.

▨ General business managers will need to be made aware
of the effect of IFRS on the business, its reporting and
planning processes.

4.2.6   Communication

▨ The financial effects of the change must be communicated
to shareholders, analysts, employees, lenders, etc. This
may require a public relations plan to advertise the adoption
of IFRS.

Example 3   Transition to IFRS

The statement of financial position of Geewiz Co at its date of transition to IFRS under local
GAAP is as follows:

	Local GAAP	Effect of transition to IFRS	IFRS
	$m	$m	$m
Property, plant and equipment	8,000		
Goodwill	2,000		
Intangible assets	1,000		
Financial assets	7,000		
Total non-current assets	18,000		
Trade and other receivables	3,000		
Inventories	5,000		
Other receivables	600		
Cash and cash equivalents	700		
Total current assets	9,300		
Total assets	27,300		
Interest-bearing loans	9,000		
Trade and other payables	4,000		
Restructuring provision	30		
Current Tax liability	40		
Deferred tax liability	600		
Total liabilities	13,670		
Total assets less total liabilities	13,630		
Issued capital	6,500		
Retained earnings	7,130		
Total equity	13,630		

© DeVry/Becker Educational Development Corp. All rights reserved.

Example 3 Transition to IFRS (continued)

Notes

(i) Depreciation was influenced by tax requirements under local GAAP. IFRS reflects the useful life of the assets. The cumulative adjustment required by IFRS increases the carrying amount of property, plant and equipment by $200 million.

(ii) Intangible assets acquired in a business combination included $300 million for items that do not qualify for recognition as intangible assets under IFRS.

(iii) Financial assets with a cost of $7,000 million are all classified as fair value through other comprehensive income under IFRS 9. Their fair value is $7,800 million.

(iv) Inventories are valued at direct manufacturing cost under previous GAAP. Fixed and variable production overhead of $1,000 million must be included to comply with IAS 2.

(v) Unrealised gains of $500 million on unmatured forward foreign exchange contracts which are not recognised under GAAP are to be recognised under IFRS.

(vi) A pension liability of $100 million is recognised under IFRS but was not recognised under GAAP. The tax base of the pension liability is zero.

(vii) A restructuring provision of $30 million relating to head office activities was recognised under previous GAAP, but does not qualify for recognition as a liability under IFRS.

(viii) The tax rate is 30%.

Required:
Show the effects of transition to IFRS on the statement of financial position.

Summary

- The objective of IFRS 1 is to ensure that an entity's first IFRS financial statements contain high-quality information which is transparent for users, comparable over all periods presented, a starting point for accounting under IFRS and generated at a cost which does not exceed the benefit (to users).

- A first-time adopter presents IFRS financial statements for the first time and includes an explicit and unreserved statement of compliance.

- Estimates used must be consistent with estimates made as at the same date under previous GAAP.

- IFRS 1 does not provide exemptions from the presentation and disclosure requirements of other accounting standards.

- IFRS 1 allows "day one" exemptions from other standards and requires mandatory exceptions to retrospective application.

- Accounting policies should be selected after a detailed review of the choices available.

- An entity must explain how the transition to IFRSs has affected its reported financial position, performance and cash flows. This is achieved through reconciliations and disclosure.

- Management must consider the effect the adoption of IFRS is going to have on the business as a whole and not just on the accounting requirements.

Session 25 Quiz
Estimated time: 15 minutes

1. State the objective of IFRS 1. (1.2)
2. Define deemed cost in accordance with IFRS 1. (1.4)
3. Identify SIX exemptions from the requirements of other IFRSs which IFRS 1 allows. (2.2)
4. Give the FOUR mandatory exceptions to retrospective application. (2.7)
5. Specify the reconciliations required by IFRS 1 in an entity's first financial statements under IFRS. (3.2)
6. State the effect that a move to IFRS will have on treasury managers. (4.2.2)

Study Question Bank
Estimated time: 50 minutes

Priority		Estimated Time	Completed
Q43	Eptilon	50 minutes	

© DeVry/Becker Educational Development Corp. All rights reserved.

EXAMPLE SOLUTIONS

Solution 1—Exclusion From Consolidation

1. It was not regarded as a subsidiary under previous GAAP—the definition of subsidiary being based on legal ownership rather than control.
2. Previous GAAP permitted that certain subsidiaries be excluded from consolidation (e.g. on the grounds that their activities are sufficiently different from those of the rest of the group).
3. The parent did not prepare consolidated financial statements (e.g. in jurisdictions where financial statements are for legal entities only).

Solution 2—Arrangements Affected

1. Bank and other loan agreements (e.g. financial ratios specified in loan covenants may be adversely affected).
2. Reporting to industry regulators.
3. Remuneration schemes and profit-related pay. Negotiations with the tax authorities may be necessary to maintain tax efficient schemes.
4. Performance-related share option schemes.

© DeVry/Becker Educational Development Corp. All rights reserved.

Solution 3—Transition to IFRS

		Previous GAAP	Effect of transition to IFRS	IFRS
		$m	$m	$m
Property, plant and equipment	(i)	8,000	200	8,200
Goodwill	(ii)	2,000	300	2,300
Intangible assets	(ii)	1,000	(300)	700
Financial assets	(iii)	7,000	800	7,800
Total non-current assets		18,000	1,000	19,000
Trade and other receivables		3,000	0	3,000
Inventories	(iv)	5,000	1,000	6,000
Other receivables	(v)	600	500	1,100
Cash and cash equivalents		700	0	700
Total current assets		9,300	1,500	10,800
Total assets		27,300	2,500	29,800
Interest-bearing loans		9,000	0	9,000
Trade and other payables		4,000	0	4,000
Employee benefits	(vi)	0	100	100
Restructuring provision	(vii)	30	(30)	0
Current Tax liability		40	0	40
Deferred tax liability (W2)		600	729	1,329
Total liabilities		13,670	799	14,469
Total assets less total liabilities		13,630	1,701	15,331
Issued capital		6,600	0	6,500
Revaluation reserve 70% × (iii)		0	560	560
Retained earnings (W1)		7,130	1,141	8,271
Total equity		13,630	1,701	15,331

© DeVry/Becker Educational Development Corp. All rights reserved.

Solution 3—Transition to IFRS (continued)

Workings

(1) Retained earnings

		$m
Depreciation	(i)	200
Production overhead	(iv)	1,000
Foreign exchange contract	(v)	500
Pension liability	(vi)	(100)
Restructuring provision	(vii)	30
		1,630
Tax effect of the above		(489)
Total adjustment to retained earnings		1,141

(2) Deferred tax liability*

		$m
Revaluation reserve	30% × (iii)	240
Retained earnings	30% × (W1)	489
Increase in deferred tax liability		729

*Commentary

*Because the tax base of the items reclassified from intangible asset to goodwill equals their carrying amount of those items at the date of transition, the reclassification does not affect deferred tax liabilities.

© DeVry/Becker Educational Development Corp. All rights reserved.

Ethics and the Accountant

FOCUS

This session covers the following content from the *ACCA Study Guide.*

A. The Professional and Ethical Duties of the Accountant

1. Professional behaviour and compliance with accounting standards

a) Appraise and discuss the ethical and professional issues in advising on corporate reporting. ☐

b) Assess the relevance and importance of ethical and professional issues in complying with accounting standards. ☐

2. Ethical requirements of corporate reporting and the consequences of unethical behaviour

a) Appraise the potential ethical implications of professional and managerial decisions in the preparation of corporate reports. ☐

b) Assess the consequences of not upholding ethical principles in the preparation of corporate reports. ☐

Session 26 Guidance

■ **Read** through this session.

■ **Revise** stakeholders (s.1.3), the different approaches to managing ethics (s.2), the main contents of the IFAC Code (s.3) and ACCA's principles-based approach (s.4). **Attempt** *Examples 1 and 2.*

(continued on next page)

VISUAL OVERVIEW

Objective: To explain the ACCA's *Rules of Professional Conduct* and IFAC's *Code of Ethics for Professional Accountants* and to consider the professional and ethical behaviour of an accountant.

INTRODUCTION
- Definition
- Background
- Stakeholders
- Individual Accountants
- Businesses and Social Responsibility
- Compliance With Accounting Standards

MANAGING ETHICS
- Compliance-Based
- Integrity-Based

ETHICS IN THE REAL WORLD
- COSO Study
- Lehman Brothers
- Parmalat
- Lessons Learnt

IFAC CODE OF ETHICS
- A Model Code
- Objectives
- The Code

ACCA CODE OF ETHICS AND CONDUCT
- Application
- Fundamental Principles
- Risks
- Safeguards
- Ethical Conflict Resolution

Session 26 Guidance

Identify the ethical issues from a practical perspective (s.5) and consider what areas, such as creative accounting, could cause conflict for an accountant. **Attempt** *Example 3*.

1   Introduction

1.1   Definition

Definition

Ethics—a set of moral principles guiding behaviour.

1.2   Background

▨ **Ethics** affect the everyday life of individuals; if we witness some form of crime we have a moral and social responsibility to do something about it.

▨ Accountants in business must also apply an ethical attitude in the performance of their work.

▨ The issue is not solely about the reporting of crime. Within our working environment we should be striving to ensure that our company is also working within an ethical code of practices.

▨ A company has a responsibility to many stakeholders and it must ensure that the interests of these stakeholders are taken into account when going about their business.

1.3   Stakeholders

▨ **Shareholders:** They invest in the business with the aim of making a profit, but a profit at what cost? Some shareholders (e.g. the church) will not invest in weapons manufacturers, while others will not invest in companies that use child labour. So a company needs to consider more than just the profit motive from the perspective of many of its shareholders.

▨ **Employees:** A company has a responsibility to pay a minimum wage to employees (UK) and to ensure that they are working in a safe environment. There is also the issue of discrimination regarding the workforce; race, gender, religion and age are not factors that should affect the employability of an individual.

▨ **The government:** The company has a responsibility to pay taxes and ensure that some of the profits it makes are fed back into government funds for the redistribution to the more needy.

▨ **Public as a whole:** The general public and the environment need to be considered by an entity when producing an ethical code. The company should be doing its utmost to prevent pollution of the environment, however if this does happen then the company must show that it is willing and able to put right its mistakes.

© DeVry/Becker Educational Development Corp. All rights reserved.

1.4   The Accountant as an Individual

▦ It is highly likely that during an accountant's career, he will encounter some form of ethical issue that he will have to face and make a difficult decision about. For example:

- Bribery by officials who want him to act in a particular way.
- Exertion of pressure by a senior employee (or client) to account for a transaction in a way that would hide its substance.
- The offer of gifts by a member of a delegation to influence, for example, voting in a particular way. It should be noted that in some cultures, such as Japan, that the giving of gifts is an accepted practice.

1.5   Businesses and Social Responsibility

1.5.1   Shareholder Wealth

▦ The role of a business is to increase the wealth of its owners, the shareholders. Or is it?

▦ Some might argue that profit maximisation will ultimately benefit all other stakeholders (e.g. through revenues raised for public spending through taxation and by the owners spending their increased wealth). However, if profit maximisation is the only criterion for business decisions, some stakeholders will certainly lose out (e.g. employees with minimum pay and working conditions).

▦ Doing what is most ethical or socially responsible invariably comes at a price. But although any cost obviously reduces shareholders' wealth, there will be benefits—even though some of these may be impossible to quantify in monetary terms and not all accrue to shareholders. For example, paying employees more than a minimum wage and providing improved working conditions have measureable costs.

 **Key Point**

A business has a social and ethical responsibility to all stakeholders and therefore it should aim to "satisfy" all stakeholders rather than focus on one group.

- Measurable benefits might include reduced costs of labour turnover and improved productivity.
- Less measurable benefits might include the reduction of risk of claims for accidents in the workplace and increased life expectancy of workers.

© DeVry/Becker Educational Development Corp. All rights reserved.

Illustration 1 Ethical Implications

Identify some of the ethical issues involved in making decisions in each of the following situations:

1. Should a company manufacture and sell recreational drugs to the general public?
2. Should a company buy shares in a tobacco company as an investment?
3. Should an energy company carry out hydraulic "fracking" in the search for fossil fuel?

Solution

1. Most people would consider this to be abhorrent even though such an activity would be very profitable. Even if the drugs were legal in a regulated industry the costs to society and the risks to individuals (turning to harder drugs, etc) are likely to be considered unacceptable. Of course, there is always another argument—that regulating the industry, etc would make the activity safer for the individual and benefit society (e.g. fewer drug-related crimes).

2. Many shareholders are likely to have strong views on smoking and might oppose shares being bought in a tobacco company. However, it is estimated that the tobacco industry employs more than 100 million people in the world, many in developing countries. Although the investment might be distasteful, opposing the investment will not bring down the industry and there will always be someone else prepared to invest. (Does that make it ethical?)

3. Environmentalists are generally against any drilling procedures that pose a risk to the environment (e.g. groundwater contamination). The local community is likely to oppose fracking (e.g. due to risk of subsidence). Shareholders would benefit from increased profits, as fracking can locate and extract natural resources that are otherwise inaccessible. But what about future generations? Should companies invest in sustainable energy solutions rather than deplete the world's natural resources?

1.5.2 Whistle-blowing

- It is an individual's responsibility not only to be ethical but also to disclose any unethical practices that one uncovers.
- The decision to be a "whistle-blower" is usually difficult:
  - The whistle-blower may expect not only to lose out financially (e.g. if he loses his job as a result and cannot find alternative employment) but suffer emotionally from the associated stigma.
  - A breach of duty of confidentiality may amount to a breach of a contact of employment. This may result in the individual being sued for considerable damages by the company.
- Although many organisations view whistle-blowing as a threat, a significant proportion of occupational fraud is detected by whistle-blowers. To be effective, a whistle-blowing policy needs to be:
  - Well implemented (a "tick box" approach will not work)
  - Well maintained (i.e. kept current in training and promotional material)
  - Well supported with "tone from the top" (i.e. encouragement to report concerns and reassurance that information will be treated seriously and in confidence).

© DeVry/Becker Educational Development Corp. All rights reserved.

1.6   Compliance With Accounting Standards

■ Incorporated businesses are required to file their financial statements with the relevant authority. This is one of the many responsibilities of company directors. These financial statements must comply with the relevant GAAP (e.g. IFRS) and company legislation.

■ The regulatory environment may allow some choices in the preparation of financial statements. For example, under IAS 16, property may be measured using a cost model or a revaluation model. Companies must disclose the policies selected by management to help the users of financial statements make decisions:

  ● A shareholder may decide to buy more shares.

  ● A supplier may decide to sell goods to the company on credit.

  ● A bank may decide to give the company a loan.

■ Preparers of financial statements must ensure that they faithfully represent the economic phenomena that have occurred in the period so that users can rely on them.

■ Professional and ethical judgement has a role to play in the preparation of the financial statements. For example, judgement must be exercised when deciding whether expenditure should be capitalised or expensed or whether an asset is impaired; users can be misled if revenue expenditure is capitalised or an impairment loss is not recognised, as profits will be overstated.

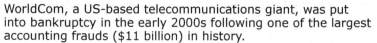

Illustration 2   WorldCom

WorldCom, a US-based telecommunications giant, was put into bankruptcy in the early 2000s following one of the largest accounting frauds ($11 billion) in history.

The financial statements were misstated to hide the company's increasingly precarious financial condition. The enormous fraud was engineered in a relatively unimaginative way by making unsupported accounting entries amounting to more than $9 billion to achieve the desired financial results.

The CEO, Bernard "Bernie" Ebbers, started to "doctor" the books when newly acquired companies failed to perform to meet expectations. Ebbers did not have the courage to face the market and explain the true financial position because, among other thing, he had pledged his investment in WorldCom's shares to secure loans.

As a result of the fraud, 30,000 employees lost their jobs, investors lost $180 billion and Ebbers is serving 25 years in prison. The Report of Investigation by the Special Investigative Committee of the board of directors of WorldCom gave rise to the following recommendations:

■ An active and independent board of directors and committees.

■ A corporate culture of openness, in which ethical conduct is encouraged and expected.

■ A corporate culture in which the advice of lawyers is sought and respected.

■ Formalised and well-documented policies and procedures, including an effective whistle-blowing policy.

© DeVry/Becker Educational Development Corp. All rights reserved.

- **Fraud** is a deliberate act to obtain unfair advantage. It is not only unethical but criminal.
  - Financial statement fraud is the most costly of frauds perpetrated by employees. Only a small proportion of these, about 10%, include financial statement manipulation.
  - Financial statement manipulation is usually perpetrated by senior management, as it requires access to and influence over the financial statements.*

*Senior management usually has the most to gain (e.g. increased performance bonuses, more valuable share options, lucrative job promotion prospects).

- The most common ways to carry out a financial statement fraud are:
  - Revenue overstatement—Sales may be inflated by recording completely fictitious sales or recognising a sale before the revenue is actually earned (i.e. a "cutoff" error).
  - Understatement of expenses—This usually involves:
    - holding over an expense incurred in the current period to a later period (i.e. a cutoff error):
    - incorrect capitalisation of revenue items.
  - Assets overstatement—This includes failure to write off irrecoverable accounts receivable or write down obsolete inventory or impaired non-current assets.
  - Understatement of liabilities—Failure to record certain liabilities or incorrectly classify as equity.
  - Recognition of "exceptional" items—Misclassification of normal, recurring expenses as one-time or non-recurring removes items from operating results.*
  - Misapplication of accounting rules, especially in grey areas—Using an accounting treatment that helps perpetrate a fraud (e.g. in concealing it) rather than determine the most appropriate treatment for a transaction.
  - Omission or misrepresentation of information—Failure to provide certain information to the users may intentionally mislead them. The absence of information may make it impossible to comprehend the entity's financial performance and position.

*Although IAS 1 effectively prohibits the designation of any item as exceptional, the term is still used in IFRS financial statements (e.g. see Diageo Annual Report 2016).

- **Insider dealing** (i.e. using "inside information" to gain advantage when dealing in securities) is a prime example of the abuse by directors or others of their position of trust and confidentiality.

Illustration 3 Insider Dealing

The CEO of HealthSouth allegedly instructed his employees to inflate the earnings figures over the period 1996—2003. This they did to the tune of $1.3 billion by "making up" the numbers in financial reports.

The fraud was discovered when the CEO sold shares for $75 million the day before the company was to report a huge loss.

© DeVry/Becker Educational Development Corp. All rights reserved.

▨ Financial statements may be manipulated to show the company in a better light; this manipulation may include:*
  - off balance sheet financing;
  - profit smoothing (e.g. through inappropriate use of provisions of reserves);
  - window dressing (e.g. presenting current liabilities as long-term or vice versa).

▨ Many companies that engage in "creative" accounting practices are "found out" because of the difficulty in sustaining fictitious levels of earnings. In the last 30 years, such companies have included Enron, WorldCom, Lehman Brothers and Polly Peck, to name but a few.*

*Financial gain through fraud may not be the principal driver (e.g. directors trying to protect themselves against claims of shortcomings in their stewardship).

2 Managing Ethics

2.1 Compliance-Based Approach

▨ This approach concentrates on acting within the law. Systems and practices should be designed in such a way that violation of the law is prevented, or if violations do occur, they are quickly detected and punished.

▨ This approach will incorporate some or all of the following into their organisation:
  - compliance procedural manuals;
  - auditing of contracts;
  - formalised disciplinary procedures; and
  - communication channels allowing individuals to report to management.

▨ The problem with this approach is that many actions may be legal but not ethical. Working in an environment that does not punish environmental pollution would mean the company could do as it liked, as it was not breaking the law.

▨ This approach also tends to work more by fear than a feeling of doing the right thing. The company will stress that this is the way things are done and failure to comply will be punished.

*At one point, HealthSouth (see *Illustration 3*) was borrowing money to pay corporate taxes that were higher than its actual revenue.

2.2 Integrity-Based Approach

▨ This approach requires acting within the law, but also requires that management take responsibility for the ethical behaviour of the company and personnel within the company.

▨ Typically, ethics programmes convey corporate values, often using codes and policies to guide decisions and behaviour, and can include extensive training and evaluating, depending on the organisation. They provide guidance in ethical dilemmas.

▨ There are many possible benefits in formally managing ethics as a programme. Ethics programmes aim to:*
  - establish organisational roles to manage ethics;
  - schedule ongoing assessment of ethics requirements;
  - establish required operating values and behaviours;
  - align organisational behaviours with operating values;
  - develop awareness and sensitivity to ethical issues;
  - integrate ethical guidelines into decision-making; and
  - structure mechanisms to resolve ethical dilemmas.

*Also to promote that attention to ethics is not just to "stay out of trouble" or improve public image.

© DeVry/Becker Educational Development Corp. All rights reserved.

- Many companies set up an ethics committee to oversee how the company meets its ethical responsibilities. Some even have an ethics ombudsman to help coordinate development of the policies and procedures to institutionalise moral values in the workplace. This position usually is directly responsible for resolving ethical dilemmas by interpreting policies and procedures.

- The integrity-based approach relies upon having a form of cultural control within the business.

3   IFAC Code of Ethics

3.1   A Model Code

- IFAC believes that, due to national differences of culture, language, legal and social systems, member bodies (e.g. ACCA) are primarily responsible for:
  - preparing detailed ethical requirement; and
  - implementing and enforcing such requirements.

- IFAC's international code (Code of Ethics for Professional Accountants) is intended to serve as a model. It sets standards of conduct and states fundamental principles to be the basis on which ethical requirements should be founded.

3.2   Objectives of the Accountancy Profession

- To work to the highest standards of professionalism.
- To attain the highest levels of performance.
- To meet the public interest requirement.

These objectives require that four basic needs be met:

- Credibility—of information and information systems provided by the professional accountant.

- Professionalism—individuals should be clearly identifiable by clients, employers and other interested parties as professional persons in the accountancy field.

- Quality of services—all services obtained from a professional accountant should be carried out to the highest standards of performance.

- Confidence—given by a framework of professional ethics which governs the provision of services.

© DeVry/Becker Educational Development Corp. All rights reserved.

3.3   The Code*

▨ IFAC's revised Code of Ethics (effective June 30, 2006) is based around a conceptual framework and guidance on the practical application of the objectives and fundamental principles to typical situations. It is divided into three sections:

*The Code of Ethics can be downloaded free from www.ifac.org.

(A) General Application

- ◉ Integrity
- ◉ Objectivity
- ◉ Professional competence and due care
- ◉ Resolution of ethical conflicts
- ◉ Confidentiality
- ◉ Professional behaviour

*(B) Professional Accountants in Public Practice***

*Additional areas of public practice include tax practice, cross-border activities and publicity.

- ◉ Professional appointment
- ◉ Conflicts of interest
- ◉ Second opinions
- ◉ Fees and other types of remuneration
- ◉ Marketing professional services
- ◉ Gifts and hospitality
- ◉ Custody of client assets
- ◉ Objectivity—all services
- ◉ Independence—assurance engagements

(C) Other Accountants Employed in Business And Industry

- ◉ Potential conflicts
- ◉ Preparation and reporting of information
- ◉ Acting with sufficient expertise
- ◉ Financial interests
- ◉ Inducements

Key Point

ACCA is a leading member of the IFAC. The codes of ACCA and the IFAC are effectively interchangeable in the majority of requirements, with the ACCA's code giving additional guidance specific to ACCA members.

4 ACCA Code of Ethics and Conduct

4.1 Application

▓ As a member of the IFAC, the ACCA's Code of Ethics and Conduct is based on the Code of Ethics of the IFAC and applies to all students and members of the Association (whether in practice, commerce, internal audit, etc) in that they are required to observe proper standards of professional conduct and refrain from misconduct. Failure to observe standards may result in disciplinary proceedings.

▓ The Codes provide five fundamental principles and a conceptual framework to assist members in applying the principles (effectively the same as the IFAC code).

4.2 Fundamental Principles

▓ Integrity—Implies honesty, fair dealing and truthfulness.

▓ Objectivity—Bias, conflicts of interest or undue influence must not override members' professional and business judgements.

▓ Professional competence and due care—reflecting current developments, sound judgements, continuing professional development (CPD) requirements, etc.

▓ Confidentiality (of information).

▓ Professional behaviour (e.g. in advertising).

4.3 Conceptual Framework—Risks

▓ The environment in which ACCA members operate may often give rise to specific threats to compliance with the Fundamental Principles.

▓ The Conceptual Framework assists members (through guidance and illustrative examples) to identify, evaluate and respond to threats to compliance with the Fundamental Principles, rather than merely following rules.

▓ If identified threats are other than clearly insignificant, members must implement safeguards to eliminate the threats or reduce them to an acceptable level so that compliance with the Fundamental Principles is not compromised.

▓ The Conceptual Framework allows members to consider the risks they face and to match those risks with the appropriate action.

▓ Although examples are used to illustrate the application of the framework, they do not cover all possibilities faced by members. The Framework should be applied to the particular circumstances faced.

Example 1 Advantages of the Principles-Based Approach

Suggest THREE advantages of the principles based approach to laying down a Code of Ethics.

© DeVry/Becker Educational Development Corp. All rights reserved.

▓ Compliance with the Fundamental Principles may potentially be threatened by a broad range of circumstances. Many threats fall into the following categories:

- self-interest (may occur as a result of the financial or other interests of members or of immediate or close family members);

- self-review (may arise when a previous judgement needs to be re-evaluated by individuals responsible for that judgement);

- advocacy (when members promote a position or opinion to the point that subsequent objectivity may be compromised);

- familiarity (where members, because of a close relationship, become too sympathetic to the interests of others); and

- intimidation (where members may be deterred from acting objectively by threats, actual or perceived, direct or indirect).

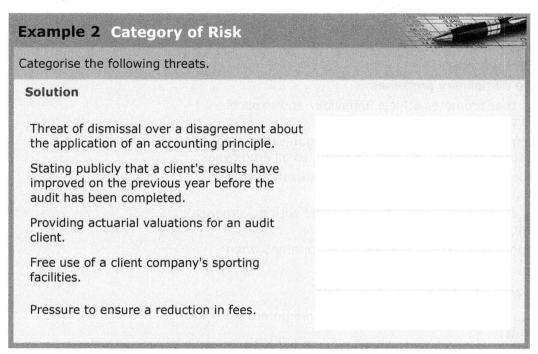

Example 2   Category of Risk

Categorise the following threats.

Solution

Threat of dismissal over a disagreement about the application of an accounting principle.

Stating publicly that a client's results have improved on the previous year before the audit has been completed.

Providing actuarial valuations for an audit client.

Free use of a client company's sporting facilities.

Pressure to ensure a reduction in fees.

4.4 Conceptual Framework—Safeguards

▓ The nature of the safeguards to be applied will vary depending on the circumstances, thus the use of a conceptual framework.

▓ In exercising their judgement, members should consider what a reasonable and informed third party, having knowledge of all relevant information, including the significance of the threat and the safeguards applied, would conclude to be unacceptable.

▓ Safeguards that may eliminate or reduce to acceptable levels the threats faced by members fall into three broad categories:

- created by the profession, legislation or regulation;
- in the work environment; and
- created by the individual.

4.4.1 Safeguards Created by the Profession, Legislation or Regulation

- Educational, training and experience requirements for entry into the profession;
- Continuing professional development (CPD) requirements;
- Corporate governance regulations;
- Professional standards;
- Professional or regulatory monitoring and disciplinary procedures; and
- External review by a legally empowered third party of the reports, returns, communications or information produced by a member.

4.4.2 Safeguards in the Work Environment

- The employing organisation's:
  - systems of corporate oversight;
  - ethics and conduct programmes; and
  - recruitment procedures.
- Strong internal controls;
- Appropriate disciplinary processes;
- Leadership that promotes ethical behaviour and expects employees to act ethically;
- Timely communication of the employing organisation's policies and procedures, and any changes to them, to all employees;
- The provision of appropriate training and education to employees;
- Discussing ethical issues with those charged with governance of the client; and
- Consultation with another professional accountant when necessary.

4.4.3 Safeguards Created by the Individuals

- Complying with continuing professional development (CPD) requirements;
- Keeping records of contentious issues and approach to decision-making;
- Maintaining a broader perspective on how similar organisations function through establishing business relationships with other professionals;
- Using an independent mentor; and
- Maintaining contact with legal advisors and professional bodies.

4.4.4 Other Safeguards

- Certain safeguards may increase the likelihood of identifying or deterring unethical behaviour. Such safeguards, which may be created by the accounting profession, legislation, regulation or an employing organisation, include, but are not restricted to:
  - effective, well-publicised complaints systems operated by the employing organisation, the profession or a regulator, which enable colleagues and employers to draw attention to unprofessional or unethical behaviour; and
  - an explicitly stated duty to report breaches of ethical requirements.

                    © DeVry/Becker Educational Development Corp. All rights reserved.

4.5   Ethical Conflict Resolution

▦ In resolving ethical conflicts, it is important to record the process and outcome. For example:

- ● relevant facts;
- ● the ethical issues involved;
- ● the fundamental principles involved;
- ● established procedures followed;
- ● action followed and outcome;
- ● alternative courses of action and their consequences; and
- ● internal and external sources of consultation (e.g. ethics partner; audit committee).

▦ Where a significant conflict cannot be resolved, consideration should be given to consulting legal advisers and/or the ACCA. This should not breach confidentiality.

▦ If, after exhausting all relevant possibilities, the ethical conflict remains unresolved, members should, where possible, refuse to remain associated with the matter creating the conflict.

▦ Members may determine that, in the circumstances, it is appropriate to withdraw from the engagement team or specific assignment, or to resign altogether from the engagement, the firm or the employing organisation.

5   Ethics in the Real World

5.1   COSO Study

▦ The Committee of Sponsoring Organisations of the Treadway Commission (COSO) has published a study, *Fraudulent Reporting: 1998–2007*, that examines 347 alleged accounting fraud cases investigated by the SEC during that period.

▦ Most of the frauds occurred before the provisions of the Sarbanes-Oxley Act had taken effect.

▦ Fraud can affect companies of any size; however, it was most common in companies having assets and revenue just under the $100 million level.

▦ The CEO or CFO was involved in some manner in 89% of the cases, with 20% of those personnel being indicted through the US courts.

▦ The average period over which the fraud was committed was just over 31 months.

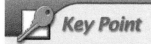 **Key Point**

The two most common fraudulent techniques used were related to improper revenue recognition and overstated asset valuations. In many cases, this involved capitalisation of costs which should have been expensed against profits.

- There did not seem to be any major differences between board of director and audit committee characteristics for those companies caught up in fraudulent activity against those companies without any instances of fraud.

- Most of the companies had received an unqualified audit opinion on their last set of misstated financial statements. However, it was likely that the audit report would contain additional explanatory language in those firms that had committed fraudulent activity.

- The share price of fraudulent companies fell on average by 16% in the first two days after public announcement of the fraud and a further 7% when news of an SEC or Department of Justice investigation was announced.

- Companies engaged in fraudulent activities often experienced bankruptcy, delisting from stock exchange or material asset sales.

5.2 Lehman Brothers

- Lehman Brothers was a global financial services firm involved in investment banking, equity and fixed income sales, private equity and private banking, to name but a few of its activities. It was a primary dealer in the US securities market.

- In September 2008, the firm filed for Chapter 11 bankruptcy protection following a mass exodus of its clients, drastic losses in its stocks and devaluation of its assets by credit rating agencies. The filing marked the largest bankruptcy in US history.

- A March 2010 report indicated that Lehman executives regularly used cosmetic accounting treatments at the end of each period to makes its finances appear better than they actually were.

- The practise was a type of repurchase agreement, called Repo 105, which temporarily removed quite risky securities from the company's statement of financial position.

- However, these deals were described as outright sales by Lehman executives and created a material misleading picture of the firm's financial condition in late 2007 and 2008.

5.3 Parmalat*

*Commentary

*Dubbed "Europe's Enron".

- Parmalat SpA is an Italy-based company which processes and distributes dairy products and fruit juices. It collapsed in 2003 with a €14 billion hole in its accounts in what remains Europe's biggest bankruptcy.

- In 1997, it moved into the world financial markets, financing several large international acquisitions with debt. By 2001, many of these acquisitions were producing losses. It then used derivative instruments which hid losses.

- In February 2003, it announced a new €500 million bond issue, much to the surprise of the markets and even the CEO. A newly-appointed CFO identified that the company's total debt was more than double what was included in the financial statements.

© DeVry/Becker Educational Development Corp. All rights reserved.

- In December 2003, the company was unable to pay its debts and meet the bond repayments. It was then found that documents showing €4 million in the bank account was a forgery. A fraud investigation was then launched, with thousands of investors losing their money. The company was officially declared bankrupt.

- Among the questionable accounting practices used by Parmalat was the selling, to itself, of credit-linked notes, effectively placing a bet on its own creditworthiness in order to conjure up an asset "out of thin air".

- The CEO later admitted diverting funds from Parmalat into other entities, which turned out to be financial disasters.

- Parmalat was rescued by the Italian government and continues to trade with operations throughout the world.

5.4   Lessons Learnt

Ethics are essential to the success or failure of any organisation as they:

- affect its reputation; and

- help to define a suitable business model that can survive in a fluctuating economic environment.

Management can be tempted to make decisions for short-term gains by ignoring ethics (despite codes of practice, regulatory oversight and increasing public pressure). Some managers believe that adhering to the law is sufficient and disregard ethical issues that can undermine the wider economy and cause irreparable damage.

However, there are many lessons to be learnt from the corporate collapses of hugely profitable entities that could not sustain the levels of performance that they first achieved.

- Strong ethical policies that go beyond upholding the law can add great value to a brand. Once adopted, demonstration of an ethical approach can result in bottom-line benefits.*

- High-quality management information is needed to monitor ethical performance. Corporate reports need to provide hard evidence to support progress on an ethical agenda (and not merely pay lip service to it).

- Finance professionals are needed to help companies operate in an ethically responsible way and avoid corporate failure, litigation and fraud. They have a particular ethical responsibility to promote a culture that does not permit practices such as bribery.

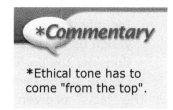

*Ethical tone has to come "from the top".

Advice for companies wishing to respond to increasing demands to be ethical might include the following:

✔ Ethics must be embedded in the business model, organisational strategy and decision-making processes.

✔ Senior management must provide "tone at the top" and create the appropriate organisational culture.

✔ Non-executive directors should have a particular duty of ensuring that the executive directors' managerial decisions are building a sustainable business.

✔ Those charged with governance must have the skills necessary to scrutinise ethical, social and environmental issues as well as financial performance.

✔ Managers must be open-minded to the opportunities and benefits of an ethical-stance approach.

✔ Finance professionals must champion ethics by challenging the assumptions upon which business decisions are made.*

✔ Management accountants are encouraged to ensure that performance is measured on a timely basis and to deliver sustained and sustainable success.

✔ Business leaders should use the skills of the finance team to evaluate and quantify reputational and other ethical risks.

✔ Finance professionals need to take social, environmental and ethical factors into account when allocating capital, so that sustainable innovation is encouraged.

*Commentary

*But at the same time uphold their valued reputation for impartiality and independence.

6 Examination Approach

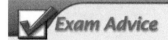
Exam Advice

It is unlikely that there will be a whole question concerning ethics in the examination. For example, in the pilot paper, there was a six-mark component on ethics in Q1.

▦ If the question is for five marks, do not write an essay. Be concise and to the point and do not regurgitate the question.

▦ To answer the question, it is likely that you will need to:
- Identify the parties involved
- Identify the event(s) that gave rise to the ethical problem
- Weigh up the possible courses of action
- Consider the professional codes that may be relevant
- Decide on the best course of action.

▦ The "facts" as given may require you to "read between the lines" to interpret what the ethical issue is.

▦ "Report the person to the relevant authority" is clearly insufficient as an answer. In the most extreme cases this may be the most appropriate conclusion, but the alternatives still need to be evaluated.

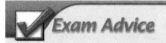
Exam Advice

There may be no one "correct" answer. Marks will be awarded for backing up an ethical stance with logical argument rather than an unsupported conclusion.

© DeVry/Becker Educational Development Corp. All rights reserved.

Illustration 4 Ethical Responsibility

Jaffa's directors are concerned about the results for the year in the statement of profit or loss and comprehensive income and the subsequent effect on the cash flow statement. They believe that the market will react badly to the results if they cannot "do something about them". They have, therefore, suggested that the proceeds of the sales of certain tangible assets and fair value through other comprehensive income financial assets should be included in "cash generated from operations".

The directors feel that making adjustments for the proceeds to enhance the "cash health" of the business would also help protect jobs.

Required:

Discuss the ethical responsibility of the company accountant in ensuring that manipulation of the statement of cash flows, such as that suggested by the directors, does not occur.

Solution

Companies can give the impression that they are generating more cash than they are, by manipulating cash flows.

Changing the way in which the sale of assets is presented in the statement of cash flows will change the amounts classified as operating and investing cash flows and hence the impression given by the financial statements.

The classification of cash flows provides useful information. Most users will be particularly interested in operating cash flows that are necessary to pay interest and tax.

There are many circumstances in which management may feel pressured into misrepresenting information. Accountants must possess a high degree of professional integrity to help managers resist such pressures; the reputation of the accounting profession depends upon it.

The company accountant has a responsibility to prevent the true nature of the statement of cash flow being masked. Showing the sale of assets as operating cash flows would mislead users even if these cash flows are correctly captioned (e.g. "proceeds of sale of equipment"). As the intention is clearly to deceive users such a classification is unacceptable.

The accountant should attempt to persuade the directors to follow acceptable accounting principles and comply with accounting standards. As there are implications for the truth and fairness of the financial statements he should point out that the auditors should challenge such blatant non-compliance with accounting standards.

Example 3 Consultancy Services

You are a professional accountant in Dedza, a firm of Chartered Certified Accountants.

The CEO of Xalam Co, an exporter of specialist equipment, has asked you for advice on the accounting treatment and disclosure of payments being made for security consultancy services. The payments, which aim to ensure that consignments are not impounded in the destination country of a major customer, may be material to the financial statements. Xalam does not treat these payments as tax deductible.

Required:

Identify and comment on the ethical issues raised by these payments and state what advice should be given to the CEO.

Example 4 Ethical Issues
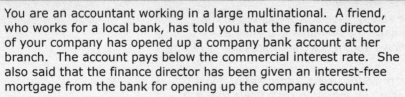

You are an accountant working in a large multinational. A friend, who works for a local bank, has told you that the finance director of your company has opened up a company bank account at her branch. The account pays below the commercial interest rate. She also said that the finance director has been given an interest-free mortgage from the bank for opening up the company account.

Required:

Identify the ethical issues in this scenario.

© DeVry/Becker Educational Development Corp. All rights reserved.

Summary

- Ethics is a set of moral principles to guide behaviour.
- The ACCA has its own code of ethics that must be followed by members and students.
- Two possible approaches to managing ethics are compliance-based and integrity-based.
- The two most common fraudulent techniques, and therefore ethical issues, relate to improper revenue recognition and overstating asset valuations.

Session 26 Quiz
Estimated time: 15 minutes

1. List the stakeholders having an interest in an entity. (1.3)

2. Name ethical issues which accountants may encounter during their career. (1.4)

3. Name the TWO methods of managing ethics that this session considers. (2)

4. State the objectives of the accountancy profession. (3.2)

5. Give the FIVE fundamental principles embodied within the ACCA Code of Ethics and Conduct. (4.2)

6. List the stages involved in the resolution of any ethical conflict. (4.5)

Study Question Bank
Estimated time: 30 minutes

Priority		Estimated Time	Completed
Q44	Happy and Healthy	30 minutes	

© DeVry/Becker Educational Development Corp. All rights reserved.

EXAMPLE SOLUTIONS

Solution 1—Advantages of the Principles-Based Approach

- Detailed rules encourage avoidance, but principles encourage compliance.
- A principles-based approach is more adaptable to meet any new potential conflicts and threats to independence.
- It is moving away from the US rule-book method approach to independence.
- It encourages firms to analyse threats to independence rather than to adopt a tick-box based approach.
- It places greater responsibility on the firms to deal with threats to independence.
- It improves self-regulation of the profession (by adopting a tougher stance).

Solution 2—Category of Risk

- Threat of dismissal over a disagreement about the application of an accounting principle.

  Intimidation/(self-interest)

- Stating publicly that a client's results have improved on the previous year before the audit has been completed.

  Advocacy

- Providing actuarial valuations for an audit client.

  Self-review

- Free use of a client company's sporting facilities.

  Self-interest/(familiarity)

- Pressure to ensure a reduction in fees.

  Intimidation/(self-interest)

© DeVry/Becker Educational Development Corp. All rights reserved.

Solution 3—Consultancy Services

- Because Xalam is not claiming these expenses as tax deductible, there are no implications for dealings with the taxation authority. However, the fact that Xalam is not treating them as tax deductible suggests that they are not legitimate in some way. It seems quite likely that they lack the supporting documentation that would be expected for bona fide business expenses.

- These payments for "security consultancy services" appear to amount to a bribe. Corruption and bribery (and extortion) are money laundering offences.*

- Xalam clearly benefits from the payments as it receives income from the contract with the major customer. This is criminal property and possession of it is a money-laundering offence.

- The CEO should be advised of the seriousness of his disclosure in the context of domestic law and encouraged to make voluntary disclosure to the relevant anti-money-laundering authority (e.g. the Financial Intelligence Unit).

- If Xalam does not, Dedza should report knowledge of a suspicious transaction.*

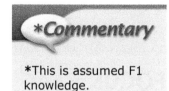

*This is assumed F1 knowledge.

Solution 4—Ethical Issues

Finance director

It is probable that the finance director would be classed as a related party of the entity, and as the opening of the bank account was not an arm's length transaction, then this should be disclosed in the financial statements.

There is a self-interest threat, as the finance director has received a benefit from an outside party.

The integrity of the director must be in doubt. Has he taken similar actions with other assets of the entity? The transaction will probably transgress the ethical code of the professional body to which the director belongs.

There is an issue of theft relating to the interest foregone.

*Making a report takes precedence over client confidentiality.

Accountant

If the accountant was party to the opening of the bank account, he should have spoken to the director before the account was opened.

He has an obligation to report the transaction to the finance director's superior. This will probably involve "whistle-blowing". However, he should be granted exemption from any involvement in the transaction.

Friend

There is an ethical issue about the friend's action as well. She has breached her duty of confidentiality of the bank by giving out information about one of the bank's customers.

© DeVry/Becker Educational Development Corp. All rights reserved.

Environmental Reporting

FOCUS

This session covers the following content from the *ACCA Study Guide.*

A. The Professional and Ethical Duties of the Accountant

3. Social Responsibility

a) Discuss the increased demand for transparency in corporate reports, and the emergence of non-financial reporting standards. ☐

b) Discuss the progress towards a framework for integrated reporting. ☐

H. Current Developments

1. Environmental and social reporting

a) Appraise the impact of environmental, social and ethical factors on performance measurement. ☐

b) Evaluate current reporting requirements in the area including the development of integrated reporting. ☐

c) Discuss why entities might include disclosures relating to the environment and society. ☐

Session 27 Guidance

- **Read** through the session paying attention to what is happening in the real world.
- **Appreciate** the reasons behind the development of environmental accounting (s.1) and **learn** the categories of GRI performance indicators (s.2.3).
- **Understand** the corporate social responsibility issues which affect corporate reporting in the modern economic environment (s.3, s.4).
- **Read** the *student accountant* article "<IR> Framework".

VISUAL OVERVIEW

Objective: To consider the environmental and social issues affecting the corporate entity.

INTRODUCTION

- Background
- Accounting
- Reasons for Environmental Accounting
- Pollution Charge

GLOBAL REPORTING INITIATIVE (GRI)

- History
- Report Content
- Performance Indicators
- BP Sustainability Report

CORPORATE SOCIAL RESPONSIBILITY (CSR)

- Background
- Business Case
- Criticisms
- Examples

CORPORATE REPORTING

- Background
- Management Commentary
- Usefulness of Corporate Reports

INTEGRATED REPORTING

- IIRC
- Integrated Framework
- Definitions of Capital
- Integrated Report
- Guiding Principles
- Content Elements
- Usefulness to Stakeholders
- Link to CSR

© DeVry/Becker Educational Development Corp. All rights reserved.

1 Introduction

1.1 Background

▣ At present, there is no compulsory requirement to present environmental reports by an entity. However, some reporting issues may be required as a result of provisions or contingencies set up in accordance with IAS 37 *Provisions, Contingent Liabilities and Contingent Assets*.*

▣ The first form of environmental reports came about in the 1980s. One of the first companies to produce a report of this nature was The Body Shop, which wanted to show that it was environmentally friendly in the production of its products.*

▣ The topic not only covers the environment but also looks at economic and social issues. These three topics are the focus of The Global Reporting Initiative (GRI).

▣ In December 2004, IFRIC (now IFRS IC) issued IFRIC 3 on accounting for emission rights arising from the Kyoto agreement. Companies are capped on the level of pollutant emissions they are allowed to make, leading to an excess for some companies and a shortage for others. Emission rights are now being traded on open markets. However, the IFRIC was quickly withdrawn as some of the requirements were fundamentally flawed.

1.2 Accounting

Key Point

Environmental accounting can be considered a subset of accounting, as it aims to incorporate both economic and environmental information into corporate reporting.

▣ An environmental accounting system identifies measures and communicates costs from a company's actual or potential impact on the environment. Costs can include clean-up costs, environmental fines and taxes, purchase of pollution prevention technologies and waste management costs.

▣ The system not only measures effects on the environment in monetary terms, but would also consider ecological accounting measures and their impact on the environment. These measures would include levels of waste products and the amount of energy consumed.

1.2.1 Environmental Management Accounting

▣ This is used by companies to make internal business strategy decisions.

*Commentary

*Many companies in the oil industry have recognised provisions for clean-up costs in their financial statements.

*Commentary

*It was subsequently identified that The Body Shop had been using cheap overseas labour in its production processes; this had a detrimental effect on its share price.

© DeVry/Becker Educational Development Corp. All rights reserved.

▩ It involves the identification, collection, analysis and use of two types of information for internal decision-making:

  ◦ physical information on the use, flows and fates of energy, water and materials, including waste; and

  ◦ monetary information on environmentally related costs, earnings and savings.

1.2.2 Environmental Financial Accounting

▩ This is used to provide information needed by external stakeholders on a company's financial status and how it is interacting with the environment.

1.3 Reasons for Environmental Accounting

▩ There are a number of reasons why an entity may adopt environmental accounting within its accounting systems:

  ◦ a reduction of environmental costs;

  ◦ the identification of environmental costs or benefits that previously may have been overlooked;

  ◦ possible revenue generation opportunities;

  ◦ improved environmental performance may have a positive effect on employees health and enhance the success of the business;

  ◦ it may lead to more accurate costing and pricing of products;

  ◦ it could give competitive advantages as customers may prefer environmentally-friendly products;

  ◦ it can support the development and running of an environment management system, which may be required by regulation for some types of businesses.

1.4 Pollution Charge

▩ There is a strong possibility that governments may start to charge companies for the pollution that they emit into the environment.

▩ The question that the accountants need to answer is how this charge should be accounted for. There are three possible options:

  (1) recognise the charge as an intangible asset;

  (2) recognise the charge as an expense for the period; or

  (3) include the charge as part of the tax expense for the period.

2 Global Reporting Initiative (GRI)

▩ GRI is a long-term, multi-stakeholder, international undertaking whose mission is to develop and disseminate globally applicable sustainability reporting guidelines for voluntary use by organisations reporting on the economic, environmental and social dimensions of their activities, products and services.

© DeVry/Becker Educational Development Corp. All rights reserved.

2.1   History

▓ The idea of a disclosure framework for the reporting of sustainability information was conceived in 1997 by a Boston-based non-profit organisation, CERES.

▓ An exposure draft of sustainability reporting guidelines was released in 1999, with the document being released in 2000.

▓ In 2001, GRI separated from CERES to become an independent body, with the board being appointed in 2002.

▓ In 2002, 150 organisations produced sustainability reports based on the GRI guidelines; by 2006, the number of organisations producing reports was in excess of 850.

▓ In 2006, the "G3" (third generation of guidelines) were produced.

2.2   Report Content

▓ To ensure a balanced and reasonable presentation of the company's performance, it is important to identify what the content of the report should cover. Consideration should be given to the purpose and experience of the company and should also take into account the expectations and interests of the stakeholders of the company.

2.2.1   Materiality

▓ The information in a report should cover topics and indicators that reflect the company's significant economic, environmental and social impacts or that would substantively influence the assessments and decisions of stakeholders.

2.2.2   Stakeholder Inclusiveness

▓ The reporting entity should identify its stakeholders and explain in the report how it has responded to their reasonable expectations and interests.

2.2.3   Sustainability Context

▓ The report should present the entity's performance in the wider context of sustainability.

2.2.4   Completeness

▓ Coverage of the material topics and indicators, and definition of the report boundary, should be sufficient to reflect significant economic, environmental and social impacts and enable stakeholders to assess the reporting entity's performance in the reporting period.

2.3   Performance Indicators

▓ The GRI guidelines identify numerous performance indicators that an entity can use to show how it has performed over the period. These indicators are broken down into three categories.

                    © DeVry/Becker Educational Development Corp. All rights reserved.

2.3.1 Economic

▦ This category includes protocols covering:
- economic performance;
- market presence; and
- indirect economic impacts.

2.3.2 Environmental

▦ This category covers protocols that include:
- materials;
- energy;
- biodiversity;
- emissions, effluents and waste;
- compliance; and
- transport.

2.3.3 Social

▦ The social category is sub-divided into four categories that deal with the following:

- Labour practices and decent work:
  employment;
  labour relations;
  occupational health and safety;
  training and education; and
  diversity and equal opportunity.
- Human rights:
  investment and procurement practices;
  non-discrimination;
  child labour;
  forced and compulsory labour; and
  indigenous rights.
- Society:
  community;
  corruption;
  anticompetitive behaviour; and
  compliance.
- Product responsibility:
  customer health and safety;
  product and service labelling;
  marketing communications; and
  customer privacy.

▦ The list is very extensive, and detailed information needs to be provided to the stakeholders. The production of a GRI-based report is therefore costly and time-consuming, but it is hoped that in the long-term, it will benefit the company.

2.4 British Petroleum Sustainability Report 2006

▦ Oil spills of one barrel or more fell to 417 spills in 2006, compared to 541 in 2005.

▦ The company is introducing dual-fuel diesel-electric propelled ships into its fleet. These ships consume between 30–40 tonnes per day less fuel.

▦ BP has a team of 136 compliance and ethics leaders who have continued embedding the compliance and ethics programme in their business areas through activities such as promoting awareness of OpenTalk and supporting the annual compliance and ethics process.*

▦ Greenhouse gas emissions were 64.4 million tonnes of CO_2 in 2006, compared to 66.8 million tonnes in 2005.

Commentary

*The BP oil spill in the Gulf of Mexico in 2010 had a major impact on the company's share price. BP set aside a $20 billion fund to compensate victims of the spill.

3 Corporate Social Responsibility CSR

3.1 Background

- The concept of CSR has been around since the early 20th century. Many individuals and organisations have tried to define what CSR is.

  - "Growth in harmony with our environment, preserving our resource base for our economic well-being, and planning for our children's future." —*Gary Filmon*

  - "Sustainable development requires environmental health, economic prosperity and social equity." —*Earth Council*

  - "Sustainable development is the achievement of continued economic and social development without detriment to the environment and natural resources. The quality of future human activity and development is increasingly seen as being dependent on maintaining this balance." —*European Foundation for the Improvement of Living and working Conditions*

- These statements highlight that CSR is about the environment, economy and social responsibility. This is what the GRI has taken forward in its mission to try to get some form of corporate responsibility amongst organisations.

3.2 Business Case for CSR

- The arguments in favour of business adopting some form of CSR will probably fall into one or more of the following issues.

3.2.1 Human Resources

- A CSR programme should be an aid to the recruitment and retention of staff, especially among today's graduate student market; during job interviews, many candidates now ask a firm about CSR policy.

- CSR can also help to improve the perception of a company among its staff, especially when staff can become involved through payroll giving, fundraising activities or community volunteering.

3.2.2 Risk Management

- Managing risk is a central part of many corporate strategies. Reputations that have taken many years to build up can be shattered through incidents such as corruption scandals or environmental incidents. These events can also draw unwanted attention from regulatory bodies, governments and the media. Being aware of these risks, and adopting a policy and culture to minimise identified risks, will lead to benefits in future periods.

3.2.3 Brand Differentiation

- In large marketplaces, companies will strive for some unique selling point in order to differentiate them from competitors. CSR can play a role of building customer loyalty based on some form of distinctive ethical values. Having a reputation for integrity and best practice will set a company above others in the same marketplace.

                              © DeVry/Becker Educational Development Corp. All rights reserved.

3.2.4 License to Operate

- By acting as good corporate citizens, a company can hope that it will be less susceptible to government intervention. By following some form of voluntary code highlighting what it is doing for the environment and economy, it may be able to save on tax bills and unwanted regulations.

3.3 Criticisms of CSR

- Some would argue that CSR hinders the workings of a free marketplace.*

- They argue that any improvements in health, longevity or infant mortality have been created by economic growth, which they attribute to free enterprise.

- This group would say that an entity pays its taxes to government to ensure that society and the environment are not adversely affected by business activities.

- There is another group who argue that the only reason companies follow any form of CSR is for purely cynical reasons (e.g. as a public relations exercise).

- They would quote examples of where companies have spent a lot of time and money on promoting CSR policies and their commitment to sustainable development on the one hand, while damaging revelations about business practices emerge on the other.

- MacDonald's, Shell and The Body Shop have all been involved in incidences of possible unethical business practices while trying to promote themselves as good corporate citizens.

*Milton Friedman (an economist) argued against CSR, saying that a company's principle objective is to maximise returns to shareholders, while obeying the laws of the countries within which it works.

3.4 Examples of CSR at Work

3.4.1 Electrolux

- Electrolux has produced a life-cycle analysis of its washing machines. It found that about 80% of total environmental impact during the life of the machine consist of water, energy and detergent consumption.

- The analysis also identified that the costs of these items exceeds the initial purchase price of the machine.

- For the customer, this means that choosing an appliance with a high environmental performance also means long-term savings. For the appliance industry, it means making consumers aware of this connection.

- Replacing old, inefficient machines with newer generation, resource-efficient appliances is beneficial for the environment.

3.4.2 Norsk Hydro

- Norsk Hydro has applied a life-cycle assessment to the workings of the whole company.

- The data show a striking overview of the company's consumption of natural resources and pollutant emissions in context of its annual profits.

3.4.3 Monsanto

- Monsanto has presented its report exclusively as an electronic document, departing from the old practice of producing paper reports.

- It has the advantage of making the report accessible to more people worldwide and creates a forum for sharing more information. It also gives access to a level of detail that was not available in a printed version.

- The downside, however, is that it cannot be seen without individuals having some form of access to a computer system. Large areas of the developing world do not have any access to computers or the Internet.

3.4.4 DuPont Canada

- DuPont has demonstrated a commitment to employee health, not only by reporting on injuries and illnesses resulting in lost time, but also employees' physical fitness levels.

- It provides data on rates of smoking, cholesterol levels, blood pressure and obesity amongst its employees.

- It also reports on the availability of on-site fitness facilities, as well as nutritional and health counselling and health information seminars that demonstrate the link between its policy and actions with regard to employees' health.

4 Corporate Reporting

4.1 Background

- This session has considered some of the issues affecting the reporting of corporate information to interested parties.

- Corporate reporting includes the periodic financial statements that a company must produce for shareholders and other users. But corporate reporting is far broader than just a set of financial statements; any press release must be produced in a manner that should not mislead those likely to be using the information.

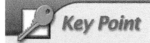 **Key Point**

The IASB is just one party involved in trying to ensure that managers are good corporate citizens working towards an environment that will be to the benefit of all, not just the chosen few.

- Unfortunately, not all entities are working towards the wider good; over the years, there have been numerous accounting scandals where individuals in power have been looking after themselves rather than the company as a whole. It is highly likely that there will always be a small number of people who are intent on defrauding the company; the aim is to keep these incidences of fraud to a minimum level.

© DeVry/Becker Educational Development Corp. All rights reserved.

4.2   Practice Statement on Management Commentary (MC)

4.2.1   Practice Statement

■ IASB published the *Practice Statement on Management Commentary* in December 2010.

■ It is a **voluntary** statement aimed initially for listed companies, but can also be adopted by other entities that follow IFRS.

■ It is **not** an IFRS and is non-binding. It proposes a framework for the presentation of management commentary that is in addition, and complimentary, to an entity's published financial statements.

■ Entities are allowed to adapt the requirements to suit their specific circumstances (e.g. the political, legal and economic environment in which the entity operates).

■ If an entity does produce management commentary, it should disclose the extent to which the statement has been followed.

Definition

Management commentary—A narrative report that relates to financial statements that have been prepared in accordance with IFRSs. It provides users with historical explanations of the amounts presented in the financial statements. It also provides commentary on an entity's prospects and other information not presented in the financial statements. It also serves as a basis for understanding management's objectives and its strategies for achieving those objectives.

■ Many countries already require an entity to produce some form of management commentary as part of their annual financial statements. In the UK, there is the "Operating and Financial Review (OFR)", and in the US, there is "Management Discussion and Analysis".

© DeVry/Becker Educational Development Corp. All rights reserved.

4.2.2 Purpose of MC

Key Point

The purpose of MC is to provide *investors (existing and future)* with decision-useful information that enables them to put the financial statements into context.

- To fulfil that objective, management should report not only upon what has happened in the period, but should also include an explanation as to why it has happened and the potential future impact.
- The information should be targeted to allow users to understand:
  - the entity's risk exposure, any strategies for managing risk, and the effectiveness of that strategy;
  - how resources that are not presented in the financial statements could affect the entity's operations; and
  - how non-financial factors have influenced the information presented in the financial statements.
- The aim of the statement is that management commentary should provide useful information to users to aid in their decision-making processes.
- Commentary should report on what has happened, why it happened and the effect(s) that may be felt in the future.
- In order to fulfil this purpose, management commentary should:
  - discuss and analyse performance, position and development from a management perspective, and identify how management plans to move the entity forward into the future;
  - supplement and complement information that is presented in the financial statements;*
  - be forward looking and at the same time assess how former forward-looking comments have borne out; and
  - possess the qualitative characteristics described in the Conceptual Framework.

*Commentary

*Management commentary is aimed at giving additional information, not merely restating what has already been said in the financial statements.

4.2.3 Elements of Management Commentary

The statement should include information that is necessary for the user to gain an understanding of:

- the nature of the business, both from a macro- and micro-level perspective;
- management strategy, to include a form of SWOT analysis;
- significant resources, both financial and non-financial, available to the entity;
- past operating results and how those results can be extrapolated into the future; and
- critical performance measures and indicators used by the entity.

© DeVry/Becker Educational Development Corp. All rights reserved.

4.3   Usefulness of Corporate Reports

▨ The aim of corporate reporting is to give information that is useful in the decision-making process to various users. (For instance, should an investor buy, sell or hold an investment? Should a creditor allow money to be lent?)

▨ Financial statements are just one of the tools to passing on information to the users. The financial statements are governed by IFRSs, but as has previously been said, the theory does not always match the practice.

▨ However, much credit must be given to the IASB and its accounting standards, as its aim is to ensure that reporting is much more risk free and that users will be able to make reliable decisions based on the information given in financial statements.

4.3.1   Risk

▨ IFRS 7 *Financial Instruments—Disclosure* requires risk disclosures based on credit risk, market risk and liquidity risk to be given within the notes to the financial statements.

▨ IFRS 8 *Operating Segments* gives some indication of the main segments of a business and should allow the user to identify any concentrations of risk or issues that may affect future operations.

▨ IAS 7 *Statement of Cash Flows* identifies the historical cash flows of an entity and will give some indication of where cash flows are going to be in the future.

▨ These standards and others will allow the reader of a set of financial statements to make some judgement decisions about how an entity has performed in the past, how it will perform in the future and what are the major areas of concern and risk that the entity will meet in its future operations.

▨ Corporate reporting will never be a foolproof method though; there will always be risk that an individual will have to take. Every answer to every question cannot be given in the financial statement; judgements will have to be made based on the knowledge the user has. The hope is that that knowledge will be as foolproof as possible if the entity has followed the principles set out within the accounting framework of the IASB.

© DeVry/Becker Educational Development Corp. All rights reserved.

5 Integrated Reporting

5.1 International Integrated Reporting Council (IIRC)

▓ Integrated reporting reflects "integrated thinking".

> **Definition**
>
> **Integrated thinking**—an application of the collective mind of those charged with governance and the ability of management to monitor, manage and communicate the full complexity of the value-creation process and how this contributes to the success of the organisation over time.

▓ The International Integrated Reporting Council (IIRC) is a global coalition of regulators, investors, companies, standard setters, the accounting profession and non-government organisations. It has a vision of a business environment in which integrated thinking is ingrained in mainstream business practice, in both public and private sectors. This would be facilitated by integrated reporting.

▓ The IIRC launched a new international framework for integrated reporting in December 2013. The document can be downloaded from the IIRC's website, www.theiirc.org.*

Commentary

*The framework is often referred to as the International <IR> Framework and integrated reporting as <IR>.

▓ A primary motivation behind the progress towards integrated reporting is that financial information alone is insufficient as an indicator of the long-term *sustainability* of a business.

▓ Integrated reporting combines *financial* and *non-financial* information in one report with the goal of maximising the value of information provided to stakeholders with a variety of interests in an organisation.

▓ Accounting for the sustainability of an organisation is important for the organisation and for those who provide financial capital to an organisation, as:

- An organisation needs a reporting environment that is conducive to comprehending and articulating its strategy to provide focus and drive internally and attract financial capital for investment.
- Investors need to understand how the strategy being pursued creates value over time.

© DeVry/Becker Educational Development Corp. All rights reserved.

- The goals of integrated reporting are:
  - to improve the quality of information available to providers of financial capital;
  - to promote a more cohesive and efficient approach to corporate reporting that better reflects all of the factors that materially affect the ability of an organisation to create value over time;
  - to enhance accountability and stewardship for all forms of capital;
  - to promote the understanding of the interdependencies among the various capitals; and
  - to support integrated thinking in decision-making and actions which create value over the short, medium and long term.

Illustration 1 "What It Is—and Is Not"

In an interview with Dr. Carol Adams, director of Integrated Horizons, the CEO of the IIRC described integrated reporting as **not** being:

1. Another report—but instead an evolution in corporate reporting.
2. Sustainability reporting. It does not create sustainability indicators.
3. A reporting process that emphasises multi-stakeholders but a reporting process emphasising integrated thinking.

C. Adams (2013, Oct 15). Integrated reporting—What it is—and is not: An interview with Paul Druckman. Source: http://drcaroladams.net/integrated-reporting-what-it-is-and-is-not-an-interview-with-paul-druckman/

5.2   The International <IR> Framework

- The purpose of the framework is to provide **principles** and **content elements** that help:
  - to shape the information provided; and
  - to explain why the inclusion of the information provided is important.
- Although the framework is written to be specifically applicable to for-profit companies of any size in the private sector, it can be adapted by not-for-profit and public sector organisations.
- Any communication which claims to be an integrated report written in conjunction with the international framework should apply the **guiding principles** (see s.5.5), unless:
  - reliable information is not available; or
  - specific legal requirements prohibit inclusion of information; or
  - disclosure of information would cause significant competitive harm.
- An integrated report should include eight **content elements**. The content elements are provided in the form of questions which can be categorised (see s.5.6).

5.3 Alternative Definitions of Capital

Integrated reporting results in a more expansive coverage of information than does traditional financial reporting. Integrated reporting more clearly demonstrates an organisation's use of and dependence on different resources and relationships or "capitals" and the organisation's access to and effect on them.*

Commentary

*IFRS currently requires extensive disclosures relating to financial capital but information about the other forms of capital would not normally be provided in annual financial statements.

- **Financial:** The pool of funds that is:
  - available for use in the production of goods or provision of services; or
  - obtained through financing.
- **Manufactured:** Manufactured physical objects that are distinct from natural physical objects (e.g. buildings, equipment and infrastructure).
- **Intellectual:** Organisational, knowledge-based intangibles.
- **Human:** People's competencies, capabilities and experience and their motivations to innovate.
- **Social and Relationship:** The institutions and the relationship within and between communities, groups of stakeholders and other networks, and the ability to share information to enhance individual and collective well-being.
- **Natural:** All renewable and non-renewable environmental resources and processes that provide goods or services that support the past, current or future prosperity of an organisation.

5.4 The Integrated Report

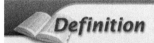

Definition

Integrated report—a concise communication about how an organisation's strategy, governance, performance and prospects, in the context of its external environment, lead to the creation of value over the short, medium and long term.

- An integrated report is prepared in accordance with the International <IR> Framework. It may be prepared in response to existing compliance requirements.*
- It is a specific and identifiable communication that may be either:
  - a standalone report; or
  - included as a distinguishable, prominent and accessible part of another report or communication (e.g. in the financial statements).
- It should be more than a summary of information available in other communications but should provide insight into the connectivity of the information and how value is created over time in an organisation.

Commentary

*South African corporate reporting, through the King Report on Governance (King III), requires all listed companies to adopt integrated reporting on a "comply or explain" basis.

© DeVry/Becker Educational Development Corp. All rights reserved.

Illustration 2 Transnet

In 2013, Transnet, a company based in South Africa,* issued an integrated report that is included in the Emerging Integrated Reporting database, which can be found at http://examples.theiirc.org/home. In this report, Transnet highlighted the company's mandate, business model, strategy, governance, performance review and future outlook. Furthermore, it aims to demonstrate how Transnet responds to its context, stakeholders, risks and opportunities in order to create sustainable value for the economy, society and the environment. Transnet's annual financial statements and sustainability report are in publications separate from the integrated report.

*The Johannesburg Stock Exchange from 1 March 2010 has required all listed companies to adopt <IR>. Transnet's report contains 140 pages of <IR> in addition to its annual financial report.

5.5 Guiding Principles

The guiding principles provide the foundation for how an organisation should consider information to be included in the report and how information should be presented. These principles are:

A. **Strategic focus and future orientation:** The report should provide insight into the organisation's strategy and how it relates to:

- the organisation's ability to create value over time; and
- its use and effect on the identified capitals.

B. **Connectivity of information:** The report should demonstrate connectivity between the factors that affect the organisation's ability to create value over time.

C. **Stakeholder relationships:** The report should provide insight into the nature and quality of the organisation's relationships with its key stakeholders.

D **Materiality:** The report should disclose information about items which significantly affect the organisation's ability to create value over time.

E. **Conciseness:** The report should be focused and avoid superfluous information that would not be relevant to stakeholders.

F. **Reliability and completeness:** The report should reflect all material items (both positive and negative) affecting the organisation and be free from material error.

G. **Consistency and comparability:** Information contained in an integrated report should be consistent over time and presented in a way which can be compared to other organisations.

5.6   Content Elements

▨ The content elements are fundamentally linked to each other and not mutually exclusive.

▨ The goal of the integrated report is not to necessarily address each content element (as a "checklist") but to ensure that the content elements are addressed in a way that demonstrates that the connections between them are logical when considering the circumstances of the organisation.*

▨ The content element categories and the question to be addressed in the integrated report when considering each category are as follows:

A. Organisational overview and external environment: What does the organisation do and what are the circumstances under which it operates?

B. Governance: How does the organisation's governance or leadership structure support its ability to create value over time?

C. Business model: What is the organisation's business model?

D. Risks and opportunities: What are the specific risks and opportunities that affect the organisation's ability to create value over time, and how is the organisation dealing with these risks and opportunities?*

E. Strategy and resource allocation: Where does the organisation want to go, and how does it intend to get there?

F. Performance: To what extent has the organisation achieved its strategic objectives for the period, and what are its outcomes in terms of effects on the capitals?

G. Outlook: What challenges and uncertainties is the organisation likely to encounter in pursuing its strategy, and what are the potential implications for its business model and future performance?

H. Basis of preparation and presentation: How does the organisation determine the issues to include in the integrated report, and how are such issues quantified or evaluated?

*IIRC does not want "boiler plate" statements that are the same for every company. The report should be entity specific and detail all event and transactions that would affect all capitals.

*Although IFRS 7 requires an entity to disclose the financial risks to which it is exposed, there is no requirement to disclose specific opportunities that might add value to the company.

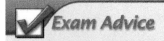

Exam Advice

The best way to understand the concept of integrated reporting is to review a typical report (e.g. Transnet) and analyse it according to the framework.

© DeVry/Becker Educational Development Corp. All rights reserved.

5.7   Usefulness to Stakeholders

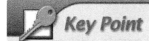

Key Point

The **primary** purpose of an integrated report is to explain to providers of financial capital how an organisation creates value over time.

- According to the framework, the creation of value is influenced by the external environment, facilitated through relationships with stakeholders and dependent on various resources.

- These external aspects to the organisation change over time and will vary in priority for different stakeholders. Therefore, focusing on just one capital while disregarding the others is unlikely to maximise value of the organisation in the long term.

- Although the report is to benefit all stakeholders interested in an organisation's ability to create value over time, the intention of the report is not to provide all information that all interested stakeholders may want.*

5.8   Link to Corporate Social Responsibility

- Because social and environmental factors must be considered in the integrated thinking process, the issues examined as part of the social and environmental audit will be important in the integrated reporting process.

- Whereas organisations in the past may have thought about sustainability issues strictly in terms of environmental preservation and awareness and separated their reporting on these factors from financial reporting, integrated reporting encourages organisations to reconsider the definition of sustainability in broader terms and how these factors contribute over time to the value in the organisation.

- The social and environmental audit can help organisations to better connect the areas examined in this type of audit to their overall strategy and creation of value.*

*Commentary

*This is impossible because different stakeholders have different information needs.

*Commentary

*Under <IR> there is currently no mandatory requirement for an independent assurance report. There is, however, a requirement for those charged with governance to acknowledge their responsibilities to ensure the integrity of the integrated report and give an opinion on whether it is presented in accordance with the International <IR> Framework.

Summary

- IFRS does not have any compulsory requirement to present environmental reports. However, IAS 37 requires disclosures relating to environmental provisions and contingent liabilities.

- Environmental accounting aims to incorporate both economic and environmental information.

- There is no one single definition that encompasses Corporate Social Responsibility (CSR).

- Not everyone is in favour of CSR; Milton Friedman thought the economy worked sufficiently well without a business taking account of CSR.

- The IASB is just one party involved in trying to ensure that management is a good corporate citizen working towards an environment that will be to the benefit of all, not just the chosen few.

- The Management Commentary aims to provide *investors* with decision-useful information that enables them to put the financial statements into context.

Session 27 Quiz
Estimated time: 20 minutes

1. Name the standard which may require some form of CSR disclosures by certain companies. (1.1)

2. Give possible reasons an entity may adopt environmental accounting within their systems. (1.3)

3. Describe how an entity might account for an environmental pollution charge introduced by a government. (1.4)

4. List the THREE categories of performance indicators identified within the GRI guidelines. (2.3)

5. Give arguments in favour of an entity adopting some form of CSR. (3.2)

6. Explain how DuPont demonstrates commitment to employee health. (3.4.4)

7. State the purpose of Management Commentary. (4.2.2)

Study Question Bank
Estimated time: 45 minutes

Priority		Estimated Time	Completed
Q45	Mucky Mining	45 minutes	

© DeVry/Becker Educational Development Corp. All rights reserved.

NOTES

Index

D

E

F

G

H

I

© DeVry/Becker Educational Development Corp. All rights reserved.

P

Q

R

S

© DeVry/Becker Educational Development Corp. All rights reserved.

T

U

V

W

ACCA

P2 CORPORATE REPORTING
(INTERNATIONAL)

STUDY QUESTION BANK

For Examinations from September 2017 to June 2018

©2017 DeVry/Becker Educational Development Corp. All rights reserved.

(i)

No responsibility for loss occasioned to any person acting or refraining from action as a result of any material in this publication can be accepted by the author, editor or publisher.

This training material has been prepared and published by Becker Professional Development International Limited: www.becker.com/acca

Copyright ©2017 DeVry/Becker Educational Development Corp. All rights reserved.
The trademarks used herein are owned by DeVry/Becker Educational Development Corp. or their respective owners and may not be used without permission from the owner.

No part of this training material may be translated, reprinted or reproduced or utilised in any form either in whole or in part or by any electronic, mechanical or other means, now known or hereafter invented, including photocopying and recording, or in any information storage and retrieval system without express written permission. Request for permission or further information should be addressed to the Permissions Department, DeVry/Becker Educational Development Corp.

Acknowledgement

Past ACCA examination questions are the copyright of the Association of Chartered Certified Accountants and have been reproduced by kind permission.

©2017 DeVry/Becker Educational Development Corp. All rights reserved.

CONTENTS

©2017 DeVry/Becker Educational Development Corp. All rights reserved.

©2017 DeVry/Becker Educational Development Corp. All rights reserved.

©2017 DeVry/Becker Educational Development Corp. All rights reserved.

Question 1 IFRS FOR SMES

International Financial Reporting Standards (IFRSs) are primarily designed for use by publicly listed companies and in many countries the majority of companies using IFRSs are listed companies. In other countries IFRSs are used as national Generally Accepted Accounting Principles (GAAP) for all companies including unlisted entities. It has been argued that the same IFRSs should be used by all entities or alternatively a different body of standards should apply to small and medium entities (SMEs).

Required:

(a)   **Discuss why there is a need to develop a set of IFRSs specifically for SMEs.**   (7 marks)

(b)   **Discuss the nature of the following issues in developing IFRSs for SMEs:**

   (i)   **the purpose of the standards and the type of entity to which they should apply;**
                                                                              (7 marks)

   (ii)   **how existing standards could be modified to meet the needs of SMEs;** (6 marks)

   (iii)   **how items not dealt with by an IFRS for SMEs should be treated.**   (5 marks)

                                                                              (25 marks)

Question 2 AUTOL

Autol, a public limited company, currently prepares its financial statements under local GAAP (Generally Accepted Accounting Principles). The company currently operates in the tele-communications industry and has numerous national and international subsidiaries. It is also quoted on the local stock exchange. The company invests heavily in research and development which it writes off immediately. The local rules in this area are not prescriptive. The company does not currently provide for deferred taxation or recognise actuarial gains and losses arising on defined benefit plans for employees. It wishes to expand its business activities and raise capital on international stock exchanges. The directors are somewhat confused over the financial reporting requirements of multi-national companies as they see a variety of local GAAPs and reporting practices being used by these companies including the preparation of reconciliations to alternative local GAAPs such as that of the United States of America, and the use of the accounting standards of the International Accounting Standards Board (IASB).

The directors have considered the use of US GAAP in the financial statements but are unaware of the potential problems that might occur as a result of this move. Further the directors are considering currently the use of the accounting standards of the IASB in the preparation of the consolidated financial statements and require advice on the potential impact on reported profit of a move from local GAAP to these accounting standards given their current accounting practice in the areas of deferred tax, research and development expenditure and employee benefits.

Required:

Write a report suitable for presentation to the directors of Autol that sets out the following information:

(a)   **the variety of local GAAPs and reporting practices currently being used by multi-national companies setting out brief possible reasons why such companies might prepare financial statements utilising a particular set of generally accepted accounting practices.**   (6 marks)

(b)   **the problems relating to the current use of GAAP reconciliations by companies and whether the use of such reconciliations is likely to continue into the future;**   (5 marks)

(c)   the potential impact on the reported profit of Autol if it prepared its consolidated financial statements in accordance with the accounting standards of the IASB in relation to its current accounting practices for deferred tax, research and development expenditure and employee benefits.   (8 marks)

                                                                                        (19 marks)

Question 3 TIMBER PRODUCTS

(a)   **Explain briefly the concept of faithful representation.**   (3 marks)

(b)   **Explain the appropriate accounting treatment for the following transactions and the entries that would appear in the financial statements of Timber Products for the year ended 31 October 2017:**

    (i)   Timber Products imports unseasoned hardwood and keeps it for five years under controlled conditions prior to manufacturing high quality furniture. In the year ended 31 October 2017 it imported unseasoned timber at a cost of $40 million. It contracted to sell the whole amount for $40 million and to buy it back in five years' time for $56.10 million.

    (ii)   Timber Products manufactures and supplies retailers with furniture on a consignment basis such that either party can require the return of the furniture to the manufacturer within a period of six months from delivery. The retailers are required to pay a monthly charge for the facility to display the furniture. The manufacturer uses this monthly charge to pay for insurance cover and carriage costs. At the end of six months the retailer is required to pay Timber Products the trade price as at the date of delivery. No retailers have yet sent any goods back to Timber Products at the end of the six month period.

            In the year ended 31 October 2017, Timber Products had supplied furniture to retailers at the normal trade price of $10 million being cost plus $33\frac{1}{3}\%$ and received $6 million from retailers.   (7 marks)

                                                                                        (10 marks)

Question 4 CREATIVE ACCOUNTING

In producing the *Conceptual Framework for Financial Reporting* (the Framework) the IASB has sought to address the potential problem that management may choose to adopt inappropriate accounting policies. These could have the effect of portraying an entity's financial position in a favourable manner. In some countries, this is referred to as "creative accounting". Embedded in the Framework, and a common feature of many recent International Accounting Standards, is the application of the principal of "substance over form".

Required:

(a)   **Describe in broad terms common ways in which management can manipulate financial statements to indulge in "creative accounting" and why they would wish to do so.**(7 marks)

(b)   **Explain the principle of substance over form and how it limits the above practice; and for each of the following areas of accounting describe an example of the application of substance over form:**

    (i)   **group accounting;**
    (ii)   **financing non-current assets;**
    (iii)   **measurement and disclosure of current assets.**   (8 marks)

                                                                                        (15 marks)

©2017 DeVry/Becker Educational Development Corp. All rights reserved.

Question 5 XYZ

XYZ, a limited company, is a well-established family company with 85% of its ordinary shares and 50% of its preferred share capital held by family members. The following summarised statement of financial position and fair value table refers to XYZ at 30 November 2017:

	Carrying amount $m	Fair value $m
Assets		
Non-current assets		
Tangible assets	45	40
Intangible assets	15	–
	60	40
Current assets	55	50
Total assets	115	90
Equity		
Issued capital – $1 ordinary shares	40	40
Accumulated losses	(21)	(57)
	19	(17)
Non-current liabilities		
10% preferred shares of $1 redeemable at a premium of 5% ($10m nominal value)	11	12
8% Unsecured loan notes 2018 repayable at a premium of 10% ($35m nominal value)	38	39
Current liabilities	47	56
Total equity and liabilities	115	90

XYZ had incurred losses for several years. In 2017 the family had sold a 5% holding in the ordinary shares to PQ and a further 10% holding to outside interests. Prior to this event, all the ordinary shares were held by the family. PQ has indicated to XYZ that they wish to increase their interest in XYZ.

XYZ has projected that it will make profits before interest and taxation in the year to 30 November 2018 of $8 million and that this will increase by 25% per annum. The directors of XYZ have decided to reconstruct the capital of the company and have suggested the following scheme of reconstruction:

(i)   The ordinary shares of $1 are to be reduced to $0.20 shares. Additionally 20 million ordinary shares of $0.20 are to be issued for cash. PQ will subscribe for 15 million of these shares and the family shareholders will purchase the balance.

(ii)   The holders of the ordinary shares not held by the family or PQ will be offered one new 7% convertible cumulative preferred share of $1 for every two ordinary shares that they own and their ordinary shares will be cancelled.

(iii) A merchant bank has agreed to subscribe in cash for $25 million of new 8% (secured on the tangible assets) loan notes and PQ and the family shareholders will subscribe equally in cash for $25 million of new unsecured 10% loan notes. Both issues are at nominal value.

©2017 DeVry/Becker Educational Development Corp. All rights reserved.

(iv)   The existing preferred shares held by the family will be cancelled and the balance not held by the family will be repaid along with the 8% loan notes on the following terms:

- Two years' arrears of accrued preferred dividends included in current liabilities to be cancelled;

- 10% preferred shares repaid at $0·80 per share;

- Loan notes repaid at par (there is no accrued interest).

(v)   The assets and liabilities are to be shown at fair value in the reconstructed statement of financial position and the directors' loans of $8 million included in short-term creditors are to be written off.

(vi)   PQ is to pay a non-equity capital contribution to shareholders funds of $10 million to XYZ in order to bolster its liquid funds.

(vii)   The bank overdraft included in current liabilities currently stands at $5 million.

(viii)   The procedures under the local companies' legislation have been followed as regards the varying of shareholders' rights.

(ix)   Assume income tax at 30%.

Required:

(a)   Prepare a statement of financial position for XYZ after the implementation of the scheme on the assumption that the proposed scheme was accepted.   (15 marks)

(b)   Discuss the fairness of the above scheme to the parties concerned and the likelihood of the scheme being accepted. (Candidates should include any relevant computations in their answers)   (10 marks)

(25 marks)

Question 6 BURLEY

Burley, a public limited company, operates in the energy industry. It has entered into the following arrangements with other entities:

(i)   Burley and Slite, a public limited company, jointly control an oilfield. Burley has a 60% interest and Slite a 40% interest and the companies are entitled to extract oil in these proportions. An agreement was signed on 1 December 2016, which allowed for the net cash settlement of any over/under extraction by one company. The net cash settlement would be at the market price of oil at the date of settlement. Both parties have used this method of settlement before. 200,000 barrels of oil were produced up to 1 October 2017 but none were produced after this up to 30 November 2017 due to production difficulties. The oil was all sold to third parties at $100 per barrel. Burley has extracted 10,000 barrels more than the company's quota and Slite has under extracted by the same amount. The market price of oil at the year end of 30 November 2017 was $105 per barrel. The excess oil extracted by Burley was settled on 12 December 2017 under the terms of the agreement at $95 per barrel.

Burley had purchased oil from another supplier because of the production difficulties at $98 per barrel and has oil inventory of 5,000 barrels at the year end, purchased from this source. Slite had no inventory of oil. Neither company had oil inventory at 1 December 2016. Selling costs are $2 per barrel.

Burley wishes to know how to account for the recognition of revenue, the excess oil extracted and the oil inventory at the year end.   (10 marks)

©2017 DeVry/Becker Educational Development Corp. All rights reserved.

(ii)   Burley has purchased a transferable interest in an oil exploration licence. Initial surveys of the region designated for exploration indicate that there are substantial oil deposits present but further surveys will be required in order to establish the nature and extent of the deposits. Burley also has to determine whether the extraction of the oil is commercially viable. Past experience has shown that the licence can increase substantially in value if further information as to the viability of the extraction of the oil becomes available. Burley wishes to capitalise the cost of the licence but is unsure as to whether the accounting policy is compliant with International Financial Reporting Standards   (4 marks)

Required:

(a)   **Discuss with suitable computations where necessary, how the above arrangements and events would be accounted for in the financial statements of Burley.**

      Note: The mark allocation is shown against the two issues above.

      Professional marks will be awarded for clarity and quality of discussion.   (2 marks)

(b)   **Discuss the implications that integrated reporting may have for the energy industry.**
                                                                                                    (9 marks)

                                                                                              (25 marks)

Question 7 ALEXANDRA

Alexandra, a public limited company, designs and manages business solutions and IT infrastructures.

(a)   In November 2017, Alexandra defaulted on an interest payment on an issued bond loan of $100 million repayable in 2023. The loan agreement stipulates that such default leads to an obligation to repay the whole of the loan immediately, including accrued interest and expenses. The bondholders, however, issued a waiver postponing the interest payment until 31 May 2018. On 17 May 2018, Alexandra felt that a further waiver was required, so requested a meeting of the bondholders and agreed a further waiver of the interest payment to 5 July 2018, when Alexandra was confident it could make the payments. Alexandra classified the loan as long-term debt in its statement of financial position at 30 April 2018 on the basis that the loan was not in default at the end of the reporting period as the bondholders had issued waivers and had not sought redemption.   (6 marks)

(b)   Alexandra enters into contracts with both customers and suppliers. The supplier solves system problems and provides new releases and updates for software. Alexandra provides maintenance services for its customers. In previous years, Alexandra recognised revenue and related costs on software maintenance contracts when the customer was invoiced, which was at the beginning of the contract period. Contracts typically run for two years.

During 2017, Alexandra had acquired Xavier, which recognised revenue, derived from a similar type of maintenance contract as Alexandra, on a straight-line basis over the term of the contract. Alexandra considered that both its own policy and the policy of Xavier comply with the requirements of IFRS 15 *Revenue from Contracts with Customers* but decided to adopt the practice of Xavier for itself and the group. Alexandra concluded that the two recognition methods did not, in substance, represent two different accounting policies and did not, therefore, consider adoption of the new practice to be a change in policy.

In the year to 30 April 2018, Alexandra recognised revenue (and the related costs) on a straight-line basis over the contract term, treating this as a change in an accounting estimate. As a result, revenue and cost of sales were adjusted, reducing the year's profits by some $6 million.   (5 marks)

(c) Alexandra has a two-tier board structure consisting of a management and a supervisory board. Alexandra remunerates its board members as follows:

- Annual base salary
- Variable annual compensation (bonus)
- Share options

In the group financial statements, within the related parties note under IAS 24 *Related Party Disclosures*, Alexandra disclosed the total remuneration paid to directors and non-executive directors and a total for each of these boards. No further breakdown of the remuneration was provided.

The management board comprises both the executive and non-executive directors. The remuneration of the non-executive directors, however, was not included in the key management disclosures. Some members of the supervisory and management boards are of a particular nationality. Alexandra was of the opinion that in that jurisdiction, it is not acceptable to provide information about remuneration that could be traced back to individuals. Consequently, Alexandra explained that it had provided the related party information in the annual accounts in an ambiguous way to prevent users of the financial statements from tracing remuneration information back to specific individuals.   (5 marks)

(d) Alexandra's pension plan was accounted for as a defined benefit plan in 2017. In the year ended 30 April 2018, Alexandra changed the accounting method used for the scheme and accounted for it as a defined contribution plan, restating the comparative 2017 financial information. The effect of the restatement was significant. In the 2018 financial statements, Alexandra explained that, during the year, the arrangements underlying the retirement benefit plan had been subject to detailed review. Since the pension liabilities are fully insured and indexation of future liabilities can be limited up to and including the funds available in a special trust account set up for the plan, which is not at the disposal of Alexandra, the plan qualifies as a defined contribution plan under IAS 19 *Employee Benefits* rather than a defined benefit plan. Furthermore, the trust account is built up by the insurance company from the surplus yield on investments. The pension plan is an average pay plan in respect of which the entity pays insurance premiums to a third party insurance company to fund the plan. Every year 1% of the pension fund is built up and employees pay a contribution of 4% of their salary, with the employer paying the balance of the contribution. If an employee leaves Alexandra and transfers the pension to another fund, Alexandra is liable for, or is refunded the difference between the benefits the employee is entitled to and the insurance premiums paid.

(7 marks)

Professional marks will be awarded for clarity and quality of discussion.   (2 marks)

Required:

Discuss how the above transactions should be dealt with in the financial statements of Alexandra for the year ended 30 April 2018.

(25 marks)

©2017 DeVry/Becker Educational Development Corp. All rights reserved.

Question 8 VENUE

The IASB has had concerns about accounting for revenue for many years. Although there were accounting standards that sought to deal with this topic, they were not sufficiently rigorous on the matter of revenue recognition and many different accounting practices had emerged. In 2014 the IASB issued IFRS 15 *Revenue from Contracts with Customers* to address this. The core principle of the standard is that an entity should recognise revenue to depict the transfer of goods or services to customers in an amount that reflects the consideration to which the entity expects to be entitled. Application of this core principle requires an entity to follow a five-step approach to revenue recognition.

Required:

(a)   **Discuss the approach to revenue recognition and measurement under IFRS 15 "Revenue from Contracts with Customers".**   (7 marks)

(b)   **(i)**   Venue enters into a contract with a customer to provide computers at a value of $1 million. The terms are that payment is due one month after the sale of the goods. On the basis of experience with other contractors with similar characteristics, Venue considers that there is a 5% risk that the customer will not pay the amount due after the goods have been delivered and the property transferred. Venue subsequently felt that the financial condition of the customer has deteriorated and that the trade receivable is further impaired by $100,000.

        (ii)   Venue has also sold a computer hardware system to a customer and, because of the current difficulties in the market, Venue has agreed to defer receipt of the selling price of $2 million until two years after the hardware has been transferred to the customer.

            Venue has also been offering discounts to customers if products were sold with terms whereby payment was due now but the transfer of the product was made in one year. A sale had been made under these terms and payment of $3 million had been received. A discount rate of 4% should be used in any calculations.

        Required:

        Discuss how both of the above transactions would be treated in subsequent financial statements under IFRS 15 and also whether there would be difference in treatment if the collectability of the debt and the time value of money were taken into account. (8 marks)

(15 marks)

Question 9 HAMILTON

Hamilton, a public listed company, owns a large 12 storey office block in the financial area of Metro City which it purchased on 1 April 2015 for $3 million. On that date it had an estimated life of 25 years. The building is currently classified in Hamilton's statement of financial position as an investment property under IAS 40 *Investment Property*. Hamilton does not intend to sell the property.

The office block has been valued annually since acquisition on an open market value basis by Platonic, a firm of professional surveyors. The values have been:

Year ended 31 March	2016	2017	2018
$ million	3.2	3.6	3.6

Hamilton has a policy of adopting these values as the carrying amount of the investment. Included in the report on the valuation for the current year end (31 March 2018) the surveyors noted that over the next few years there is expected to be a surplus of rented property space in the City and sub-lease rentals are expected to fall. This in turn is expected to lead to a serious decline in the value of properties like Hamilton's.

In view of this the directors of Hamilton wish to change the accounting policy for the office block to the cost model as described in IAS 16 *Property, Plant and Equipment*.

You are given the following extra information:

■ An article in "Accountancy Update" reported that an important paper in the "Journal of Valuation Surveyors" had reported dramatic falls averaging 25% in the value of office property in the City during the last six months of Hamilton's current reporting year

■ The draft statement of profit or loss for the year to 31 March 2018 showed profit (after tax) of $180,000. In the financial statements for 2017 the profit before any adjustments in respect of the investment property was $200,000. The retained profit brought forward at 1 April 2016 was $110,000 before any adjustments for the property revaluation. No dividends have been paid in either year.

Required:

(a) **Describe the circumstances in which companies are permitted to change their accounting policies, and explain whether the change proposed by Hamilton would be allowed under International Financial Reporting Standards.** (7 marks)

(b) **Suggest reasons why the management of Hamilton may wish to change the policy and present extracts from the financial statements under both possible models to show the effect two policies would have on the financial statements for the year to 31 March 2018 (include one year's comparatives) if the value of the property had fallen by 25% (to $2.7 million) in the year to 31 March 2018.** (8 marks)

(15 marks)

Question 10 SPONGER

Sponger has been having financial difficulties recently due to the economic climate in its industry sector. However, its financial director Mr Philip Tislid has discovered that there are a number of schemes by which he can obtain government financial assistance. Details of the assistance obtained are as follows:

(a) Sponger has received three grants of $10,000 each in the current year relating to on-going research and development projects. One grant relates to the Cuckoo project which involves research into the effect of various chemicals on the pitch of the human voice. No constructive conclusions have been reached yet.

The second relates to the development of a new type of hairspray which is expected to be extremely popular. Commercial production will commence in 2019 and large profits are foreseen. The third relates to the purchase of high powered microscopes.

(b) In 2016 Sponger's premises were entirely isolated from the outside world for four months due to the renovation of roads by the local council. All production was lost in that period. Mr Tislid has been assured by the council's officers that a $25,000 compensation grant will be paid on submission of the relevant triplicate form. Mr Tislid had not yet filled in the form by 31 December 2017.

©2017 DeVry/Becker Educational Development Corp. All rights reserved.

(c)   Sponger entered into an agreement with the government that, in exchange for a $60,000 grant, it will provide "vocational experience" tours around its factory, for 12 young criminals per month over a five year period starting 1 January 2017. The grant was to be paid on the date Sponger purchased a minibus (useful life three years) to take the inmates to the factory and back. The bus was bought and the grant received on 1 January 2017.

The grant becomes repayable on a pro rata basis for every monthly visit not fulfilled. During 2017 five visits did not take place due to the pressure of work and this pattern is expected to be repeated over the next four years.

No repayments have yet been made.

Mr Tislid is totally confused about how to account for these grants.

Required:

Write a memorandum to Mr Tislid explaining to him how he should account for the above grants in the accounts for the year ended 31 December 2017.

(12 marks)

Question 11 MOORE

Moore, an investment property company, has been constructing a new building for the last 18 months. At 31 December 2016, the cinema was nearing completion, and the costs incurred to date were:

	$m
Materials, labour and sub-contractors	14.8
Other directly attributable overheads	2.5
Interest on borrowings	1.3

The building is deemed to be a qualifying asset and therefore any borrowing costs are capitalised as part of the cost of the building. The amount of borrowings outstanding at 31 December 2016 in respect of this project is $18m, and the interest rate is 9.5%pa.

During the three months to 31 March 2017 the project was completed, with the following additional costs incurred:

	$m
Materials, labour and sub-contractors	$1.7
Other overhead	$0.3

The company were not able to determine the fair value of the property reliably during the construction period and so used the allowance within IAS 40 *Investment Property* to value at cost until construction was complete.

On 31 March 2017, the company obtained a professional appraisal of the cinema's fair value, and the valuer concluded that it was worth $24m. The fee for his appraisal was $0.1m, and has not been included in the above figures for costs incurred during the 3 months.

The cinema was taken by a national multiplex chain on an operating lease as at 1 April 2017, and was immediately welcoming capacity crowds. The lease agreement allows for annual revisions, and thus it was clear that it was worth even more than the valuation at 31 March 2017. Following a complete valuation of the company's investment properties at 31 December 2017, the fair value of the cinema was established at $28m.

Required:

Set out the accounting entries in respect of the cinema complex for the year ended 31 December 2017.

(10 marks)

Question 12 HEYWOOD

The problems of identifying and valuing intangible assets with a view to recognising them on the statement of financial position has been an area of inconsistent practice that has led to great debate within the accountancy profession. IAS 38 *Intangible Assets* was issued in order to try and eliminate these inconsistent practices.

Required:

(a) **Discuss the recognition and initial measurement criteria for intangible assets contained in IAS 38.**   **(9 marks)**

(b) On 1 July 2017 Heywood, a company listed on a recognised stock exchange, was finally successful in acquiring the entire share capital of Fast Trak. The terms of the bid by Heywood had been improved several times as rival bidders also made offers for Fast Trak. The terms of the initial bid by Heywood were:

    ■   20 million $1 ordinary shares in Heywood. Each share had a market price of $3·50 immediately prior to the bid;

    ■   a cash element of $15 million.

The final bid that was eventually accepted on 1 July 2017 by Fast Trak's shareholders. Heywood had improved the cash offer to $25million and included a redeemable loan note of a further $25 million that will be redeemed on 30 June 2021. It carried no interest, but market rates for this type of loan note were 13% per annum. There was no increase in the number of shares offered but at the date of acceptance the price of Heywood's shares on the stock market had risen to $4·00 each.

The present value of $1 receivable in a future period where interest rates are 13% can be taken as:

          at end of year three $0·70
          at end of year four $0·60

The fair value of Fast Trak's net assets, other than its intangible long-term assets, was assessed by Heywood to be $64million. This value had not changed significantly throughout the bidding process. The details of Fast Trak's intangible assets acquired were:

(i) The brand name "Kleenwash"; a dish washing liquid. A rival brand name thought to be of a similar reputation and value to Kleenwash had recently been acquired for a disclosed figure of $12 million.

(ii) A Government licence to extract a radioactive ore from a mine for the next ten years. The licence is difficult to value as there was no fee payable for it. However, as Fast Trak is the only company that can mine the ore, the directors of Heywood have estimated the licence to be worth $9 million. The mine itself has been included as part of Fast Trak's property, plant and equipment.

(iii) A fishing quota of 10,000 tonnes per annum in territorial waters. A specialist company called Quotasales actively trades in these and other quotas. The price per tonne of these fishing quotas at the date of acquisition was $1,600. The quota is for an indefinite period of time, but in order to preserve fish stocks the Government has the right to vary the weight of fish that may be caught under a quota. The weights of quotas are reviewed annually.

(iv) The remainder of the long-term intangible assets is attributable to the goodwill of Fast Trak.

©2017 DeVry/Becker Educational Development Corp. All rights reserved.

Required:

Calculate the purchase consideration and prepare an extract of the intangible assets of Fast Trak that would be separately recognised in the consolidated financial statements of Heywood on 1 July 2017. Your answer should include an explanation justifying your treatment of each item. (8 marks)

(c) On the same date, but as a separate purchase to that of Fast Trak, Heywood acquired Steamdays, a company that operates a scenic railway along the coast of a popular tourist area. The summarised statement of financial position at fair values of Steamdays on 1 July 2017, reflecting the terms of the acquisition was:

	$000
Goodwill	200
Operating licence	1,200
Property – train stations and land	300
Rail track and coaches	300
Steam engines (2)	1,000
Purchase consideration	3,000

The operating licence is for ten years. It has recently been renewed by the transport authority and is stated at the cost of its renewal. The carrying amounts of the property and rail track and coaches are based on their estimated replacement cost. The carrying amount of the engines closely equates to their fair value less any disposal costs.

On 1 August 2017 the boiler of one of the steam engines exploded, completely destroying the whole engine. Fortunately no one was injured, but the engine was beyond repair. Due to its age a replacement could not be obtained. Because of the reduced passenger capacity the estimated value in use of the business after the accident was assessed at $2 million.

Passenger numbers after the accident were below expectations even after allowing for the reduced capacity. A market research report concluded that tourists were not using the railway because of the fear of a similar accident occurring to the remaining engine. In the light of this the value in use of the business was re-assessed on 30 September 2017 at $1·8 million. On this date Heywood received an offer of $900,000 in respect of the operating licence (it is transferable).

Required:

Briefly describe the basis in IAS 36 *Impairment of Assets* for allocating impairment losses; and show how each of the assets of Steamdays would be valued at 1 August 2017 and 30 September 2017 after recognising the impairment losses. (8 marks)

(25 marks)

Question 13 WILDERNESS

(a) IAS 36 *Impairment of Assets* prescribes the procedures that should ensure that assets are included in a statement of financial position at no more than their recoverable amounts. Where an asset is carried at an amount in excess of its recoverable amount, it is said to be impaired and IAS 36 requires an impairment loss to be recognised.

Required:

(i) **Define an impairment loss explaining the relevance of fair value less costs of disposal and value in use, and state how frequently assets should be tested for impairment.** (5 marks)

(ii) **Explain how an impairment loss is accounted for.** (4 marks)

(b) Wilderness owns and operates an item of plant that cost $640,000 and had accumulated depreciation of $400,000 at 1 October 2016. It is being depreciated at 12½% on cost. On 1 April 2017 the plant was damaged when a factory vehicle collided into it. Due to the unavailability of replacement parts, it is not possible to repair the plant, but it still operates, albeit at a reduced capacity. Also it is expected that as a result of the damage the remaining life of the plant from the date of the damage will be only two years. Based on its reduced capacity, the estimated present value of the plant in use is $150,000. The plant has a current disposal value of $20,000 (which will be nil in two years' time), but Wilderness has been offered a trade-in value of $180,000 against a replacement machine which has a cost of $1 million (there would be no disposal costs for the replaced plant). Wilderness is reluctant to replace the plant as it is worried about the long-term demand for the product produced by the plant. The trade-in value is only available if the plant is replaced.

Required:

Prepare extracts from the statement of financial position and statement of profit or loss of Wilderness in respect of the plant for the year ended 30 September 2017. Your answer should explain how you arrived at your figures. (6 marks)

(15 marks)

Question 14 ARTRIGHT

Artright, a public limited company, produces artefacts made from precious metals. Its customers vary from large multinational companies to small retail outlets and mail order customers.

(i) On 1 December 2016, Artright has a number of finished artefacts in inventory which are valued at cost $4 million (selling value $5·06 million) and whose precious metal content was 200,000 ounces. The selling price of artefacts produced from a precious metal is determined substantially by the price of the metal. The inventory value of finished artefacts is the metal cost plus 5% for labour and design costs. The selling price is normally the spot price of the metal content plus 10% (approximately). The management were worried about a potential decline in the price of the precious metal and its effect on the selling price of the inventory. Therefore it sold futures contracts for 200,000 ounces in the metal at $24 an ounce at 1 December 2016. The contracts mature on 30 November 2017.

The management have designated the futures contracts as cash flow hedges of the anticipated sale of the artefacts. Historically this has proved to be highly effective in offsetting any changes in the selling price of the artefacts. The finished artefacts were sold for $22·8 per ounce on 30 November 2017. The costs of setting the futures contracts in place were negligible.

The metal's spot and futures prices were as follows:

	Spot price $ per ounce	Futures price ($) per ounce for delivery 30 November 2017
1 December 2016	23	24
30 November 2017	21	21

©2017 DeVry/Becker Educational Development Corp. All rights reserved.

(ii)   The company also trades with multi-national corporations. Artright often has cash flow problems and factors some of its trade receivables. On 1 November 2017 it sold trade receivables of $500,000 to a bank for a cash settlement of $440,000. The portfolio of trade receivables sold is due from some of the company's best customers who always pay their debts but are quite slow payers. Because of the low risk of default, Artright has guaranteed 12% of the balance outstanding on each receivable and the fair value of this guarantee is thought to be $12,000.

Required:

Discuss, using the principles of IFRS 9 *Financial Instruments*:

(a)   **whether the cash flow hedge of the sale of the inventory of artefacts is effective and how it would be accounted for in the financial statements for the year ended 30 November 2017;**   (6 marks)

(b)   **whether the sale of the trade receivables would result in them being derecognised in the statement of financial position at 30 November 2017 and how the sale of the trade receivables would be recorded.**   (5 marks)

(11 marks)

Question 15 AMBUSH

Ambush, a public limited company, is assessing the impact of implementing the accounting standards relating to financial instruments. The directors realise that significant changes may occur in their accounting treatment of financial instruments, however, there are certain issues that they wish to have explained and these are set out below.

Required:

(a)   **Outline for inclusion in a report to the directors of Ambush the following information how financial assets and liabilities are measured and classified, briefly setting out the accounting method used for each category. (Hedging relationships can be ignored.)**
                                                                                            (10 marks)

(b)   Ambush loaned $200,000 to Bromwich on 1 December 2015. The effective and stated interest rate for this loan was 8%. Interest is payable by Bromwich at the end of each year and the loan is repayable on 30 November 2019. At 30 November 2017, the directors of Ambush have heard that Bromwich is in financial difficulties and is undergoing a financial reorganisation. The directors feel that it is likely that they will only receive $100,000 on 30 November 2019 and no future interest payment. Interest for the year ended 30 November 2017 had been received. The financial year end of Ambush is 30 November 2017.

Required:

(i)   **Outline the requirements of IFRS 9** *Financial Instruments* **for the impairment of financial assets.**   (6 marks)

(ii)   **Explain the accounting treatment under IFRS 9 of the loan to Bromwich in the financial statements of Ambush for the year ended 30 November 2017.**
                                                                                            (4 marks)

(20 marks)

©2017 DeVry/Becker Educational Development Corp. All rights reserved.

Question 16 ARROCHAR

Arrochar is about to undertake a sale and leaseback arrangement on 1 January 2017 in respect of an item of plant and machinery, which has a remaining life of six years, and has two lease options available.

Option 1: Sell the asset at a profit of $1 million and lease it back for its remaining life; paying a nominal amount at the end of the lease to purchase legal title to it.

Option 2: Sell the asset at a profit of $400,000 and lease it for three years; the buyer will take physical possession of the asset at the end of the lease contract.

Required:

Advise Arrochar on the accounting implications of the two lease options in accordance with IFRS 16 *Leases.*

(10 marks)

Question 17 ROUTER

(a)   Router, a public limited company operates in the entertainment industry. It recently agreed with a television company to make a film which will be broadcast on the television company's network. The fee agreed for the film was $5 million with a further $100,000 to be paid every time the film is shown on the television company's channels. It is hoped that it will be shown on four occasions. The film was completed at a cost of $4 million and delivered to the television company on 1 April 2018. The television company paid the fee of $5 million on 30 April 2018 but indicated that the film needed substantial editing before they were prepared to broadcast it, the costs of which would be deducted from any future payments to Router. The directors of Router wish to recognise the anticipated future income of $400,000 in the financial statements for the year ended 31 May 2018.   (5 marks)

(b)   Router has a number of film studios and office buildings. The office buildings are in prestigious areas whereas the film studios are located in "out of town" locations. The management of Router wish to apply the "revaluation model" to the office buildings and the "cost model" to the film studios in the year ended 31 May 2018. At present both types of buildings are valued using the "revaluation model". One of the film studios has been converted to a theme park. In this case only, the land and buildings on the park are leased on a single lease from a third party. The lease term was 30 years in 2001. The lease has been correctly accounted for in accordance with IFRS 16 *Leases*.

The terms of the lease were changed on 31 May 2018. Router is now going to terminate the lease early in 2026 in exchange for a payment of $10 million on 31 May 2018 and a reduction in the monthly lease payments. Router intends to move from the site in 2026. The revised lease terms have not resulted in a change of classification of the lease in the financial statements of Router.   (8 marks)

(c)   At 1 June 2017, Router held a 25% shareholding in a film distribution company, Wireless, a public limited company. On 1 January 2018, Router sold a 15% holding in Wireless thus reducing its investment to a 10% holding. Router no longer exercises significant influence over Wireless. Before the sale of the shares the net asset value of Wireless on 1 January 2018 was $200 million and goodwill relating to the acquisition of Wireless was $5 million. Router received $40 million for its sale of the 15% holding in Wireless. At 1 January 2018, the fair value of the remaining investment in Wireless was $23 million and at 31 May 2018 the fair value was $26 million.   (6 marks)

©2017 DeVry/Becker Educational Development Corp. All rights reserved.

(d)   Additionally Router purchased 60% of the ordinary shares of a radio station, Playtime, a public limited company, on 31 May 2018. The remaining 40% of the ordinary shares are owned by a competitor company who owns a substantial number of warrants issued by Playtime which are currently exercisable. If these warrants are exercised, they will result in Router only owning 35% of the voting shares of Playtime.   **(4 marks)**

Required:

Discuss how the above items should be dealt with in the group financial statements of Router for the year ended 31 May 2018.

(23 marks)

Question 18 AZ

For entities that are engaged in different businesses with differing risks and opportunities, the usefulness of financial information concerning these entities is greatly enhanced if it is supplemented by information on individual business segments.

Required:

(a)   **Explain why the information content of financial statements is improved by the inclusion of segmental data on individual business segments.**   **(5 marks)**

(b)   AZ, a listed entity, operates in the global marketplace.

(i)   The major revenue-earning asset is a fleet of aircraft which are registered locally and its other main source of revenue comes from the sale of holidays. The directors are unsure how to identify business segments.   **(3 marks)**

(ii)   The company also owns a small aircraft manufacturing plant which supplies aircraft to its domestic airline and to third parties. The preferred method for determining transfer prices for these aircraft between the group companies is market price, but where the aircraft is of a specialised nature with no equivalent market price the companies negotiate a price for the aircraft.   **(2 marks)**

(iii)   The company has incurred an exceptional loss on the sale of several aircraft to a foreign government. This loss occurred due to a fixed price contract signed several years ago for the sale of second hand aircraft and resulted through the fluctuation of the exchange rates between the two countries.   **(3 marks)**

(iv)   During the year the company decided to discontinue its holiday business due to competition in the sector. This plan had been approved by the board of directors and announced in the press.   **(3 marks)**

(v)   The company owns 40% of the ordinary shares of Eurocat, an unlisted company which specialises in the manufacture of aircraft engines and has operations in China and Russia. The investment is accounted for by the equity method and it is proposed to exclude the company's results from segment assets and revenue. **(2 marks)**

Required:

Discuss the implications of each of the above points for the determination of the segmental information required to be prepared and disclosed under relevant International Financial Reporting Standards.

Note: The mark allocation is shown against each point.

(18 marks)

Question 19 KELLY

IAS 19 *Employee Benefits* is applied to all employee benefits other than those to which IFRS 2 *Share-based Payment* applies. Accounting for short-term employee benefits is relatively straightforward. However, accounting for post-employment benefits can be rather more complex. This particularly applies where post-employment benefits are provided through defined benefit plans.

Required:

(a) State the meaning of post-employment benefits and the manner in which such benefits that are provided through defined contribution plans should be measured and recognised in the financial statements of employers. (3 marks)

(b) Explain why accounting for defined benefit plans is more complex than accounting for defined contribution plans in the financial statements of employers. (2 marks)

(c) Explain the amounts that should be included in the financial statements of employers defined benefit plans. (6 marks)

(d) Kelly provides post-employment benefits to its employees through a defined benefit plan. The following data relates to the plan:

| | Year ended 31 March | |
| | 2018 | 2017 |
	$000	$000
Present value of obligation at year end	36,000	33,000
Fair value of plan assets at year end	31,000	30,000
Current service cost	6,000	5,700
Benefits paid by plan	8,000	7,500
Contributions paid into plan	5,800	5,600
Discount rate at the start of the year	10%	9%

Required:

Prepare extracts of Kelly's statement of financial position at 31 March 2017 and statement of profit or loss and other comprehensive income for the year ended 31 March 2018 relating to the defined benefits plan. (8 marks)

(19 marks)

Question 20 DERRY

Derry, a public limited company, operates a defined benefit plan. A full actuarial valuation by an independent actuary revealed that the value of the asset at 31 May 2017 was $1,500 million. This was updated to 31 May 2018 by the actuary and the value of the asset at that date was $2,000 million. The value of the pension obligation at 31 May 2017 was $1,970 million and this had increased to $2,950 million at 31 May 2018.

The scheme had been altered during the year with improved benefits arising for the employees and this had been taken into account by the actuaries. The increase in the actuarial liability in respect of employee service in prior periods was $30 million (past service cost). The increase in the actuarial liability resulting from employee service in the current period was $110 million (current service cost).

The company had paid contributions of $60 million to the scheme during the period. The discount rate to be used to discount post-employment benefit obligations, as determined by high quality corporate bonds, is 10%.

©2017 DeVry/Becker Educational Development Corp. All rights reserved.

Required:

Calculate the amount which will be shown as the plan liability in the statement of financial position of Derry as at 31 May 2018, showing a reconciliation of the movement in the plan deficit during the year and a statement of those amounts which would be charged to profit or loss and those included in other comprehensive income.

(8 marks)

Question 21 KERENSKY

The following information relates to Kerensky:

(a) The company made an accounting profit of $900,000.

(b) Properties were revalued from $240,000 to $300,000 in the period.

(c) The remaining non-current assets comprised plant and machinery. On 1 July 2017 this amounted to:

	$
Tax base	500,000
Carrying amount	1,300,000

During the year to 30 June 2018, depreciation amounted to $260,000 and tax allowable depreciation of $175,000 was claimed.

(d) The company entered into a five year lease on 1 July 2017. The lease expense charged to profit or loss in the year was $72,000 and the rental paid was $160,000. The lease has been accounted for in accordance with IFRS 16 *Leases* and, according to tax legislation; a taxable temporary difference of $88,000 has been recognised.

(e) Kerensky now realises that a programme of research and development is essential to set itself apart from its competition. In the current year (the first year in which capitalisation has occurred) expenditure of $80,000 was capitalised in accordance with IAS 38 *Intangible Assets*.

Required:

(a) **Calculate the corporate income tax liability for the year ended 30 June 2018.**

(b) **Calculate the deferred tax balance that is required in the statement of financial position as at 30 June 2018.**

(c) **Prepare a note showing the movement on the deferred tax account and thus calculate the deferred tax charge for the year ended 30 June 2018.**

(d) **Prepare the disclosure note which shows the compilation of the tax expense for the year ended 30 June 2018.**

(e) **Prepare a note which reconciles accounting profit multiplied by the applicable tax rate and the tax expense.**

(f) **Prepare a disclosure note showing the movement on deferred tax in respect of each type of temporary difference.**

Assume a corporation tax rate of 30%.

(20 marks)

Question 22 GENPOWER

IAS 37 *Provisions, Contingent Liabilities and Contingent Assets* is concerned with the accounting treatment of provisions and contingencies.

Required:

(a) **(i)** **Explain the need for an accounting standard in respect of provisions.** (5 marks)

(ii) **Describe the principles in IAS 37 of accounting for provisions. Your answer should refer to definitions and recognition and measurement criteria.** (7 marks)

(b) Genpower is a company involved in the electricity generating industry. It operates some nuclear power stations for which environmental clean-up costs can be a large item of expenditure. The company operates in some countries where environmental costs have to be incurred as they are written into the licensing agreement, and in other countries where they are not a legal requirement. The details of a recent contract Genpower entered into are:

A new nuclear power station has been built at a cost of $200 million and was brought into commission on 1 October 2016. The licence to produce electricity at this station is for 10 years. This is also the estimated economic life of the power station. The terms of the licence require the power station to be demolished at the end of the licence. It also requires that the spent nuclear fuel rods (a waste product) have to be buried deep in the ground and the area "sealed" such that no contamination can be detected. Genpower will also have to pay for the cost of cleaning up any contamination leaks that may occur from the water cooling system that surrounds the fuel rods when they are in use.

Genpower estimates that the cost of the demolition of the power station and the fuel rod "sealing" operation will be $180 million in ten years' time. The present value of these costs at an appropriate discount rate is $120 million. From past experience there is a 30% chance of a contaminating water leak occurring in any 12 month period. The cost of cleaning up a leak varies between $20 million and $40 million depending on the level of the contamination.

Extracts from Genpower's draft financial statements to 30 September 2017 relating to the contract after applying the company's normal accounting policy for this type of power station are:

Statement of profit or loss	$m
Non-current asset depreciation (power station) (10% × $200 million)	20
Provision for demolition and "sealing" costs (10% × $180 million)	18
Provision for cleaning up contamination due to water leak (30% × an average of $30 million)	9
	47

Statement of financial position	
Tangible non-current assets	
Power station at cost	200
Depreciation	(20)
	180

Non-current liabilities	
Provision for environmental costs ($18 + $9 million)	27

Note: No contamination from water leakage occurred in the year to 30 September 2017.

Genpower is concerned that its current policy does not comply with IAS 37 *Provisions, Contingent Liabilities and Contingent Assets* and has asked for your advice.

©2017 DeVry/Becker Educational Development Corp. All rights reserved.

Required:

(i)   **Comment on the acceptability of Genpower's current accounting policy, and redraft the extracts of the financial statements in line with the regulations of IAS 37.**   (8 marks)

      Note: Your answer should ignore the "unwinding" of the discount to present value.

(ii)   **Assuming Genpower was operating the nuclear power station in a country that does not legislate in respect of the above types of environmental costs;**

      Explain the effect this would have on your answer to (i) above.   (5 marks)

Note: your answer should include a consideration of what Genpower's environmental policy might be.

                                                          (25 marks)

Question 23 CONNECT

Connect, a public limited company is quoted on the local stock exchange. This exchange is a member of IOSCO and has recently announced that it is going to change its listing regulations to require all registrants to prepare financial statements in accordance with IFRS instead of local GAAP for all accounting periods beginning on or after 1 January 2018. Furthermore it will require members of the exchange to use IFRS for filing purposes with immediate effect. Connect has decided to adopt IFRS immediately.

Local GAAP has undergone considerable convergence with IFRS in recent years and there are no major recognition and measurement implications for existing members. However the local GAAP disclosure requirements are less demanding than IFRS in several areas. One of these is that there is no local regulation on the need to disclose related party transactions.

Connect has asked for your help in identifying relevant related party transactions in accordance with IFRS and for guidance on the disclosures that need to be made. Mr Joint, the finance director of Connect, has provided the following information:

(1)   The two major shareholders of Connect are Big Boy Investment Fund (BBIF) which holds 45% of the share capital and Mr Big who holds 10%. Mr Big is a multimillionaire. He set up BBIF several years ago and is the majority investor in the fund. No other shareholder owns more than 1%.

(2)   Connect has 14 subsidiaries. There is considerable inter-company trading between the members of this group. Transfer prices are generally below market rates for members of the group. The total inter-group sales in the period are $110 million. This is at cost plus 10%. Normal trading terms would be at cost plus 30%. The group revenue was over $800 million in the last financial year.

(3)   Connect has recently signed an advertising contract with JJ Advertising. JJ Advertising is an agency owned by Janet Joint. She is the wife of the finance director. The contract is worth $10 million per annum. This contract was won in a competitive tender.

(4)   Connect has recently sold a tract of land to Weld. Weld is an incorporated entity. The land was sold for $4.5 million (net of a selling cost of $100,000). The market value of the land was $5.3 million and its value in use was $3.8 million. It was carried at a value of $5.8 immediately prior to the sale. Mr Big is a director and major investor in Weld.

(5)   Three of the directors of Connect have set up a consultancy which provides services to Connect. Connect paid $2.6 million in respect of these services in the last financial year.

Required:

Set out, for inclusion in a report to the directors, the reasons why it is important to disclose related parties and related party transactions and the nature of any disclosure required for the above transactions under IAS 24 *Related Party Disclosures*.

(25 marks)

Question 24 LIMA

In recent years it has become increasingly common for entities to enter into transactions with third parties that are settled by means of a share based payment. IFRS 2 *Share-based Payment* was issued in order to provide a basis of accounting for such transactions. Share based payments can be equity settled or cash settled.

Required:

(a)   **Define cash and equity settled share based payments.**   (3 marks)

(b)   **Explain the basis of measurement of the fair value of equity settled share based payments.**   (3 marks)

(c)   **Explain the accounting treatment of both equity and cash settled share based payment transactions with employees.**   (8 marks)

(d)   Lima prepares financial statements to 30 September each year. Lima has a number of highly skilled employees that it wishes to retain and has put two schemes in place to discourage employees from leaving:

Scheme A

On 1 October 2015 Lima granted share options to 200 employees. Each employee was entitled to 500 options to purchase equity shares at $10 per share. The options vest on 30 September 2018 if the employees continue to work for Lima throughout the three-year period. Relevant data is as follows:

	Date Share price ($)	Fair value of option ($)	Expected number of employees for whom 500 options will vest
1 October 2015	10	2·40	190
30 September 2016	11	2·60	185
30 September 2017	12	2·80	188

Scheme B

On 1 October 2014 Lima granted two share appreciation rights to 250 employees. Each right gave the holder a cash payment of $100 for every $0.50 increase in the share price from the 1 October 2014 value to the date the rights vest. The rights vest on 30 September 2017 for those employees who continue to work for Lima throughout the three-year period. Payment is due on 31 January 2018.

Relevant data is as follows:

	Date Share price ($)	Fair value of right ($)	Expected number of employees for whom two rights will vest	
1 October 2014	9	500	240	
30 September 2015	10	520	235	
30 September 2016	11	540	240	
30 September 2017	12	600	238	(the actual number in whom two rights vested)

©2017 DeVry/Becker Educational Development Corp. All rights reserved.

Required:

Explain:

(i)   For both schemes, compute the charge to profit or loss for the year ended 30 September 2017. (8 marks)

(ii)   For both schemes, compute the amount that will appear in the statement of financial position of Lima at 30 September 2017 and state where in the statement the relevant amount will appear. (3 marks)

(25 marks)

Question 25 DANNY

The directors of Danny are concerned that Toots, currently recognised as a subsidiary, has been making losses since acquisition. They would prefer not to include these losses in the consolidated financial statements and have heard that International Financial Reporting Standards allow the results of subsidiaries to be omitted in certain circumstances. They have indicated that Toots supplies customers that operate mainly in the retail sector, whilst Danny and Smiffy, another subsidiary of Danny, have customers that operate mainly in the manufacturing sector. Therefore they have suggested that consolidation of Toots would be misleading in such circumstances.

Required:

Write a memorandum to the directors of Danny that:

(i)   Describes the circumstances in which non-consolidation of subsidiaries is appropriate under International Financial Reporting Standards.

(ii)   Responds to the issues they have raised in the above note.

(5 marks)

Question 26 PICANT

Picant has been approached by a potential new customer, Trilby, to supply it with a substantial quantity of goods on three months credit terms. Picant is concerned at the risk that such a large order represents in the current difficult economic climate, especially as Picant's normal credit terms are only one month's credit. To support its application for credit, Trilby has sent Picant a copy of Tradhat's most recent audited consolidated financial statements. Trilby is a wholly-owned subsidiary within the Tradhat group. Tradhat's consolidated financial statements show a strong statement of financial position including healthy liquidity ratios.

Required:

Comment on the importance that Picant should attach to Tradhat's consolidated financial statements when deciding on whether to grant credit terms to Trilby.

(4 marks)

Question 27 BACUP

The summarised statements of financial position of Bacup, Townley and Rishworth as at 31 March 2018 are as follows:

	Bacup $000	Townley $000	Rishworth $000
Non-current assets:			
Tangible assets	3,820	4,425	500
Development expenditure	–	200	–
Investments	1,600	–	–
	5,420	4,625	500
Current assets			
Inventory	2,740	1,280	250
Receivables	1,960	980	164
Cash at bank	1,260	–	86
	5,960	2,260	500
Total assets	11,380	6,885	1,000
Equity			
Ordinary shares of $0.25 each	4,000	500	200
Share premium	800	125	
Retained earnings at 31 March 2017	2,300	380	450
Profit for the year	1,760	400	150
	8,860	1,405	800
Current liabilities			
Trade payables	2,120	3,070	142
Bank overdraft	–	2,260	–
Taxation	400	150	58
	2,520	5,480	200
Total equity and liabilities	11,380	6,885	1,000

The following information is relevant:

(i)   Bacup acquired 1.6 million shares in Townley on 1 April 2017 paying $0.75 per share. On 1 October 2017 Bacup acquired 40% of the share capital of Rishworth for $400,000.

(ii)   Group accounting policies

The development expenditure in the statement of financial position of Townley does not meet the recognition criteria for intangible assets as prescribed by IAS 38 *Intangible Assets*. It relates to a project that was commenced on 1 April 2016. At the date of acquisition the value of the capitalised expenditure was $80,000. No development expenditure of Townley has yet been depreciated.

The fair value of the non-controlling interest on acquisition was $285,000. The goodwill was tested for impairment at the year end and it was found that the goodwill in respect of Townley was impaired by $90,000.

As the carrying amount of the investment in Rishworth is less than its recoverable amount there is no impairment to recognise in the consolidated accounts.

©2017 DeVry/Becker Educational Development Corp. All rights reserved.

(iii)   Intra-group trading

The inventory of Bacup includes goods at a transfer price of $200,000 purchased from Townley after the acquisition. The inventory of Rishworth includes goods at a transfer price of $125,000 purchased from Bacup. All transfers were at cost plus 25%.

The receivables of Bacup include an amount owing from Townley of $250,000. This does not agree with the corresponding amount in the books of Townley due to a cash payment of $50,000 made on 29 March 2018, which had not been received by Bacup at the year end.

(iv)   The share premium account of Townley arose prior to the acquisition by Bacup.

Required:

(a)   Prepare a consolidated statement of financial position of the Bacup group as at 31 March 2018.   **(18 marks)**

(b)   Norden Manufacturing has been approached by Mr Long, a representative of Townley. Mr Long is negotiating for Norden to supply Townley with goods on six-month credit. Mr Long has pointed out that Townley is part of the Bacup group and provides the consolidated statement of financial position to support the credit request.

Required:

Briefly discuss the usefulness of the group statement of financial position for assessing the creditworthiness of Townley and describe the further investigations you would advise Norden Manufacturing to make.   **(7 marks)**

(25 marks)

Question 28 HOLDING

Holding acquired 18 million of Subside's equity shares on 1 January 2017 at a cost of $10 per share. Holding's accounting year end is 30 September; the year end of Subside prior to its acquisition had been 30 June. In order to facilitate the consolidation process Subside has changed its year end to 30 September and prepared its financial statements for the 15 months period to 30 September 2017. The following are the statements of profit or loss of both companies:

	Holding 12 months to 30 September 2017 $m	Subside 15 months to 30 September 2017 $m
Revenue	350	280
Cost of sales	(200)	(170)
Gross profit	150	110
Operating expenses	(72)	(35)
Interest payable	(10)	(5)
Dividend from Subside	15	–
Profit before tax	83	70
Income tax expense	(22)	(10)
Profit after tax	61	60
Extracts from statement of changes in equity:		
Dividends – final payable	(25)	
– final paid (15 September 2017)		(20)

The share capital and reserves of Subside at 30 June 2016 were:

	$m	$m
Equity shares of $1 each		24
Retained earnings	64	
Revaluation surplus	20	84
		108

The following information is relevant:

(i) In the post-acquisition period Holding sold goods to Subside at a price of $30 million. Holding had marked up the cost of these goods by 25%. One third of these goods were still held in inventory by Subside at 30 September 2017.

(ii) The revaluation surplus of Subside relates to land carried at its fair value. It was last revalued on 30 June 2016. At the date of acquisition the value of the land had increased by a further $4 million.

(iii) The only other fair value adjustment that is required in respect of the acquisition is in relation to the plant and equipment of Subside. The details of this as at 30 June 2016 are:

	$m
Cost on 1 July 2014	100
Depreciation (2 years)	(40)
Carrying amount	60

The plant is being depreciated over a 5-year life using the straight-line method. This is in line with group policy. The cost of sales expense of Subside contains an amount of $25 million in respect of depreciation on the plant for the 15 months to 30 September 2016. The replacement cost of the type of plant used by Subside has increased dramatically since it was acquired and Holding estimated that the fair value of Subside's plant at the date of acquisition was $90 million. The estimate of its remaining life was unaltered.

(iv) Subside's business activities are not seasonal in nature and therefore it can be assumed that profits, and related dividends, accrued evenly throughout the 15 month period to 30 September 2017. Dividends paid out of pre-acquisition profits are to be treated as income and should not be deducted from the cost of acquiring the shares in the subsidiary.

(v) The fair value of the non-controlling interests on acquisition was $56 million. The value of goodwill was $54 million at 30 September 2017. Any impairment should be treated as an operating expense.

Required:

(a) **Calculate the consolidated goodwill in respect of the acquisition of Subside.** (8 marks)

(b) **Prepare the consolidated statement of profit or loss and other comprehensive income of Holding for the year to 30 September 2017.** (17 marks)

(25 marks)

©2017 DeVry/Becker Educational Development Corp. All rights reserved.

Question 29 GUIDO ELECTRICALS

In January 2017 Guido Electricals made an offer of $20,000 for patent rights owned by Chuck, a small family company. Rather than accept the offer the directors of Chuck announced to Guido Electricals that the whole company was available for sale. Consequently the share capital of Chuck was acquired by Guido Electricals in exchange for consideration of $220,000.

The statement of financial position of Chuck at the time of its acquisition was as follows:

	Electricals $	Rope-making $	Total $
Property	80,000	30,000	110,000
Plant and machinery			
Cost	20,000	10,000	30,000
Depreciation	(8,000)	(5,000)	(13,000)
Motor vehicles			
Cost	10,000	–	10,000
Depreciation	(6,000)	–	(6,000)
Inventory	32,000	18,000	50,000
Receivables	9,000	–	9,000
Cash	3,000	1,000	4,000
Payables	(6,000)	(2,000)	(8,000)
	134,000	52,000	186,000
Share capital			50,000
Retained earnings			136,000
			186,000

Guido Electricals intended to sell off the rope-making segment of the business as soon as possible after the acquisition had been completed. The segment was sold late in 2017 for $50,000. The segment made a profit after tax of $5,000 for the period up to the date of sale.

Guido Electricals integrated the electricals segment of the business into its existing operations, except that it did not require the motor vehicles. These were sold to the directors of Chuck shortly after the acquisition for $1,500.

The properties were valued on an existing use basis at the time of the acquisition at $77,000 (electricals) and $27,000 (rope-making). The gross replacement cost of the electricals plant and machinery was $30,000, of the rope-making plant and machinery was $12,000, and of the motor vehicles was $15,000. There is no evidence of market value due to the specialist nature of the plant.

The inventory may be analysed as follows:

	Electricals $	Rope-making $
Raw materials	2,000	18,000
Work in progress	20,000	–
Finished goods	10,000	–
	32,000	18,000

The replacement cost of the Electricals raw materials was not materially different from their historical cost. The replacement cost of the rope-making raw materials was $21,000. All electricals are made to customers' own specifications from standard raw materials.

The directors of Guido Electricals calculate that 10% of their time and therefore payroll costs (amounting to $57,000) has been spent on work related to the acquisition. In addition legal fees of $10,000 were incurred.

Required:

In accordance with the provisions of IFRS 3 *Business Combinations* calculate the goodwill arising on the acquisition of Chuck which will be reflected in the financial statements of Guido Electricals for the year ended 31 December 2017.

(12 marks)

Question 30 H, S AND T

(a)   **Statements of financial position at 31 December 2017**

	P $	S $	T $
Shares in S (75%)	65,000	–	–
Shares in T (60%)	–	50,000	–
Sundry net assets	145,000	70,000	75,000
	210,000	120,000	75,000
Ordinary share capital	120,000	70,000	40,000
Reserves	90,000	50,000	35,000
	210,000	120,000	75,000

Both investments were acquired on 31 December 2010 when S reserves were $10,000 and T reserves were $12,000. Goodwill was written off prior to 1 January 2017. The fair value of the non-controlling interest on acquisition of S was $21,000. The fair value of the 55% non-controlling interest in T was $44,500.

Required:

Prepare the consolidated statement of financial position at 31 December 2017.   (8 marks)

(b)   Facts as in (a) above except that the investments were acquired with the following reserve balances:

		S $	T $
(i)	P in S on 31 December 2014	12,000	14,000
	S in T on 31 December 2015	13,000	15,000
or			
(ii)	S in T on 31 December 2014	14,000	16,000
	P in S on 31 December 2015	15,000	17,000

Required:

Determine which of the above amounts should be used as the pre-acquisition reserves of S and T in (i) and (ii).   (4 marks)

(12 marks)

©2017 DeVry/Becker Educational Development Corp. All rights reserved.

Question 31 JANE

Jane holds 90% of the ordinary shares of Prue and 20% of the ordinary shares of Elizabeth. Prue also holds 60% of the ordinary shares of Elizabeth.

Jane acquired its holding in Prue on 1 January 2004 when the reserves of that company were $201,000. On the same date both companies acquired their shares in Elizabeth when the balance on retained profits was $67,000.

The statements of financial position of the three companies at 31 December 2017 are as follows:

	Jane	Prue	Elizabeth
	$	$	$
Investments at cost			
in Prue	600,000	–	–
in Elizabeth	40,000	120,000	–
Sundry assets	1,336,000	717,000	213,000
			————p
	1,976,000	837,000	213,000
Share capital (ordinary $1 shares)	500,000	400,000	100,000
Reserves	1,476,000	437,000	113,000
	1,976,000	837,000	213,000

Non-controlling interest <u>is</u> valued at the proportional share of the identifiable net assets; it is not credited with any goodwill. Goodwill had been fully impaired prior to 1 January 2008.

Required:

Prepare the consolidated statement of financial position at 31 December 2017.

(12 marks)

Question 32 HARLEY

On 30 June 2017 Harley had net assets of $1,052,000. These comprised $22,000 in cash, $650,000 of net current assets, and the balance represented the cost of investment in Davidson.

Harley's share capital at the year ended 30 June 2017 comprised 220,000 $1 ordinary shares. Harley's retained earnings reserves were $732,000 at that date.

Harley had acquired 40% of Davidson on 1 July 2009, when Davidson's reserves were $100,000, and a further 30% of Davidson on 1 July 2010, when Davidson's reserves were $124,000. The cost of the two acquisitions was $160,000 and $220,000 respectively in cash.

On 1 July 2010 the fair value of the initial 40% shareholding was $175,000 and the fair value of non-controlling interest was $157,200. Harley has chosen to value non-controlling interest at fair value, and incorporate its share of goodwill into the acquisition process. The fair value of the identifiable net assets on acquisition was $252,200.

At the year ended 30 June 2017, Davidson's reserves were $255,000.

Davidson's share capital was 100,000 $1 ordinary shares.

Goodwill has been impaired by $60,000 since acquisition.

Required:

Prepare the consolidated statement of financial position of the Harley group at 30 June 2017.

(14 marks)

Question 33 RENEWAL

Renewal was incorporated in 2007 to carry on business as manufacturers of designer jewellery. The company has incurred recent trading losses but has now returned to modest profitability. The directors estimate that raising new capital for additional investment in plant would produce an increase in profit from $1,000,000 to $1,750,000 per year but in order to be able to pay dividends it is necessary to eliminate the debit balance on the accumulated profits.

The draft statement of financial position of Renewal as at 31 May 2018 showed:

	$000	$000
Assets		
Non-current assets		
Premises		2,890
Plant and machinery		2,040
Patents		578
Development expenditure		408
		5,916
Current assets		
Inventory	2,108	
Receivables	2,720	
		4,828
Total assets		10,744
Equity and liabilities		
Ordinary shares of $1 each – $0.80 paid up		4,080
Accumulated profits/(losses)		(5,046)
Profit attributable to arrears of preference dividends		1,306
		340
Non-current liabilities		
8% Cumulative preference shares of $1 each		5,440
Current liabilities		
Trade payables	2,176	
Overdraft	1,768	
Loans from directors	1,020	
		4,964
Total equity and liabilities		10,744

©2017 DeVry/Becker Educational Development Corp. All rights reserved.

The directors have formulated the following scheme:

(a)   The unpaid capital on the $1 ordinary shares to be called up.

(b)   The ordinary shareholders to agree to a reduction of $0.70 on each share held with new shares having a nominal value of $0.50 and treated as $0.30 paid up.

(c)   The preference shareholders to agree to the cancellation of their three years' arrears of dividend.

(d)   The preference shareholders to agree to a reduction of $0.20 on each share held with the new shares having a nominal value of $.80 and treated as fully paid up.

(e)   The dividend rate on preference shares to be increased from 8% to 11%.

(f)   The debit balance on accumulated profits to be eliminated.

(g)   The premises have been professionally valued at $3,800,000.

(h)   Plant is to be written down by $850,000; patents are to be written down to $340,000; development expenditure is to be written off; inventory is to be written down by $406,000; an allowance for irrecoverable debts of 10% is to be created.

(i)   New capital to be raised by a rights issue with existing ordinary shareholders subscribing for two shares for every one share held, $0.30 payable on application, and preference shareholders subscribing for one new $0.80 preference share for every four preference shares held.

(j)   The directors to agree to $420,000 of their loans to be written off and to accept ordinary shares of $0.50 each, at a value of $0.30 (paid up), in settlement of the balance of their loans. These shares are not affected by the rights issue in (i) above.

Required:

(a)   Prepare the statement of financial position for Renewal on the assumption that the directors' scheme has been put into effect.   (7 marks)

(b)   Advise the preference shareholders whether they should participate in the scheme.
                                                                                                 (8 marks)

                                                                                          (15 marks)

Question 34 HOLLY

Statements of financial position at 31 December 2017

	Holly group $000	Ivy $000
Non-current assets		
Tangible (carrying amount)	4,400	2,500
Investment in Ivy at cost	600	–
	5,000	2,500
Current assets	3,460	1,520
	8,460	4,020
Equity		
$1 ordinary shares	2,000	800
Retained earnings	1,560	900
	3,560	1,700
Non-controlling interests	500	–
Non-current liabilities	2,000	1,680
Current liabilities	2,400	640
	8,460	4,020

Holly acquired a 40% interest in Ivy on 1 January 2013 when the retained profits of Ivy were $70,000.

There is no impairment in the investment in Ivy.

Required:

Prepare a consolidated statement of financial position at 31 December 2017.

(7 marks)

Question 35 ASSOCK

The draft statements of profit or loss for the year ending 30 June 2018 of Assock and its subsidiary and associated undertakings, Curly and Tiny, appear below.

Assock's investments in these companies were made as follows:

(a)   On 1 July 2017 40% of the ordinary share capital of Tiny. A director of Assock has been appointed to the board of Tiny to take an active part in its management.

(b)   On 1 November 2017 75% of the ordinary share capital of Curly.

The following additional information is relevant:

(a)   Assock has no other investments.

(b)   During the year Curly had sold goods to Assock amounting to $255,000. Of these $176,000 had been sold in the period 1 November 2017 to 30 June 2018.

At the year end, Assock held unsold goods with a sales value of $17,000. These were included in the calculation of Assock's cost of sales. Curly's mark-up was 20% on cost price.

©2017 DeVry/Becker Educational Development Corp. All rights reserved.

It is Assock's policy to eliminate unrealised profit in full but to charge the non-controlling interest with their share as appropriate.

(c)   In addition Assock had bought for $150,000 goods from Tiny at a margin of 30% on sales price. Half of these remained unsold at the year end.

	Assock $	Curly $	Tiny $
Revenue	2,600,000	1,100,000	1,600,000
Cost of sales	(2,167,000)	(901,500)	(1,315,400)
Gross profit	433,000	198,500	284,600
Distribution costs	(88,400)	(32,700)	(35,900)
Administration expenses	(104,600)	(48,800)	(38,700)
Operating profit	240,000	117,000	210,000
Dividends from			
Subsidiaries	24,000	–	–
Associates	18,800	–	–
Profit before taxation	282,800	117,000	210,000
Income tax expense	(90,000)	(51,000)	(85,000)
Profit after taxation	192,800	66,000	125,000
Statement of changes in equity (extract)			
Dividends – ordinary paid	132,000	32,000	47,000

Required:

Prepare the consolidated statement of profit or loss of Assock for the year ending 30 June 2018. (Ignore any issues relating to goodwill).

(10 marks)

Question 36 BERTIE

The following transactions took place at Bertie, a limited liability company, a company reporting in dollars, in the year ended 31 December 2017:

(a)   Sale of goods on credit on 1 October 2017 for £50,000. The customer paid on 3 December 2017.

(b)   Purchases of goods on credit for £60,000. The goods were received by Bertie on 15 December 2017 and the account had not been settled by the year end.

(c)   A non-current asset was purchased on 1 January 2017 for £200,000 cash. The asset has a life of five years.

(d)   A long term loan of £800,000 was taken out with a bank on 3 December 2017 for the purpose of improving the company's working capital.

Relevant exchange rates in 2017 are:

	$1 =
1 January	£1.70
1 October	£1.65
3 December	£1.50
15 December	£1.40
31 December	£1.35

Required:

Show how each of the above transactions would be represented in the statement of profit or loss and other comprehensive income and/or statement of financial position of Bertie in the year ended 31 December 2017.

(8 marks)

Question 37 MEMO

Memo, a public limited company, owns 75% of the ordinary share capital of Random, a public limited company which is situated in a foreign country. Memo acquired Random on 1 May 2017 for 120 million krowns (KR) when the retained profits of Random were KR80 million. Random has not revalued its assets or issued any share capital since its acquisition by Memo. The following financial statements relate to Memo and Random:

Statements of financial position at 30 April 2018

	Memo $m	Random KRm
Tangible non-current assets	297	146
Investment in Random	48	–
Loan to Random	5	–
Current assets	355	102
	705	248
Equity		
Ordinary shares of $1/1KR each	60	32
Share premium account	50	20
Retained earnings	360	95
	470	147
Non-current liabilities	30	41
Current liabilities	205	60
	705	248

Statements of profit or loss for year ended 30 April 2018

	Memo $m	Random KRm
Revenue	200	142
Cost of sales	(120)	(96)
Gross profit	80	46
Distribution and administrative expenses	(30)	(20)
Operating profit	50	26
Interest receivable	4	–
Interest payable	–	(2)
Profit before taxation	54	24
Income tax expense	(20)	(9)
Profit after taxation	34	15

©2017 DeVry/Becker Educational Development Corp. All rights reserved.

The following information is relevant to the preparation of the consolidated financial statements of Memo:

(a)   Non-controlling interest is valued at the proportionate share of the identifiable net assets. Goodwill has fallen in value by 20% since the acquisition occurred.

(b)   During the financial year Random has purchased raw materials from Memo and denominated the purchase in krowns in its financial records.   The details of the transaction are set out below:

	Date of transaction	Purchase price $m	Profit percentage on selling price
Raw materials	1 February 2018	6	20%

At the year end, half of the raw materials purchased were still in the inventory of Random. The inter-company transactions have not been eliminated from the financial statements and the goods were recorded by Random at the exchange rate ruling on 1 February 2018. A payment of $6 million was made to Memo when the exchange rate was KR2·2 to $1. Any exchange gain or loss arising on the transaction is still held in the current liabilities of Random.

(c)   Memo had made an interest free loan to Random of $5 million on 1 May 2017. The loan was repaid on 30 May 2018. Random had included the loan in non-current liabilities and had recorded it at the exchange rate at 1 May 2017.

(d)   The fair value of the net assets of Random at the date of acquisition is to be assumed to be the same as the carrying amount.

(e)   The following exchange rates are relevant to the financial statements:

	KR to $
30 April/1 May 2017	2·5
1 November 2017	2·6
1 February 2018	2
30 April 2018	2·1
Average rate for year to 30 April 2018	2

(g)   Memo has paid a dividend of $8 million during the financial year.

Required:

Prepare a consolidated statement of profit or loss for the year ended 30 April 2018 and a consolidated statement of financial position at that date in accordance with International Financial Reporting Standards.

(25 marks)

Question 38 LADWAY

(a)   The draft statements of financial position for the years to 31 March 2018 and 2017 of Ladway, a company listed on a recognised stock exchange, are shown below:

	$m	2017 $m	$m	2016 $m
Assets				
Non-current assets				
Tangible assets		2,480		1,830
Intangibles		450		410
		2,930		2,240
Current assets				
Inventories	920		763	
Trade receivables	642		472	
Cash and cash equivalents	–		34	
		1,562		1,269
Total assets		4,492		3,509
Equity and liabilities				
Equity capital		500		400
Share premium		90		70
Revaluation surplus		170		–
Retained earnings		1,871		1,732
		2,631		2,202
Non-current liabilities				
8% Loan note	200		–	
10% preferred capital	350		350	
Government grants	210		160	
Deferred tax	52		30	
Environmental provision	76		24	
		888		564
Current liabilities				
Trade payables	680		518	
Accrued interest	4			
Operating overdraft	63		–	
Taxation	176		185	
Government grants	50		40	
		973		743
Total equity and liabilities		4,492		3,509

©2017 DeVry/Becker Educational Development Corp. All rights reserved.

The draft statement of profit or loss for Ladway for the year to 31 March 2018 is as follows:

	$m	$m
Revenue		3,655
Cost of sales:		
Depreciation of tangibles	366	
Amortisation of intangibles	36	
Other costs	2,522	
		(2,924)
Gross profit for period		731
Other operating income – government grant		50
		781
Distribution costs	75	
Administration	56	
Environmental provision	67	
		(198)
		583
Interest – loan notes		(12)
Preferred dividend		(35)
Profit before income tax		536
Income tax expense		(177)
		359
Statement of changes in equity (extract)		
Dividend paid		220

The following information is relevant:

Tangible non-current assets

(i) these include land which was revalued giving a surplus of $170 million during the period;

(ii) the company's motor vehicle haulage fleet was replaced during the year. The fleet originally cost $42 million and had been written down to $11 million at the date of its replacement. The gross cost of the fleet replacement was $180 million and a trade-in allowance of $14 million was given for the old vehicles;

(iii) the company acquired some new plant on 1 July 2017 at a cost of $120 million from Bromway. An arrangement was made on the same day for the liability for the plant to be settled by Ladway issuing at par an 8% loan note dated 2018 to Bromway. The value by which the 8% loan note exceeded the liability for the plant was received from Bromway in cash.

Provision

The provision represents an estimate of the cost of environmental improvements relating to the company's mining activities.

Equity share issues

During the year Ladway made a bonus issue from the share premium reserve of one share for every ten shares held. Later Ladway made a further share issue for cash.

Required:

A statement of cash flows for Ladway for the year to 31 March 2018 prepared in accordance with IAS 7 *Statement of Cash Flows*. (20 marks)

(b) IAS 7 encourages companies to disclose, usually in the notes, additional information on:

(i) aggregate cash flows relating to an expansion of operating capacity separate to those required to maintain operating capacity; and

(ii) cash flows arising from each reported operating segment.

Required:

Discuss the relevance and usefulness of the above information to users of accounts.
(5 marks)

(25 marks)

Question 39 LOVEY

The draft statement of profit or loss, statements of financial position and notes of Lovey group are as follows:

Consolidated statement of profit or loss for the year ended 31 December 2017

	$000
Group operating profit (after goodwill impairment of $15,000)	385
Income from interest in associated undertaking	21
Interest payable and similar charges	(25)
Group profit before tax	381
Taxation	(170)
Group profit after tax	211
Non-controlling interest	(29)
Profit for the financial year	182
Statement of changes in equity (extract)	
Dividends paid	100

©2017 DeVry/Becker Educational Development Corp. All rights reserved.

Consolidated statements of financial position as at 31 December

	2017 $000	2017 $000	2016 $000	2016 $000
ASSETS				
Non-current assets				
Intangible assets		58		-
Tangible non-current assets (Note 1)		933		520
Interest in associate		90		75
Current assets				
Inventory	119		106	
Receivables	205		180	
Cash at bank and in hand	96		290	
		420		576
Total assets		1,501		1,171
Equity				
Ordinary shares		90		60
Share premium		243		40
Retained earnings		627		545
Non-controlling interest		98		90
Non-current liabilities				
Loan notes		100		100
Current liabilities				
Trade payables	165		196	
Corporation tax	170		135	
Accruals for interest	8		5	
		343		336
Total equity and liabilities		1,501		1,171

Notes:

(1)   Tangible non-current assets

	$000
Carrying amount at start of year	520
Additions	505
Carrying amount of disposals	(45)
Depreciation charge	(47)
Carrying amount at end of year	933

Non-current assets disposed of comprise assets sold during the year for $18,000 cash and $15,000 trade-in allowances against new non-current assets.

(2) **Acquisition of subsidiary**

During the year an 80% holding in Newhall was acquired. Details of the acquisition are as follows:

	$000
Non-current assets	129
Inventory	30
Receivables	25
Cash	83
Payables	(17)
	250
Non-controlling interest (20%)	(50)
	200
Goodwill	73
	273
Shares	233
Cash	40
	273

Required:

Prepare the group statement of cash flows and notes for Lovey for the year ended 31 December 2017 in accordance with IAS 7 *Statement of Cash Flows*.

(25 marks)

Question 40 HEYWOOD BOTTLERS

Below are the financial statements for the years to 31 March 2017 and 2018 of Heywood Bottles, a company which manufactures bottles for many different drinks companies:

Statements of profit or loss for the years to 31 March

	2017 $m	2017 $m	2018 $m	2018 $m
Sales revenues		120		300
Manufacturing costs	83		261	
Depreciation	7	(90)	9	(270)
Gross profit		30		30
Other expenses	10		28	
Interest	2	(12)	10	(38)
Profit/(loss) before tax		18		(8)
Tax		(6)		(4)
Profit/(loss) after tax		12		(12)
Extract from statement of changes in equity:				
Dividends paid		8		8

©2017 DeVry/Becker Educational Development Corp. All rights reserved.

Statements of financial position as at 31 March

	2017		2018	
	$m	$m	$m	$m
Non-current assets:				
Land and buildings		5		5
Plant and Equipment		38		58
		——		——
		43		63
Current assets				
Inventory	12		18	
Receivables	25		94	
Deferred expenditure	–		6	
Bank	8		–	
	——	45	——	118
		——		——
Total assets		88		181
		——		——
Equity				
Ordinary shares		25		25
Capital reserves	11		10	
Retained earnings	8	19	(12)	(2)
	——	——	——	——
		44		23
Non-current liabilities		19		32
Current liabilities				
Trade payables	15		80	
Others	10		12	
Bank	–		34	
	——	25	——	126
		——		——
Total equity and liabilities		88		181
		——		——

Notes:

(1) Plant and equipment is made up as follows:

	$m	$m
At 31 March	2017	2018
Owned plant	10	18
Leased plant	28	40

(2) Non-current liabilities are leasing obligations.

The directors were disappointed in the profit for the year to 31 March 2017 and held a board meeting in April 2017 to discuss future strategy. The Managing Director was insistent that the way to improve the company's results was to increase sales and market share. As a result the following actions were implemented.

(i) An aggressive marketing campaign through trade journals cost $12 million was undertaken. Due to expected long-term benefits $6 million of this has been included as a current asset in the statement of financial position at 31 March 2018;

(ii) A "price promise" to undercut any other supplier's price was announced in the advertising campaign;

©2017 DeVry/Becker Educational Development Corp. All rights reserved.

(iii)   A major contract with Koola Drinks was signed that accounted for a substantial proportion of the company's output. This contract was obtained through very competitive tendering.

(iv)   The credit period for customers was extended from two months to three months.

A preliminary review by the Board of the accounts to 31 March 2018 concluded that the company's performance had deteriorated rather than improved. There was particular concern over the prospect of renewing the bank overdraft facility because the maximum legal agreed level of $30 million had been exceeded. The Board decided that it was time to seek independent professional advice on the company's situation.

Required:

In the capacity of a business consultant, prepare a report for the Board of Heywood Bottles analysing the company's performance for the year to 31 March 2018 in comparison with the previous year. Particular emphasis should be given to the effects of the implementation of the effects of the actions referred to in points (i) to (iv) above.

(15 marks)

Question 41 NFP ORGANISATIONS

Not-for-Profit (NFP) organisations share many characteristics with those organisations whose main aim is to generate profits. NFPs include government bodies, museums and charities.

Required:

(a)   Explain the main aims of a NFP organisation and those of a profit orientated entity.
(5 marks)

(b)   Discuss the different approaches that may be required when assessing the performance of a NFP organisation.   (5 marks)

(10 marks)

Question 42 RADAN

Extracts from the statement of financial position of Radan as at 1 April 2017 are:

	$000	$000
Ordinary shares of $0.25 each		4,000
Share premium	700	
Capital redemption reserve	1,300	
Revaluation surplus	90	
Retained earnings	750	
		2,840
		6,840
10% Convertible loan notes		2,000
8% Preference shares		1,000

Note: The above are extracts from the **opening** statement of financial position for the current reporting year.

©2017 DeVry/Becker Educational Development Corp. All rights reserved.

The following draft statement of profit or loss has been prepared for the year to 31 March 2018, prior to the declaration of the proposed final ordinary dividend for the year:

	$000	$000
Profit before interest and tax		1,800
Loan interest		(200)
Preference dividend		(80)
Profit before tax		1,520
Taxation		
– provision for 2018	300	
Deferred tax	390	
		(690)
Profit for year		830
Extract from statement of changes in equity:		
Dividends paid Ordinary		320

The following information is relevant:

(i)   A bonus issue of 1 new share for every 8 ordinary shares held was made on 7 September 2017.

(ii)   A fully subscribed rights issue of 1 new share for every 5 ordinary shares held at a price of $0.50 each was made on 1 January 2018. Immediately prior to the issue the market price of Radan's ordinary shares was $1.40 each.

(iii)   The terms of conversion of the 10% loan notes are:

Year	Loan notes	Ordinary shares
2020 to 2024	$100	100
2025	$100	120

Income tax is to be taken as 33%.

(iv)   Profit before interest and taxation includes the following items:

- stage profits of $150,000 relating to construction contracts that have been calculated in accordance with IFRS 15 *Revenue from Contracts with Customers;*

- an exchange gain of $25,000 on a long-term foreign currency loan.

(v)   The statement of financial position includes an asset of deferred development expenditure of $114,000. The directors are confident that the development project will be a success.

(vi)   Plant and equipment was revalued on 1 April 2015 giving a surplus of $150,000. At that time it had a remaining life of five years. It is being depreciated, based on its revalued amount, on a straight-line basis. The excess depreciation for the years to 31 March 2016 and 2017 has been transferred from the revaluation surplus to retained earnings.

(vii) Earnings per share (EPS) was correctly reported in last year's accounts at $0.08.

Required:

(a) Calculate the earnings per share (EPS) for Radan for the year ended 31 March 2018:

(i) on a basic basis (including the comparative figure);

(ii) on a diluted basis (ignore the comparative figure);

and state which figures need to be disclosed in the financial statements (ignore comparatives). (11 marks)

(b) Explain why it is useful to disclose the EPS calculated on a diluted basis in addition to the basic basis. (6 marks)

(c) Discuss the principles underlying the calculation of the distributable profit of Radan at 31 March 2018 prior to the deduction of any dividends relating to the current year; and explain how you have treated the items in notes (iv), (v) and (vi) above. (8 marks)

(25 marks)

Question 43 EPTILON

Eptilon is listed in a jurisdiction that allows entities to file financial statements that are prepared under either local accounting standards or International Financial Reporting Standards (IFRSs). The stock exchange on which Eptilon is listed does not require any interim financial statements and Eptilon does not currently produce such statements. Eptilon is seeking a listing on another stock exchange that also allows financial statements to be filed that are prepared under IFRSs but would not accept financial statements that are prepared under the local accounting standards that are relevant to Eptilon. This stock exchange requires comparative figures for the previous year only and interim financial reports, prepared in accordance with IFRSs, on a half-yearly basis. Therefore Eptilon wishes to adopt IFRSs for the first time in its financial statements for the year ending 31 December 2017. The Chief Executive Officer has three questions regarding the adoption of IFRSs in 2017:

(1) I am aware that the adoption of IFRSs will require us to make a number of changes to our existing accounting practices and that the IASB has issued IFRS 1 *First time Adoption of IFRS* detailing the procedures that need to be undertaken when adopting IFRSs for the first time. I know very little about this standard and need a summary of what IFRS 1 requires us to do together with an indication of any practical difficulties this will give us. Please provide me with this information addressing issues concerning the annual financial statements.

(12 marks)

(2) I don't know anything about interim financial reports. Please outline what we will need to disclose when we prepare our first interim report for the six months to June 2017. (6 marks)

(3) One of the most sensitive aspects of the change we are making is the future need to disclose transactions with certain related parties. Please outline the disclosures that are needed and the parties that the disclosures apply to. (7 marks)

Required:

Draft a reply that answers the questions raised by the Chief Executive Officer. Your answer should refer to specific International Financial Reporting Standards where relevant.

(25 marks)

©2017 DeVry/Becker Educational Development Corp. All rights reserved.

Question 44 HAPPY AND HEALTHY

"Happy and healthy" is a traditional independent health food business that has been run as a family company for 40 years by Ken and Steffi Potter. As a couple they have always been passionate campaigners for healthy foods and are more concerned about the quality of the foods they sell than the financial detail of their business. Since the company started in 1970, it has been audited by Watson Shreeves, a local audit firm. Mr Shreeves has overseen the Potters' audit for all of the 40 year history (rotating the engagement partner) and has always taken the opportunity to meet with Ken and Steffi informally at the end of each audit to sign off the financial statements and to offer a briefing and some free financial advice in his role as what he calls, "auditor and friend". In these briefings, Mr Shreeves, who has become a close family friend of the Potters over the years, always points out that the business is profitable (which the Potters already knew without knowing the actual figures) and how they might increase their margins. But the Potters have never been too concerned about financial performance as long as they can provide a good service to their customers, make enough to keep the business going and provide continued employment for themselves and their son, Ivan. Whilst Ken and Steffi still retain a majority shareholding in "Happy and healthy" they have gradually increased Ivan's proportion over the years. They currently own 60% to Ivan's 40%. Ivan was appointed a director, alongside Ken and Steffi, in 2015.

Ivan grew up in the business and has helped his parents out since he was a young boy. As he grew up, Ken and Steffi gave him more and more responsibility in the hope that he would one day take the business over. By the end of 2014, Ken made sure that Ivan drew more salary than Ken and Steffi combined as they sought to ensure that Ivan was happy to continue in the business after they retired.

During the audit for the year ended 31 March 2018, a member of Watson Shreeves was performing the audit as usual when he noticed a dramatic drop in the profitability of the business as a whole. He noticed that whilst food sales continued to be profitable, a large amount of inventory had been sold below cost to Barong Company with no further explanation and it was this that had caused the reduction in the company's operating margin. Each transaction with Barong Company had, the invoices showed, been authorised by Ivan.

Mr Shreeves was certain Ken and Steffi would not know anything about this and he prepared to tell them about it as a part of his annual end of audit meeting. Before the meeting, however, he carried out some checks on Barong Company and found that it was a separate business owned by Ivan and his wife. Mr Shreeves' conclusion was that Ivan was effectively stealing from "Happy and healthy" to provide inventory for Barong Company at a highly discounted cost price. Although Mr Shreeves now had to recommend certain disclosures to the financial statements in this meeting, his main fear was that Ken and Steffi would be devastated if they found out that Ivan was stealing and that it would have long-term implications for their family relationships and the future of "Happy and healthy".

Required:

(a)   **Mr Shreeves is a professional accountant and auditor. Explain why he is considered a professional by society and describe the fundamental principles (or responsibilities) of professionalism that society expects from him and all other accountants.**   (7 marks)

(b)   **Discuss the professional and ethical dilemma facing Mr Shreeves in deciding whether or not to tell Ken and Steffi about Ivan's activity. Advise Mr Shreeves of the most appropriate course of action.**   (8 marks)

(15 marks)

Question 45 MUCKY MINING

Mucky Mining, a company listed on a recognised stock exchange, is a minerals exploration, development and production company with global operations.

The company is highly successful with a strong financial position, consistently positive cash flow and profitability and production sustainability from its ever increasing minerals reserves.

Mucky Mining recently won the LAQH LLP and Monetary Times "transparency" award for its financial statements for the most recent year.

The Chairman, Connie Flikt, described this award as "a great honour and a mark of our objectivity and integrity in financial reporting evidenced by our informative and relevant reporting".

On the same day as winning the transparency award a newspaper report in *The Daily Moon* newspaper ran with the headline "Kids dig gold for pennies" in which it set out use and abuse of children in appalling working conditions in a mine owned by Mucky Mining.

In an interview with an independent TV news Connie Flikt is asked to comment on the Daily Moon report and on an article in the magazine *Green is Good* that criticises the company's mining operations that are scarring the landscape and its careless disregard for reinstatement and decommissioning. Connie makes a brief statement "Mucky Mining is committed to high standards in its employment policies and supports environmental improvement and all stakeholders can rest assured that our business is sustainable and successful and a major contributor to economic, social and environmental improvement that delivers long term growth and return for our shareholders".

Required:

(a)   **Explain and assess the concept of sustainability in the conduct of business and ethical behaviour referring to the scenario as necessary.**   (9 marks)

(b)   **Explain what is meant by a stakeholder contrasting the responsibilities of listed companies towards stakeholders and shareholders.**   (8 marks)

(c)   **Critically evaluate the role of accountants as a profession in society by reference to relevant issues in the scenario.**   (8 marks)

(25 marks)

©2017 DeVry/Becker Educational Development Corp. All rights reserved.

Answer 1 IFRS FOR SMES

(a) **Need for IFRS for SMEs**

IFRSs were not designed specifically for listed companies. However, in many countries the main users of IFRS are listed companies. Until recently SMEs who adopt IFRS had to follow all the requirements and not all SMEs take exception to applying IFRS because it gives their financial statements enhanced reliability, relevance and credibility, and results in fair presentation. However, other SMEs will wish to comply with IFRS for consistency and comparability purposes within their own country and internationally but wish to apply simplified or different standards relevant to SMEs on the grounds that some IFRS are unnecessarily demanding and some of the information produced is not used by users of SME financial statements.

The objectives of general purpose financial statements are basically appropriate for SMEs and publicly listed companies alike. Therefore there is an argument that there is a need for only one set of IFRS which could be used nationally and internationally. However, some SMEs require different financial information than listed companies. For example expanded related party disclosures may be useful as SMEs often raise capital from shareholders, directors and suppliers. Additionally directors often offer personal assets as security for bank finance.

The cost burden of applying the full set of IFRS may not be justified on the basis of user needs. The purpose and usage of the financial statements, and the nature of the accounting expertise available to the SME, will not be the same as for listed companies. These circumstances themselves may provide justification for a separate set of IFRSs for SMEs. A problem which might arise is that users become familiar with IFRS as opposed to local GAAP thus creating a two tier system which could lead to local GAAP being seen as an inferior or even a superior set of accounting rules.

One course of action would be for GAAP for SMEs to be developed on a national basis with IFRS being focused on accounting for listed company activities. The main issue here would be that the practices developed for SMEs may not be consistent and may lack comparability across national boundaries. This may mean that where SMEs wish to list their shares on a capital market, the transition to IFRSs may be difficult. It seems that national standards setters are strongly supportive of the development of IFRSs for SMEs.

(b) **Issues to be addressed when developing IFRSs for SMEs**

(i) *The purpose of the standards and type of entity*

The principal aim of the development of an accounting framework for SMEs is to provide a framework which generates relevant, reliable and useful information. The standards should provide high quality and understandable accounting standards suitable for SMEs globally. Additionally they should meet the needs set out in (a) above. For example reduce the financial reporting burden for SMEs. It is unlikely that one of the objectives would be to provide information for management or meet the needs of the tax authorities as these bodies will have specific requirements which would be difficult to meet in an accounting standard. However, it is likely that the standards for SMEs will be a modified version of the full IFRSs and not an independently developed set of standards in order that they are based on the same conceptual framework and will allow easier transition to full IFRS if the SME grows or decides to become a publicly listed entity.

It is important to define the type of entity for which the standards are intended. Companies who have issued shares to the public would be expected to use full IFRS. The question arises as to whether SME standards should apply to all unlisted entities or just those listed entities below a certain size threshold. The difficulty with size criteria is that it would have to apply worldwide and it would be very difficult to specify such criteria.

©2017 DeVry/Becker Educational Development Corp. All rights reserved.

Additionally some unlisted companies (e.g. public utilities) have a reporting obligation that is equivalent to that of a listed company and should follow full IFRS.

The main characteristic which distinguishes SMEs from other entities is the degree of public accountability. Thus the definition of what constitutes an SME could revolve around those entities that do not have public accountability.

Indicators of public accountability will have to be developed. For example, a listed company or companies holding assets in a fiduciary capacity (e.g. a bank) or a public utility or an entity with economic significance in its country. Thus all entities that do not have public accountability may be considered as potential users of IFRSs for SMEs.

Size may not be the best way to determine what constitutes an SME. SMEs could be defined by reference to ownership and the management of the entity. SMEs are not necessarily just smaller versions of public companies.

(ii) The development of IFRSs for SMEs as a modification of existing IFRSs

Most SMEs have a narrower range of users than listed entities. The main groups of users are likely to be the owners, suppliers and lenders. In determining the modifications to make to IFRS, the needs of the users will need to be taken into account as well as the costs and other burdens imposed on SMEs by the IFRS. There will have to be a relaxation of some of the measurement and recognition criteria in IFRS in order to achieve the reduction in the costs and the burdens. Some disclosure requirements, such as segmental reports and earnings per share, are intended to meet the needs of listed entities, or to assist users in making forecasts of the future. Users of financial statements of SMEs often do not make such kinds of forecasts. Thus these disclosures may not be relevant to SMEs, and a review of all of the disclosure requirements in IFRS will be required to assess their appropriateness for SMEs.

The difficulty is determining which information is relevant to SMEs without making the information disclosed meaningless or too narrow/restricted. It may mean that measurement requirements of a complex nature may have to be omitted.

There are, however, rational grounds for justifying different treatments because of the different nature of the entities and the existence of established practices at the time of the issue of an IFRS.

(iii) The treatment of items not dealt with by an IFRS for SMEs

IFRSs for SMEs would not necessarily deal with all the recognition and measurement issues facing an entity but the key issues should revolve around the nature of the recognition, measurement and disclosure of the transactions of SMEs. In the case where the item is not dealt with by the standards there are three alternatives:

(1)   the entity can look to the full IFRS to resolve the issue;

(2)   management's judgement can be used with reference to the Framework and consistency with other IFRSs for SMEs;

(3)   existing practice could be used.

The first approach is more likely to result in greater consistency and comparability. However, this approach may also increase the burden on SMEs as it can be argued that they are subject to two sets of standards.

An SME may wish to make a disclosure required by a full IFRS which is not required by the SME standard, or a measurement principle is simplified or exempted in the SME standard, or the

©2017 DeVry/Becker Educational Development Corp. All rights reserved.

IFRS may give a choice between two measurement options and the SME standard does not allow choice. Thus the issue arises as to whether SMEs should be able to choose to comply with a full IFRS for some items and SME standards for other items, allowing an SME to revert to IFRS on a principle by principle basis. The problem which will arise will be a lack of consistency and comparability of SME financial statements.

Answer 2 AUTOL

Report to the Directors of Autol, a public limited company
International Reporting Practice

Although some multi-national companies still prepare their financial statements in accordance with local GAAP, this practice can be a major disadvantage if the company wishes to raise capital internationally. Local GAAPs do not command the same confidence internationally as US GAAP or IFRS.

(a)   Current Reporting Practices

Global capital markets and multi-national companies are requiring a uniform set of accounting practices for comparability purposes. It is unfortunate that different accounting practices are used in different geographical locations. It is time for consensus and the production of one international GAAP. However, there are a variety of GAAPs currently in use by multinational companies. Some companies simply prepare their financial statements under US GAAP as this gives access to the US capital markets. In certain industrial sectors this can be beneficial as the US rules (e.g. in the area of revenue recognition) may be geared more specifically to the nature of their business (e.g. in the case of software development companies); although revenue recognition rules in US GAAP will be changing as the new revenue recognition standard (Topic 606) is introduced, this is the US equivalent to IFRS 15 *Revenue from Contracts with Customers*. Additionally, companies may use US GAAP because it was seen as the most detailed and stringent regulatory system in operation and for many analysts was seen as a much clearer accounting framework. This opinion is still shared by many users and thus would appear to reduce the risk of investment. Also if financial statements are prepared under local GAAP, a US GAAP reconciliation would have to be prepared in order to access the US capital markets.

However, the reliance on US GAAP has been tarnished over the years since 2000 with the accounting scandals relating to Enron, Worldcom and other major companies being identified as slightly frugal with their accounting practices.

Some companies publish dual financial statements prepared under local and US GAAPs. Other companies produce reconciliations from local GAAP to IAS/IFRS but this latter practice is somewhat rare at the moment. Finally GAAP reconciliations are not exclusively to US GAAP as some companies, reflecting their listing or operating environments, provide reconciliations to other GAAPs. For example HSBC used to discuss different treatments of impairment and long term investments under local and Hong Kong GAAP and provides a full local to US GAAP reconciliation; its latest financials no longer include this reconciliation.

Some companies produce one set of accounts using local GAAP for compliance purposes and another set of financial statements utilising US GAAP or IAS/IFRS for international purposes. This happens for example in Germany.

Thus it can be seen that a variety of practices are in use by multi-national companies. The vast majority of companies who want access to international capital markets prepare reconciliations to US GAAP. This practice will make any transition to IFRS more difficult as the cost of developing the expertise and training required in order to utilise US GAAP has been already incurred by many companies and there will be a reluctance to incur the additional cost to convert to IFRS.

©2017 DeVry/Becker Educational Development Corp. All rights reserved.

The SEC in USA now allows companies presenting their financial statements under IFRS a US listing without the need for a 20F reconciliation to US GAAP. There are also many accountants in the US who believe that the way forward is for the US to fully adopt IFRS and do away totally with US GAAP. There was a roadmap in place that would have seen US companies fully adopting IFRS by 2014, however, with a change in government in the USA and as a result of the financial crisis it now looks unlikely that there will be full convergence in the near future.

(b)   Use of GAAP reconciliations

The use of GAAP reconciliations is varied and not controlled by any form of regulation. Many reconciliations are not included in the scope of the auditor's report which should reduce their credibility although in reality it does not appear that this is the case.

It is likely that GAAP reconciliations will be used for several years to come. There is little hope of complete consensus on international accounting practice in the short term, particularly in view of the differences in US GAAP, local GAAP and IFRS. The IASB are working closely to eliminate local differences but it seems that even in this environment, differences in practice are bound to remain (e.g. in the area of deferred taxation).

In Europe, the European Commission has endorsed the use of IFRS throughout the European Union and since 2005 has required IFRS be used for the consolidated financial statements. This "Euro GAAP" will aid the harmonisation process but the next step is to align US GAAP with "Euro GAAP". This will involve a significant degree of detailed discussion which will not be easily resolved. Hence, companies that wish to utilise the capital markets in the US will have little option but to provide reconciliations to alternative GAAPs.

It should be noted that Europe has not endorsed all documentation issued by the IASB meaning that there are in effect two versions of IFRS, those issued by the IASB and those issued by the IASB that have been endorsed by the European Union.

The location and nature of the information disclosed about alternative GAAPs is varied and diffuse. Companies generally show these disclosures in the notes to the financial statements or in an appendix but many scatter the information throughout the accounts. The nature of the financial information varies also; some companies show merely a reconciliation of profit whilst others show a reconciliation of shareholders' funds, or a statement of cash flows, or a discussion of the differences, or a statement of financial position or even other non-financial information. The lack of consensus about the location and nature of the information shown is a problem area.

(c)   Potential impact

Being in the telecommunications industry, having a group structure will mean that there may be significant effects on the financial statements under IFRS. The main areas relating to your company where divergence may occur in respect of three areas are:

(i)   Development expenditure – under IFRS development expenditure must be capitalised. However, under IFRS, the criteria for recognition are quite rigorous and the development expenditure may not qualify. In any event as your company currently writes off development expenditure, the impact of the IFRS may be to equalise the development expenditure and match it against future revenues, thus possibly reducing the volatility of this element of the financial statements.

(ii)   Employee benefits – the IFRS requires service cost (current and past) and net interest on the net opening liability or asset related to any defined benefit obligations to be recognised in profit or loss, with any other changes recognised in other comprehensive income, this will include actuarial gains or losses on fund liabilities and actual gains or losses on fund assets.

©2017 DeVry/Becker Educational Development Corp. All rights reserved.

The difference in the present value of the plan obligation and the fair value of the plan assets will be recognised as a net asset/liability in the entity's own statement of financial position. Thus it can be seen that this recognition and disclosure could have a major impact on the reported profit under IFRS.

(iii) Deferred Tax – the IFRS uses the full provision method to determine the liability and the IFRS is based on temporary differences. The potential impact on profitability could be quite significant as the IFRS requires a provision for deferred tax based on a "balance sheet" approach whereby most temporary differences are recognised in the financial statements. Some accounting systems would not require the recognition of deferred tax on revaluation of assets, if there was no intent on realising the revaluation surplus, IAS 12 would require recognition of this temporary difference.

I hope that the above discussion helps in the understanding of the current complex reporting structures being used by multi-national companies.

Answer 3 TIMBER PRODUCTS

(a) Concept of faithful representation

Faithful representation is one of the two fundamental qualitative characteristics, the other being relevance, incorporated in the IASB's *Conceptual Framework for Financial Reporting*. Information should faithfully represent the events and transactions (economic phenomena) that it purports to represent.

Information should be neutral, complete and free from error if it is to faithfully represent the economic phenomena. Information can never be 100% neutral, complete and free from error; choices have to be made in selecting and applying accounting policies, for information to be complete would take too much time and there can be no absolute guarantee that information is 100% correct.

Faithful representation encapsulates the concept of substance over form. This concept was core to the previous version of the framework but is now embedded in the characteristic of faithful representation.

The objective of the substance over form principle is to ensure that the substance (i.e. the economic reality) of an entity's transactions is reported in its financial statements. The commercial effect of transactions, and any resulting assets, liabilities, gains or losses should be faithfully represented in its financial statements. Application of this principle ensures that arrangements are not accounted for in accordance with their strict legal form in a manner that would inappropriately omit assets and liabilities from the statement of financial position.

(b) Accounting treatment and entries in the financial statements

(i) Sale and buy-back

The legal form of this transaction is that it is a sale. The issue is to decide whether this is the substance of the contract or whether it is in fact a financing transaction.

Legal form Dr Cash and Cr Sales

No inventory on the statement of financial position at the year end.

Alternative? Dr Cash and Cr Loan

Inventory retained on the statement of financial position. Interest charged through the statement of profit or loss.

This decision requires an analysis of the terms of the contract. Usually this involves an examination of:

- the main feature of the transaction to decide if it is a real sale or not (e.g. sale to a bank; banks do not buy wood they lend money); and

- which party has access to the risks and benefits of ownership.

IFRS 15 *Revenue from Contracts with Customers* states that where an entity is obliged to buy back the goods this is a forward contract and must be accounted for as either:

- a lease, if the buy-back price is below the selling price; or
- a finance arrangement where the buy-back price is greater that the selling price.

The latter applies in the case of Timber Products.

The contract specifies that the timber will be repurchased. Therefore it is not a real sale in the first place. Timber Products has not transferred the risks and rewards of ownership of the timber and this transaction is a financing transaction. Timber products have in fact borrowed money using the timber as security. The timber will therefore appear as inventory in the statement of financial position and the loan will appear as a liability.

Carrying amount of the liability

The liability is a financial liability within the definition in IFRS 9. This standard requires that liabilities (other than those classified as fair value through profit or loss) are carried at their amortised cost using the effective interest rate method. This means that the carrying amount of the liability will be increased by the interest charge based on the rate that is inherent in the contract and reduced by any cash flows (though in this case there are none). Each year there will be an interest element charged to profit or loss and added to the liability.

Calculation of the effective interest rate

Total finance charge over the term of the loan is:

	$m
Total repayments	56.1
Amount borrowed	(40)
Interest	16.1

This must be spread to profit or loss using the effective rate. This is calculated as the internal rate of return of the loan as follows:

$$\sqrt[5]{56.1/40} - 1 = 0.07 \text{ or } 7\%$$

The annual interest cost and the carrying amount of the loan at each year end over the life of the loan is given below. (This is not required but provided for tutorial purposes.)

Period	Opening balance	Interest @ 7%	Cash flow	Closing balance
1	40	2.8	–	42.8
2	42.8	3.0	–	45.8
3	45.8	3.2	–	49
4	49	3.4	–	52.4
5	52.4	3.7	(56.1)	–

©2017 DeVry/Becker Educational Development Corp. All rights reserved.

The statement of financial position as at 31 October 2017 will show:

	$m
Inventory	40.0
Loan payable after more than one year	42.8

Note: The loan is secured by inventory of $40 million at cost.

The statement of profit or loss will show:

Interest payable (7% of $40m)	$2.8m

Tutorial note: *This transaction is a sale and repurchase agreement. It could be possible to include the interest cost as part of the inventory, if the inventory falls to be a qualifying asset in accordance with IAS 23 "Borrowing Costs".*

(ii)   Consignment sales

The problem in this transaction is to determine at which point Timber Products should recognise the sale. Is the substance of the transaction such that it is right to recognise the sale on delivery of the furniture or at a later date?

If the sale is recognised on delivery of the furniture then the financial statements of Timber Products should recognise revenue of $10m for the year and its closing statement of financial position will show a receivable of $4m ($10m – $6m).

If the sale is not recognised at delivery, but at some later date then Timber Products should recognise revenue of $6m for the year. The inventory held by the retailers at the year-end would be treated as that of Timber products and appear in its statement of financial position at cost of $3 million ($4m × 100/133$^1/_3$)

The decision as to when the sale is recognised requires an examination of the terms of the contract. The contract contains some terms that support recognition at delivery and some that suggest a later date to be appropriate.

Factors supporting recognition at delivery

- Retailer pays insurance (bears the risk of ownership).
- Price fixed at delivery (retailer has risks and benefits of price change).

Factors supporting recognition at a time after delivery

- Retailer may return the goods (Timber Products retains risk and rewards of ownership).

However, this right has never been exercised.

On balance it seems that this sale should be recognised at delivery. In substance once the goods leave Timber products they never return.

©2017 DeVry/Becker Educational Development Corp. All rights reserved.

Answer 4 CREATIVE ACCOUNTING

(a)   Manipulation of financial data

Creative accounting is not a term that has a definition; however various commentators have described some doubtful accounting practices as "creative accounting". Such practices may be used by a company's management to make its financial statements appear more favourably different from what would be commonly acceptable. It must be appreciated that the accounting policies in question are not "illegal" and they may even be permitted by accounting standards. The problem lies in their inappropriate application. For example, if management classifies debt as equity this could dramatically change solvency (gearing) ratios derived from the statement of financial position. Creative accounting is undesirable and, at its worst, is a form of deception.

In the statement of profit or loss and other comprehensive income there are generally two aspects to profit manipulation or creative accounting; inflating profits and profit smoothing.

Inflating profit

There are several techniques used to achieve this (e.g. management may attempt to avoid certain costs being expensed in the statement of profit or loss). Reserve accounting for losses is a good example of this, however IAS 1 *Presentation of Financial Statements* aims to reduce the incidence of reserve accounting as all gains and losses must now be included in the statement of profit or loss and other comprehensive income. Another example is treating future reorganisation costs relating to an acquisition as a reduction of the acquired entity's net assets. One area that has caused concern in the past is the capitalisation of costs that should have been expensed to profit or loss, which in effect classifies revenue expenditure as capital expenditure.

Profit smoothing

The timing of revenue recognition can lead to profit smoothing. Some examples of profit smoothing are regarded as acceptable. For example recognising stage profits in relation to construction contracts (IFRS 15) is common practice, whereas other methods such as "selling" and later repurchasing maturing inventories are generally considered undesirable. IFRS 15 *Revenue from Contracts with Customers* was issued by the IASB in 2014 to clarify when revenue should be recognised. Although the standard is principal based it has much more detail than the previous revenue standards. The standard should minimise an entity's ability to smooth profits.

In the statement of financial position creative accounting has mainly been used to improve "key" reporting ratios such as financial gearing, profitability and liquidity ratios.

It is important to stress that such accounting policies and practices are not illegal and must be distinguished from fraud. Deliberately overvaluing closing inventories would improve profits and liquidity but this would be fraud, not creative accounting. Although creative accounting may not be illegal, it generally prevents the financial statements of an entity from "faithful representation" of the events and transactions that occurred in the period.

Creative accounting has also been used to describe less sinister practices. There are many new and complex financial transactions for which existing standards may not be appropriate because such transactions did not exist when the statements were produced. As a company's management has to account for these complex transactions it has to "create" an accounting policy.

There are obvious explanations of why management may participate in manipulating financial statements. Perhaps the most obvious is that of self-interest: management may be remunerated (partly) in the form of a bonus based on the level of profit. Other reasons may be that creative accounting can, in the short term, increase the market price of a company's shares, again with obvious benefits.

©2017 DeVry/Becker Educational Development Corp. All rights reserved.

A company with high gearing will find further borrowing difficult and expensive. In extreme cases high gearing may breach debt covenants. It is therefore beneficial to the company and its shareholders to reduce gearing in these circumstances.

(b) **Principles of substance over form**

Accounting standards and corporate laws have to be written in "legal form" which describes the issues and defines accounting treatments for particular topics. In addition to the legal form, they often have a spirit or "substance". The IASB believes that in order for financial statements to represent faithfully that which they purport to represent, accounting transactions should be recorded by reflecting their substance or economic reality whether or not it this is also the legal form of the transaction. The substance of a transaction is not always easy to determine, for guidance it is necessary to look at which parties to the transaction bear the substantial risks and rewards relating to it.

(i)   *Group accounting*

Areas of current group accounting regulations that are based on the concept of substance include:

■   probably the most important is that the definition of a subsidiary (IFRS 10) is based on control rather than purely ownership. Where an entity is controlled by another, the controlling entity can ensure that the benefits accrue to itself and not to other parties.

■   IFRS 3 *Business Combinations* states that a business combination must be accounted for as an acquisition using acquisition accounting and the results of the combining entities amalgamated as if they were one.

(ii)   *Financing non-current assets*

The most common example of the application of the principle of substance over form in relation to the financing of non-current assets is in the area of leasing (IFRS 16 *Leases*). In the legal form the hirer of an asset (lessee) under a lease does not own the asset until an option to purchase is exercised. Where this occurs, it is normally at the end of the agreement. Regardless of the legal position, IFRS 16 requires recognition of the right-of-use asset and corresponding liability in the lessee's statement of financial position. This is despite the fact that the lessee does not currently, or may even never, legally own the asset.

Sometimes an entity may sell a non-current asset that it owns to a finance house and lease it back for use in the business. If the seller retains all risks and rewards associated with the asset, the asset is effectively treated as not having been sold and the transaction is treated as a secured loan.

In 2016 the IASB issued a new accounting standard on leases which will require the majority of leases to be "on-balance sheet" and therefore reduce management's ability to be creative.

(iii)   *Measurement and disclosure of current assets*

Factoring of trade receivables is an area where close attention must be paid to the substance of the arrangements. When trade receivables are "sold" to a factor, often a finance house, the substance is usually determined by examining which party will bear the risk of no or slow collection. If the trade receivables are sold without recourse this would mean the finance house must bear the cost of the bad debts. As such this would be a genuine sale and the trade receivables would be removed from the seller's statement of financial position. If the receivables are sold "with recourse" then the seller must bear the expense of bad debts. In this case the "sale" is simply a financing arrangement and the proceeds of the "sale" should be shown as a liability. The above is a simplification of what in practice are often very complex arrangements.

Another common example in relation to the current assets is the sale and repurchase of inventories. A company that deals in maturing inventories may sell them, while they are maturing, to a finance house with an option to repurchase them at some future date. The repurchase price will be designed to repay the original "sale proceeds" and give the finance house a return on funds lent to the seller. The inventories are not likely to leave the premises of the seller. Clearly this is a financing arrangement, not a commercial sale, and should be treated as such.

Answer 5 XYZ

(a)   **Statement of Financial Position after reconstruction**

	$m	$m
Non-current assets		40
Current assets		70
		——
Total assets		110
		——
Equity and liabilities		
Share capital		11.2
Capital contribution	10	
Less capital reserve	(4.2)	
	——	5.8
		17
Non-current liabilities		52
Current liabilities		41
		——
Total equity and liabilities		110
		——

WORKINGS

(1)   Capital reduction

	$m
Ordinary shares of $1	32
Preferred shares dividend	2
Outside shareholders holding of ordinary shares	0.8
Directors' loans	8
Family preferred shares	5.5
Preferred shares redeemed – balance	1.5
Loan notes balance	3
	——
	52.8
Less:	
Outside shareholders holding converted to preferred shares (4m × 0.5)	(2)
Net assets written down – intangible	(15)
– tangible	(5)
– current assets	(5)
Increase in current liabilities	(9)
Accumulated losses	(21)
	——
	57
	——
Balance	(4.2)
	——

©2017 DeVry/Becker Educational Development Corp. All rights reserved.

(2)   Ordinary shares

	$m
Opening balance	40
Less	
Reduction to $0.20 shares	(32)
Outside shareholders offered preferred shares	(0.8)
Add shares issued for cash	4
	11.2

(3)   Redeemable preferred shares

	$m
Opening balance	11
Less	
Capital reduction – family shares	(5.5)
Preferred shares redeemed – cash	(4)
Outside preferred shares capital reduction	(1.5)
Closing balance	0

(4)   Cash (overdraft)

Opening balance		(5)
Cash from ordinary shares		4
Loan notes proceeds	– bank	25
	– family	25
Capital contribution – PQ		10
		59
Less:		
Preferred shares (5m at $0.80)		(4)
Loan notes		(35)
		20

(5)   Current liabilities

Balance	47
Fair value adjustment	9
Directors' loans	(8)
Bank overdraft	(5)
Arrears of preferred dividend	(2)
	41

(6)   Non-current liabilities

Non-current liabilities comprise the two issues of loan notes $50m and the new preferred shares $2m i.e. $52m.

(b) **Fairness of the scheme**

The proposed capital reduction scheme has a different effect depending on the nature of the relationship with XYZ.

Preferred shareholders (outside)

At present the preferred shareholders are not receiving payment of dividends although, if the profit forecast is accurate, dividends may become payable in several years' time. There is no asset backing for the preferred shareholders as the creditors will require payment before any excess is paid to the preferred shareholders and given the fair values of the assets, this seems to be unlikely. Thus a payment of $0.80 per share seems to be quite acceptable in the light of the above comments.

8% Unsecured loan notes

The future cover for loan interest will be $\dfrac{\$8\,\text{million}}{\$2.8\,\text{million}} = 2.86$

This cover is reasonably satisfactory but depends on future profits being earned. Conversely, the asset cover for the loan notes is quite poor as the loan is unsecured and would rank alongside the other creditors in the event of liquidation.

	Historic $m	Fair value $m
Total assets (excluding intangible)	100	90
Total liabilities	85	95
Cover	1.25	0.95

Thus when the asset cover is based on fair values there are not sufficient assets to cover the loan notes and current liabilities. Additionally some of the short-term current liabilities (tax, wages) may rank for priority of repayment before the loan note holders. Thus an offer of redemption at par value without any premium would seem to be acceptable.

Non-controlling interest (10%) – ordinary shares

There will be no asset backing for the ordinary shares and possible future earnings without the reconstruction scheme would be:

	$m
Profit before tax and interest	8
Less: Loan note interest	(2.8)
	5.2
Less: Taxation (at 30%)	(1.6)
	3.6
Less: Preferred dividend	1.0
	2.6
Earnings per share (40 million shares)	6.5 cents

However the debit balance on the accumulated reserves is likely to have to be eliminated before any dividends are paid and together with the lack of asset backing, the non-controlling interest are unlikely to object to the scheme especially as there are conversion rights attached to the preferred shares and the fact that the preferred shares are cumulative.

©2017 DeVry/Becker Educational Development Corp. All rights reserved.

Majority shareholding

These persons are subscribing the additional risk capital. The control of the company is likely to change.

	Before scheme		After scheme	
	Shares (m)	%	Shares (m)	%
Family	34	85	7.8	70
PQ	2	5	3.4	30
Others	4	10	–	–
	40	100	11.2	100

Although the family still maintains control, PQ now has a substantial interest in the company and is likely to want representation on the board of directors. Additionally the family is loaning the company $12.5 million without any security and similarly PQ is giving the company a capital contribution of $10 million and loaning the company $12.5 million without security. The family and PQ are receiving a higher rate of interest than the merchant bank because of a lack of security on the loans.

The forecast profit for the future based on the projected profit would be:

	2018 $000	2019 $000	2020 $000
Profit before interest and tax	8,000	10,000	12,500
Loan stock interest (2,500 + 2,000)	(4,500)	(4,500)	(4,500)
	3,500	5,500	8,000
Taxation 30%	(1,050)	(1,650)	(2,400)
	2,450	3,850	5,600
Preferred dividend	(140)	(140)	(140)
Available for ordinary shareholders	2,310	3,710	5,460
Capital invested	11,200		
Return on capital invested	20.6%	33.1%	48.8%

Thus if the projected profit is accurate, the return on capital invested is good. PQ must presumably be looking to take over the company, particularly as it has been prepared to make a capital contribution without any interest. (In PQs books this contribution will be included in the –cost of the investment– in XYZ) It appears therefore that the scheme will be acceptable to all parties including the merchant bank which is providing a secured loan. The scheme also provides sufficient working capital for the maintenance of operations.

©2017 DeVry/Becker Educational Development Corp. All rights reserved.

Answer 6 BURLEY

(a) **Accounting for arrangements and events**

(i) *Oil revenue and inventory*

In accordance with IFRS 15 *Revenue from Contracts with Customers* revenue is recognised once the five steps enabling revenue recognition have been fulfilled:

Step 1 – Identify the contract with the customer, the contract must create enforceable rights and obligations;

Step 2 – Identify the performance obligations in the contract, if there are two or more distinct performance obligations in the contract then they need to be accounted separately;

Step 3 – Determine the transaction price, this will be the consideration an entity expects to be entitled in exchange for transferring promised goods or services to a customer;

Step 4 – Allocate the transaction price to the performance obligations in the contract, if the contract has two or more obligations then the transaction price will normally be allocated based on the stand-alone price of the individual obligations of the contract; and

Step 5 – Recognise revenue when the entity satisfies the performance obligation, this could be at a point in time or over a period of time.

Burley should recognise a purchase from Slite for the amount of the excess amount extracted (10,000 barrels × $100). The substance of the transaction is that Slite has sold the oil to Burley at the point of production at market value at that time. Burley should recognise all the oil sold to the third parties as revenue including that purchased from Slite as the criteria in IFRS 15 have been met and the performance obligation, the sale of oil, has been performed. The amount payable to Slite will change with movements in the oil price. The balance at the year-end is a financial liability, which should reflect the best estimate of the amount of cash payable, which at the year-end would be $1,050,000. The best estimate will be based on the price of oil on 30 November 2017. At the year-end there will be an expense of $50,000 as the liability will have increased from $1 million. The amount payable will be revised after the year end to reflect changes in the price of oil and would have amounted to $950,000. Thus a gain of $100,000 to profit or loss arises in the following accounting period.

Events after the reporting period are events, which could be favourable or unfavourable, and occur between the end of the reporting period and the date that the financial statements are authorised for issue.

An adjusting event is an event after the reporting period that provides further evidence of conditions that existed at the end of the reporting period, including an event that indicates that the going concern assumption in relation to the whole part or part of the entity is not appropriate. A non-adjusting event is an event after the reporting period that is indicative of a condition that arose after the end of the reporting period.

Inventories are required to be stated at the lower of cost and net realisable value (NRV). NRV is the estimated selling price in the ordinary course of business, less the estimated cost of completion and the estimated costs necessary to make the sale. Any write-down to NRV should be recognised as an expense in the period in which the write-down occurs. Estimates of NRV are based on the most reliable evidence available at the time the estimates are made. These estimates consider fluctuations in price directly relating to events occurring after the end of the financial period to the extent that they confirm conditions at the end of the accounting period.

©2017 DeVry/Becker Educational Development Corp. All rights reserved.

Burley should calculate NRV by reference to the market price of oil at the reporting date. The price of oil changes frequently in response to many factors and therefore changes in the market price since the reporting date reflect events since that date. These represent non-adjusting events. Therefore the decline in the price of oil since the date of the financial statements will not be adjusted in those statements. The inventory will be valued at cost of $98 per barrel as this is lower than NRV of $103 ($105 – 2) at the year end.

WORKING

(1)   Revenue recognition

	Dr $000	Cr $000
Purchases/Inventory (10,000 × 100)	1,000	
Slite – financial liability		1,000
At year end		
Expense	50	
Slite – financial liability (10,000 × $(105 – 100))		50
After year end		
Slite – financial liability (10,000 × $(105 – 95))	100	
Profit or loss		100

Cash paid to Slite is $950,000 on 12 December 2017

(ii)   Intangible assets

An asset is a resource controlled by the entity as a result of past events and from which future economic benefits are expected to flow to the entity. An asset is recognised in the statement of financial position when it is probable that the future economic benefits will flow to the entity and the asset has a cost or value that can be measured reliably.

IAS 38 *Intangible Assets* also requires an entity to recognise an intangible asset, whether purchased or self-created (at cost) if, and only if:

(a)   it is probable that the future economic benefits that are attributable to the asset will flow to the entity; and

(b)   the cost of the asset can be measured reliably.

The probability of future economic benefits must be based on reasonable and supportable assumptions about conditions that will exist over the life of the asset. The probability recognition criterion is always considered to be satisfied for intangible assets that are acquired separately or in a business combination. IAS 36 *Impairment of Assets* also says that at each reporting date, an entity should review all assets to look for any indication that an asset may be impaired (its carrying amount may be in excess of the greater of its fair value less costs of disposal and its value in use). IAS 36 has a list of external and internal indicators of impairment. If there is an indication that an asset may be impaired, the asset's recoverable amount must be calculated. Thus the licence can be capitalised and if the exploration of the area does not lead to the discovery of oil, and activities are discontinued in the area, an impairment test will be performed.

(b)   Integrated Reporting and the energy industry

Integrated reporting refers to a reporting process based on integrated thinking. Integrated thinking is the active consideration by an organisation of the relationships between its various operating and functional units and the capitals that the organisation uses or affects.

Integrated thinking leads to integrated decision-making and actions that consider the creation of value over the short, medium and long term.

The International Integrated Reporting Council (IIRC) is a global coalition of regulators, investors, companies, standard setters, the accounting profession and non-government organisations. It has a vision of a business environment in which integrated thinking is ingrained in mainstream business practice, in both the public and private sectors. In December 2013, the IIRC launched the International Integrated Reporting Framework (<IR> Framework) which established the guiding principles and content elements for the integrated report. The integrated report is a periodic report prepared for stakeholders that communicates how an organisation creates value over time.

The integrated report is not merely a summary of information provided in other reports. It is a standalone report or a prominent and accessible part of another report or communication. Integrated reporting is most widely adopted in South Africa at this time. The King Report on Governance (King III) in South Africa recommends integrated reporting. This means that listed companies must submit an integrated report in compliance with the recommendation or explain non-compliance. Many companies throughout the world, however, are implementing the integrated reporting process on a voluntary basis.

Improves public perception of companies in the energy sector

One goal of integrated reporting is to improve relationships and communication between an organisation and its stakeholders through presenting how the organisation creates value over time. Given the scrutiny typically placed on the energy industry, it is understandable that a move towards integrated reporting for companies in the energy industry can help improve public perception of the industry and relationships with stakeholders.

Mindful of external environment

The integrated report is used to show that value of an organisation can be created through the organisation's interaction with its external environment. This is important for companies in the energy sector. The International <IR> Framework states "The external environment, including economic conditions, technological change, societal issues and environmental challenges, sets the context within which the organisation operates".

Focus on natural capital

Integrated reporting supports an organisation to report on multiple capitals and not just financial capital. One of these capitals is natural capital. The integrated report would provide a company in the energy sector the opportunity to explain to its stakeholders the means by which it makes the best uses of its natural capital and how it affects natural capital.

Entry point into other corporate communications

A company in the energy sector may cover information such as sustainability and environmental issues in the integrated report that are an introduction or entry point to other more detailed communications on sustainability and the organisation's impact on the environment.

Conclusion

Many companies in the energy sector are leading the way in the process of integrated reporting. Companies throughout the world in the energy industry are voluntarily self-reporting using the integrated report format. This is understandable given an increased focus in recent years on corporate mindfulness of the environment and sustainability. The integrated report helps an organisation in the energy industry to communicate to stakeholders information that would not otherwise be provided in traditional financial statements.

©2017 DeVry/Becker Educational Development Corp. All rights reserved.

Answer 7 ALEXANDRA

(a) **Loan classification**

The loan should have been classified as short-term debt. According to IAS 1 *Presentation of Financial Statements*, a liability should be classified as current if it is due to be settled within 12 months after the date of the statement of financial position. If an issuer breaches an undertaking under a long-term loan agreement on or before the date of the statement of financial position, such that the debt becomes payable on demand, the loan is classified as current even if the lender agrees, after the statement of financial position date, not to demand payment as a consequence of the breach. It follows that a liability should also be classified as current if a waiver is issued before the date of the statement of financial position, but does not give the entity a period of grace ending at least 12 months after the date of the statement of financial position.

The default on the interest payment in November represented a default that could have led to a claim from the bondholders to repay the whole of the loan immediately, inclusive of incurred interest and expenses. As a further waiver was issued after the date of the statement of financial position, and only postponed payment for a short period, Alexandra did not have an unconditional right to defer the payment for at least 12 months after the date of the statement of financial position as required by the standard in order to be classified as long-term debt. Alexandra should also consider the impact that a recall of the borrowing would have on the going concern status.

If the going concern status is questionable then Alexandra would need to provide additional disclosure surrounding the uncertainty and the possible outcomes if waivers are not renewed. If Alexandra ceases to be a going concern then the financial statements would need to be prepared on a break-up basis.

(b) **Prior period error**

The change in accounting treatment should have been presented as a correction of an error in accordance with IAS 8 *Accounting Policies, Changes in Accounting Estimates and Errors*, as the previous policy applied was not in accordance with IFRS 15 *Revenue from Contracts with Customers*, which requires revenue arising from transactions involving the rendering of services to be recognised with reference to the stage of completion at the date of the statement of financial position. The change in accounting treatment should not be accounted for as a change in estimate.

According to IAS 8 changes in an accounting estimate result from changes in circumstances, new information or more experience, which was not the case. Alexandra presented the change as a change in accounting estimate as, in its view, its previous policy complied with the standard and did not breach any of its requirements. However, IFRS 15 requires that revenue associated with performance obligations settled over time (e.g. for a service based contract) should be recognised by reference to the stage of completion of the transaction.

Given that the maintenance contract with the customer involved the rendering of services over a two-year period, the previous policy applied of recognising revenue on invoice at the commencement of the contract did not comply with IFRS 15. The subsequent change in policy to one which recognised revenue over the contract term, therefore, was the correction of an error rather than a change in estimate and should have been presented as such in accordance with IAS 8 and been effected retrospectively.

In the opening balance of retained earnings, the income from maintenance contracts that has been recognised in full in the year ended 30 April 2017, needs to be split between that occurring in the year and that to be recognised in future periods. This will result in a net debit to opening retained earnings as less income will be recognised in the prior year. Comparative figures for the profit or loss require restatement accordingly.

In the current year, the maintenance contracts have already been dealt with following the correct accounting policy. The income from the maintenance contracts deferred from the revised opening balance will be recognised in the current year as far as they relate to that period. As the maintenance contracts only run for two years, it is likely that most of the income deferred from the prior year will be recognised in the current period. The outcome of this is that there will be less of an impact on the profit or loss as although this year's profits have reduced by $6m, there will be an addition of profits resulting from the recognition of maintenance income deferred from last year.

(c) **Related party disclosures**

The exclusion of the remuneration of the non-executive directors from key management personnel disclosures did not comply with the requirements of IAS 24 which defines key management personnel as those persons having authority and responsibility for planning, directing and controlling the activities of the entity, directly or indirectly, including any director (whether executive or otherwise) of that entity. Alexandra did not comply with the standard, which also requires key management personnel remuneration to be analysed by category. The explanation of Alexandra is not acceptable. IAS 24 states that an entity should disclose key management personnel compensation in total and for each of the following categories:

- short-term employee benefits;
- post-employment benefits;
- other long-term benefits;
- termination benefits; and
- share-based payment.

Providing such disclosure will not give information on what individual board members earn as only totals for each category need be disclosed, hence will not breach any cultural protocol. However legislation from local government and almost certainly local corporate governance will require greater disclosure for public entities such as Alexandra.

By not providing an analysis of the total remuneration into the categories prescribed by the standard, the disclosure of key management personnel did not comply with the requirements of IAS 24.

(d) **Pension plan**

Alexandra's pension arrangement does not meet the criteria as outlined in IAS 19 for defined contribution accounting on the grounds that the risks, although potentially limited, remained with Alexandra. Alexandra has to provide for an average pay pension plan with limited indexation, the indexation being limited to the amount available in the trust fund. The pension plan qualifies as a defined benefit plan under IAS 19.

The following should be taken into account:

The insurance contract is between Alexandra and the insurance company, not between the employee and the insurer; the insurance contract is renewed every year. The insurance company determines the insurance premium payable by Alexandra annually.

The premium for the employee is fixed and the balance of the required premium rests with Alexandra, exposing the entity to changes in premiums depending on the return on the investments by the insurer and changes in actuarial assumptions. The insurance contract states that when an employee leaves Alexandra and transfers his pension to another fund, Alexandra is liable for, or is refunded, the difference between the benefits the employee is entitled to, based on the pension formula, and the entitlement based on the insurance premiums paid. Alexandra is exposed to actuarial risks (i.e. a shortfall or over funding as a consequence of differences between returns compared to assumptions or other actuarial differences).

©2017 DeVry/Becker Educational Development Corp. All rights reserved.

There are the following risks associated with the pension plan:

- Investment risk: the insurance company insures against this risk for Alexandra. The insurance premium is determined every year; the insurance company can transfer part of this risk to Alexandra to cover shortfalls. Therefore, the risk is not wholly transferred to the insurance company.

- Individual transfer of funds: on transfer of funds, any surplus is refunded to Alexandra while unfunded amounts have to be paid; a risk that can preclude defined contribution accounting.

- The agreement between Alexandra and the employees does not include any indication that, in the case of a shortfall in the funding of the plan, the entitlement of the employees may be reduced. Consequently, Alexandra has a legal or constructive obligation to pay further amounts if the insurer did not pay all future employee benefits relating to employee service in the current and prior periods. Therefore the plan is a defined benefit plan.

Answer 8 VENUE

(a)   IFRS 15 approach to revenue recognition and measurement

IFRS 15 requires that before an entity can recognise revenue there must be a contract; the standard defines a contract as "an agreement between two or more parties that creates enforceable rights and obligations"; the entity has a performance obligation that must be fulfilled and the seller has an enforceable right to receive consideration from the customer. The contract does not need to be in writing but must be enforceable within the context of the relevant legal framework of a jurisdiction.

An entity must recognise revenue if **all** the following criteria are met:

(1)   The parties to the contract have approved it and are committed to fulfil their obligations;

(2)   The entity can identify each parties' rights regarding the goods or services to be transferred;

(3)   The entity can identify the payment terms;

(4)   The contract has commercial substance; commercial substance exists if the risk, timing or amount of future cash flows is expected to change as a result of the contract; and

(5)   It is probable that the entity will collect the consideration to which it is entitled.

Once the contract has been identified IFRS 15 follows a five-step approach to the recognition and measurement of revenue.

Step 1 – is to identify the specific contract with the customer by considering the above five criteria. If two or more contracts are entered into at the same time with the same customer and if they share the same characteristics they may be combined and accounted for as a single contract. If contracts are subsequently modified the modification may be treated as a distinct contract or as an extension of the original contract depending on the relevant circumstances.

Step 2 – is to identify the performance obligations embedded in the contract. Any contracts with two or more obligations may need to be separated and accounted for as distinct contracts. For example, the sale of a computer with a three-year servicing contract would need to be accounted for as two distinct contracts as the entity has two performance obligations, the sale of the computer and the three-year service agreement. Another example that would require "unbundling" is in the mobile telephone industry where providers regularly bundle together the phone and air time as part of a single contract; under IFRS 15 the two obligations must be separated and accounted for as individual contracts.

Step 3 – is to determine the contract price. The time value of money must be taken into account if there is a financing agreement built into the contract. Any variable consideration should also be considered when identifying the contract price, this will require either an expected value approach or a most likely outcome approach to be applied; any subsequent changes will be treated as a change in estimate. Consideration might be variable due to performance bonuses or penalties; it is common in the construction industry for the building contractor to earn a bonus if the contract is completed early or suffer a penalty if the contract is not completed on time. This means that the measurement of the contract can be quite complex if it has unusual features.

Step 4 – is to allocate the contract price between the performance obligations inherent in the contract. Where this is a single performance obligation this step is not required. However, if the contract includes a sale of goods and a follow up servicing contract, as mentioned above, then the contract price must be allocated between the two obligations. Wherever possible the stand-alone selling price of the component parts will be used to measure the various obligations. The allocation is made at the inception of the contract and will not be subsequently adjusted for any changes to the stand-alone selling prices. In the context of a mobile telephone contract revenue will be recognised for the handset immediately (on inception of the contract) and over the period of the contractual obligation for the airtime.

Step 5 – is to recognise revenue once the performance obligation has been satisfied. The entity must assess whether the obligation is to be satisfied over a period of time or at a point in time. Revenue will be recognised over a period of time if one of the following criteria is met:

- The customer simultaneously receives and consumes benefits;
- Performance either creates or enhances an asset that is controlled by the customer; or
- The asset does not have an alternative use and the entity has an enforceable right to payment.

If none of the above criteria are relevant then revenue will be recognised at a point in time.

(b)   Revenue contracts

(i)   Sale of computers

Following the five step principles:

(1)   Venue has a contract with a customer, it can be identified.

(2)   The performance obligation is the transfer of goods, this obligation has been fulfilled by Venue.

(3)   The transaction price is $1 million as this is the invoiced value of the computers.

(4)   There is only one performance obligation so the full amount of the transaction price is allocated to the sale of computers.

(5)   Venue has satisfied the performance obligation by transferring the goods.

©2017 DeVry/Becker Educational Development Corp. All rights reserved.

The issue with this transaction is that there is a 5% risk that the customer will not pay, but that also means that there is a 95% chance that the customer will pay. In deciding if the five steps have been met Venue should consider the expected value (if the contract has a number of possible outcomes) or the most likely amount, as in this situation. The most likely outcome is that the customer will make the payment due, so revenue should be recognised in full.

This gives rise to a trade receivable of $1 million. If Venue is of the opinion that the amount is not recoverable in full it should apply the impairment requirements of IFRS 9 *Financial Instruments* to the receivable. The receivable will be classified as a financial asset at amortised cost and therefore must be considered for any impairment loss using the expected loss approach. Venue is of the opinion that the customer will not pay the full amount and therefore an impairment loss of $100,000 must be recognised. This would be an expense in the statement of profit or loss and not a reduction in revenue.

(ii)   Discounting

Where payment is deferred, the substance of the arrangement is that there is both a sale and a financing transaction. Under IFRS 15 it is necessary to discount the consideration to present value in order to arrive at fair value.

Venue would recognise revenue of $2 million $\div$ ($1\cdot04 \times 1\cdot04$), i.e. $1\cdot85 million. The interest would then be unwound over the period of the credit given and should be recognised as interest income over the two year financing period. In many situations, entities will sell the same type of goods on a cash or credit basis. In such cases, the cash price equivalent may normally be the more readily determinable indicator of fair value.

In terms of the cash payment in advance, under IFRS 15, cash would be debited with $3 million and a deferred income liability set up in the financial statements of the same amount. No revenue is immediately recorded but when delivery has occurred in one year's time, revenue is recognised of $3 million.

If the time value of money was taken into account, Venue would recognise a contract liability of $3 million and cash of $3 million. During the year to the date of the transfer of the product, an interest expense of ($3 million $\div$ $1\cdot04$) – $3 million, i.e. $120,000 would be recognised and the liability would be increased to $3\cdot12 million. When the product is transferred to the customer, Venue would recognise revenue of $3\cdot12 million.

Answer 9 HAMILTON

(a)   Change in accounting policy

IAS 40 requires that all investment properties be measured at cost at initial recognition.

An entity with an investment property then has a policy choice for subsequent measurement. Investment properties must be carried using either the "fair value model" or the "cost model" as described in the standard. Hamilton appears to be using the fair value model. Under this model the carrying amount of the property is its fair value at each reporting date. Any changes in fair value are taken to profit or loss.

Tutorial note: *This process is known as "marking to market".*

IAS 8 *Accounting Policies, Changes in Accounting Estimates and Errors* advocates that in order for financial statements to be comparable over a period of time the consistent application of accounting policies is important.

©2017 DeVry/Becker Educational Development Corp. All rights reserved.

However there are circumstances where the principle of consistency should be departed from:

■ a new accounting standard may render a previous accounting policy no longer appropriate/acceptable; or

■ if the change will result in a more appropriate presentation of events and transactions leading to more relevant and reliable financial statements.

In this case Hamilton has proposed a change in policy. The only grounds for this change are that the new policy will result in a fairer presentation. However this is unlikely to be the case in the circumstances described. The motivation of the directors seems to be to protect the statement of profit or loss from adverse movements rather than to achieve fairer presentation.

(b) **Reasons and effect**

From the information in the question it seems that the future fall in the value of the property is prompting the change in policy. Because the company is carrying the property as an investment at its market value, any fall in the market value must be recognised.

However, if the property was classified as property under IAS 16 then, although the asset must be depreciated, it need only be written down if its value is impaired. Thus the directors of Hamilton may be intending to avoid a write down against profits on the basis that the fall in the market value is not a decline in the recoverable amount of the properly. The directors may expect the market value to recover in the future, or that the value in use (based on receipt of rental income) of the asset has not fallen below the carrying amount. Thus a change in accounting policy would avoid reporting a loss in the year to 31 March 2018.

The effect on the financial statements would be:

Fair value model

The retained profit at the start of year ended 31 March 2017 should be $310,000 if the property is accounted for using the fair value model. This is $110,000 plus the surplus on the property ($3.2m – 3.0m).

Assuming the properly had fallen in value by 25% this would mean a fall of $900,000 (25% of $3.6m) in the year to 31 March 2018. This should be charged to profit or loss as shown below:

	$000 2018	$000 2017
Profit or loss		
Profit before revaluation profit	180	200
Revaluation surplus/(loss) on investment	(900)	400
Profit/(loss) for year	(720)	600
Retained profit b/f	910	310
Retained profit c/f	190	910
Statement of financial position:		
Investment property (3,600 – 900)	2,700	3,600
Retained profit	190	910

©2017 DeVry/Becker Educational Development Corp. All rights reserved.

Change in accounting policy to cost model

IAS 8's treatment of a change in accounting policy is to prepare the financial statements as if the new policy had always existed. This involves restating the comparative accounts, and the retained profits b/f in the comparative accounts:

Profit or loss	*2018*	*2017*
Profit before depreciation (per question)	180	200
Depreciation	(120)	(120)
Profit for year	60	80
Retained profit b/f	70	110
Prior period adjustment (2016 depreciation)	–	(120)
Restated loss b/f		(10)
Retained (restated) profit c/f	130	70
Statement of financial position		
Property, plant and equipment at cost	3,000	3,000
Accumulated depreciation	(360)	(240)
	2,640	2,760
Retained profits	130	70

Answer 10 SPONGER

MEMORANDUM

To	Philip Tislid, Sponger
From	Bill Smith, Accountant
Date	27 January 2018

Subject   Accounting for government assistance received by Sponger

IAS 20 *Accounting for Government Grants and Disclosure of Government Assistance* requires that no grant should be recognised until there is reasonable assurance that the entity will comply with the conditions attaching to them and that the grants will actually be received. The IAS covers forgivable loans and non-monetary grants.

(a)   Research and development grants

The general principle of *IAS 20* is that grants should be matched in the profit or loss with the expenditure to which they are intended to contribute. They should not be credited directly to shareholders interests.

Cuckoo project

The expenditure on the Cuckoo project is research and therefore is written off as incurred under IAS 38 *Intangible Assets*. Accordingly the grant of $10,000 should be credited to profit or loss in the years in which the expenditure to which it relates is incurred.

Hairspray project

The Hairspray project appears to satisfy the criteria of *IAS 38* for deferral of development expenditure, and thus may be carried forward as an intangible asset until commercial production commences (2019). It will then be amortised to profit or loss over the period of successful production. Technological and economic obsolescence create uncertainties that restrict the time period over which development costs should be amortised.

As the project is not yet fully completed the costs that have been capitalised as an intangible asset will be tested for impairment at each period end.

The grant of $10,000 relating to it will therefore also be carried forward as deferred income, and will be released to profit or loss in line with the amortisation of the development expenditure. The balance of $10,000 will appear in the statement of financial position at 31 December 2017 under current and non-current liabilities as appropriate.

Grants relating to assets can either be:

–   set up as deferred income and recognised in profit or loss over the useful life of the asset (to match the depreciation charge), or

–   deducted from the carrying amount of the asset (i.e. being recognised over the useful life of the asset by means of a reduced depreciation charge).

(b)   Compensation grant

IAS 20 states that grants receivable as compensation for expenses or losses already incurred should be recognised as income when they become receivable. They cannot be taken back to prior periods, as their receipt does not constitute correction of a prior period error or a change in accounting policy.

However, the standard requires grants not to be recognised until conditions for receipt have been satisfied and receipt is reasonably assured.

In this case the conditions for receipt, namely completing the triplicate form, have not been fully satisfied and therefore the grant should not be recognised as at 31 December 2017.

(c)   "Vocational experience" grants

(i)   General accounting

This grant relates not to specific expenditure but to a non-financial objective.

The terms of the grant suggest that it is effectively earned at a rate of $1,000 per visit, and therefore it should be credited to income at that rate. In the year to 31 December 2017 the credit will be $7,000. Amounts to be recognised in future periods will be carried forward as deferred income.

The grant is not spread over the life of the bus as it does not specifically contribute to its cost.

(ii)   Repayments

A repayment of $5,000 relating to unfulfilled visits in the current year should be provided for. However, as this is expected to recur in each of the next four years, provision also needs to be made in total for repayments relating to 20 further unfulfilled visits.

A contingent liability should be disclosed relating to the potential repayment of the grant relevant to the visits in future periods which are expected to take place.

©2017 DeVry/Becker Educational Development Corp. All rights reserved.

(iii)   *Amounts for the financial statements*

Statement of profit or loss

	$
Grants received (7 × $1,000)	7,000

Statement of financial position

	$
Current liabilities (1 × 7 × $1,000)	7,000
Non-current liabilities (3 × 7 × $1,000)	21,000
Provision for grant repayment (5 × 5 × $1,000)	25,000

Note to the financial statements

There is a contingent liability in respect of potentially repayable government grants of $28,000.

Answer 11 MOORE

Costs incurred in the 3 months to 31 March 2017

		$m	$m
Dr	Asset under construction	1.7	
	Cr Cash/Creditors		1.7
Dr	Asset under construction	0.3	
	Cr Cash/Creditors		0.3
Dr	Asset under construction	0.43	
	Cr Interest expense		0.43

WORKING

Outstanding borrowings	$18m
Interest for 3 months	$18m × $^3/_{12}$ × 9.5% = 0.43m

Accumulated costs at the date of transfer into investment properties

	$m
Costs to 31 December 2016 (14.8 + 2.5 + 1.3)	18.6
Costs to 31 March 2017 (1.7 + 0.3 + 0.43)	2.43
Investment property at cost	21.03

		$m	$m
Dr	Investment property	2.97	
	Cr Profit or loss		2.97

Being the increase from cost to fair value on completion of the property.

Tutorial note: *The receipt of the professional valuation at 31 March 2017 has not improved the profit earning potential of the asset. The valuation itself is also irrelevant since IAS 40 states that initial recognition should be at cost.*

At 31 December 2017

			$m	$m
Dr	Investment property	(28 – 24)	4	
	Cr Profit or loss			4

Being the increase in fair value following first subsequent re-measurement.

Answer 12 HEYWOOD

(a) **Recognition criteria**

An intangible asset should only be recognised (IAS 38) if:

■ it is probable that future economic benefits specifically attributable to the asset will flow to the entity; and

■ the cost of the asset can be measured reliably.

The recognition and initial measurement of intangible assets is considered in the following circumstances:

As separate acquisitions

This is where an intangible asset is purchased separate to any accompanying assets. This is the most straightforward circumstance and there are no particular difficulties in describing and recognising the asset. There may be some complications in determining the purchase consideration for the intangible asset if it is in the form of shares or other non-cash consideration. However in most circumstances it is usually readily determinable and is often in cash. Examples of this type of acquisition would be the purchase of the copyright to a song or book, or some computer software.

As part of a business combination

This situation is more complex. The acquiring company will usually obtain all of the net assets of the acquired company for an amount of purchase consideration. The basic principle in IFRS 3 *Business Combinations* is that all assets, including intangibles, should be recorded at their fair values at the date of acquisition. It is often difficult to determine whether the fair value of an intangible asset can be measured with sufficient reliability for the purpose of separate recognition. If there is a separate and active market in the intangible asset this could be used to determine its fair value. However, most intangibles do not have an active market as they are unique (e.g. brand names) and a condition for an active market is that the assets are homogeneous. Another possible method of estimating the cost of an intangible is to discount the net future cash flows attributable to it. The problem with this approach is that it is rare for cash flows to be attributable to a single asset; they are usually earned from assets in combination (tangible and intangible). Thus, while it may be possible to identify separate intangibles in an acquisition, it is often difficult to reliably attach a cost or fair value to them. In these circumstances such intangible assets cannot be separately recognised and will be included in goodwill.

Internally generated goodwill

There is no doubt that internally generated goodwill and other intangibles exist (e.g. a brand name), but in order for them to be recognised a cost would have to be placed on them. This is difficult. In the past costs such as advertising and even staff training have been suggested as examples forming part of the cost of internal goodwill. Alternatively the difference between the market value of a business as a whole, often based on a total market capitalisation figure, and the carrying amount of its identifiable assets could be considered to be a measure of the internal goodwill of the business.

©2017 DeVry/Becker Educational Development Corp. All rights reserved.

However this value could fluctuate greatly in a short space of time and cannot be considered as the "cost" of the goodwill. IAS 38 does not consider that any of these methods can be used to reliably measure internal goodwill and therefore concludes that it cannot be recognised.

Granted intangible assets

An intangible asset may be acquired from a government or other third party for a nominal fee or even for free. An example of this may be aircraft landing rights. If an active market, as described above, exists for such rights, this may be used to determine its fair value. This is likely to be rare. In the absence of an active market the cost (which may be zero) together with any expenses that are directly attributable to preparing the asset for use will be the carrying amount on initial recognition of the asset.

(b)   **Fast Trak**

	$m	$m
Net tangible assets		64
Intangible assets – fishing quota	16	
– brand	12	
– licence	9	
– goodwill	19	56
Net assets/purchase consideration		120

Notes:
Purchase consideration:

	$m
shares 20 million × $4	80
cash	25
loan note 25 million ×$0·60	15
	120

IFRS 3 *Business Combination* requires intangible assets acquired as part of a business combination to be recognised separately from goodwill. The standard requires that any intangible that is identifiable, either through separation or contractually, and whose fair value is identifiable at the date of acquisition will be recognised as a separate asset and not subsumed in the value of goodwill.

Kleenwash

A brand, almost by definition, is unique; however IAS 38 says that where similar assets have been bought recently this may be used as a basis for determining a "reliable" value. Presumably this applies to brands.

Government licence

Under previous accounting models it is highly likely that this licence would not have been recognised as an identifiable intangible asset; the licence would have been subsumed in the goodwill value.

IFRS 3 requires an acquirer to recognise, separately from goodwill, the identifiable intangible assets acquired in a business combination. An intangible asset is identifiable if it meets either the separability criterion or the contractual-legal criterion. In this situation the licence is not capable of separation but has arisen due to a legal contract.

©2017 DeVry/Becker Educational Development Corp. All rights reserved.

IFRS 3 requires the intangible to be recognised at its fair value. In this example the only value is the $9 million arrived at by the directors. If this can be justified, maybe through future cash flows, the licence can be recognised at this value. However, it is highly likely that some form of external verification of the value should be sought before accepting the director's value.

The standard does also say that it is possible that the value of the licence and the asset to which it relates (mine) could be recognised as a single asset for reporting purposes if the useful lives of the two assets are similar.

Fishing quota

This appears to satisfy the definition of an active market, therefore the fair value is 10,000 × $1,600 = $16 million. The quota may well be classified as an intangible asset with an indefinite life as the quota is for an indefinite period of time. If this were the case the quota would be capitalised and tested annually for impairment, the quota would not be amortised. If Heywood followed the revaluation model for subsequent measurement then if the price per tonne were to increase above $1,600 the asset would be revalued with any increase in value being recognised in other comprehensive income.

If the government were to impose a finite life on the quota then from that point in time the asset would have a finite life and would be amortised over the life of the quota imposed by the government.

Goodwill

This is the excess of the purchase consideration over the net tangible and separate intangible assets.

(c)   Steamdays

IAS 36 *Impairment of Assets* says that an impairment loss for a cash-generating unit should be recognised if its recoverable amount is less than its carrying amount. An impairment loss for a cash-generating unit should be allocated in the following order:

(i)   to the goodwill of the unit; then
(ii)   to other asset on a pro rata basis, based on their carrying amounts.

In allocating an impairment loss as above, the carrying amount of an individual asset should not be reduced to less than the highest of:

(i)   its fair value less costs to sell;
(ii)   its value in use (if separately determinable); and
(iii)   zero

The IASB has concluded that there is no practical way to estimate the recoverable amount of each individual asset (other than goodwill) as they all work together as a single unit. Nor do they believe that the value of an intangible asset is necessarily more subjective than a tangible asset.

©2017 DeVry/Becker Educational Development Corp. All rights reserved.

	Assets: 1 July $000	First loss $000	Revised assets: 1 August $000	Second loss $000	Revised assets: 30 Sept $000
Goodwill	200	(200)	nil		nil
Operating licence	1,200	(200)	1,000	(100)	900
Property					
– train stations					
and land	300	(50)	250	(50)	200
Rail track and coaches	300	(50)	250	(50)	200
Steam engines	1,000	(500)	500		500
	3,000	(1,000)	2,000	(200)	1,800

Notes:

The first impairment loss of $1 million:

■ $500,000 must be written off the engines as one of them no longer exists and is no longer part of the cash-generating unit

■ the goodwill of $200,000 must be eliminated; and

■ the balance of $300,000 is allocated pro rata to the remaining net assets other than the engine which must not be reduced to less than its fair value less costs to sell of $500,000.

The second impairment loss of $200,000:

■ the first $100,000 is applied to the licence to write it down to its fair value less costs to sell;

■ the balance is applied pro rata to assets carried at other than their fair value less costs to sells (i.e. $50,000 to both the property and the rail track and coaches).

Answer 13 WILDERNESS

(a) Impairment loss

(i) Definition

An impairment loss arises where the carrying amount of an asset is higher than its recoverable amount. The recoverable amount of an asset is defined in IAS 36 *Impairment of Assets* as the higher of its fair value less costs of disposal and its value in use. Thus an impairment loss is simply the difference between the carrying amount of an asset and the higher of its fair value less costs of disposal and its value in use.

Fair value is defined in IFRS 13 *Fair Value Measurement* as "the price that would be received to sell an asset or paid to transfer a liability in an orderly transaction between market participants at the measurement date". IFRS 13 applies a hierarchy to the measurement of fair value, with level 1 inputs being the most objective, and therefore requiring less verification, to level 3 inputs which are the most subjective and will require more verification.

The *value in use* of an asset is the estimated future net cash flows expected to be derived from the asset discounted to a present value. The estimates should allow for variations in the amount, timing and inherent risk of the cash flows.

A major problem with this approach in practice is that most assets do not produce independent cash flows (i.e. cash flows are usually produced in conjunction with other assets). For this reason IAS 36 introduces the concept of a cash-generating unit (CGU) which is the smallest identifiable group of assets, which may include goodwill, which generates (largely) independent cash flows.

Frequency of testing for impairment

Goodwill, intangibles not yet ready for use and any intangibles that are deemed to have an indefinite useful life should be tested for impairment at least annually. In addition, at each period end an entity must consider if there has been any indication that other assets may have become impaired and, if so, an impairment test should be done. If there are no indications of impairment, testing is not required.

(ii)   *Accounting*

Once an impairment loss for an individual asset has been identified and calculated it is applied to reduce the carrying amount of the asset, which will then be the base for future depreciation charges. The impairment loss should be charged to profit or loss immediately. However, if the asset has previously been revalued upwards, the impairment loss should first be charged to the revaluation surplus, through other comprehensive income. The application of impairment losses to a CGU is more complex. They should first be applied to eliminate any goodwill and then to the other assets on a pro rata basis to their carrying amounts. However, an entity should not reduce the carrying amount of an asset (other than goodwill) to below the higher of its fair value less costs of disposal and its value in use if these are determinable.

Tutorial note: *The requirements do not call for a description of indicators of impairment.*

(b)   **Impairment of plant**

The plant had a carrying amount of $240,000 on 1 October 2016. The accident that may have caused impairment occurred on 1 April 2017 and an impairment test would be done at this date. The depreciation on the plant from 1 October 2016 to 1 April 2017 would be $40,000 (640,000 × $12\frac{1}{2}\% \times {}^6/_{12}$) giving a carrying amount of $200,000 at the date of impairment. An impairment test requires the plant's carrying amount to be compared with its recoverable amount. The recoverable amount of the plant is the higher of its value in use of $150,000 or its fair value less costs of disposal. If Wilderness trades-in the plant it would receive $180,000 by way of a part exchange, but this is conditional on buying new plant which Wilderness is reluctant to do. A more realistic fair value is the plant's current disposal value of only $20,000. Thus the recoverable amount would be its value in use of $150,000 giving an impairment loss of $50,000 ($200,000 – $150,000). The remaining effect on profit or loss would be a depreciation charge for the last six months of the year. As the damage has reduced the remaining life to only two years (from the date of the impairment) the remaining depreciation would be $37,500 ($150,000 ÷ 2 years × ${}^6/_{12}$). Thus extracts from the financial statements for the year ended 30 September 2017 would be:

Statement of financial position
	$
Non-current assets	
Plant (150,000 – 37,500)	112,500

Statement of profit or loss
Plant depreciation (40,000 + 37,500)	77,500
Plant impairment loss	50,000

©2017 DeVry/Becker Educational Development Corp. All rights reserved.

Answer 14 ARTRIGHT

(a) Futures contracts and sale of inventory

The hedge is a cash flow hedge of the metal inventory. Hedge accounting must follow strict criteria before it can be used. Management must identify, document and test the effectiveness of the hedge. The hedged item and instrument must be specifically identified. The gains and losses on the hedged item and instrument should almost fully offset each other over the life of the hedge. To qualify for hedge accounting the hedge relationship must meet the hedge effectiveness requirements. One of these requirements is that there is an economic relationship between the hedged item and the hedging instrument; which is the case in this situation as the hedging instrument is a derivative based on the movement in price of the hedged item. Hedge effectiveness is the extent to which changes in fair value or cash flows related to the hedging instrument offset changes in fair value or cash flows associated with the hedged item. This normally means that the value changes in respect of the hedged item and hedging instrument move in opposite directions; movement in the same direction is rare. The change in value will not necessarily be an exact match (i.e. a perfect hedge) and many hedges are effective even when they do not match exactly. The effectiveness must be identified at the outset of the hedge and on an on-going basis throughout the life of the hedge.

For Artright the change in fair value of the futures contract is $600,000 (200,000 ounces × $24–$21) and the change in cash flows expected from the sale of inventory is $500,000 i.e. $5·06m minus $4·56m (200,000 × $22·8). There is no information to assess hedge effectiveness at the start of the hedge but on an on-going basis it appears to be an effective (albeit imperfect) hedge.

Thus if hedge accounting is used the futures contracts would be recorded at fair value when taken out on 1 December 2016 ($4·8 million). On the subsequent settlement of the contracts for $21 per ounce a gain of $600,000 would be recorded in profit or loss having been transferred from the hedging reserve. The purpose of hedge accounting is to ensure that gains and losses on the hedging instrument are recognised in the same performance statement as the gains and losses on the hedged item. Hence the gains and losses on the instrument will be recorded in the hedging reserve until the sale of the artefacts.

Statement of profit or loss (extract)	$000
Revenue – artefacts ($22·8 × 200,000)	4,560
Cost of sales	(4,000)
	560
Profit on futures contracts from Hedging reserve (200,000 × $24 – $21)	600
	1,160

(b) Derecognition of a financial asset – factoring of receivables

The question arises as to whether the sale of the receivables should result in them being derecognised in the statement of financial position. Artright has in effect transferred control of a financial asset and in doing so has created a new financial liability. The new liability should be recognised at fair value. The provision of the limited guarantee creates the new liability. Because Artright has transferred control over the receivables and the bank has the contractual right to receive cash payments from the trade receivables and Artright, the transaction should be derecognised and treated as a sale.

The sale would be recorded as follows:

	DR $000	CR $000
Cash received	440	
Loss on disposal – profit or loss	72	
Receivables (sold)		500
Liabilities (fair value of guarantee)		12
	512	512

Answer 15 AMBUSH

(a) **Classification of financial instruments and their measurement**

Financial assets and liabilities are initially measured at fair value which will normally be the fair value of the consideration given or received. Transaction costs are included in the initial carrying amount of the instrument unless it is carried at "fair value through profit or loss" when these costs are recognised in profit or loss.

Financial assets

Financial assets and financial liabilities are covered by IFRS 9, which requires that all financial assets are classified into one of three categories. The standard states the following:

On initial recognition a financial asset should be measured at fair value.

For any asset that is not measured at fair value through profit or loss then the initial value of the asset will include transaction costs that are directly attributable to the acquisition of the asset.

Subsequent measurement

An entity must then measure the financial asset at either fair value or amortised cost, depending on the entity's business model.

Categories of financial assets

Amortised cost

The asset is measured at amortised cost if both of the following conditions are met:

(1)   The asset is held within a business model whose objective is to hold assets in order to collect their contractual cash flows.

(2)   The contractual terms of the asset give rise to cash flows that are solely payments of principal and interest on the principal.

On initial recognition an asset may be designated at fair value through profit or loss if it will eliminate or significantly reduce an accounting mismatch.

Any gain or loss on derecognition, impairment or reclassification must be recognised in profit or loss along with any investment income generated by the asset.

©2017 DeVry/Becker Educational Development Corp. All rights reserved.

Fair value through other comprehensive income (1)

The asset is measured at fair value through other comprehensive income if both the following conditions are met:

(1)   The asset is held within a business model whose objective is achieved by both collecting contractual cash flows and selling financial assets.

(2)   The contractual terms of the asset give rise to cash flows that are solely payments of principal and interest on the principal.

This category differs from the amortised cost category in that an entity may decide to sell the asset before maturity if that will be beneficial (financially); there is no requirement to hold to maturity.

For this category any changes in fair value need to be split, with impairment gains and losses and foreign exchange gains and losses taken to profit or loss and other changes in fair value taken to other comprehensive income. When the asset is derecognised the cumulative gain or loss in other comprehensive income will be reclassified to profit or loss.

Fair value through profit or loss

All other financial assets will subsequently be measured at fair value. Any changes in fair value will be recognised in profit or loss as well as any profit or loss on derecognition.

Fair value through other comprehensive income (2)

At initial recognition an entity may elect to present any changes in fair value through other comprehensive income in respect of an investment in equity instruments of another entity, as long as the investment is not held for trading.

This election is permanent and cannot be changed at a later date.

Any changes in fair value will be recognised in other comprehensive income, on disposal of the asset any cumulative gain or loss will **not** be reclassified through profit or loss.

Financial liabilities

IFRS 9 states the following about the measurement and recognition of financial liabilities:

A financial liability is recognised only when an entity becomes a party to the contractual provisions of the instrument.

The liability, if classified at amortised cost, will initially be recognised at fair value less any directly attributable transaction costs.

If the liability is classified at fair value through profit or loss any relevant transaction costs will be charged immediately to profit or loss.

Subsequent measurement

Most financial liabilities will subsequently be measured at amortised cost using the effective interest method. Interest expense based on the effective interest method will be charged to profit or loss.

The groups of financial liabilities that are not measured at amortised cost will include:

■ Those at fair value through profit or loss (including derivatives) – these must be measured at fair value.

■ Commitment to provide a loan at below-market interest rate – these liabilities will be measured at the higher of the amount determined under IAS 37 and the initial amount recognised less any cumulative amortisation.

■ Financial liabilities that are designated (irrevocably) at fair value through profit or loss on initial recognition. This should result in more relevant information, because either:

(i) It eliminates or significantly reduces a measurement or recognition inconsistency (an accounting mismatch); or

(ii) The group of financial liabilities is managed (and performance evaluated) on a fair value basis.

Any change in fair value due to credit risk associated with the liability is presented in other comprehensive income and all other changes in fair value will be presented in profit or loss.

(b) *(i) Impairment of financial assets*

IFRS 9 adopts an "expected loss" approach to the recognition of impairment losses in respect of financial assets. This will usually advance the recognition of impairment losses as compared with its predecessor (IAS 39) which followed an incurred loss approach.

Financial assets measured at amortised cost and financial assets measured at fair value through other comprehensive income according to the entity's business model are subject to impairment testing.

A loss allowance for any expected credit losses must be recognised in **profit or loss**.

The loss allowance is measured at each reporting date. The amount depends on whether or not the instrument's credit risk has *increased significantly* since initial recognition:

■ If significant, the loss allowance is the amount of the lifetime expected credit losses;
■ If not significant, the loss allowance is 12-month expected credit losses.

The credit risk associated with a financial asset must be assessed at each reporting date:

■ If it has increased significantly the loss is measured based on the lifetime of the asset;
■ Otherwise the loss is measured based on the 12-month expected credit losses.

The probability of a significant increase in credit risk will be higher for assets with a low credit risk on initial recognition than for those with a high credit risk on initial recognition.

©2017 DeVry/Becker Educational Development Corp. All rights reserved.

Factors that could significantly increase credit risk include:

■　An actual or forecast deterioration in the economic environment which is expected to have a negative effect on the debtor's ability to generate cash flows.

■　The debtor is close to breaching covenants which may require restructuring of the loan.

■　A decrease in the trading price of the debtor's bonds and/or significant increases in credit risk on other bonds of the same debtor.

■　The fair value of an asset has been below its amortised cost for some time.

■　A reassessment of the entity's own internal risk grading of loans given.

■　An actual or expected decline in the debtor's operating results.

The standard allows a simplified impairment approach to an entity's trade receivables. The simplification allows the entity to measure the loss allowance as an amount equal to lifetime expected credit losses for trade receivables or contract assets resulting from transactions under IFRS 15 *Revenue from Contracts with Customers.*

(ii)　Accounting for impairment loss

Bromwich has suffered financial difficulties and is in the process of reorganising its business. As a result of the reorganisation it is unlikely that it will be able to meet all its obligations and therefore an impairment loss must be recognised in respect of the financial asset held by Ambush. The impairment loss on the loan will be calculated by discounting the estimated future cash flows. The future cash flows will be $100,000 on 30 November 2019. This will be discounted at an effective interest rate of 8% to give a present value of $85,733. The loan will, therefore, be impaired by ($200,000 – $85,733) i.e. $114,267.

The difference between the expected proceeds of $100,000 and the new valuation of $85,733 will be recognised as interest income over the following two years remaining life of the asset, this will increase the value of the asset to the expected proceeds of $100,000 by the settlement date.

Answer 16　ARROCHAR

IFRS 16 *Leases* and IFRS 15 *Revenue from Contracts with Customers* are the relevant standards. Initially, Arrochar must apply IFRS 15 first as this will dictate the accounting treatment. If the five-steps of revenue recognition are met, a sale is recognised and the asset derecognised. (A right-of-use asset and a lease liability will then be recognised in accordance with IFRS 16.) If the revenue recognition requirements are not met, the contract is accounted for as a financing arrangement; a sale cannot be recognised and the asset is not derecognised.

One of the steps to revenue recognition is that a contract promises to transfer goods (or services) to a customer; if the contract does not identify a performance obligation to be satisfied by the seller, revenue cannot be recognised.

Option 1

Arrochar will retain possession of the asset and have the use of it for the remainder of its useful life. There is also an option to buy back the legal title for a nominal amount. Arrochar will not relinquish any of the risks or rewards associated with the asset so there is no performance obligation to be satisfied. The "lease" should be treated as a financing arrangement; the "sale proceeds" give rise to a financial liability that should be measured at amortised cost.

Option 2

As the risks and rewards will pass to the buyer and a performance obligation will be satisfied, this contract will be treated as a sale and the asset derecognised. Instead of the physical asset, Arrochar will recognise a right-of-use asset and a lease liability. The lease liability will be measured at the present value of future lease payments discounted at the interest rate implicit in the lease (or Arrochar's incremental cost of borrowing). The right-of-use asset will initially be measured at the present value of the liability plus any up-front payments and direct costs. It will then be depreciated over the term of the lease (i.e. three years). Lease rentals will be analysed between the repayment of capital and the interest element, using the discount rate applied in the initial calculation of the lease liability.

Arrochar can only recognise a gain on the sale that relates to the proportion of rights transferred to the buyer.

Answer 17 ROUTER

(a)   **Revenue recognition**

IFRS 15 *Revenue from Contracts with Customers* deals with revenue recognition, both in terms of when and how much. It requires fulfilment of a five-step process:

- ■ Step 1 – Identify the contract with the customer. The contract must create enforceable rights and obligations;

- ■ Step 2 – Identify the performance obligations in the contract. If there are two or more distinct performance obligations in the contract they need to be accounted separately;

- ■ Step 3 – Determine the transaction price. This will be the consideration an entity expects to be entitled to in exchange for transferring promised goods or services to a customer;

- ■ Step 4 – Allocate the transaction price to the performance obligations in the contract. If the contract has two or more obligations then the transaction price will normally be allocated based on the stand-alone price of the individual obligations of the contract; and

- ■ Step 5 – Recognise revenue when the entity satisfies the performance obligation. This could be at a point in time or over a period of time.

Router has a contract with the customer, the performance obligation being to deliver the film; the contract price is $5 million with a further variable element of $100, 000 for each showing, there is a degree of uncertainty as to how many times the film will be shown and therefore there is uncertainty about the total amount of revenue to recognise. As there appears to be just one performance obligation there is no question of allocating the transaction price. The main issue seems to be whether or not Router has satisfied its performance obligation to deliver a film to the customer that will allow the customer to broadcast it on its network.

Although the film has been delivered to the customer, indicating the customer has control, the customer appears unwilling to accept the film in its present format stating that a major editing process needs to be carried out before it is suitable for showing.

IFRS 15 requires the goods or services provided to a customer must be in accordance with agreed-upon specifications; Router does not appear to have met those specifications at this point in time and therefore revenue should not be recognised in year ending 31 May 2018 but deferred until the customer has carried out the editing process to meet the contact specifications. The payment made by the customer should be recognised as a liability until the specifications have been met and only then should revenue be recognised.

©2017 DeVry/Becker Educational Development Corp. All rights reserved.

There is also an issue about the amount of revenue that should be recognised; the $5 million is fairly obvious but Router cannot be certain of how many viewings there will be and will not be certain, therefore, of the additional $100,000 per viewing. Router may need to make a best estimate of the amount receivable but will also need to take account of the time value of money (if the broadcasts are to be some time in the future) and also the costs to be incurred by the customer which will reduce the expected future payments.

(b)   Land and buildings

IAS 16 *Property, Plant and Equipment* permits assets to be revalued on a class by class basis. The different characteristics of the buildings allow them to be classified separately. Different measurement models can, therefore, be used for the office buildings and the film studios. However, IAS 8 *Accounting Policies, Changes in Accounting Estimates and Errors* says that once an entity has decided on its accounting policies, it should apply them consistently from period to period and across all relevant transactions. Accounting policies can only be changed in specific circumstances:

(a)   where there is a new accounting standard or interpretation or changes to an accounting standard;

(b)   where the change results in the financial statements providing reliable and more relevant information about the effects of transactions, other events or conditions on the financial position, financial performance or cash flows. Voluntary changes are quite rare but may occur when an accounting policy is no longer appropriate.

Router will have to ensure that the change in accounting policy meets the criteria in IAS 8. Additionally, depreciated historical cost will have to be calculated for the film studios at the commencement of the period and the opening balance on the revaluation reserve and any other affected component of equity adjusted. The comparative amounts for each prior period should be presented as if the new accounting policy had always been applied. There are limits on retrospective application on the grounds of impracticability.

IFRS 16 *Leases* prescribes the accounting treatment for the initial recognition of a lease and any subsequent modification to the lease terms. Router has correctly accounted for the lease initially, by recognising the theme park as a right-of-use asset along with the lease liability.

The modification should be treated as a separate lease if both:

■   the modification increases the scope of the lease to use additional assets; and
■   the consideration increases by a commensurate amount with the stand-alone selling price for the increase in the scope.

In Router's case no additional asset has been included in the terms of the lease and therefore the modification is not treated as a separate lease.

When a modification is not treated as a separate lease, the lease liability should be remeasured based on the modified lease term using a revised discount rate, if relevant. Any change in the value of the lease liability will be adjusted against the carrying amount of the lease liability. Any gain or loss relating to the partial or full termination of the lease will also be recognised.

(c)   Partial disposal

The investment in Wireless is currently accounted for using the equity method of accounting under IAS 28 *Investments in Associates and Joint Ventures*. On the sale of a 15% holding, the investment in Wireless will be accounted for in accordance with IFRS 9. Router should recognise a gain, in profit or loss, on the sale of the holding in Wireless of $8 million.

The gain is calculated as the proceeds on disposal (40) plus the fair value of the remaining investment (23) less the carrying amount of the investment on disposal of 55 ((200 × 25%) + 5).

The remaining 10% investment will be classified as a financial asset at "fair value through profit or loss" or "fair value through other comprehensive income". Changes in fair value for these categories are reported in profit or loss or other comprehensive income (then equity) respectively. At 1 January 2018, the investment will be recorded at fair value of $23 million. At 31 May 2018 a further gain of $3 million ($26m – 23m) will be recorded. IFRS 9 requires all investments in equity instruments of another entity to be measured at fair value through profit or loss unless designated, on initial recognition, at fair value through other comprehensive income. Once the designation has been made the classification of the investment cannot be changed.

(d)   Potential voting rights

This is quite a complex situation and the respective rights of both parties would need to be understood before making a final decision. IFRS 10 *Consolidated Financial Statements* deals with a parent's ability to control a subsidiary.

Normally the holding of 60% of voting rights would tend to indicate that control exists but, where another party has potential voting rights that are "substantive", the ability to control would be called into question. For rights to be "substantive" the holder must have the practical ability to exercise its right.

Based on the above it would appear that Router does not have the power to exercise control over the radio station as the other party, if they exercised their rights, would then be the majority shareholder and would have dominant influence over the radio station.

Therefore Router should either account for its shareholding in the radio station in accordance with IAS 28 *Investments in Associates and Joint Ventures*, if significant influence exists, and value using the equity method, or in accordance with IFRS 9 *Financial Instruments* and measure the asset at fair value.

Answer 18 AZ

(a)   Why segmental data improves information

Many companies and groups of companies conduct their business in several industrial sectors and in a number of different countries. Such companies also may manufacture in one country and supply goods to customers in another country. These different parts of the business will be subject to different risks determined by the business environment in which they are operating. Additionally each segment may have a different growth potential because of the region of the world in which it is trading and may have different regional problems to deal with. For example, there may be high inflation in that part of the world, or currency problems. There is greater awareness of cultural and environmental differences between countries by investors and therefore geographical knowledge of business operations is increasingly important.

The provision of segmental information will enable users to better understand the company's past performance and to make more informed judgements about the company as a whole. If users are to be able to assess the performance of a company and attempt to predict likely future results, data in the financial statements needs to be disaggregated. It is important that users are aware of the impact that changes in significant components of the business may have on the business as a whole. Several companies are currently demerging their activities and as a result of this, the provision of segmental information becomes increasingly important. The computation of key accounting ratios for the different segments is important information for potential investors in the demerged activities.

©2017 DeVry/Becker Educational Development Corp. All rights reserved.

(b)   **Transactions**

(i)   Fleet of aircraft

IFRS 8 requires disclosure of information relating to operating segments that are based on components of the entity that report directly to the Chief Operating Decision Maker. This position is responsible for managing and allocating resources to the segment.

If the two business's report separately to management for internal purposes and management view the business's as two separate components then it is highly likely that they will be classified as operating segments under IFRS 8.

Information would need to be presented to users of accounts relating to the revenue, profit, assets and liabilities of the segments. The information provided is based on that given to the Chief Operating Decision Maker, which may be measured in a manner different to that required for the full IFRS financial statements. Where there is a difference in the method of measurement then IFRS 8 requires reconciliation between that disclosed under IFRS 8 and the figures presented in the full financials.

IFRS 8 not only concerns itself with the quantitative disclosures but also requires a number of qualitative disclosures to be made to users, giving the users the information that is available to the internal management of the business.

(ii)   Manufacturing plant

IFRS 8 requires that in measuring and reporting segment revenue from transactions with other segments, inter-segment transfers should be measured on the basis that the entity actually used to price the transfers. The basis of pricing inter-segment transfers and any change is disclosed in the financial statements. Thus the fact that market prices are used to price intra-group transfers except where such a price is not available, will give important information to users of financial statements.

(iii)   Material items

A segment expense is one which results from the operating activities of a segment that is directly attributable to that segment or the relevant portion of an expense that can be allocated on a reasonable basis to that segment. Any material items relating to a specific segment should be disclosed as part of the disclosure requirements of IFRS 8.

IAS 1 *Presentation of Financial Statements* requires an entity to disclose information of a material nature, either due to the size or nature of the transaction. IFRS 8 is carrying this principle forward into the disclosure requirements for individual operating segments, allowing users to make their own decisions about the events that have affected that segment of the business.

(iv)   Holiday business

IFRS 8 does not deal specifically with the segmental disclosure of a discontinued operation. IFRS 5 *Non-current Assets Held for Disposal and Discontinued Operations* requires NCA or groups of assets that are held for disposal to be presented separately in the financial statements. Assets are to be classified as held for disposal if the economic benefits from that asset will primarily be generated through its disposal.

It would seem the disposal or discontinuance of the holiday business may well meet the definition of held for disposal, requiring the assets to be presented separately in the statement of financial position and to be valued at the lower of the current carrying amount and fair value less costs to sell.

(v)   Unquoted investment

IFRS 8 requires that an entity should disclose for each reportable segment the aggregate of the entity's share of the profit or loss of associates accounted for using the equity method.

The entity should also disclose the amount of any investment in associates accounted for using the equity method that is reported within the operating segment.

Answer 19 KELLY

(a)   Post-employment benefits

Meaning

Post-employment benefits are employee benefits (other than termination benefits and short-term employee benefits) that are payable after completion of employment. Examples of such benefits include lump sum payments on completion of employment and ongoing cash sums payable on a monthly basis in the form of a pension. Such benefits are often (but not necessarily) payable via post-employment benefit plans.

Measurement and recognition – defined contribution plans

Where such plans are defined contribution plans the obligation of the entity is limited to the amount that it agrees to contribute to the plan. Therefore the related employee benefit is measured at the amount of contributions payable by an entity (and perhaps also the employee) to the fund. Unless another standard requires or permits the inclusion of the benefits in the cost of an asset the benefits should be recognised as an expense in profit or loss. Any unpaid or prepaid contributions should be recognised in the statement of financial position as a liability or an asset.

(b)   Why accounting for defined benefit plans is more complex

Where post-employment benefits are provided via defined benefit plans then the basis of measuring the benefit payable differs from defined contribution plans. The benefit is typically based on the length of service and the final salary of the former employee. There is no guarantee that the contributions paid plus associated investment income will be sufficient to fund the benefit payable. In such circumstances the contributing entity has a legal or constructive obligation to provide additional resources to the plan to ensure that the benefit can be paid. In addition these benefits are often payable on a regular basis until the death of the employee. Therefore measuring the cost of the benefit to the contributing entity is more complex.

(c)   Amounts that should be included in financial statements

IAS 19 requires entities to initially focus on amounts in the statement of financial position when accounting for benefits provided via defined benefit plans. The essential principle is that, in the statement of financial position, entities should measure the net obligation to provide benefits based on service provided up to the reporting date. This obligation should be measured at the net of the following amounts:

■   The present value of the defined benefit obligation at the reporting date, less;
■   The fair value at the reporting date of any plan assets out of which the obligations are to be settled directly.

Where the net obligation is negative then IAS 19 allows entities to recognise an asset provided this amount is recoverable either by receiving refunds from the plan or from reducing future contributions that would otherwise be payable to the plan.

©2017 DeVry/Becker Educational Development Corp. All rights reserved.

The amounts that should be recognised in profit or loss as costs (or in certain circumstances in the cost of an asset) are:

- The current service cost.
- Any past service cost.
- The net interest on the net defined benefit liability or asset.

The amounts that should be recognised in other comprehensive income are:

- Remeasurements of the net defined liability or asset

    Remeasurements comprise any actuarial gains or losses and the return of the plan assets, excluding any amounts included in the net interest on the net defined benefit liability or asset that has been included in profit or loss.

(d)   **Financial statement extracts**

Statement of financial position at 31 March 2018

	$000
Obligation at reporting date	36,000
Fair value of plan assets at reporting date	(31,000)
	5,000

Profit or loss – year ended 31 March 2018

	$000
Current service cost	6,000
Net interest on opening net liability (10% × 3,000)	300
	6,300

Other comprehensive income – year ended 31 March 2018

	$000
Remeasurements	
Actuarial loss on liability (W1)	1,700
Return on plan assets not included in profit or loss (W2)	(200)
	1,500

Tutorial note: *Returns on assets will depend on the type of asset held: if property, returns will include rent and fair value changes; if shares, returns will be dividends and fair value changes and if debt, returns will be interest. The amount included in OCI will be the actual returns earned less any interest already included in profit or loss.*

Journal (not required, but included for completeness)

		$000	$000
Dr	Profit or loss	6,300	
	Other comprehensive income	1,500	
Cr	Cash		5,800
	Net liability (5,000 – 3,000)		2,000

WORKINGS

(1) Actuarial gains/losses on liability arising in the year

	$000
Opening liability	33,000
Current service cost	6,000
Interest cost	3,300
Benefits paid	(8,000)
Expected liability	34,300
Actuarial loss in the period (to OCI remeasurement)	1,700
Closing liability	36,000

(2) Actual return on plan assets

	$000
Opening asset	30,000
Cash contribution	5,800
Benefits paid	(8,000)
Actual return	3,200
Closing asset	31,000

Of the actual return of $3,200, $3,000 ($30,000 × 10%) has already been included in the net interest which has been charged to profit or loss.

Therefore $200 is part of the remeasurement figure included in other comprehensive income (OCI).

Answer 20 DERRY

Defined benefit scheme

Statement of financial position

Closing net defined liability (2,950 – 2,000)	950

Statement of comprehensive income

Service cost (110 current + 30 past)	140
Net interest (W1)	47
Profit or loss	187
Other comprehensive income:	
Remeasurements (W2)	353
Total comprehensive income	540

©2017 DeVry/Becker Educational Development Corp. All rights reserved.

WORKINGS

(1)   10% × 470 opening net defined benefit liability (i.e. 1,970 – 1,500).

(2)   Remeasurements:

Actuarial gain or loss on defined benefit liability:

Opening liability	1,970
Current service cost	110
Past service cost	30
Interest on opening liability (1,970 × 10%)	197
Actuarial loss (to balance)	643
Closing liability	2,950

Actual return on plan assets:

Opening asset	1,500
Cash contribution	60
Actual return (to balance)	440
Closing asset	2,000

Net interest on opening plan asset is 150 (1,500 × 10%) and so increase in plan assets due to remeasurement is 290 (440 – 150).

Net remeasurement is 353 (643 losses on liability + 290 return on assets).

Journal entries

Dr	Profit or loss	187	
Dr	Other comprehensive income	353	
Cr	Cash (contribution)		60
Cr	Net defined benefit liability (W)		480

WORKING

Opening net liability (1,970 – 1,500)	470
Closing net liability (as per statement of financial position)	950
Increase in liability	480

Answer 21 KERENSKY

(a)   Corporate income tax liability – year ended 30 June 2018

		$000
Profit per accounts		900
Add Depreciation		260
Lease expense		72
		1,232
Less Tax allowance (given)		(175)
Lease rentals paid		(160)
Development costs		(80)
Taxable profits		817
Tax payable @ 30%		245.1

(b)   Deferred tax liability

	Carrying amount $000	Tax base $000	Temporary difference $000
Tangible assets			
Carrying amount (1,300 – 260)	1,040		
Tax base (500 – 175)		325	715
Properties	300	240	60
Lease	88	–	88
Development expenditure	80	–	80
	1,508	565	943
Deferred tax @30%			282.9

(c)   Movement on the deferred tax liability

	$000
Balance b/f ((1,300 – 500) × 30%)	240
To Other comprehensive income (60 × 30%)	18
Profit or loss (balancing figure)	24.9
Balance c/f	282.9

(d)   Profit or loss note

	$000
Current tax expense	245.1
Deferred tax on temporary differences originating in the period	24.9
Tax expense	270

©2017 DeVry/Becker Educational Development Corp. All rights reserved.

(e)   Reconciliation of accounting profit multiplied by the applicable tax rate to the tax expense

	$000
Accounting profit	900
Tax @ 30 %	270
Tax expense	270

(f)   Movement on deferred tax by each category of temporary difference

	B/f $000	Other compre- hensive income $000	Profit or loss $000	C/f $000
Tangible assets	240	18	(25.5)	232.5
Lease	–	–	26.4	26.4
Deferred development costs	–	–	24.0	24.0
	240	18	24.9	282.9

Answer 22 GENPOWER

(a)   IAS 37

(i)   Need for a standard

The use of provisions can have a significant effect on a company's financial statements. They arise in many areas of business and often relate to controversial areas such as restructuring costs, environmental and decommissioning liabilities, and guarantees and warranties. Provisions have often been based on management's intentions rather than on the existence of a relevant liability.

In the recent past there has been much criticism of the use and abuse of provisions. The main area of abuse has been that of "profit smoothing" or creating artificial growth. In essence this amounts to creating a provision, usually for some future intended expenditure, when a company's profits are healthy, and subsequently releasing the provision through profit or loss to offset the expenditure when it occurs. This has the effect of reducing the profit in the years in which provisions are made and increasing profits in the years in which they are released. A common complaint is that provisions created for a specific purpose (or type of expenditure) are aggregated with other provisions and subsequently used to offset expenditures of future years that were not (and should not have been) provided for. Such provisions were often very large and treated as extraordinary or exceptional items. This treatment may have caused some users to disregard the expense in the belief that it was a non-recurring item thus minimising the adverse impact of the provision. Extreme cases occurred where provisions were deliberately over provided with the intention that their release in future years would boost profits.

In some cases provisioning was used to "create" profits rather than just smooth them. This occurs if a provision is created without it being charged to profit or loss before its subsequent release. The most common examples of this were provisions for restructuring costs as a consequence of an acquisition. The effect of such provisions was that they added to the goodwill rather than being debited to profit or loss. This practice created the ironic situation that (given an agreed purchase price) the more restructuring a company needed and the larger its anticipated losses were, the greater was the reported value of the acquired company's goodwill.

Many commentators, including the IASB, thought this perverse and IFRS 3 *Business Combinations* has now eliminated this practice completely.

Some of the above practices are often referred to as "big bath" provisioning.

(ii) Principles of accounting for provisions

IAS 37 is intended to establish appropriate recognition and measurement criteria for provisions and contingent assets and liabilities. It also requires much more detailed disclosure of provisions. Although not specifically referred to in the IAS, it does not apply to the "traditional" type of provision that is used to write down the value of an asset (e.g. bad debts allowances or allowances for depreciation of non-current assets) nor does it apply to executory contracts or provisions required by other accounting standards such as a deferred tax provision. The main thrust of IAS 37's definition of a provision is that it represents a liability of uncertain timing or amount. This is expanded further in that a liability is an obligation (which may be legal or constructive) which will probably require an entity to transfer economic benefits that result from a past transaction or event.

This definition relies heavily on the IASB's "Framework". The distinction between a provision and a liability (or accrual) is the degree of uncertainty in the timing or amount of the liability. A contingent liability is (i) a possible obligation which will be confirmed only by the occurrence of uncertain future events that are not wholly within the entity's control, or (ii) where there is an obligation but it is not possible to measure it with sufficient reliability. In essence, if an obligation is probable it is a liability, if it is only possible (presumably less than a 50% chance) then it is a contingent liability. The definition of a contingent asset "mirrors" that of a liability.

An event is an obligating one if there is no realistic possibility of it being avoided. This is obviously the case if it is enforceable by law, but IAS 37 adds to this the concept of a constructive obligation. A constructive obligation derives from an established pattern of past practice or some form of public commitment to accept certain responsibilities that creates a valid expectation on the part of other parties that the entity will discharge them. Although the concept of a constructive obligation does introduce an element of subjectivity, the new definition is intended to prevent provisions being made as a result of future intentions by management.

The last element of the definition is that of reliable measurement. This is taken to be the best estimate of the expenditure required to settle the obligation at the end of the reporting period. The estimate may be based on a range of possible outcomes and it should take into account any surrounding risk and uncertainty and the time value of money if it is material (i.e. settlement may be some years ahead). Also where there are a number of similar obligations (e.g. product warranties) the estimate should be based (often statistically) on the class as a whole. The IAS considers that the circumstances in which a reliable estimate cannot be made will be extremely rare, but if they do exist the liability should be treated as a contingent liability and given appropriate disclosures in the notes to the financial statements.

(b) Genpower

(i) Acceptability of current accounting policy

Genpower's current policy of providing for environmental costs relating to the demolition of the power station and "sealing" the fuel rods on an annual basis is no longer acceptable under the requirements of IAS 37 *Provisions, Contingent Liabilities and Contingent Assets*. If a present obligation will (probably) require the transfer of economic benefits as a result of a past event, a provision is required for the best estimate of the full amount of the liability. If the liability is measured in expected future prices this should be discounted at a nominal rate.

©2017 DeVry/Becker Educational Development Corp. All rights reserved.

Applying these principles means the company would provide for $120 million (not $180 million) for environmental costs on 1 October 2016 as this is the date the obligation arose. An interesting aspect of the provision is the accounting entries to record it. The credit entry is shown in the statement of financial position under "non-current liabilities" as would be expected, but the debit is included as part of the cost of the asset (i.e. the power station). This is a relatively controversial treatment. In effect it is "grossing up" the statement of financial position (initially) by the amount of the liability and creating an asset of equivalent value. Understandably, some commentators believe that non-current assets that have been increased by the cost of a future liability will confuse many users of accounts and calls into question the nature of an asset. The effect on the statement of profit or loss of IAS 37's requirements is not too different from the company's current treatment (ignoring the error of using $180 million). As the carrying amount of the power station (which now includes the amount of the provision as well as the cost of the asset) is depreciated over its 10 year life, the provision is effectively charged to income over the life of the asset. This has the same effect on profit as the previous policy.

The treatment of the provision for contamination leaks needs careful consideration. It could be argued that the obligating event relating to such a cost is the occurrence of a leak. As this has not happened there is no liability and therefore a provision should not be made. An alternative view is that it is the generation of electricity that creates the possibility of a leakage and, as this has occurred, a liability should be recognised. The difference between a liability and a contingent liability is one of probability. If it is probable (presumably more than a 50% chance) then it is a liability that should be provided for, conversely if it is not probable, it is a contingent liability which should be disclosed by way of a note to the financial statements. In any 12 month period there is only a 30% chance of a contamination occurring. It could be argued that the liability is therefore not probable, as turned out to be the case in the current year. Again there is an alternative view. Over the expected period of electricity generation (of 10 years), statistically there will be three leakages causing contamination that will cost a total of $90 million. As the company has produced a tenth of the electricity, it should provide for a tenth of the expected contamination costs. On balance and applying prudence it would be acceptable to provide $9 million for contamination costs each year.

Applying the above would give the following revised extracts:

Statement of profit or loss

	$m
Non-current asset depreciation	
10% × ($200 million + $120 million)	32
Provision for clean-up of contamination leaks	
10% × $90 million (or 30% × $30 million)	9
	41

Statement of financial position
Non-current assets

	$m
Power station at "cost" ($200 million + $120 million)	320
Depreciation	(32)
	288

Non-current liabilities

	$m
Provision for environmental costs ($120 million + $9million)	129

(ii)   *Explanation of effect*

In part (i) the environmental legislation in relation to this industry created an obligation which led to a provision for the consequent liability. In the absence of environmental legislation there would be no legal or enforceable obligation. However, IAS 37 refers to a "constructive" obligation. This occurs where there is a valid expectation by other parties that an entity will discharge its responsibilities. A constructive obligation usually derives from a company's actions. These may be in the form of an established pattern of past practice, a published policy statement or by indications to other parties that it will accept certain responsibilities. Thus if it can be established that Genpower has a publicly-known policy of environmental cleaning up, or a past record of doing so when it is not legally required to, this could be regarded as a constructive obligation and the treatment of the environmental costs would be the same as in part (i). If there is no legal requirement to incur the various environmental costs, and Genpower has not created an expectation that it will be responsible for such costs, there is no obligation and no provision should be made. The power station would be recorded at a cost of $200 million and depreciated at $20 million per annum.

Answer 23 CONNECT

Reasons for the importance of related party disclosures

Related party relationships are a normal feature of commerce and business. Entities frequently carry on separate parts of their activities through subsidiary or associated entities and acquire interests in other entities – for investment purposes or for trading reasons – that are of sufficient proportions that the investing company can control or exercise significant influence on the financial and operating decisions of its investee.

A related party relationship could have an effect on the financial position and operating results of the reporting entity:

- related parties may enter into transactions that unrelated parties would not enter into;
- transactions between related parties may not be effected at the same amounts as between unrelated parties.

Note that the operating results and financial position of an entity may be affected by a related party relationship even if related party transactions do not occur. The mere existence of the relationship may be sufficient to affect the transactions of the reporting entity with other parties. For example:

- A subsidiary may terminate relations with a trading partner on acquisition by the parent of a fellow subsidiary engaged in the same trade as the former partner.

- Alternatively, one party may refrain from acting because of the significant influence of another (e.g. a subsidiary may be instructed by its parent not to engage in research and development).

Sometimes, transactions would not have taken place if the relationship had not existed. For example, a company that sold a large proportion of its production to its parent company at cost might not have found an alternative customer if the parent company had not purchased the goods.

IAS 24 requires that entities disclose information about related parties and related party transactions so that users of the financial statements can better understand its position and performance. Information about related parties can be an important element of any investment decision and regulatory authorities consider disclosure of such information to be of paramount importance.

©2017 DeVry/Becker Educational Development Corp. All rights reserved.

The main issues in determining such disclosures are:

- the identification of related parties,
- the types of transactions and arrangements, and
- the information to be disclosed.

The following specific comments relate to the list of transactions with connected persons which you supplied to us.

Specific guidance – Overview of IAS 24 requirements

IAS 24 requires disclosure of any related party relationship where control exists irrespective of whether there have been transactions with the related parties.

If there have been transactions between related parties, the reporting entity should disclose the nature of the related party relationships as well as the types of transactions and the elements of the transactions necessary for an understanding of the financial statements.

The elements of transactions necessary to understand the financial statements would normally include:

- any key management personnel compensation for employment;

- amount of transactions undertaken;

- amount of outstanding balances, including terms and conditions, nature of consideration and any guarantees of collateral;

- allowances for receivables in respect of outstanding balances; and

- expense in the period for bad debts.

Identification of related parties

Parties are considered to be related if one party has the ability to control the other party or exercise significant influence over the other party in making financial and operating decisions.

IAS 24 applies to specific related parties. Based on the information provided Connect's related parties in the context of IAS 24 are as follows:

- Mr Big. Mr Big has effective control over Connect. He holds 10% directly and controls 45% through his holding in BBIF.

- BBIF. A 45% holding gives BBIF significant influence over the group.

- All 14 of its subsidiaries. Any entity that is controlled by or controls Connect is its related party.

- Mr Joint and all of the other directors. IAS 24 specifically includes key management personnel as related parties and goes onto say that these are those persons having authority and responsibility for planning, directing and controlling the activities of the reporting entity, including directors and officers of companies and close members of the families of such individuals.

- Mrs Joint. See above. Mrs Joint is the wife of the finance director.

- Weld. This company is owned by the Mr Big who has effective control over Connect.

Transactions and disclosures

Mr Big and BBIF

IAS 24 requires disclosure of any related party relationship where control exists. Connect should disclose the fact of Mr Big's control over the organisation. This disclosure must be made regardless of whether there have been any transactions involving Mr Big.

Group transactions

The subsidiaries of Connect are all related parties of Connect and also to each other. However IAS 24 does not require disclosure of related party transactions in consolidated financial statements in respect of group transactions, but they are required in the separate financial statements of the parent. In short IAS 24 does not require disclosure of inter-company transactions described in the engagement information in the consolidated financial statements.

Note however that Connect will be subject to the requirements of IFRS 8 *Operating Segments*. This requires analysis of revenue of the organisation from sales to external customers and to internal customers (i.e. other members of the group). IFRS 8 also requires a reconciliation of these figures to the consolidated revenue figure. Thus inter-company items will appear as a reconciling item in the IFRS 8 disclosures.

Advertising contract

Mrs Joint is a related party and there have been transactions with her advertising agency. Connect should disclose the nature of the related party relationship (i.e. director's spouse), the type of the transaction (i.e. contract) and elements of the transaction. In general, IFRSs require disclosure of any element of a transaction necessary for an understanding of the financial statements to be disclosed.

IAS 24 does not specify which elements of a transaction must be disclosed but simply sets out what they would normally include. In this case Connect should probably disclose:

- the existence of the contract, when it was entered and its duration;
- the price of the contract;
- the fact that it has been won in competitive tender.

Tutorial note: *The fact that the contract was awarded through competitive tender is not grounds for non-disclosure (as JJ Advertising might not have been invited to tender had it not been for the relationship).*

Sale of land to Weld

Weld is a related party and there has been a transaction with it. Connect must disclose the nature of the related party relationship (i.e. ownership by Mr Big and his effective control of Connect), the type of the transaction (i.e. a sale of property) and elements of the transaction.

The land sold to Weld is a related party transaction which appears to have been undertaken at below market price. The disclosure of the facts of the transaction alone would not reflect the reality of Connect's position. IAS 24 also requires disclosure of any elements of the transaction that are necessary for an understanding of it.

The carrying amount of the land must be adjusted as it has become impaired. According to IAS 36 *Impairment of Assets* it should have been shown in Connect's records at the lower of carrying amount ($5.8 million) and the recoverable amount (higher of fair value less costs to sell ($5·3 million less $0·1 million, i.e. $5·2 million) and value in use $3·8 million). Thus the land should have been written down by $0.6 million to $5·2 million.

©2017 DeVry/Becker Educational Development Corp. All rights reserved.

The land has been sold for $4.5 million. This is $700,000 below the impaired value.

IAS 24 does not specify which elements of a transaction must be disclosed but simply sets out what they would normally include. In this case Connect should probably disclose:

- that there was a transaction involving the sale of land;
- the sale was for $4.5 million;
- that this transaction was $0.7 million below market price;
- any non-cash consideration;
- payment terms etc.

Consultancy services

The directors are all a related parties and there have been transactions with three of them who are operating in the capacity of consultants for the company. As before Connect should disclose the nature of the related party relationship, the type of the transaction and elements of the transaction. In general, IFRSs require disclosure of any element of a transaction necessary for an understanding of the financial statements to be disclosed.

Connect should probably disclose:

- the existence of the consultancy arrangements;
- the nature of the consultancy service provided;
- names of the directors involved;
- the fees paid (i.e. $2.6 million).

Answer 24 LIMA

(a) **Cash and equity settled share-based payments**

A share-based payment arises out of a transaction where a third party:

- Receives equity instruments of the entity (including share options) in exchange for goods or services – equity-settled share-based payment; or

- Receives cash or other assets of the entity of a value that is based on the value of the equity shares of the entity – cash-settled share-based payment.

(b) **Basis of measurement of fair value of equity-settled share-based payments**

In all cases other than transactions with employees, the fair value of equity-settled share-based payments should be measured with reference to the value of the goods or services provided by the third party. For transactions with employees' fair value should be measured with reference to the value of the equity instruments granted.

(c) **Accounting treatment of share-based payment transactions with employees**

Equity-settled share-based payments

The amounts recognised should be based on the fair value (see (b)) of the payments at the grant date, with no adjustments to subsequent changes to fair value. The total cost should be built up over the vesting period (the period between the grant date and the date the third party is unconditionally entitled to the relevant equity instruments). The annual charge to profit or loss is the difference between the cumulative amount recognised at the beginning and end of the period. The cumulative balance at the end of the period will be shown in equity.

Where the vesting is subject to conditions the cumulative cost should be based on the number expected to vest based on information available at the date the financial statements are authorised for issue. After the vesting date there will be no further increase or decrease in equity. However there may be a transfer from one component of equity to another relating to the exercising or lapsing of equity options.

Cash-settled share-based payments

The liability should be recognised over the vesting period based on its fair value at the date the financial statements are authorised for issue. After the vesting date the liability will continue to be re-measured at fair value until settled.

(d)(i)   Charge to profit or loss

Scheme A

The total expected cost of the scheme at 30 September 2017 was $225,600 (500 × 188 × $2·40). So the cumulative charge to profit or loss up to that date was $150,400 ($225,600 × $^2/_3$).

The total expected cost of the scheme at 30 September 2016 was $222,000 (500 × 185 × $2·40). So the cumulative charge to profit or loss to that date was $74,000 ($222,000 × $^1/_3$).

Therefore the charge to profit or loss for the year is $76,400 ($150,400 – $74,000)

Tutorial note: *The movement in fair value of the share options is irrelevant as the amount charged to profit or loss is based on the grant date fair value.*

Scheme B

The final cost of the scheme at vesting date (30 September 2017) was $285,600 (2 × 238 × $600).

The total expected cost of the scheme at 30 September 2016 was $259,200 (2 × 240 × $540). So the cumulative charge to profit or loss up to that date was $172,800 ($259,200 × $^2/_3$).

Therefore the charge to profit or loss for the year is $112,800 ($285,600 – $172,800).

Tutorial note: *The fair value of share appreciation rights will reflect all variables that affect the amount of cash bonus. Any change in fair value must be reflected in the year-end liability.*

(ii)   Statement of financial position

Scheme A

The amount recognised in the statement of financial position is the cumulative amount recognised in profit or loss to date – $150,400 (see (d)(i) above). This amount will be recognised in equity.

Scheme B

Again the cumulative amount is recognised – in this case $285,600 (see (d)(i) above). This amount will be recognised as a current liability.

©2017 DeVry/Becker Educational Development Corp. All rights reserved.

Answer 25 DANNY

Memorandum to directors of Danny regarding exclusion of Smiffy

The only circumstances in which the income and net assets of individual subsidiaries are not line by line consolidated is where the parent's control is intended to be temporary, because the subsidiary is acquired and held exclusively with a view to its subsequent disposal in the near future. This means that the decision to dispose of the subsidiary must have been taken prior to the date of acquisition. Such a scenario could occur if the parent acquires a group of entities with the intention of disposing of one of the subsidiaries of that group. In such circumstances an excluded subsidiary is accounted for as a financial asset in accordance with the provisions of IFRS 5 *Non-current assets Held for Sale and Discontinued Operations*.

The basic requirement of IFRS 10 *Consolidated Financial Statements* is that the income and net assets of all group members [parent and subsidiary entities] should be included in the consolidated financial statements [CFS]. The rationale for this requirement is that the CFS should include the resources that are under the control of the parent and the return generated by those resources. Where a particular subsidiary makes losses then the return generated by those resources is negative but this does not alter the basic principle that this amount should be reflected in the CFS. There is an argument that, where the business of an individual subsidiary is different from the core business of the group, line by line consolidation is misleading. However IFRS10 states that this issue should be addressed by the provision of additional disclosure in the notes to the CFS, for example the information required by IFRS 8 *Operating Segments*.

Answer 26 PICANT

Importance of consolidated financial statements

Although the concept behind the preparation of consolidated financial statements is to treat all the members of the group as if they were a single economic entity, it must be understood that the legal position is that each member is a separate legal entity and therefore the group itself does not exist as a separate legal entity. This focuses on a criticism of group financial statements in that they aggregate the assets and liabilities of all the members of the group. This can give the impression that all of the group's assets would be available to discharge all of the group's liabilities. This is not the case.

Applying this to the situation in the question, it would mean that any liability of Trilby to Picant would not be a liability of any other member of the Tradhat group. Thus the fact that the consolidated statement of financial position of Tradhat shows a strong position with healthy liquidity is not necessarily of any reassurance to Picant. Any decision on granting credit to Trilby must be based on Trilby's own (entity) financial statements (which Picant should obtain), not the group financial statements. The other possibility, which would take advantage of the strength of the group's statement of financial position, is that Picant could ask Tradhat if it would act as a guarantor to Trilby's (potential) liability to Picant. In this case Tradhat would be liable for the debt to Picant in the event of a default by Trilby.

Answer 27 BACUP

(a)   **Consolidated statement of financial position**

Statement of financial position as at 31 March 2018

	$000	$000
Non-current assets:		
Tangible assets (3,820 + 4,425)		8,245
Goodwill (W2)		470
Investment in associate (W5)		420
		9,135
Current assets:		
Inventory (2,740 + 1,280 – 40)	3,980	
Receivables (1,960 + 980 – 250)	2,690	
Bank (1,260 + 50 cash in transit)	1,310	
		7,980
		17,115
Equity and liabilities		
Ordinary shares ($0.25)		4,000
Share premium	800	
Retained earnings (W4)	4,200	
		5,000
		9,000
Non-controlling interest (W3)		315
		9,315
Current liabilities		
Trade payables (2,120 + 3,070 – 200)	4,990	
Bank overdraft	2,260	
Taxation (400 + 150)	550	
		7,800
Total equity and liabilities		17,115

(b)   **Usefulness of the group statement of financial position**

The group statement of financial position is of little use in assessing the liquidity of any member of the group. It must be appreciated that the group does not exist as a legal entity; it is an economic reporting entity. For example it is not possible to sue a group; one would have to sue the relevant member of the group.

Even if the liquidity position shown by calculations using the group statement of financial position is favourable (for the statement of financial position in the answer to (a) they are not good at all), it implies nothing about the individual members of the group. A criticism often levelled at group statements of financial position is that they can give the impression that all of the group's assets are available to meet all of the group's liabilities. The reality is that only the assets of an individual member of the group are available to discharge the liabilities of that individual member.

©2017 DeVry/Becker Educational Development Corp. All rights reserved.

Occasionally some lenders, usually banks, will obtain guarantees from the parent when advancing loans or overdrafts to subsidiaries. When this occurs it contradicts the above paragraph. Sometimes a parent will support a subsidiary that is in financial difficulties when it has no legal obligation to do so. It does this to preserve the value, reputation and goodwill of the group.

Further investigations

■ Norden's management must obtain the separate financial statements of Townley in order to calculate appropriate liquidity ratios. From the information in the question Townley's liquidity position is a cause of serious concern. However, the usefulness of this could be questioned even if the liquidity position was more favourable. This is due to the limitations of such ratios (e.g. they are open to "window dressing" and "creative accounting" techniques).

■ The above should be supplemented by the use of a credit reference agency to obtain a report on the position of Townley.

■ Discreet enquiries should be made with existing customers and suppliers to see if they have had any unsatisfactory dealings with Townley.

■ It is always worth trying to get the parent (i.e. Bacup) to guarantee any liability that Townley may incur to Norden.

■ As a further precaution, Norden could sell goods "subject to reservation of title".

WORKINGS

(1)   Net assets summary

Townley	At date of consolidation		At date of acquisition	
	$000	$000	$000	$000
Share capital		500		500
Share premium		125		125
Retained earnings;				
Per question: (400 + 380)	780		380	
Development expenditure	(200)		(80)	
Unrealised profit	(40)			
	——	540	——	300
		1,165		925

(2)   Goodwill

	$000
Cost	1,200
Fair value of non-controlling interest	285
Net assets on acquisition	(925)
	560
Retained earnings/Non-controlling interest (impairment)	90
Statement of financial position	470

(3)   Non-controlling interest

	$000
Fair value on acquisition	285
Share of post-acquisition profits $(1,165 - 925) \times 20\%$	48
Goodwill impaired $(90 \times 20\%)$	(18)
	315

(4)   Consolidated retained earnings

	$000
All of Bacup per question $(2,300 + 1,760)$	4,060
Share of Townley $(80\% \times (1,165 - 925))$	192
Share of Rishworth $(40\% \times (775 - 725))$	20
Goodwill impaired $(90 \times 80\%)$	(72)
	4,200

(5)   Investment in the associate

	$000
Cost of investment	400
Share of post-acquisition profits $(40\% \times (775 - 725))$	20
	420

Answer 28 HOLDING

(a)   Goodwill

Holding has acquired 18 million of Subside's 24 million equity shares which represents 75% ownership. The consolidated goodwill is calculated as follows:

			$
Cost of shares	(18 m × $10)		180
Non-controlling interest			56
Less Net assets on acquisition			
Share capital		24	
Revaluation surplus (W1)		64	
Pre-acquisition profits (W2)		88	
		—	(176)
Goodwill			60

Holding has included in its profit or loss $15 million ($20m × 75%) which is the whole of its share of Subside's dividend. This dividend is deemed to accrue evenly during the reporting period of 15 months. Therefore $^6/_{15}$ of this amount = $6 million is a dividend payable out of pre-acquisition profits.

Consolidated goodwill at the date of acquisition is $60 million.

©2017 DeVry/Becker Educational Development Corp. All rights reserved.

(b) **Consolidated profit or loss of Holding for the year to 30 September 2017**

	$million
Revenue (W3)	488
Cost of sales (W4)	(286)
Gross profit	202
Operating expenses (W5)	(99)
Interest payable ($10 + 60\% \times 5$)	(13)
Profit before tax	90
Income tax expense ($22 + 60\% \times 10$)	(28)
Profit for year	62
Attributable to:	
Owners of Holding	57.5
Non-controlling interests (W6)	4.5
	62

WORKINGS

(1) **Fair value gains/revaluation surplus**

	$m
Investment property	
– at 30 June 2016	20
– increase up to 1 January 2017	4
	24
Plant:	
Carrying amount 30 June 2016	60
Depreciation 6 months to date of acquisition ($20 \times {}^{6}/_{12}$)	(10)
Carrying amount at date of acquisition	50
Fair value at date of acquisition	(90)
Fair value increase	40
Total revaluation gains ($24 + 40$)	64

(2) **Pre-acquisition profits**

	$m
Retained earnings at 30 June 2016	64
Retained profit for period $60m, of which ${}^{6}/_{15}$ is earned to 1 January 2017	24
Total pre-acquisition profits	88

(3) Most of the figures in the consolidated profit or loss are based on the parent's figures plus the post-acquisition figures of the subsidiary. The results of the subsidiary are for a 15 month period, of which nine months is post acquisition. Thus the post-acquisition results would be $^9/_{15}$ or 60% of Subside's relevant figures.

	$m
Revenue	
Holding	350
Subside (60% × 280)	168
Intra-group sales	(30)
	────
	488
	────

(4) **Cost of sales**

	$m
Holding	200
Subside (60% × 170)	102
Intra-group sales	(30)
Unrealised profit in inventory (see below)	2
Additional depreciation (see below)	12
	────
	286
	────

Unrealised profit

A mark-up of 25% on cost is equivalent to 20% of the selling price. Holding has $10 million ($30 m × $^1/_3$) of inventories at the transfer price, thus the unrealised profit is ($10 m × 20%) $2 million.

Additional depreciation (plant of Subside)

At the date of the acquisition (1 January 2017) the plant is two and a half years old and has a remaining life also of two and a half years. Therefore the revaluation gain of $40 million will be amortised at $16 million per annum ($40 m ÷ 2.5). The post-acquisition period is 9 months and would thus require additional depreciation of $12 million ($^9/_{12}$ × $16)

(5) **Operating expenses**

	$m
Holding	72
Subside (60% × 35)	21
Goodwill amortisation ($60 – $54)	6
	────
	99
	────

(6) **Non-controlling interests**

The profit after tax of Subside is $60 million of which $36 million ($^9/_{15}$) is post acquisition. The depreciation adjustment of $12 million (see (3) above) and goodwill impairment of $6 million (see (a) above) is deducted from this to give an adjusted figure of $18 million. The non-controlling interests has a 25% interest in this profit = $4.5 million.

©2017 DeVry/Becker Educational Development Corp. All rights reserved.

Answer 29 GUIDO ELECTRICALS

	$	$
Fair value of consideration (W1)		220,000
Fair value of identifiable assets and liabilities		
Electricals segment (W2)	159,000	
Rope-making segment (W3)	45,000	
		(204,000)
Goodwill on acquisition		16,000

WORKINGS

(1)   Consideration

	$
Per question	220,000

IFRS 3 requires that all transaction costs related to an acquisition must be recognised as an expense in the period they are incurred, they cannot be included in the consideration.

(2)   Electricals

	$	*Tutorial note*
Patent rights	20,000	*Market value*
Property	77,000	*Market value*
Plant and machinery		
Gross replacement cost	30,000	
Depreciation $(8,000 \times \dfrac{30,000}{20,000})$	(12,000)	*Depreciated replacement cost*
Motor vehicles		
Gross replacement cost	15,000	
Depreciation $(6,000 \times \dfrac{15,000}{10,000})$	(9,000)	*Depreciated replacement cost*
Raw materials	2,000	*Replacement cost*
WIP and Finished goods	30,000	
Receivables	9,000	*Carrying amount (no discount rate given)*
Cash	3,000	
Payables	(6,000)	*Carrying amount (no discount rate given)*
	159,000	

(3)   Rope-making segment

Sold by the end of the financial year: therefore should be included at the net proceeds of the sale, adjusted for the fair value of any assets or liabilities transferred into or out of the business between the date of acquisition and the date of disposal.

	$
Net proceeds	50,000
Increase in assets in period up to date of sale	(5,000)
	45,000

©2017 DeVry/Becker Educational Development Corp. All rights reserved.

Answer 30 H, S AND T

(a)   **Statement of financial position as at 31 December 2017**

	$
Sundry net assets (145,000 + 70,000 + 75,000)	290,000
Share capital	120,000
Reserves (W5)	112,350
Non-controlling interests (W4)	57,650
	290,000

(1)   **Group structure**

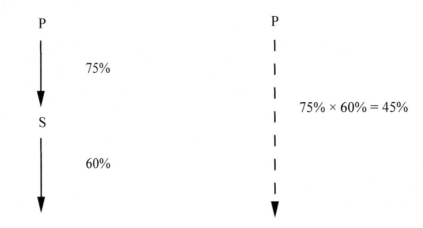

Non-controlling interest = 55%

(2)   **Net assets summaries**

(a)   **S**

	At date of consolidation	At date of acquisition
	$000	$000
Share capital	70	70
Reserves	50	10
	120	80

(b)   **T**

	At date of consolidation	At date of acquisition
	$000	$000
Share capital	40	40
Reserves	35	12
	75	52

©2017 DeVry/Becker Educational Development Corp. All rights reserved.

(3) Goodwill

	On acquisition of	
	S	T
	$000	$000
Cost		
of S	65	
of T (75% × 50)		37.5
Non-controlling interest	21	44.5
Net assets on acquisition (W2)	(80)	(52)
	6	30

Tutorial note: *All would have been written off to the statement of profit or loss (and thus to reserves).*

(4) Non-controlling interest

	$000
In S on acquisition	21
Share of post-acquisition profits (25% × 40)	10
Share of goodwill impaired (25% × 6)	(1.5)
Non-controlling in S's share of cost of investment in T (25% × 50%)	(12.5)
In T on acquisition	44.5
Share of post-acquisition profits (55% × 23)	12.65
Share of goodwill impaired (55% × 30)	(16.5)
	57.65

(5) Consolidated reserves

		$000
All of P		90
Share of S (75% × (50 – 10)) (W2a)		30
Share of T (45% (35 – 12)) (W2b)		10.35
Goodwill		
on S (75% × 6)	4.5	
on T (45% × 30)	13.5	(18)
		112.35

(b) Pre-acquisition profits for consolidation with P

(i) S $12,000
   T $15,000 since T became a subsidiary undertaking of both P and S on 31 December 2015

(ii) S $15,000
   T $17,000 since T became a subsidiary undertaking of P on 31 December 2015

Answer 31 JANE

Consolidated statement of financial position as at 31 December 2017

		$
Sundry assets		
$(1,336,000 + 717,000 + 213,000)		2,266,000
		2,266,000
Share capital – ordinary $1 shares		500,000
Reserves (W5)		1,638,920
		2,138,920
Non-controlling interests (W4)		127,080
		2,266,000

WORKINGS

(1)

(a)   Group structure

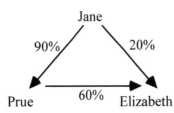

Jane
90%   20%
Prue   60%   Elizabeth

(b)   Group interests

		Prue %		Elizabeth %
Group				
Direct		90		20
Indirect		–	(90% × 60%)	54
		90		74
Non-controlling interest		10		26
		100		100

(2)   Net assets summaries

(a)   Prue

	At date of Consolidation $000	At date of acquisition $000
Share capital	400	400
Reserves	437	201
	837	601

©2017 DeVry/Becker Educational Development Corp. All rights reserved.

(b)   *Elizabeth*

	At date of consolidation $000	At date of acquisition $000
Share capital	100	100
Reserves	113	67
	213	167

(3)   **Goodwill**

	Prue $000	On acquisition of Elizabeth (direct) $000	Elizabeth (indirect) $000
Cost			
of Prue	600		
of Elizabeth		40	
90% × 120			108
Share of net assets			
90% × 601 (W2a)	(540.9)		
20% × 167 (W2b)		(33.4)	
54% × 167 (W2b)			(90.18)
	59.1	6.6	17.82

(4)   **Non-controlling interest**

		$000
In Prue	(10% × 837) (W2a)	83.7
Non-controlling interest in Prue's share of cost of investment in Elizabeth (10% × 120)		(12)
In Elizabeth	26% × 213 (W2b)	55.38
		127.08

(5)   **Consolidated reserves**

		$000
All of Jane		1,476
Share of Prue		
90% (437 – 201) (W2a)		212.4
Share of Elizabeth		
Direct 20% (113 – 67) (W2b)		9.2
Indirect 54% (113 – 67) (W2b)		24.84
Goodwill		
Prue	59.1 (W3)	
Elizabeth (6.6 + 17.82)	24.42 (W3)	
		(83.52)
		1,638.92

Answer 32 HARLEY

Consolidated statement of financial position at 30 June 2017

	$
Goodwill	240,000
Net assets (1,052,000 – 380,000) + (100,000 + 255,000))	1,027,000
	1,267,000
Share capital	220,000
Share premium (1,052 – 220 – 732)	100,000
Consolidated reserves (W3)	776,960
	1,096,960
Non-controlling interest (W4)	170,040
	1,267,000

WORKINGS

(1)   Group structure

	%	
	40	(1.7.2009)
	30	(1.7.2010)
	70	
Non-controlling interest	30	
	100	

(2)   Goodwill

	At date of acquisition 1 July 2010
	$
Cost of investment 1 July 2010	220,000
Fair values	
Original 40% holding	175,000
Non-controlling interest	157,200
Davidson's identifiable net assets	(252,200)
	300,000

The date of acquisition is the date that Harley gains control of Davidson, being 1 July 2010. On that date the original 40% holding is measured to fair value and the non-controlling interest are also measured to fair value, which is now an option available under IFRS 3.

Goodwill has been impaired by $60,000 since acquisition, of this amount 30% (18,000) will be charged to non-controlling interest and 70% (42,000) will be charged to consolidated retained earnings.

©2017 DeVry/Becker Educational Development Corp. All rights reserved.

(3)   Consolidated reserves

	$
All of Harley	732,000
Gain on fair value of original 40% (175,000 – 160,000)	15,000
Share of Davidson (355,000 – 252,200) × 70%	71,960
Goodwill impaired (W2)	(42,000)
	776,960

Of the gain in fair value of the original 40%, $9,600 ((124,000 – 100,000) × 40%) would have been recognised by equity accounting for the investment and the remaining $6,400 would be the gain recognised on remeasuring the investment at the date of acquisition.

(4)   Non-controlling interest

	$
Fair value on acquisition	157,200
Increase in value of net assets since acquisition (355,000 – 252,200) × 30%	30,840
Goodwill impaired	(18,000)
	170,040

Answer 33 RENEWAL

(a)   Statement of financial position as at 31 May 2018

	$000	$000
Assets		
Non-current assets		
Premises at valuation		3,800
Plant and machinery [2,040 – 850]		1,190
Patents [578 – 238]		340
		5,330
Current assets		
Inventory [2,108 – 406]	1,702	
Receivables [2,720 – 272]	2,448	
Bank (W4)	3,400	
		7,550
Total assets		12,880
Equity and liabilities		
Ordinary shares (17,300,000 shares of $0.50; $0.30 paid) (W1)		5,190
Capital reserve (W3)		74
		5,264
Non-current liabilities		
11% cumulative preference shares		
6,800,000 shares of $0.80 fully paid (W2)		5,440
Current liabilities – Trade payables		2,176
Total equity and liabilities		12,880

WORKINGS

(1) Ordinary shares

	$000
Opening balance (5,100,000 shares × $0.80 paid up)	4,080
Balance (5,100,000 shares × $0.20)	1,020
	5,100
Less: Capital reduction ($0.70 per share)	(3,570)
Transferred to ordinary shares ($0.50 par value)	1,530

Ordinary $0.50 shares

5,100,000 shares ($0.30 paid up)	1,530
New shares (10,200,000 × $0.30 paid up)	3,060
Issued to directors (2,000,000 × $0.30 paid up)	600
Total (17,300,000 shares of $0.50 each; $0.30 paid)	5,190

(2) Preference shares

	$000
Opening balance (5,440,000 shares of $1 each)	5,440
Less: Capital reduction ($0.20 per share)	(1,088)
5,440,000 11% preference shares of $0.80 each	4,352
New shares (1,360,000 × $0.80)	1,088
New balance	5,440

(3) Capital reduction

	$000	$000
Ordinary shares $1 each		3,570
Preference shares $1 each		1,088
Premises		910
Directors' loans		420
Profit attributable to preference dividend arrears		1,306
		7,294
Accumulated losses	5,046	
Plant	850	
Patents	238	
Development expenses	408	
Inventory	406	
Receivables	272	
		(7,220)
Capital reserve		74

©2017 DeVry/Becker Educational Development Corp. All rights reserved.

(4)   Bank

	$000	$000
Overdraft (as given)		(1,768)
Less Ordinary shares $0.80 paid up – balance	1,020	
10,200,000 new ordinary shares of $0.50	3,060	
1,360,000 new preference shares	1,088	
		5,168
Closing bank balance		3,400

(b)   Advise preference shareholders

Preference shareholders need to consider two aspects of the scheme, namely, the capital and income implications.

Considering the capital implications and basing it on the information on current values implied in the scheme, it would appear that the preference shareholders could receive approximately $0.80 per share. This means that they have already suffered a reduction in the asset backing for their shares below their par value.

	$000
Non-current assets	5,330
Current assets	4,150
	9,480
Less Current liabilities	(4,964)
Available for members	4,516

The asset backing has been calculated on the assumption that the values in the scheme could be achieved on liquidation. In reality they might be substantially lower on a forced sale.

Considering the income implications, it is helpful to consider the position before and after the reduction and reconstruction.

	Income without reconstruction	Income with reconstruction
Total	$1,000,000	$1,750,000
Preference shareholders		
5,440,000 at 8%	435,200	
5,440,000 at 11%		598,400
Ordinary shareholders	564,800	
Directors	2,000,000	133,133
Other ordinary	15,300,000	1,018,467

This shows an increase of $163,200. However, preference shareholders will have put in $1,088,000 additional capital. If the increase is related to that figure it shows a return of approximately 15% on the new funds.

©2017 DeVry/Becker Educational Development Corp. All rights reserved.

From the preference shareholders point of view the scheme is fair. If they were to be unable to take up the rights issue, the increase in the dividend rate would still leave them in a better position (i.e. 11% of the reduced capital of $4,352,000 produces $478,720 which exceeds the current dividend of $435,200).

The preference shareholders would not get a better deal in a voluntary liquidation and should accept the scheme.

Answer 34 HOLLY

Consolidated statement of financial position as at 31 December 2017

ASSETS	$000
Non-current assets	
Tangible	4,400
Interest in associate (W2)	932
	5,332
Current assets	3,460
	8,792
EQUITY AND LIABILITIES	
Ordinary shares	2,000
Retained earnings (W2)	1,892
	3,892
Non-controlling interests	500
Non-current liabilities	2,000
Current liabilities	2,400
	8,792

WORKINGS

(1)   Net assets summary

	At date of consolidation $000	At date of acquisition $000
Share capital	800	800
Retained earnings	900	70
	1,700	870

(2)   Investment in associate

	$000
Cost of investment	600
Post-acquisition profits (40% (900 – 70) W1)	332
	932

©2017 DeVry/Becker Educational Development Corp. All rights reserved.

(3) **Consolidated reserves**

	$000
All of Holly	1,560
Share of Ivy (40% (900 – 70) W1)	332
	1,892

Answer 35 ASSOCK

Consolidated statement of profit or loss for the year ended 30 June 2018

	$
Revenue	3,157,333
Cost of sales	(2,594,833)
Gross profit	562,500
Distribution costs	(110,200)
Administrative expenses	(137,133)
Group profit before taxation	315,167
Income from interests in associate	41,000
	356,167
Group taxation	(124,000)
Profit for year	232,167
Attributable to:	
Non-controlling interests (W3)	10,292
Profit attributable to members of Assock	221,875
	232,167

Statement of changes in equity (extract)

Profit for year	221,875
Dividend	(132,000)
Retained profit for the financial year	89,875

WORKINGS

(1) **Shareholdings**

	Curly	Tiny
	%	$
Assock	75	40
Non-controlling/other	25	60
	100	100

$8/12^{ths}$ of Curly's profits are post-acquisition.

©2017 DeVry/Becker Educational Development Corp. All rights reserved.

(2)   Profit or loss

	Assock	Curly $^{8}/_{12}$	Tiny (associated undertaking) 40%	Adjust-ments	Consolidated
	$	$	$	$	$
Revenue	2,600,000	733,333	–	(176,000)	3,157,333
Cost of sales	(2,167,000)	(601,000)	–	176,000	(2,594,833)
Provision for unrealised profit		(2,833)			
Gross profit	433,000	129,500	–		562,500
Distribution costs	(88,400)	(21,800)	–		(110,200)
Administrative expenses	(104,600)	(32,533)	–		(137,133)
	240,000	75,167	–		315,167
Share of Tiny 40% × $(125,000 – 22,500)			41,000		41,000
Taxation	(90,000)	(34,000)	–		(124,000)
	150,000	41,167	41,000		232,167

(3)   Non-controlling interests in Curly

25% × $41,167   10,292

(4)   Provision for unrealised profit

Curly	$^{20}/_{120}$ × $17,000 =	2,833	
Tiny	½ × $150,000× 30% =	22,500	

Tutorial note: *Assuming FIFO, goods from Curly held by Assock were purchased post-acquisition.*

Answer 36 BERTIE

Profit or loss		**Statement of financial position**	
(a) Revenue (W1)	$30,303		
Exchange differences (W1)	$3,030		
(b) Purchases (W2)	$42,857	Trade payables (W2)	$44,444
Exchange differences (W2)	$1,587		
(c) Depreciation	$23,529	Tangible asset	$
$\left(\dfrac{\$117,647}{5}\right)$		Cost $\left(\dfrac{£200,000}{1.70}\right)$	117,647
		Depreciation	(23,529)
		NBV	94,118
(d) Interest payable charges (W3)	$59,260	Loan (W3)	$592,593

©2017 DeVry/Becker Educational Development Corp. All rights reserved.

WORKINGS

(1) **Customer**

		£	$			£	$
1 Oct	Sales	50,000	30,303	3 Dec	Cash	50,000	33,333
31 Dec	Ex gain		3,030				
		50,000	33,333			50,000	33,333

(2) **Supplier**

		£	$			£	$
				15 Dec Purchases		60,000	42,857
31 Dec	c/f	60,000	44,444	31 Dec Ex loss			1,587
		60,000	44,444			60,000	44,444
				1 Jan	b/f	60,000	44,444

(3) **Loan**

		£	$			£	$
				3 Dec	Cash	800,000	533,333
31 Dec	c/f	800,000	592,593	31 Dec	Ex loss		59,260
		800,000	592,593			800,000	592,593
				1 Jan	b/f	800,000	592,593

Answer 37 MEMO

Consolidated statement of financial position for the year ended 30 April 2018

	$m
Tangible non-current assets	366.5
Goodwill	8
Current assets	403
	777.5
Ordinary shares of $1	60
Share premium account	50
Retained earnings	372.2
	482.2
Non-controlling interest	17.6
	499.8
Non-current liabilities	43.6
Current liabilities	234.1
	777.5

**Consolidated statement of profit or loss and other comprehensive income
for the year ended 30 April 2018**

	$m
Revenue	265
Cost of sales	(162.6)
	———
Gross profit	102.4
Distribution and administrative expenses	(40)
Goodwill impairment	(2)
Interest payable	(1)
Interest receivable	4
Exchange gains	0.4
	———
Profit before taxation	63.8
Tax	(24.5)
	———
Profit for year	39.3
Other comprehensive income:	
Exchange gain on translation of Random	9.7
Exchange gain on translation of goodwill	1.6
	———
Total comprehensive income for year	50.6
	———
Attributable to:	
Non-controlling interest (2 (W6) + 2.4 (W10))	4.4
Shareholders of Memo (balance)	46.2
	———
	50.6
	———

WORKINGS

(1)   Consolidated statement of financial position

	KRm	Adjustment	Rate	$m	Notes
Tangible non-current assets	146		2·1	69·5	
Current assets	102		2·1	48·6	
Current liabilities	(60)	(1·2)	2·1	(29·1)	Exchange loss on inter-company debt
Non-current liabilities	(41)	2	2·1	(18·6)	Exchange gain on inter-company loan
	———			———	
	147			70·4	
	———			———	
Ordinary share capital	32		2·5	12·8	
Share premium account	20		2·5	8·0	
Retained earnings:					
Pre-acquisition	80		2·5	32	
	———				
	132			52·8	Net assets at acquisition
Post-acquisition	15	0·8		17·6	Balance
	———	———		———	
	147	–		70·4	
	———	———		———	

©2017 DeVry/Becker Educational Development Corp. All rights reserved.

(2) Goodwill

	$m	KRm
Cost of acquisition (120 ÷ 2·5)	48	120
Less Net assets acquired: 75% of $52·8 million (above)	(39·6)	(99)
Goodwill	8·4	21

Goodwill is treated as a foreign currency asset which is translated at the closing rate. Essentially under this method, goodwill is being included in the retranslation of the opening net investment with any gain or loss going to reserves. Therefore, goodwill is KR21m ÷ 2·1 = $10 million.

Therefore a gain of $1·6 million will be recorded directly in equity: $2 million will be written off as an impairment loss through profit or loss, giving a balance of $8 million for goodwill.

(3) Non-controlling interest

	$m
Net assets of Random at 30 April 2018	70·4
Non-controlling interest 25% thereof	17·6
Proof:	
Net assets on acquisition $52.8 (W1) × 25%	*13.2*
Share of total comprehensive income for period	*4.4*
	17.6

(4) Post-acquisition reserves

75% of $17·6 million (W1)	13·2

(5) Consolidated statement of financial position at 30 April 2018

	Memo $m	*Random* $m	*Adjustment* $m	*Total* $m
Tangible non-current assets	297	69·5		366·5
Goodwill				8
Loan to Random	5		(5)	
Current assets	355	48·6	(0·6)	403
				777·5
Ordinary share capital	60			60
Share premium account	50			50
Retained earnings	360	13·2	(0·6)	
			(0·4)	
				372·2
				482·2
Non-controlling interest				17·6
Non-current liabilities	30	18·6	(5)	43·6
Current liabilities	205	29·1		234·1
				777·5

Adjustments are the elimination of inter-company loan ($5m), inter-company profit in inventory ($0·6m) and goodwill gain on retranslation of $0·4 million ($1·6m less amortisation $2m).

©2017 DeVry/Becker Educational Development Corp. All rights reserved.

(6) **Profit or loss**

	Memo $m	Random KRm	Random $m	adjustment $m	Total $m
Revenue	200	142 ÷ 2	71	(6)	265
Cost of sales	(120)	(96) ÷ 2	(48)	6	(162·6)
Inventory inter-company profit (W8)	(0·6)				
Distribution and Administrative Expenses	(30)	(20) ÷ 2	(10)		(40)
Goodwill				(2)	(2)
Interest receivable	4				4
Interest payable		(2) ÷ 2	(1)		(1)
Exchange gain – loan (W7)		2 ÷ 2	1		1
Exchange loss – purchases (W8)		(1.2) ÷ 2	(0·6)		(0·6)
Taxation	(20)	(9) ÷ 2	(4·5)		(24·5)
	33.4		7·9	(2)	39·3
Non-controlling interest			(2)		(2)
	33.4		5·9	(2)	37·3

Tutorial note: *The income and expenses of Random have been translated at KR2 = $1 (i.e. the average rate). The closing rate is not allowed under IAS 21.*

Non-controlling interest is $2 million ($7·9 million × 25%).

(7) **Loan to Random**

There is no exchange difference in the financial statements of Memo as the loan is denominated in dollars. However, there is an exchange gain arising in the financial statements of Random.

	KRm
Loan at 1 May 2017 ($5m at 2·5)	12·5
Loan at 30 April 2018 ($5m at 2·1)	10·5
Exchange gain	2·0

This will be translated into dollars at 30 April 2018 and will appear in the consolidated statement of profit or loss as income of $1 million (KR2m ÷ 2). This is because the loan was carried in the currency of the parent and the subsidiary was exposed to the foreign currency risk.

©2017 DeVry/Becker Educational Development Corp. All rights reserved.

(8) **Purchase of raw materials**

	$m
Profit made by Memo ($6m × 20%)	1·2
Profit remaining in inventory at year end (½)	0·6

	KRm
Purchase from Memo ($6m × 2)	12
less payment made ($6m × 2·2)	(13·2)
Exchange loss to profit/loss	(1·2)

The exchange loss will be translated at the average rate (KR2 to $1) into dollars, i.e. $0·6 million. Again the fact that the group cash flows have been affected by foreign currency fluctuations could mean that this loss will be reported in the group statement of profit or loss.

(9) **Movement on consolidated reserves**

	$m
Balance at 1 May 2017 (360 – (34 – 8))	334
Consolidated profit for the period	37·3
Dividend paid	(8)
Exchange gain on translation	7·3
Exchange gain on goodwill	1·6
Balance at 30 April 2018	372·2

Analysis of exchange gain

	$m
Gain on retranslation of opening equity interest (132 ÷ 2·5 – 132 ÷ 2·1)	10·1
Loss on translation of profit for period (7·9 – (7·9 × 2 ÷ 2·1))	(0·4)
Exchange gain	9·7

75% of exchange gain $9·7 million is <u>$7·3 million</u>, with non-controlling interest of <u>$2.4 million.</u>

OR

Opening net assets (W1)	52.8
Profit for year (W6)	7.9
Exchange gain (balance)	9.7
Closing net assets (W1)	70.4

Answer 38 LADWAY

(a)   **Statement of cash flows**

Statement of cash flows of Ladway for the Year to 31 March 2018

	$m	$m
Cash flows from operating activities		
Profit before interest and income tax		583
Adjustments for:		
depreciation – property, plant and equipment	366	
– intangibles	36	
profit on disposal of plant (14 – 11)	(3)	
		399
government grants		(50)
non-cash environmental provision (67 – 15) (W1)		52
		───
Operating profit before working capital changes		984
Increase in inventories		(157)
Increase in trade receivables		(170)
Increase in trade payables		162
		───
Cash generated from operations		819
Interest paid (12 – 4 accrued + 35 preferred dividend)		(43)
Income taxes paid (W2)		(164)
Dividends paid		(220)
		───
Net cash from operating activities		392
Investing activities		
Purchase of property, plant and equipment (W3)	(723)	
Receipt of government grant (W4)	110	
Purchase of intangibles [(450 – 410) + 36]	(76)	
	───	
Net cash used in investing activities		(689)
Cash flows from financing activities		
Proceeds from issue of share capital (W5)	120	
Proceeds from long-term borrowings (W6)	80	
	───	
Net cash received from financing activities		200
		───
Net decrease in cash and cash equivalents		(97)
Cash and cash equivalents at beginning of period		34
		───
Cash and cash equivalents at end of period		(63)
		───

©2017 DeVry/Becker Educational Development Corp. All rights reserved.

WORKINGS

		$m
(1)	**Environmental provision**	
	Balance b/f	24
	Charged to profit or loss	67
	Balance c/f	(76)
	Cash payments during year	15
(2)	**Income taxes**	
	Income tax provision b/f	185
	Deferred tax b/f	30
	Profit or loss charge	177
	Income tax provision c/f	(176)
	Deferred tax c/f	(52)
	Difference cash paid	164
(3)	**Property, plant and equipment**	
	Balance b/f	1,830
	Revaluation surplus	170
	Trade in allowance (non-cash)	14
	Plant acquired in exchange for loan note	120
	Depreciation	(366)
	Disposal at carrying amount	(11)
	Balance c/f	(2,480)
	Difference cash purchases	723
(4)	**Government grant**	
	Balances b/f – current	40
	– non-current	160
	Credit to profit or loss	(50)
	Balances c/f – current	(50)
	– non-current	(210)
	Difference cash receipt	110

©2017 DeVry/Becker Educational Development Corp. All rights reserved.

(5) **Share capital**

Equity capital b/f	400
Bonus issue (from share premium)	40
Difference issue for cash	60
Equity capital c/f	500
Share premium b/f	70
Bonus issue	(40)
	30
Difference premium on issue of equity	60
Share premium c/f	90
Total cash proceeds of issue (60 + 60)	120

(6) **Loan note**

Total value issued	200
Exchanged for plant (non-cash)	(120)
Balance cash proceeds	80

(b) **Relevance and usefulness**

The separate disclosure of cash flows relating to the maintenance of operating capacity is useful in enabling the user to determine whether the company is investing adequately in the future of the company. Without such investment, which is often capped when companies are under liquidity pressures, the company's future prosperity is threatened. The disclosure of cash flows representing increases in operating capacity adds to the information regarding the continued success of the company. Prospective investors are much more likely to be attracted to companies that are expanding than those which are merely maintaining their current levels of operations. The statement of cash flows also shows how these investing activities are being financed: by generating excess cash from operations, by raising loans or by issuing new equity.

The disclosure of cash flow information relating to operating segments of a company supplements the information in other parts of the financial statements relating to segments, and in many ways has the same usefulness:

- the ultimate success of the company as a whole is a function of the success of its individual components. It is not usually possible to appreciate the financial position of a diversified business without information relating to its individual segments;

- a change in the cash flows of a significant component of the business (say if it is going to be sold) may have considerable impact on the cash flows of the business as a whole. Without segmental cash flows users could not assess the impact of a (segment) disposal;

- segmental cash flows provide users with information on the relative size, growth, future prospects and cash generating capacity of the different operations of the business.

©2017 DeVry/Becker Educational Development Corp. All rights reserved.

Answer 39 LOVEY

	$	$
Cash flows from operating activities		
Profit before taxation	381	
Adjustments for		
Impairment of goodwill	15	
Depreciation	47	
Loss on sale of non-current asset	12	
Income from investment in associate	(21)	
Interest expense	25	
Operating profit before working capital changes	459	
Increase in trade and other receivables	-	
Decrease in inventories	17	
Decrease in trade payables	(48)	
Cash generated from operations	428	
Interest paid (25 – 8 + 5)	(22)	
Income taxes paid	(135)	
Dividend from associate	6	
Net cash from operating activities		*277*
Cash flows from investing activities		
Purchase of property, plant and equipment (505 – 129 – 15)	(361)	
Proceeds from sale of equipment	18	
Acquisition of subsidiary (83 – 40)	43	
Net cash used in investing activities		*(300)*
Cash flows from financing activities		
Dividends paid	100	
Dividends paid to the non-controlling interest	71	
Net cash used in financing activities		*(171)*
Net decrease in cash and cash equivalents		**(194)**
Cash and cash equivalents at beginning of period (Note)		**290**
Cash and cash equivalents at end of period (Note)		**96**

©2017 DeVry/Becker Educational Development Corp. All rights reserved.

Notes to the statement of cash flows

(1) Financing

	Share capital (including premium) $000
Balance at 1 January 2017	100
Issue of shares on acquisition	233
Cash flow	–
Balance at 31 December 2017	333

(2) Major non cash transactions

Shares with a market value of $233,000 were issued as consideration for the acquisition of a new subsidiary (see Note 3).

(3) Acquisition of subsidiary undertaking

	$000
Net assets	
Non-current assets	129
Inventory	30
Receivables	25
Cash	83
Payables	(17)
	250
Non-controlling interest	(50)
	200
Goodwill	73
	273
Shares	233
Cash	40
	273

WORKINGS

(1) **Associate**

	$000		$000
Balance b/f	75		
Profit or loss	21	Dividend received(to balance)	6
		Balance c/f	90
	96		96

©2017 DeVry/Becker Educational Development Corp. All rights reserved.

(2) **Non-controlling interest**

	$000		$000
Dividend paid		Balance b/f	90
(to balance)	71	Profit or loss	29
Balance c/f	98	Acquisition	50
	169		169

Answer 40 HEYWOOD BOTTLERS

The Directors, Heywood Bottles

From: ....

Date   30 June 2018

Company performance for the year to 31 March 2018

The following report is submitted in accordance with your request to assess the financial performance of Heywood Bottles for the year to 31 March 2018 in light of the strategic action implemented in April 2017.

The report considers key areas of profitability, liquidity and solvency: It is based on selected ratios calculated in the Appendix.

Profitability

The primary measure of profitability, the return on capital employed (ROCE), has declined from a healthy 32% to a poor 3.6%. The actions taken by the Board to reduce prices to beat the competition would obviously be expected to have squeezed margins and thus stimulate greater sales and more efficient use of assets. All these factors have occurred, the gross margin declined from 25% to only 10%, sales increased by 150% and net asset turnover increased from 1.9 to 5.5 times. Unfortunately the improvement on the sales side has not compensated for the very large decline in the gross margin. At the net profit level this has led to losses.

The deferring of the marketing costs is controversial. It has effectively reduced the current year's loss by $6m less than it would have been had the marketing costs been written off as incurred.

Liquidity and working capital

The current and liquid (acid test) ratios have deteriorated from acceptable figures of 1.8 and 1.3 in 2017 to dangerous figures of 0.9 and 0.8 in 2018. The causes of this lie principally in the new credit policy. In 2017 customers were taking 76 days to pay; this was actually two weeks longer than the two months (61 days) they were supposed to take. The increasing of the allowed credit period to three months (91 days) has actually led to customers taking 114 days to pay. This has been financed by delaying payments to suppliers and a decline in the bank balance from $8 million in hand to a $34 million overdraft.

It is not possible to calculate payable days from the information you have provided. However as a percentage of manufacturing costs (excluding depreciation) they have increased from 18% to 31% and have gone from representing 125% of inventory to 444% of inventory. From this it is possible to conclude that the payables period must have increased dramatically.

©2017 DeVry/Becker Educational Development Corp. All rights reserved.

The inventory turnover has improved, doubling from 7.5 to 15 times. On the surface this is indicative of efficient low inventory levels but it may be that suppliers are becoming unwilling to supply goods due to the time Heywood Bottles is taking to pay them. Therefore the inventory may be artificially low. This could lead to serious problems in the near future.

Solvency

The company has gone from having an acceptable level of gearing (leverage) in 2017 to a high level in 2018. The figures given in the appendix would be worse if the overdraft was considered as part of long-term borrowing. This is a realistic suggestion as there seems little prospect of it being paid off in the near future. The increase in production has led to a requirement for more investment in non-current assets. From the information provided, the overdraft has exceeded its agreed limit and therefore it may be assumed that this is the main reason for the assets having been acquired through lease contracts. The more worrying aspect of this is that, due to poor profitability, interest payments which were covered by a factor of 10 in 2017 are not covered in 2018. This position cannot be maintained for very long.

Conclusion

The present trading position is unsustainable. Unless dramatic action is taken, coupled with an injection of capital, the company is likely to fail in the near future: The actions implemented by the Board in April 2017 have turned out to be little short of disastrous. There is little point increasing sales and market share if there is no profit in it. It is advisable to reverse the marketing strategy. However the company will find it much more difficult to increase prices and keep customers than it was to attract customers with loss making prices. Other methods of developing sales and customer loyalty must be implemented. A meeting to discuss the above findings and related matters is advisable. Your early response would be appreciated.

Business Consultant

Appendix

For the calculation of appropriate ratios the lease obligations falling due after more than one year have been treated as debt finance and included in capital employed and excluded from the net assets.

		2017		2018
ROCE	$(20 \div (44 + 19))$	31.7%	$(2 \div (23 + 32))$	3.6%
Net asset turnover	$(120 \div 63)$	1.9	$(300 \div 55)$	5.5
Non-current asset turnover	$(120 \div 43)$	2.8	$(300 \div 63)$	4.8
Gross profit %	$(30 \div 120)$	25%	$(30 \div 300)$	10%
Net profit % (before interest and taxation)				
	$(20 \div 120)$	16.7%	$(2 \div 300)$	0.7%
Current ratio	$(45 \div 25)$	1.8	$(118 \div 126)$	0.9
Acid test	$(33 \div 25)$	1.3	$(100 \div 126)$	0.8
Inventory turnover	$(90 \div 12)$	7.5	$(270 \div 18)$	15
Receivable days	$(25 \div 120 \times 365)$	76	$(94 \div 300 \times 365)$	114
Payables (as a % of manufacturing costs excluding depreciation)				
	$(15 \div 83)$	18%	$(80 \div 261)$	31%
Gearing (i)	$(19 \div 44)$	43%	$(32 \div 23)$	139%
Gearing (ii)	$(19 \div (44 + 19))$	30%	$(32 \div (23 + 32))$	58%
Interest cover	$(20 \div 2)$	10	$(2 \div 10)$	0.2

Note: ROCE is calculated as:

$$\frac{\text{Profit before interest and tax}}{\text{Equity} + \text{Debt (finance obligations) at the year end}}$$

©2017 DeVry/Becker Educational Development Corp. All rights reserved.

Answer 41 NFP ORGANISATIONS

(a)   **Main aims**

A profit-orientated entity will have a primary aim of increasing the wealth of its owners. The best way of increasing this wealth is to be profitable and thereby increase the entity's share price and also distribute the profits to the owners by way of a dividend payment. In fulfilling this primary aim the entity will also have to consider other stakeholders of the entity, employees, the local environment and government bodies to name a few. The considerations of these other stakeholders may well have an impact on the entity's primary aim, employees will want a satisfactory return for the labour they provide and governments will want a share of the entity's profits by way of taxation. So as well as maximising profits an entity will have to consider, maybe as secondary objectives, the other stakeholders that have a say in the business. An entity will make profits by selling its goods or services to its customers and thereby earn revenues.

A NFP does not have the primary objective of making profits; the main objective of a NFP will be to provide a service for the community it serves. For example, a government body is responsible for providing a policing service in the local community; a museum will have one of its primary objectives to educate the people by allowing them to see the various exhibits. There are no specific owners of a NFP, so there is no need to make profits; that is not to say that a NFP can continually make losses. A NFP must work in a given budget and must recognise if it exceeds that budget there will be consequences to the future income and costs. Income for a NFP may be in the form of government funding or donations from sponsors or by asking the public to make a contribution to the running costs of the organisation.

(b)   **Assessing performance**

Assessing the performance of a profit-orientated entity is generally done by analysing the financial statements of the entity. Calculating various ratios and comparing those ratios with budget, prior years or other similar entities will give the analyst an idea of how the entity has performed. The analyst will consider whether the entity has made adequate returns on funds invested, that the entity is able to meet its commitments and that the market perceives that the entity is meeting expectations through various stock market ratios.

Some of the ratios used in assessing a profit based entity will still be useful in assessing a NFP organisation. However, as the main aim of an NFP is to provide a service, rather than make profits, profit-based ratios may not be as relevant. One of the most critical ways of assessing an NFP is to ensure it has met its budget. The budget of an NFP is far more relevant is assessing performance than the budget of a profit based entity. The NFP must stay within its budget and analysts of a NFP will be focusing more on this factor than its statement of income and expenses. Assessment of a NFP tends to be based on the "3 Es":

(i)   Efficiency is measured by considering what inputs have been used to generate the respective output, and managers should be trying to minimise the level of inputs to perform the task.

(ii)   Effectiveness considers whether the objectives and targets have been met. Management must give clear objectives to the workforce so that those objectives can be seen and attained.

(iii)   Economy is considered by looking at the cost of the resources consumed against the value of the output delivered. Economy is very much linked to the efficiency of the task.

A NFP must ensure that it can meet any obligations that it may have and so liquidity is just as important for a NFP as it is for a profit orientated entity. If a NFP has borrowed monies then it must be in a situation that will allow it to repay those funds on the due date. Cash is possible more important for a NFP than profit, so an assessment of the cash flow statement of a NFP will be extremely important when considering its performance. Considerations will include, have cash inflows met budgeted expectations, have funds been used for the correct purpose.

For both types of entities it is very important to assess performance so that if the entity is not performing as expected then steps can be taken to ensure that in the future the entity is able to meet its objectives, whether they be making a profit or providing a service.

Answer 42 RADAN

(a)   Earnings per share

Radan

Earnings per share (EPS) for the year ended 31 March	2018	2017
(i) Basic basis (W1)	$0.04	$0.063
(ii) Diluted basis (W2)	$0.042	

(b)   Usefulness of diluted EPS

The figure for the basic EPS reflects the earnings performance of the company for the year taking into account all costs and revenues that have occurred during the year. In some circumstances further figures for the EPS may be of informational value to investors and analysts.

Diluted basis

The basic EPS is based on the current year's profit. Investors and analysts are more interested in the future performance of a company: They often use trends of past profits/EPS as a basis for assessing the future performance. Circumstances may exist whereby a company has entered into obligations that may dilute the EPS in the future. Such obligations may adversely affect existing shareholders in terms of a potential reduction in future EPS. One example of such circumstances is the convertible loan notes of Radan. Other examples are share option schemes. Where these circumstances exist the basic EPS can be misleading. The diluted EPS is a measure of what the current year's EPS would be if all relevant diluting circumstances had matured or were exercised. It is important however to realise that the diluted EPS is not a prediction of future EPS.

(c)   Principles of calculation of distributable profit

	$000	$000
Distributable profit of Radan		
Retained earnings 1 April 2017		750
After tax profit in draft accounts to 31 March 2018	910	
Adjustments:		
IFRS 15 profit	no effect	
Exchange gain	(25)	
Development expenditure	no effect	
Excess depreciation (150 ÷ 5)	30	
	———	915
Distributable profit before dividends		1,665

Explanations

IFRS 15 accepts stage profits as being realised when the performance obligation on the contract will be satisfied over a period of time.

Exchange gains are included in reported profit, to reflect the fact that exchange movements can be favourable as well as unfavourable, but they are not realised.

Development expenditure properly carried forward in accordance with IAS 38 is not a realised loss.

Any "excess" depreciation is not treated as a realised loss for the purposes of determining distributable profit.

WORKINGS

Note: all $ figures are in $000, and all numbers of shares are in thousands.

(1)   Basic basis

Ordinary shares 1 April 2017 = 4,000 × 4	16,000
Bonus issue of 1 for 8	2,000
	18,000
Rights issue 1 for 5	3,600
Ordinary shares at 31 March 2018	21,600
Price 100 shares at $1.40	140
Rights issue 20 new shares at $0.50	10
	150

Therefore the 120 shares have a theoretical value of $1.25 each ($150 ÷ 120).

Weighted average number of shares:

$18,000 \times {}^{9}/_{12} \times 1.40 \div 1.25$	15,120
$21,600 \times {}^{3}/_{12}$	5,400
	20,520

Earnings:

Profit after tax	830

Therefore EPS is $830 ÷ 20,520 = $0.04

Comparative figure:

Reported in 2017, EPS $0.08 × $^{8}/_{9}$ (bonus) × 1.25 ÷ 1.40 (rights) restated as $0.063

(2)   Diluted EPS

Assuming the greatest dilution, the 10% loan notes will be converted to ($2,000 × 120 ÷ 100) 2,400 ordinary shares

The effect on earnings will be the interest saved net of tax $2,000 × 10% × (100 – 33)% = $134

Therefore EPS is (830 + 134) ÷ (20,520+ 2,400) = $0.042

Answer 43 EPTILON

(1)   IFRS 1

The International Accounting Standards Board (IASB) addressed this issue in International Financial Reporting Standard (IFRS) 1 *First Time Adoption of International Financial Reporting Standards*. IFRS 1 states that the starting point for the adoption of IFRSs for the year ended 31 December 2017 is to prepare an opening IFRS statement of financial position at 1 January 2016 (the beginning of the earliest comparative period). The general rule is that this statement of financial position will need to comply with each IFRS effective at 31 December 2017 (the reporting date). This means that the opening IFRS statement of financial position should:

- Recognise all assets and liabilities whose recognition is required by IFRSs.
- Not recognise items as assets or liabilities if IFRSs do not permit such recognition.
- Apply IFRSs in the measurement of all recognised assets and liabilities.

This requirement causes a number of practical difficulties:

- At the effective date of transition to IFRSs (1 January 2016) it is not totally clear which IFRSs will be in force two years later so the originally prepared statement of financial position may well need to be amended several times prior to the publication of the first IFRS financial statements.

- The costs of retrospectively applying the recognition and measurement principles of IFRSs might well be considerable. As far as this issue is concerned IFRS 1 grants a limited number of exemptions from the general requirements where the cost of complying with them would be likely to exceed the benefits to users. For example:

    - There is no need to retrospectively apply IFRS 3 *Business Combinations* to combinations that occurred before the date of transition to IFRSs.

    - An entity can elect to measure an item of Property, Plant and Equipment at the date of transition at its fair value and use that fair value as its deemed cost going forward. This is not a revaluation and any difference between the carrying amount under previous GAAP and the carrying amount for IFRS will be taken to retained earnings.

In general the transitional provisions in other IFRSs do not apply to first time adoption. However IFRS 1 does not allow full retrospective application of IFRSs in the following areas:

- Any financial assets or liabilities derecognised under our existing accounting standards in a period beginning before 1 January 2004 do not need to be recognised even if standards relating to Financial Instruments would normally require such recognition.

- The hedge accounting rules of IFRS 9 *Financial Instruments* are not applied to existing contracts.

The 2016 financial statements will need to be prepared under two different sets of accounting standards and resources (both human and capital) must be available to complete this task.

©2017 DeVry/Becker Educational Development Corp. All rights reserved.

(2)   IAS 34

IAS 34 *Interim Reporting* does not oblige entities to publish interim financial reports but when they are published and purport to comply with IFRSs then IAS 34 governs their content. An interim report should be a condensed version of the full financial statements, and should include an explanation of the events and transactions that are significant to an understanding of the interim financial statements. According to IAS 34 our first interim report (for the six months to 30 June 2017) should contain, as a minimum:

■   a condensed statement of financial position at 30 June 2017;
■   a condensed statement of total profit or loss and other comprehensive income for six months to 30 June 2017;
■   a condensed statement of changes in equity for the six months to 30 June 2017;
■   a condensed statement of cash flows for the six months to 30 June 2017;
■   relevant explanatory notes.

Condensed statements should include, as a minimum, each of the headings and sub-totals that would have been included in the 2017 financial statements based on IFRSs. The recognition and measurement principles should be the same as those used in the main financial statements.

The requirements for comparative information on first time adoption of IFRSs depend on whether or not interim reports have been prepared previously. Comparative information is only required if previously prepared. Therefore, comparative information does not need to be prepared for inclusion in the interim financial report.

(3)   IAS 24

IAS 24 *Related Party Disclosures* deals, as its name suggests, with the disclosure of matters concerning related parties. Broadly the disclosures fall into two parts:

(i)   It is always necessary to disclose related party relationships when control exists even if there have been no transactions between the parties.

(ii)   In other circumstances disclosure is only required where there have been related party transactions. A related party transaction is the transfer of resources or obligations between related parties, regardless of whether a price is charged. Where such transactions have occurred entities should disclose the nature of the related party relationship as well as the types of transactions and the elements of the transaction necessary for an understanding of the financial statements. This would normally include:

❑   the monetary amounts of the transactions;
❑   the monetary amounts of any outstanding items;
❑   any irrecoverable debts expense associated with the transactions.

Parties are considered to be related if one party has the ability to control or exercise significant influence over the other party in making financial and operating decisions. A related party may be another entity or an individual. An entity is usually a related party to its key management personnel and also to fellow members of the same group.

©2017 DeVry/Becker Educational Development Corp. All rights reserved.

Answer 44 HAPPY AND HEALTHY

(a)   **Accountants as professionals**

Society accords professional status to those that both possess a high level of technical knowledge in a given area of expertise (accounting, engineering, law, dentistry, medicine) on the understanding that the expertise is used in the public interest. The body of knowledge is gained through passing examinations and gaining practical expertise over time. Acting in the public interest means that the professional always seeks to uphold the interests of society and the best interests of clients (subject to legal and ethical compliance).

Fundamental principles (responsibilities) of professionalism

Society has reasonable expectations of all professionals. The major professional responsibilities of any professional are as follows:

Integrity. The highest levels of probity in all personal and professional dealings. Professionals should be straightforward and honest in all relationships. This has clear implications for Mr Shreeves in his dealings with Ken and Steffi.

Objectivity. Professionals should not allow bias, conflicts of interest or undue influence to cloud their judgements or professional decisions. In this case, Mr Shreeves should not allow his friendship with the Potters to affect his judgement as an auditor.

Professional competence and due care. Professionals have a duty to ensure that their skills and competences are continually being updated and developed to enable them to serve clients and the public interest. This includes continuing to study and scrutinise ethical guidance from Mr Shreeves' own professional accounting body and also IFAC.

Confidentiality. Professionals should, within normal legal constraints, respect the confidentiality of any information gained as a result of professional activity or entrusted to them by a client.

Professional behaviour. Professionals should comply fully with all relevant laws and regulations and avoid acting in any way that might discredit the profession or bring it into disrepute.

(b)   **Professional and ethical dilemma facing Mr Shreeves**

The normal behaviour for the auditor, regardless of the options available in this situation, would be to initially seek representations from Ivan to establish whether there is an explanation that has so far been overlooked or not known about. Following that, Mr Shreeves' options are: to tell or not tell Ken and Steffi about Ivan's behaviour. *Issues*

Mr Shreeves is clearly in a difficult situation but he must be aware of his duty as a professional accountant which includes, in his role as auditor, a duty to the public interest. He has a duty of due care and diligence to society and government as well as the shareholders of a company being audited. Being complicit in Ivan's activity is clearly not an option as this would be incompatible with his duties to the shareholders and to society in his role as auditor. Furthermore, he has realised a disclosure of such transactions is required and it would be unprofessional not to discuss this with his clients.

©2017 DeVry/Becker Educational Development Corp. All rights reserved.

He feels he owes a debt to the Potter family as a long-standing family friend and this has the potential to cloud his judgement as the company's auditor. The effect of Ken and Steffi finding out about Ivan's theft could be "devastating" and this is bound to weigh heavily on Mr Shreeves' mind. In getting too close to the family, Mr Shreeves has compromised his duty as auditor as he is probably less objective than he should be. He should probably have chosen between being a family friend and being the auditor some years ago and that would have made his resolution of the dilemma somewhat easier.

Ivan has been unprofessional and has acted fraudulently in his dealings with "Happy and healthy". In such a situation, the auditor does not have latitude in how he or she deals with such a discovery. It is a very serious breach of trust by Ivan, regardless of whether he is the Potters' son or not, and it would be inexcusable to withhold this information from the owner-managers of the business.

Advice

Given that the auditor has a duty to the public interest and the company shareholders, he should inform the majority shareholders (Ken and Steffi) what he has found during the audit. To do anything other than this would be to act unprofessionally and irresponsibly towards the majority shareholders of the company. Family relationships or friendships must never be allowed to interfere with an auditor's professional duty and independence. This approach need not be in the form of a blunt confrontation, however, and it would not be unprofessional to speak with Ivan before he spoke to his parents in order to convey to him the potential seriousness of his actions.

Answer 45 MUCKY MINING

(a)   Sustainability

Sustainability is a term with several meanings, even in this context. A sustainable business could mean a successful business with tangible and intangible assets and future cash flows that, in the current environment (or any predicted changes or foreseeable uncertainties), is able to continue to operate successfully in business in the long term.

A sustainable business may also be seen as one that recognises ethical obligations towards society through it social and environmental policies. It could be regarded as a business that recognises and balances economic, social and environmental objectives. In this context the business is sustainable in the long-run because it meets the requirement of a very broad range of stakeholders both now and in the future. Sustainability implies that it protects society and environment by not compromising future generations in its activities and use of resources.

Sustainability may also be seen as doing those things economic, social and environmental that supports the long-run maximisation of profit or shareholder value. This is the so called "ethics pays" view.

The term ethics used in the question is concerned with what is right and wrong in terms of business decision-making, behaviour and activity. An ethical business is an honest and transparent business that meets the moral requirements of society and operates in a socially and environmentally acceptable way.

There are inevitably some potential conflicts between achieving objectives in terms of return, growth and risk and achieving social and environmental objectives. Focus on economic objectives may be a short-term view that is not sustainable in the long run. Shareholders, customers and other stakeholders may not be supportive of a pure profit maximisation if they have "ethical", social and environmental concerns. This could lead to a falling or static share price or revenues.

In the scenario it is clear that Mucky Mining is economically successful. The company does however have social and environmental issues with its potentially immoral labour practices and potential disregard for the environment in its mining operations. The media reports are however unconfirmed.

As a listed company shareholders may express their dissatisfaction orally, in writing, at votes or by walking away and selling their shares.

The scenario does not give information regarding the legality of the social and environmental issues but putting the morals to one side both issues could give rise to economic cost for the company beyond reputation damage in terms of potential fines and damages.

Ultimately a sustainable business contributes to the economic and social success of a nation in a way that does not compromise future generations.

(b)   Stakeholders

A stakeholder is a person, organisation, individual or group who has a legitimate interest in, is affected by or affects an entity or its activities or operations. Some stakeholders have legal interests, some have contractual interests and some impose their interests on the entity. Stakeholders may be internal (e.g. directors and employees), connected (e.g. shareholders, suppliers and customers) or external (e.g. government, lobby groups and society or communities). Stakeholders have varying power to influence and interests that connect them to an entity.

Listed companies can be regarded as firms with a purely economic purpose or entities with economic, social and environmental purposes.

Listed companies have a particular issue in that ownership and control are largely separated. The directors who run or control the business do not usually have significant shareholdings that give them ownership or effective legal entity voting control. Whilst directors can be removed shareholders rarely take such action and directors are generally promoted from within or selected from outside by the board.

When the question refers to responsibilities of listed companies this could be seen as the responsibilities of the board.

Legally directors must act in good faith in what they believe are the interests of the company. UK law requires consideration of social and environmental matters but leaves it up to directors to determine what they wish to do to promote the success of the company.

Shareholders are particularly important to listed company directors since the directors will actively operate to deliver shareholder value in terms of return and growth at an acceptable risk to the shareholders. They will to some extent be judged on the share price performance.

Delivering these objectives may however require social and environmental concern to create a sustainable business. Ethic does tend to pay.

Some shareholders may also be "ethical" members who are willing to pay a premium for high standards of social and environmental performance.

Stakeholders other than shareholders may therefore be seen as a key to maximising long-term shareholder value. Satisfied customers, suppliers, employees and society may support this.

Listed companies are likely to put shareholders at the top of their stakeholder priority list. This is due to the fundamentals of traditional and legal company purpose.

Other stakeholders' legitimacy may be judged by their power, or influence, and interest or willingness to engage.

©2017 DeVry/Becker Educational Development Corp. All rights reserved.

(c)   **Accountants as a profession**

Professionally qualified accountants take on many roles in industry, commerce, the public sector and the accounting profession itself. Traditionally accountants are the preparers of financial information and the professionals who give assurance through opinions on financial information prepared by others.

Accountants are also businessmen when they take up senior managerial roles or run their own practices or businesses. Many accountants have specialist expertise in areas such as tax and insolvency. Accountants undergo a broad business based examination and practical training underpinned by excellence in accounting, auditing, tax and law.

The general public see accountants as professionals and expect expertise, knowledge and strong ethics.

The chartered accountancy bodies in the UK received their Royal Charters because they demonstrated excellence in examinations, training, continuing professional development and had well enforced standards and ethical codes.

At the heart of our ethical approach, as illustrated by the IFAC Ethical Code is the concept of the public interest. Accountants work for their employers or clients but put the public interest first.

The public interest arises because of the "reserved" nature of much of an accountant's work. In areas such as insolvency and auditing legal restrictions exist on carrying out such work. As professionals accountants have earned the right to undertake such work largely because of their ethical codes.

The IFAC code contains five fundamental principles that are essential to giving confidence in the work of accountants. Following these as non-negotiable universal moral principles means that their work and the information they provide (e.g. in a tax return, annual return, annual report and financial statements or an audit opinion) can be relied on.

The principle of integrity implies absolute honesty, indeed it goes beyond this to include being straightforward in business dealings. The principle of objectivity implies being totally unbiased in applying accounting principles, laws and regulations whatever the circumstances, whatever the pressures and whatever the temptations and interests involved, true objectivity means transparency and reliability. These are supported by ethical obligations of confidentiality in keeping client and employer affairs private unless a public interest demands disclosure, due care in adhering to standards and professional behaviour in not bringing the profession into disrepute.

Accountants are a key part of corporate governance whether they are inside business ensuring honesty and transparency or outside the business reporting robustly on the honesty and transparency of corporate reporting.

In the scenario the professional accountants appear to be upholding these principles in that Mucky Mining has won awards for the quality of its financial statements. This implies adherence to generally accepted accounting principles and that the financial statements are not just true and fair as assured by the audit opinion but clear and understandable in presenting the business results. However we should be careful in drawing such conclusions since audit reports only give reasonable assurance that financial statements are free from material error and fraud.

There are, however, other ethical issues of a social and environmental nature in the scenario.

It can be argued that there is a difference between business ethics and the professional ethics of an accountant. Professional ethics almost exclusively is concerned with our roles in compiling and reporting on financial information.

Professional ethics does extend to our business role as explained in the concept of integrity where we are required to be "honest and straightforward in all business dealings". Integrity here is concerned with deals, contracts, proposals, tenders and the like rather than the more fundamental "morality" of business and business activities, or at least that is the current generally held view.

Professional ethics however always implies acting lawfully. Business ethics arguably has boundaries beyond being lawful, honest and fair and includes social and environmental responsibilities. These are the "grey areas" where laws and regulations do not exist but where society has expectations regarding issues of employment conditions, working conditions, responsible use of resources and responsible activities.

Some argue that accountants may act against the public interest since we do not "professionally" embrace social and environmental responsibilities. Most professional accountants would argue that these issues are outside our "professional" domain and covered by our more general "citizens" domain.

As citizens we may have social and environmental responsibilities beyond upholding the law, moral standards and expectations. Our professional ethical understanding does however give us a mature understanding of the meaning of morality and applying the Kohlberg view we are maybe more likely than non-professionals to adopt a stage 4 "law and order" view that requires respect for human dignity, social responsibility and environmental responsibility in order to support the sustainable and successful workings of economies and societies.

Our ethical approach does not however really encourage us to be post-conventional since we rarely "challenge" laws and regulations as being "wrong" since most of the laws we deal with are "morally right" in a democracy.

Some also argue that the accounting profession is a "value laden" profession that through its accounting principles focuses attention on profit and measurement of profit rather than on social and environmental good performance.

Ultimately our role is best seen as being the upholders of lawful behaviour, honesty and transparency in reporting. Society relies on us to challenge those who breach laws and regulations and those who fail to report their business affairs reliably.

©2017 DeVry/Becker Educational Development Corp. All rights reserved.

ABOUT BECKER PROFESSIONAL EDUCATION

Becker Professional Education provides a single solution for students and professionals looking to advance their careers and achieve success in:

- Accounting

- International Financial Reporting

- Project Management

- Continuing Professional Education

- Healthcare

For more information on how Becker Professional Education can support you in your career, visit www.becker.com/acca.

Becker Professional Education
is an ACCA approved content provider

Lightning Source UK Ltd.
Milton Keynes UK
UKOW07f2245050717

304699UK00007B/181/P

9 781785 663970